ONE WEEK LOAN

Machine Learning and
Data Mining

To my wife, Ela
R.S.M.

To my parents, Angela and Ivan
I.B.

To my wife, Verunka
M.K.

Machine Learning and Data Mining

Methods and Applications

Edited by

Ryszard S. Michalski
George Mason University, Fairfax, USA

Ivan Bratko
University of Ljubljana, Ljubljana, Slovenia

Miroslav Kubat
University of South Western Louisiana, Lafayette, USA

JOHN WILEY & SONS LTD

Chichester · New York · Weinheim · Brisbane · Toronto · Singapore

Other Wiley Editorial Offices

John Wiley & Sons, Inc., 605 Third Avenue,
New York, NY 10158-0012, USA

WILEY-VCH Verlag GmbH
Pappelallee 3, D-69469 Weinheim, Germany

Jacaranda Wiley Ltd, 33 Park Road, Milton,
Queensland 4064, Australia

John Wiley & Sons (Canada) Ltd, 22 Worcester Road,
Rexdale, Ontario, M9W 1L1, Canada

John Wiley & Sons (Asia) Pte Ltd, 2 Clementi Loop #02-01,
Jin Xing Distripark, Singapore 129 809

British Library Cataloguing in Publication Data

A catalogue record for this book is available from the British Library

ISBN 0 471 97199 5

Produced from camera ready copy supplied by the authors
Printed and bound in Great Britain by Bookcraft (Bath) Ltd, Midsomer Norton, Somerset
This book is printed on acid-free paper responsibly manufactured from sustainable forestry, in which at least two trees are planted for each one used for paper production.

Contents

Preface   xi

List of contributors   xiii

PART I   **GENERAL TOPICS**   1

Chapter 1   **A Review of Machine Learning Methods**   3
Miroslav Kubat, Ivan Bratko and Ryszard S. Michalski

1.1	Introduction	3
1.2	The machine learning task	5
1.3	Search through the space of generalizations	12
1.4	Classic methods of learning	17
1.5	How can predicate logic be used?	31
1.6	Artificial discovery	42
1.7	How to cope with the vastness of the search space?	53
1.8	Close neighborhood of machine learning	56
1.9	Hybrid systems and multistrategy learning	61
1.10	Perspectives	65
	References	66

Chapter 2   **Data Mining and Knowledge Discovery:**
A Review of Issues and a Multistrategy Approach   71
Ryszard S. Michalski and Kenneth A. Kaufman

2.1	Introduction	72
2.2	Machine learning and multistrategy data exploration	73
2.3	Classification of data exploration tasks	83
2.4	Integration of many operators in INLEN	87
2.5	Illustration of clustering and learning operators	90
2.6	Data and rule visualization	92
2.7	Learning rules with structured attributes	94
2.8	Learning decision structures from decision rules	97
2.9	Automatic improvement of representation spaces	98
2.10	Exemplary application: discovery in economic and demographic data	99
2.11	Summary	104
	Acknowledgements	105
	References	105

Chapter 3   Fielded Applications of Machine Learning   113
Pat Langley and Herbert A. Simon

3.1   Introduction   113
3.2   Fielded applications of rule induction   114
3.3   Other applied work on rule induction   120
3.4   Some strategies and lessons   123
Acknowledgements   127
References   127

Chapter 4   Applications of Inductive Logic Programming   131
Ivan Bratko, Stephen Muggleton and Aram Karalič

4.1   Introduction   131
4.2   ILP compared to other approches to ML   132
4.3   Predicting the mutagenicity of chemical compounds   134
4.4   Skill reconstruction in electrical discharge machining   136
4.5   Some other applications of ILP   139
4.6   Conclusion   141
Acknowledgements   142
References   142

PART II   DESIGN AND ENGINEERING   145

Chapter 5   Application of Machine Learning in Finite Element Computation   147
Bojan Dolšak, Ivan Bratko and Anton Jezernik

5.1   Introduction   148
5.2   Adding an expert system to FEM generator   149
5.3   The learning problem, examples and background knowledge   150
5.4   Previous experiments   155
5.5   Selection of an appropriate learning algorithm   158
5.6   Learning with CLAUDIEN   159
5.7   Post-processing of the induced rules   162
5.8   Results   164
5.9   Conclusions   168
Acknowledgements   170
References   170

**Chapter 6   Application of Inductive Learning and Case-Based Reasoning for
Troubleshooting Industrial Machines   173**
Michel Manago and Eric Auriol

6.1   Introduction   174
6.2   Inductive learning and case-based reasoning   174
6.3   Obtaining better feedback from experience   176
6.4   Applications   177
References   183

**Chapter 7   Empirical Assembly Sequence Planning: A Multistrategy
               Constructive Learning Approach**   **185**
               Heedong Ko

               7.1   Introduction   185
               7.2   Representation and planning in NOMAD   187
               7.3   Multistrategy constructive learning   191
               7.4   Learning scenario by NOMAD   193
               7.5   Comparison with previous research   198
               7.6   Conclusion   200
               Acknowledgements   200
               References   201

**Chapter 8   Inductive Learning in Design: A Method and Case Study
               Concerning Design of Antifriction Bearing Systems**   **203**
               Wojciech Moczulski

               8.1   Introduction   204
               8.2   A method for learning design rules   204
               8.3   Description of an exemplary problem   207
               8.4   Application of the induction method   209
               8.5   Training and testing events   211
               8.6   Results obtained   212
               8.7   Recapitulation and conclusions   216
               Acknowledgements   218
               References   218

PART III   DETECTION OF PATTERNS IN TEXTS, IMAGES AND MUSIC   221

Chapter 9   Finding Associations in Collections of Text   **223**
               Ronen Feldman and Haym Hirsh

               9.1   Introduction   223
               9.2   The FACT system architecture   225
               9.3   Associations   229
               9.4   The query language   230
               9.5   Query execution   232
               9.6   Presentation of associations   234
               9.7   Applying FACT to newswire data   235
               9.8   Final remarks   238
               Acknowledgements   239
               References   240

Chapter 10 Learning Patterns in Images   **241**
Ryszard S. Michalski, Azriel Rosenfeld, Zoran Duric,
Marcus Maloof and Qi Zhang

    10.1 Introduction   241
    10.2 Previous work on machine learning in computer vision   242
    10.3 Semantic interpretation of color images of outdoor scenes   245
    10.4 Detection of blasting caps in x-ray images of luggage   249
    10.5 Recognizing actions in video image sequences   255
    10.6 Conclusions and future research   264
    Acknowledgements   266
    References   266

Chapter 11 Applications of Machine Learning to Music Research: Empirical
Investigations into the Phenomenon of Musical Expression   **269**
Gerhard Widmer

    11.1 Introduction   270
    11.2 The object of study: expressive music performance   271
    11.3 The nature and importance of background knowledge   271
    11.4 Approach I: learning at the note level   273
    11.5 Approach II: learning at the structure level   280
    11.6 A machine learning analysis of real artistic performances   284
    11.7 Discussion of experimental results   288
    11.8 Conclusion   291
    Acknowledgements   291
    References   292

PART IV   COMPUTER SYSTEMS AND CONTROL SYSTEMS   **295**

Chapter 12 WebWatcher: A Learning Apprentice for the World Wide Web **297**
Robert Armstrong, Dayne Freitag, Thorsten Joachims
and Tom Mitchell

    12.1 Overview   297
    12.2 WebWatcher   298
    12.3 Learning   304
    12.4 Results   307
    12.5 Conclusions   310
    Acknowledgements   310
    Appendix   311
    References   312

Chapter 13 Biologically Inspired Defences Against Computer Viruses   313
J. O. Kephart, G. B. Sorkin, W. C. Arnold, D. M. Chess,
G. J. Tesauro and S. R. White

    13.1 Introduction   314
    13.2 Background   315
    13.3 Generic detection of viruses   317
    13.4 A computer immune system   323
    13.5 Conclusion and perspective   332
    References   333

Chapter 14 Behavioural Cloning of Control Skill   335
Ivan Bratko, Tanja Urbančič and Claude Sammut

    14.1 Introduction   335
    14.2 Behavioural cloning   337
    14.3 Pole balancing   338
    14.4 Learning to fly   340
    14.5 Container cranes   343
    14.6 Production line scheduling   347
    14.7 Discussion   348
    Acknowledgements   349
    References   350

Chapter 15 Acquiring First-order Knowledge About Air Traffic Control 353
Yves Kodratoff and Christel Vrain

    15.1 Introduction   353
    15.2 Knowledge intensive relational generalization   356
    15.3 Application of ATC   366
    15.4 Conclusion   383
    Acknowledgements   384
    References   384

PART V   MEDICINE AND BIOLOGY   387

Chapter 16 Application of Machine Learning to Medical Diagnosis   389
Igor Kononenko, Ivan Bratko and Matjaž Kukar

    16.1 Introduction   389
    16.2 Medical diagnosis   390
    16.3 Diagnostic performance of physicians vs. machine learning 391
    16.4 Selecting the appropriate ML system   393
    16.5 Acceptance in practice   401
    16.6 Conclusion   403
    Acknowledgements   403
    Appendix: information score   404
    References   405

Chapter 17 Learning to Classify Biomedical Signals   **409**
            Miroslav Kubat, Irena Koprinska and Gert Pfurtscheller

            17.1 Introduction   409
            17.2 Two medical domains   410
            17.3 Decision-tree based initialization of neural networks   414
            17.4 Tree-based initialization of RBF networks   419
            17.5 Experiments   422
            17.6 Discussion   425
            Acknowledgements   426
            References   426

**Chapter 18 Machine Learning Applications in Biological Classification of
            River Water Quality**   **429**
            Sašo Džeroski, Jasna Grbović and William J. Walley

            18.1 Introduction   430
            18.2 Learning rules for biological classification of British rivers   431
            18.3 Analysis of data about Slovenian rivers   436
            18.4 Discussion   445
            Acknowledgements   447
            References   447

Index   **449**

Preface

This book is intended for a wide audience of readers who are not necessarily experts in machine learning or data mining, but are interested in receiving a general introduction to these areas and their many practical applications. Machine learning is a field dedicated to the development of computational methods underlying learning processes and to applying computer-based learning systems to practical problems. A significant part of research in machine learning has been concerned with developing methods for determining general descriptions of concepts from examples. Examples can be expressed in various forms, in particular, in the form of relational data tables, therefore many machine learning methods have an important and direct application to the problems of data mining, that is, problems of searching for interesting patterns and important regularities in large databases. Particularly challenging, and not yet widely addressed problems in the latter area, are those concerned with extracting patterns or rules from text, images or sound sequences (music), which are discussed in one of the book's sections.

The first part of the book reviews fundamental concepts and methods of machine learning, and discusses issues and multistrategy methodology for data mining and knowledge discovery. It also reviews selected fielded applications of machine learning and of inductive logic programming – an important modern subarea of machine learning.

Subsequent chapters have been structured into several general application themes. These themes include design and engineering, detection of patterns or rules in texts, images and music, computer systems and control systems, and medicine and biology. Some of the applications described in the book are in everyday use, some have the status of research experiments. Our guiding criterion for including an application in the book was that a machine learning method had to be applied to a difficult and interesting real-world problem, and produced satisfactory or at least truly promising results.

This book has been written by a truly international team of scientists. Authors of individual chapters are leading experts in machine learning or related areas, representing major research groups from eleven countries – Australia, Austria, Bulgaria, Canada, France, Israel, Korea, Poland, Slovenia, the United Kingdom and the USA. The editors are obliged to mention, however, that because there are so many excellent researchers now working in the areas of machine learning and data mining, it was not possible for them to select some 'representative' authors. Many of those who have been invited to contribute to this book are simply current or former collaborators or associates of the editors. However, all the selected authors are outstanding scientists whose work covers a very wide range of topics, and the editors feel very privileged to have been able to assemble in this book contributions from them.

The editors wish to express their gratitude to many people who helped in the preparation of this book. Special thanks go to the researchers at the Machine Learning and Inference Laboratory of George Mason University, who provided invaluable help in various technical and editorial matters, in particular to Zoran Duric, Ken Kaufman, Seokwon Lee and Qi Zhang. We also thank Roslyn Meredith and Gaynor Redvers-Mutton of John Wiley & Sons for their collaboration in this project.

In conclusion, we hope that the reader will find this book a truly helpful guide and a valuable source of information about machine learning and data mining, and their numerous practical applications.

Ryszard S. Michalski
Ivan Bratko
Miroslav Kubat

Contributors

Robert Armstrong
School of Computer Science, Carnegie Mellon University, 5000 Forbes Ave., Pittsburgh, PA 15213, USA.

William C. Arnold
IBM TJ Watson Research Center, USA

Eric Auriol
AcknoSoft, 58 rue du Dessous des Berges, 75 013 Paris, France.

Ivan Bratko
Faculty of Computer and Information Science, University of Ljubljana, Trzaska 25, 1000 Ljubljana, Slovenia.

David M. Chess
High Integrity Computing Laboratory, IBM TJ Watson Research Center, USA

Bojan Dolšak
Faculty of Mechanical Engineering, University of Maribor, Smetanova 17, 2000 Maribor, Slovenia.

Zoran Duric
Machine Learning and Inference Laboratory, M.S. 4A5, George Mason University, Fairfax, VA 22030-4444, USA.

Sašo Džeroski
Jozef Stefan Institute, Jamova 39, 1000 Ljubljana, Slovenia.

Ronen Feldman
Math and Computer Science Department, Bar-Ilan University, Ramat-Gan, Israel 52900.

Dayne Freitag
School of Computer Science, Carnegie Mellon University, 5000 Forbes Ave., Pittsburgh, PA 15213, USA.

Jasna Grbović
Hydrometerological Institute, Vojkova 1B, 1001 Ljubljana, Slovenia.

Haym Hirsh
Department of Computer Science, Rutgers University, New Brunswick, NJ 08903, USA.

Anton Jezernik
*Laboratory for Technical Software, Faculty of Mechanical Engineering,
University of Maribor, Smetanova 17, 2000 Maribor, Slovenia.*

Thorsten Joachims
FB Informatik VIII, Universitaet Dortmund, 44221 Dortmund, Germany.

Ken A. Kaufman
*Machine Learning and Inference Laboratory, M.S. 4A5, George Mason University,
Fairfax, VA 22030-4444, USA.*

Aram Karalič
*Department of Intelligent Systems, Jozef Stefan Institute, Jamova 39, 1000 Ljubljana,
Slovenia.*

Jeffrey O. Kephart
*IBM TJ Watson Research Center, 30 Saw Mill River Rd., Hawthorne,
NY 10532, USA.*

Heedong Ko
Korea Institute of Science and Technology, PO Box 131, Cheongryang, Seoul, Korea.

Yves Kodratoff
LRI, Blg 490, Universite de Paris Sud, F-91405 Orsay cedex, France.

Igor Kononenko
*Faculty of Computer and Information Science, University of Ljubljana, Trzaska 25,
1000 Ljubljana, Slovenia.*

Irena Koprinska
*Institute for Information Technologies, Bulgarian Academy of Sciences, Acad.
G. Bonchev Str., Bl. 29A, 113 Sofia, Bulgaria.*

Miroslav Kubat
*Center for Advanced Computer Studies, University of South Western Louisiana,
Lafayette, LA 70504-4330, USA.*

Matjaž Kukar
*Faculty of Computer and Information Science, University of Ljubljana, Trzaska 25,
1000 Ljubljana, Slovenia.*

Pat Langley
Intelligent Systems Laboratory, Daimler-Benz Research & Technology,
1510 Page Mill Road, Palo Alto, CA 94304, USA.

Marcus A. Maloof
Computational Learning Laboratory, Center for the Study of Language and Information,
Ventura Hall, Stanford University, Stanford, CA 94305-4115, USA.

Michel Manago
AcknoSoft, 58 rue du Dessous des Berges, 75 013 Paris, France.

Ryszard S. Michalski
Machine Learning and Inference Laboratory, M.S. 4A5, George Mason University, Fairfax,
VA 22030-4444, USA.

Tom M. Mitchell
School of Computer Science, Carnegie Mellon University, 5000 Forbes Ave., Pittsburgh,
PA 15213, USA.

Wojciech Moczulski
Department of Fundamentals of Machine Design, Technical University of Silesia,
Konarskiego 18a, 44-100 Gliwice, Poland.

Stephen Muggleton
Department of Computer Science, University of York, Heslington, York, YO1 5DD, UK.

Gert Pfurtscheller
Department of Medical Informatics, Graz University of Technology, Brockmanngasse 41,
A-8010 Graz, Austria.

Azriel Rosenfeld
Center for Automation Research, University of Maryland, College Park, MD 20742-3275,
USA.

Claude Sammut
School of Computer Science and Engineering, University of New South Wales,
Sydney 2052, Australia.

Herbert A. Simon
Department of Psychology, Carnegie-Mellon University, Pittsburgh, PA 15213, USA..

Gregory B. Sorkin
IBM TJ Watson Research Center, USA.

Gerald J. Tesauro
IBM TJ Watson Research Center, USA.

Tanja Urbančič
Jozef Stefan Institute, Jamova 39, 1000 Ljubljana, Slovenia.

Christel Vrain
LIFO, Universite d'Orleans, rue Leonard de Vinci, BP 6759, F-45067 Orleans cedex 2, France.

William Walley
School of Computing, University of Staffordshire, UK.

Steve R. White
IBM TJ Watson Research Center, USA.

Gerhard Widmer
Department of Medical Cybernetics and Artificial Intelligence, University of Vienna, Freyung 6/2, A-1010 Vienna, Austria.

Qi Zhang
Machine Learning and Inference Laboratory, M.S. 4A5, George Mason University, Fairfax, VA 22030-4444, USA.

PART I

General Topics

1

A Review of Machine Learning Methods

Miroslav Kubat, Ivan Bratko and Ryszard S. Michalski

1.1 INTRODUCTION

The field of machine learning was conceived nearly four decades ago with the bold objective to develop computational methods that would implement various forms of learning, in particular mechanisms capable of inducing knowledge from examples or data. As software development has become one of the main bottlenecks of today's computer technology, the idea of introducing knowledge into computers by way of examples seems particularly attractive and appealing to common sense. Such a form of knowledge induction is particularly desirable in problems that lack algorithmic solutions, are ill-defined, or only informally stated. Medical or technical diagnosis, visual concept recognition, engineering design, material behavior, chess playing, or the detection of interesting reqularities in large data sets are examples of such problems.

One of the vital inventions of artificial intelligence research is the idea that formally intractable problems can be solved by extending the traditional scheme

$$program = algorithm + data$$

to the more elaborate

$$program = algorithm + data + domain\ knowledge$$

Applying domain knowledge, encoded in suitable data structures, is fundamental for solving problems of this kind. Anyone who has taken a course on artificial intelligence knows the power of production rules, frames, semantic networks, and uncertainty propagation in expert systems. Machine learning systems, too, profit from this idea.

Nevertheless, the use of knowledge only shifts the bottleneck from the programmer to the

Machine Learning and Data Mining: Methods and Applications
Edited by R.S. Michalski, I Bratko and M. Kubat
© 1997 John Wiley & Sons Ltd

knowledge engineer, who has to elicit it from an expert and encode it into the system. The process of knowledge acquisition and encoding is, in any real-world application, far from being easy. For example, specialists in computer chess know that the brute-force approach has led to more powerful programs than the artificial intelligence methods because the knowledge needed to make the program beat a grandmaster is very difficult to formulate; grandmasters use their experience intuitively and are, in most cases, unable to convey it to an artificial intelligence system in the form of production rules or other representational systems. Chess textbooks are full of abstract concepts such as initiative, cooperation of pieces, weak pawn structures, good bishops, and well-protected king; and chess players need years of experience to develop their understanding. Such concepts usually lack precise definition, and encoding them in a computer is very difficult.

Thus a tempting idea springs to mind: employ a learning system that will acquire such higher-level concepts and/or problem-solving strategies through examples in a way analogical to human learning.

Most research in machine learning has been devoted to developing effective methods to address this problem. Although progress has been slow, many significant results have been achieved. The main argument of the opponents of the field is now: if, in expert systems, programming has been replaced by knowledge-encoding, then in machine learning knowledge encoding is supposed to be replaced by induction from examples; however, available learning systems are not powerful enough to succeed in realistic domains.

The objective of this book is to demonstrate that in many practical domains the application of machine learning leads to useful practical results. We demonstrate on presented case studies that the field has reached the state of development in which existing techniques and systems can be used for the solution of many real-world problems.

Two groups of researchers need to be put together if the application of machine learning is to bear fruit: those that are acquainted with existing machine learning methods, and those with expertise in the given application domain to provide training data. This book aims at attracting the attention of potential users from disciplines outside computer science. If it can arouse their interest and make them consider an application of machine-learning to problems in their fields that resist traditional approaches, it will be worth the authors' effort.

To initiate non-specialists into the field of machine learning, this chapter surveys methods that are necessary to develop a general understanding of the field and which have been used in the case studies presented in this volume. Section 1.2 discusses the meaning of a concept and its use as a basic unit of knowledge. It then briefly elaborates on issues related to the problem of concept representation in computer memory. Section 1.3 formulates the generic machine learning task as a search through the space of representations. Upon these basic considerations, Section 1.4 discusses two fundamental approaches to concept learning, thus preparing the ground for Section 1.5, which outlines more sophisticated methods based on a subset of first-order logic.

To deepen the reader's understanding of the general way of thinking of machine learning researchers, Section 1.6 describes some approaches to discovery. Section 1.7 briefly reviews two methods to save effort in building concept descriptions in rich representation languages— analogy and the use of examples themselves as knowledge representation.

The next two sections, 1.8 and 1.9, briefly cover techniques that are not usually included in traditional symbolic machine learning texts, but whose knowledge is, nevertheless, indispensable for any specialist in this domain: neural networks, genetic algorithms, and various hybrid systems. The objective of this introduction is to arm the reader with the basic knowledge necessary for forthcoming chapters, rather than to provide a comprehensive coverage of the discipline. For a more detailed coverage, the reader is referred to various books devoted to this field such as Michalski, Carbonell, and Mitchell, (1983, 1986), Kodratoff and Michalski (1990), Michalski and Tecuci (1994), Langley (1996), or Mitchell (1996).

1.2 THE MACHINE LEARNING TASK

The general framework for machine learning is depicted in Figure 1.1. The learning system aims at determining a description of a given concept from a set of concept examples provided by the teacher and from the background knowledge.

Concept examples can be positive (e.g., a dog, when teaching the concept of a mammal) or negative (e.g., a scorpion). Background knowledge contains the information about the language used to describe the examples and concepts. For instance, it can include possible values of variables (attributes) and their hierarchies, predicates, auxiliary syntactic rules, subjective preferences, and the like. The learning algorithm then builds on the type of examples, on the size and relevance of the background knowledge, on the representational issues, on the presumed nature of the concept to be acquired, and on the designer's experience.

An important requirement is that the learning system should be able to deal with imperfections of the data. Examples will often contain a certain amount of *noise*—errors in the descriptions or in the classifications. For instance, a classification error will be if 'scorpion' is classified by the absent-minded teacher as 'mammal'. Moreover, examples can be incomplete in the sense that some attribute values are missing. Also, the background knowledge need not necessarily be perfect.

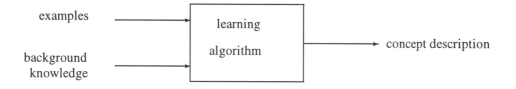

Figure 1.1   Machine learning task.

Learning algorithms can generally be classified into one of two major categories: *black-box* methods, such as neural networks or mathematical statistics, and *knowledge-oriented* methods. The black-box approaches develop their own concept representation that is to be used for concept recognition purposes. However, this internal description cannot be easily interpreted by the user, and provides neither insight nor explanation of the recognition process. Black-box methods typically involve numeric calculations of coefficients, distances, or weights.

On the other hand, knowledge-oriented methods aim at creating symbolic knowledge structures that satisfy the principle of comprehensiblity (Michalski, 1983). Michie (1988) formulated the distinction between black-box and knowledge-oriented concept learning systems in the terms of three criteria. These criteria—weak, strong and ultra-strong—differ in their aspirations regarding the comprehensibility of learned descriptions:

1. *Weak criterion*: the system uses sample data to generate an updated basis for improved performance on subsequent data.
2. *Strong criterion*: weak criterion is satisfied. Moreover, the system can communicate its internal updates in explicit symbolic form.
3. *Ultrastrong criterion*: weak and strong criteria are satisfied. Moreover, the system can communicate its internal updates in an *operationally effective* symbolic form.

Any approach to learning, including artificial neural networks and statistical methods, satisfies the weak criterion. Methods of machine learning that have been inspired by artificial intelligence research have been particularly concerned with the strong criterion. The last, ultrastrong, criterion requires that the user not only understands the induced description, but can also *use* this description without being aided by a computer. That is, the user can execute all the corresponding computations required to apply the induced descriptions in his or her mind.

This chapter, and this book in general, is mainly concerned with the *knowledge-oriented* algorithms capable of developing descriptions understandable to the user. Most of these methods are based on manipulating symbolic structures. Before proceeding further, let us explore the cognitive perspective and the representation issues related to the crucial notion of this approach to machine learning: concept.

1.2.1 Cognitive Perspective

The notion of a *concept* is as vital to machine learning as is chemical compound to chemistry, force field to physics, number to mathematics, and knowledge to artificial intelligence. Throughout this book, we will understand a concept as an abstraction standing for a set of objects sharing some properties that differentiate them from other concepts.

'Bird,' 'tiger,' 'vertebrate,' 'aminoacid,' 'car,' 'rainy day,' 'mathematics,' 'prime number,' 'leukemia,' 'galaxy,' 'despotic ruler,' or 'fertile land' are concepts. Note that their boundaries are not always clear. While no serious problems are posed by 'bird' or 'prime number,' any attempt to define precisely what is meant by a 'despotic ruler' will turn out to be rather tricky because this concept is subjective and context-dependent. Other concepts, such as 'mathematics' or 'galaxy,' have fuzzy boundaries. Even when concepts can be defined precisely (e.g., leukemia), a correct classification of an object (e.g., a patient) based on the available data may present a difficult problem.

In statistics, the notion of a *cluster* is often used. Its meaning is related but different. By a cluster, statisticians usually mean a group of objects that are relatively close to each other according to a chosen numerical distance (which does not need to be Euclidean). A group of students sitting close to each other in the lecture hall represent a cluster. On the other hand, 'students of machine learning' is a concept defined by characteristic features such as the shared interest in the indicated discipline.

In the real world, concepts are never isolated. Groups of related concepts can often be organized into a generalization hierarchy represented by a tree or graph (Figure 1.2). At a given level of the hierarchy, concepts are usually disjoint, but sometimes they can overlap; the difference between them may be small or large. In a generalization hierarchy, a concept can be exemplified not only by the objects at the bottom level, but also by subconcepts at any level below the concept in question. For example, the concept 'bird' is an example of a 'vertebrate', and so is 'eagle.'

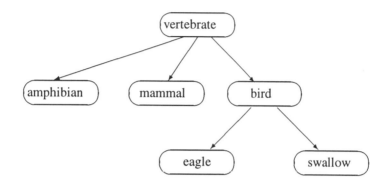

Figure 1.2   Generalization hierarchy.

Three important notions that are germane to the mutual relations among concept deserve brief exposition: basic-level effect, typicality, and contextual dependency.

Psychological findings indicate that in an ordered hierarchy of concepts (e.g., a branch in Figure 1.2), one level can be understood as *basic*. This means that the concept on this level shares with its subconcepts a large number of features that can be described in sensorially recognizable terms.

For illustration, consider the sequence

eagle → bird → animal → living being

Here, the basic-level concept is 'bird' because its subconcepts ('eagle,' 'blackbird,' 'ostrich,' etc.) share features that can be detected by sensors (e.g., wings, feathers, beak). Note that the subconcepts of 'animal'—e.g. reptiles, birds, or mammals—do not share such features and, therefore, the level of 'animal' is not basic. The same goes for 'living being.'

The basic-level concepts can be found in many concept hierarchies. After some thought, the reader will agree that in

BMW → car → transportation means

such a concept is 'car.'

The fact that basic-level concepts are described by features that can be readily identified makes them easy to learn for humans. The concepts on lower levels can then be understood as specializations of the basic-level concepts (e.g., 'birds that can sing'), whereas concepts on higher levels are often defined as groups of basic-level concepts sharing some important feature.

The second useful aspect says how *typical* an instance is for a given concept. In learning, the typicality of instances plays a crucial role—to exemplify 'bird' by penguin, ostrich, and goose will hardly lead to good learner's understanding of the concept. In psychological literature, two ways to measure typicality have been suggested: by the number of features shared with other subconcepts, and by the number of features inherited from superconcepts (the greater the number of inherited features that can be found in the instance, the more typical the instance is).

The third aspect to be considered is *context dependency*. When speaking about students, the speaker can have different concepts in mind: students from the given university, students of computer science, or students from the high school in the neighborhood. Each of them has different connotations, as far as their knowledge, age, and interests are concerned. Obviously, real-world concepts are learnable only in an appropriate context.

Readers interested in more details related to psychological and cognitive aspects of concept acquisition, remembering, and recalling will find a profound analysis in Klimesch (1988).

1.2.2 Representational Issues

The first question to be posed whenever a task is to be solved by a computer is how to translate the problem into computational terms. In machine learning, this means how to represent concepts, examples, and the background knowledge. To describe concepts and examples, *representation languages* are used. In the sequel, some languages encountered in machine learning are outlined. In ascending order of complexity and expressive power, they include zero-order logic, attribute-value logic, Horn clauses, and second-order logic. To avoid unnecessary mathematical complexity, we just give intuitional explanations of these languages.

From now on, we will say that a description *covers* an example if it is true for (or satisfied by) the example. Thus the description has_four_legs covers a lion, but does not cover a goose.

1.2.2.1   ZERO ORDER LOGIC: PROPOSITIONAL CALCULUS

In zero-order logic, also called propositional calculus, examples and concepts are described by conjunctions of Boolean *constants* that stand for the individual features (attribute values). In mathematical terms, this type of description can look something like:

$$c \Leftarrow x \wedge y \wedge z$$

which reads: an object is an instance of the concept c whenever the conditions x, y, and z hold simultaneously.

For illustration, consider the following naïve description of a potential husband for Jane:

$$can\_marry\_jane \Leftarrow male \wedge grown\_up \wedge single$$

Other connectives include negation and disjunction.

The zero-order logic is capable of describing only simple concepts, and the reader will find it difficult to capture in this way complex concepts encountered in daily life. In other words, the zero-order logic has low *descriptive power*. The low descriptive power excludes widespread application of zero-order logic in machine learning, and can only be used to illustrate simple algorithms.

1.2.2.2   ATTRIBUTIONAL LOGIC

Formally, attributional logic is roughly equivalent to zero-order logic but employs a much richer and more flexible notation. The basic idea is to characterize examples and concepts by values of some predefined set of *attributes*, such as color or height. The improvement over the zero-order logic (where concepts are characterized by conjunctions of constants) is that the attributes are *variables* that can take on various values. For instance, the value of the attribute 'color' can be 'green,' 'red,' 'blue,' 'blue or green,' or '*' which stands for *any* color (the 'or' linking two or more attribute values is called *internal disjunction*.

Examples are often presented in a table where each row represents an example and each column stands for an attribute. Thus Table 1.1 contains positive (⊕) and negative (⊖) examples of a car attractive for a young enterpreneur.

Table 1.1   Positive and negative examples of the concept *big* ∨ *(medium ∧ expensive).*

Object	*Make*	*Size*	*Price*	Classification
*car*1	European	big	affordable	⊕
*car*2	Japanese	big	affordable	⊕
*car*3	European	medium	affordable	⊖
*car*4	European	small	affordable	⊖
*car*5	European	medium	expensive	⊕
*car*6	Japanese	medium	affordable	⊖
*car*7	Japanese	medium	expensive	⊕
*car*8	European	big	expensive	⊕

Boolean, numeric, symbolic, or mixed-valued attributes can be considered, and the scope of their values is often constrained by background knowledge. The legal values can often be ordered or partially ordered. Intuitively, ordered values are those that can be expressed by integers, for instance, the length and height as measured in some properly chosen units. Partially ordered values are those that form a hierarchy. For illustration, consider the possible values of the variable 'animal' in Figure 1.2. Note that 'eagle' is more specific than 'bird' but is unrelated to 'amphibian.'

As a description language, attributional logic is significantly more practical than zero-order logic, although in a strict mathematical sense they have equivalent expressiveness. For this reason, attribute-value logic has received considerable attention from machine-learning researchers and provides the basis for such well-known algorithms as TDIDT (Quinlan, 1986) or AQ (Michalski, 1983a). A formal basis for such a description language was defined in *variable-valued logic* (Michalski, 1973a).

1.2.2.3   FIRST ORDER PREDICATE LOGIC: HORN CLAUSES

First order logic provides a formal framework for describing and reasoning about objects, their parts, and relations among the objects and/or the parts. An important subset of first order logic is Horn clauses. A Horn clause consists of a head and a body, as illustrated by the following definition of a grandparent:

```
grandparent(X,Y) :- parent(X,Z), parent(Z,Y)
```

which says that the person X is a grandparent of the person Y if a person Z can be found such that X is a parent of Z, and Z is a parent of Y. The part to the left from ':-' is called the *head* and the part to the right from ':-' is called the *body* of the clause. The commas stand for conjunctions and X, Y, and Z are universally quantified variables.

The words 'grandparent' and 'parent' are called *predicates* and the variables in the parentheses are called *arguments*. The number of arguments can be, in general, arbitrary but is fixed for a given predicate. If all predicates have precisely one argument, the language reduces into the attribute-value logic. If all predicates have precisely zero arguments, the language reduces into zero-order logic.

Horn clauses constitute an advanced representation language that facilitates very complex descriptions. They form the basis of the programming language Prolog and are used, for instance, in the learning system FOIL (Quinlan, 1990).

1.2.2.4   SECOND ORDER LOGIC

Second order logic builds on the idea that the predicate names themselves can be considered as variables. Thus, for instance, the schema

$$p(X,Y) :- q(X,XW) \wedge q(Y,YW) \wedge r(XW,YW)$$

can be instantiated to

```
brothers(X,Y) :- son(X,XW) ∧ son(Y,YW) ∧ equal(XW,YW)
```

by means of the substitution

$$\Theta = \{p = \text{brothers}, q = \text{son}, r = \text{equal}\}$$

Another possible instantiation is

```
lighter(X,Y) :- weight(X,XW) ∧ weight(Y,YW) ∧ less(XW,YW)
```

with the substitution

$$\Theta = \{p = \text{lighter}, q = \text{weight}, r = \text{less}\}$$

So the skeleton of the clause remains untouched and only the predicate names can vary. The rationale behind this idea is that groups of concepts often share the same structure of admissible descriptions. The *second-order schemata* are used to store the most successful of such structures to assist the search for the concept. However, this representation language is rather complex and is rarely used. For an exception, see the program CIA, described in de Raedt (1992).

1.2.2.5 EXPLICITLY CONSTRAINED LANGUAGES

Representation languages based on logic are sometimes so rich and flexible that their use for machine learning is computationally intractable. Therefore, a common practice is to introduce various constraints, such as a limited number of predicates in the clause, a limited number of predicate arguments, or excluded recursive definitions.

Limited occurence of variables in a clause means that the number of variables in the body of the clause is not allowed to exceed a predefined threshold. For instance, only those variables can appear in the body that have already appeared in the head of the clause. Alternatively, precisely one variable not appearing in the head can be allowed to appear in the body. A number of similar constraints of this kind can easily be introduced.

Another restriction can exclude *functions* from predicate arguments. This can become a severe limitation because, in general, an argument need not necessarily be a simple variable but also a calculation, complex algebraic or logic expression, or an n-ary function. The presence of functions significantly increases the space of all possible descriptions.

Finally, an important restriction can exclude *recursive descriptions*. Expressed in first-order logic, the power of recursive descriptions is often demonstrated by the definition of the predicate ancestor:

```
ancestor(X,Y)  :- parent(X,Y).
ancestor(X,Y)  :- parent(X,Z), ancestor(Z,Y).
```

which reads: X is an ancestor of Y either if X is parent of Y or if a person Z can be found such that X is parent of Z and Z is an ancestor of Y.

Although recursively described concepts are sometimes unavoidable, they tend to complicate the learner's task and be difficult to comprehend. Hence, recursions are sometimes explicitly forbidden by the language definition (Michalski, 1980).

1.2.2.6 ALTERNATIVE REPRESENTATIONS

Theoretically, also, some extra-logical representational schemes are possible candidates for concept characterization. Among them, Minsky's *frames* (Minsky, 1975) have been very popular in the artificial intelligence community. Abstract mathematical structures such as *grammars* or *finite automata*, too, can be recommended because they possess structural properties that have been widely explored by mathematicians and are useful for some applications.

However, these representations received relatively limited attention in machine learning. The reader should only bear in mind that even though logical schemes currently prevail in the relevant literature, other options can be considered in future research.

1.3   SEARCH THROUGH THE SPACE OF GENERALIZATIONS

Suppose that a representation language has been selected and that the learner wants to learn a concept from a set of positive and negative examples. Even if the descriptions are based on attribute-value logic, the space of all discernible concepts is surprisingly large. Ten attributes with five possible values for each of them amount to $5^{10} = 9,765,625$ possible vectors. Any subset of such vectors can correspond to a concept, which means that $2^{9,765,625}$ concepts can be defined over these attributes. In more complex languages this number grows even faster, even though background knowledge can limit the size of the representation space.

To cope with the problem of computational tractability, the learner mostly combines two powerful techniques: induction and heuristic search. The discussion of the relevant techniques, together with the analysis of the fundamental reasoning principles employed by the learner, is the task of subsequent subsections.

1.3.1   Inductive Essence of Learning

Imagine that an extraterrestrial scientist lands in the vicinity of your town with the intention of studying terrestrial living forms. The scientist has some preliminary linguistic knowledge which, however, needs polishing. This is why he contacts you as one of the informed aborigines with the question what is 'bird.'

To start with, you point to a 'blackbird' as a positive example of the concept. Nevertheless, simply memorizing all the features of blackbirds will hardly be sufficient to recognize other birds as instances of the same category. Obviously, a generalization of this example is necessary. But how strong a generalization? To establish its limits, the ET will need a negative example, something which is *not* a bird. Knowing that, you suggest a 'dog.' Apparently, one of the differences between dogs and blackbirds is that dogs do not possess wings. (Suppose that, at the beginning, the ET is interested in easily recognizable discriminators.)

To check whether all creatures with wings are birds, the ET will ask whether 'flies' also belong to the same category. Obviously they do not, which is a good indication that the possession of wings is a too general feature for proper discrimination between positive and negative instances. A specialization of this description is necessary. This can be accomplished by way of adding one more feature from an example to the current description. A noticable feature of the blackbird—absent in dogs and flies—is the yellow beak. ET might then assume that a 'crow' is not a bird because it does not have the yellow beak.

The fact that this feature is found only in some of the birds signals that this time the description has become too specific and, again, a proper generalization should be considered. Thus the scientist drops the requirement of the yellow color of the beak and concludes simply that birds are winged creatures with beaks. This description facilitates the recognition of a 'sparrow' as a positive example of a 'bird.'

This simple story illustrates an elementary machine-learning strategy. Let us recapitulate the procedure with a more scientific vocabulary. After the first example (blackbird), the idea of birds is very specialized. ET only knows the *most specific* description of this single example and nothing more. This description can become the first member of the set of the most specific descriptions, denoted by S. Any generalization of the most specific description is possible at this point. Only after the arrival of the first negative example (dog) is the learner able to impose a limit on the generalization, thus obtaining a set of the *most general* descriptions (denoted by G) that correctly cover the positive but not the negative example. From the set G, the scientist selects 'has-wings' as the most appealing.

The next negative example (fly) reveals that the description is *overgeneralized*: wings do not represent a sufficient discriminator between blackbird (positive) and fly (negative). Therefore, the set G has to be specialized. On the other hand, the next positive example (crow) enriches the set S with another most specific description, which calls for another generalization, accomplished by replacing the description 'has-wings' with 'has-wings' and 'has-yellow-beak.'

To summarize, generalization is applied to the set S whenever a new positive example arrives. Conversely, a negative example can necessitate the specialization of the set G. This principle underlies a family of techniques—called Version Space algorithms—that build on the idea of gradual reduction of the space of current *versions* of the concept description. The method was invented and published by Mitchell (1982); for a more recent treatise with extensive bibliography, see Hirsh (1990). An earlier method that viewed concept learning as a series of generalizations and specializations of a single hypothesis (rather than two sets of hypotheses) was presented in a well-known paper by Winston (1970).

For our needs, the details of the algorithm and of its many derivatives are not so important. The above story was meant to demonstrate the fact that concept learning can be conceived as a search through the space of descriptions, the essential search operators being *generalization* and *specialization.*

A good deal of this chapter will deal, directly or indirectly, with this kind of operator. For instance, a description in Horn clauses can be generalized by turning a constant into a variable or by dropping a condition. Hence the clause:

```
p(X,Y)  :- q(X, 2), r(Y, 2).
```

can be generalized into

```
p(X,Y)  :- q(X,Z), r(Y,Z).
```

or into

```
p(X,Y)  :- q(X,2).
```

Specialization can be understood as the complementary operation. In this sense, a Horn clause can be specialized by turning a variable into a constant, or by adding a literal to the clause.

Proper selection of the search operators is (besides the choice of the representation language) the critical task of the designer of a learning program. One of the first attempts to systemize generalization operators was made by Michalski (1983).

1.3.2   Exhaustive Search

A widespread framework for concept learning is *search* through the space of descriptions permitted by the learner's representation language. The merit of this philosophy is obvious: search techniques have been widely investigated by artificial intelligence researchers and are widely understood. The following terms are requisite in the definition of a search technique.

In general, a search process explores *states* in a search space according to the following:

- *Initial state* is the starting position of the search. In machine learning, initial states of-ten correspond to the most specific concept descriptions, i.e., to the positive examples themselves.
- *Termination criterion* is the objective to be arrived at. States that satisfy the termination criterion are referred to as *final states*. In machine learning, the termination criterion can require that the description covers all positive and no negative examples.
- *Search operators* advance the search from one state to another. In machine learning, these operators are mostly generalizations and/or specializations of concept descriptions.
- *Search strategy* determines under what conditions and to which state an operator is to be applied.

The two fundamental strategies of systematic search are depth-first and breadth-first search. These can be easily explained if we visualize the space of all possible states as an oriented graph whose nodes represent the individual states and whose edges represent the search operators.

In *depth-first search* an operator is applied to the initial state S_1, arriving at a new state S_2. If S_2 is not recognized as the final state, then, again, an operator is applied to S_2, thus arriving at a new state S_3. If no new state can be reached in this way and the final state has not yet been found, the system *backtracks* (returns) to the previous state and applies some other operator. If this is not possible, the system backtracks further, until a state is found that allows the application of some of the operators. If no such state can be found, the search terminates. The principle is depicted in Figure 1.3. The numbers in the rectangles indicate the order in which the states are visited.

Breadth-first search constitutes the complementary approach. First, all operators are applied, one by one, to the initial state. The resulting states are then tested. If some of them are recognized as the final state, the algorithm stops. Otherwise, the operators are applied to all subsequent states, then again to the subsequent states, and so on, until the termination criterion is satisfied. The principle is depicted in Figure 1.4.

Note that, unlike depth-first search, breadth-first search assumes no backtracking, which is a slight simplification of the task. On the other hand, the searcher must store many intermediate states, which can render the system much too expensive.

1.3.3   Heuristic Search

The fundamental search techniques are not very efficient in large search spaces, where *heuristics* guiding the search must be considered. The task of the heuristics is to decide which of

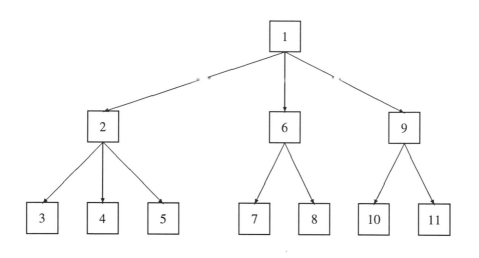

Figure 1.3 Depth-first search.

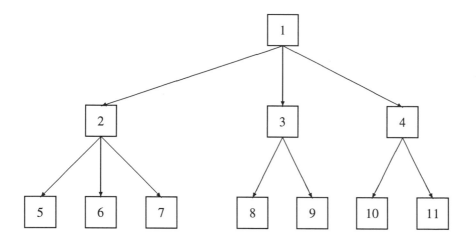

Figure 1.4 Breadth-first search.

the available operators will lead the search to the closest proximity of the final state. This requires an evaluation function to assess the value of each of the states reached. Assume, for the moment, that the evaluation function is given.

1.3.3.1   BEST-FIRST SEARCH ALGORITHM

1. Let the initial state be referred to as the *best* state and let the set of *current states* consist of this single state;
2. If the best state satisfies the given termination criterion, then stop (the best state is the solution of the search);
3. Apply all applicable operators to the best state, thus creating a set of new states that are added to the set of current states;
4. Evaluate all current states. Decide which is the best state and go to 2.

This algorithm differs from the breadth-first algorithm in that it always extends only the most promising state, thus hopefully speeding up the search. The price is the danger of falling to a local maximum of the evaluation function.

The algorithm is illustrated by the following example.

Example

The learner tries to derive the concept description from the set of eight positive and negative examples described by the attribute values as shown in Table 1.2. '$\oplus$' stands for 'positive example' and '$\ominus$' stands for 'negative example.' Assume two operators: 'specialize the current description by adding a conjunction' and 'generalize the current description by adding a disjunction.'

Table 1.2   Positive and negative examples for concept learning.

example	$at1$	$at2$	$at3$	classif.
$e1$	a	x	n	$\oplus$
$e2$	b	x	n	$\oplus$
$e3$	a	y	n	$\ominus$
$e4$	a	z	n	$\ominus$
$e5$	a	y	m	$\oplus$
$e6$	b	y	n	$\ominus$
$e7$	b	y	m	$\oplus$
$e8$	a	x	m	$\oplus$

Let the initial state be 'any description.' The application of the specialization operator (generalization has no sense, here) will produce the following descriptions: $at1 = a, at1 = b, at2 = x, at2 = y, at2 = z, at3 = m$, and $at3 = n$. Among them, $at2 = x$ and $at3 = m$ do not cover any $\ominus$ and will probably achieve the highest value of a reasonable evaluation function. Suppose that, for some reason, $at2 = x$ is preferred and will thus become the *best* description.

Since some $\oplus$'s in the table are now not covered, the learner will try to apply the search operators to the best description. Applying the specialization operator only worsens the situation by reducing the number of $\oplus$'s covered. However, by generalizing the description into $at2 = x \vee at2 = y$ the number of $\oplus$'s covered increased. Suppose that the evaluation function confirms this description as better than $at2 = x$.

The new description covers all $\oplus$'s but, on the other hand, it also covers two $\ominus$'s. Thus, in the next step, the description is specialized into $at2 = x \vee [(at2 = y) \wedge X]$, where X stands for any of the following conjuncts. $at1 = a, at1 = b, at3 = m$, and $at3 = n$.

Among the new states, the best one is $at2 = x \vee [(at2 = y) \wedge (at3 = m)]$. As it covers all $\oplus$'s and no $\ominus$'s, the search terminates.   □

The best-first search may require excessive memory because it stores all the generated states. A more economical approach is the *beam-search* that only retains N best states at any time.

1.3.3.2   BEAM-SEARCH ALGORITHM

1. Let the initial state be the *best* state;
2. If the best state satisfies some termination criterion, stop;
3. If the number of current states is larger than N, keep only the N best states and delete all others;
4. Apply the search operators to the best state, and add the newly created states to the set of current states;
5. Evaluate all states and go to 2.

A popular instantiation of the beam-search algorithm is defined by $N = 1$ and is sometimes called *hill-climbing* algorithm. The name is meant to emphasize the resemblance to hill climbers striving to find the shortest trajectory to the peak and always picking the steepest path.

Readers interested in more detailed information about search techniques are referred to the artificial intelligence literature, for instance, Charniak and McDermott (1985) or Bratko (1990).

1.4   CLASSIC METHODS OF LEARNING

Having explained the principles of generalization and specialization operators as well as some basic search techniques, we can proceed with two essential learning principles, namely divide-and-conquer learning and the AQ-philosophy. Both are crucial for the understanding of more advanced methods.

1.4.1   Divide-and-Conquer Learning

The essence of this method is very simple: the entire set of examples is split into subsets that are more easy to handle. In attributional logic, the partitioning is carried out along attribute values so that all examples in a subset share the same value of the given attribute.

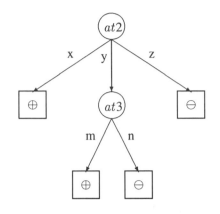

Figure 1.5   A decision tree.

In Table 1.2, the attribute $at1$ splits the set of eight examples into the subset defined by $at1 = a$ and the subset defined by $at1 = b$. Similarly, $at3$ imposes an alternative split into two subsets, one defined by $at3 = m$ and the other defined by $at3 = n$. Finally, $at2$ imposes decomposition into three subsets defined by $at2 = x$, $at2 = y$, and $at2 = z$, respectively.

This principle underlies the popular algorithm for induction of decision trees (see Breiman *et al.*, 1984; and Quinlan, 1986), known under the acronym TDIDT (Top-Down Induction of Decision Trees) or ID3. With a properly defined evaluation function, the TDIDT-algorithm described below will derive the decision tree in Figure 1.5 from the examples in Table 1.2. The reader is encouraged to check that the concept description in the tree is really consistent with the table. For instance, the example $e1$ has $at2 = x$, which sends it downward along the leftmost branch, only to end up in the box labeled with $\oplus$. The example $e3$ has $at2 = y$ and will be passed down the middle branch, arriving at the test on attribute $at3$; having the value $at3 = n$, the example follows the right-hand branch, ending up at the box labeled with $\ominus$.

Note that the tree can be rewritten into the following logical expressions:

$$(class = \oplus) \leftarrow (at2 = x) \vee [(at2 = y) \wedge (at3 = m)]$$
$$(class = \ominus) \leftarrow (at2 = z) \vee [(at2 = y) \wedge (at3 = n)]$$

Any future example will be classified according to these two formulae or the decision tree. The classification of examples that do not satisfy either of these rules (for instance, if the example has $at2 = w$ which is a value unseen during training) can be based on the distance between the example description and the rules. Alternatively, an 'I-don't-know' answer can be issued.

1.4.1.1   TDIDT ALGORITHM

S ... the set of examples

1. Find the 'best' attribute at;

2. Split the set S into the subsets $S_1, S_2, \ldots$, so that all examples in the subset S_i have $at = v_i$. Each subset constitutes a node in the decision tree;
3. For each S_i: if all examples in S_i belong to the same class ($\oplus$ or $\ominus$), then create a leaf of the decision tree and label it with this class label. Otherwise, perform the same procedure (go to 1) with $S = S_i$.

The algorithm terminates when all subsets are labeled or when no further attributes splitting the unlabeled sets are available (in this case, some leaves of the tree will cover examples of both classes).

1.4.1.2 HOW TO FIND THE 'BEST' ATTRIBUTE?

Assume two classes ($\oplus$ and $\ominus$) of examples described by attribute values. The task is to find the best attribute for step 1 in the previous algorithm. A plausible criterion is based on the number of $\oplus$'s and $\ominus$'s in each of the subsets generated by the different attribute values.

After some thought, the reader will agree that we need a function satisfying the following requirements:

1. The function reaches its maximum when all subsets are homogeneous, i.e., all examples in S_i are $\oplus$ or all examples in S_i are $\ominus$. In this case, the information about the attribute value is sufficient to decide whether the example is positive or negative;
2. The function reaches its miminum when 50% of the examples in each of the subsets are positive and 50% are negative;
3. The function should be steep when close to the extremes (100% positives and 0% negatives or *vice versa*) and flat when in the 50%–50% region.

Mathematicians know that information is maximized when another important quantity, *entropy*, is minimized. Entropy determines the extent of randomness, 'unstructuredness', and chaos in the data. In our context, the entropy of the subset S_i can be calculated by means of the following formula:

$$H(S_i) = -p_i^+ \log p_i^+ - p_i^- \log p_i^-$$

where p_i^+ is the probability that a randomly taken example in S_i is $\oplus$ and can be estimated by the relative frequency $p_i^+ = \frac{n_i^+}{n_i^+ + n_i^-}$; similarly, p_i^- is the probability that a randomly taken example in S_i is $\ominus$ and can be estimated by $p_i^- = \frac{n_i^-}{n_i^+ + n_i^-}$. Here, n_i^+ is the number of $\oplus$'s in S_i and n_i^- is the number of $\ominus$'s in S_i.

Let the values of attribute *at* split the set S of examples into the subsets $S_i, i = 1, \ldots K$. Then the entropy of the system of subsets S_i is:

$$H(S, at) = \Sigma_{i=1}^{K} P(S_i) \cdot H(S_i)$$

where $H(S_i)$ is the entropy of the subset S_i; $P(S_i)$ is the probability of an example belonging to S_i and can be estimated by the relative size of the subset S_i in S: $P(S_i) = \frac{|S_i|}{|S|}$.

The information gain achieved by the partitioning along *at* is measured by the entailed decrease in entropy:

$$I(S, at) = H(S) - H(S, at)$$

where $H(S)$ is the *a priori* entropy of S (before the splitting) and $H(S, at)$ is the entropy of the system of subsets generated by the values of *at*.

Let us demostrate the use of these formulae by building a decision tree from the examples in Table 1.2.

Since there are 5 positives and 3 negatives among the 8 examples in S, the *a priori* entropy of the system S is:

$$
\begin{aligned}
H(S) &= -p^+ \log p^+ - p^- \log p^- \\
&= -(5/8) \log(5/8) - (3/8) \log(3/8) \\
&= 0.954 bits
\end{aligned}
$$

Note that this entropy is close to its maximum ($0.954 \doteq 1$) because the number of $\oplus$'s is about the same as the number of $\ominus$'s. If the number of $\oplus$'s were much larger than that of $\ominus$'s (or *vice versa*), than we would have a high chance of a correct guess of the class by simply assuming that it is always $\oplus$. This would correspond to small entropy.

What will be the entropy of the different partitions as generated by the individual attributes? For instance, attribute *at2* can acquire three different values, x, y, and z. For each of them, we obtain the entropies of the related subsets S_x, S_y, and S_z:

$$
at2 : \quad
\begin{aligned}
H(S_y) &= -(2/4) \log(2/4) - (2/4) \log(2/4) = 1 \ bit \\
H(S_x) &= -1 \cdot \log 1 - 0 \cdot \log 0 = 0 \ bit \\
H(S_z) &= -0 \cdot \log 0 - 1 \cdot \log 1 = 0 \ bit
\end{aligned}
$$

and determine the overall entropy as their weighted sum:

$$H(S, at2) = (3/8) \cdot 0 + (1/8) \cdot 0 + (4/8) \cdot 1 = 0.5 \ bit$$

Calculating the entropies for the remaining attributes similarly, we will arrive at the following information gains:

$$
\begin{aligned}
I(S, at2) &= H(S) - H(S, at2) = 0.954 - 0.500 = 0.454 \ bits \\
I(S, at1) &= H(S) - H(S, at1) = 0.954 - 0.951 = 0.003 \ bits \\
I(S, at3) &= H(S) - H(S, at3) = 0.954 - 0.607 = 0.347 \ bits
\end{aligned}
$$

Evidently, *at2* yields the highest information gain (0.454 bits), and thus ought to be selected as the root of the tree. This is how the tree from Figure 1.5 was created.

The use of entropy is just one of many possibilities. Several alternative attribute-selection criteria have been suggested. Some can be found in Breimann *et al.* (1984) and in Mingers (1989a).

1.4.1.3 PROBABILITY ESTIMATION

Estimating the probabilities p_i^+ and p_i^- by relative frequencies is far from ideal because the estimates are reliable only with sufficiently large sets of examples. However, in the process of a decision-tree generation, the number of examples quickly decreases with each subsequent splitting. Assume that only two examples are left and that both of them have the class of $\oplus$. Then, a naïve learner will conclude that the probability of the class $\oplus$ is 100%, which may not be true.

For this reason, improved methods to estimate probabilities have been put forward. For instance, the m-estimate (Cestnik, 1990) calculates the probabilities by the following formula:

$$p_\oplus = \frac{n_\oplus + m p_a}{N + m}$$

where $n_\oplus$ is the number of $\oplus$'s, N is the total number of examples in the subset ($N = n_\oplus + n_\ominus$), p_a is the *prior* probability of $\oplus$, and m is the parameter of the estimate. In the case of much noise in the examples, m should be set high, and for low noise m is set low. In any case, the user or the expert who understands the domain and the level of noise should recommend a corresponding setting for m and p_a.

A special case of the m-estimate is the Laplace law of succession (or simply Laplace estimate) which is for two classes, $\oplus$ and $\ominus$, given by:

$$p_\oplus = \frac{n_\oplus + 1}{N + 2}$$

The appropriateness of this formula is illustrated by the simple experiment in Table 1.3. Suppose you are tossing a coin, each time arriving at one of the two possible outcomes, heads and tails. The table gives the probabilities of heads (in percent) obtained from relative frequencies and from the Laplace estimate. Clearly, the Laplace estimate gives more realistic results.

Table 1.3 Probability (in percentage) of heads in tossing a coin.

toss No.	1	2	3	4	5
outcome	heads	heads	tails	heads	tails
relative frequency	100	100	67	75	60
Laplace estimate	67	75	60	67	57

1.4.1.4 PRUNING THE TREES

A few pitfalls can put the use of a decision tree in question. One of them is *overfitting*. A tree branch (ending with a class label) might have been created from examples that are noisy, in the sense that the attribute values or class labels are erroneous. Obviously, this branch, or rather some of its decision tests, will be misleading. Second, if the number of attributes is large, the tree may contain tests on random features that are actually irrelevant for correct classifications.

Thus, for instance, the color of a car does not matter if we are interested in the principle of the engine. In spite of that, the attribute can appear in the trees whenever many cars with, say, combustion-based engines happen to be red. Finally, very large trees are hard to interpret and the user will perceive them as a black box representation.

For all these reasons, it may be beneficial to prune the resulting tree by the method indicated in Figure 1.6.

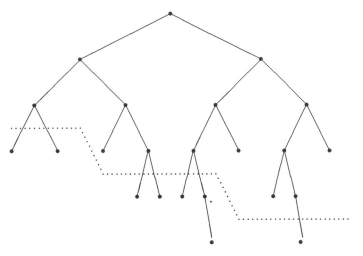

Figure 1.6   Pruning decision trees.

In principle, two approaches to pruning are possible: on-line pruning and post-pruning. The essence of *on-line pruning* is to stop the tree growing when the information gain caused by the partitioning of the example set falls below a certain threshold. *Post-pruning* methods prune out some of the branches after the tree has been completed.

A popular approach to pruning, known as *minimal-error* pruning, was designed by Niblett and Bratko (1986). This technique aims at pruning the tree to such an extent that the overall expected classification error on new examples is minimized. For this purpose, the classification error is estimated for each node in the tree. In the leaves, the error is estimated using one of the methods for estimating the probability that a new object falling into this leaf will be misclassified. Suppose that N is the number of examples that end up in the leaf, and e is the number of these examples that are misclassified at this leaf. Niblett and Bratko (1986) used the Laplace estimate $(e + 1)/(N + k)$ (where k is the number of all the classes) to estimate the expected error. Cestnik and Bratko (1991) showed that using the m-estimate instead of the Laplace estimate gives better results. For a non-leaf node of the decision tree, its classification error is estimated as the weighted sum of the classification errors of the node's subtrees. The weights are calculated as relative frequencies of the examples passing from the node into the corresponding subtrees. This non-leaf error estimate is called a backed-up error. Now the classification error in a non-leaf node is also estimated for the case when its subtrees were pruned out, and the non-leaf would thus become a leaf. If this error estimate is lower than the backed-up error, the subtrees will be pruned out. This process of pruning subtrees starts at the bottom levels of the tree and propagates upwards as long as the backed-up errors are higher than the 'static estimates'.

Several alternative approaches to pruning are reviewed by Mingers (1989b) and Esposito *et al.* (1993).

1.4.1.5   OTHER MOTIVATIONS FOR TREE SIMPLIFICATION

Figure 1.7 illustrates another type of tree simplification, this time with the objective to carry out a kind of *constructive induction* (Michalski, 1983a). The learning system strives to create new attributes as logical expressions over the attributes provided by the teacher. Constructive induction can be profitable in situations where a subtree is replicated in more than one position in the tree—see Figures 1.8 and 1.9.

1.4.1.6   COPING WITH NUMERIC DATA

So far, the analysis has been restricted to symbolic attributes. However, decision trees can also be induced from numerical attributes. One possibility is to provide one additional step, the *binarization* of the numeric attributes, that means thresholding their numerical ranges into pairs of subintervals to be treated as symbols. Figure 1.10 shows a decision tree built from numeric data. At each node, the respective attribute value is tested against threshold T_i.

The threshold position in the range of values can, again, be determined by entropy. Suppose that attribute $at1$ is to be discretized. First, we order all the examples according to the value of $at1$ and observe the classification values. In the case illustrated by Figure 1.11, the classification values $\oplus$ and $\ominus$ decompose the set of 80 examples into four regions (in realistic settings, the number of such regions is likely to be larger). The candidate splitting cuts lie on the boundaries between the regions. Then, the information gain of each of these cuts is calculated as explained earlier, and the cut providing the highest information gain is selected (for a detailed and rigorous discussion of this mechanism see Fayyad and Irani, 1992).

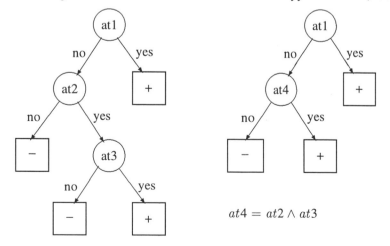

Figure 1.7   Constructive induction in decision trees. A new attribute, *at4*, is constructed.

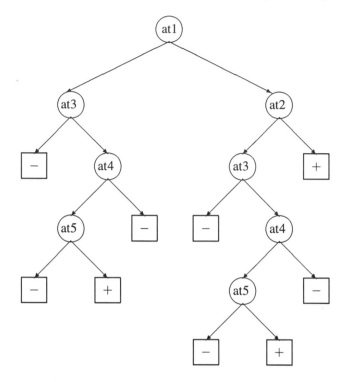

Figure 1.8   The replication problem in decision trees.

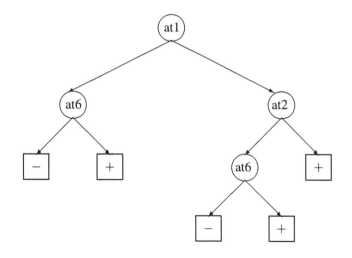

Figure 1.9   Simplified version of the tree from the previous figure.

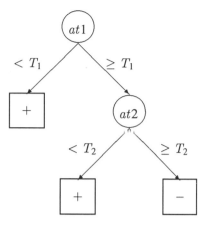

Figure 1.10   Decision tree induced from numeric attributes.

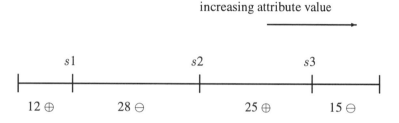

Figure 1.11   Examples sorted by the values of an attribute; $s1$, $s2$, and $s3$ are candidate split points.

The numeric version of the TDIDT algorithm will thus look as follows:

Algorithm for numeric TDIDT

1. Use the entropy measure to find the optimal split for each of the numeric attributes;
2. Determine the attribute whose optimal split maximizes entropy and partition the example set along this attribute into two subsets;
3. If the termination criterion is not satisfied, repeat the procedure recursively for each subset.

Note that with each new subtree, the splitting cuts must be re-calculated. The optimal position for a cut is likely to be different in a different subset of examples.

1.4.2   Progressive Coverage: AQ Learning

The AQ learning is based on the idea of progressive coverage of the training data by consecutively generated decision rules. The approach has been implemented in a whole family of methods derived from an algorithm that was first published by Michalski (1969) and then adapted for machine learning purposes by Michalski (1973b). One of the most recent versions of the family is described by Wnek *et al.* (1995).

The essence is to search for a set of rules (conjunctions of attribute-value pairs or, generally, arbitrary predicates) that covers all $\oplus$'s but none of the $\ominus$'s. Instead of partitioning the example sets, the AQ algorithm generalizes, step-by-step, the descriptions of selected positive examples, called *seeds*. This allows the rules to logically intersect whenever desirable.

1.4.2.1   BASIC PRINCIPLE

The principle is summarized in a simplified version of the algorithm presented below. Assume that the goal is to find a minimal set of *decision rules* characterizing the given concept. Decision rules will acquire the form:

$$\text{if } A_1 \text{ and } A_2 \text{ and} \dots \text{and } A_n \text{ then } C$$

where C is the concept, and conditions A_i can acquire the common attribute-value form of $at_i = V$, or the more general form of $at_i = v_1 \lor v_2 \lor v_3 \dots$, where an attribute can take on one of several values (linked by 'internal' disjunctions).

AQ Algorithm (simplified version)

1. Divide all examples into the subsets *PE* of $\oplus$'s and *NE* of $\ominus$'s;
2. Choose randomly or by design one example from *PE* and call it the *seed*;
3. Find a set of maximally general rules characterizing the seed. The limit of the generalization is defined by the set *NE*: a generalized description of the seed is not allowed to cover any object from *NE*. The set of rules obtained is called the *star*;
4. According to some *preference criterion*, select the best rule in the star;
5. If this rule, jointly with all previously generated rules, covers all objects from *PE*, then stop. Otherwise, find another seed among the uncovered examples in *PE* and go to 3.

Step 3 is done by a special *star generation procedure* (Wnek *et al.*, 1995). The *rule preference criterion* in step 4 should reflect the needs of the problem at hand. To this end, it can be a combination of various elementary criteria such as requirements to maximize the number of $\oplus$'s covered by the rule, minimize the number of attributes involved, maximize the estimate of generality (the number of $\oplus$'s covered divided by the number of all examples covered by the rule), minimize the costs of attribute-value measurements, and the like. It can also use attribute selection criteria used in decision tree learning, such as entropy, gain ratio, etc. The algorithm also makes it possible to construct a set of decision rules with different relationships among the individual rules. Rules may be logically intersecting, logically disjoint, or linearly ordered (which requires their evaluation in a sequential order).

The next example illustrates this simple version of the algorithm.

Example

Suppose that the examples, described in terms of attributes $at1, at2$, and $at3$, are those listed in Table 1.4 and visualized in Figure 1.12. In Table 1.4, each row corresponds to one vector of attribute-values. Rows corresponding to positive examples are labeled by $\oplus$ and rows

Table 1.4 A specification of a sample training set.

example		at1	at2	at3	classification
	e1	y	n	r	⊕
PE	e2	x	m	r	⊕
	e3	y	n	s	⊕
	e4	x	n	r	⊕
	f1	x	m	s	⊖
	f2	y	m	t	⊖
NE	f3	y	n	t	⊖
	f4	z	n	t	⊖
	f5	z	n	r	⊖
	f5	x	n	s	⊖

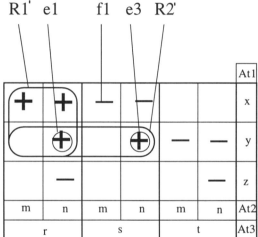

Figure 1.12   Visualization of the examples from Table 1.4.

corresponding to negative examples are labeled by ⊖. Assume that the preference criterion favors rules that cover the maximum possible number of positive examples, and that the rules can intersect each other. The program leading to rule acquisition from the above examples will consist of the following steps:

Select 1st seed: e1
   Pick the first negative example: $f1$. To create the star of seed $e1$ (that is the set of maximally general descriptions of $e1$), begin by creating the set of all descriptions of $e1$ that do not cover $f1$. They are:

$R1$: $(at3 = r \lor t)$
$R2$: $(at1 = y \lor z)$
$R3$: $(at2 = n)$

However, each of these descriptions also covers some of negative examples. Therefore, these rules are specialized so as to exclude these negative examples, which is done by multiplying out the current rules by the negations of the negative examples, and applying absorption laws. The results are:

$R1'$: $(at1 = x \lor y)$ & $(at3 = r)$
$R2'$: $(at1 = y)$ & $(at3 = r \lor s)$

This is the star of $e1$. Suppose that the preference criterion recommends choosing from the star the rule that covers the most positive examples. Thus, $R1'$ is selected (it covers three examples while $R2'$ covers only two). The next step is to select a new seed from still uncovered positive examples. Only one such example exists, $e3$.

Select next seed: $e3$
Again, determine the star for the new seed. Two rules are generated. The one that covers more examples is the same as $R2'$ shown above.

As there are no uncovered examples left, the selected rules $R1'$ and $R2'$ constitute a complete and consistent description of the concept, which optimizes the assumed preference criterion:

$R1'$ $(at1 = x \lor y)$ & $(at3 = r)$
$R2'$ $(at1 = y)$ & $(at3 = r \lor s)$

Learning systems based on the AQ-algorithm can easily incorporate background knowledge because such knowledge is often also represented by decision rules. Nevertheless, we will not deal with this feature here because the employment of background knowledge is more typical for predicate-logic-based learning systems that will be addressed later.

1.4.2.2   THE TWO-TIERED APPROACH

In AQ-based methods, the output has the form of decision rules. To handle context imprecision and noise in the data, the *two-tiered* approach has been invented (for a detailed treatise, see Michalski, 1990). This approach also facilitates handling context sensitivity and improves comprehensibility in the AQ-paradigm.

The principal idea is to split the concept description into two parts: *base concept representation* (BCR) containing the explicit concept characterization stored in the learner's memory; and the *inferential concept interpretation* (ICI) containing a set of inference rules to be applied in the recognition phase.

For illustration, the BCR can contain the production rule

if A_1 *and* A_2 *and ... and* A_n **then** X

and the ICI can contain the interpretational rule

'at least 3 conditions out of $A_1 \ldots A_n$ must be satisfied.'

A very simple example of the two-tiered approach is the TRUNC method, which consists of the following general steps:

1. Use AQ to derive the initial set of rules;
2. Determine the 'importance' of each rule. A simple measure of importance is the number of positive examples covered by the rule. Save only the most important rules in BCR;
3. Define the ICI procedure for the correct recognition of uncovered examples by the rules in BCR.

When the induced representation is used for recognition, the new example is assigned the class of that rule in BCR that provides the 'best match' according to ICI. A *flexible matching* procedure was proposed for that purpose.

Readers interested in more details about the two-tiered approach and some of its implementation are referred to Michalski (1990), Zhang and Michalski (1991), Bergadano *et al.* (1992), or Kubat (1996).

1.4.3   Assessment of Learning Algorithms

During the last two decades, machine learning researchers have come up with so many learning algorithms that criteria for their assessment and taxonomization are indispensable. Some of them are summarized in Table 1.5.

Table 1.5   Assessment of ML-algorithms.

criterion	comments
accuracy	percentage of correctly classified $\oplus$'s and $\ominus$'s
efficiency	# examples needed, computational tractability
robustness	against noise, against incompleteness
special requirements	incrementality, concept drift
concept complexity	representational issues (examples and *BK*)
transparency	comprehensibility for the human user

Perhaps the most important criterion is *accuracy*. As the usual motivation of concept learning is the correct identification of future instances, the success of learning is quite straightforwardly measured by the percentage of correctly classified testing examples. Suppose that the learner is asked to classify a set of 200 examples, out of which 100 are $\oplus$ and 100 are $\ominus$. If the learner correctly classifies 80 $\oplus$'s and 60 $\ominus$'s, then the accuracy is $\frac{80+60}{200} = 0.7$, that is 70%.

Sometimes it is more important to know how many times the system recognizes the positives, while the negatives can be much less critical (or *vice versa*). In that case we draw distinction between two kinds of error: negatively classified positives (erros of omission) and positively classified negatives (errors of commision). These errors can tell the user that the learned

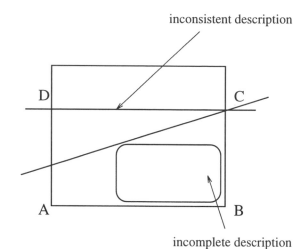

Figure 1.13   Illustration of incompleteness and inconsistency.

concept description is too specialized or too general. In the case of overspecialization, the learner will tend to misclassify positive testing examples more often than negatives. In the case of overgeneralization, the learner will more frequently fail by misclassifying negative examples (classifying them as positives).

Ideally, the learner should develop a hypothesis (internal description of the concept) that is *consistent* (does not cover any ⊖) and *complete* (covers all ⊕'s). Inconsistency and incompleteness are illustrated in Figure 1.13. In the space described by two numeric variables (one represented by the horizontal axis and the other by the vertical axis) the concept to be found is the shaded area below the oblique line separating the upper and the lower part of the rectangle. The description represented by the oval is incomplete because it does not cover the entire area of the concept. The rectangle *ABCD* is inconsistent because it also covers a part of the negative area.

Classification accuracy is only one of the criteria for the assessment of machine learning algorithms. The learner should also be efficient—able to achieve a certain level of accuracy with the *minimum* number of learning examples. The teacher might not be always able to provide many examples and, anyway, the ability to learn fast is a sign of intelligence. Also, *computational requirements* are of interest—how much time the computer needs to arrive at a good hypothesis.

Another criterion is concerned with the *comprehensibility* of the induced concept description. It is often important that the description generated be understandable so that the user learns something new from it about the application domain. Such a description can be used by humans directly and understood as an enhancement to their own knowledge. This criterion also applies when the induced descriptions are to be employed in a knowledge-based system whose behaviour should be transparent. The criterion of comprehensility typically separates machine learning in artificial intelligence from other forms of learning, including neural networks and statistical methods. As mentioned in Section 1.2 of this chapter, Michie (1988) further elaborated criteria that are germane to comprehensibility. Early effort in this direction was reported by Michalski (1983).

A serious intricacy in learning is the presence of noise (error) in the examples and/or in their class labels. The measurement devices providing the attribute values may be imprecise or improperly adjusted, the attribute values supplied by the teacher may be too subjective, an accident can damage the data, or some of the data may get lost. Many unpleasant misfortunes can happen to the examples before their presentation to the machine. Quite logically, *robustness against noise* and *robustness against missing information* (e.g., missing attribute values) is required. However, this is no dogma! Some learning tasks are characterized by the presence of noise and missing information, and others are characterized by perfect examples. The concrete application must decide whether this criterion matters.

The specific conditions of the application should really be taken seriously. For instance, the user can demand that the learner be able to acquire the knowledge on-line from a stream of examples arriving one by one (as opposed to the situation where all examples are present from the very beginning). Imagine that a new example is presented at the moment when an initial concept description has already been developed. In traditional batch algorithms, this would mean re-running the entire learning procedure on all data. Such behavior can hardly be called intelligent. The learner should be capable of refining the previous knowledge, to *learn incrementally*, like humans.

Incremental learning is particularly important in the presence of *concept drift* or *evolution* (Widmer and Kubat, 1993, 1996). In some domains, the meaning of a concept changes from time to time. This can be illustrated by such terms as 'fashionable dress' or 'democracy.' The learner should be able to follow the drift in the same way as humans do.

Finally, the designer must consider the representational issues, which means respecting the language used to describe the examples as well as the language in which the background knowledge has been encoded. The reader has already seen that various representational languages differ in their expressiveness. For instance, while the TDIDT algorithm pertains to attribute-value logic, more advanced systems that will be discussed in the next section are able to learn concepts from examples described by predicate expressions.

1.5   HOW CAN PREDICATE LOGIC BE USED?

As already mentioned, attribute-value languages are very useful but have their limitations. Even though a lot can be described in this way, logical descriptions with predicates that describe relations among objects or their parts are certainly more powerful. Consider the background knowledge about family relations shown in Figure 1.14 (for simplicity, the names of the persons are '1,' '2,' ... instead of 'John,' 'Bill,' ...). Here, the family relations are described by the single predicate parent(X,Y), for instance, parent(1,2) means 1 is the parent of 2.

The family tree can be encoded by the following set of relationships:

$$\texttt{parent} = \{(1,2)(1,3)(3,4)(3,5)(3,6)(4,7)\}$$

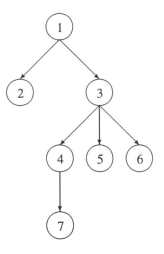

Figure 1.14 Family relations.

Suppose that with these relationships in the background knowledge, the system wants to learn the meaning of grandparent (X, Y). Suppose, further, that the teacher provides the following positive examples of the concept:

```
grandparent(1,4)
grandparent(1,5)
grandparent(1,6)
grandparent(3,7)
```

Again, these are easier to encode by the set of relationships:

$$\text{grandparent} = \{(1,4)(1,5)(1,6)(3,7)\}$$

All other family relations among the persons $1, \ldots 7$ are assumed to be negative examples of grandparent.

Of course, these relations can also be described by attribute values. For instance, each possible pair of persons (X, Y) can be represented by a Boolean attribute whose truth value is determined by the truth value of the predicate relation parent (X, Y). However, such descriptions are rather cumbersome and inflexible.

Higher-level description languages require more sophisticated algorithms, and the task of the next section is to present a few ideas for learning in predicate logic. Effort will be made to begin with principles that are already known, and gradually proceed to more elaborate techniques.

The most popular approach to learning in predicate logic is Inductive Logic Programming (ILP), which is currently an intensively studied branch of machine learning. For more detailed coverage, see the books by Muggleton (1992) or Lavrač and Džeroski (1994).

1.5.1   Learning Horn Clauses from Relations

Suppose you are asked to write a program capable of learning the concept of `grandparent` from examples of family relationships. The concept is to be described by Horn clauses. What learning strategies would you apply?

Trying to express the concept in the simplest possible way, you will start with the language where only those arguments are allowed in the body that also appear in the head. Assume that the concept description is a set of Horn clauses in the form of:

$$C_1 :\text{-} L_{11}, L_{12}, \ldots L_{1m}$$
$$C_2 :\text{-} L_{21}, L_{22}, \ldots L_{2m}$$
$$\ldots$$

where the predicate C_i is the head of a clause and the literals L_{ij} form the body of the clause. The commas separating the literals in the body indicate that they are linked by conjunction. Each of the literals represents a relation that has $n \geq 0$ arguments.

Recall the divide-and-conquer principle or the AQ method, where the learner started with a relatively general description involving a single attribute, and then gradually specialized by adding more conditions. Why not use the same principle here as well?

Since adding a literal to a clause body has a similar specializing effect as adding a condition to a decision rule in AQ or appending a node at the bottom of a decision tree, a good strategy is to start with a clause consisting solely of the head and then specialize it by adding literals to its body.

As there are no other predicates in the background knowledge except for *parent*, and as only those variables are allowed in the body that also appear in the head, possible clauses to define grandparent in this language are:

```
grandparent(X,Y)  :- parent(X,Y).
grandparent(X,Y)  :- parent(Y,X).
grandparent(X,Y)  :- parent(X,X).
grandparent(X,Y)  :- parent(Y,Y).
```

Unfortunately, none of these clauses covers any of the positive examples. Obviously, the restriction should be relaxed allowing also for one argument that does not appear in the head of the clause. Four literals of this kind can be constructed: `parent(X,Z)`, `parent(Y,Z)`, `parent(Z,X)` and `parent(Z,Y)`. Suppose that the system selects the following option:

```
grandparent(X,Y)  :- parent(X,Z).
```

Let us now examine for which triplets (X,Z,Y), satisfying this clause, the head of the clause represents a positive example and for which it represents a negative example. Note that there are $7^3 = 343$ possible triplets (X,Z,Y).

$\oplus$: (1,2,4) (1,2,5) (1,2,6) (1,3,4) (1,3,5) (1,3,6) (3,4,7) (3,5,7) (3,6,7)
$\ominus$: (1,2,1) (1,2,2) (1,2,3) (1,2,7) (1,3,1) (1,3,2) (1,3,3) (1,3,7) (3,4,1)

(3,4,2) (3,4,3) (3,4,4) (3,4,5) (3,4,6) (3,5,1) (3,5,2) (3,5,3) (3,5,4)
(3,5,5) (3,5,6) (3,6,1) (3,6,2) (3,6,3) (3,6,4) (3,6,5) (3,6,6) (4,7,1)
(4,7,2) (4,7,3) (4,7,4) (4,7,5) (4,7,6) (4,7,7)

A closer look reveals that the positive triplets include all four positive examples and the negative triplets include 17 negative examples: (1,1) (1,2) (1,3) (1,7) (3,1) (3,2) (3,3) (3,4) (3,5) (3,6) (4,1) (4,2) (4,3) (4,4) (4,5) (4,6) (4,7).

We say that the clause grandparent(X,Y) :- parent(X,Z) is inconsistent because it also covers negative examples. The inconsistenty can be reduced by a properly chosen specialization of the clause. This can be accomplished by adding some of the other permitted literals to it. Let us try the following:

```
grandparent(X,Y) :- parent(X,Z), parent(Z,Y).
```

This clause covers the following triplets (X,Z,Y):

⊕: (1,3,4) (1,3,5) (1,3,6) (3,4,7)
⊖: none

Since all of the positives and none of the negatives are covered, the learner is satisfied with this clause and stops here.

What if some other literal instead of parent(Z,Y) were added? Consider the next clause:

```
grandparent(X,Y) :- parent(X,Z), parent(Y,Z).
```

Despite the fact that the clause does not cover any negative examples, the use of the clause is questionable because it does not cover any positives either. Obviously, a suitable criterion to decide what literal to add to a clause is needed.

Let us examine a more complicated concept, say, ancestor. Based on the seven persons whose family relations are known from Figure 14, the following positive examples are provided:

```
ancestor = {(1,2) (1,3) (1,4) (1,5) (1,6) (1,7) (3,4) (3,5) (3,6) (3,7) (4,7)}
```

The search for the best literal (involving the same arguments as the head) arrives at the following description:

```
ancestor(X,Y) :- parent(X,Y).
```

This clause is consistent, so there is no need for specialization. The system will store it and—because the description is incomplete—will attempt to find an alternative clause covering those positives that lie outside the reach of the first clause. The result is then interpreted in such a way that at least one of the clauses should cover the example if it is to be a positive instance of the concept. Repeating the procedure, the following three clauses can be determined:

```
ancestor(X,Y) :- parent(X,Y).
```

```
ancestor(X,Y) :- parent(X,Z), parent(Z,Y).
ancestor(X,Y) :- parent(X,Z), parent(Z,W), parent(W,Y).
```

Even though these clauses cover all learning examples, we know that they are not complete because they cover only four generations. A reader acquainted with logic programming, would recommend a *recursive* description:

```
ancestor(X,Y) :- parent(X,Y).
ancestor(X,Y) :- parent(X,Z), ancestor(Z,Y).
```

A learning system can find this description only if it is allowed to define the predicate `ancestor` in terms of the initial understanding of the concept. This is the principle of recursion. To start with, the learner uses the predicate `parent`. After formulating the first clause, the learner also uses the predicate `ancestor`.

The procedure just outlined forms the kernel of the FOIL system, developed by Quinlan (1990b). The following algorithm formalizes the approach:

Algorithm FOIL

1. Initialize the clause by defining the head that represents the name of the concept to be learned and leave the body empty;
2. While the clause covers negative examples do:
       Find a 'good' literal to be added to the clause body;
3. Remove all examples covered by the clause;
4. Add the clause to the emerging concept definition. If there are any uncovered positive examples then go to 1.

The only remaining problem at this moment is how to find a 'good' literal to be added to the clause (step 2 of the algorithm). To this end, FOIL makes use of an information criterion similar to that employed in the induction of decision trees.

Denote by T_i^+ the number of $\oplus$'s covered by the conjunction $L_1, L_2, \ldots, L_{i-1}$ and denote by T_i^- the number of $\ominus$'s covered by the same conjunction. Then the information provided by signalling a positive example among all the examples covered by this clause is:

$$I_i = -\log\left(\frac{T_i^+}{T_i^+ + T_i^-}\right)$$

After adding a new literal L_i this information becomes:

$$I_{i+1} = -\log\left(\frac{T_{i+1}^+}{T_{i+1}^+ + T_{i+1}^-}\right)$$

The success of the literal L_i is measured by two factors:

1. The remaining information I_{i+1} (the smaller, the better);

2. The number T_i^{++} of $\oplus$ that remain covered by the clause after adding L_{i+1} (the higher, the better).

Accordingly, FOIL's measure of success is defined as:

$$Gain(L_i) = T_i^{++} \times (I_i - I_{i+1})$$

It is instructive to observe how FOIL combines the two approaches outlined in the previous section. In principle, the program carries out the AQ-algorithm, trying to cover the positive space by a set of clauses. In the inner loop, a clause is stepwise specialized by a procedure controlled by a function similar to that used in the divide-and-conquer method.

1.5.2   Inverse Resolution

Returning to our search-oriented conception of learning, we can easily see that FOIL exploits two search operators: the generalizing *add_a_clause* operator and the specializing *add_a_literal* operator. Providing the complementary operators *delete_a_clause* for specialization and *delete_a_literal* for generalization, we arrive at the elementary repertoir of learning in first-order logic. The operators can be exemplified by the following four steps, gradually changing the clause x :- a,b into x :- d,e:

– add a clause x :- a,b $\Rightarrow \left\{ \begin{array}{l} x \text{ :- } a,b \\ x \text{ :- } c,d \end{array} \right\}$

– delete a clause $\left\{ \begin{array}{l} x \text{ :- } a,b \\ x \text{ :- } c,d \end{array} \right\} \Rightarrow x$:- c,d

– add a literal x :- c,d $\Rightarrow x$:- c,d,e

– delete a literal x :- c,d,e $\Rightarrow x$:- d,e

The main task of this subsection is to show how this collection can be extended by the following alternative inductive search operators:

– identification $\left\{ \begin{array}{l} a \text{ :- } b,x \\ a \text{ :- } b,c,d \end{array} \right\} \Rightarrow \left\{ \begin{array}{l} a \text{ :- } b,x \\ x \text{ :- } c,d \end{array} \right\}$

– absorption $\left\{ \begin{array}{l} x \text{ :- } c,d \\ a \text{ :- } b,c,d \end{array} \right\} \Rightarrow \left\{ \begin{array}{l} x \text{ :- } c,d \\ a \text{ :- } b,x \end{array} \right\}$

– inter-construction $\left\{ \begin{array}{l} a \text{ :- } v,b,c \\ a \text{ :- } w,b,c \end{array} \right\} \Rightarrow \left\{ \begin{array}{l} a \text{ :- } u,b,c \\ u \text{ :- } v \\ u \text{ :- } w \end{array} \right\}$

– intra-construction
$$\left\{ \begin{array}{l} a :\text{-}\ v,b,c \\ a :\text{-}\ w,b,c \end{array} \right\} \quad \Rightarrow \quad \left\{ \begin{array}{l} a :\text{-}\ v,u \\ a :\text{-}\ w,u \\ u :\text{-}\ b,c \end{array} \right\}$$

All of these operators can be derived from the *resolution principle* that is very popular in artificial intelligence. Denote two disjunctions of predicates by C_1 and C_2 and denote an arbitrary predicate by l. The resolution principle is deductive, and states the following:

If $(C_1 \vee l)$ is true and $(C_2 \vee \neg l)$ is true, then $(C_1 \vee C_2)$ is also true.

Put another way, two disjunctive expressions are assumed. One of them contains the literal l and the other one contains its negation $\neg l$. The disjunction of the two expressions, where l and $\neg l$ have been deleted, is also true and is called *resolvent*. The principle is depicted in Figure 1.15.

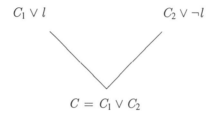

$$C_1 \vee l \qquad\qquad\qquad C_2 \vee \neg l$$

$$C = C_1 \vee C_2$$

Figure 1.15 Resolution principle.

Interestingly, the basic schema of resolution can be reversed. Knowing the resolvent and one of the original strings, we construct the other original string. Depending on whether the available clause contains the positive or the negated form of the predicate l, we speak about *identification* or *absorption*, respectively. The whole derivation scheme for both of them is shown in Figure 1.16. We will explain only identification, the derivation of absorption is analogous. The operators of inter- and intra-construction can be derived by slightly more complicated procedures that will not be described here.

Suppose we are given two clauses, $a :\text{-}\ b,x$ and $a :\text{-}\ b,c,d$. Let the former be called 'original' and the latter be called 'resolvent.' The task is to find the unknown clause that would, together with the original, produce the resolvent. For simplicity, no arguments of the predicates are assumed.

Knowing that the formula $A :\text{-}\ B$ can be rewritten as $A \vee \neg B$, we transform the two clauses into $a \vee \neg b \vee \neg x$ and $a \vee \neg b \vee \neg c \vee \neg d$. Both of the two clauses share the substring $a \vee \neg b$. Furthermore, the resolvent also contains the substring $\neg c \vee \neg d$ that might have been inherited from the unknown clause. The original, in turn, also contains the predicate $\neg x$ and hence its negation, x, is expected to appear in the unknown clause. Concatenating the contribution of the resolvent and the original, we will arrive at the string $\neg c \vee \neg d \vee x$. Turned back into the Horn clause, the string will change into $x :\text{-}\ c,d$. This newly created clause replaces the resolvent.

38

M. KUBAT, I. BRATKO, R.S. MICHALSKI

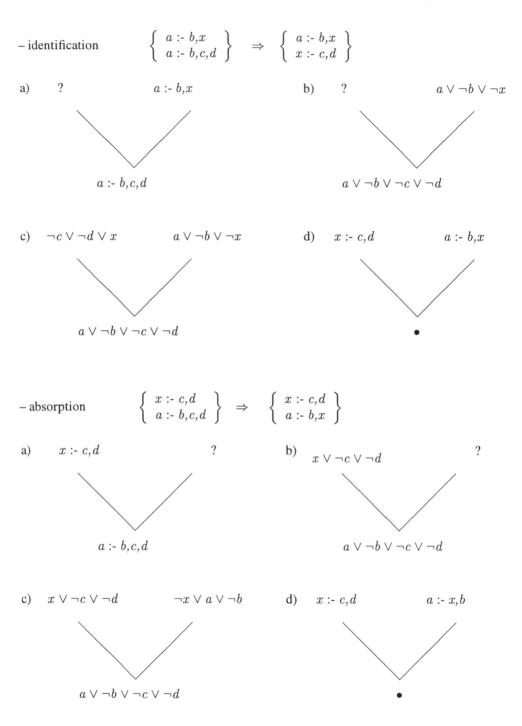

Figure 1.16 Derivation of the *identification* and *absorption* operators.

Unfortunately, in real-world applications the task gets complicated. Thus in the case of the reversed resolution, the learner will have to find proper substitutions of the arguments in the predicates l and $\neg l$ so that they are compatible. For instance, the predicates $p_1 =$ parent(john,bill) and $p_2 =$ parent(X,eve) are compatible only under the substitutions $\theta_1 = \{$john/X, bill/Y$\}$ in the first predicate, and $\theta_2 = \{$eve/Y$\}$ in the second predicate. The reader is referred to Muggleton (1991) for a more detailed discussion of this and related problems.

1.5.3 Theory Revision

Sometimes a body of *background knowledge* is available to guide the learning process. For illustration, suppose that the background knowledge contains partial information about the family relations similar to those in Figure 1.14, and that the additional information about the sex of the individual persons is provided in terms of the predicates male and female. Being told that Jack is the father of Bill, the learner is expected to derive the definition of the predicate father, previously not present in the background knowledge. The approach described here roughly builds on the algorithm that forms the core of the system CLINT—see de Raedt (1992).

The learner starts with some strongly restricted language, for instance, with the initial constraint demanding that each literal in the clause body is allowed to contain as arguments only those constants and variables that also appear in the head, as in p(X,Y) :- q(X,Y),r(X). In the case of father(jack,bill), this means that the system searches for all literals containing no other arguments except for jack and bill. Having found such literals, the system connects them with conjunctions.

For illustration, suppose that the system's background knowledge contains, among other things, the following predicates:

```
          ⋮
parent(jack,bill).
parent(tom,jack).
parent(tom,eve).
parent(eve,bill).
male(tom).
male(jack).
male(bill).
female(eve).
painter(bill).
singer(jack).
          ⋮
```

If there are no other predicates containing either of the arguments jack or bill, the attempt to construct the concept in terms of the above simple language will end up in the following description:

```
father(jack,bill) :- parent(jack,bill), male(jack), male(bill),
                    painter(bill), singer(jack).
```

Having found this concrete clause, the learner will generalize it by turning constants into variables, thus obtaining what is referred to as the *initial clause*:

```
father(X,Y) :- parent(X,Y), male(X), male(Y), painter(Y),
              singer(X).
```

Obviously, this method of clause construction is inevitably rather blind, and even a superficial look at the 'invented' clause reveals that there is something wrong with it: the fact that `jack` is `bill`'s father has nothing to do with `bill` being male, much less with his profession. To address this issue, the authors of CLINT provided the learner with the ability to refine the initial description of the concept by way of a simple dialog with the user.

During the dialog, the learner examines each predicate in turn and checks its necessity by creating new examples and asking the user to classify them. For instance, the question

Is `father(tom,jack)` true?

is positively answered by the user, indicating that the literal `painter(Y)` is unnecessary (`jack` is singer and, still, `tom` is his father).

The next question should check whether it is necessary that Y be male. Knowing that `eve` is female, the learner finds in the background knowledge the literal `parent(tom,eve)` and asks the user the following question:

Is `father(tom,eve)` true?

A positive answer indicates that `male(Y)` was also unnecessary. On the other hand, the question:

Is `father(eve,bill)` true?

will be answered negatively, which means that `male(X)` cannot be discarded from the clause.

Obviously, in the course of this verification, the original clause can totally alter or, even, all literals will be deleted from the body. Alternatively, it can happen that no initial clause is found. In both of these cases, the system proceeds by alleviating some of the constraints, for instance, the one imposed on the predicate arguments. Then the body predicates will be allowed to contain one and only one argument that does not appear in the head, as is the case of the clause:

```
grandparent(X,Y) :- parent(X,Z), parent(Z,Y).
```

In this way, the system generalizes the concept description with the objective to cover also those positive instances (created by the system and presented to the user) that have not been covered by the previous description.

Of course, the description can become too general in the sense that it also covers negative examples. In this case, respective measures must be taken to rectify this inconvenience. The solution implemented in CLINT consists of building the explanation tree for the negative example, identifying the culprit clause c responsible for the coverage of the negative example, deleting c from the knowledge base, and re-generalizing the resulting knowledge structure so that all positive examples that have previously been covered by c become covered again.

For more about the CLINT system see de Raedt (1992).

1.5.4 Constructive Induction

Let us now turn our attention to the problem of determining the appropriate representation space for learning, that is attributes or predicates relevant to the problem at hand. In standard methods, the learner analyzes the examples, describes them in terms of some predefined set of attributes or predicates, and produces the expected concept description using the operators of the description language, for instance, conjunctions, disjunctions, and negations of the attribute values or predicates. Michalski (1991) calls this simple kind of induction *empirical*. It is carried out by the simplest versions of the TDIDT and AQ algorithms, where the concept was described by a subset of the attributes that have been used to describe the learning examples.

In some approaches, such as inverse resolution, the learning algorithm itself constructs new predicates that are to facilitate the learning process. Often, this method necessitates an interactive learning procedure. Since the concept is invented by the machine, the user (possessing more knowledge about which predicates make sense) is asked to acknowledge the new predicate and assign it a name. Meat-eating animals with claws can be accepted and given the name `predators`; big animals with yellow skin will probably not make a useful concept, and will be rejected by the user in the belief that the two features have appeared together by mere coincidence.

At this point, constructive induction in *analogy-based* learning should be mentioned. Although the issue of analogy is discussed later, the idea of *second-order schemata* as implemented in the CIA system (see de Raedt, 1992) falls into the context of constructive induction.

The essence of the system consists in storing typical schemata of predicate expressions, such as:

```
p(X,Y)  :- q(X, XW), q(Y, YW), r(XW, YW)
```

where not only the arguments X, XW, Y, and YW, but also the predicates p, q, and r represent variables. Thus the previous schema can, by suitable substitutions, be instantiated into the following clauses (the respective substitutions are also provided):

```
lighter(X,Y) :- weight(X,XW), weight(Y,YW), less(XW,YW)
```
$\Theta = \{p/\text{lighter}, q/\text{weight}, r/\text{less}\}$

```
same-color(X,Y) :- color(X,XC), color(Y,YC), eq(XC,YC)
```
$\Theta = \{p/\text{same-color}, q/\text{color}, r/\text{eq}\}$

```
brothers(X,Y) :- son(X,XP), son(Y,YP), eq(XP,YP)
```
$\Theta = \{p/\text{brothers}, q/\text{son}, r/\text{eq}\}$

The second-order schemata lend themselves quite straightforwardly to constructive induction. In CIA's setting, this happens whenever the system finds out that, after proper substitutions, the body of a schema becomes a subset of the body of some clause whose head is unknown. For illustration, the schema:

```
p(X,Y) :- q(X, XW), q(YW, Y), r(XW, YW))
```

can become a subset of the clause

```
:- male(F), male(C),  parent(F,M1), parent(M2,C), eq(M1,M2)
```

after the substitutions:

$\Theta = \{q/\text{parent}, r/\text{eq}\}$ and
$\rho = \{\text{X/F, Y/C, XW/M1, YW/M2}\}$

The instantiated schema is:

```
p(F,C) :- parent(F,M1), parent(M2,C), eq(M1,M2)
```

If prompted, the user will certainly acknowledge the new clause as sensible, and will suggest the name `grandparent` for predicate p.

To conclude, the principle of constructive induction is very powerful and, combined with deeper studies of the nature of various representation languages, is generally considered as a very important research topic.

1.6   ARTIFICIAL DISCOVERY

The issue of artificial discovery is an instructive illustration of the general way of thinking in machine learning and, as such, deserves a brief elaboration here, even though it does not directly relate to the applications reported in the subsequent chapters.

So far, our interest has focused on *supervised* learning, where the learner seeks to develop a concept description from examples that have been preclassified by the teacher. The present section departs from this path in that it concentrates on *unsupervised* learning, whose task is to generate conceptual taxonomies from non-classified objects.

Actually, this is what scientists (say, biologists) have been doing for centuries, developing such categories as vertebrates, subcategories as mammals or birds, and the like. The utility of the taxonomies and categories is obvious: any object that has been recognized as a member of a certain category inherits the general properties of the category. Being told that a horse is a mammal, we immediately know whether the animal lays eggs, whether it can fly, or whether its skin is covered with fur or feathers.

A related task is carried out by some traditional statistical techniques such as *cluster analysis*. The dots in Figure 1.17 represent objects described by two numeric attributes, x and y. Apparently, the objects can be partitioned into two groups which are easy to discover by relatively simple algorithms exploiting the notion of similarity, as measured by the numeric distance between objects. Unfortunately, not every kind of similarity can be assessed numerically. Indeed, is the distance between cat and giraffe greater than the distance between dog and elephant? Even though these distances can be transformed into numbers, any such a transformation would be difficult and subjective.

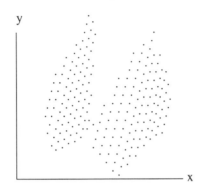

Figure 1.17   Traditional task for cluster analysis.

To come to understand another important issue, consider the task depicted in Figure 1.18. Here, the objects are already pre-ordered in a way that can be described conceptually, and several interpretations can be offered depending on the particular context. Obviously, traditional distance-based cluster analysis will hardly produce reasonable outcomes on these data and yet,

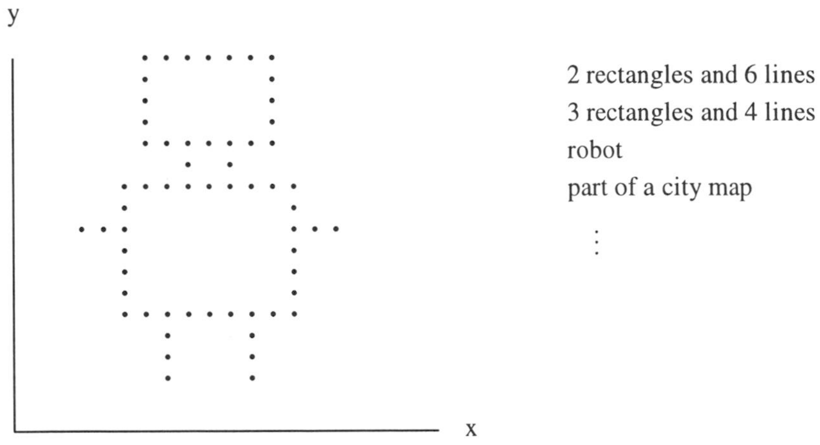

y

2 rectangles and 6 lines
3 rectangles and 4 lines
robot
part of a city map

$\vdots$

x

Figure 1.18   Concept-discovery task of machine learning.

for humans, this task appears to be trivial. In machine learning, the search for concepts hidden in a set of objects is studied by the discipline known under the name of *Concept Formation*.

To proceed one step further, one might want to discover not only concepts but also laws defining the relations among them, with the ambition of creating a computer-based system to assist human researchers in such disciplines as chemistry or biology. Even though to expect the implementation of artificial scientists would perhaps be too optimistic, a few remarkable systems addressing simple discovery tasks have already been developed.

Below, we devote one subsection to Concept Formation and one to Automated Discovery.

1.6.1   Concept Formation

Gennari *et al.* (1989) divide the field of unsupervised concept learning into two different sub-fields: *Concept Discovery*, deriving concepts from a batch, and incremental *Concept Formation* that gradually forms the concepts from a stream of examples.

1.6.1.1   CONCEPT DISCOVERY BY CONCEPTUAL CLUSTERING

Conceptual clustering has been introduced as a novel form of clustering in which clusters are not just collections of entities possessing numerical similarity. Rather, the clusters are understood as groups of objects that together represent a concept. Conceptual clustering produces not only clusters, but also descriptions of the related concepts. The *CLUSTER* system (see Michalski and Stepp, 1983) is anchored in the same seed-and-star philosophy as AQ, and can actually be considered as its extension to the realm of non-classified examples.

A simple task for concept discovery is depicted in Figure 1.19. Eight non-classified examples are described by three attributes. Attribute *at1* is symbolic, attribute *at2* acquires integer values, and attribute *at3* acquires integer values that can be decomposed into three symbolic values. Background knowledge provides the type and range for each of the attributes and defines the decomposition of *at3*.

Michalski and Stepp's idea is that the learner picks k seeds and treats them as if they represented k different clusters. In a simplified version, the procedure can be summarized by the following algorithm:

CLUSTER-Algorithm

1. Pick k seeds, where k is a user-specified parameter;
2. Build k stars, each star being understood as a collection of the most general descriptions of one seed; the limits for the seed generalization are all the other seeds;
3. Select from each star one rule so that each rule in the generated rule-set has the minimum logical intersection with the remaining rules, and the logical union of these rules covers the maximum number of instances;
4. If there are any uncovered instances, find rules with which they have the best 'fit'. Refine the rules so that together they cover all instances and are all logically disjoint. Instances that belong to an intersection of rules are redistributed so that each is covered by one and only one rule. At this moment, each rule represents a set of examples. From each of these sets, select a new seed;

example	at1	at2	at3
e1	a	2	110
e2	b	4	100
e3	b	2	9
e4	b	3	10
e5	c	5	20
e6	c	4	15
e7	b	5	200
e8	b	4	50

Background Knowledge:

$at1 : [a,b,c]$

$at2 : [2..6]$

$at3 : [1..300]$

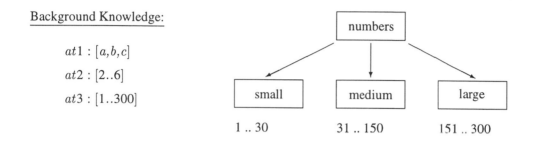

Figure 1.19   Simple task for concept discovery.

5. Repeat the above procedure for the new seeds and keep repeating the entire procedure as long as each new solution makes an improvement over the previous solutions. Repeat for several different values of k, e.g., $k = 2,3,\ldots 7$, and determine the highest 'quality' solution, the quality being determined on the basis of various criteria such as the simplicity of the rules in a clustering and their sparseness (measuring the degree of generalization of each rule over the instances covered by the rule; Michalski and Stepp, 1983).

Let us now apply this algorithm to the data from Figure 1.19. For simplicity, assume that numerical values have been replaced by symbolic values 'small', 'medium' or 'large', according to Figure 1.19 (normally, CLUSTER itself proposes the most appropriate clusters of numerical values). The algorithm will roughly perform the following steps (k is assumed to be 2):

Choose randomly 2 seeds, say, *e1* and *e5*. Their descriptions are:

des(e1): $(at1 = a)\&(at2 = 2)\&(at3 = large)$
des(e5): $(at1 = c)\&(at2 = 5)\&(at3 = small)$

The initial stars are:

star(e1): $(at1 \neq c),(at2 \neq 5),(at3 \neq small)$
star(e5): $(at1 \neq a),(at2 \neq 4),(at3 \neq large)$

Each star has three one-condition rules and rules from different stars intersect. From each star, one rule is selected and modified in such a way that the rules in the rule-set obtained are logically disjoint and their union covers all instances (this is done by the NID and PRO procedures described in Michalski and Stepp, 1983). The result is the following solution:

Cluster 1: $(at1 = a \lor b)\&(at2 = 2 \lor 3)$
        Instances: e1, e3, e4

Cluster 2: $(at1 = b \lor c)\&(at2 = 4 \lor 5)$
        Instances: e2, e5, e6, e7, e8

Snce selecting new seeds from the above rules does not lead to an improved clustering, the above rules constitute the proposed solution for $k = 2$. A repetition of the algorithm for higher values of k also does not improve the solution, so that the above is the final result. For more details, see Michalski and Stepp (1983).

1.6.1.2   CRISP CONCEPTUAL HIERARCHIES

The algorithms for concept discovery from fixed sets of non-classified examples tend to be prohibitively expensive. On the other hand, concept formation algorithms attempt to simulate the development of taxonomies in humans as closely as possible, in the sense that this process is supposed to be incremental. Moreover, emphasis is usually (not always) laid on generating *hierarchically ordered* concepts.

Most of these systems combine the process of classification and learning: whenever a new example arrives, the system integrates it (classifies) into the current knowledge structure. This is depicted in Figure 1.20, where the UNIMEM system (Lebowitz, 1987) has developed a taxonomy from six examples of cells, described by their size, number of nuclei, and number of tails. When another example arrives (small, two-tailed, one nucleus), it is found to be most similar to the triplet in the right-hand branch of the knowledge tree. Confronted with this new experience, the system creates a new subclass, as shown in Figure 1.21.

Concept-formation algorithms have typically been conceived as search systems—defined by initial state, termination criterion, search operators, search strategy, and, of course, representational issues. The initial state is given by the description of the first example whereas the final state is the knowledge structure after the last example—the system is supposed to learn as long as the examples keep coming. The most common search policy is hill-climbing driven by a properly chosen criterion to determine the quality of the current structure.

The representation used by UNIMEM, as seen in Figures 1.20 and 1.21, is self-explanatory. Each node (representing a concept formed by the system) is defined by a set of features such as `size(big)` (in the picture, the literal is reduced to the attribute value). Each feature is accompanied by an integer called `score` which tells the learner how many times the feature has so far been encountered. Note that the score also reflects examples that have been placed in other clusters—see, for instance, the score of the '2-tails' feature in the right-hand category. The score determines the strength of the feature. A small score indicates that the feature is rather irrelevant and should perhaps be discarded. Conversely, a high score suggests that the feature should be 'fixed' in the structure and no longer threatened by deletion.

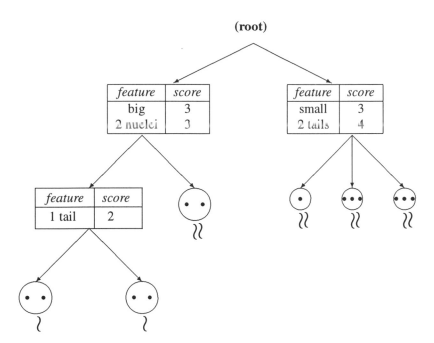

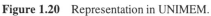

Figure 1.20 Representation in UNIMEM.

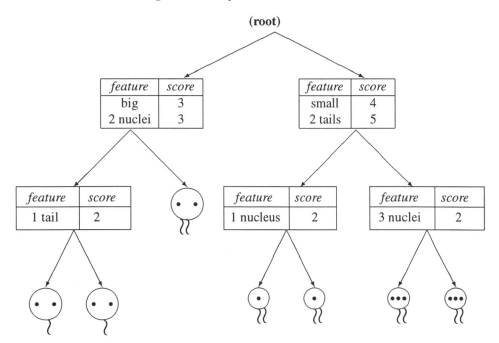

Figure 1.21 Absorbing a new example in the structure from the previous figure.

In principle, the following search operators underly the concept-formation process in UNIMEM:

1. Store a new instance in the closest node;
2. Create a new node if it improves the value of some general criterion assessing the quality of the conceptual structure created;
3. Fix a feature if its score exceeds a predefined threshold;
4. Delete a feature if its score is lower than the scores of the other features;
5. Delete an overly general node (containing only a few features).

For more detailed information about the procedure carried out by the UNIMEM system see Lebowitz (1987).

1.6.1.3   PROBABILISTIC CONCEPTUAL HIERARCHIES

Other concept-formation systems differ from UNIMEM in the internal representational structure, in the description language (e.g., symbolic versus numeric attributes), in the search operators, and in the evaluation function guiding the search.

Thus in the COBWEB system, each node in the hierarchy contains complete information about the probability of the individual attribute values, as shown in Figure 1.22, where the probabilities are estimated simply as relative frequencies.

What is peculiar about this representation is that the system does not store crisp descriptions. Rather, each attribute-value pair is accompanied by a number giving the probability that an instance of the concept will possess this particular attribute value. Each node in Figure 1.22 consists of a heading and a 3-column table. The heading contains information about the frequency, $P(N_i)$, with which an example falls into this category. The table contains the relative frequency of the occurence of any attribute-value pair.

COBWEB uses the following search operators:

1. *Incorporate* the new example into some of the existing nodes;
2. *Create* a new node for the example;
3. *Merge* two nodes into one;
4. *Split* a node into two nodes.

Whenever a new example is encountered, the learner must decide which of the operators applies best. Knowing that each operator can change the conceptual hierarchy, the system uses the formula assessing the *utility* of each of the potential new hierarchies:

$$\frac{IG - UG}{N}$$

where *UG* (*Uninformed Guess*) is the expected number of attribute values that can be correctly guessed from an unordered set of objects; *IG* (*Informed Guess*) is the expected number of attribute values that can be correctly guessed, given the conceptual hierarchy; and N is the number of categories that are currently present in the hierarchy.

More specifically, the following formula has been recommended (see Fisher, 1987, for a detailed derivation):

objects: 1 tail, light color, 1 nucleus
2 tails, light color, 2 nuclei
2 tails, dark color, 2 nuclei
1 tail, dark color, 3 nuclei

$P(N_1) = 4/4$		$P(V/C)$
tails	one	0.5
	two	0.5
color	light	0.5
	dark	0.5
nuclei	one	0.25
	two	0.5
	three	0.25

$P(N_2) = 1/4$		$P(V/C)$
tails	one	1.0
	two	0.0
color	light	1.0
	dark	0.0
nuclei	one	1.0
	two	0.0
	three	0.0

$P(N_3) = 2/4$		$P(V/C)$
tails	one	0.0
	two	1.0
color	light	0.5
	dark	0.5
nuclei	one	0.0
	two	1.0
	three	0.0

$P(N_6) = 1/4$		$P(V/C)$
tails	one	1.0
	two	0.0
color	light	0.0
	dark	1.0
nuclei	one	0.0
	two	0.0
	three	1.0

$P(N_4) = 1/2$		$P(V/C)$
tails	one	0.0
	two	1.0
color	light	1.0
	dark	0.0
nuclei	one	0.0
	two	1.0
	three	0.0

$P(N_5) = 1/2$		$P(V/C)$
tails	one	0.0
	two	1.0
color	light	0.0
	dark	1.0
nuclei	one	0.0
	two	1.0
	three	0.0

Figure 1.22 Representational structure of *COBWEB*.

$$\frac{\Sigma_{k=1}^{N} P(C_k) \Sigma_i \Sigma_j P(A_i = V_{ij} \mid C_k)^2 - \Sigma_i \Sigma_j P(A_i = V_{ij})^2}{N}$$

where $P(C_k)$ is the relative frequency of class C_k; $P(A_i = V_{ij})$ is the probability that attribute A_i will acquire the value V_{ij}; and $P(A_i = V_{ij} \mid C_k)$ is the corresponding conditional probability.

The point of this probabilistic approach is to create a conceptual hierarchy that maximizes the number of attribute values which can be predicted in an unseen example, given the information about the category into which the example falls.

1.6.2 Quest for Natural Laws

Many researchers claim that having powerful algorithms for concept formation at hand is not enough, that one should actually attempt to go one step further and try to build a system capable not only of constructing new concepts, but also of describing their relations in terms of laws, as is the case in chemistry and physics.

Several reasons support activities in this field:

1. Nowadays, huge databases from many scientific fields are available, waiting for someone to analyze them;
2. Powerful techniques in machine learning and artificial intelligence have been developed so that one can hope for a kind of 'intelligent' analysis;
3. Even if intelligent automatic analyzers are not constructed, the research into artificial discovery may help to ellucidate some of the mysteries of human invention (e.g., inspiration, analogy, and abstraction).

1.6.2.1 QUANTITATIVE EMPIRICAL LAWS

Suppose the task is to re-discover the ideal gas. The reader will recall from high school that this law has the form $PV = 8.32NT$, where P is pressure, V is volume, N is gas amount, and T is temperature. A system capable of accomplishing this task has been proposed by Langley *et al.* (1987) and given the name BACON. Here, only a brief overview is possible; for more details see their paper.

BACON starts by suggesting a series of experiments that will provide the measurement data. The human operator carries them out and supplies the computer with the outcomes. As soon as enough data have been gathered, the system searches the space of mathematical functions with the objective of finding an equation consistent with the data. One method of searching for the equation is to make one of the variables dependent while the others remain independent. Let the system have a repertoir of typical law-forms such as

$$y = ax^2 + bx + c$$
$$\sin(y) = ax + b$$
$$y^{-1} = ax + b$$

Table 1.6 Sample data for the BACON system.

quantity	temperature	pressure	volume
N=1	T=10	P=1000	V=2.36
.	.	P=2000	V=1.18
.	.	P=3000	V=0.78
,	T=20	P=1000	V=2.44
.	.	P=2000	V=1.22
.	.	P=3000	V=0.81
.	T=30	P=1000	V=...
.	.	P=2000	V=...
.	.	P=3000	V=...
.			
N=2	⋮		
.			
.			
N=3	⋮		
.			

The principle consists in selecting the best law-form and tuning the parameters $a, b, \ldots$, with the objective of finding an equation that best describes the observed data.

Suppose the equation $y^{-1} = ax + b$ has been selected. At the beginning, the parameters a and b are initialized to the values 1,0, and -1, so that the following combinations are considered as a set of initial states: $[a = 1, b = 1], [a = 1, b = 0], [a = 1, b = -1], [a = 0, b = 1], [a = 0; b = 0]$, etc.

In the search process, the parameters are tuned by adding or subtracting one parameter value at a time, starting with 0.5, then 0.25, 0.125, ... The evaluation function assessing the quality of each subsequent equation is defined by the correlation between the measured data and the values implied by the equation.

Suppose the values in Table 1.6 have been measured. BACON will investigate them in the following steps:

1. Find a function describing $V = f(P)$ for the triplets of examples assigned, in Table 1.6, to each of the three temperatures, $T = 10, T = 20$, and $T = 30$.

Suppose that $V^{-1} = aP + b$ with the following parameters provides the best fit:

$T = 10$: $a = 0.000425$, thus $V^{-1} = 0.000425P$
$T = 20$: $a = 0.000410$, thus $V^{-1} = 0.000410P$
$T = 30$: $a = 0.000396$, thus $V^{-1} = 0.000396P$

2. Since the parameter values evidently depend on the temperature T, the next task is to find the function relating a to T. Again, the best fit is achieved by the form $a^{-1} = cT + d$ with the values of the parameters, c and d, depending on N:

$N = 1$: $c = 8.32$ and $d = 2271.4$, thus $a^{-1} = 8.32\,T + 2271.4$
$N = 2$: $c = 16.64$ and $d = 4542.7$, thus $a^{-1} = 16.64\,T + 4542.7$
$N = 3$: $c = 24.96$ and $d = 6814.1$, thus $a^{-1} = 24.96\,T + 6814.1$

3. Find functions relating c to N and d to N. The best fit is achieved by $c = eN$ and $d = fN$, respectively, with $e = 8.32$ and $f = 2271.4$. These parameters do not depend on any other variable.

4. Substituting the equation into those equations found in the previous steps, the system obtains:

$$V^{-1} = (8.32NT + 2271.4N)^{-1}P$$

and this last expression can easily be transformed into:

$$PV = 8.32NT + 2271.4N$$

Factoring out $8.32N$ on the right-hand side, we arrive at:

$$PV = 8.32N(T + 273)$$

which, indeed, is the standard form of the ideal gas law. Note that BACON has found that the Celsius temperature scale is improper. As a matter of fact, the system introduced the Kelvin scale, adding 273 to the observed Celsius value.

To conclude, the essence of BACON is to apply common search principles in the quest for an ideal *form* of a quantitative law, rather than just find the best fitting parameters, as is the case of traditional regression techniques.

The qualitative counterpart of the previous quantitative discoverer is the GLAUBER system, which attempts to form qualitative chemical laws and concepts. GLAUBER turned out to be able to re-discover the concepts of acids and alkalis, and to postulate some basic properties of these concepts. For more details, as well as for other interesting systems capable of automated discovery, see Langley *et al.* (1987). To conclude this subsection, let us briefly mention a slightly more advanced variation on the principles just outlined.

1.6.3   Discovery in Dynamic Systems

LAGRANGE is a program for discovering numerical laws in the submitted data, as was the case in BACON. However, LAGRANGE differs in that it generates models from data measured on *dynamic* systems. LAGRANGE's models have the form of differential equations. As opposed to traditional system identification techniques used in control engineering, LAGRANGE finds the *structure* of the equations, not only the values of the parameters.

As an illustration, consider an application from the domain of ecological modelling. Two variables, x and c, are assumed. x is the concentration of bacteria in a test-tube, and c is the concentration of nutrition for bacteria. The task for LAGRANGE is: given the tabular representation of the two curves in time $x(t)$ and $c(t)$, find a differential equation whose numerical solution corresponds to the two given behaviors. For the case of this particular biological domain—reported by Džeroski and Todorovski (1994)—LAGRANGE found the following differential equations:

$$\mathcal{L} = -\frac{1}{60}x - \frac{10}{6}x$$

$$c\mathcal{x} = -x - 100x + 0.09\,cx$$

For the concrete values of the system's parameters, such as the growth rate, this corresponds to the Monod model, well known from ecological modelling.

In general, the discovery problem for LAGRANGE is stated as follows:

Given:

Trace in time of a dynamic system:

$$\vec{x}(t_0),\ \vec{x}(t_0 + h),\ \dots$$

Parameters:

      o = order of differential equations
      d = maximum depth of newly generated terms
      r = maximum number of 'independent regression variables'
      t_R = significance threshold

Find:

Differential equations within the parameters (o,d,r) that match the data within significance threshold t_R.

As reported by Džeroski and Todorovski (1994), LAGRANGE successfully discovered (again, it should be admitted: *re*-discovered) differential equations for: a chemical reaction with three chemical substances, modelling the predator-prey chain, the so-called Brusselator chemical reactor, the pole-cart system, etc.

1.7 HOW TO COPE WITH THE VASTNESS OF THE SEARCH SPACE?

One of the principal problems of machine learning is that the space of all possible descriptions is often so large that the search either has to rely on heuristics, or becomes computationally intractable. Also, the danger of converging to local maxima of evaluation functions is in large spaces more serious.

Two techniques to attack this problem deserve a special section: the use of analogy and the idea of storing the original examples instead of their generalized descriptions.

1.7.1 Analogy Providing Search Heuristics

The principle of analogy has been extensively studied in the artificial intelligence community because of the widespread belief that the ability to find proper analogies is one of the secrets of intelligence. Much work has been devoted to analogy-based reasoning.

Figure 1.23   General scheme of analogy.

What is the essence of this mechanism as viewed from the machine-learning perspective? Kodratoff (1988) coined the scheme depicted in Figure 1.23 as the general framework of analogy. Here, S stands for source, SC for source concept, T for target, and TC for target concept. The task is to derive the target concept from T in a way that is analogous to the way source concept was derived from the source. Thus, having the target, the learner must find a proper source.

Greiner (1988) suggests the following general procedure for any reasoning by analogy:

Reasoning-by-Analogy Algorithm

1. *Recognition.* Given a target concept, find in the background theory a source S that is 'similar' to T. The similarity can be measured by syntactic distance, by the existence of common generalization or of a pair of unifying substitutions, or by some hint supplied by the user;
2. *Elaboration.* Find SC, together with the inference chain $\vdash_S$ leading to it from S. Note that, for each S, a collection of SC's usually exist;
3. *Evaluation.* Among the SC's, find the one that best satisfies given criteria;
4. Apply to T an inference chain $\vdash_T$ 'similar' to $\vdash_S$, thus obtaining TC. Assess the utility of TC;
5. If necessary, repeat iteratively steps 1–4 to find S, SC, $\vdash_S$, and $\vdash_T$ that yield the most promising (useful) TC;
6. *Consolidation.* Include TC together with the inference chain $\vdash_T$ into the background theory.

Since the above framework is somewhat too general, reasonable constraints are usually needed. Thus the source S can be explicitly supplied by the user telling the system that if the task is to calculate the flowrate through a pipelining structure, then the laws analogical to those used in electrical engineering (Kirchhoff's laws) should be used. Another possibility is that the user takes over the evaluation process and selects a proper SC for the source that has been suggested by the system. Greiner (1988) describes a system that was capable of learning to solve fluid flow problems, using as analogy prior knowledge about electrical circuits.

1.7.2   Instance-Based Learning

An explicit concept description is not always explicitly required. If the only reason for learning is the need to identify future examples, then the learner can adopt an alternative policy: instead of descriptions, store typical examples. This can preclude many troubles potentially entailed by the search through a prohibitively large space of generalizations. Note that a similar idea has already been adopted by some of the concept-formation systems treated earlier.

This section outlines the principle of the IBL system (Aha *et al.* 1991) which is able to store selected examples (described by attribute values) and use them according to the so-called *nearest-neighbor* principle: the newly arrived example is assigned the class of the closest one among the stored examples.

A simple formula to calculate the similarity between the examples x and y is used (x_i and y_i are the respective values of the i-th attribute):

$$\text{similarity}(x,y) = -\sqrt{\sum_{i=1}^{n} f(x_i, y_i)}$$

where the function f is calculated for numeric attributes by:

$$f(x_i, y_i) = (x_i - y_i)^2$$

and for symbolic and Boolean attributes by:

$$f(x_i, y_i) = \begin{cases} 1 & x_i \neq y_i \\ 0 & x_i = y_i \end{cases}$$

The principle is illustrated in Figure 1.24, where four examples described by two numeric variables are depicted, together with the discrimination function separating the space of positive examples from the space of negative examples.

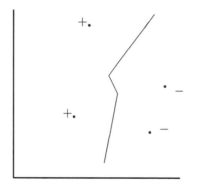

Figure 1.24 $\oplus$ and $\ominus$ examples defining the positive and negative space.

The learning assumes the availability of a feedback that will immediately inform the learner about the success or failure of each single classification attempt. A very simplified version of the IBL-algorithm involves the following steps:

Instance-Based-Learning Algorithm

1. Define the *set of representatives* containing, at the beginning, the first example;
2. Read a new example x;
3. For each y in the set of representatives, determine *similarity(x,y)*;
4. Label x with the class of the closest example in the set of representatives;
5. Find out from the feedback whether the classification was correct;
6. Include x in the set of representatives and go to 2.

Two shortcomings degrade the utility of this elementary version: excessive storage require-ments caused by the fact that *all* examples are stored; and sensitivity to noise.

The rectification consists of a selective storage of the examples by a 'wait-and-see' strategy whose essence can be summarized by the following principles:

1. Whenever a new instance has been classified, the 'significance-score' of each of the previous instances is updated (see below) and the instance is stored;
2. Instances with *good* scores are used for the classifications; instances with *bad* scores are deleted;
3. *Mediocre* instances are retained as potential candidates. However, they are not used for classification.

In the classification phase, the new arrival is assigned the class of the nearest *good* instance if a *good* instance exists. Otherwise, the new arrival is assigned the class of the nearest *mediocre* instance.

Then, the system increments the scores of those *mediocres* that are closer to the new arrival than the closest *good* instance. If no *good* instance is available, the system updates *mediocres* inside a randomly chosen hypersphere arround the new arrival.

A score is considered as *good* whenever the classification accuracy achieved by this instance is higher than the frequency of the example's class. The *classification accuracy* of class $\oplus$ is the percentage of correctly recognized positive examples in the set of *all* examples.

Instance-based learning has been reported to achieve a significant recognition power in attribute-value domains, especially when the number of examples is large and the attributes describing them are properly chosen. Also, the robustness against noise is satisfactory. On the other hand, the power of the system degrades if the descriptions of the examples contain irrelevant attributes and/or if the number of examples available to the learning procedure is small.

1.8   CLOSE NEIGHBORHOOD OF MACHINE LEARNING

The general label of machine learning is usually reserved for artificial intelligence-related techniques, especially for those whose objective is to induce symbolic descriptions that are *meaningful* and *understandable* and at the same time help improve performance. In a broader understanding, though, the machine-learning task can be defined as any computational pro-cedure leading to an increased knowledge or improved performance of some process or skill such as object recognition.

Particularly the learn-to-recognize task is often addressed by methods that are traditionally not strictly included in machine-learning paradigms but which have the same or similar objective. Thus a statistical data analysis (see Everit, 1981) and traditional pattern recognition (see Duda and Hart, 1973) spawned many useful techniques. Even though a detailed discussion of the many alternative approaches would prohibitively extend the scope of this chapter, two techniques must be briefly mentioned because of their popularity, and because of the many attempts to combine them with machine-learning algorithms: neural networks and genetic algorithms.

1.8.1 Artificial Neural Networks

In the late fifties, Mark Rosenblatt suggested to use, for pattern-recognition purposes, a simple device, inspired by early mathematical models of biological neurons. In his famous paper (Rosenblatt, 1958) and book (Rosenblatt, 1962), he dubbed this device a *perceptron*, and showed how it can be trained for the recognition job simply by automatic adjustments of its parameters, based on a set of preclassified examples. The principle is shown in Figure 1.25. Several input signals, x_i, each multiplied by a weight w_i, are attached to a summation unit. The resulting $sum = \Sigma_i w_i \cdot x_i$ is subjected to a step function ensuring that if the sum exceeds a certain threshold θ, the output of the peceptron is 1, otherwise the output is 0. As an alternative to the values 1 and 0, any other pair of outputs can be considered, say 1 and -1.

input

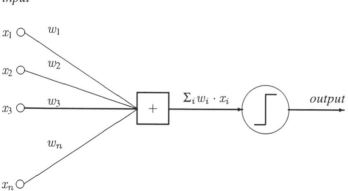

Figure 1.25   General scheme of a perceptron.

Proper adjustments of the weights w_i and of the threshold θ ensure that the perceptron will react to input vectors with the required output value. The information is thus encoded in the weights assigned to each individual input, each input representing an attribute. More relevant attributes are assigned more weight and less relevant attributes have less weight. Perceptron's learning algorithm seeks such weight values that will accomplish the requested mapping from the space of input vectors to the set of two binary values, $R^n \rightarrow \{0,1\}$.

Unfortunately, some concepts cannot be acquired by the perceptron, among them, for instance, *exclusive* OR, as has been shown by Minsky and Papert (1969). That is why perceptrons

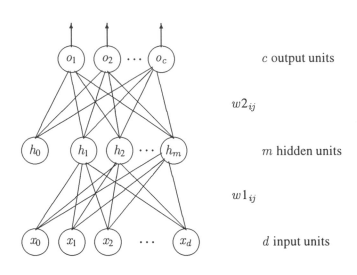

Figure 1.26   Multilayer perceptron.

are only rarely used in isolation. Rather, they are interconnected in structures such as the *Multilayer Perceptron*, depicted in Figure 1.26 (for an analysis of multilayer perceptrons, see Rumelhart *et al.*, 1986).

In principle, the multilayer perceptron consists of one layer of input nodes, one layer of output nodes, and one or more 'hidden' layers between them. During the recognition phase, the components of the input vector are clamped to the input layer. Obviously, some of the perceptrons 'fire' (their output is 1), when the weighted sum of their inputs exceeds the particular threshold. The value 1 or 0 is then propagated to the next layer, until the output of the network is reached.

As the basic threshold function is too rigid (it does not tolerate noise and does not facilitate learning), usually the *sigmoid function* is used to calculate the output of a single unit from its inputs:

$$f(sum) = \frac{1}{1 + e^{-sum}}$$

where *sum* is the weighted sum of the signals at the unit input. According to this formula, the unit will output a real value between 0 and 1. For $sum = 0$, the output is 0.5; for large negative values of *sum* the output converges to 0; and for large positive values of *sum* the output converges to 1. The formula is more tolerant than the step function with respect to noisy signals.

Usually, only a single hidden layer is employed, as is the case in Figure 1.26. However, in many complicated tasks, researchers made good experience when they used two or more hidden layers.

The procedure for automatic adjustment of the weights is provided below without any further discussion. The interested reader is referred to some of the many monographs on neural networks. Among the many existing textbooks of neural networks, perhaps Beale and Jackson (1990) can be recommended as an easy-to-read introduction. For more comprehensive treatment, see, for instance, Haykin (1994).

Backpropagation Learning Algorithm

1. Define the configuration of the neural net in terms of the number of units in each layer;
2. Set the initial weights $w1_{ij}$ and $w2_{ij}$ to small random values, say, from the interval $[-0.1, 0.1]$;
3. Select an example and denote its attribute values by $x_1, \ldots, x_k$. Attach the example to the input layer;
4. *Propagate* the input values from the input layer to the hidden layer. The output value of the j-th unit is calculated by the function $h_j = \dfrac{1}{1 + e^{-\sum_i w1_{ij} \cdot x_i}}$.

   Propagate the values thus obtained to the output layer. The output value of the j-th unit in this layer is caluculated by the function: $o_j = \dfrac{1}{1 + e^{-\sum_i w2_{ij} \cdot h_i}}$;

5. Compare the outputs o_j with the teacher's classifications y_j; calculate the correction error as $\delta 2_j = o_j(1 - o_j)(y_j - o_j)$ and adjust the weights $w2_{ij}$ by the following formula:

$$w2_{ij}(t + 1) = w2_{ij}(t) + \delta 2_j \cdot h_i \cdot \eta$$

   where $w2_{ij}(t)$ are the respective weight values at time t and η is a constant such that $\eta \in (0,1)$;
6. Calculate the correction error for the hidden layer by means of the formula $\delta 1_j = h_j(1 - h_j) \sum_i \delta 2_i \cdot w2_{ij}$ and adjust the weights $w1_{ij}$ by:

$$w1_{ij}(t + 1) = w1_{ij}(t) + \delta 1_j \cdot x_i \cdot \eta$$

7. Go to step 3.

   The above algorithm captures only the fundamental principle of learning in multilayer perceptrons, and its practical use in many realistic applications suffers from various shortcomings and pitfalls that the user must be acquainted with. However, these caveats have been studied in great detail and, nowadays, neural networks represent a well-established scientific discipline.

1.8.2   Genetic Algorithms

The reader has seen that the learning procedure is in many cases conceived as a search through the space of representations permitted by the given language. This subsection presents a surprisingly powerful alternative to the traditional heuristic search techniques: the *genetic algorithm* that has been inspired by a similar principle in nature.

   Generally speaking, the evolution in nature is controlled by three fundamental principles:

1. *Survival of the fittest* means that the strongest specimens have the highest chance to survive and reproduce, whereas the weak ones are likely to die before they reach the reproduction stage;

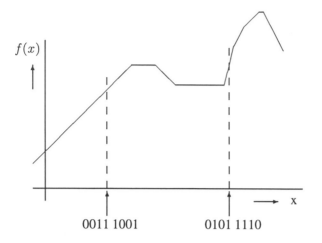

Figure 1.27   Evaluation function $f(x)$ and two binary specimens.

2. In *sexual reproduction* the specimens find the partners they consider to be the best ones, thus further contributing to the survival-of-the-fittest principle. Then they recombine their genetic information, thus creating new specimens with somewhat different characteristics;
3. *Mutations* cause random, and relatively rare, changes in the genetic information.

The unquestionable success that this 'search technique' has in nature inspired some researchers to investigate methods to turn it into algorithms that can be encoded in computer programs. A lucid introduction to the discipline of genetic algorithms has been written by Goldberg (1989).

In this chapter we present only the basic principles that are necessary for the implementation of a working version of this mechanism. At the beginning of any successful attempt to cast a technological problem in a setting that facilitates its solution by means of a genetic algorithm, two questions must be answered. How to encode the search space in chromosomes; and how to define the *fitness function* (see Figure 1.27) that plays the role of evaluation function in heuristic search? In most implementations, the chromosomes are represented by bit strings. Each bit can stand for a binary attribute, the presence of a multivalued attribute, the presence of a predicate, etc. The fitness function, measuring the survival chance of the specimen, can be defined as the accuracy of the description derived from the chromosome, the entropy of the partitioning imposed by this description (examples satisfying the description versus example that do not satisfy it), and the like.

The principle of the genetic algorithm is illustrated by the example in Table 1.7. Here, the fitness function is defined as $f(x) = 1/(x + 1)$, where x is the number represented in the chromosome in binary form (e.g., '111' = 7). Obviously, the maximum value of $f(x)$ will be reached for the string '000000.'

The table shows one step of the algorithm. The old generation contains four numbers: 37, 11, 20, and 7. The maximum value of the fitness function is reached for $f(7) = 1/(7 + 1) = 0.125\%$, so the chromosome representing $x = 7$ has the highest chance of survival. Conversely, the number $x = 37$ has the smallest fitness function, $f(37) = 1/(37 + 1) = 0.027$, and consequently, has a negligent chance to survive. This chance is given by a random number

Table 1.7 One step in the genetic search for the maximum of the function $1/(x+1)$ (no mutation).

	old gener.	x	$1/(x+1)$		survivors	new gener.	x	$1/(x+1)$
(1)	1 0 0 1 0 1	37	0.026	(4)	0 0 0 | 1 1 1	0 0 0 0 1 1	3	0.250
(2)	0 0 1 0 1 1	11	0.083	(2)	0 0 1 | 0 1 1	0 0 1 1 1 1	15	0.063
(3)	0 1 0 1 0 0	20	0.048	(4)	0 0 0 1 | 1 1	0 0 0 1 0 0	4	0.200
(4)	0 0 0 1 1 1	7	0.125	(3)	0 1 0 1 | 0 0	0 1 0 1 1 1	23	0.042

generator ensuring that the strongest specimens can be replicated more than once in the space of survivors (here, the 'technical' genetic algorithm somewhat departs from the 'natural' one) while the weakest specimens die out. This step is called *reproduction*.

In the next step, each survivor chooses a mating partner and exchanges with it part of their genetic information. This step is called *recombination*, and is modeled as the exchange of random substrings. For simplicity, the chromosomes in Table 1.7 exchange only tails of random length. After this step, a new generation of stronger specimens comes into being. Indeed, the values of the fitness function indicate that its maximum as well as the average value increased.

The *mutation* operator (not applied in Table 1.7) is modeled quite straightforwardly: with a very small likelihood, a bit is flip-flopped to its opposite value. The likelihood constant is usually adjusted so that in one generation no more than just a few (say, 0 through 5) mutations appear.

GA-Algorithm

1. Define the initial population as a set of binary strings generated randomly or by some pre-specified mechanism;
2. Replicate the specimens in the population into the set of survivors by a mechanism that ensures that specimens with a high value of fitness function have higher chances of survival (and can be replicated more than once);
3. For each survivor, find a mate with which it exchanges part of the information encoded in the binary strings. With a very low frequency, a single bit is flip-flopped to model random mutations;
4. If the fitness function has not increased throughout several cycles, stop. Otherwise go to step 2.

The interested reader is referred to the monograph by Goldberg (1989), where a detailed analysis with extensive bibliography can be found.

1.9 HYBRID SYSTEMS AND MULTISTRATEGY LEARNING

The real world often poses problems that cannot be successfully tackled by one of the basic techniques described above. Each of these techniques has its assets and liabilities. For instance, TDIDT has been designed for attribue-valued data and is much less valuable when more sophisticated description languages together with substantial background knowledge are required. Likewise, systems based on predicate logic are good at dealing with Horn clauses but pay the price of high computational demands; neural nets are excellent at pattern recognition but suffer from their sensitivity to the initial topology and weights, as well as proper selection of attributes; and genetic algorithms, albeit surprisingly powerful, require smart encoding into chromosomes and can be very slow learners.

It is only natural that machine-learning researchers experiment with combinations of the individual approaches to bridge some of the chronical pitfalls. Research on building systems that combine different strategies or methods is at its very early stage and falls into a new subarea of machine learning, called multistrategy learning (Michalski and Tecuci, 1994; Wnek *et al.*, 1995

1.9.1 Entropy Networks

As already mentioned, the performance of neural networks tends to degenerate whenever the input vector contains irrelevant features. Conversely, TDIDT-related systems, though good at pruning out noise and useless attributes, tend to build too rigid descriptions based on the strict ordering of attributes. These complementary deficiencies inspired successful attempts to merge the two approaches. An impressive simplicity and convincing results characterize the idea of *entropy nets* that was first introduced by Sethi (1990). The system was designed primarily for learning in domains where examples are described by numeric attributes.

The procedure for the generation of entropy nets consists of three steps: tree growing, translation of the tree into a neural net (which is then called an entropy net), and training the entropy net.

For the decision-tree growing, the procedure described earlier in this chapter can be used. The fact that proper attributes are selected by a measure based on entropy has given the system its name.

The mapping of the decision tree to a neural network is facilitated by the observation that conjunctions and disjunctions of Boolean attributes are easy to implement by simple models of neurons. Suppose that all weights are equal to 1. Then setting the neuron's threshold value to $n - 0.5$ ensures that the neuron can be activated only if all inputs are 1. In this case, the weighted sum of the inputs is $\Sigma w_i a_i = n$, which exceeds the threshold value. Similarly, setting the neuron's threshold to 0.5 makes it carry out disjunction of the inputs.

Figure 1.28 illustrates the mapping. The bottom layer of the network simply contains the inputs. Each of the units in the first hidden layer (called the *partitioning layer*) carries out one of the decision tests (such as $a_1 < t_1$) at the internal nodes of the tree. Each leaf of the decision tree is mapped to a corresponding unit in the second hidden layer, called the AND-layer. These units perform the conjunction of the tests along the tree branch. Finally, each unit of the output layer (OR-layer) stands for one classification value and models the disjunction of the leaves with the same class label.

The subsequent training of the net uses the backpropagation algorithm that has been described in a previous section. The idea is to further increase the classification accuracy of the system as compared to the original decision tree. The trade-off is that the interpretability of the encoded knowledge vanishes.

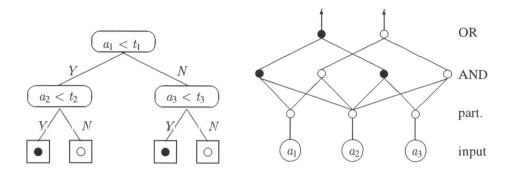

Figure 1.28 Functional decision tree and the corresponding entropy net.

1.9.2 Knowledge-Based Neural Nets

Another shortcoming of neural nets is their negligence of background knowledge and complications with the search for the ideal topology. This is why Towell *et al.* (1990) experimented with their KBANN system, which is able to learn in logic and then tune the acquired knowledge by way of neural network training.

Suppose that the background knowledge contains the following rules which, taken together, define some concept a:

```
a  :- b, c.
b  :- g, not(f).
b  :- not(h).
c  :- i, j.
```

a is defined as the conjunction of *intermediate concepts* b and c. These, in turn depend on the *supporting facts* g, f, h, i, and j. Supporting facts are those features that can be directly measured on the objects serving as examples. Intermediate concepts are defined by the supporting facts and, potentially, by other intermediate concepts.

Two steps characterize the system. First, the knowledge is translated into the network where the supporting facts are modeled by input units, intermediate concepts by hidden units, and the final concepts by output units. The dependencies between units in different layers are represented by weights. At this stage, each of the weights has the same absolute value. In the second step, the net is enlarged to also give a chance to those predicates and facts that have not explicitly appeared in the background knowledge. Then, the weights are slightly perturbed by random numbers and the net is trained by the backpropagation algorithm.

Figure 1.29 illustrates the principle. The rules are translated into the rough topology in the left-hand part of the figure, where the dotted lines represent links with negative weights (e.g., in the rule b :- not(h)). This topology is then refined by introducing supplementary low-weighted connections, shown in the right-hand part of the figure. For more details see Towell *et al.* (1990). An approach to initialize neural networks with an AQ-based algorithm is studied by Bala *et al.* (1994).

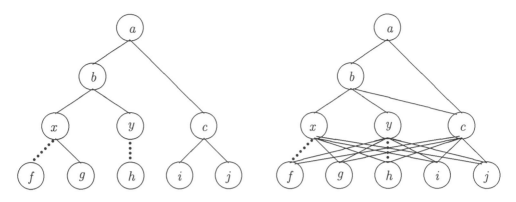

Figure 1.29   Translation of knowledge into a neural net.

We have already mentioned that as the network is a black-box system, an unpleasant consequence of the refinement of knowledge by neural-net training is that the user loses the interpretation of the results. To tackle this problem, Towell *et al.* (1991) suggested a method to extract knowledge in the form of production rules from a trained neural network.

1.9.3   Genetic Search for Generalizations in AQ

One of the vulnerable aspects of the AQ-algorithm is the search for the optimal generalization of seeds. The reason is that the number of all possible generalizations can be so high that the computational tractability of the whole program might become an issue.

This problem motivated Venturini (1993) to develop the SIA system, where the search for the ideal seed generalization is carried out by a mechanism inspired by the genetic algorithm. Each chromosome represents one production rule. However, the reproduction scheme as well as mutation are the same as described above. The recombination uses the crossover operator only in a relatively small proportion of the specimens, just to supplement the traditional generalization. The population size is variable.

To find the ideal generalization, SIA starts with a population containing only the most specific description of the seed (the initial size of the population is, therefore, $N = 1$). In each of the subsequent generations, one of the following operators is randomly chosen and applied with the probability indicated in the parentheses:

1. *Create* a new rule (probability of 10%);
2. Select an arbitrary rule and *generalize* it (probability of 80%);
3. Perform the traditional *crossover* of two rules by exchanging some conjuncts between them (probability of 10%).

For a more detailed explanation, see the original paper by Venturini (1993).

1.9.4   Combination of GA and Neural Nets

Finally, several researchers investigated the possibilities of the use of genetic algorithms to find the architecture and/or weights of neural networks. The work by Bornholdt and Graudenz

(1992) can serve as an illustration of these efforts. Here, the genetic algorithm searches for the ideal topology of the network. The individul positions of the chromosome represent neurons, and each of them contains pointers to other neurons, so the chromosome is more complicated than a simple bit string. The fitness function measures the quality of a given network.

However, more detailed discussion of these efforts would depart from the main stream of the learning algorithms described in this chapter.

1.10 PERSPECTIVES

As shown above, the field of machine learning has developed a great variety of approaches and techniques. A brief historical review of the evolution of many of them can be found in Cohen and Feigenbaum (1982) and Michalski *et al.* (1983).

The methods presented here fall into the general category of inductive concept learning, which perhaps constitutes the most advanced task in machine learning. The underlying assumption for most of these methods is that the learner induces a concept description from given concept instances. Such a process is inherently inductive, and the correctness of the descriptions created cannot be guaranteed. Therefore, the descriptions created by these techniques always have to be tested on new data.

Since these descriptions represent generalizations of given facts and can be incorrect, in many applications it is crucial that they be interpreted and understood by a human expert before they can be used. Therefore, we have pointed to the importance of the comprehensibility condition in concept learning.

The descriptions can be expressed in different forms, such as decision trees, decision rules, neural nets, Horn clauses, grammars, etc. Each representation requires a somewhat different method of information processing, and has its own advantages and disadvantages. To apply any of them to a given problem requires an analysis of the problem at hand and a decision on which representation and learning strategy would be most appropriate.

For completness, it should be mentioned in conclusion, that there have been several other general approaches developed in the field, that are not covered in this chapter. They include:

1. *Explanation-based learning*, a methodology that deductively derives operational knowledge from a concept example and some *a priori* known abstract concept description—see, for instance DeJong and Mooney (1986) or Mitchell *et al.* (1986);
2. *Case-based learning*, a learning method in which concept examples are stored, and new cases are recognized by determining the class of the closest past case (or cases)—see, for instance, Bareiss *et al.* (1987) or Rissland and Ashley (1989);
3. *Reinforcement learning*, in which numerical feedback about the performance at a given step is used to modify the parameters of the learning system—see, for instance, Sutton (1988).

Machine learning is a relatively young discipline and it is likely that many new, more powerful methods will be developed in the future. The following chapters of this book demonstrate, however, that the existing techniques can already be successfully applied to many practical problems.

References

Aha, D.W., Kibler, D., and Albert, M.K. (1991). Instance-Based Learning Algorithms. *Machine Learning*, 6:37–66

Bala J.W., Michalski, R.S., and Pachowicz, P.W. (1994). Progress on Vision through Learning at George Mason University. *Proceedings of ARPA Image Understanding Workshop* 191–207

Bareiss, E.R., Porter, B., and Wier, C.C. (1987). PROTOS: An Exemplar-Based Learning Apprentice. *Proceedings of the Fourth International Workshop on Machine Learning*, Irvine, CA, Morgan Kaufmann, 12–23

Beale, R. and Jackson, T. (1990). *Neural Computing: An Introduction*. Adam Hilger, Bristol

Bergadano, F., Matwin, S., Michalski, R.S., and Zhang, J. (1992). Learning Two-Tiered Descriptions of Flexible Concepts: The POSEIDON System. *Machine Learning*, 8, 5–43

Bornholdt, S., and Graudenz, D. (1992). General Asymmetric Neural Networks and Structure Design by Genetic Algorithms. *Neural Networks*, 5:327–334

Bratko, I. (1990). *PROLOG Programming for Artificial Intelligence*, Addison-Wesley (Second Edition)

Breiman, L., Friedman, J., Olshen, R., and Stone, C.J. (1984). *Classification and Regression Trees*. Belmont, California, Wadsworth Int. Group

Cestnik, B. (1990). Estimating probabilities: a crucial task in Machine Learning. *Proc. ECAO 90*, Stockholm, August

Cestnik, B., and Bratko, I. (1991). On estimating probability in decision tree pruning. *Proc. EWSL-91*, Porto, Portugal, March. Springer-Verlag

Cestnik, B., and Karalič, A. (1991). The Estimation of Probabilities in Attribute Selection Measures for Decision Tree Induction. *Proceedings of the Information Technologies Interface, ITI-91*, Cavtat, Croatia, June

Charniak, E., and McDermott, D. (1985). *Introduction to Artificial Intelligence*. Addison-Wesley

Cohen, P.R., and Feigenbaum, E. (eds.) (1992). *The Handbook of Artificial Intelligence*, vol. III, sec. XIV (written by T. Dietterich), 323–494

DeJong, G.F., and Mooney, R.J. (1986). Explanation-Based Learning: An Alternative View. *Machine Learning*, 1:145–176

de Raedt, L. (1992). Interactive Concept-Learning and Constructive Induction by Analogy. *Machine Learning*, 8:107–150

Duda, R.O., and Hart, P.E. (1973). *Pattern Classification and Scene Analysis*. New York, John Wiley & Sons

Džeroski, S., and Todorovski, L. (1994). Discovering dynamics. *J. Intelligent Information Systems*

Esposito, F., Malerba, D., and Semeraro, D. (1993). Decision tree pruning as a search in the state space. *Machine Learning: ECML-93* (ed. P. Brazdil), *Proc. European Conf. Machine Learning*, Vienna, April

Everitt, B. (1981). *Cluster Analysis*. London, Heinemann

Fayyad, U.M., and Irani, K.B. (1992). On the Handling of Continuous-Valued Attributes in Decision Tree Generation. *Machine Learning*, 8:87–102

Fisher, D.H. (1987). Knowledge Acquisition via Incremental Conceptual Clustering. *Machine Learning*, 2:139–172

Fisher, D.H., Pazzani, M.J., and Langleym, P. (eds.) (1991). *Concept Formation: Knowledge and Experience in Unsupervised Learning*. San Mateo, Morgan Kaufmann

Gennari, J., Langley, P., and Fisher, D. (1989). Models of Incremental Concept Formation. *Artificial Intelligence*, 40:11–62

Goldberg, D.E. (1989). *Genetic Algorithms in Search, Optimization, and Machine Learning*. Reading, MA, Addison-Wesley

Greiner, R. (1988). Learning by Understanding Analogies. *Artificial Intelligence*, 35:81–125

Haykin, S. (1994). *Neural Networks, A Comprehensive Foundation*. New York, Maxmillan College Publishing Company

Hirsh, H. (1990). *Incremental Version-Space Merging: A General Framework for Concept Learning*. Kluwer Academic

Klimesch, W. (1988). *Struktur und Aktivierung des Gedächtnisses. Das Vernetzungsmodell: Grundlagen und Elemente einer übergreifenden Theorie*. Bern, Verlag Hans Huber, 1984

Kodratoff, Y. (1988) *Introduction to Machine Learning*, London, Pitman

Kodratoff, Y., and Michalski, R.S. (eds.) (1990). *Machine Learning: An Artificial Intelligence Approach*, Vol. 3, Morgan Kaufmann

Kubat, M. (1996). Second Tier for Decision Trees. *Machine Learning: Proceedings of the 13th International Conference*, Morgan Kaufmann, 293–301

Langley, P. (1996). *Elements of Machine Learning*, San Francisco, CA, Morgan Kaufmann

Langley, P., Zytkow, J.M., Simon, H.A., and Bradshaw, G.L. (1986). The Search for Regularity: Four Aspects of Scientific Discovery. In: R.S. Michalski, J.G. Carbonell, and T.M. Mitchell (eds.), *Machine Learning: An Artificial Approach*, Vol 2, Los Altos, CA, Morgan Kaufmann

Langley, P., Simon, H.A., Bradshaw, G.L., and Zytkow, J.M. (1987). *Scientific Discovery: Computational Explorations of the Creative Processes*. MIT Press

Lavrač, N., and Džeroski, S. (1994). *Inductive Logic Programming: Techniques and Applications*. Hertfordshire, Ellis Horwood

Lebowitz, M. (1987). Experiments with Incremental Concept Formation: UNIMEM. *Machine Learning*, 2:103–138

Michalski, R.S. (1969). On the Quasi-Minimal Solution of the General Covering Problem. *Proceedings of the 5th International Symposium on Information Processing (FCIP'69)*, Vol. A3, Bled, Slovenia, 125–128

Michalski, R.S. (1973a). Discovering Classification Rules Using Variable-Valued Logic System CL1. *Proceedings of the 3rd International Conference on Artificial Intelligence, IJCAI*, 162–172

Michalski, R.S. (1973b), AQVAL/1–Computer Implementation of a Variable-Valued Logic System VL1 and Examples of its Application to Pattern Recognition, *Proceedings of the First International Joint Conference on Pattern Recognition*, Washington, DC, 3–17, October 30–November 1

Michalski, R.S. (1980). Pattern Recognition as Rule-Guided Inductive Inference. *IEEE Transactions on Pattern Analysis and Machine Intelligence*, 2(4):349–361, July

Michalski, R.S. (1983). A Theory and Methodology of Inductive Learning. *Artificial Intelligence*, 20:111–161

Michalski, R.S. (1990). Learning Flexible Concepts: Fundamental Ideas and a Method Based on Two-Tiered Representation. In: Y. Kodratoff and R.S. Michalski (eds.), *Machine Learning: An Artificial Intelligence Approach*, Volume III. Morgan Kaufmann, 63–102

Michalski, R.S. (1991). Toward a Unified Theory of Learning: An Outline of Basic Ideas. *Proceedings of the First World Conference on the Fundamentals of Artificial Intelligence*, Paris, July 1–5

Michalski, R.S., Carbonell, J.G., and Mitchell, T.M. (eds.) (1983). *Machine Learning: An Artificial Intelligence Approach*, Morgan Kaufmann

Michalski, R.S., Carbonell, J.G., and Mitchell, T.M. (eds.) (1986). *Machine Learning: An Artificial Intelligence Approach*, Vol. 2, Morgan Kaufmann

Michalski, R.S., and Stepp, R. (1983). Learning from Observation: Conceptual Clustering. In: R.S. Michalski, J.G. Carbonnell, and T.M. Mitchell (eds.), *Machine Learning: An Artificial Intelligence Approach*. Morgan Kaufmann

Michalski, R.S., and Tecuci, G. (eds.) (1994) *Machine Learning: A Multistrategy Approach*, Volume IV, Morgan Kaufmann.

Michie, D. (1988). Machine learning in the next five years. *EWSL-88 – Proc. 3rd European Working Session on Learning*, Glasgow, London, Pitman

Mingers, J. (1989a). An Empirical Comparison of Selection Measures for Decision Tree Induction. *Machine Learning*, 3:319–342

Mingers, J. (1989b). An empiricial comparison of pruning methods for decision-tree induction. *Machine Learning*, 4(2)

Minsky, M. (1975). A Framework for Representing Knowledge. In: P.H. Winston (ed.), *The Psychology of Computer Vision*. New York, McGraw-Hill, 221–277

Minsky. M., and Papert, S. (1969). *Perceptrons*. Cambridge, MA, MIT Press

Mitchell, T.M. (1982). Generalization as Search. *Artificial Intelligence*, 18:203–226

Mitchell, T.M. (1996). *Machine Learning*. McGraw-Hill

Mitchell, T.M., Keller, R.M., and Kedar-Cabelli, S.T. (1986). Explanation-Based Generalization: A Unifying View. *Machine Learning*, 1:47–80

Muggleton, S. (1991). Inductive Logic programming. *New Generation Computing*, 8:295–318

Muggleton S. (ed.) (1992). *Inductive Logic Programming*. Academic Press.

Niblett, T. (1987). Constructing Decision Trees in Noisy Domains. In: I. Bratko and N. Lavrač (eds.), *Progress in Machine Learning*. Wilmslow, England, Sigma Press

Niblett, T. and Bratko, I. (1986) Learning decision trees in noisy domains. In: M. Bramer (ed.), *Expert Systems 86: Proc. Expert Systems 86 Conf.* Cambridge University Press

Núñez, M. (1991). The Use of Background Knowledge in Decision Tree Induction. *Machine Learning*, 6:231–350

Quinlan, J.R. (1986). Induction of Decision Trees. *Machine Learning*, 1:81–106

Quinlan, J.R. (1990a). Probabilistic Decision Trees. In: Kodratoff, Y., and Michalski, R.S. (eds.), *Machine Learning: An Artificial Intelligence Approach*, Volume III. Morgan Kaufmann, 140–152

Quinlan, J.R. (1990b). Learning Logical Definitions from Relations. *Machine Learning*, 5:239–266 XXXX

Quinlan, J.R., and Cameron-Jones, R.M. (1993). FOIL: A Midterm Report. *Proceedings of the European Conference on Machine Learning*, 3–20

Rissland, E., and Ashley, K. (1989). A Case-Based System for Trade Secrets Law. *Proceedings of the First International Conference on Artificial Intelligence and Law*, Boston, MA: ACM Press, 60–66

Rosenblatt, M. (1958). The Perceptron: A Probabilistic Model for Information Storage and Organization in the Brain. *Psychological Review* 65:386–408

Rosenblatt, M. (1962). *Principles of Neurodynamics: Perceptrons and the Theory of Brain Mechanisms*. Spartan Books, Washington, D.C.

Rumelhart, D., Hinton, G. and Williams, J. (1986). Learning Internal Representations by Error Propagation. In: D. Rumelhart and J. McClelland (eds.), *Parallel Distributed Processing*, MIT Press, Cambridge, Vol.1, 318–362

Sethi, I.K. (1990). Entropy Nets: From Decision Trees to Neural Networks. *Proceedings of the IEEE*, 78:1605–1613

Sethi, I.K., and Sarvarayudu, G.P.R.(1982). Hierarchical Classsifier Design Using Mutual Information. *IEEE Transactions on Pattern Analysis and Machine Intelligence*, PAMI-4: 441–445

Sutton, R.S. (1988). Learning to Predict by the Methods of Temporal Differences. *Machine Learning* 3:9–44

Towell, G.G., Shavlik, J., and Noordewier, M.O. (1990). Refinement of Approximate Domain Theories by Knowledge-Based Networks. *Proceedings of the Eight National Conference on Artificial Intelligence*, 861–866

Towell, G.G., Craven, M.W., and Shavlik, J. (1991). Constructive Induction in Knowledge-Based

Neural Networks. *Proceedings of the 8th International Workshop on Machine Learning*, San Mateo, 213–217.

Vafaie, H., and De Jong, K.A. (1994). Improving the Performance of a Rule Induction System Using Genetic Algorithms. In: R.S. Michalski and G. Tecuci (eds.), *Machine Learning: A Multistrategy Approach, Vol. IV*. San Mateo, CA, Morgan Kaufmann

Venturini, G. (1993). SIA: a Supervised Inductive Algorithm with Genetic Search for Learning Attributes Based Concepts. *Proceedings of the European Conference on Machine Learning*, Vienna, April, 280–296.

Widmer, G., and Kubat, M. (1993). Effective Learning in Dynamic Environments by Explicit Context Tracking. *Proceedings of the European Conference on Machine Learning ECML'93*, Vienna, 3–7 April, 227–243

Widmer, G., and Kubat, M. (1996). Learning in the Presence of Concept Drift and Hidden Contexts. *Machine Learning*, 23:69–101

Winston, P.H. (1970). Learning Structural Descriptions from Examples. *Technical report AI-TR-231*, MIT Cambridge, MA, September

Wnek, J., Kaufman, K., Bloedorn, E., and Michalski, R.S. (1995). Selective Induction Learning System AQ15c: The Method and User's Guide. *Reports of the Machine Learning and Inference Laboratory, MLI 95-4*, Machine Learning and Inference Laboratory, George Mason University, Fairfax, VA

Zhang, J. (1991). Integrating Symbolic and Subsymbolic Approaches in Learning Flexible Concepts. *Proceedings of the 1st International Workshop on Multistrategy Learning*, Harpers Ferry, USA, November 7–9, 289–304

2

Data Mining and Knowledge Discovery: A Review of Issues and a Multistrategy Approach

Ryszard S. Michalski and Kenneth A. Kaufman

ABSTRACT

An enormous proliferation of databases in almost every area of human endeavor has created a great demand for new, powerful tools for turning data into useful, task-oriented knowledge. In efforts to satisfy this need, researchers have been exploring ideas and methods developed in machine learning, pattern recognition, statistical data analysis, data visualization, neural nets, etc. These efforts have led to the emergence of a new research area, frequently called data mining and knowledge discovery. The first part of this chapter is a compendium of ideas on the applicability of symbolic machine learning methods to this area. The second part describes a multistrategy methodology for *conceptual data exploration*, by which we mean the derivation of high-level concepts and descriptions from data through symbolic reasoning involving both data and background knowledge. The methodology, which has been implemented in the INLEN system, combines machine learning, database and knowledge-based technologies. To illustrate the system's capabilities, we present results from its application to a problem of discovery of economic and demographic patterns in a database containing facts and statistics about the countries of the world. The results presented demonstrate a high potential utility of the methodology for assisting in solving practical data mining and knowledge discovery tasks.

Machine Learning and Data Mining: Methods and Applications
Edited by R.S. Michalski, I Bratko and M. Kubat
© 1997 John Wiley & Sons Ltd

2.1 INTRODUCTION

The current information age is characterized by an extraordinary expansion of data that are being generated and stored about all kinds of human endeavors. An increasing proportion of these data is recorded in the form of computer databases, in order that the computer technology may easily access it. The availability of very large volumes of such data has created a problem of how to extract from them useful, task-oriented knowledge.

Data analysis techniques that have been traditionally used for such tasks include regression analysis, cluster analysis, numerical taxonomy, multidimensional analysis, other multivariate statistical methods, stochastic models, time series analysis, nonlinear estimation techniques, and others (e.g., [DW80], [Tuk86], [MT89], [Did89], and [Sha96]). These techniques have been widely used for solving many practical problems. They are, however, primarily oriented toward the extraction of quantitative and statistical data characteristics, and as such have inherent limitations.

For example, a statistical analysis can determine covariances and correlations between variables in data. It cannot, however, characterize the dependencies at an abstract, conceptual level, and produce a causal explanation of reasons why these dependencies exist. Nor can it develop a justification of these relationships in the form of higher-level logic-style descriptions and laws. A statistical data analysis can determine the central tendency and variance of given factors, and a regression analysis can fit a curve to a set of datapoints. These techniques cannot, however, produce a qualitative description of the regularities and determine their dependence on factors not explicitly provided in the data, nor can they draw an analogy between the discovered regularity and a regularity in another domain.

A numerical taxonomy technique can create a classification of entities, and specify a numerical similarity among the entities assembled into the same or different categories. It cannot, however, build qualitative descriptions of the classes created and hypothesize reasons for the entities being in the same category. Attributes that define the similarity, as well as the similarity measures, must be defined by a data analyst in advance. Also, these techniques cannot by themselves draw upon background domain knowledge in order to automatically generate relevant attributes and determine their changing relevance to different data analysis problems.

To address such tasks as those listed above, a data analysis system has to be equipped with a substantial amount of background knowledge, and be able to perform symbolic reasoning tasks involving that knowledge and the data. In summary, traditional data analysis techniques facilitate useful data interpretations, and can help to generate important insights into the processes behind the data. These interpretations and insights are the ultimate knowledge sought by those who build databases. Yet, such knowledge is not created by these tools, but instead has to be derived by human data analysts.

In efforts to satisfy the growing need for new data analysis tools that will overcome the above limitations, researchers have turned to ideas and methods developed in machine learning. The field of machine learning is a natural source of ideas for this purpose, because the essence of research in this field is to develop computational models for acquiring knowledge from facts and background knowledge. These and related efforts have led to the emergence of a new research area, frequently called data mining and knowledge discovery, e.g., [Lbo81], [MBS82], [ZG89], [Mic91b], [Zag91], [MKKR92], [VHMT93], [FPSU96], [EH96], [BKKPS96], and [FHS96].

The first part of this chapter is a compendium of ideas on the applicability of symbolic machine learning methods to data mining and knowledge discovery. While this chapter concentrates on methods for extracting knowledge from numeric and symbolic data, many techniques can also be useful when applied to text, speech or image data (e.g., [BMM96], [Uma97], [CGCME97], [MRDMZ97]).

The second part of this chapter describes a methodology for *conceptual data exploration*, by which we mean the derivation of high-level concepts and descriptions from data. The methodology, stemming mainly from various efforts in machine learning, applies diverse methods and tools for determining task-oriented data characterizations and generalizations. These characterizations are expressed in the form of logic-style descriptions, which can be easily interpreted and used for decision-making. The term *task-oriented* emphasizes the fact that an exploration of the same data may produce different knowledge; therefore, the methodology tries to connect the task at hand with the way of exploring the data. Such task-orientation naturally requires a multistrategy approach, because different tasks may need to employ different data exploration and knowledge generation operators.

The aim of the methodology is to produce knowledge in a form that is close to data descriptions that an expert might produce. Such a form may include combinations of different types of descriptions, e.g., logical, mathematical, statistical, and graphical. The main constraint is that these descriptions should be easy to understand and interpret by an expert in the given domain, i.e., they should satisfy the "principle of comprehensibility" [Mic93]. Our first efforts in developing a methodology for multistrategy data exploration have been implemented in the INLEN system [MKKR92]. The system combines a range of machine learning methods and tools with more traditional data analysis techniques. These tools provide a user with the capability to make different kinds of data explorations and to derive different kinds of knowledge from a database.

The INLEN methodology for intelligent data exploration directly reflects the aims of the current research on data mining and knowledge discovery. In this context, it may be useful to explain the distinction between the concepts of data mining and knowledge discovery, as proposed in [FPS96]. According to this distinction, data mining refers to the application of machine learning methods, as well as other methods, to the "enumeration of patterns over the data," and knowledge discovery refers to the process encompassing the entire data analysis lifecycle, from the identification of data analysis goals and the acquisition and organization of raw data to the generation of potentially useful knowledge, its interpretation, and its testing. According to these definitions, the INLEN methodology incorporates both data mining and knowledge discovery techniques.

2.2 MACHINE LEARNING AND MULTISTRATEGY DATA EXPLORATION

This section shows a close relationship between ideas and methods developed in the field of machine learning to the goals of data mining and knowledge discovery. Specifically, it describes how methods of symbolic machine learning can be used for automating or semi-automating a wide range of tasks concerned with conceptual exploration of data and a generation of task-oriented knowledge from them. Let us briefly review some of these methods.

2.2.1 Determining General Rules from Specific Cases

A major class of tools for multistrategy data exploration is based on methods for symbolic inductive learning from examples. Given collections of examples of different decision classes (or cases of a relationship), and problem-relevant knowledge ("background knowledge"), an inductive learning method hypothesizes a general description of each class. Some methods use a fixed criterion for choosing the description from a large number of possibilities, and some allow the user to define a criterion that reflects the problem at hand. A description can be in the form of a set of decision rules, a decision tree, a semantic net, etc. A decision rule can also take on many different forms. Here we will assume the following form:

CLASS ⇐ CONDITION

where CLASS is a statement indicating a class, decision, or a concept name to be assigned to an entity (an object or situation) that satisfies CONDITION; CONDITION is a conjunction of elementary conditions on the values of attributes characterizing the objects; and ⇐ denotes implication.

We will also assume that if CLASS requires a disjunctive description, then several such (conjunctive) rules relate to the same CLASS. To illustrate this point, Figure 2.1 gives an example of a disjunctive description of a class of robot-figures in EMERALD (a large system for demonstrating machine learning and discovery capabilities [KM93]).

Rule A: *Class 1* ⇐   *Jacket Color is Red, Green or Blue &*
                                        Head Shape is Round or Octagonal

Rule B: *Class 1* ⇐   *Head Shape is Square &*
                                        Jacket Color is Yellow

Figure 2.1   A two-rule description of Class 1.

To paraphrase this description, a robot belongs to *Class 1* if the color of its jacket is red, green or blue, and its head is round or octagonal, or, alternatively, its head is square and the color of its jacket is yellow.

The EMERALD system, mentioned above, combines five programs that display different kinds of learning capabilities [KM93]. These capabilities include rule learning from examples (using program AQ15), learning distinctions between structures (INDUCE), conceptual clustering (CLUSTER/2), prediction of object sequences (SPARC), and derivation of equations and rules characterizing data about physical processes (ABACUS). Each of these programs is directly applicable to conceptual data exploration. For example, the rules in Figure 2.1 were generated by the AQ15 rule module [MMHL86], [HMM86] from a set of "positive" and "negative" examples of Class 1 of robot-figures.

AQ15 learns *attributional* descriptions of entities, i.e., descriptions involving only their attributes. More general descriptions, *structural* or *relational*, also involve relationships among components of the entities, the attributes of the components, and quantifiers. Such descriptions are produced, for example, by the INDUCE module of EMERALD [Lar77], [BMR87]. Constructing structural descriptions requires a more complex description language that includes multi-argument predicates, for example, PROLOG, or Annotated Predicate Calculus [Mic83], [BMK97].

For database exploration, attributional descriptions appear to be the most important and the easiest to implement, because typical databases characterize entities in terms of attributes, not relations. One simple and popular form of attributional description is a decision or classification tree. In such a tree, nodes correspond to attributes, branches stemming from the nodes correspond to attribute values, and leaves correspond to individual classes (e.g., [Qui86]). A decision tree can be transformed into a set of decision rules (a ruleset) by traversing all paths from the root to individual leaves. Such rules can often be simplified by detecting superfluous conditions in them (e.g., [Qui93]). The opposite process of transforming a ruleset into a decision tree is not so direct [Ima95], because a rule representation is more powerful than a tree representation. The term "more powerful" means in this context that a decision tree representing a given ruleset may require superfluous conditions (e.g., [Mic90]).

The input to an attributional learning program consists of a set of examples of individual classes and "background knowledge" (BK) relevant to the given learning problem. The examples (cases of decisions) are in the form of vectors of attribute-value pairs associated with some decision class. Background knowledge is usually limited to information about the legal values of the attributes, their type (the scale of measurement), and a *preference criterion* for choosing among possible candidate hypotheses. Such a criterion may refer to, for example, the computational simplicity of the description, and/or an estimate of its predictive accuracy. In addition to BK, a learning method may have a *representational bias*, i.e., it may constrain the form of descriptions to only a certain type of expressions, e.g., single conjunctions, decision trees, sets of conjunctive rules, or DNF expressions.

In some methods, BK may include more information, e.g., constraints on the interrelationship between various attributes, rules for generating higher level concepts, new attributes, as well as some initial hypothesis [Mic83]. Learned rules are usually *consistent* and *complete* with regard to the input data. This means that they completely and correctly classify all the original "training" examples. Sections 2.5 and 2.8 present consistent and complete example solutions from the inductive concept learning program AQ15c [WKBM95]. In some applications, especially those involving learning rules from noisy data or learning *flexible* concepts [Mic90], it may be advantageous to learn descriptions that are incomplete and/or inconsistent [BMMZ92].

Attributional descriptions can be visualized by mapping them into a planar representation of a discrete multidimensional space (a diagram) spanned over the given attributes [Mic78], [WSWM90]. For example, Figure 2.2 shows a diagrammatic visualization of the rules from Figure 2.1. The diagram in Figure 2.2 was generated by the concept visualization program DIAV [WSWM90], [Wne95].

Each cell in the diagram represents one specific combination of values of the attributes. For example, the cell marked by an X represents the vector: (HeadShape=$\underline{S}$quare, Holding=$\underline{S}$word, JacketColor=$\underline{R}$ed, IsSmiling=$\underline{F}$alse). The four shaded areas marked Class1 (A) represent rule A, and the shaded area marked Class 1 (B) represents rule B. In such a diagram, conjunctive rules correspond to certain regular arrangements of cells that are easy to recognize [Mic78].

The diagrammatic visualization can be used for displaying the *target concept* (the concept to be learned), the training examples (the examples and counter-examples of the concept), and the actual concept learned by a method. By comparing the target concept with the learned concept, one can determine the *error area*, i.e., the area containing all examples that would be incorrectly classified by the learned concept. Such a diagrammatic visualization method can illustrate any kind of attributional learning process [WSWM90].

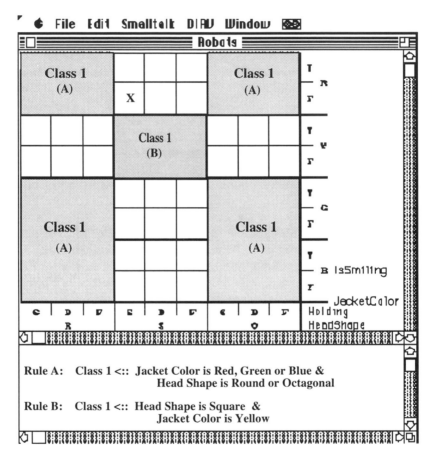

Figure 2.2   A diagrammatic visualization of rules from Figure 2.1.

Two types of data exploration operators can be based on methods for learning concept descriptions from examples:

• Operators for determining general symbolic descriptions of a designated group or groups of entities in a data set. Such descriptions express the common properties of the entities in each group. The operators can use abstract concepts that are not present in the original data via the

mechanism of *constructive induction* (see below). These operators are based on programs for learning *characteristic concept description*s.
• Operators for determining differences between different groups of entities. Such differences are expressed in the form of rules that define properties that characterize one group but not the other. These operators are based on programs for learning *discriminant concept descriptions*.

Section 2.5 will illustrate these two types of descriptions. For more details and their definitions see [Mic83]. Basic methods for concept learning assume that examples do not have errors, that all attributes have a specified value in them, that all examples are located in the same database, and that concepts to be learned have a precise ("crisp") description that does not change over time. In many situations one or more of these assumptions may not hold. This leads to a variety of more complex machine learning and data mining problems:

• *Learning from incorrect data*, i.e., learning from examples that contain a certain amount of errors or noise (e.g., [Qui90], [MKW91]). These problems are important to learning from complex real-world observations, where there is always some amount of noise.

• *Learning from incomplete data*, i.e., learning from examples in which the values of some attributes are unknown (e.g., [Don88], [LHGS96]).

• *Learning from distributed data*, i.e., learning from separate collections of data that must be brought together if the patterns within them are to be exposed (e.g., [RKK95]).

• *Learning drifting or evolving concepts*, i.e., learning concepts that are not stable but changing over time, randomly or in a certain general direction. For example, the "area of interest" of a user is often an evolving concept (e.g., [WK96]).

• *Learning concepts from data arriving over time*, i.e., incremental learning in which currently held hypotheses characterizing concepts may need to be updated to account for the new data (e.g., [MM95]).

• *Learning from biased data*, i.e., learning from a data set that does not reflect the actual distribution of events (e.g., [Fee96]).

• *Learning flexible concepts*, i.e., concepts that inherently lack precise definition and whose meaning is context-dependent; some ideas concerned with this topic include *fuzzy sets* (e.g., [Zad65], [DPY93]), *two-tiered concept representations* (e.g., [Mic90], [BMMZ92]), and *rough sets* (e.g., [Paw91], [Slo92], [Zia94]).

• *Learning concepts at different levels of generality*, i.e., learning descriptions that involve concepts from different levels of generalization hierarchies representing background knowledge (e.g., [KM96]).

• *Integrating qualitative and quantitative discovery*, i.e., determining sets of equations that fit a given set of data points, and qualitative conditions for the application of these equations (e.g., [FM90]).

• *Qualitative prediction*, i.e., discovering patterns in sequences or processes and using these patterns to qualitatively predict the possible continuation of the given sequences or processes (e.g., [Dav81], [MKC85], [MKC86], [DM86]).

Each of these problems is relevant to the derivation of useful knowledge from a collection of data (static or dynamic). Therefore, methods for solving these problems developed in the area of machine learning are directly relevant to data mining and knowledge discovery, in particular, to conceptual data exploration.

2.2.2 Conceptual Clustering

Another class of machine learning methods relevant to data mining and knowledge discovery concerns the problem of building a conceptual classification of a given set of entities. The problem is similar to that considered in traditional cluster analysis, but is defined in a different way. Given a set of attributional descriptions of some entities, a description language for characterizing classes of such entities, and a classification quality criterion, the problem is to partition entities into classes in a way that maximizes the classification quality criterion, and simultaneously to determine general (extensional) descriptions of these classes in the given description language. Thus, a conceptual clustering method seeks not only a classification structure of entities (a dendrogram), but also a symbolic description of the proposed classes (clusters). An important, distinguishing aspect of conceptual clustering is that, unlike in cluster analysis, the properties of class descriptions are taken into consideration in the process of determining the classes (clusters).

To clarify the difference between conceptual clustering and conventional clustering, notice that a conventional clustering method typically determines clusters on the basis of a similarity measure that is a function solely of the properties (attribute values) of the entities being compared, and not of any other factors:

$$Similarity(\text{A, B}) = f(\text{properties}(\text{A}), \text{properties}(\text{B}))$$

where A and B are entities being compared.

In contrast, a conceptual clustering program clusters entities on the basis of a *conceptual cohesiveness*, which is a function of not only properties of the entities, but also of two other factors: the *description language* L, which the system uses for describing the classes of entities, and of the *environment*, E, which is the set of neighboring examples:

$$Conceptual\ cohesiveness(\text{A, B}) = f(\text{properties}(\text{A}), \text{properties}(\text{B}), \text{L, E})$$

Thus, two objects may be similar, i.e., close according to some distance (or similarity) measure, while having a low conceptual cohesiveness, or *vice versa*. An example of the first situation is shown in Figure 2.3. The points (black dots) A and B are "close" to each other; they would therefore be placed into the same cluster by any technique based solely upon the distances between the points. However, these points have small conceptual cohesiveness due to the fact that they belong to configurations representing different concepts. A conceptual clustering method, if equipped with an appropriate description language, would cluster the points in Figure 2.3 into two "ellipses," as people normally would.

A classification quality criterion used in conceptual clustering may involve a variety of factors, such as the *fit* of a cluster description to the data (called sparseness), the *simplicity* of the description, and other properties of the entities or the concepts that describe them [MSD81]. An example of conceptual clustering is presented in Section 2.5.

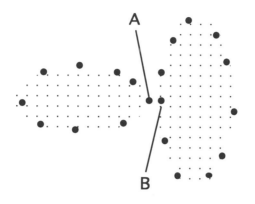

Figure 2.3   An illustration of the difference between closeness and conceptual cohesiveness.

Some new ideas on employing conceptual clustering for structuring text databases and creating concept lattices for discovering dependencies in data are in [CR95a] and [CR95b]. The concepts created through the clustering are linked in lattice structures that can be traversed to represent generalization and specialization relationships.

2.2.3 Constructive Induction

Most methods for learning rules or decision trees from examples assume that the attributes used for describing examples are sufficiently relevant to the learning problem at hand. This assumption does not always hold in practice. Attributes used in the examples may not be directly relevant, and some attributes may be irrelevant or *nonessential*. An important advantage of symbolic methods over statistical methods is that they can relatively easily determine irrelevant or nonessential attributes. An attribute is *nonessential* if there is a complete and consistent description of the classes or concepts to be learned that does not use this attribute. Thus, a nonessential attribute may be either irrelevant or relevant, but will by definition be dispensable. Inductive learning programs such as the rule-learning program AQ, or the decision tree-learning ID3, can cope relatively easily with a large number of nonessential attributes in their input data.

If there are very many nonessential attributes in the initial description of the examples, the complexity of a learning process may significantly increase. Such a situation calls for a method that can efficiently determine the most relevant attributes for the given problem from among all those given initially. Only the most relevant attributes will be used in the description learning process. Determining the most relevant attributes is therefore a useful data exploration operator. Such an operator can also be useful for the data analyst on its own merit, as it may be important to know which attributes are most discriminatory for a given set of classes. By removing less relevant attributes, the representation space is reduced, and the problem becomes simpler. Thus, such a process can be viewed as a form of improving the representation space. Some methods for finding the most relevant attributes are described in [Zag72] and [Bai82].

In many applications, the attributes originally given may only be weakly or indirectly relevant to the problem at hand. In such situations, there is a need for generating new, more relevant attributes that may be functions of the original attributes. These functions may be simple, e.g., a product or sum of a set of the original attributes, or very complex, e.g., a Boolean attribute based on the presence or absence of a straight line or circle in an image [Bon70]. Finally, in some situations, it will be desirable to abstract some attributes, that is, to group some attribute values into units, and thus reduce the attribute's range of possible values. A quantization of continuous attributes is an example of such an operation.

All the above operations—removing less relevant attributes, adding more relevant attributes, and abstracting attributes—are different forms of improving the original representation space for learning. A learning process that consists of two (intertwined) phases, one concerned with the construction of the "best" representation space, and the second concerned with generating the "best" hypothesis in the found space is called *constructive induction* [Mic78], [Mic83], [WM94]. An example of a constructive induction program is AQ17 [BWM93], which performs all three types of improvements of the original representation space. In this program, the process of generating new attributes is done by combining initial attributes by mathematical and/or logical operators and selecting the "best" combinations, and/or by obtaining advice from an expert [BWM93], [BM96].

2.2.4 Selection of the Most Representative Examples

When a database is very large, determining general patterns or rules characterizing different concepts may be very time-consuming. To make the process more efficient, it may be useful to extract from the database the most representative or important cases (examples) of given classes or concepts. Most such cases are those that are either most typical or most extreme (assuming that there is not too much noise in the data). One method for determining the latter ones, the so-called "method of outstanding representatives," is described in [ML78].

2.2.5 Integration of Qualitative and Quantitative Discovery

In a database that contains numerical attributes, a useful discovery might be an equation binding these attributes. For instance, from a table of planetary data including planets' masses, densities, distances from the sun, periods of rotation, and lengths of local years, one could automatically derive Kepler's Law that the cube of the planet's distance from the sun is proportional to the square of the length of its year. This is an example of quantitative discovery. The application of machine learning to quantitative discovery was pioneered by the BACON system [LBS83], and then explored by many systems since, such as COPER [Kok86], FAHRENHEIT [Zyt87], and ABACUS [FM90]. Similar problems have been explored independently by Zagoruiko [Zag72] under the name of empirical prediction.

Some equations may not apply directly to data, because of an inappropriate value of a constant, or different equations may apply under different qualitative conditions. For example, in applying Stoke's Law to determine the velocity of a falling ball, if the ball is falling through a vacuum, its velocity depends on the length of time it has been falling and on the gravitational force being exerted upon it. A ball falling through some sort of fluid will reach a terminal velocity dependent on the radius and mass of the ball and the viscosity of the fluid.

A program ABACUS [Gre88], [FM90], [Mic91a] is able to determine quantitative laws under different qualitative conditions. It partitions the data into example sets, each of which adheres to a different equation determined by a quantitative discovery module. The qualitative discovery module can then determine conditions/rules that characterize each of these example sets (in the case of Stoke's Law, the rules would be based on the medium of descent).

2.2.6 Qualitative Prediction

Most programs that determine rules from examples determine them from instances of various classes of objects. An instance of a concept exemplifies that concept regardless of its relationship to other examples. Contrast that with a sequence prediction problem, in which a positive example of a concept is directly dependent on the position of the example in the sequence. For example, Figure 2.4 shows a sequence of seven figures. One may ask what object plausibly follows in the eighth position? To answer such a question, one needs to search for a pattern in the sequence, and then use the pattern to predict a plausible sequence continuation. In *qualitative prediction*, the problem is not to predict a specific value of a variable (as in time series analysis), but to *qualitatively* describe a plausible future object, that is, to describe plausible properties of a future object.

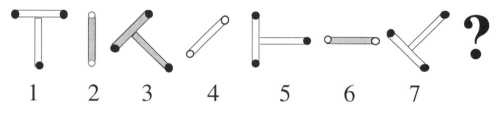

Figure 2.4   An example of a sequence prediction problem.

In the example in Figure 2.4, one may observe that the sequence consists of T-shaped figures with black tips and I-shaped figures with white tips. The figures may be white or shaded, and may be rotated in different orientations at 45-degree intervals. But is there a consistent pattern?

To determine such a pattern, one can employ different *descriptive models*, and instantiate the models to fit the particular sequence. The instantiated model that best fits the data is then used for prediction. Such a method is described in [DM86]. The method employs three descriptive models—periodic, decomposition, and DNF.

The *periodic model* is used to detect repeating patterns in a sequence. For example, Figure 2.4 depicts a recurring pattern that alternates T-shaped and I-shaped objects. In general, there can also be periodic sequences within the periodic sequences. In the figure, the T-shaped objects form a subsequence in which individual objects rotate leftward by 45 degrees.

The second model, the *decomposition model*, is used to characterize a sequence by decision rules in the following general form: "If one or more of the previous elements of the sequence have a given set of characteristics, then the next element will have the following characteristics." One such rule that applies to the sequence in Figure 2.4 would state that if an element in the sequence has a vertical component, then the next element in the sequence will have a shaded component; otherwise it will have no shaded components.

The third model, the DNF (disjunctive normal form) or "catch-all" model, tries to capture general properties characterizing the whole sequence. For example, for the sequence in Figure 2.4, it could instantiate to a statement such as "all elements in the sequence are T-shaped or I-shaped, they have white or shaded interiors, white or black tips, etc.

The program SPARC/G [MKC86] employs these three descriptive models to detect patterns in a sequence of arbitrary objects, and then uses the patterns to predict a plausible continuation for the sequence. For the sequence in Figure 2.4, SPARC/G found the following strong pattern based on the periodic model:

Period< [Shape=T-shape] & [orientation(i+1)=orientation(i) - 45],
        [Shape = I-shape] & [orientation(i+1)=orientation(i) + 45] &
        [shaded(i+1)=unshaded(i)]>

The pattern can be paraphrased: there are two phases in a repeating period (their descriptions are separated by a comma). The first phase involves a T-shaped figure, and the second phase an I-shaped figure. The T-shaped figure rotates to the left, and the I-shaped figure rotates to the right by 45 degrees in relation to its predecessor. I-shaped figures are alternatingly shaded and unshaded. Based on this pattern, a plausible next figure in the sequence would be an unshaded I-shaped figure rotated clockwise 45 degrees in relation to the previous I-shaped figure.

The qualitative prediction capabilities described above can be useful for conceptual exploration of temporal databases in many application domains, such as agriculture, medicine, robotics, economic forecasting, etc.

2.2.7 Summarizing the Machine Learning-Oriented Approach

To help the reader develop a rough sense of what is different and new in the above, let us summarize operations typically performed by traditional multivariate data analysis methods. These include computing mean-corrected or standardized variables, variances, standard deviations, covariances and correlations among attributes; principal component analysis (determining orthogonal linear combinations of attributes that maximally account for the given variance); factor analysis (determining highly correlated groups of attributes); cluster analysis (determining groups of data points that are close according to some distance measure); regression analysis (fitting an equation of an assumed form to given data points);

multivariate analysis of variance; and discriminant analysis. All these methods can be viewed as primarily oriented toward a numerical characterization of a data set.

In contrast, the machine learning methods described above are primarily oriented towards developing symbolic logic-style descriptions of data, which may characterize one or more sets of data qualitatively, differentiate between different classes (defined by different values of designated output variables), create a "conceptual" classification of data, select the most representative cases, qualitatively predict sequences, etc. These techniques are particularly well suited for developing descriptions that involve nominal (categorical) and rank variables in data.

Another important distinction between the two approaches to data analysis is that statistical methods are typically used for globally characterizing a class of objects (a table of data), but not for determining a description for predicting class membership of future objects. For example, a statistical operator may determine that the average lifespan of a certain type of automobile is 7.3 years. Knowledge of the average lifespan of automobiles in a given class does not allow one to recognize the type of a particular automobile for which one obtained information about how long this automobile remained driveable. In contrast, a symbolic machine learning approach might create a description such as "if the front height of a vehicle is between 5 and 6 feet, and the driver's seat is 2 to 3 feet above the ground, then the vehicle is likely to be a minivan." Such descriptions are particularly suitable for assigning entities to classes on the basis of their properties.

The INLEN methodology integrates a wide range of strategies and operators for data exploration based on machine learning research, as well as statistical operators. The reason for such a multistrategy approach is that a data analyst may be interested in many different types of information about the data. Different types of questions require different exploratory strategies and different operators.

2.3 CLASSIFICATION OF DATA EXPLORATION TASKS

The problems described above can be simply illustrated by means of a *general data table* (GDT). Such a table is a generalization of a standard data table used in data analysis (Figure 2.5). It consists of a collection of relational tables (data tables) arranged in layers ordered by the time instance associated with each table. A GDT is used to represent a sequence of entities as they change over time. Examples of a GDT are a sequence of medical records of a patient (when each record is represented as a table of test results), a sequence of descriptions of a crop as it develops in the field, a sequence of data tables characterizing the state of a company during selected time instances, etc.

Columns in the tables correspond to attributes used to characterize entities associated with the rows. These may be initial attributes, given *a priori*, or additional ones generated through a process of *constructive induction* (e.g., [WM94]). Each attribute is assigned a *domain* and a *type*. The *domain* specifies the set of all legal values that the attribute can be assigned in the table. The *type* defines the ordering (if any) of the values in the domain. For example, the AQ15 learning program [MMHL86] allows four types of attributes: nominal (no order), linear (total order), cyclic (cyclic total order), and structured (hierarchical order; see [KM96]).

The attribute type determines the kinds of operations that are allowed on this attribute's values during a learning process.

Entries in each row are values of the attributes for the entity associated with the row. Typically, each row corresponds to a single entity. However, in large databases whose records represent common, repeatable transactions, a column can be added to represent the number of occurrences of that particular transaction. With such information, discovery tools can incorporate a bias based on the frequency of instances.

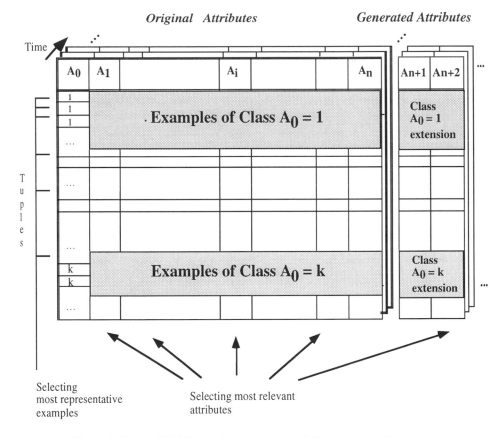

Figure 2.5   A GDT illustrating the role of different symbolic operators.

Entries in the various columns of the table can be specific values of the corresponding attributes, the symbol "?," meaning that a value of this attribute is unknown for the given entity, or the symbol N/A, if an attribute does not apply to a specific entity. For example, "number of legs" usually applies to an animal, but would not apply to a plant.

An important problem of conceptual data exploration is to determine which attribute or attributes in a table functionally depend on other attributes. A related problem is to determine a general form of this relationship that would enable one to predict values of some attributes for future entities. For instance, when it is known that a nominal-scale attribute depends on other (independent) attributes, the problem is to hypothesize a general description of this relationship so that one can predict values of the nominal-scale attribute for future combinations of values of the independent attributes. This problem is equivalent to the problem of concept learning from examples, so methods developed in machine learning directly apply. In such a case, the column in the data table that corresponds to the dependent attribute represents the *output attribute*. The values of that variable are classes whose descriptions are to be learned. In Figure 2.5, for illustration, it was assumed that the first column (attribute A_0) represents values of the output variable. When there are no *a priori* classes to which entities belong, there is no such designated column. In this case, methods of conceptual clustering can be applied to determine a classification of entities.

Below we use the GDT (Figure 2.5) to relate machine learning techniques described in the previous section to data exploration problems.

Learning rules from examples:

Suppose that one discrete attribute in the GDT has been designated as the output attribute, and all or some of the remaining attributes as input (independent) attributes. A set of rows in the table for which the output attribute takes the same value can be viewed as a set of training examples of the decision class (concept) symbolized by this value. Any of the conventional concept learning techniques can be directly applied for determining a rule relating the output attribute to the input attributes. For a general analysis of the data set, every discrete attribute (and continuous attributes as well after quantization) can be considered as an output attribute, and a machine learning method can be applied to determine a relationship between that attribute and other attributes. The determination of such relationships (rules) can be guided by different rule quality criteria, for example, simplicity, cost, predictive accuracy, etc. In the INLEN system, the AQ learning method was applied due to the simplicity and the high comprehensibility of decision rules it generates [WKBM95], [BM96].

Determining time-dependent patterns:

This problem concerns the detection of temporal patterns in sequences of data arranged along the time dimension in a GDT (Figure 2.5). Among the novel ideas that could be applied for analyzing such time-dependent data is a multi-model method for qualitative prediction [DM86], [MKC85], [MKC86]. Another novel idea is a temporal constructive induction technique that can generate new attributes that are designed to capture time-dependent patterns [Dav81], [BM96].

Example selection:

The problem is to select rows from the table that correspond to the most representative examples of different classes. When a datatable is very large, is it important to concentrate the analysis on a representative sample. The "method of outstanding representatives" selects examples (tuples) that are most different from the other examples [ML78].

Attribute selection:

When there are many columns (attributes) in the GDT, it is often desirable to reduce the data table by removing columns that correspond to the least relevant attributes for a designated learning task. This can be done by applying one of many methods for attribute selection, such as Gain Ratio [Qui93] or Promise level [Bai82].

Generating new attributes:

The problem is to generate additional columns that correspond to new attributes generated by a constructive induction procedure. These new attributes are created by using the problem's background knowledge and/or special heuristic procedures as described in papers on constructive induction, e.g., [BWM93].

Clustering:

The problem is to automatically partition the rows of the table into groups that correspond to "conceptual clusters," that is, sets of entities with a high conceptual cohesiveness [MSD81]. Such a clustering operator will generate an additional column in the table that corresponds to a new attribute "cluster name." The values of this attribute for each tuple in the table indicate the assigned class of the entity. Rules that describe clusters are stored separately in the Knowledge Base and linked to the entities via *knowledge segments* (see Section 2.4). An example of a clustering is presented in Section 2.5.

Determining attribute dependencies:

The problem is to determine relationships, such as correlations, causal dependencies, logical or functional dependencies among the attributes (columns) in the given GDT, using statistical and logical methods.

Incremental rule update:

The problem is to update working knowledge (in particular, rulesets characterizing relationships among attributes in the GDT) to accommodate new instances or time slices in the table. To do so, an incremental learning program must be applied to synthesize the prior knowledge with the new information. The incremental learning process may be *full-memory*, *partial-memory*, or *no-memory*, depending on how much of the original training data is maintained in the incremental learning process [HMM86], [RM88], [MM95].

Searching for approximate patterns in (imperfect) data:

For some GDTs, it may not be possible (or useful) to find complete and consistent descriptions. In such cases, it is important to determine patterns that hold for a large number of cases, but not necessarily for all. An important case of this problem is when some entries in the table are missing or incorrect. The problem is then to determine the best (i.e., the most plausible) hypothesis that accounts for most of the available data.

Filling in missing data:

Given a data table in which some entries are missing, determine plausible values of the missing entries on the basis of an analysis of the currently known data. An interesting approach to this problem is to apply a multi-line reasoning, based on the core theory of human plausible reasoning [CM81], [Don88], [CM89].

Determining decision structures from declarative knowledge (decision rules):

Suppose that a set of general decision rules (a declarative form of knowledge) has been hypothesized for a given data set (GDT). If this ruleset is to be used for predicting new cases (by a computer program, or by an expert), it may be desirable to convert it into the form of a decision tree (or a more general form, a decision structure) that is tailored to a given decision-making situation (e.g., by taking into consideration the cost of measuring attributes). A methodology for doing this and arguments for and against using such an approach (as opposed to the traditional method of learning of decision trees directly from examples) are discussed in [IM93], [Ima95], and [MI97].

Methods for performing the above operations on data tables have been implemented in various machine learning programs (e.g., [MCM83], [MCM86], [FR86], [Kod88], and [KM90]). Below we describe the INLEN system that aims at ultimately incorporating all of these programs as operators in one integrated system for the generation of knowledge from data.

2.4 INTEGRATION OF MANY OPERATORS IN INLEN

To make the data exploration operations described above easily available to a data analyst, and applicable in sequences in which the output from one operation is an input to another one, programs performing these operations need to be integrated into one system. This idea underlies the INLEN system [KMK91], [MKKR92], [MK97]. The name INLEN is derived from **in**ference and **lear**ning. The system integrates machine learning programs, statistical data analysis tools, a database, a knowledge base, inference procedures, and various supporting programs under a unified architecture and graphical interface. The knowledge base is used for storing, updating and applying rules and other forms of knowledge that may be employed for assisting data exploration, and for reporting results from it.

The general architecture of INLEN is presented in Figure 2.6. The system consists of a database (DB) connected to a knowledge base (KB), and a set of operators. The operators are divided into three classes:

- *DMOs:* Data Management Operators, which operate on the database. These are conventional data management operators that are used for creating, modifying and displaying relational tables.
- *KMOs:* Knowledge Management Operators, which operate on the knowledge base. These operators play a similar role to the DMOs, but apply to the rules and other structures in the knowledge base.
- *KGOs:* Knowledge Generation Operators, which operate on both the data and knowledge bases. These operators perform symbolic and numerical data exploration tasks. They are based on various machine learning and inference programs, on conventional data exploration techniques, and on visualization operators for displaying graphically the results of exploration. The diagrammatic visualization method DIAV [Wne95] is used for displaying the effects of symbolic learning operations on data.

The KGOs are the heart of the INLEN system. To facilitate their use, the concept of a *knowledge segment* was introduced [KMK91], [MK97]. A knowledge segment is a structure that links one or more relational tables from the database with one or more structures from the knowledge base. KGOs can be viewed as modules that perform some form of inference or transformation on knowledge segments and, as a result, create new knowledge segments. Knowledge segments are both inputs to and outputs from the KGOs. Thus, they facilitate the passage of data and knowledge from one knowledge generation operator to another.

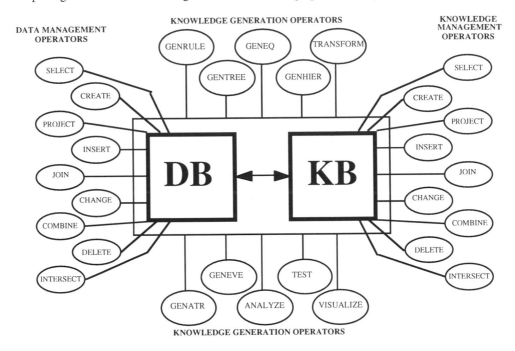

Figure 2.6   An architecture of the INLEN system for multistrategy data exploration.

The execution of a KGO usually requires some background knowledge, and is guided by control parameters (if some parameters are not specified, default values are used). The background knowledge may contain some general knowledge as well as knowledge specifically relevant to a given application domain, such as a specification of the value sets and types of attributes, the constraints and relationships among attributes, initial rules hypothesized by an expert, etc. The KGOs can be classified into groups, based on the type of operation they perform. Each group includes a number of specific operators that are instantiated by a combination of parameters. The basic operator groups are as follows:

• GENRULE operators generate different kinds of decision rules from given facts. A specific operator may generate rules characterizing a set of facts, discriminating between groups of facts, characterizing a sequence of events, and determining differences between sequences, based on programs such as AQ15c [WKBM95] and SPARC/G [MKC86]. A KGO for learning rules can usually work in either incremental or batch mode. In the incremental mode, it tries to improve or refine the existing knowledge, while in the batch mode, it tries to create entirely new knowledge based on the facts in the database, and knowledge in the knowledge base.

- GENTREE operators build a decision structure from a given set of decision rules (e.g., [IM93]), or from examples (e.g., [Qui93]). A decision structure is a generalization of the concept of a decision tree in which nodes can be assigned an attribute or a function of attributes. Individual branches may be assigned a set of attribute values. Leaves may be assigned a set of decisions [IM93], [Ima95].

- GENEQ operators generate equations characterizing numerical data sets and qualitatively describing the conditions under which these equations apply (e.g., [FM90]).

- GENHIER operators build conceptual clusters or hierarchies. They are based on the program CLUSTER methodology [MSD81]. The operator in INLEN is based on the reimplementation in C of the program CLUSTER/2 [Ste84].

- TRANSFORM operators perform various transformations on the knowledge segments, e.g., generalization or specialization, abstraction or concretion, optimization of given rules, etc. according to user provided criteria. For instance, one such operator climbs an attribute's generalization hierarchy to build more general decision rules [KM96].

- GENATR operators generate new attribute sets by creating new attributes [BM96], selecting the most representative attributes from the original set [Bai82], or by abstracting attributes [Ker92].

- GENEVE operators generate events, facts or examples that satisfy given rules, select the most representative events from a given set [ML78], determine examples that are similar to a given example [CM89], or predict the value of a given variable using an expert system shell or a decision structure.

- ANALYZE operators analyze various relationships that exist in the data, e.g., determining the degree of similarity between two examples, checking if there is an implicative relationship between two variables, etc. Statistical and symbolic operators alike may perform these tasks.

- TEST operators test the performance of a given set of rules on an assumed set of facts. The output from these operators is a confusion matrix—a table whose (i,j)th element shows how many examples from the class i were classified by the rules to be in class j. These operators can also be used to apply the rules to any given situation to determine a decision. The TEST operator implemented in INLEN is based on the ATEST program [Rei84].

- VISUALIZE operators are used to present data and/or knowledge to the user in a convenient, easy-to-understand format [Wne95].

Summarizing, INLEN integrates a large set of operators for performing various types of operations on the data base, on the knowledge base, or the data and knowledge bases combined.

2.5 ILLUSTRATION OF CLUSTERING AND LEARNING OPERATORS

Among the most important knowledge generation operators implemented in INLEN are the operator for creating a classification of data (clustering), and the operator for learning general rules relating a designated concept (attribute) to other designated attributes. The first operator is realized by the CLUSTER/2 program for conceptual clustering [Ste84]. The second operator is realized by the AQ15c rule learning program [WKBM95]. This section illustrates these operators through an application to a datatable characterizing hard drives (Figure 2.7). The datatable is based on information published in the October 1994 issue of *MacUser*.

Hard Drive	AC Outlet	SCSI 50-Pin	FCC Class B	Passwd Protect	Encrypt	5yr Warranty	Toll-free Support	Guarantee	Loaners	Capacity	Group
Apple 1050	no	yes	yes	yes	no	no	yes	by dealer	by dealer	low	1
Micropolis	no	yes	yes	yes	yes	yes	no	no	no	low	2
SLMO 1000	no	yes	Class A	yes	no	yes	no	no	yes	low	2
Focus 1G	yes	yes	yes	yes	no	no	yes	yes	yes	low	1
GHD 1200S	no	yes	yes	no	no	yes	no	no	no	low	2
Joule 1080	yes	no	yes	yes	no	yes	yes	yes	no	low	1
Liberty 1GB	no	25 pin	yes	yes	no	no	no	yes	yes	low	3
Spitfire 1GB	yes	yes	yes	yes	no	yes	no	yes	no	low	2
PowerUser 1070	no	yes	yes	no	no	no	yes	yes	no	low	1
P1000	no	yes	yes	yes	no	no	yes	yes	no	low	1
Seagate 1075	yes	yes	yes	yes	no	no	yes	yes	no	low	1
Minipak 1000	no	yes	yes	yes	no	no	no	yes	yes	low	3
PowerCity 1GB	yes	yes	yes	yes	no	on mech.	yes	yes	no	low	1
Spin 1021	no	yes	yes	yes	no	yes	yes	yes	no	low	1
APS MS 1.7	no	yes	yes	yes	no	yes	yes	yes	no	high	1
Seagate 2GB	no	yes	yes	yes	yes	yes	no	no	no	high	2
SLMO 2000	no	yes	no	yes	no	yes	no	no	yes	high	2
Focus 2G	yes	yes	yes	yes	no	no	yes	yes	yes	high	1
FWB 1760MF	no	68 pin SCSI2	yes	yes	yes	no	no	no	if avail.	high	3
Liberty 2GB	no	no	yes	yes	no	no	no	yes	yes	high	3
Loviel L2000	yes	yes	yes	yes	no	yes	no	yes	yes	high	2
Seagate 2.1	yes	yes	yes	yes	no	yes	no	yes	no	high	2
PowerUser 1801	no	yes	yes	no	no	no	yes	yes	no	high	1
MacP Sg 28	no	yes	yes	yes	no	yes	no	yes	no	high	2

Figure 2.7   A datatable characterizing hard drives.

In the table presented in Figure 2.7, each row (except for the first one) describes a hard drive in terms of the attributes specified in the first row. Suppose that the task of data exploration is to develop a classification of the hard drives into some meaningful categories. For this task, the operator CLUSTER is applied. Let us assume that the operator will seek a clustering that maximizes the quality of classification, as defined by two criteria: the simplicity of the descriptions of generated categories, and the cohesiveness of the descriptions (measured by the ratio of the number of instances in the datatable covered by a given description to the number of possible instances covered by the description). The input to the conceptual clustering operator is the table in Figure 2.7 (without the rightmost column, which, for the sake of saving space, already represents the result of clustering).

The result of applying the clustering operator is a knowledge segment containing two components—a new, extended datatable, and a set of rules. The new table, in comparison to the input table, has an additional column—the rightmost column in Figure 2.7, labeled "Group," which represents the category assignments of the drives by the clustering operator. The second component is the set of rules describing the categories that were generated. Here are the rules describing the categories created by the operator:

[Class 1] ⇐ [Toll_free_Support is yes] & [FCC_Class-B is yes] & [Encryption is no] & [SCSI_50-Pin is yes or no] & [Guarantee is yes or by dealer]

[Class 2] ⇐ [Toll_free_Support is no] & [SCSI_50-Pin is yes] & [5yr_Warranty is yes] & [Guarantee is yes or no] & [Loaners is yes or no]

[Class 3] ⇐ [Toll_free_Support is no] & [FCC_Class-B is yes] & [AC outlet is yes] & [Passwd_Protect is yes] & [5yr_Warranty is no] & [Guarantee is not by dealer] & [Loaners is yes or if available]

Thus, the operator created three categories of hard drives and described each category in the form of rules. Each rule shows all the characteristics common to a given category, that is, it represents a *characteristic description* of a category [Mic83]. (Note that some of the conditions in these rules appear to be redundant. For example, the last condition of the Class 2 rule says that Loaners is yes or no. This can be explained by the presence of a third value, "by dealer," that neither guarantees nor rules out a loaner.) These characterizations do not point out the most significant distinctions between a given category and other categories.

To create a description that points out the most significant distinctions, one needs to apply the operator that creates *discriminant descriptions* [Mic83]. The operator (GENRULE) is applied to the extended datatable in Figure 2.7, using the "Group" column as its output attribute. The result is a set of new decision rules:

[Class 1] ⇐ [Toll_free_Support is yes]
[Class 2] ⇐ [Toll_free_Support is no] & [5yr_Warranty is yes]
[Class 3] ⇐ [Toll_free_Support is no] & [5yr_Warranty is no]

The rules obtained are much simpler and easier to interpret than the rules generated by the CLUSTER operator that invented the three classes. The reason is that a discriminant description lists only those characteristics that are necessary to discriminate a given category from the other categories. Discriminant descriptions are designed to provide the minimum information needed for distinguishing between entities of different categories. Both characteristic and discriminant descriptions are *complete* and *consistent* with all the examples in Figure 2.7, i.e., they classify all examples in the same way.

2.6   DATA AND RULE VISUALIZATION

It is desirable for data analysts to be able to visualize the results of different operators in order to relate visually the input data to the rules that have been learned from them, to see which datapoints would corroborate or contradict these rules, to identify possible errors, etc. To this end, INLEN supports the visualization of data and knowledge through the *diagrammatic visualization* method implemented in the DIAV program [Mic78], [Wne95].

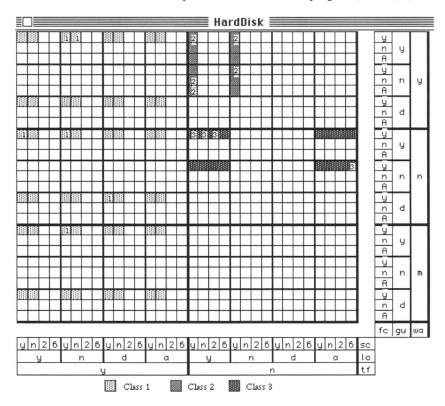

Figure 2.8   A visualization of the *characteristic description* created by the conceptual clustering operator.

Let us illustrate the method with the hard disk classification problem presented in the previous section. The representation space, projected onto six attributes, is pictured in Figure 2.8. To simplify the visualization, the attributes used to span the diagram, Toll_free_Support (tf), Loaners (lo), SCSI_50-Pin (sc), FCC_Class-B (fc), Guarantee (gu), and 5yr_Warranty (wa), are only those that appeared most frequently in the characteristic descriptions created by the conceptual clustering operator. Each cell in the diagram corresponds to one combination of attribute values, specified by the annotations of the columns and rows. Thus the upper-leftmost cell corresponds to a datapoint in which all six of these attributes have the value yes (y).

The 24 examples from Figure 2.7 have been projected onto this space, and are represented by placing their class number in the corresponding cells. The shaded areas represent the characteristic descriptions of the classes generated by the clustering operator, the lightest color indicates Class 1, the intermediate shade represents Class 2, and the darkest one indicates Class 3. As can be seen in the diagram, the descriptions generated by the clustering operator are generalizations of the input instances, as they also cover instances that have not yet been observed (shaded areas without a number).

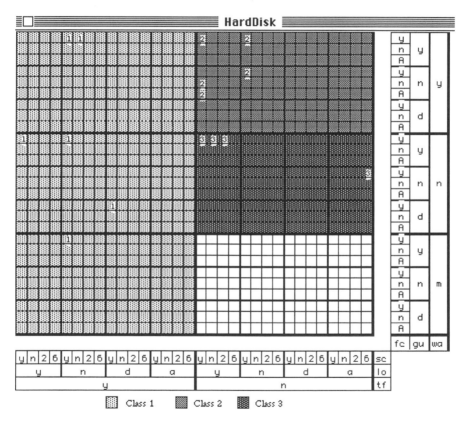

Figure 2.9 A visualization of the *discriminant rules* created by the inductive generalization operator.

For comparison, Figure 2.9 is a visualization of the discriminant descriptions generated by the rule_learning operator from the input examples classified according to the previously generated clustering. The organization of the diagram in Figure 2.9 is the same as in Figure 2.8 with regard to the labeling of examples, classes, rows and columns. Because discriminant descriptions focus only on features that distinguish among the classes, they cover broader sections of the representation space. Thus, they are much more general than characteristic descriptions.

The discriminant descriptions obtained divide the representation space into four sections, three corresponding to the rules for the three classes, and the fourth to the indeterminate portion of the event space, containing none of the known instances of the three categories. This latter section is defined by the combination of characteristics: Toll_free_Support = no and 5yr_Warranty = on_mechanism.

Note also that due to the greater generality of the discriminant descriptions, the indeterminate area is much smaller than in the case of characteristic descriptions (the blank area in Figure 2.8).

As can be seen from the diagram, the discriminant descriptions generated are consistent and complete with regard to all of the examples presented, that is, they preserve the classification of cases created by the clustering operator. Summarizing, the visualization method presented above makes it very easy to see how generated descriptions relate to the cases from which they were generated.

2.7 LEARNING RULES WITH STRUCTURED ATTRIBUTES

In addition to conventional symbolic and numerical attributes, INLEN supports a new kind of attribute, called *structured*. Such attributes have value sets ordered into hierarchies [Mic80]. To take advantage of the properties of structured attributes in executing inductive learning, new inductive generalization rules have been defined.

An inductive generalization rule (or transmutation) takes an input statement and relevant background knowledge, and hypothesizes a more general statement [Mic80], [Mic83], [Mic94]. For example, removing a condition from the premise of a decision rule is a generalization transmutation (this is called a *dropping condition* generalization rule), since if the premise has fewer conditions, a larger set of instances can satisfy it.

A powerful inductive generalization operator used in the AQ learning programs is the *extension-against* operator. If rule **R1: C ⇐ [x_i = A] & CTX1** characterizes a subset of positive concept examples, **E⁺**, of the concept **C**, and rule **R2: C ⇐ [x_i = B] & CTX2** characterizes negative examples, **E⁻** (where **A** and **B** represent disjoint subsets of the values of x_i, and the CTXs stand for any additional conditions), then the *extension of R1 against R2 along dimension x_i*

$$C \Leftarrow R1 \text{ —| } R2 / x_i$$

produces a new rule **R3: [$x_i \neq B \cup \varepsilon$]**, which is a *consistent generalization* of **R1**, that is, a generalization that does not intersect logically with **R2** [MM71], [Mic83]. The value of the parameter ε controls the degree of generalization. If ε is ∅ (the empty set), then **R3** is the *maximal consistent generalization* of **R1**. If ε is $D(x_i) \setminus (A \cup B)$ (where $D(x_i)$ is the domain of x_i), then **R3** is the minimal consistent generalization of **R1** involving only x_i. In AQ programs, the extension-against operator is typically used with $\varepsilon = ∅$.

By repeating the extension-against operator until the resulting rule no longer covers any negative examples, a consistent concept description (one that covers no negative examples) can be generated. Such a process can be applied to generate a description (cover) that is complete and consistent with regard to all the training examples.

By applying the extension-against operator with different values of the parameter ε, one can generate descriptions with different degrees of generality. For instance, in AQ15c, in order to learn a characteristic rule, the output of the operator with ε initially set to ∅ is maximally specialized in such a way that it continues to cover all of the positive examples described by the initial extension. If discriminant rules are desired, the extension will be maximally generalized so long as it continues not to cover any negative examples of the concept.

To effectively apply the extension-against operator to structured attributes, new generalization rules need to be defined. Let us illustrate the problem by an example that uses a structured attribute "Food" shown in Figure 2.10. Each non-leaf node denotes a concept that is more general than its children nodes. These relationships need to be taken into consideration when generalizing given facts. Suppose that the concept to be learned is exemplified by statements: "John eats strip steak" and "John doesn't eat vanilla ice cream." There are many consistent generalizations of these facts, for example, "John eats strip steak," "John eats steak," "John eats cattle," "John eats meat," "John eats meat or vegetables," or "John eats anything but vanilla ice cream." The first statement represents the maximally specific description (no generalization), the last statement represents the maximally general description, and the remaining ones represent intermediate levels of generalization. A problem arises in determining the generalization of most interest for a given situation. We approach this problem by drawing insights from human reasoning.

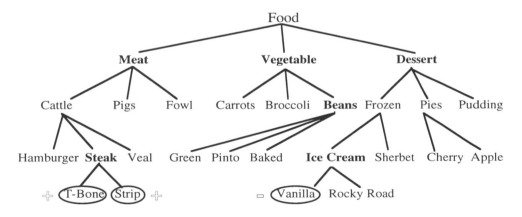

Anchor nodes are shown in bold. Nodes marked by ✛ and – are values occurring in positive and negative examples, respectively.

Figure 2.10 The domain of a structured attribute "Food."

Cognitive scientists have noticed that people prefer certain nodes in a generalization hierarchy (concepts) over other nodes when creating descriptions (e.g., [RMGJB76]). Factors that influence the choice of a concept (node) include the concept typicality (how common are a concept's features among its sibling concepts), and the context in which the concept is being used. For instance, upon seeing a robin (a typical bird), we may say, "There is a bird," rather than "There is a robin," assuming that the given situation does not require a specification of the type of bird. On the other hand, when we see a penguin, a much less typical bird, we are more likely to say "There is a penguin," rather than "There is a bird". This way a listener (who is not an observer) will not assign to the unseen bird characteristics typical to a bird, but rather the special characteristics of a penguin. This facilitates communication. Context also comes into play; at a gathering of bird watchers, the robin will probably not be called simply a bird, but rather will be referred to by its taxonomic name.

To provide some mechanism for capturing such preferences, INLEN allows a user to define *anchor nodes* in a generalization hierarchy. Such nodes should reflect the interests of a given application [KM96]. To illustrate this idea, consider Figure 2.10 again. In this hierarchy, vanilla and rocky road are kinds of ice cream; ice cream is a frozen dessert, which is a dessert, which is a type of food. In everyday usage, depending on the context, we will typically describe vanilla or rocky road as ice cream or dessert, but less likely as frozen dessert or food. Hence, we can designate dessert and ice cream as anchor nodes in the Food hierarchy. Using information about anchor nodes, different rule preference criteria can be specified, such as selecting the rule with the most general anchor nodes, or the one that generalizes positive examples to the next higher anchor node(s).

INLEN supports the use of structured attributes both as *independent* (input) and *dependent* (output) variables. Structured independent attributes represent hierarchies of values that are used to characterize entities. Structured dependent attributes represent hierarchies of decisions or classifications that can be made about an entity. Through the use of structured output attributes, INLEN's learning module can determine rules at different levels of generality.

While dependent attributes, like independent ones, can in principle take on different types (nominal, linear, cyclic or structured), in practical applications they are frequently either nominal or linear. A nominal output attribute is most frequently used in concept learning; its values denote concepts or classes to be learned. A linear output attribute (which is typically a measurement on a ratio scale) is used to denote a measurement whose values are to be predicted on the basis of the past data.

In many applications, it is desirable to use a structured attribute as a dependent variable. For example, when deciding which personal computer to buy, one may first decide on the general type of the computer—whether it is to be IBM PC-compatible or Macintosh-compatible. After deciding the type, one can focus on a specific model of the chosen type. The above two-level decision process is easier to execute than a one-level process in which one has to directly decide which computer to select from a large set.

When a dependent variable is structured, the learning operator focuses first on the top-level values (nodes), and creates rules for them. Subsequently, it creates rules for the descendant nodes in the context of their ancestors. This procedure produces decision rules that are simpler and easier to interpret than rules learned with a flat (nominal) organization of the decision attribute.

2.8 LEARNING DECISION STRUCTURES FROM DECISION RULES

One of the main reasons for data exploration is to learn rules or patterns in data that will enable a data analyst to predict future cases. Thus, when such rules are learned, one needs a method for efficiently applying the rules for prediction. Since a convenient structure for implementing a decision process is a decision tree, the problem of how to transfer knowledge to a decision tree arises. In the conventional machine learning approach, decision trees are learned directly from training examples, thus avoiding the step of first creating rules [HMS66], [Qui86], [Qui93].

Learning a decision tree directly from examples, however, may have serious disadvantages in practice. A decision tree is a form of procedural knowledge. Once it has been constructed, it is not easy to modify it to accommodate changes in the decision-making conditions. For example, if an attribute (test) assigned to a high-level node in the tree is impossible or too costly to measure, the decision tree offers no alternative course of action other than probabilistic reasoning [Qui86].

In contrast, a human making the decision would probably search for alternative tests to perform. People can do this because they typically store decision knowledge in a declarative form. From a declarative form of knowledge, such as a set of decision rules, one can usually construct many different, but logically equivalent, or nearly equivalent, decision trees. One such decision tree may be preferable to another in a given decision-making situation. Therefore, it is desirable to store knowledge decoratively and to transfer it only when the need arises to the procedural form that is most appropriate to the given situation.

Another weakness of decision trees is that they may become unwieldy and incomprehensible because of their limited knowledge representational power. To overcome the above limitations, a new approach has been developed that creates task-oriented *decision structures* from decision rules [Ima95], [MI97]. A decision structure is a generalization of a decision tree in which tests associated with nodes can refer not only to single attributes, but also to functions of multiple attributes; branches may be associated not only with single values/results of these tests, but also with a set of such values; and leaves can be assigned not only a single decision, but also a set of alternative decisions with appropriate probabilities.

This approach has been implemented in the AQDT-2 program, and employs an AQ-type learning algorithm (AQ15c and AQ17-DCI) for determining decision rules from examples. Among its advantages are the ability to generate a decision structure that is most suitable to a particular task and the ability to avoid or delay measuring costly attributes. Different users may want to generate different decision structures from a given set of rules, so that the structures are tailored to their individual situations. Furthermore, if an attribute is difficult to measure, or cannot be measured at all, the program can be instructed to build a decision structure from rules that tries to avoid this attribute, or measure it only when necessary.

Another advantage of this methodology is that once a rule set is determined, a decision structure can be generated from it far more rapidly than if it has to be determined from examples, hence processing time is very small. Also, a set of rules will take up less storage space than the data set from which it was learned.

Experiments with AQDT-2 indicate that decision structures learned from decision rules tend to be significantly simpler than decision trees learned from the same data, and frequently also have a higher predictive accuracy. For example, a decision structure learned by AQDT-2 for a wind bracing design problem had 5 nodes and 9 leaves, with a predictive accuracy of 88.7% when tested against a new set of data, while the decision tree generated by the popular program C4.5 had 17 nodes and 47 leaves with a predictive accuracy of 84% [MI97]. In another experiment, a decision tree learned from decision rules by AQDT to analyze Congressional voting patterns had 7 nodes and 13 leaves, with a predictive accuracy of 91.8% (when AQDT built an equivalent decision structure by combining some branches, the number of leaves was reduced to 8), while the decision tree learned by C4.5 from the same set of training examples had 8 nodes and 15 leaves, with a predictive accuracy of 85.7% [IM93].

This methodology directly fits the philosophy of INLEN. A rule base may be provided either from an expert or through the use of a rule learning operator, thereby allowing for the generation of decision structures from rules.

2.9 AUTOMATIC IMPROVEMENT OF REPRESENTATION SPACES

2.9.1 Determining Most Relevant Attributes

In a large database, many attributes may be used to characterize given entities. For any specific problem of determining rules characterizing the relationship between a designated output attribute and other attributes, it may be desirable to limit the independent attributes to the most relevant ones. To this end, one may use many different criteria for evaluating the relevance of an attribute for a given classification problem, such as gain ratio [Qui93], gini index [BFOS84], PROMISE [Bai82], and chi-square analysis [Har84], [Min89].

These criteria evaluate attributes on the basis of their expected global performance, which means that those attributes with the highest ability to discriminate among *all* classes are selected as the most relevant.

When determining a declarative knowledge representation, such as decision rules, the goal is somewhat different. Here, each class is described independently from other classes, and the simplest and most accurate rules for each class are desired. Hence, if an attribute has a single value that characterizes very well just one specific class, the attribute with this value will be used effectively in a corresponding decision rule. In contrast, such an attribute may have a low global discriminating value, and is thus ignored in building a decision tree. It follows that the determination of attributes for decision trees and for decision rules needs to follow different criteria.

To illustrate this point, consider the problem of recognizing the upper-case letters of the English alphabet. Two of the attributes to be considered might be whether the letter has a tail and whether it is made up exclusively of straight lines. In a rule-based (declarative) representation, the letter Q can be distinguished from the rest of the alphabet by a simple and concise property, *if the letter has a tail, it is a Q*. Conversely, the straight line condition is alone insufficient to discriminate any specific letter, but is useful overall.

Thus, the attribute *has-tail* is very useful for learning one specific class, although not very useful for characterizing other classes. It is thus appropriate for use in rule learning. In decision-tree learning, however, it may be evaluated as having a relatively low overall utility and replaced by other attributes. This will most likely happen if Qs are relatively rare. Hence, testing the letter for a tail will be considered a wasted operation, as it only serves to eliminate the possibility of it being a Q, without making any progress in distinguishing between the other 25 letters. Meanwhile, testing the condition *all-straight-lines* immediately bisects the search space. It is better to pare down the set of hypotheses more rapidly, and only check for a tail as a last step when the set of possible letters has been reduced to O and Q. This way, the recognition of Q will require more tests than necessary, but at no expense to the recognition of other letters.

INLEN supports both global and local attribute evaluation criteria for selecting the most relevant attributes. The former is based on the PROMISE methodology [Bai82], while the latter employs a variation of PROMISE that is oriented toward the maximum performance of some attribute value, rather than on the attribute's global performance.

2.9.2 Generating New Attributes

When the original representation space is weakly relevant to the problem at hand, or the concept to be learned is difficult to express in the from of attributional decision rules such as those employed in INLEN, there is a need to generate new attributes that are functions of the original ones and better suited to the given problem. This is done by a *constructive induction* operator based on the program AQ17-DCI [BM96].

In the case of a database that contains information on objects changing over time, one needs a mechanism for constructive induction that can take advantage of the time data ordering. For example, the database may contain information on the maximum temperature at a given location each day, with a field in each record indicating the day on which its temperature was recorded. Inherent in a timestamped representation are many attributes that can be generated through constructive induction, for example, date of the highest temperature, the minimum population growth rate during some period, weediness on date of planting, etc.

CONVART [Dav81] uses user-provided and default system suggestions to search for useful time-dependent attributes that are added to the representation space. It uses the items on the suggestion list to generate new attributes and to test them for likely relevance to the problem. If they exceed a relevance threshold, it adds them to the representation space, repeating this procedure until a desired number of new attributes have been constructed. As part of its attribute construction capability, INLEN will incorporate such techniques for the generation of time-dependent attributes.

2.10 EXEMPLARY APPLICATION: DISCOVERY IN ECONOMIC AND DEMOGRAPHIC DATA

2.10.1 Motivation

Economic analysis is one domain in which conceptual data exploration tools can be of great value. The following example illustrates the role an intelligent data exploration system can play in the extraction of knowledge from data.

The United States government maintains records of the import and export of goods from various countries of the world. The different products and raw materials are divided and subdivided into different categories. In the early 1980s the data showed a sharp decline in the import of trucks from Japan and a corresponding increase in the import of auto parts from Japan. It took several years before analysts noticed that fact and concluded that Japan was shipping the chassis and truck beds separately to the US, where they would be subsequently assembled, thereby avoiding a high US tariff on imported trucks that was directed primarily at Europe and had been on the books since World War II. When United States analysts inferred this explanation, the US and Japan commenced trade negotiations pertaining to the import of trucks.

How much sooner would that trend have been noticed had a conceptual data exploration program been applied to the data and pointed out the opposite changes in two related categories to an analyst? How much revenue did the undiscovered truth cost the US before they could finally work out a new agreement with Japan? Noticing economic trends and patterns like the one above is a difficult task, as humans can easily get overwhelmed by the amount of data.

Based on such motivation, the analysis of economic and demographic data has become one of the focus domains for INLEN development and testing. We illustrate some of its discovery capabilities through experiments involving two similar data sets: one provided by the World Bank consisting of information on 171 countries for the period of 1965 to 1990 (in terms of 95 attributes), and one extracted from the 1993 World Factbook (published by the Central Intelligence Agency) containing several databases of information on 190 countries (in terms of 17 attributes).

2.10.2   Experiment 1: Integration of Multiple Operators

The World Bank data enabled us to conduct a number of experiments for testing INLEN capabilities. One experiment focused on distinguishing between development patterns in Eastern Europe and East Asia, first by identifying such patterns, and then by generating discriminant rules [Kau94].

A conceptual clustering operator determined a way of grouping the countries, based on each country's change in the percentage of its population in the labor force between 1980 and 1990. In this classification, the typical Eastern European country and the typical East Asian country fell into separate groups. Most of the European countries had a labor force change below a threshold determined for the region by the clustering program, while most of the Asian countries had changes in labor force participation above the threshold determined for their region.

Based on this grouping, the rule learning operator (using the AQ15c inductive learning program) was called upon first in characteristic mode to characterize the Asian-like countries (those above their regional thresholds) and the European-like countries (those below their regional thresholds), and then in discriminant rule-optimizing mode to condense those characterizations into simple discriminant rules. The discriminant rules obtained were:

Country is Asian-Like if:

A.1   Change in Labor Force Participation ≥ slight_gain,   *(9 countries)*
      or
B.1   Life Expectancy is in 60s, and
  2   Working Age Population ≤ 64%,   *(2 countries)*

Country is European-Like if:

A.1   Change in Labor Force Participation is near 0 or decreasing, and
  2   Life Expectancy is not in 60s,   *(7 countries)*
      or
B.1   Percentage of Labor Force in Industry ≥ 40.   *(1 country)*

The rules show that of the 10 attributes in the original data set, only four attributes are instrumental in distinguishing between the European-style and Asian-style development patterns, namely *Change in Labor Force Participation, Life Expectancy, Working Age Population* and *Percentage of Labor Force in Industry*. In both the Asian- and European-Like cases, the first rule accounted for most of the countries fitting the class, while the second one described the remainder.

This experiment demonstrated one of the cornerstone features of the methodology – an integration of different learning and discovery strategies that allows knowledge to be passed from one operator to another in a seamless way, leading to conclusions unreachable by any one individual program. It also shows that the rules created by the system are easy to understand and interpret.

2.10.3   Experiment 2: Detecting Anomalies in Subgroups

Another experiment with INLEN investigated the problem of detecting interesting regularities within the subgroups it creates. While the subgroups in a demographic domain may indicate that member countries or regions have something in common, notable exceptions may be exposed when a member of these constructed subsets shows a marked dissimilarity to the rest of the group. These exceptions in turn may prove to be a springboard for further discovery.

INLEN discovered several rules from the World Factbook PEOPLE database characterizing the 55 countries with low (less than 1% per year) population growth rates by invoking the rule learning operator in characteristic mode. One of the characteristic descriptions (Figure 2.11) had three conditions that together characterized 19 low growth countries and only one with higher population growth rates.

In the characterization shown in Figure 2.11, the columns Pos and Neg respectively represent the number of positive and negative examples satisfying the condition. The *support level* (Supp) is defined as *Pos / (Pos + Neg)*, giving an indication of how much support the condition lends to the suggestion that a country's Population Growth Rate is less than 1%. The *commonality level* (Comm) is defined as *Pos / Total_Pos*, giving an indication of how commonly the condition occurs in countries with Population Growth Rates below 1% (in this example, Total_Pos = 55).

Characteristic Description of Countries with Population Growth Rate below 1 per 1000 people:	**Pos**	**Neg**	**Supp**	**Comm**
1 Birth Rate = 10 to 20 or Birth Rate ≥ 50	46	20	69%	84%
2 Predominant Religion is Orthodox or Protestant or Hindu or Shinto	40	68	37%	73%
3 Net Migration Rate ≤ +20	32	104	23%	58%
All 3 conditions:	19	1	95%	35%

Figure 2.11   A characterization of countries with low population growth.

The first condition (and thus the strongest in terms of support level) states that countries with population growth rate below 1% have a low (under 20 per 1000 population) or very high (over 50 per 1000 population) birth rate. The presence of a very high birth rate in countries with low population growth is highly counterintuitive; examination of the 19 countries covered by the description pointed out that 18 had birth rates below 20, while only one, Malawi, had the high birth rate. When further attention was focused on Malawi, the explanation was clear. Malawi had a massive outward net migration rate of over 30 per 1000 population, by far the most extreme migration rate in the world. INLEN thus facilitated a discovery of a surprising exception to a normal pattern.

2.10.4   Experiment 3: Utilizing Structured Attributes

The rule shown in the previous example contained an attribute "predominant religion." This attribute was presented as a nominal attribute in the initial dataset. To examine how the structuring of attributes affects knowledge discovery, INLEN was applied to identical data sets with and without the Religion attribute being structured [KM96]. A portion of the attribute domain structure is shown in Figure 2.12.

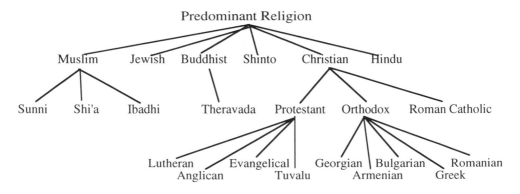

Figure 2.12   Part of the structure of the PEOPLE database's *Religion* attribute.

One strong argument for structuring is that if the Predominant Religion attribute has been set up in an unstructured (nominal) manner, the statement "Predominant Religion is Lutheran" would be regarded as being as antithetical to "Predominant Religion is Christian" as it is to the statement "Predominant Religion is Buddhist," since "Lutheran," "Christian" and "Buddhist" are all considered equally different in a "flat" domain. This would lead to the possibility that some contradictions such as "Predominant Religion is Lutheran, but not Christian" might be generated.

Experiments using INLEN-2 have lent support to this and other hypotheses regarding the use of structured and non-structured attributes. Among the findings regarding their use as independent variables was that structuring attributes leads to simpler rules than when not structuring them. For example, when INLEN learned rules to distinguish the 55 countries with low population growth rate (less than 1%) from other countries, in a version of the PEOPLE database in which the attribute "Predominant Religion" was not structured, one of the rules it found was:

Population Growth Rate < 1% if: (20 examples)
1   Literacy = 95% to 99%,
2   Life Expectancy is 70 to 80 years,
3   Predominant Religion is Roman Catholic or Orthodox or Romanian or Lutheran or Evangelical or Anglican or Shinto,
4   Net Migration Rate ≤ +20 per 1000 population.

This rule was satisfied by 20 of the 55 countries with low growth rates. When the same experiment was run with "Religion" used as a structured attribute, a simpler pattern was discovered:

Population Growth Rate < 1% if: (21 examples, 1 exception)
1   Literacy = 95% to 99%,
2   Life Expectancy is 70 to 80 years,
3   Predominant Religion is Christian or Shinto,
4   Net Migration Rate ≤ +10 per 1000 population.

This rule has one exception (the United States, whose 1993 population growth rate was between 1% and 2%). If full consistency is required, the third condition could still be expressed in a simpler form than in an unstructured religion domain by performing a minimal specialization operation on the node Christian so that the rule would cover the same positive examples, but not the exception.

Similar differences were obtained by structuring dependent attributes. By arranging events into different levels of generality, rules classified them accordingly, which reduced the complexity and increased the informational significance of the rules at different levels of generalization.

These effects were especially visible at the lower levels of the hierarchy. In the unstructured dataset, five rules, each with two to five conditions, were required to define the 11 Sunni Muslim countries. The only one to describe more than two of the 11 countries was a rule with quite fragmented conditions:

Predominant Religion is Sunni_Muslim if: (4 examples)
1   Literacy ≠ 30% to 99%,

2   Infant Mortality Rate is 25 to 40 or greater than 55 per 1000 population
3   Fertility Rate is 1 to 2 or 4 to 5 or 6 to 7 per 1000 population,
4   Population Growth Rate is 1% to 3% or greater than 4%.

The value ranges in these conditions are divided into multiple segments, suggesting that this is not a strong pattern. In contrast, using a structured religion attribute, the learning operator produced two simple and easily understood patterns, each with one only condition:

Predominant Religion is Sunni_Muslim if: (10 examples, 1 exception)
1   Infant Mortality Rate ≥ 40 per 1000 population.

Predominant Religion is Sunni_Muslim if: (4 examples)
1   Birth Rate is 30 to 40 per 1000 population.

As described above, these rules apply only in the context of predominantly Islamic countries, and are based on the assumption that that determination has already been made.

2.10.5   Experiment 4: Applying Constructive Induction Operators

An experiment chronicled by Bloedorn and Michalski [BM96] demonstrates the power of utilizing constructive induction as a knowledge discovery operator. Working from 11 economic attributes sampled over each of five consecutive years, 1986–1990 (for a total of 55 available attributes per record), the learning program attempted to discover rules to predict countries' changes in gross national product over the 5-year period. By applying three data-driven constructive induction operators—generating new attributes based on the existing attribute set, removing attributes less relevant to the goal concept, and abstracting numerical attributes into a small number of intervals—the predictive accuracy on new data increased by nearly half (from 41.7% to 60.5%).

Among the newly constructed highly relevant attributes were *Change in Energy Consumption Between 1986 and 1988*, *Ratio of Birth Rate in 1989 to Energy Consumption in 1990*, and *Average Annual Energy Consumption Over the 5-year Period*.

These results demonstrated that constructive induction can be a very useful tool for analyzing data, as it can build more adequate representation spaces for knowledge discovery.

2.11   SUMMARY

The main thesis of this chapter is that modern methods developed in symbolic machine learning have a direct and important application to the development of new operators for conceptual data exploration. A wide range of ideas on the applicability of various machine learning methods to this area were presented.

Two highly important operators are the construction of conceptual hierarchies (conceptual clustering), and the inductive derivation of general rules characterizing the relationship between designated output and input attributes. These rules represent high-level knowledge that can be of great value to a data analyst and directly usable in human decision-making.

Other important operators include construction of equations along with logical preconditions for their application, determination of symbolic descriptions of time sequences, selection of most relevant attributes, generation of new, more relevant attributes, and selection of representative examples.

In contrast to many data mining approaches, the methodology presented requires a considerable amount of background knowledge regarding the data and the domain of discourse. This background knowledge may include, for example, a specification of the domain and the type of the attributes, the relationships among them, causal dependencies, theories about the objects or processes that generated the data, goals of the data analysis and other high-level knowledge. An important aspect of the methodology is its ability to take advantage of this knowledge.

The machine learning techniques implemented in the INLEN system allow a user to easily perform a wide range of symbolic data manipulation and knowledge generation operations. The illustrative examples demonstrate a significant potential utility of the described multistrategy methodology in solving problems of data mining and knowledge discovery.

ACKNOWLEDGEMENTS

The authors thank Eric Bloedorn, Vinh Duong, Scott Fischthal, Seok Won Lee, Elizabeth Marchut-Michalski, Jim Mitchell, and Qi Zhang for useful comments and criticism on earlier drafts of this chapter. This research was done in the Machine Learning and Inference Laboratory of George Mason University. The Laboratory's research activities are supported in part by the National Science Foundation under Grants No. DMI-9496192 and IRI-9020266, in part by the Office of Naval Research under Grant No. N00014-91-J-1351, in part by the Defense Advanced Research Projects Agency under Grant No. N00014-91-J-1854 administered by the Office of Naval Research, and in part by the Defense Advanced Research Projects Agency under Grants No. F49620-92-J-0549 and F49620-95-1-0462 administered by the Air Force Office of Scientific Research.

REFERENCES

[Bai82]   Baim, P.W. The PROMISE Method for Selecting Most Relevant Attributes for Inductive Learning Systems. Report No. UIUCDCS-F-82-898, Department of Computer Science, University of Illinois, Urbana, 1982.

[BMR87]   Bentrup, J.A., Mehler, G.J. and Riedesel, J.D. INDUCE 4: A Program for Incrementally Learning Structural Descriptions From Examples. *Reports of the Intelligent Systems Group*, ISG 87-2. UIUCDCS-F-87-958, Department of Computer Science, University of Illinois, Urbana, 1987.

[BMMZ92]   Bergadano, F., Matwin, S., Michalski, R.S. and Zhang, J. Learning Two-Tiered Descriptions of Flexible Concepts: The POSEIDON System. *Machine Learning*, 8, pp. 5-43, 1992.

[BMM96]   Bloedorn, E., Mani, I. and MacMillan, T.R. Machine Learning of User Profiles: Representational Issues. *Proceedings of the Thirteenth National Conference on Artificial Intelligence (AAAI-96)*, Portland, OR, 1996.

[BM96]   Bloedorn, E. and Michalski, R.S. The AQ17-DCI System for Data-Driven Constructive Induction and Its Application to the Analysis of World Economics. *Proceedings of the 9th International Symposium on Methodologies for Intelligent Systems*, Zakopane, Poland, 1996.

[BWM93]   Bloedorn, E., Wnek, J. and Michalski, R.S. Multistrategy Constructive Induction. *Proceedings of the Second International Workshop on Multistrategy Learning*, Harpers Ferry, WV, pp. 188-203, 1993.

[Bon70]   Bongard, N. *Pattern Recognition*. Spartan Books, New York (a translation from Russian), 1970.

[BKKPS96]   Brachman, R.J., Khabaza, T., Kloesgen, W., Piatetsky-Shapiro, G. and Simoudis, E. Mining Business Databases. *Communications of the ACM*, 39:11, pp. 42-48, 1996.

[BMK97]   Bratko, I., Muggleton, S. and Karalic, A. \ Applications of Inductive Logic Programming. In: Michalski, R.S., Bratko, I. and Kubat, M. (eds.), *Machine Learning and Data Mining: Methods and Applications*, London, John Wiley & Sons, 1997.

[BFOS84]   Breiman, L., Friedman, J.H., Olshen, R.A. and Stone, C.J. *Classification and Regression Trees*, Belmont, CA, Wadsworth Int. Group, 1984.

[CR95a]   Carpineto, C. and Romano, G. Some Results on Lattice-based Discovery in Databases. *Workshop on Statistics, Machine Learning and Knowledge Discovery in Databases*, Heraklion, pp. 216-221, 1995.

[CR95b]   Carpineto, C. and Romano, G. Automatic Construction of Navigable Concept Networks Characterizing Text Databases. In: Gori, M. and Soda, G. (eds.), *Topics in Artificial Intelligence*, LNAI 992-Springer-Verlag, pp. 67-78, 1995.

[CGCME97]   Cavalcanti, R.B., Guadagnin, R., Cavalcanti, C.G.B., Mattos, S.P. and Estuqui, V.R. A Contribution to Improve Biological Analyses of Water Through Automatic Image Recognition. *Pattern Recognition and Image Analysis*, 7:1, pp. 18-23, 1997.

[CM81]   Collins, A. and Michalski, R.S. Toward a Formal Theory of Human Plausible Reasoning. *Proceedings of the Third Annual Conference of the Cognitive Science Society*, Berkeley, CA, 1981.

[CM89]   Collins, A. and Michalski, R.S. The Logic of Plausible Reasoning: A Core Theory. *Cognitive Science*, 13, pp. 1-49, 1989.

[DW80]   Daniel, C. and Wood, F.S. *Fitting Equations to Data*. New York, John Wiley & Sons, 1980.

[Dav81]   Davis, J. CONVART: A Program for Constructive Induction on Time-Dependent Data. M.S. Thesis, Department of Computer Science, University of Illinois, Urbana, 1981.

[Did89]   Diday, E. (ed.) *Proceedings of the Conference on Data Analysis, Learning Symbolic and Numeric Knowledge.* Nova Science Publishers, Inc., Antibes, 1989.

[DM86]   Dieterrich, T. and Michalski, R.S. Learning to Predict Sequences. In: Michalski, R.S., Carbonell, J.G. and Mitchell, T.M. (eds.), *Machine Learning: An Artificial Intelligence Approach Vol. 2*, Morgan Kaufmann, pp. 63-106, 1986.

[Don88]   Dontas, K. APPLAUSE: An Implementation of the Collins–Michalski Theory of Plausible Reasoning. M.S. Thesis, Computer Science Department, The University of Tennessee, Knoxville, TN, 1988.

[DPY93]   Dubois, D., Prade, H. and Yager, R.R. (eds.). *Readings in Fuzzy Sets and Intelligent Systems*, Morgan Kaufmann, 1993.

[EH96]   Evangelos S. and Han, J. (eds.) *Proceedings of the Second International Conference on Knowledge Discovery and Data Mining.* Portland, OR, 1996.

[FM90]   Falkenhainer, B.C. and Michalski, R.S. Integrating Quantitative and Qualitative Discovery in the ABACUS System. In: Kodratoff, Y. and Michalski, R.S. (eds.), *Machine Learning: An Artificial Intelligence Approach Vol. III*, San Mateo, CA, Morgan Kaufmann, pp. 153-190, 1990.

[FHS96]   Fayyad, U., Haussler, D. and Stolorz, P. Mining Scientific Data. *Communications of the ACM*, 39:11, pp. 51-57, 1996.

[FPS96]   Fayyad, U., Piatetsky-Shapiro, G. and Smyth, P. Knowledge Discovery and Data Mining: Toward a Unifying Framework. *Proceedings of the Second International Conference on Knowledge Discovery and Data Mining*, Portland, OR, pp. 82-88, 1996.

[FPSU96]   Fayyad, U.M., Piatetsky-Shapiro, G., Smyth, P. and Uhturusamy, R. (eds.), *Advances in Knowledge Discovery and Data Mining*, San Mateo, CA, AAAI Press, 1996.

[Fee96]   Feelders, A. Learning from Biased Data Using Mixture Models. *Proceedings of the Second International Conference on Knowledge Discovery and Data Mining*, Portland, OR, pp. 102-107, 1996.

[FR86]   Forsyth, R. and Rada, R. *Machine Learning: Applications in Expert Systems and Information Retrieval*, Pitman, 1986.

[Gre88]   Greene, G. The Abacus.2 System for Quantitative Discovery: Using Dependencies to Discover Non-Linear Terms. Reports *of the Machine Learning and Inference Laboratory*, MLI 88-4, Machine Learning and Inference Laboratory, George Mason University, Fairfax, VA, 1988.

[Har84]   Hart, A. Experience in the Use of an Inductive System in Knowledge Engineering. In: Bramer, M. (ed.), *Research and Developments in Expert Systems*, Cambridge, Cambridge University Press, 1984.

[HMM86]   Hong, J., Mozetic, I. and Michalski, R.S. AQ15: Incremental Learning of Attribute-Based Descriptions from Examples: The Method and User's Guide.

Reports of the Intelligent Systems Group, ISG 86-5, UIUCDCS-F-86-949, Department of Computer Science, University of Illinois, Urbana, 1986.

[HMS66]   Hunt, E., Marin, J. and Stone, P. *Experiments in Induction*, Academic Press, New York, 1966.

[Ima95]   Imam, I.F. Discovering Task-Oriented Decision Structures from Decision Rules. Ph.D. dissertation, School of Information Technology and Engineering, George Mason University, Fairfax, VA, 1995.

[IM93]   Imam, I.F. and Michalski, R.S. Should Decision Trees be Learned from Examples or from Decision Rules? *Proceedings of the Seventh International Symposium on Methodologies for Intelligent Systems (ISMIS-93)*, Trondheim, Norway, 1993.

[Kau94]   Kaufman, K.A. Comparing International Development Patterns Using Multi-Operator Learning and Discovery Tools. *Proceedings of AAAI-94 Workshop on Knowledge Discovery in Databases*, Seattle, WA, pp. 431-440, 1994.

[KM93]   Kaufman, K.A. and Michalski, R.S. EMERALD: An Integrated System of Machine Learning and Discovery Programs to Support Education and Experimental Research. *Reports of the Machine Learning and Inference Laboratory*, MLI 93-10, Machine Learning and Inference Laboratory, George Mason University, Fairfax, VA, 1993.

[KM96]   Kaufman, K.A. and Michalski, R.S. A Method for Reasoning with Structured and Continuous Attributes in the INLEN-2 Multistrategy Knowledge Discovery System. *Proceedings of the Second International Conference on Knowledge Discovery and Data Mining*, Portland, OR, pp. 232-237, 1996.

[KMK91]   Kaufman, K.A., Michalski, R.S. and Kerschberg, L. Mining for Knowledge in Databases: Goals and General Description of the INLEN System. In: Piatetsky-Shapiro, G. and Frawley, W.J. (eds.), *Knowledge Discovery in Databases,* AAAI Press, Menlo Park, CA, pp. 449-462, 1991

[Ker92]   Kerber, R. ChiMerge: Discretization of Numeric Attributes. *Proceedings of the Tenth National Conference on Artificial Intelligence (AAAI-92)*, San Jose, CA, pp. 123-127, 1992.

[Kod88]   Kodratoff, Y. *Introduction to Machine Learning*, Pitman, 1988.

[KM90]   Kodratoff, Y. and Michalski, R.S. (eds.). *Machine Learning: An Artificial Intelligence Approach, Vol. III*, San Mateo, CA, Morgan Kaufmann, 1990

[Kok86]   Kokar, M.M. Coper: A Methodology for Learning Invariant Functional Descriptions. In: Michalski, R.S., Mitchell, T.M and Carbonell, J.G. (eds.), *Machine Learning: A Guide to Current Research*, Kluwer Academic, Boston, MA 1986.

[LHGS96] Lakshminarayan, K., Harp, S.A., Goldman, R. and Samad, T. Imputation of Missing Data Using Machine Learning Techniques. *Proceedings of the Second International Conference on Knowledge Discovery and Data Mining*. Portland, OR, pp. 140-145, 1996.

[LBS83]   Langley, P., Bradshaw G.L. and Simon, H.A. Rediscovering Chemistry with
           the BACON System. In: Michalski, R.S., Carbonell, J.G. and Mitchell, T.M.
           (eds.), *Machine Learning: An Artificial Intelligence Approach*, Morgan
           Kaufmann, San Mateo, CA, pp. 307-329, 1983.

[Lar77]   Larson, J.B. INDUCE-1: An Interactive Inductive Inference Program in VL21
           Logic System. Report No. 876, Department of Computer Science, University
           of Illinois, Urbana, 1977.

[Lbo81]   Lbov, G.S. *Mietody Obrabotki Raznotipnych Ezperimentalnych Danych
           (Methods for Analysis of Multitype Experimental Data)*. Akademia Nauk
           USSR, Sibirskoje Otdielenie, Institut Matiematikie, Izdatielstwo Nauka,
           Novosibirsk, 1981.

[MM95]   Maloof, M.A. and Michalski, R.S. Learning Evolving Concepts Using Partial
           Memory Approach. Working Notes of the *1995 AAAI Fall Symposium on
           Active Learning*, Boston, MA, pp. 70-73, 1995

[Mic91a]   Michael, J. Validation, Verification and Experimentation with Abacus2.
           Reports of the Machine Learning and Inference Laboratory, MLI 91-8, Machine
           Learning and Inference Laboratory, George Mason University, Fairfax, VA,
           1991.

[Mic78]   Michalski, R.S. A Planar Geometrical Model for Representing Multi-
           Dimensional Discrete Spaces and Multiple-Valued Logic Functions. ISG
           Report No. 897, Department of Computer Science, University of Illinois,
           Urbana, 1978.

[Mic80]   Michalski, R.S. Inductive Learning as Rule-Guided Generalization and
           Conceptual Simplification of Symbolic Descriptions: Unifying Principles and
           a Methodology. *Workshop on Current Developments in Machine Learning*,
           Carnegie Mellon University, Pittsburgh, PA, 1980.

[Mic83]   Michalski, R.S. A Theory and Methodology of Inductive Learning. *Artificial
           Intelligence*, 20, pp. 111-161, 1983.

[Mic90]   Michalski, R.S. Learning Flexible Concepts: Fundamental Ideas and a Method
           Based on Two-tiered Representation. In: Kodratoff, Y. and Michalski, R.S.
           (eds.), *Machine Learning: An Artificial Intelligence Approach, Vol. III*, San
           Mateo, CA, Morgan Kaufmann, pp. 63-102, 1990.

[Mic91b]   Michalski, R.S. Searching for Knowledge in a World Flooded with Facts.
           Applied Stochastic Models and Data Analysis, 7, pp. 153-163, January 1991.

[Mic94]   Michalski, R.S. Inferential Theory of Learning: Developing Foundations for
           Multistrategy Learning. In: Michalski, R.S. and Tecuci, G. (eds.), *Machine
           Learning: A Multistrategy Approach*, San Francisco, Morgan Kaufmann, pp.
           3-61, 1994.

[MBS82]   Michalski, R.S., Baskin, A.B. and Spackman, K.A. A Logic-based Approach
           to Conceptual Database Analysis. *Sixth Annual Symposium on Computer
           Applications in Medical Care* (SCAMC-6), George Washington University,
           Medical Center, Washington, DC, pp. 792-796, 1982.

[MCM83]   Michalski, R.S., Carbonell, J.G. and Mitchell, T.M. (eds.). *Machine Learning: An Artificial Intelligence Approach*, Palo Alto, CA, Tioga Publishing, 1983.

[MCM86]   Michalski, R.S., Carbonell, J.G. and Mitchell, T.M. (eds.). *Machine Learning: An Artificial Intelligence Approach Vol. 2*, San Mateo, CA, Morgan Kaufmann, 1986.

[MI97]   Michalski, R.S. and Imam, I.F. On Learning Decision Structures. *Fundamenta Matematicae*, Polish Academy of Sciences, 1997 (in press).

[MK97]   Michalski, R.S. and Kaufman, K.A. Multistrategy Data Exploration Using the INLEN System: Recent Advances. *Sixth Symposium on Intelligent Information Systems (IIS '97)*, Zakopane, Poland, 1997.

[MKW91]   Michalski, R.S., Kaufman, K. and Wnek, J. The AQ Family of Learning Programs: A Review of Recent Developments and an Exemplary Application. *Reports of the Machine Learning and Inference Laboratory*, MLI 91-11, Machine Learning and Inference Laboratory, George Mason University, Fairfax, VA, 1991.

[MKKR92] Michalski, R.S., Kerschberg, L., Kaufman, K. and Ribeiro, J. Mining for Knowledge in Databases: The INLEN Architecture, Initial Implementation and First Results. *Journal of Intelligent Information Systems: Integrating AI and Database Technologies*, 1, pp. 85-113, 1992.

[MKC85]   Michalski, R. S., Ko, H. and Chen, K. SPARC/E(V.2), An Eleusis Rule Generator and Game Player. *Reports of the Intelligent Systems Group*, ISG No. 85-11, UIUCDCS-F-85-941, Department of Computer Science, University of Illinois, Urbana, 1985.

[MKC86]   Michalski, R.S., Ko, H. and Chen, K. Qualitative Prediction: A Method and a Program SPARC/G. In: Guetler, C. (ed.), *Expert Systems*, Academic Press, London, 1986.

[ML78]   Michalski, R.S. and Larson, J.B. Selection of Most Representative Training Examples and Incremental Generation of VL1 Hypotheses: The Underlying Methodology and the Description of Programs ESEL and AQ11. Report No. 867, Department of Computer Science, University of Illinois, Urbana, 1978.

[MM71]   Michalski, R.S. and McCormick, B.H. Interval Generalization of Switching Theory. *Proceedings of the 3rd Annual Houston Conference on Computer and System Science*, Houston, TX, 1971.

[MMHL86] Michalski, R.S., Mozetic, I., Hong, J. and Lavrac, N. The AQ15 Inductive Learning System: An Overview and Experiments. ISG Report 86-20, UIUCDCS-R-86-1260, Department of Computer Science, University of Illinois, Urbana, 1986.

[MRDMZ97] Michalski, R.S., Rosenfeld, A., Duric, Z., Maloof, M. and Zhang, Q. Application of Machine Learning in Computer Vision. In: Michalski, R.S., Bratko, I. and Kubat, M. (eds.), *Machine Learning and Data Mining: Methods and Applications*, London, John Wiley & Sons, 1997.

[MSD81]   Michalski, R.S., Stepp, R. and Diday, E. A Recent Advance in Data Analysis: Clustering Objects into Classes Characterized by Conjunctive Concepts. In:

Kanal, L. and Rosenfeld, A. (eds.), *Progress in Pattern Recognition, Vol. 1*, Amsterdam, North-Holland, pp. 33-55, 1981.

[Min89]   Mingers, J. An Empirical Comparison of Selection Measures for Decision-Tree Induction. *Machine Learning*, 3, pp. 319-342, 1989.

[MT89]   Morgenthaler, S. and Tukey, J.W. The Next Future of Data Analysis. In: Diday, E. (ed.), *Proceedings of the Conference on Data Analysis, Learning Symbolic and Numeric Knowledge*, Nova Science Publishers, Antibes, 1989.

[Paw91]   Pawlak, Z. *Rough Sets: Theoretical Aspects of Reasoning about Data*, Kluwer Academic, Dordrecht, 1991.

[Qui86]   Quinlan, J.R. Induction of Decision Trees. *Machine Learning*, 1, pp. 81-106, 1986.

[Qui90]   Quinlan, J.R. Probabilistic Decision Trees. In: Kodratoff, Y. and Michalski, R.S. (eds.), *Machine Learning: An Artificial Intelligence Approach. Volume III*, Morgan Kaufmann, San Mateo, CA, pp. 140-152, 1990.

[Qui93]   Quinlan, J.R. *C4.5: Programs for Machine Learning*, Morgan Kaufmann, Los Altos, CA, 1993.

[Rei84]   Reinke, R.E. Knowledge Acquisition and Refinement Tools for the ADVISE Meta-Expert System. Master's Thesis, Department of Computer Science, University of Illinois, Urbana, 1984.

[RM88]   Reinke, R.E. and Michalski, R.S. Incremental Learning of Concept Descriptions: A Method and Experimental Results. *Machine Intelligence*, 11, pp. 263-288, 1988.

[RKK95]   Ribeiro, J.S., Kaufman, K.A. and Kerschberg, L. Knowledge Discovery From Multiple Databases. *Proceedings of the First International Conference on Knowledge Discovery and Data Mining*, Montreal, PQ, pp. 240-245, 1995.

[RMGJB76]   Rosch, E., Mervis, C., Gray, W., Johnson, D. and Boyes-Braem, P. Basic Objects in Natural Categories. *Cognitive Psychology*, 8, pp. 382-439, 1976.

[Sha96]   Sharma, S. *Applied Multivariate Techniques*, London, John Wiley & Sons, 1996.

[Slo92]   Slowinski, R. (ed.). *Intelligent Decision Support: Handbook of Applications and Advances of the Rough Sets Theory*, Dordrecht/Boston/London, Kluwer Academic, 1992.

[Ste84]   Stepp, R. A Description and User's Guide for CLUSTER/2, A Program for Conjunctive Conceptual Clustering. Report No. UIUCDCS-R-83-1084, Department of Computer Science, University of Illinois, Urbana, 1984.

[Tuk86]   Tukey, J.W. *The Collected Works of John W. Tukey, Vol. V, Philosophy and Principles of Data Analysis: 1965-1986*. Jones, L.V. (ed.), Wadsworth & Brooks/Cole, Monterey, CA, 1986.

[Uma97]   Umann, E. Phons in Spoken Speech: A Contribution to the Computer Analysis of Spoken Texts. *Pattern Recognition and Image Analysis*, 7:1, pp. 138-144, 1997.

[VHMT93]   Van Mechelen, I., Hampton, J., Michalski, R.S. and Theuns, P. (eds.), *Categories and Concepts: Theoretical Views and Inductive Data Analysis*, London, Academic Press, 1993.

[WK96]   Widmer, G. and Kubat, M. Learning in the Presence of Concept Drift and Hidden Concepts. *Machine Learning*, 23, pp. 69-101, 1996.

[Wne95]   Wnek, J. DIAV 2.0 User Manual, Specification and Guide through the Diagrammatic Visualization System. *Reports of the Machine Learning and Inference Laboratory*, MLI 95-5, George Mason University, Fairfax, VA, 1995.

[WKBM95]   Wnek, J., Kaufman, K., Bloedorn, E. and Michalski, R.S. Selective Induction Learning System AQ15c: The Method and User's Guide. *Reports of the Machine Learning and Inference Laboratory*, MLI 95-4, Machine Learning and Inference Laboratory, George Mason University, Fairfax, VA, 1995.

[WM94]   Wnek, J. and Michalski, R.S. Hypothesis-driven Constructive Induction in AQ17-HCI: A Method and Experiments. *Machine Learning*, 14, pp. 139-168, 1994.

[WSWM90]   Wnek, J., Sarma, J., Wahab, A. and Michalski, R.S. Comparing Learning Paradigms via Diagrammatic Visualization: A Case Study in Single Concept Learning using Symbolic, Neural Net and Genetic Algorithm Methods. *Reports of the Machine Learning and Inference Laboratory*, MLI 90-2, Machine Learning and Inference Laboratory, George Mason University, Fairfax, VA, 1990.

[Zad65]   Zadeh, L. Fuzzy Sets. *Information and Control*, 8, pp. 338-353, 1965.

[Zag72]   Zagoruiko, N.G. *Recognition Methods and Their Application*. Sovietsky Radio, Moscow (in Russian), 1972.

[Zag91]   Zagoruiko, N.G. Ekspertnyie Sistemy I Analiz Dannych (Expert Systems and Data Analysis). *Wychislitielnyje Sistemy*, N.144, Akademia Nauk USSR, Sibirskoje Otdielenie, Institut Matiematikie, Novosibirsk, 1991.

[ZG89]   Zhuravlev, Y.I. and Gurevitch, I.B. Pattern Recognition and Image Recognition. In: Zhuravlev, Y.I. (ed.), *Pattern Recognition, Classification, Forecasting: Mathematical Techniques and their Application. Issue 2*, Nauka, Moscow, pp. 5-72 (in Russian), 1989.

[Zia94]   Ziarko, W.P. (ed.). *Rough Sets, Fuzzy Sets and Knowledge Discovery*, Berlin, Springer-Verlag, 1994.

[Zyt87]   Zytkow, J.M. Combining Many Searches in the FAHRENHEIT Discovery System. *Proceedings of the Fourth International Workshop on Machine Learning*, Irvine, CA, pp. 281-287, 1987.

3

Fielded Applications of Machine Learning

Pat Langley and Herbert A. Simon

ABSTRACT

An important area of application for machine learning involves automating the acquisition of knowledge bases required for expert systems. We review some recent applications of decision-tree and rule induction, in each case stating the problem, how machine learning was used, and the status of the resulting expert system. In closing, we identify the main stages in fielding an applied learning system and draw some lessons from successful applications.

3.1 INTRODUCTION

Expert performance requires domain-specific knowledge, and although knowledge engineering has produced hundreds of industrial expert systems, this process remains a time-consuming human activity. Machine learning, as one of its central aims, hopes to automate the knowledge engineering process, replacing it with techniques that improve accuracy or efficiency by discovering regularities in training data. The ultimate test of machine learning is its ability to produce systems that are used regularly in industry, education, and elsewhere.

In fact, the past decade has seen many applications of machine learning that have led to fielded knowledge-based systems. Some of this work has focused on structures like neural networks and induction methods like backpropation; Widrow *et al.* (1994) review recent work in this tradition. Other applied work has used instance-based representations and learning methods like nearest neighbor; Allen (1994) reviews some fielded applications within this framework.

Machine Learning and Data Mining: Methods and Applications
Edited by R.S. Michalski, I Bratko and M. Kubat
© 1997 John Wiley & Sons Ltd

Table 3.1   Highlights of Leech's (1984) work on fuel processing for Westinghouse

---

PROBLEM: Improve yield in fuel processing for nuclear power plants
FORMULATION: Learn rules for predicting pellet quality
REPRESENTATION: Pelleting quality and manufacturing control settings
DATA COLLECTION: Interaction with expert, results from pellet batches
EVALUATION: Presented rules to experienced process engineers
STATUS: Fielded in 1984, giving increased throughput, higher yield, and reduced inventory

---

In this chapter, we examine similar applications of methods for decision-tree and rule induction. We focus on this approach not because it is more central to machine learning or more robust than others, but rather to complement the reviews of applied work on neural networks and case-based learning mentioned above.[1] We assume readers already have a basic understanding of methods for learning logical descriptions, including decision-tree algorithms like C4.5 (Quinlan, 1993) and rule-induction techniques like AQ (Michalski & Chilausky, 1980). We focus instead on eight fielded knowledge bases that have been developed using methods of this sort, as well as discussing other applications efforts in less detail. We conclude by discussing some of the lessons suggested by these projects.

Before proceeding, we should note that nearly all applied work on machine learning has focused on simple classification or prediction tasks. This should not cause much surprise, because the most robust learning methods were designed for just such problems. Nor should this restriction to learning one-step decisions cause great concern, since one can usually decompose a complex process such as design, control, or planning into a sequence of individual steps, each of which involves simple classification or prediction. We will see that many efforts have taken exactly this approach.

3.2   FIELDED APPLICATIONS OF RULE INDUCTION

To clarify the potential for decision-tree and rule induction in real-world problems, in this section we consider some fielded applications of these methods. In each case we describe the problem, its reformulation in terms of supervised learning, and the status of the resulting knowledge base; tables highlight these and other factors for each effort. However, this sample hardly exhausts the fielded applications, and in closing we mention briefly some other recent uses of the rule-induction approach.

3.2.1   Increasing Yield in Chemical Process Control

Fuel for nuclear power plants is commonly generated by transforming Uranium hexafloride gas into pellets of Uranium dioxide powder. These pellets must be high in quality, but experts cannot predict when a batch of pellets will be good or bad. Researchers at Westinghouse used

---

[1] Some other paradigms, including analytic learning (e.g., Samuelson & Rayner, 1991) and probabilistic learning (e.g., Manganaris & Fisher, 1994), have produced applied research but, to our knowledge, no deployed systems.

Table 3.2   Highlights of Michie's (1989) work on loan decisions for American Express UK

PROBLEM: Reduce losses on defaulted loans from borderline applicants
FORMULATION: Learn decision trees to predict whether applicants would default
REPRESENTATION: Standard descriptive attributes for applicants
DATA COLLECTION: Sample of 1014 cases from company records
EVALUATION: Substantially higher accuracy than loan officers
STATUS: Adopted by American Express UK after a week's dvelopment effort

---

statistical methods to predict pellet quality with partial success, but interactions among the predictive attributes limited the effectiveness of this approach.

Leech (1984) followed a different path in which decision-tree induction played a central role. He collected samples of pellet batches of high and low quality, along with their manufacturing control settings (e.g., pelleting parameters and powder characteristics), some numeric and others symbolic. He ran these training data through a decision-tree algorithm, then transformed the resulting tree into rules that predicted pellet quality. He repeated this process to find rules for predicting qualitative powder attributes, which were then used in the top-level rules, giving a structured knowledge base.

After careful evaluation, Leech presented these rules to experienced process engineers, who found them acceptable, and plant technicians began using them to control the pelleting process. As new data became available, he repeated the induction process to produce more accurate rules. The fielded expert system led to increased throughput, higher pellet yield, and reduced inventory, increasing Westinghouse's business (in 1984) by over ten million dollars per year.

3.2.2   Making Credit Decisions

Loan companies regularly use questionnaires to collect information about people applying for credit, which they then use in deciding whether to make loans. This process has long been partially automated. For example, American Express UK used a statistical decision process based on discriminant analysis to reject applicants falling below a certain threshold and to accept those exceeding another. The remaining 10 to 15 percent of the applicants fell into a "borderline" region and were referred to loan officers for a decision. However, records showed that the loan officers were no more than 50% accurate in predicting whether these borderline applicants would default on their loans.

These observations motivated American Express UK to try methods from machine learning to improve the decision process. Starting with 1014 training cases and 18 descriptive attributes (such as age and years with an employer), Michie (1989) and his colleagues used an induction method to produce a decision tree, containing around 20 nodes and ten of the original features, that made correct predictions on 70% of the borderline applicants. In addition to achieving improved accuracy, the company found the rules attractive because they could be used to explain the reasons for decisions to applicants. Although this project was intended as exploratory and took under a week's effort by the development team, American Express UK was so impressed that they put the resulting knowledge base into use without further development.

Table 3.3 Highlights of Giordana *et al.*'s (in press) work on preventive maintenance for Enichem

---

PROBLEM: Prevent breakdowns of motor pumps in a large chemical plant
FORMULATION: Learn rules for predicting the type of fault about to occur
REPRESENTATION: Fourier analysis of vibrations, augmented by causal knowledge
DATA COLLECTION: Gathered 209 examples of pump measurements, labeled by expert
EVALUATION: Learned rules were more accurate than hand-crafted expert system
STATUS: Fielded in plant, reduction in idle times due to improper halting of pumps

---

3.2.3   Diagnosis of Mechanical Devices

Electric motor pumps play an important role in the chemical industry, and preventive maintenance has become a common strategy for reducing interruptions. At Enichem, a chemical branch of a large Italian oil company, diagnosticians regularly check each pump and measure vibrations at various points to determine whether it needs repairs. The machinery includes a motor and a pump, whose shafts are connected by an elastic joint; both motor and pump are anchored to the ground by elastic supports containing bearings. Typical faults include an unbalanced pump, faulty bearings, and distortion of the base. Domain experts at Enichem rely on Fourier analysis of the vibrations to aid them in their diagnostic decisions.

Giordana *et al.* (in press) believed that this task would benefit from the use of machine learning. Previously, they had worked with an expert at Enichem to produce an expert system for the diagnosis of motor pumps, representing knowledge in terms of rules, using traditional interviewing techniques to infer the knowledge and coding the information manually to construct the rule base. During this process, the researchers found that the expert measured vibrations at different places on the pump, then used the resulting mathematical analyses in his diagnosis.

After collecting 209 examples of pump measurements and getting the domain expert to label instances as examples of various faults, Giordana *et al.* ran these data through an induction algorithm to produce a new set of diagnostic rules. Their method used causal knowledge, also gleaned from the expert, to constrain the rule-induction process and increase the likelihood that he would accept the results. Experiments indicated that the learned knowledge base was more accurate than the hand-crafted one, and the induced rules have now replaced the original ones in the diagnostic system. Since their installation, there has been a noticeable reduction in idle times due to improper halting of machines; moreover, the learned rules have greatly aided the less experienced person who replaced the human expert upon his retirement.

3.2.4   Automatic Classification of Celestial Objects

The second Palomar Observatory Sky Survey has produced about three terabytes of image data, containing nearly two billion sky objects. In the past, astronomers have classified and catalogued the objects in photographic plates manually. However, here the aim was to handle stars and nebulae considerably fainter than either visual inspection or existing computer methods could support, and attempts to handcraft expert systems for the task had not produced reliable advances.

Table 3.4   Highlights of Fayyad *et al.*'s (1995) work for the Palomar Sky Survey

PROBLEM: Catalog two billion sky objects in the Palomar Observatory Sky Survey
FORMULATION: Learn decision trees that distinguish stars from galaxies
REPRESENTATION: standard numerical attributes combined with higher-order features
DATA COLLECTION: Samples from the sky survey, labeled by experts
EVALUATION: Accuracy of 94%, above that required by astronomers for data analysis
STATUS: Embedded in database management system, used to catalog objects in survey

In response, Fayyad *et al.* (1995) adapted a machine learning approach to the problem. First they used image-processing techniques to describe each object in a set of images in terms of standard numerical attributes, such as object magnitude, area, ellipticity, and statistical moments of object and core brightness. After astronomers assigned a label to each described object (star, galaxy, etc.), the researchers ran these training data through a decision-tree algorithm that produced a tree for classifying new objects. Initial results were discouraging, yielding low accuracies on novel test objects. However, Fayyad *et al.* worked with the astronomers to devise additional predictive attributes, defined in terms of the others, which increased the accuracy of the induced knowledge base to 94%—above the level specified by astronomers as necessary for scientific data analysis.

The researchers embedded the resulting classifier in a database management system that supports a variety of uses by astronomers, such as statistical analyses of stellar and galactic distributions. The system is being used to classify all objects in the Sky Survey image automatically, a task that would be impractical for humans. The system classifies objects ranging down to some that are one magnitude fainter than any cataloged in large-scale surveys to date, producing a catalog at least three times the size achievable without machine learning.

3.2.5   Monitoring Quality of Rolling Emulsions

The Sendzimir mill, commonly used to roll cold steel, is cooled and lubricated by an emulsion of water and oil, on whose properties the quality of the steel depends critically. For this reason, the Steel Works Jesenice (located in Jesenice, Slovenia) continuously monitors such properties as the oil concentration, the concentration of iron, and the presence of bacteria. Based on these measurements, the factory staff determine the quality of the emulsion and any necessary treatments, such as increasing the magnetic filtering or replacing the emulsion. In complex situations, the staff would consult an expert chemist, but as he was not always available, they sought to manually elicit his expertise through dialogue with him.

When this approach did not succeed, the developers collaborated with local university researchers on an inductive approach, using examples of the expert's decisions as training data (Karba & Drole, 1989). The induced decision tree was installed in the steel works, but later, after a change in the emulsion and its supplier, the knowledge ceased to perform satisfactorily. When attempts at manual adaptation did not work, the developers collected new examples of the expert's decisions and used the same induction method to obtain a revised decision tree. However, they were successful only after formulating a new set of attributes in collaboration with the expert. The resulting knowledge base has been used at the factory since 1989.

Table 3.5 Karba and Drole's (1989) work on emulsion quality for the Steel Works Jesenice

PROBLEM: Maintain the quality of rolling emulsions in a steel mill
FORMULATION: Induce decision trees that predict appropriate actions
REPRESENTATION: Properties of the emulsion obtained from expert
DATA COLLECTION: Records of mill's operation, including expert's actions
EVALUATION: Unknown
STATUS: Fielded in steel mill, later changes required reengineering features

3.2.6 Reducing Banding in Rotogravure Printing

Rotogravure printing involves pressing a continuous supply of paper against a chrome-plated, engraved copper cylinder that has been bathed in ink. Unfortunately, grooves or bands sometimes develop on the cylinder during the printing process and appear on the printed pages. The print run must then be halted and in some cases the cylinder replaced, at a substantial cost. The reasons for banding are largely unknown, and experts cannot predict reliably when it will occur.

Evans and Fisher (1994) decided that decision-tree induction might be useful in reducing banding, which had become a significant problem at a plant of R. R. Donnelley, a large U.S. printing company. Working with technicians at the plant, they collected positive and negative cases of banding, along with environmental factors (suggested as potentially relevant by the technicians) present in each case. Evans and Fisher ran these data through an induction algorithm that constructed a decision tree to predict the probability of banding in various classes of situations.

The researchers translated the induced decision tree into a small set of rules, which they posted on one Donnelley plant floor for use by printing teams. Technicians now use these rules to set ink viscosity and other factors under their control, and this new procedure has greatly reduced the frequency of banding effects. For example, banding incidents dropped from 384 in 1990 to 135 in 1991, and went down still further to 66 in the following year, as printing teams came to accept the value of the rules.

3.2.7 Improving Separation of Gas from Oil

When crude oil is extracted from the ground, the oil is usually admixed with natural gas, and before a refinery can begin to process the oil, it must first be separated from the gas. However, one can configure in different ways the size, weight, geometry, and components of the separation vessel. British Petroleum used decision-tree induction to determine the best settings for these parameters as a function of the relative amounts of gas, oil, and water, the pressure, viscosity, and temperature of the mixture, and similar factors.

The complexity of the configuration task led the developers to use an approach called *structured induction*. This scheme incorporates the decisions made by some trees as tests on branches in higher-level trees, but decomposes the learning task by inducing each decision tree separately. Guilfoyle (1986) reports that the British Petroleum developers collected 1600

Table 3.6 Highlights of Evans and Fisher's (1994) work on banding reduction for R. R. Donnelley

---

PROBLEM: Reduce banding during process of rotogravure printing
FORMULATION: Learn decision trees to predict when banding will occur
REPRESENTATION: Environmental and control variables known to experts
DATA COLLECTION: Manual collection by technicians operating printers
EVALUATION: Experiments suggested ability to predict banding accurately
STATUS: Fielded in 1991, followed by major reductions in banding events

---

training instances, providing a knowledge base of some 2500 rules organized into 25 sets, which the company subsequently translated into 14,000 lines of Fortran code. By 1987, the software was in regular use at four different sites, dealing with a task in ten minutes that had previously taken human experts over a day.

3.2.8 Preventing Breakdowns in Electrical Transformers

Utility companies often use large, oil-filled electrical transformers to distribute power. However, deteriorating insulation, overheating, joint failure, and other problems can cause very costly breakdowns. Experts can predict failures accurately from gas chromatographs that reveal chemical traces in the transformer oil. To reduce these experts' workloads, Hartford Steam Boiler, an insurer of industrial equipment, funded development of an expert system for this task using rule induction. The resulting system, described by Riese (1984), contains 27 sets of rules that check the validity of data, identify the presence of symptoms, infer faults from symptoms, and suggest corrective actions. Experimental evaluation on 859 test cases showed the induced rules agreed with the expert's diagnosis in all but four cases. In 1990, the system was in regular use, automatically producing reports for clients of the insurance company.

3.2.9 Additional Fielded Applications of Rule Induction

The above examples constitute only a fraction of the fielded applications of decision-trees and rule induction, though few results are published in the scientific literature. For instance, Donald Michie (1987) reports four induced knowledge bases for diagnosing faults in circuit boards that are in routine use in a European electronics laboratory and that save millions of dollars a year. Hayes-Michie (1990) reviews an expert system, again developed through decision-tree induction, regularly used by Siemens to configure fire-detection equipment for buildings. Gill Mowforth (personal communication, 1993) mentions another system, developed partly with decision-tree methods, now used by a South African bank to evaluate applications for credit cards. And David Stirling (personal communication, 1994) has used a similar approach to develop rules for predicting effects in a rolling steel mill, now used by BHP Stainless in Australia.

A few software companies actually specialize in the application of decision-trees and rule induction. For example, David Isherwood (personal communication, 1994) of Attar Software reports a system that provides advice on share trading, currently used by over 20 security

Table 3.7   Highlights of British Petroleum effort in configuring separation vessels (Guilfoyle, 1986)

PROBLEM: Configure vessels for separating natural gas from oil
FORMULATION: Learn decision trees to predict the best vessel parameters
REPRESENTATION: Characteristics of gas/oil mixture at multiple levels of abstraction
DATA COLLECTION: Acquired 1600 cases with input from experts
EVALUATION: Accuracy unknown, but much faster than experts
STATUS: Rules translated into Fortran, fielded at four sites by 1987

---

dealers in six European countries; a system that predicts which overdue mortgages are likely to be paid, used by the Leeds Permanent Building Society; a fault-diagnosis system for public pay phones that reduces visits by engineers and speeds repairs; a system that predicts the likelihood of retaining good salespeople for an insurance company; and a system that profiles average claims for different medical treatments, used by a health insurance company to monitor excessive claims from both clients and providers.

In a similar vein, Rudolph Sillen (personal communication, 1995) of Novacast describes a support tool for advising administrators on value-added taxes, in use at several Swedish sites since 1992; a thermal analysis system that controls the treatment of iron alloys, used by a Swedish foundry since 1994 and saving $50 per ton by minimizing scrap, increasing yield, and reducing energy and additives; an advisory system for selecting paints for metals and other coating processes, in commercial use in Sweden since 1993; a system for evaluating the capabilities of military units that saves the Swedish Defence Material Administration ten million Crowns a year; and a system that predicts whether breast cancer patients will develop new tumors within five years after an operation, used since 1993 by doctors at the Central Hospital in Karlstad, Sweden. Thamir Hassan (personal communication, 1994) at Infolink Decision Services reports that his company has also fielded a number of systems developed through similar methods.

3.3   OTHER APPLIED WORK ON RULE INDUCTION

In addition to the fielded applications described in the previous section, we should mention a number of other efforts that have a strong applied flavor. Although these systems are not currently in regular use, the range of tasks covered gives additional evidence of the robustness and flexibility of decision-tree and rule induction methods.

3.3.1   Automated Completion of Repetitive Forms

Completing forms is a tedious activity that continues to occupy an enormous amount of time in both business and government. Even partial automation of the process would produce substantial savings, but the cost of writing a separate expert system for each form often forestalls this approach. Hermens and Schlimmer (1994) have developed a form-filling advisory system that learns to predict its users' preferences through observation. They used an incremental

Table 3.8 Highlights of Riese's (1984) work on preventive diagnosis for Hartford Steam Boiler

PROBLEM: Decide whether to insure large, oil-filled electrical transformers
FORMULATION: Learn rules for predicting failures from chemical traces in oil
REPRESENTATION: Symptoms that appear in gas chromatograph readings
DATA COLLECTION: Historical data from company records
EVALUATION: Very close agreement with expert on 859 test cases
STATUS: Fielded in 1990, producing reports for insurance customers

version of decision-tree induction to find rules for predicting the default entry for each field in terms of other fields already specified. The user can always override the predicted value and revise the rules learned. Experiments showed that the form-filling apprentice saved up to 87% in keystroke effort and correctly predicted nearly 90% of the entries on the form. The system was used by administrative staff in Hermens and Schlimmer's university department for eight months, until changes in hardware ended the project.

3.3.2 Supporting Maintenance of Knowledge Bases

One of the earliest sets of expert systems (for the automatic design of motors, generators, and transformers in operation at the Westinghouse Corporation in 1956) went out of use after a few years because of the recurring cost of revising them manually to incorporate new design knowledge (Simon, 1993). As the technology of expert systems has matured, it has become clear that approximately half of their lifetime cost is incurred in maintaining the knowledge base. Regular maintenance is needed not only because of errors introduced at coding time, but also because the problem itself changes over time, as devices and users evolve.

For instance, Langley *et al.* (1994) describe a diagnostic system for computerized tomography scanners that is used on a regular basis by technicians at a Siemens operating company, but in which errors in the knowledge base have started to emerge. Langley *et al.* considered using existing induction algorithms for theory revision to handle this problem, but the available theory-revision methods were designed for knowledge represented either as Horn clauses or decision trees, whereas the existing diagnostic system uses a fault hierarchy. However, the researchers borrowed a search framework from existing methods, while replacing the learning operators with ones appropriate to fault hierarchies. This method has not yet been tested in the field, but preliminary evaluations with synthetic but realistic data have been encouraging.

3.3.3 Testing Engines for the Space Shuttle

The main engines for the space shuttle require extensive testing before they become operational. Each test firing produces over 100 megabytes of data from pressure, temperature, velocity, strain, and acceleration sensors located throughout the engine. Teams of engineers examine these data to determine whether enough tests have been run and whether the engine's performance meets stringent criteria. They must decide whether another test firing is needed, whether to replace engine components, and so forth.

Because this evaluation process itself is expensive, Rocketdyne used structured induction methods (similar to those used in the British Petroleum effort) to construct recursively structured decision trees for the task. Modesitt (1990) describes one of the resulting systems, designed to handle data from static-fire tests, which contained over 1500 rules organized into 48 rule sets. Another knowledge base, constructed to analyze dynamic data such as frequencies and vibrations, was induced in a similar fashion. Both were embedded in a larger software system for supporting the testing process. Field tests of the various modules were encouraging, but also suggested extensions to the overall system.

3.3.4   Forecasting Severe Thunderstorms

Although numerical models can predict large-scale weather patterns a day in advance, local forecasting still relies on the expertise of human meteorologists. For example, to determine the chance of severe thunderstorms they use factors like the amount of low-level moisture and the destabilization potential at low and high levels, which they in turn analyze using such data as the dew point, advection variables, and stability indices. Zubrick and Riese (1985) describe an expert system for this task developed, using decision-tree induction, by a meteorologist at the National Severe Storms Forecast Center. The system's hierarchical structure supports explanation of its predictions, and in tests during a one-week period in which five severe thunderstorms occurred, it made more accurate predictions than the traditional methods.

3.3.5   Repair of Helicopter Blades

Repairing a helicopter blade typically takes six months and involves a number of work groups. To reduce the cost of this activity Eurocopter developed an expert system that suggested repairs for their entire line of helicopters. However, experience with the system showed that new faults and new repairs continued to occur, requiring updates of the knowledge base. El Attar and Hamery (1994) decided that rule induction could provide an appropriate solution for the updating problem, and data from previous repairs were readily available. Whereas the original expert system contained 800 rules having two to eight attributes each, the induced knowledge base contained only 300 rules having two to four attributes each, which were more understandable to the expert. Moreover, in 88% of the cases in which the hand-crafted system was incorrect, the learned rules were able to predict the correct repair.

3.3.6   Predicting the Structure of Proteins

One largely unsolved problem in molecular biology involves predicting the secondary structure (folding) of proteins from information about their primary amino acid sequences. Some hand-crafted theories exist, but their predictive abilities are disappointing. Muggleton *et al.* (1992) attacked this problem using inductive logic programming, which they felt was appropriate for such a relational domain. Taking 16 proteins that contained only α helices, they treated each position in these proteins as a training instance. They also included background facts about the residues at each position and about the physical and chemical properties of those residues. The initial rules generated by the induction algorithm were moderately accurate but, after adding these rules' predictions as background facts and repeating the induction process, the second rule set produced better results. Another repetition of this strategy gave predictive rules that were 81% accurate on four separate test proteins, considerably higher than other results in the protein literature.

3.3.7 Automation of Scheduling in a Steel Mill

Materials scheduling in steel mills is a complex task that experts divide into three major components: receiving incoming materials into stockpiles; transferring materials from stockpiles to plants for crushing, blending, or blasting; and routing iron ore through screening or crushing plants. For example, depending on the size of ore lumps in a batch, one may crush them, blend them with other material, or send them directly to the blast furnace. Michie (1992) describes an effort by Pohang Iron and Steel Company, in South Korea, to construct an expert system for this process using structured decision-tree induction. The applications team interviewed experts to determine potentially relevant attributes for each component task, then ran training data through a decision-tree algorithm to produce a structured knowledge base. The resulting scheduling system, which includes 40 rule sets, performed comparably to domain experts during operational tests.

3.3.8 Additional Applications and Related Approaches

Naturally, the above list does not exhaust the examples applied work on decision-tree and rule induction, as the other chapters in this book attest. For instance, the research literature abounds with examples of machine induction for medical diagnosis of humans (e.g., Kononenko *et al.*, 1984; Quinlan *et al.*, 1987), and many of the online data sets used for experimental studies fall into this area. Readers should view the systems in this chapter as representative samples rather than exhaustive.

Also, we have focused on techniques that come from the machine learning community, but independent developments in statistics have produced similar methods. Breiman *et al.*, (1984) describe a set of methods for inducing decision trees, which they tested on a variety of applied problems, such as predicting the survival of recent heart-attack patients. A related line of statistical work, known as *automated interaction detection* (Biggs *et al.*, 1991) has been widely used in the analysis of survey data. Similar techniques are now included in SPSS, a widely available statistical package, making the technology of rule induction accessible to a wide audience.

3.4 SOME STRATEGIES AND LESSONS

Efforts to apply machine learning follow a standard pattern, but one that has seldom been made explicit in the literature. In this section we attempt to characterize the main stages of the process (reflected in the tables presented earlier), while noting some lessons from the examples presented earlier. In closing, we draw some tentative conclusions about the sources of power in successful applications.

We should emphasize that, although these steps typically occur in the order specified, the overall process is iterative in nature. That is, developers usually progress through some of the stages, uncover some problem, and return to a previous stage to revisit decisions made earlier. Development of a fielded application may require many cycles of this sort, with feedback from later stages informing revised choices about earlier ones.

3.4.1 Formulating the Problem

The first step in using machine learning to solve any real-world problem is to reformulate the problem in terms that can be handled by some induction method. Process control, diagnosis, and scheduling are complex tasks, yet one can identify components that involve simple classification, a task for which there exist robust induction algorithms. Repeatedly we see developers transforming an apparently difficult problem into a one-step classification task. In the applications we examined, only the work by Langley *et al.* employed learning methods that dealt directly with more complex performance elements. But this project has not yet produced a fielded knowledge base, whereas the simpler approaches have.

A number of developers have relied on a technique known as *structured induction*, which involves dividing a complex task into subproblems, then providing training data for each one separately. Zubrick and Reese (1985), Leech (1986), and Modesitt (1990) all took this approach, producing performance systems that carry out multi-step inference, but, by factoring it, avoid this complexity during the induction process. Muggleton *et al.*'s (1992) scheme, which added predictions produced by learned rules as background knowledge for later rounds of induction, provides an alternative way of decomposing the learning task.

The best formulation of the problem may not always be the one most intuitive to a machine-learning researcher. In process-control domains, it seems natural to search for rules or trees that directly predict the values of process variables, such as ink viscosity in printing, from environmental ones like humidity. However, on two of the control tasks we examined (Leech, 1986; Evans & Fisher, 1994), developers instead used induction to find rules to predict directly the effects of both process and environmental variables, apparently because users were more familiar with this formulation. On the other hand, similar work reported by Michie (1992) took the more 'natural' approach, so no general conclusions can be drawn.

3.4.2 Determining the Representation

The second step in applying machine learning techniques is to settle on an effective representation for both training data and the knowledge to be learned. We are not referring here to the representational formalism, such as decision trees or neural networks, but to the attributes or features used to describe examples and to characterize the result of learning.

Representation engineering—finding an effective representation of the phenomena—was central to most of the projects we examined. In some cases, this involved little more than talking with domain experts and getting their advice on attributes that were likely to have predictive value. In other cases (e.g., Fayyad *et al.*, 1995), it involved a painstaking search of the feature space, looking for descriptors that could provide the discriminating power the more obvious features lacked.

In some cases the "primitive" features may be computed by already established methods. Fayyad *et al.* relied heavily on established techniques for image processing to transform their digital images into attribute-value descriptions that could be handled by decision trees. Zubrick and Reese (1985) incorporated traditional statistical measures in their work on forecasting thunderstorms, and Giordana *et al.* (in press) used the output of Fourier analysis as primitive attribute values.

3.4.3   Collecting the Training Data

After settling on a task and a representation, one can collect the training data needed for the induction process. In some domains, this process is straightforward and can even be automated, but in others it can pose a significant challenge. In Evans and Fisher's (1994) work on banding in rotogravure printing, the researchers asked the printing technicians to record periodically the values of the process variables and the outcome, but the technicians were reluctant to waste time collecting data on a machine that was working well. Only after considerable effort were they persuaded to record values when the machine was working properly as well as when it failed. Most application domains fall somewhere between these two extremes, with some help from the experts being needed to classify training data or to generate them.

The availability of data depends heavily on the instrumentation of the systems that are being studied. In the ideal situation, the expert system can be tied directly into the flow of data from the operating system's instruments. As expert systems become more common, instrumentation for them will increasingly be designed into the machines they are guiding; however, for the foreseeable future, accessing the available data streams and generating data where they have been lacking will be an important part of applied work in machine learning.

3.4.4   Evaluating the Learned Knowledge

Rules induced from training data are not necessarily of high quality. The performance of knowledge acquired in this way is an empirical question that must be answered before that knowledge can be used on a regular basis. One standard approach to evaluation involves dividing the data into two sets, training on the first set, and testing the induced knowledge on the second. One can repeat this process a number of times with different splits, then average the results to estimate the rules' performance on completely new problems. Kibler and Langley (1988) review experimental methods of this sort for a broad class of learning algorithms.

However, human experts are available in many domains, and it would be foolhardy to ignore their opinions, even when they cannot articulate their knowledge fully. Thus, an important part of the evaluation process is the experts' examination of the learned knowledge. If significant problems emerge at this stage, they may suggest revisions to the problem formulation or representation. Evans and Fisher (1994) encourage such an iterative process in developing a fielded application, and other work we have seen took similar approaches.

3.4.5   Fielding the Knowledge Base

The final stage in applications is fielding the learned knowledge base. We intend this term in the broadest possible sense. In some cases, the knowledge acquired can be used without even embedding it in a computer system. In Evans and Fisher's (1994) work, a simple rule set written on paper was enough for humans to use in making decisions that alleviated their banding problem. In other cases, as in Fayyad *et al.*'s (1995) and Modesitt's (1990) domains, users expected not only computer implementation of the learned knowledge, but also considerable software support that had nothing to do with machine learning.

The important consideration is that the learned knowledge be *used*. Graphical interfaces may increase the chances of use in some domains but hurt them in others. Explanation capabilities may be welcomed by some users but not by others. In some cases (Giordana *et al.*, in press), the existence of a fielded hand-crafted expert system has been useful in fielding the learned knowledge base. Users who are already convinced that a knowledge-based system is beneficial are unlikely to object to having an improved knowledge base, although the fact that machine learning generated this knowledge may have had little meaning to them. For this reason, it is easier to introduce machine learning systems as extensions of expert systems that are already in place than to introduce both the expert system and its learning component at the same time.

We have made a number of comments on the role of users and experts both in designing the learning system and in securing its actual use. Everything that has been written and said about the importance of motivating users and domain experts, the need for their participation in the design and application processes, and the need to introduce computer interfaces that are usable and convenient for them applies in spades to the design and application of machine learning to industrial and other real-life situations.

3.4.6   Sources of Power in Applied Machine Learning

In this chapter we examined a number of applications of decision-tree and rule induction, some in regular use and others moving toward that goal. Most of these application efforts have used well-understood, established induction algorithms that operate on supervised, attribute-value data, and do not employ the more sophisticated techniques that dominate the research literature. Developers need not be ashamed of this fact; it is quite appropriate that applications draw on methods that have proved their power, reliability, and versatility in other applications or in laboratory tests, and if simple methods are available that have these properties, so much the better.

In fact, close inspection of these projects suggests that much of the power comes not from the specific induction method, but from proper formulation of the problems and from crafting the representation to make learning tractable. In these cases, machine learning has not completely automated the knowledge engineering process, but it *has* replaced knowledge engineering with two simpler tasks: characterizing the problem and designing a good representation. Developers need not play down this fact; reducing the time and effort needed to develop knowledge-based systems, however short this may fall of complete automation, can produce systems of great practical value, as we have seen.

Although we have concentrated on rule-induction methods, one might question—given our comments about sources of power—whether equivalent results would not emerge if one replaced the rule-induction algorithms with neural network, genetic, or case-based learning techniques. Recent comparatives studies in the literature, which show roughly equivalent performance across many domains, are consistent with this prediction. Consequently, given equivalent tools, each person may well want to use the ones with which they are most comfortable and familiar.

It is probably not an accident that quite different procedures produce similar results in application. Similar phenomena have been noticed in applying diverse management science tools to problems like scheduling. Where this occurs, it may result from the nature of the problem space. If global optima are easy to find or if local optima are nearly as good as the global one, then many methods may produce comparable performance. Engineers, accustomed to working in complex situations that do not admit analytic solutions, have long been aware of these facts. Rivers can be spanned with suspension bridges, trusses, cantilevers, and other radically different designs, and often there is no conclusive reason for choosing one over another.

Machine learning may never entirely replace knowledge engineering as a framework for constructing knowledge-based systems, but our examples show that significant progress toward automation has already been made, and we anticipate that rule induction and other learning methods will become increasingly prevalent as their benefits become better known.

ACKNOWLEDGEMENTS

We thank Peter Clark, Donald Michie, and Steve Muggleton for pointing us toward many of the application efforts we have reported; Donald Michie deserves a large share of credit for fostering many of these projects and advising their developers. Comments from Ivan Bratko, Donald Michie, and two anonymous reviews improved an earlier draft of this chapter, which appeared in the *Communications of the ACM*. This work was funded in part by Grants N00014-94-1-0505 and N00014-94-1-0746 from the Office of Naval Research to the Institute for the Study of Learning and Expertise and in part by Grant F49620-94-1-0118 from the Air Force Office of Scientific Research to Stanford University.

REFERENCES

Allen, B. P. (1994). Case-based reasoning: Business applications. *Communications of the ACM, 37*, 40–42.

Biggs, D., de Ville, B., & Suen, E. (1991). A method of choosing multiway partitions for classification and decision trees. *Journal of Applied Statistics, 18*, 49–62.

Bratko, I., & Muggleton, S. (1995). Applications of inductive logic programming. *Communications of the ACM, 38*, November.

Breiman, L., Friedman, J. H., Olshen, R. A., & Stone, C. J. (1984). *Classification and regression trees*. Belmont: Wadsworth.

El Attar, M., & Hamery, X. (1994). Industrial expert system acquired by machine learning. *Applied Artificial Intelligence, 8*, 497–542.

Evans, B., & Fisher, D. (1994). Overcoming process delays with decision-tree induction. *IEEE Expert, 9*, 60–66.

Fayyad, U. M., Smyth, P., Weir, N., & Djorgovski, S. (1995). Automated analysis and exploration of image databases: Results, progress, and challenges. *Journal of Intelligent Information Systems, 4*, 1–19.

Giordana, A., Neri, F., & Saitta, L. (in press). Automated learning for industrial diagnosis. In P. Langley & Y. Kodratoff (Eds.), *Fielded applications of machine learning*. San Francisco: Morgan Kaufmann.

Goldberg, D. E. (1994). Genetic and evolutionary algorithms come of age. *Communications of the ACM*, *37*, 113–119.

Guilfoyle, C. (1986). Ten minutes to lay the foundations. *Expert Systems User*, August, 16–19.

Hayes-Michie, J. (1990). News from companies. *Pragmatica: Bulletin of the Inductive Programming Special Interest Group*, Spring, 10–12.

Hermens, L. A., & Schlimmer, J. C. (1994). A machine-learning apprentice for the completion of repetitive forms. *IEEE Expert*, *9*, 28–33.

Hertz, D. B. (1987). *Applied AI Reporter*, *4*. Miami, NJ: University of Miami.

Karba, N., & Drole, R. (1989). Expert system for the cold rolling mill of the Steel Works Jesenice. *Proceedings of the Thirteenth Symposium on Information Technologies*. Sarajevo, Yugoslavia.

Kibler, D., & Langley, P. (1988). Machine learning as an experimental science. *Proceedings of the Third European Working Session on Learning* (pp. 81–92). Glasgow: Pittman.

Kononenko, I., Bratko, I., Roskar, E. (1984). *Experiments in automatic learning of medical diagnostic rules* (Technical Report). Jozef Stefan Institute, Ljubljana, Slovenia.

Langley, P., Drastal, G., Rao, B., & Greiner, R. (1994). Theory revision in fault hierarchies. *Proceedings of the Fifth International Workshop on Principals of Diagnosis*. New Paltz, NY.

Leech, W. J. (1986). A rule-based process control method with feedback. *Advances in Instrumentation*, *41*, 169–175.

Manganaris, S., & Fisher, D. (1994). Learning time series for intelligent monitoring. *Proceedings of the Third International Symposium on Artificial Intelligence, Robotics, and Automation for Space* (pp. 71–74). Pasadena, CA.

Michalski, R. S., & Chilausky, R. L. (1980). Learning by being told and learning by examples. *International Journal of Policy Analysis and Information Systems*, *4*.

Michie, D. (1987). Current developments in expert systems. In J. R. Quinlan (Ed.), *Applications of expert systems*. Wokingham, UK: Addison-Wesley.

Michie, D. (1989). Problems of computer-aided concept formation. In J. R. Quinlan (Ed.), *Applications of expert systems* (*Vol. 2*). Wokingham, UK: Addison-Wesley.

Michie, D. (1992). Directions in machine intelligence. *Computer Bulletin*, September/October, 9–11.

Modesitt, K. L. (1990). Inductive knowledge acquisition: A case study of SCOTTY. In K. L. McGraw & C. R. Westphal (Eds.), *Readings in knowledge acquisition: Current practices and trends*. Chichester, UK: Ellis Horwood.

Muggleton, S., King, R. D., & Sternberg, M. J. E. (1992). Protein secondary structure prediction using logic-based machine learning. *Protein Engineering*, *5*, 647–657.

Quinlan, J. R. (1993). *C4.5: Programs for machine learning*. San Francisco: Morgan Kaufmann.

Quinlan, J. R., Compton, P. J., Horn, K. A., & Lazarus, L. (1987). Inductive knowledge acquisition: A case study. In J. R. Quinlan (Ed.), *Applications of expert systems*. Wokingham, UK: Addison-Wesley.

Riese, C. (1984). *Transformer fault detection and diagnosis using RuleMaster by Radian* (Technical Report). Austin, TX: Radian Corporation.

Samuelson, C., & Rayner, M. (1991). Quantitative evaluation of explanation-based learning as an optimization tool for a large-scale natural language system. *Proceedings of the Twelfth International Joint Conference on Artificial Intelligence* (pp. 609–615). Sydney: Morgan Kaufmann.

Simon, H. A. (1993). A very early expert system. *Annals of the History of Computing, 15,* 63-68.

Widrow, B., Rumelhart, D. E., & Lehr, M. A. (1994). Neural networks: Applications in industry, business, and science. *Communications of the ACM, 37,* 93–105.

Zubrick, S. M., & Riese, C. E. (1985) An expert system to aid in severe thunderstorm forecasting. *Proceedings of the Fourteenth Conference on Severe Local Storms*. Indianapolis.

4

Applications of Inductive Logic Programming

Ivan Bratko, Stephen Muggleton and Aram Karalič

ABSTRACT

A logic-based approach to machine learning, called Inductive Logic Programming (ILP), is outlined, and several applications of ILP are reviewed. These benefit from the ability of ILP to flexibly use background knowledge in the learning process. The results from a variety of experimental applications of ILP are presented together with a discussion of the relative advantages of ILP and other machine learning approaches. Experience shows that ILP is a powerful tool for "knowledge-intensive" data mining.

4.1 INTRODUCTION

Inductive Logic Programming (ILP) is a combination of inductive machine learning and logic programming. In ILP, logic-based representation is used to carry out induction of rules from examples. ILP benefits from the solid theoretical framework provided by logic and logic programming.

Recently, a number of programs that learn at the level of first order logic have been developed. These include FOIL [Qui90], Golem [MF90] and Progol [SMKS94]. Shapiro's program MIS is one of their early predecessors [Sha83]. These developments have led to the inception of a new area of machine learning named *Inductive Logic Programming* [Mug91]. For recent developments see [Mug92, LD94, MDR94].

The learning problem in ILP is normally stated as follows: given *background knowledge* B, expressed as a set of predicate definitions, positive examples E^+ and negative examples E^-, an ILP system will construct a predicate logic formula H such that:

Machine Learning and Data Mining: Methods and Applications
Edited by R.S. Michalski, I Bratko and M. Kubat
© 1997 John Wiley & Sons Ltd

1. all the examples in E^+ can be logically derived from $B \wedge H$, and
2. no negative example in E^- can be logically derived from $B \wedge H$.

This definition is similar to the general problem of inductive learning, but it insists on predicate logic representation of B and H.

Typically, in ILP systems B, H, E^+ and E^- will each be Prolog programs. $B \wedge H$ is simply the Prolog program B extended by the Prolog program H. Stated this way, the ILP problem can be viewed as the following exercise in (automatic) Prolog programming. We have a Prolog program called B. This program is incomplete and needs to be extended to correctly handle the given examples E^+ and E^-. These examples can be viewed as Prolog queries. When a query from E^+ is asked, program B will answer "no". Program B is to be extended by a set of clauses H so that this new program $B \wedge H$ will answer "yes" to the queries in E^+ and "no" to the queries in E^-. A common ILP exercise of this kind is the induction of the quick-sort program from examples, saying for instance that the list `[f,e,g]` sorts into `[e,f,g]`. Suitable background knowledge contains the definition of the predicates for list concatenation, and for partitioning of a list, with respect to some value, into the lists of "small" and "big" elements. Using this background knowledge and some ten examples and counter examples, a typical ILP system will induce the known Prolog program for quick-sort in a few seconds of CPU time. Figure 4.1 shows examples and background knowledge that suffice for learning about quicksort with difference lists, using Grobelnik's ILP system Markus [Gro92].

The use of Prolog throughout has advantages in integrating techniques and theory with those inherited from the logic programming school. Also, logic allows for a highly versatile representation language for all constituents of the problem. This versatility is reflected in the wide variety of ILP applications.

4.2   ILP COMPARED TO OTHER APPROACHES TO ML

Let us now consider the relative advantages and disadvantages with respect to more common approaches to machine learning.

The majority of machine learning applications rely on attribute-based learning, exemplified by the induction of decision trees as in the well-known programs CART [BFOS84] and C4.5 [Qui93]. Broadly speaking, attribute-based learning also includes such approaches to learning as neural networks and nearest neighbour techniques. The advantages of attribute-based learning are: relative simplicity, efficiency, and the existence of effective techniques for handling noisy data. However, attribute-based learning is limited to non-relational descriptions of objects in the sense that the learned descriptions do *not* specify *relations* among the objects' parts. Attribute-based learning thus has the following strong limitations:

*   the background knowledge can be expressed in rather limited form,
*   the lack of relations makes the concept description language inappropriate for some domains.

Examples of such domains are presented in this chapter.

```
% EXAMPLES

example( qsort( [], [a], [a] ), true ).
example( qsort( [a], [a], [a] ), false ).
example( qsort( [d,f,b,e,c,g,a], [a,b,c,d,e,f,g], [] ), true ).
example( qsort( [f,e,g], [e,f,g], [] ), true ).
example( qsort( [b,c,a], [a,b,c,d,e,f,g], [d,e,f,g] ), true ).

% BACKGROUND KNOWLEDGE

partition( X, [], [], []).

partition( X, [Y | Rest], [Y | Smalls], Bigs)   :-
  gt( X, Y), !,
  partition( X, Rest, Smalls, Bigs).

partition( X, [Y | Rest], Smalls, [Y | Bigs])   :-
  partition( X, Rest, Smalls, Bigs).

% INDUCED DEFINITION

qsort( [], L, L).
qsort( [X | L], SL1A, SL2B)   :-
  partition( L, X, L1, L2),
  qsort( L2, SL2A, SL2B),
  qsort( L1, SL1A, [X | SL2A]).
```

Figure 4.1   Learning quicksort with difference lists with the ILP program Markus.

One of the main advantages of ILP over attribute-based learning is ILP's generality of representation for background knowledge. This enables the user to provide, in a more natural way, domain-specific background knowledge to be used in learning. The use of background knowledge enables the user both to develop a suitable problem representation and to introduce problem-specific constraints into the learning process. By contrast, attribute-based learners can typically accept background knowledge in rather limited form only. This means that in attribute-based learning, induction almost has to start from scratch. In ILP, on the other hand, knowledge that is known prior to induction can be fully exploited. So in ILP, if the problem is to learn about properties of chemical compounds, the molecular structures can be introduced as background knowledge in terms of the atoms and bonds between them. If the task is to automatically construct a model of a physical system from the observed behaviours, complete mathematical apparatus that is considered relevant to the modelling domain is included in background knowledge. Application of ILP involves the development of a good representation of the examples together with relevant background knowledge. A general purpose ILP system is then applied.

Of course, the price for these benefits of ILP includes ILP's greater logical and computational complexity.

In the sequel we describe selected applications of ILP. Those applications are chosen that specifically benefit from the ILP's predicate logic descriptions, and from the background facility in ILP.

4.3   PREDICTING THE MUTAGENICITY OF CHEMICAL COMPOUNDS

The construction of new scientific knowledge from real-world data remains an active focus for machine learning. One such problem is the Structure/Activity Relationships (SAR) of chemical compounds. This forms the basis of rational drug design. One widely used method of SAR stems from the work of Hansch [HMFM62] and uses regression/discrimination to predict activity from molecular properties such as hydrophobicity, sigma effect, molar reflectivity and LUMO (the energy of the Lowest Unoccupied Molecular Orbital). This and many other traditional approaches are limited in their representation of molecular connectivity and structure. They take into account the global attributes of a molecule, but do not comprehensively consider the *structural relationships* in the molecule. Thus some possibly important information, comprised as patterns in the molecular structure, may remain unexploited.

The ILP approach allows, however, that the complete structural information is taken into account. An ILP system *Progol* has been applied to the problem of identifying Ames test mutagenicity within a series of heteroaromatic nitro compounds [Mug94, SMKS94]. Hansch and coworkers have studied 230 compounds using classical regression [DLdCD+91]. For 188 compounds, they successfully obtained a linear regression function using hydrophobicity, LUMO and two hand-crafted binary attributes indicative of some structural properties. This regression formula predicts high mutagenicity with very acceptable accuracy. However, the remaining 42 compounds could not be successfully modelled by regression and no structural principles were proposed. This subset of 42 compounds will be therefore referred to as "regression unfriendly". *Progol* was applied to this mutagenicity data using the split of the compounds into those with high mutagenicity and the rest as suggested by Hansch and coworkers. All the compounds were represented relationally in terms of atoms, bonds and their partial charge. This information was automatically generated by the modelling program QUANTA^{TM}, and was represented as about 18300 Prolog facts (unit Horn clauses) for the entire set of 230 compounds. For the 188 compounds found to be amenable to regression, the additional Hansch attributes of LUMO and hydrophobicity were also provided. All this was supplied to *Progol* as background knowledge for learning. For these compounds, *Progol* constructed the following theory. A compound is highly mutagenic if it has (1) a LUMO value $\leq$ -1.937; or (2) a LUMO value $\leq$ -1.570 and a carbon atom merging six-membered aromatic rings; or (3) a LUMO value $\leq$ -1.176 and an aryl-aryl bond between benzene rings; or (4) an aliphatic carbon with partial charge $\leq$ -0.022. The theory has an estimated accuracy of 89%. This matches the accuracy of both the regression analysis of Hansch and coworkers, and a more recent effort using neural networks [VCJ93]. It should be noted, however, that *Progol*'s theory is easier to comprehend and was generated automatically, without access to any structural indicator variables hand-crafted by experts specifically for this problem.

The advantage of ILP, however, became particularly clear on the remaining subset of the 42 "regression unfriendly"' compounds. For these, *Progol* derived a single rule with an accuracy of 88% estimated from a leave-one-out validation (Figure 4.2). This is significant at $P < 0.001$. In contrast, linear regression and linear discrimination on the parameters used by Hansch and coworkers yield theories with accuracies estimated at 69% and 62% which are no better than random guesses supplied with the default accuracy of 69%. Perhaps even more important than the predictive accuracy, *Progol*'s rule provides the new chemical insight that the presence of a five-membered aromatic carbon ring with a nitrogen atom linked by a single bond followed by a double bond indicates mutagenicity. *Progol* has therefore identified a new structural feature that is an alert for mutagenicity.

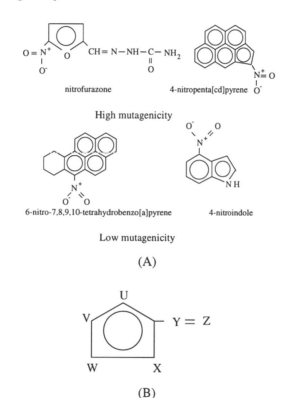

Figure 4.2 "Regression unfriendly" compounds and the structural feature found by *Progol*. (A) Some of the compounds found not to be amenable to analysis by statistical methods of regression or discrimination. No structural rules/alerts have previously been proposed for mutagenesis in these compounds. (B) *Progol* identified the alert of a double bond conjugated to a five membered aromatic ring via a carbon atom. The atoms U–Z do not necessarily have to be carbon atoms. This is the most compressive explanation for mutagensis for the 42 compounds possible within the hypothesis language used by *Progol*. The alert is present in the two high mutagenic compounds shown in (A) and not present in the two low mutagenic compounds.

4.4 SKILL RECONSTRUCTION IN ELECTRICAL DISCHARGE MACHINING

In *electrical discharge machining* (EDM), the workpiece surface is machined by electrical discharges occurring in the gap between two electrodes — the tool and the workpiece. The gap is continuously flushed by the third element, the dielectricum [JFv93]. The process consists of numerous randomly ignited monodischarges generating crater-textured surface. Stability and quality of the process depend on various parameters: type of dielectricum, workpiece material, required surface roughness, size of the gap between the electrodes (that is, between the electrode and the workpiece), servomechanism strengthening, period of discharges, duration of discharges, electric current upper limit, open voltage.

Some parameters can be controlled during the process (gap, flow), some require process interruption (duration of discharges, ...), and some of them are inherent to the particular machining task and cannot be changed (e.g., required workpiece roughness). For a standard set of workpiece types there exist predefined (recommended by the manufacturer of an EDM machine) sets of values for the process parameters, which guarantee certain degree of generated surface quality. However, the parameter settings are very conservative and do not yield really good performance in terms of the time needed to accomplish the task. Therefore, a human operator is normally employed to control the process parameters and minimize the machining time.

One immediately sees the potential importance of automatically reproducing operator's behavior: an EDM machine assisted by an "automatic operator". So in this domain the goal of induction was not to model the physics of a dynamic system, but to reconstruct an operator's skill from examples.

4.4.1 Developing the Representation

During the conversations with the operator, it was found that he monitors the following characteristics: (i) Relative share of different kind of pulses generated during dischargement. (There are three kinds of pulses: A (*empty*) pulses, B (*effective*) pulses, and C (*arc*) pulses.) (ii) average electric current, (iii) gap, and (iv) flow. The operator controls only gap and flow, therefore they were chosen to be the control parameters — input variables. Values of other quantities remained fixed through all experiments. Mean values and deviations of the observed quantities for the last 5 and the last 20 seconds were chosen as the attributes. The name of an attribute consists of three letters. The first letter indicates the parameter (A, B, C for the three kinds of pulses and I for the electric current). The second letter describes time interval: L is used for attributes describing state of the process in the last 20 seconds (Long-term) while S (for Short-term) is used to describe the last 5 seconds. The third letter is M for the Mean value or D for the standard Deviation.

It is interesting that during the process of attribute identification the operator frequently monitored some quantities which he claimed he monitored only occasionally or that he didn't monitor at all. This showed up when the operator was observed during one of the test runs.

To enable the detection of the rate of change of the attributes, the predicate "<" was defined as background knowledge. The attributes were given appropriate types, so that the comparison of their values (through background knowledge) was possible only for the attributes describing the same quantity.

Since we tried to model control by two variables (gap and flow), the learning task was decomposed in two learning tasks — learning gap control and learning flow control separately.

For each control variable three actions were possible: increase the control variable (the action was assigned a numerical value +1.0), no action (value 0.0), and decrease the control variable (value −1.0).

For each action (gap or flow change) a learning example was generated *in each domain*. If, for example, gap was increased, one example was generated for the "gap" (sub)domain, with action +1.0 and one example was also generated for the "flow" (sub)domain, with action 0.0. Additionally, to provide learning examples also in the areas of relatively stable process behavior, for each 60 seconds elapsed without an action, an example was generated with action 0.0 for both subproblems.

4.4.2 Results of Learning and Expert's Evaluation

Several models of operator's skill were generated using the FORS program (First Order Regression [Kar95]). FORS is an ILP system with numerical capabilities. These include numerical regression and arithmetic and standard numerical functions introduced through background knowledge. Models of skill were induced at various degrees of pruning. As an example we present below part of an induced model of skill:

```
f(DGap,ASM,ASD,BSM,BSD,CSM,CSD,ISM,ISD,ALM,ALD,BLM,BLD,CLM,CLD,ILM,ILD)  :-
                ILD >= 0.55, DGap is 0.3,!.
f(DGap,...) :- CLM >= 5.6300, DGap is 0.7,!.
f(DGap,...) :- BSM =< 1.1000, DGap is -0.2,!.
f(DGap,...) :- DGap is -0.5,!.

f(DFlow,...) :- ASD =< 0.0100, DFlow is 0.0,!.
f(DFlow,...) :- ALD =< 0.0800, DFlow is 0.0,!.
f(DFlow,...) :- ASM < ALM, ISD < ILD, BSD < BLD, DFlow is 0.1,!.
f(DFlow,...) :- BLM < BSM, DFlow is 0.5,!.
f(DFlow,...) :- DFlow is 0.1,!.
```

DGap means *change of gap*, DFlow means *change of flow*. Notice that the induced model may instantiate DGap and DFlow to values *between* −1.0 and 1.0 although in the learning examples these values were only −1.0, 0.0, and 1.0. In an automatic controller, the rules could be interpreted probabilistically, determining the *proportion* of the corresponding directions of change of gap and flow. The operator's and expert's [Kom95] comments on the model were that most of the induced actions were logical. However, there were some comments about the understandability of the models:

- In operator's opinion the decomposition of the problem (separate control rules for gap and flow) degraded model's understandability. A combination of gap and flow actions would be more intuitive.
- Clauses which appear late in the hierarchy of clauses tend to be less comprehensible, because one must remember the negations of all the clauses that appeared before.

- There were also situations where simple post-processing of the clause bodies (in combination with a solution to previous remark) would improve their comprehensibility. For example, in the situation

```
f(...) :- ALM =< 0.10,...,ALM =< 0.05
```

the first literal is obviously redundant. In fact, domain expert usually rewrote the rules prior to their evaluation.

To improve model comprehensibility, the two induced submodels were combined together to reveal the combined strategy for simultaneous control of gap and flow. The combination of the models was done in the following way:

1. Every clause in the model was expanded, so that clauses explicitly included negations of the conditional parts of previous clauses' bodies. This step ensured that each model consisted of mutually exclusive clauses independent of the order of evaluation.
2. Each clause in the gap model was combined with each clause of the flow model to produce new set of rules for every possible combination of conditional parts of clauses' bodies.

The above procedure resulted in a model consisting of 20 disjoint clauses, each predicting gap *and* flow actions. As an illustration, we present the clause constructed from the last clause of the gap submodel and the last clause of the flow submodel:

```
f(DG/DF,...):-
    ILD  < 0.55, CLM  < 5.63, BSM  > 1.10, ASD  > 0.01,
    ALD  > 0.08, ASM >= ALM,  ISD >= ILD,  BSD >= BLD, BLM > BSM,
    DG is -0.5, DF is 0.1,!.
```

Despite the fact that the new model contained more than twice as many clauses as the original and that all the clauses were longer, the operator and the expert claimed that this model is more comprehensible than the first one.

The domain expert qualitatively defined the relation between the effectiveness of the process and the control parameters — gap and flow. The qualitative states of the process are presented in two dimensions on the left diagram of Figure 4.3. The diagram defines two states of the process: stable state and arcing state. The effectiveness of the process decreases with the distance of the process from the boundary between the two regions. The arcing state is to be avoided, because it can damage the workpiece. The stable process region, on the other hand, is not harmful to the workpiece. It is, however, not recommendable to stay in the stable process region, because its characteristic is very low process effectiveness. So, the goal of the control should be to guide the process as close as possible to the boundary between the arcing and the stable region. More precisely: even on the boundary the performance is not constant. There is a (small) region on the boundary, which represents the region of the best process performance. The region is marked with an asterisk. The state diagram was further divided into six regions, representing qualitatively different process behaviors.

The induced model was evaluated by plotting the suggested actions into the state diagram of the process. For each rule in the model, at least one vector representing the combination of suggested gap and flow actions was drawn, representing the suggested action. For some rules, more than one vector was drawn, because very general rules cover more than one region of the state diagram. The right side of the Figure 4.3 depicts actions suggested by the induced model. One can immediately see that most of the vectors point towards the boundary between the

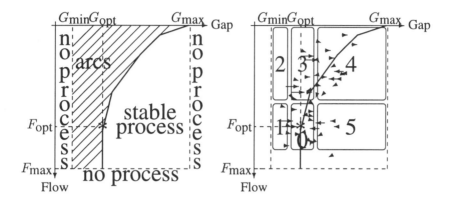

Figure 4.3 State space of the EDM process and control actions predicted by the model induced by FORS.

regions — the optimal working region. Additionally, we see that many of them point towards the point of optimal performance. It seems that the model correctly reproduces the operator's skill. The model has been installed on the actual machine to successfully replace the human operator.

4.5   SOME OTHER APPLICATIONS OF ILP

Finite element mesh design. Finite element (FE) methods are used extensively by engineers and modelling scientists to analyse stresses in physical structures. Finite element methods require that the structures being modelled are partitioned into a finite number of elements, resulting in a finite element mesh. In order to design a numerical model of a physical structure it is necessary to decide the appropriate resolution of the mesh. Considerable expertise is required in choosing these resolution values. Too fine a mesh leads to unnecessary computational overheads when executing the model. Too coarse a mesh produces intolerable approximation errors.

Normally some regions of the object require a denser mesh, whereas in other regions a coarser mesh still suffices for good approximation. There is no known general method that would enable automatic determination of optimal, or even reasonably good, meshes. However, many examples of successful meshes for particular objects have been accumulated in the practice of FE computations. These meshes can be used as sources of examples for learning about the construction of good meshes.

The mesh density in a region of the object also depends on the adjacent regions. Because of these relational dependences, the ILP approach most naturally applies to the mesh design problem. Dolšak [Dol96] has applied various ILP systems to the learning of rules about good FE meshes (see also [DBJ94] and [DJB96]).

Biological classification of river water quality. River water quality can be monitored and assessed by observing various biological species present in the river. In particular, the river-bed macro-invertebrates are considered to be suitable indicators of the quality of water. Different species have different sensitivity to pollutants, and therefore the structure of the macro-invertebrate community in a river is well correlated with the degree and type of pollution. Džeroski *et al.* [DDHRW94] used ILP to analyse the relation between the samples of macro-invertebrates and the quality class of water. For learning, they used 292 field samples of benthic communities taken from British Midlands rivers, classified by an expert river ecologist into five water quality classes. They constructed a relational representation of these samples and used the ILP systems Golem [MF90] and CLAUDIEN [DB93] for inducing logic clauses from the data. The induced clauses were judged by experts to be intuitively appealing and largely consistent with their knowedge. In particular, the experts appreciated the symbolic explicitness of the generated descriptions. They considered this as a major advantage over neural net learning that was also applied to the same data.

Inducing program invariants with ILP. In formally proving the correctness of procedural programs, one needs to find suitable conditions that always hold at given points in the program. Such a precondition has to be sufficiently strong to imply the postcondition of the program. Of particular interest is the problem of finding suitable conditions that are true inside program loops, called loop invariants. In general, the construction of loop invariants is considered difficult, and is usually done simply by guessing. Bratko and Grobelnik [BG93] explored the idea that ILP techniques can be used for automatically constructing loop invariants. A program that is to be proved correct can be executed, and the resulting execution traces can be used as learning examples for an ILP system. The states of the program variables at a given point in the program represent positive examples for the condition associated with that point in the program. Negative examples can be generated by employing a kind of "controlled closed-world assumption". In [BG93] suitable loop invariants were straightforwardly induced for simple programs that are used in typical correctness proof exercises. The automatic induction of an invariant for a parallel program was also demonstrated. The scaling up of this approach to larger programs has not been investigated yet.

Data refinement in program design. In program construction from higher order specification, functions in the specification language (higher level) are to be implemented in the target language (lower level). Thereby abstract data types at the higher level are to be refined into concrete data types at the target language level. For example, sets can be reified into lists. In [BG93] this refinement problem is formulated in the ILP framework. As an illustration, the general ILP program Markus [Gro92] was used to implement by induction the set union operation from abstract, high level specification.

Innovative design from first principles. Bratko [Bra93] formulated an approach to innovative design as an ILP problem. The design process is viewed as the process of structuring available elementary components in such a way that they together realize some specified target behaviour. The approach addresses the design from "first principles" in the sense that the functional behaviour of an artifact is derived from the *physics* of the elementary components available to the designer. The approach involves: specification of the target artifact by examples of its intended behaviour, *qualitative physics* definition of the behaviour of the elementary components available, and ILP as the mechanism for conceptually constructing the device. As an illustration, the Markus program [Gro92] was applied to constructing simple electric circuits from examples of their intended behaviour and the qualitative physics of some simple electrical components.

Qualitative system identification. A fundamental problem in the theory of dynamic systems is system identification. This can be defined as follows: given examples of the behavior of a dynamic system, find a model that explains these examples. Motivated by the hypothesis that it should be easier to learn qualitative than quantitative models, Bratko *et al.* [BMV92] formulated the qualitative identification problem as an ILP problem. In their work, models are sets of Qualitative Differential Equations (QDEs) that constrain the values of the system variables. A Prolog implementation of QDE constraints normally used in qualitative physics is provided as background knowledge for learning. Example behaviors of the modelled system are used as positive training examples, while negative examples are generated as near misses. Models of simple dynamical systems have been induced using general ILP systems.

4.6   CONCLUSION

ILP has been applied to difficult, industrially or scientifically relevant and not yet satisfactorily solved problems. In some of the applications described (mutagenicity in particular), the results obtained with ILP using real industrial or environmental data are better than with any other known approach, with or without ML. Mesh design and mutagenicity are good examples of problems where relational background knowledge is most natural, and converting this into attribute-value form would be at least rather awkward, if possible. In many of these applications, the users – domain specialists – are becoming increasingly interested in the understandability, or meaningfulness, of the induced concept descriptions. This helps them to obtain new insights in their problem domains. The representational flexibility in ILP helps the issue of understandability. Experience shows that ILP is a powerful tool for "knowledge-intensive" data mining.

In all applications, general purpose ILP systems were used. Accordingly, a typical ILP application amounts to designing a good relational representation of the problem, including the definition of relevant background knowledge. A major strength of ILP systems, compared with other machine learning approaches, is that they accept background knowledge in the form as general as Prolog programs. This often completely changes the nature of representational engineering, which is essential part of machine learning applications as observed by Langley and Simon [LS95].

On the other hand, a major obstacle to more effective use of ILP at present is the relative inefficiency of the existing ILP systems, and their presently rather limited facilities for handling numerical data. Therefore, in problems for which attribute-value representation is adequate, attribute-based learning is more practical simply for efficiency reasons.

ACKNOWLEDGEMENTS

The authors would especially like to acknowledge the input of Ashwin Srinivasan, Ross King and Michael Sternberg for their involvement in experimental results on structural molecular biology applications, Mihael Junkar and Igor Komel for their involvement in the electric discharge machining application, and Bojan Dolšak for the mesh design application. This work was supported partly by the Esprit Basic Research Action ILP (Inductive Logic Programming) and ILP^2, the Slovenian Ministry for Science and Technology, a SERC Advanced Research Fellowship held by Stephen Muggleton and a Research Fellowship supporting Stephen Muggleton at Wolfson College, Oxford.

REFERENCES

[BFOS84] L. Breiman, J.H. Friedman, R.A. Olshen, and C.J. Stone. *Classification and Regression Trees.* Wadsworth, Belmont, CA, 1984.

[BG93] I. Bratko and M. Grobelnik. Inductive learning applied to program construction and verification. In J. Cuena, editor, *Knowledge-based Techniques for Software Engineering.* North-Holland, 1993. Also in: *Proc. ILP'93 Workshop,* Bled, Slovenia, April 1993.

[BMV92] I. Bratko, S. Muggleton, and A. Varšek. Learning qualitative models of dynamic systems. In S. Muggleton, editor, *Inductive Logic Programming,* London, 1992. Academic Press.

[Bra93] I. Bratko. Innovative design as learning from examples. In *Proc. Int. Conf. Design to Manufacture in Modern Industries,* 1993. Bled, Slovenia.

[DB93] L. De Raedt and M. Bruynooghe. A theory of clausal discovery. In *Proc. Thirteenth International Joint Conference on Artificial Intelligence,* pages 1058–1063, San Mateo, CA, 1993. Morgan Kaufmann.

[DBJ94] B. Dolšak, I. Bratko, and A. Jezernik. Finite-element mesh design: an engineering domain for ILP application. In *Proc. Fourth Int. Workshop on Inductive Logic Programming ILP-94,* 1994. Bad Honnef/Bonn.

[DDHRW94] S. Džeroski, L. De Haspe, B.M. Ruck, and W.J. Walley. Classification of river water quality data using machine learning. In *Proc. Fifth International Conference on the Development and Application of Computer Techniques to Environmental Studies (ENVIROSOFT'94),* 1994.

[DJB96] B. Dolšak, A. Jezernik, and I. Bratko. Application of machine learning in finite element computation. 1996. This volume.

[DLdCD+91] A.K. Debnath, R.L. Lopez de Compadre, G. Debnath, A.J. Schusterman, and C. Hansch. *Jnl. Medicinal Chemistry,* 34:786–797, 1991.

[Dol96] Dolšak. *Contribution to Intelligent Mesh Design for Finite Element Analysis,* 1996. Univ. of Maribor: Ph.D. Thesis (in Slovenian).

[Gro92] M. Grobelnik. Markus: an optimized model inference system. In *Logic Approaches to Machine Learning Workshop,* 1992. ECAI-92 Workshop, Vienna.

[HMFM62] C. Hansch, P.P. Malong, T. Fujita, and M. Muir. *Nature,* 194:178–180, 1962.

[JFv93] M. Junkar, B. Filipič, and M. Žnidaršič. An AI approach to the selection of dielectricum in electrical discharge machining. In *Proc. Third International Conference on Advanced*

Manufacturing Systems and Technology AMST'93, 1993. Udine, Italy.

[Kar95]   A. Karalič. *First Order Regression*, 1995. Univ. of Ljubljana, Faculty of Computer and Information Sc.: Ph.D. Thesis.

[Kom95]   I. Komel, 1995. Univ. of Ljubljana, Faculty of Mechanical Eng., Laboratory of Alternative Technologies (personal communication.

[LD94]   N. Lavrač and S. Džeroski. *Inductive Logic Programming: Techniques and Applications.* Ellis Horwood, Chichester, England, 1994.

[LS95]   P. Langley and H. Simon. Applications of machine learning and rule induction. *Communications of the ACM*, 38(11):55–64, 1995.

[MDR94]   S. Muggleton and L. De Raedt. Inductive logic programming: theory and methods. *Journal of Logic Programming*, 19:629–679, 1994.

[MF90]   S. Muggleton and C. Feng. Efficient induction of logic programs. In S. Arikawa, S. Goto, S. Ohsuga, and T. Yokomori, editors, *Proc. First Conference on Algorithmic Learning Theory*, pages 368–381, 1990. Japanese Society for Artificial Intelligence, Tokyo.

[Mug91]   S. Muggleton. Inductive logic programming. *New Generation Computing*, 8(4):295–318, 1991.

[Mug92]   S. Muggleton, editor. *Inductive Logic Programming*. Academic Press, 1992.

[Mug94]   S. Muggleton. Bayesian inductive logic programming. In W. Cohen and H. Hirsh, editors, *Proc. eleventh international conference on machine learning*, pages 371–379, 1994.

[Qui90]   J.R. Quinlan. Learning logical definitions from relations. *Machine Learning*, 5:239–266, 1990.

[Qui93]   J.R. Quinlan. *C4.5: Programs for Machine Learning*. Morgan Kaufmann, San Francisco, 1993.

[Sha83]   E. Shapiro. *Algorithmic Program Debugging*. MIT Press, Cambridge, MA, 1983.

[SMKS94]   A. Srinivasan, S.H. Muggleton, R.D. King, and M.J.E. Sternberg. Mutagenesis: ILP experiments in a non-determinate biological domain. In *Proc. Fourth Int. Workshop on Inductive Logic Programming ILP-94*, 1994. Bad Honnef/Bonn.

[VCJ93]   D. Villemin, D. Cherqaoui, and Cense J.M. *J. Chim. Phys.*, 90:1505–1519, 1993.

PART II

Design and Engineering

5

Application of Machine Learning in Finite Element Computation

Bojan Dolšak, Ivan Bratko and Anton Jezernik

ABSTRACT

The Finite Element Method (FEM) is the most successful numerical method used extensively by engineers to analyse stresses and deformations in physical structures. In FEM, such structures have to be represented as finite element meshes. Defining an appropriate geometric mesh model that ensures low approximation errors and avoids unnecessary computational overheads is a very difficult and time consuming task. It is the major bottleneck in the FEM analysis process. In practice, FE mesh design is based on the user's experience. No satisfactory general method exists for the automatic construction of FE meshes. Here we describe applications of several ML systems to learning how to design FE meshes from examples of known good meshes. In the most recent experiments, the Inductive Logic Programming (ILP) system CLAUDIEN has been employed to construct rules for determining the appropriate mesh resolution values. Ten cylindrical mesh models have been used as a source of training examples. An evaluation of the resulting knowledge base shows that the mesh design patterns are captured well by the induced rules. A comparison between the results obtained by this knowledge base and conventional mesh generation techniques confirms that ILP is an effective approach to the problem of mesh design.

Machine Learning and Data Mining: Methods and Applications
Edited by R.S. Michalski, I Bratko and M. Kubat
© 1997 John Wiley & Sons Ltd

5.1   INTRODUCTION

The *Finite Element Method* (*FEM*), in the last 30 years the most successful numerical method in design, has been used extensively by engineers and modelling scientists to analyse stresses in physical structures. The effects of a specific loading case and support of such a structure can be expressed as a set of differential equations. However, it is not possible to solve that kind of equation in a reasonable amount of computer time for arbitrarily complex structures. Therefore we have to approximate the structure (Figure 5.1a) with a *mesh model*, that is with a set of *Finite Elements* (*FE*) interconnected in the nodal points (Figure 5.1b).

Displacements in the nodal points are then adopted as the basic unknown parameters of the problem. A set of functions is chosen to approximate the displacement within each FE in terms of its nodal displacements. As a consequence of such a discretisation, a set of linear algebraic equations, instead of differential equations, has to be solved. In detail, FEM is described in Zienkiewicz and Taylor (1988).

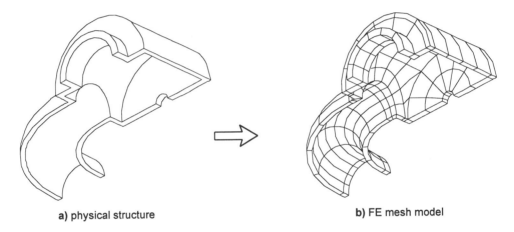

a) physical structure   b) FE mesh model

Figure 5.1   FEM discretisation.

A FE mesh should correspond to the geometric shape of the structure. In the areas where high deformations are expected a fine mesh is required to ensure low approximation errors. On the other hand, a coarse mesh is adequate for the rest of the structure to avoid unnecessary computational overheads, since each additional FE adds new equations to the set that has to be solved. Thus the "optimal" mesh model is the coarsest one that still ensures a satisfactory accuracy of the results. Figure 5.1b shows an example of that kind of the mesh model (Dolšak, 1996).

A lot of experience and knowledge about FEM is required to know in advance where the mesh should be fine and where it should be coarse. A number of parameters like the shape of the structure, loads and supports have to be considered. Most of the FEM packages on the market have the ability to build the FE mesh automatically.

Yet, this option only considers the geometric shape of the structure, which is one of the influential parameters, but certainly not the only one and, in many cases, also not the most important one. Usually it is necessary to design a few different meshes until we find the right one through experimentation (Figure 5.2).

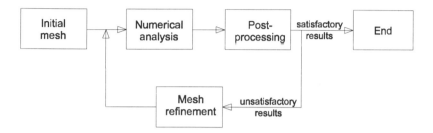

Figure 5.2   FE mesh design process.

The trouble is that each mesh must be analysed, since the next mesh should be generated with respect to the results derived from the previous one. If we consider that one FEM analysis can take from a few minutes to several hours (and even days) of computer time, it is obvious that there exists a great motivation to build an Expert System (ES) which would be able to design "optimal" FE meshes in the first iteration, or at least in less trials.

In this chapter, a basic idea for the development of such an ES is described, as well as an attempt to induce a knowledge base for FE mesh design using Machine Learning (ML) techniques. This study illustrates well the typical procedure of applying ML tools. This includes experimenting with several ML tools to develop the feeling for the domain and the data, improving the data set according to the shortcomings exposed by the initial experiments, detection of desirable domain-specific properties of ML tools, and accordingly, the choice of a tool satisfying these properties for further improved application. The structure of this chapter follows this paradigm of ML application. But first, in the next section, we discuss how this ML application combines with the existing, conventional FEM software.

5.2   ADDING AN EXPERT SYSTEM TO FEM GENERATOR

Besides the automatic mesh design, all FEM packages have the alternative option to build a FE mesh manually. The user is asked to specify the resolution values, such as the global size of the elements or the number of elements on the edges of the structure. Since the automatic mesh design in most cases does not give satisfactory results, manual mesh design is the usual way to build the FE mesh.

With respect to the resolution values, a FEM pre-processor is able to generate the FE mesh using some built-in rules and algorithms.

If the user specifies the number of elements on the edges of the structure, it may happen that some elements will have a geometric shape that is considerably different from the ideal one. In this case adaptive meshing is required. It is a built-in option in most of the FEM packages.

The basic problem in manual mesh design is the selection of correct resolution values to ensure the "optimal" FE mesh. We envisage this could be done by an ES linked with an appropriate FEM pre-processor, as shown in Figure 5.3.

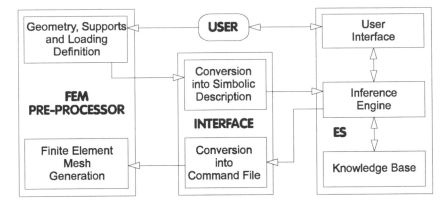

Figure 5.3   An integrated ES for FE mesh design.

In any case, the user has to define the problem (geometry, loads, supports). The data about the problem are converted from the FEM pre-processor format into the symbolic qualitative description to be used by the ES. The ES should be able to determine the mesh resolution values. A command file for the mesh generator can be constructed according to the resolution values obtained by the ES.

The main question is how to build a mesh design knowledge base? FEM has been applied extensively for the last 30 years. Still, there is no clear and satisfactory formalisation of the mesh design know-how. Mesh design is still a mixture of art and experience. However, a lot of published reports exist in terms of the problem definition, an adequate FE mesh (chosen after several trials) and the results of the analysis. These reports can be used as a source of training examples for ML. This provides an opportunity for automated knowledge acquisition for FE mesh design. Problem definitions and FE meshes from the reports can be presented to a learning program to construct rules for FE mesh design by generalising the given examples. In the sequel we describe such an application of ML.

5.3   THE LEARNING PROBLEM, EXAMPLES AND BACKGROUND KNOWLEDGE

5.3.1   Relational Nature of the Problem

A FE model consists of a network of edges. Relations between edges are important with respect to an appropriate resolution of the FE mesh. To take into account this relational information among the edges, relational learning techniques apply most naturally to the learning about mesh design.

Therefore we applied several Inductive Logic Programming (ILP) systems as they realise a form of relational learning. In general, the ILP problem statement involves positive and negative examples, and background knowledge (see the chapter on applications of ILP). In this section we develop a suitable representation for learning about mesh design in terms of examples and background knowledge.

5.3.2 Source of Examples

Ten different FE mesh models are comprised in the present learning set. It is impossible to take into consideration all different structures that can appear in practice. The FE mesh models in our learning set represent a family with the following common features:

- all structures are cylindrical,
- loads are only due to forces or pressures (there are no thermal influences, etc.),
- highly local mesh refinement is not required.

A detailed description of the FE mesh models used can be found in Dolšak (1996). Figure 5.1b shows one of the models. The FE meshes for all the structures were 'hand-constructed' and modified several times until the numerical results were accurate enough at acceptable computer time consumption.

A single edge can be described much more easily than the whole structure. Individual edges represent a lower level of the problem. The same type of edge can be found in many different structures, which allows us to describe a wide set of possible structures with a relatively small number of edge types. Therefore all the FE mesh models were put together as a collection of edges. The edges were labelled by a combination of a letter and a number. The letter (a – i) denotes a mesh model while the consecutive numbers denote individual edges in the model. Figure 5.4 shows some labelled edges in the FE mesh model from Figure 5.1b.

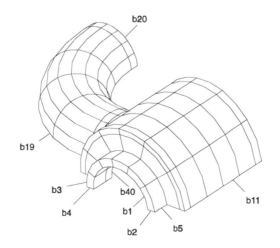

Figure 5.4   Some labelled edges in the FE mesh model **b.**

The geometric form, loads and supports are defined for all the edges in the training set. In addition, certain important topological relations between the edges are also defined. Because of these relations, a relational learning algorithm suits this problem most naturally. The FE mesh is defined by stating the number of finite elements along the edges.

5.3.3   Positive Examples

The relation to be learned is mesh(E,N), where E is the name of an edge in the structure and N is the recommended number of finite elements along this edge. For each edge in the training set the number of finite elements is given as a positive example. Some deviations are allowed. So for N≥8, for each example mesh(E,N), additional examples mesh(E,N1), N1=N±1 are added. We sometimes refer to the number N of finite elements along an edge as the *class* of the edge.

Since edges with more than 12 finite elements are quite rare, we decided to induce the rules only for classes from 1 to 12. Thus it may happen that the induced rules will not be able to classify all the edges of the structure. Yet this should not be a serious problem, since one does not have to specify the number of finite elements for all the edges in order to build a FE mesh. In such cases, the FEM pre-processor constructs a FE mesh with respect to the given resolution values using some built-in rules to determine the missing values.

5.3.4   Negative Examples

Basically, negative examples were constructed according to the closed-world assumption. So the negative examples are constructed as the combinations of the names of the edges with all the numbers between 1 and 12 other than those found in the positive examples. Again, some deviations from this are considered. For all the edges with 5 to 7 finite elements, deviations by 1 element are not stated as the negative examples. For the edges with 8 or more elements, deviations by up to 2 elements are tolerated.

An alternative set of negative examples has been built up for single class learning. In this case the positive examples for all other classes except the actual class are considered as negative examples. Thus, for example, for learning the rules for class 1, all the examples specifying 1 FE on the edge are considered as positive examples. All other examples are considered in that case as negative.

5.3.5   Background Knowledge

Background knowledge contains definitions of the predicates that can be used in the hypotheses about the target relation mesh/2. It can be divided into two parts:

- attribute-value description of the edges,
- topological relations between the edges.

5.3.5.1 ATTRIBUTE-VALUE DESCRIPTION OF THE EDGES

The following attributes of the edges that pertain to the FE mesh are described as background facts:

- the type of the edge using predicates:
  `long, usual, short, circuit, half_circuit, quarter_circuit, short_for_hole, long_for_hole, circuit_hole, half_circuit_hole, quarter_circuit_hole, not_important,`
- the supports using predicates:
  `free, one_side_fixed, two_side_fixed, fixed,`
- the loads using predicates:
  `not_loaded, one_side_loaded, two_side_loaded, cont_loaded.`

There are special predicates describing the type of an edge for those edges that have the circular shape (we have described a family of cylindrical structures). The other edges are classified regarding their length with qualitative values "long", "usual" and "short". Special predicates are also used for the edges that are a part of a hole in the structure, since those places are usually important for the analysis. Short edges that do not belong to an important part of the structure are described with the predicate not_important.

There are four predicates to describe the supports. Only the property of an edge being fixed (completely or at the end-points) or free is considered, without distinguishing the supports with respect to the number of degrees of freedom. Similarly, a description of a load only states the position of a load.

Each predicate that defines an attribute of an edge has one argument – the name of the edge. All the edges in the training set are described by one predicate for each attribute. It could happen that an edge would be loaded with a combination of pressure (continuously) and force, which can be described by two predicates, yet in our training set such an example does not exist.

5.3.5.2 TOPOLOGICAL RELATIONS BETWEEN THE EDGES

A topological representation is needed because of the *relationships* between the edges that also pertain to the FE mesh. We believe there is a connection between the edges that are *neighbours* or *opposite* (parallel) to each other, which affects the appropriate number of finite elements on those edges. A third interesting relation concerns the edges that are not only opposite but also have the same length or form. For instance, concentric circles have the same form. Such pairs of edges have been described using the predicate equal. All three predicates are binary.

An edge can also be a neighbour, or opposite or equal to more than one edge. Because of that, it is best to use an ILP learning algorithm that allows *nondeterminate* literals. A literal such as neighbour(a3,X) is called nondeterminate because the "input" argument a3 does not necessarily determine the "output" argument X (if a3 has several neighbours X can be any one of them).

In spite of this, a "determinate" version of background knowledge description was also used in our earlier experiments (Dolšak and Muggleton, 1992; Dolšak *et al.*, 1994) with the ILP program GOLEM (Muggleton and Feng, 1990), which is restricted to determinate literals only.

5.3.6 Summary of the Learning Set

The learning set used in the present experiments comprises 4029 facts in the nondeterminate version of background knowledge (Table 5.1) and 644 positive examples (Table 5.2).

Table 5.1   Background facts distribution

Background description	Training models										Σ
	a	b	c	d	e	f	g	h	i	j	
long	3				2		6	2	2	2	17
usual	2	6	6	4	59	6	18	21	16	14	152
short	14	10	2	15	20	10	8	18	4	8	109
circuit			10	28							38
half_circuit	11	8				10	20	2	2	2	55
quarter_circuit		4			6			10			20
short_for_hole	4	4	2		2			2			14
long_for_hole	1		1		2			2		2	8
circuit_hole			4			9			2		15
half_circuit_hole	4	6			4	2		3		2	21
quarter_circuit_hole											0
not_important	16	4	3	10	1	4	8	11			57
free	2		13	53	34	9		16	10	14	151
one_side_fixed	3		6		24			8	8	8	57
two_side_fixed	15	12			4	10	18	10	2	2	73
fixed	35	30	9	4	34	22	42	37	6	6	225
not_loaded	21	23	17	50	88	19	52	63	10	14	357
one_side_loaded	5			4	4	6	4	4	8	8	43
two_side_loaded					1				2	2	5
cont_loaded	29	19	11	3	3	16	4	4	6	6	101
neighbour	220	168	84	168	382	116	240	280	96	120	1874
opposite	28	38	28	12	24	10	54	34	6	8	242
equal	34	32	32	20	19	38	80	68	34	38	395
Total	**447**	**364**	**228**	**371**	**713**	**287**	**554**	**595**	**214**	**256**	**4029**

The only proposed predicate that is not represented in the background knowledge is quarter_circuit_hole. Such edges are scarce enough, so this omission was considered non-critical.

Table 5.2 Positive examples distribution

Class (No. of FE)	Training models										Σ
	a	b	c	d	e	f	g	h	i	j	
1	21	9	6	14	23	12	10	16	8	4	123
2	9	9	6	13	36	4	10	21		2	110
3	3	4	2		11	4	4	4		6	38
4	2	1		2	3		8	3	12	14	47
5	3				9	2		5			19
6		11			4	5	2	2		2	26
7		4					4	6	2		16
8	1	4	14		6		20	5	2	2	54
9	1	4	14		7	4	20	12	2	2	66
10	2				7	4	2	7	2	2	26
11	15			28	2	4	2	7			58
12	15			28	1		2				46
13								1			1
14								1			1
15						10					10
16									2		2
17	1										1
Total	73	46	42	85	111	49	84	90	30	34	644
Original	55	42	28	57	96	41	60	71	26	30	506
Additional	18	4	14	28	15	8	24	19	4	4	138

5.4 PREVIOUS EXPERIMENTS

The mesh data set was probably the first real-world relational data set. This contributed to the fact that mesh design became one of the most widely used domains for experimenting with ILP systems. So several learning systems have been applied to the FE mesh design problem in the last few years. Most of them are relational learning algorithms. As already mentioned, the first experiments with GOLEM were done using a smaller training set (Dolšak and Muggleton, 1992). After that the training set has been expanded and changed into the form that is described in Dolšak et al. (1994). Basically, the form of the training set was the same as discussed in the previous section, yet only first five training models (a – e) were described in it. In the rest of this section, the main points of the ML experiments with such a learning set are discussed.

5.4.1 Experiments with GOLEM

GOLEM (Muggleton and Feng, 1990) is an ILP algorithm based on Relative Least General Generalisation (RLGG) (Plotkin, 1969). It was applied several times to the finite element mesh design problem. The best results obtained in this domain so far are reported in Dolšak et al. (1994). GOLEM was run several times with the following experimental set-up:

- a determinate version of the background knowledge was used;
- the negative examples, constructed according to the close-world assumption, were used;
- some of the induced rules were accepted, although they were covering a negative example.

Provision was made to eliminate induced rules that were useless from the practical point of view of their application to classifying new edges. The accuracy of the induced rules was measured by ten-fold cross validation. According to this evaluation method, the complete set of examples was partitioned randomly into ten equally sized subsets. Then ten learning-testing iterations were performed. In each iteration, a different subset was removed from the training set. The learning was then performed on the so obtained 90% of the examples, and the accuracy of the induced rules tested on the removed 10% of examples. The average classification accuracy on the test set over the ten iterations was 78%, with a rather large standard deviation (5.7).

A similar experimental set-up was used in experiments done by Sašo Džeroski, described in Lavrač and Džeroski (1993, Section 9.2). In his experiments with GOLEM, recursive clauses were not allowed at all. Rules that were useless from a practical point of view were not eliminated. In classification, the rules were ordered according to their expected classification accuracy estimated by the Laplace probability estimate. In one experiment (Džeroski, 1991), the clauses with an accuracy of less than 75% were discarded while in his second experiment (Lavrač and Džeroski, 1993), the classification accuracy threshold was raised to 80%.

The accuracy was estimated by the "leave-one-structure-out" method, which became generally accepted in later experiments. This is a variation of k-fold cross validation. However, instead of a random k-way partition of the available example set, here the partition is done according to the structures to which the edges belong. Each subset of the example edges belongs precisely to one of the structures (five in these initial experiments). This "leave-one-structure-out" test is considered to be the most natural in the mesh design domain, because the rules induced from the training structures are applied to designing a mesh for the remaining, testing structure. In the sequel we will be referring to this test also simply as "leave-one-out".

The accuracy measured by the leave-one-out test was low. Džeroski reported 29% accuracy on the test set in the case of 75% accuracy threshold on the training set.

5.4.2　Experiments with FOIL

FOIL (Van Laer et al., 1994) extends some ideas from attribute-value learning algorithms to the ILP paradigm. In particular, it uses a covering approach similar to AQ's (Michalski, 1983) and an information-based search heuristic similar to ID3's (Quinlan, 1996). FOIL can deal with non-determinate literals. So do all the other algorithms applied to the finite element mesh design problem, except GOLEM. FOIL was run by Sašo Džeroski with the same settings that have been used in his experiments with GOLEM. Performing the leave-one-out test, the classification accuracy was only around 12% (Džeroski, 1991). The predicate neighbour was almost never used in the induced clauses, probably due to FOIL's myopic heuristic for choosing from among the candidate literals.

An additional problem with FOIL turned out to be its encoding length restriction, which apparently prevented the induction of some useful clauses.

5.4.3 Experiments with mFOIL

The ILP system mFOIL (Džeroski, 1991) is based on FOIL. It uses the accuracy of a clause (estimated by the m-probability estimate) as a search heuristic, instead of the entropy-based information gain heuristic implemented in FOIL. As a result of this improvement, classification accuracy increased to 22% (Džeroski, 1991). Similar to FOIL, mFOIL had problems with the relation neighbour.

5.4.4 Experiments with CLAUDIEN

CLAUDIEN looks for valid rules in the whole space of solutions without a guarantee that the induced hypotheses will cover all positive examples. Also, a hypothesis may cover a positive example several times. The main characteristic of the CLAUDIEN algorithm (De Raedt and Bruynooghe, 1993) is an elegant mechanism that allows a specification of the language bias. It is very useful in our case, since the induction of rules that are practically useless can easily be prevented. However, this was not exploited in the experiment (Van Laer *et al.*, 1994) carried out by the authors of CLAUDIEN. Nevertheless, the results of the leave-one-out test are better than those obtained by FOIL and mFOIL. The reported classification accuracy is 28%. In this experiment a time limit of 1000 CPU seconds on a Sparc workstation was used to terminate the learning process.

5.4.5 Experiments with MILP

The MILP algorithm (Kovačič, 1994) is an implementation of the stochastic search technique as a substitution for greedy search techniques, implemented in existing ILP algorithms. The finite element mesh design domain was used as one of the examples for testing the efficiency of this approach. MILP outperformed FOIL, mFOIL and GOLEM. The reported classification accuracy of the induced rules, performing the leave-one-out test, was about 32%.

5.4.6 Experiments with FOSSIL

FOSSIL (Fürnkranz, 1994a) is a FOIL-like ILP system that uses a search heuristic based on statistical correlation. Johannes Fürnkranz, the author of FOSSIL, made some experiments to induce classification rules from the described five-structure dataset using FOSSIL. Again, using the leave-one-out test, rules were learned from four of the five structures and then tested on the remaining fifth structure. The best classification accuracy was around 35% (Fürnkranz, 1994b).

5.4.7 Experiments with Attribute-value Algorithms

Some experiments with attribute-based learning algorithms have also been made (Kononenko *et al.*, 1994). By using only the attribute description and ignoring the relational description of the edges, the percentage of the correct classified edges was between 27 and 34%, performing the leave-one-out test! With an additional twelve attributes, derived from the relational background knowledge, the results were significantly improved even further. The best results in that case (44%) were obtained by using the ASSISTANT-R program, which is an improvement, with the RELIEFF approach to attribute evaluation of the ASSISTANT learning system for top down induction of decision trees (Cestnik *et al.*, 1987). These accuracy results, achieved by attribute-value learning, are surprisingly high for a domain that appears to naturally require relational learning. This point will be discussed later in the light of more recent results, when it will still be argued that relational learning is more appropriate in this domain than attribute-value learning.

5.5 SELECTION OF AN APPROPRIATE LEARNING ALGORITHM

The results of the preliminary ML experiments to the finite element mesh design problem seem excessively variable. Yet, the results of our experiment with GOLEM, described in Dolšak *et al.* (1994), have to be treated separately, for two reasons:

1. Only in this experiment was the leave-one-out strategy not used for testing the classification accuracy.
2. The additional knowledge about the engineering aspect of the problem was used to eliminate / prevent the rules that are useless from a practical point of view.

By ignoring this experiment, the evaluation of the results, obtained in the rest of the experiments that are described in the previous section can be summarised as follows:

- The classification accuracy, measured by performing a leave-one-out test, is under 50% (12 to 44). Practical applicability of the rules is therefore very limited.
- The results, obtained by attribute-value algorithms, outperform almost all the ILP results.

One can argue that a relational description in the background knowledge is not relevant! On the other hand, in the knowledge base induced by GOLEM (Dolšak *et al.*, 1994), 55 out of 62 rules contain topological relations. It is also the fact that the results of the experiments with attribute-value learners were significantly improved by the introduction of twelve additional attributes that have been derived from the background relational description. All this leads us to the conclusion that the relational description is beneficial. Furthermore, the conversion of some of the relational representations into equivalent attributes produces a description that is less meaningful than the original, relational one: the ensuing attribute description can no longer be interpreted so naturally. Therefore the relational learning algorithm is preferred in this domain.

Yet, there still remains a doubt about the poor performance of the ILP algorithms in comparison with attribute-value learners. The reason for that lies in the nature of the training set. A closer look at the distribution of the training instances for only the first five training models (Tables 5.1 and 5.2) shows that each structure is in a way unique and has contributed a significant number of examples to the training set. The leave-one-out test was therefore not appropriate, since it can easily be that by leaving the complete structure out of the learning set, no learning examples will remain with characteristics similar to the testing examples. This dissimilarity between the five structures shows that the leave-one-structure-out test was not very appropriate in this case. In attribute-based learning, this problem of dissimilarity between the structures was handled better by the naive Bayes formula applied to the cases not "covered" by the induced decision tree.

To ensure the necessary conditions for the leave-one-out test, which is indeed the most natural in this case, a distribution of training examples was improved by the extension of the training set. Five additional structures (f – i) are included in the present training set. To ensure good results with ML with the new training set, the following features were considered important in the choice of an appropriate learning algorithm:

- relational learning,
- capability for dealing with non-determinate literals,
- noise tolerance; both the number of positive and negative examples covered by the clause have to be considered,
- induction of practically useless rules should be prevented during the learning process.

The ILP system CLAUDIEN (De Raedt and Bruynooghe, 1993) has all the desired properties. Furthermore, it does not require (in our case a huge) set of negative examples. Therefore, CLAUDIEN was chosen to be applied on the described new training set. A very useful feature of CLAUDIEN is that it allows the user to loosely specify the general form and contents of rules to be potentially generated by the induction algorithm.

5.6   LEARNING WITH CLAUDIEN

The learning of the rules for determining the resolution values for the finite element mesh was carried out in six stages. In each learning stage a different form of rules was specified to be induced by CLAUDIEN. Furthermore, we also influenced the learning process by setting the required accuracy (percentage of positive examples among those covered) and coverage (the number of covered ground "cases"; this is understood as the number of substitutions from the training set that make the body of the induced clause true; so a case does not necessarily correspond to an example).

In the following paragraphs these six stages are described. We give examples of induced rules and rule schemas. They have a Prolog syntax as generated or accepted by CLAUDIEN.

In the first stage CLAUDIEN induced 17 classification rules that contain only attribute description of the edges. The following rule schema was specified for this purpose:

```
clausemodel('mesh(Edge1,[1,2,3,4,5,6,7,8,9,10,11,12]) <-\
    +1{(Type(Edge1),Support(Edge1),Load(Edge1)}').
```

This says that the conclusion part of an induced rule is a literal of the form mesh/2 specifying up to 12 finite elements on Edge1. The condition part of the rule may mention at least one and at most three attributes of Edge1 (Type, Support and Load). For example, rule number 10 with 100% accuracy (perc_cov(1)), which was induced in little more than 14 CPU seconds, is :

```
        rule(10,[perc_cov(1),body(4),cpu(14.1667)],
             (mesh(Edge1,11) :-
                  long(Edge1),
                  one_side_loaded(Edge1))).
```

It specifies 11 finite elements on the long edges, loaded at one side. From the rule description it can also be seen that there are four substitutions in the training set that make the body of the rule true.

In the second stage of the learning process the use of a single topological relation was allowed. To prevent the induction of practically useless rules, the following conditions were also specified by the language for the target hypothesis:

- the rules must contain at least one attribute description of the actual edge;
- the new edge, introduced by the topological relation, has to be further described by at least one attribute.

```
clausemodel( 'mesh(Edge1,[1,2,3,4,5,6,7,8,9,10,11,12]) <-\
     < +1{Type(Edge1),Support(Edge1),Load(Edge1)},\
     {<Relation(Edge1,Edge2),\
     +1{Type(Edge2),Support(Edge2),Load(Edge2)}>}').
```

The predicate variable Relation was defined as one of: neighbour, opposite or equal. Limited by this specification, 351 rules were induced in the second learning stage. Here is an example of a rule that specifies seven finite elements for the "usual" edges, which have a continuously loaded and both sided fixed neighbour of the quarter circuit geometric form:

```
        rule(340,[perc_cov(1),body(4),cpu(19375.2)],
             (mesh(Edge1,7) :-
                  usual(Edge1),
                  neighbour(Edge1,Edge2),
                  quarter_circuit(Edge2),
                  two_side_fixed(Edge2),
                  cont_loaded(Edge2))).
```

Classification rules with two topological relations were induced in two learning stages. First, rules with two topological relations, both referring to the "target" edge, were built. For example the following rule, induced in the third learning stage, contains two topological relations (neighbour and opposite) with an actual edge (Edge1) as the first argument in both cases:

```
rule(166,[perc_cov(0.909091),body(22),cpu(1026)],
        (mesh(Edge1,9)  :-
                half_circuit(Edge1),
                not_loaded(Edge1),
                neighbour(Edge1,Edge2),
                usual(Edge2),
                opposite(Edge1,Edge3),
                half_circuit(Edge3),
                not_loaded(Edge3))).
```

CLAUDIEN induced 1988 rules of that type in 128207 CPU seconds on a SUN Sparc workstation! Yet, the search space was even more complex in the fourth stage of the learning process, when the rules with two topological relations, describing a chain of edges, were sought. Despite the fact that the required accuracy and coverage of the rules were increased (Table 5.3), almost 300000 CPU seconds were spent in the fourth learning step to built 1700 rules. An example is:

```
rule(1535,[perc_cov(1),body(8),cpu(64226)],
        (mesh(Edge1,3)  :-
                cont_loaded(Edge1),
                neighbour(Edge1,Edge2),
                half_circuit(Edge2),
                cont_loaded(Edge2),
                neighbour(Edge2,Edge3),
                not_important(Edge3),
                one_side_loaded(Edge3))).
```

In this case, two new edges Edge2 and Edge3 are introduced as a chain of neighbours together with the target edge Edge1.

In the fifth learning stage we allowed the induced rules to specify more than one class. The use of one topological relation was also allowed. In this case we considered all 17 classes that appear in the training set. On the other hand, the required accuracy and coverage of the rules were further increased. CLAUDIEN spent more than 10 days of CPU time to induce 395 rules that meet the given specification in this stage of learning. Most of them specify an interval over the classes, although there are also examples with some missing classes, for example:

```
rule(362,[perc_cov(1),body(26),cpu(775726)],
        (one(A);two(A);four(A)  :-
        mesh(Edge1,A),
                one_side_fixed(Edge1),
                neighbour(Edge1,Edge2),
                free(Edge2),
                cont_loaded(Edge2))).
```

The rule specifies one, two or four finite elements for edges that are fixed on one side and have a neighbour, which is free and continuously loaded.

In the last, sixth stage, interval specifications were again allowed. This time only the type of the edge was considered in the body of a clause.

For each type description predicate, one rule was induced specifying the possible numbers of finite elements corresponding to that type of edge. Thus, for example, the following rule says that short edges in the training set have between one and four finite elements:

```
rule(2,[perc_cov(1),body(109),cpu(13.9333)],
        (one(A);two(A);three(A);four(A)  :-
      mesh(Edge1,A),
            short(Edge1))).
```

The basic parameters of the overall learning process are presented in the Table 5.3. CLAUDIEN induced 4462 rules altogether in some 15 days of effective CPU time! The learning process could be terminated after a specified CPU time, however this option was not applied, since there is no connection between the order of the induced rules and their quality.

Table 5.3   Learning the rules – basic parameters

Step	The form of the rules	Accuracy	Coverage	Rules	CPU sec.
1	Class rules without relations	≥ 0.90	≥ 3	17	79
2	Class rules with one relation	≥ 0.90	≥ 3	351	26657
3	Class rules with two relations (Edge1)	≥ 0.90	≥ 3	1988	128207
4	Class rules with two relations in chain	≥ 0.95	≥ 10	1700	299833
5	Interval rules with one relation	≥ 0.98	≥ 20	395	894573
6	Limits depending on the edge type	1	≥ 8	11	8666
				4462	**1356237**

The induced rules mention all the background predicates, as well as all the classes represented in the training set.

5.7   POST-PROCESSING OF THE INDUCED RULES

The induced rules were found to be inappropriate to be placed directly into the knowledge base. Many of them were subsequently eliminated, while the form and order of the remaining rules were adjusted to meet the application requirements. In post-processing, the rules that specify an exact number of finite elements were treated separately from the interval rules. Rules were eliminated considering the following conditions:

- if they covered less than three positive examples,
- if they were duplicated,
- if they were subsumed by a more general rule for the same class,
- if they covered only additional positive examples,
- if they were merged with other rules that had the same body but specified different classes (in the case of interval rules).

The first condition seems to be redundant, since the minimum number three of substitutions from the training set that make the body of the clause true has already been considered in the learning process. Yet, it must be taken into account that the number of substitutions is not always the same as the number of positive examples covered by the rule. One positive example may cause more than one successful substitution. For example, one edge can have up to four neighbours with the same attributes.

After the learning process 2686 rules were eliminated in total. To ensure the best possible efficiency, all the elements of the remaining 1776 rules that are not necessary for practical application were abandoned. On the other hand a mechanism for preventing the infinite loops was implemented to handle the recursive rule that was induced in one of the previous learning experiments (Dolšak *et al.*, 1994) and was added to the knowledge base.

In the FEM pre-processor environment one has to define the exact number of finite elements on each edge of the structure to be idealised. Therefore rules for determining the most appropriate class from the proposed list of classes, specified by the interval rules, were also added to the knowledge base. Basically, these rules compare the geometric type of two edges and give the difference between the average classes used in the training set for that kind of edge. For example, the following rule says that usual edges have on average six finite elements less than long edges:

```
compare_type(Edge1,Edge2,-6) :-
        usual(Edge1),
                long(Edge2).
```

The comparison rules were built on the basis of simple statistics on the training set. The comparison rules in the knowledge base enable the inference engine to choose the class out of the proposed list of classes considering the type of the opposite edge. If there is no opposite edge, a single class is calculated as an arithmetic mean value of the proposed classes.

Finally, rules for determining the appropriate type of the finite elements were also added to the knowledge base. They were built manually and specify the primary and secondary type of elements to be used, considering the space dimension, complexity of the geometry and loading case, as well as the thickness in the case of a three dimensional structure. Denotations of the elements are adopted from the FEM package BERSAFE (Hellen, 1970). Here, for example, is the rule for solid elements with a second order approximation function:

```
finite_element(ez60,ez45) :-
        space_dimension(3),
        thickness(thick),
        ( geometry_complexity(high) ;
          loading_case(complex) ).
```

All the rules in the knowledge base were ordered to optimise the effectiveness and accuracy of the ES. Because of the top-down search strategy implemented in Prolog, which was used as a programming language for the ES shell, the most reliable rules were placed on top of the knowledge base.

This is especially important in the case of classification rules to ensure that the best rule is executed to determine the number of finite elements for each particular edge of the structure. There were several criteria used to define a proper order of the classification rules in the knowledge base:

- Rules that classify single classes were placed in the knowledge base before interval rules to minimise the need for selection of the most appropriate class from the proposed list of classes with the comparative rules. For the same reason, the recursive rule is placed just after the rules for single classes.
- Rules without negative covers had priority.
- Rules describing the type of the actual edge were placed before the rest of the rules, since the type of the edge (relative length) is most obviously related to the number of finite elements.
- Rules with 100% accuracy (on training data) were ordered from simple attribute rules to more complex rules with one and two geometric relations. The opposite ordering was used for the rules that cover negative examples.

5.8   RESULTS

5.8.1   Knowledge Base and ES Shell

Finally, 1873 rules and 31 facts were accepted into the knowledge base as described in the previous section. The quantity and order of the rules/facts in the knowledge base are shown in Table 5.4. The presented knowledge base is the most comprehensive one considering all the experiments in this field. Undoubtedly the reason for that is the extension of the training set. It should also be noted that the interval classification rules were induced for the first time, and some additional rules were put into the knowledge base after the learning process. The knowledge base is written in Prolog syntax in the form of Prolog rules and facts. Thus it is sufficiently transparent and can be easily extended if necessary.

The ES shell is also written in Prolog. It facilitates a proper use of the knowledge base for finite element mesh design, as well as communication between the user and the system. One of the more interesting features of the user interface is its capability to explain the inference process.

Table 5.4 The number and order of the rules and facts in the knowledge base

Classification rules for single classes	**1538**	**rules**
Acc = 1		
Attribute rules with type description for the actual edge	9	rules
Rules with one geometric relation and with type description for the actual edge	114	rules
Rules with two geometric relations and with type description for the actual edge	768	rules
Rules with two geometric relations, without type description for the actual edge	417	rules
Rules with one geometric relation, without type description for the actual edge	44	rules
0.9 ≤ Acc < 1		
Attribute rules with type description for the actual edge	1	rule
Rules with one geometric relation and with type description for the actual edge	19	rules
Rules with two geometric relations and with type description for the actual edge	89	rules
Rules with two geometric relations, without type description for the actual edge	71	rules
Rules with one geometric relation, without type description for the actual edge	6	rules
Recursive classification rule	**1**	**rule**
Interval classification rules	**227**	**rules**
Acc = 1		
Attribute rules with type description for the actual edge	9	rules
Rules with one geometric relation and with type description for the actual edge	114	rules
Rules with one geometric relation, without type description for the actual edge	44	rules
0.9 ≤ Acc < 1		
Attribute rules with type description for the actual edge	1	rule
Rules with one geometric relation and with type description for the actual edge	19	rules
Rules with one geometric relation, without type description for the actual edge	6	rules
Classification limits	**11**	**facts**
Comparative rules	**102**	**rules**
Comparative fact	**1**	**fact**
Facts about finite elements	**11**	**facts**
Introduction of the finite elements, considered in the system	1	fact
Facts about compatible finite elements	18	facts
Rules for finite elements selection	**5**	**rules**

TOTAL: 1873 rules + 31 facts

5.8.2   Evaluation of the Expert System

A comprehensive evaluation of the ES was carried out. First of all, the classification accuracy was tested in various ways. Furthermore an additional, more informative criterion of success, called classification cost, was introduced. This takes into account the size of error in the case of misclassification. Misclassification cost was defined as:

$$\text{Cost} = |N1\text{-}N2| / \max(N1, N2)$$

N1 is the reference number of finite elements, and N2 is the number prescribed by the ES. Misclassification cost is normalised between 0 and 1, where a smaller cost means better classification performance. In our domain, the worst possible error is to classify a 1-element edge into "class" 17. This would incur a misclassification cost of $|17\text{-}1|/17 = 0.94$.

The results of the ES have been used in practice as the resolution values for real-life mesh generation with the FEM pre-processor. The results of these tests are also presented in this section.

5.8.2.1   TEST ON THE EDGES FROM THE TRAINING SET

The ES presented was used to determine the number of finite elements for all the edges from the training set. The classification accuracy was 78.26%, and the misclassification cost was 0.092.

5.8.2.2   LEAVE-ONE-OUT TEST

Here the classification accuracy and cost were measured for each training model, which was for that purpose effectively eliminated from the training set. Because of its time complexity, the learning process was not actually repeated each time with a different training set. Instead, the rules that could not be induced if the current structure would not be a part of the training set, were eliminated from the knowledge base. A detailed description of the elimination process can be found in Dolšak (1996). Although this process does not guarantee exactly the same results as would be obtained by repeated induction without the eliminated structure, any differences in results are unlikely.

The classification accuracy was between 40.48 and 80.46%, and 59.09% on average. The lowest misclassification cost for single structure was 0.064, and the highest 0.244.

The results of the ES for the "eliminated" structure were also used as basic parameters for mesh generation with the well known FEM pre-processor within the popular computer aided design package I-DEAS (I-DEAS, 1993). Let us consider the structure with the lowest classification performance as an example. To meet the requirements of the built-in mapped meshing method, the structure was partitioned into six sub-volumes (Figure 5.5).

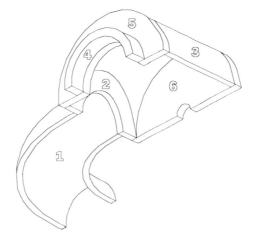

Figure 5.5   Partitioning of the part for mapped meshing procedure.

In spite of quite low classification accuracy, the mesh built on the basis of the results of the ES (Figure 5.6a) is not bad, at least as an initial attempt. A comparison with the reference, manually designed mesh (Figure 5.6b), which was used for the numerical analysis, shows that the ES proposed a few more elements on some of the edges, but the overall pattern of the mesh was almost the same.

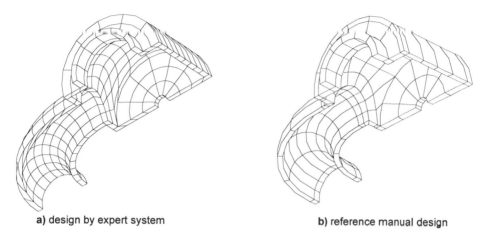

a) design by expert system   **b) reference manual design**

Figure 5.6   A comparison between knowledge-based and manual mesh design.

5.8.2.3   TEN-FOLD CROSS-VALIDATION TEST ON RANDOMLY SELECTED SUBSETS

The training set was randomly divided into ten subsets. The elimination of each subset from the training set was simulated in the same way as in the case of the leave-one-out test. On average, 70.16% of the edges were correctly classified. The average misclassification cost was 0.127.

5.8.2.4   TEST ON AN UNSEEN STRUCTURE

In the final test, the ES was employed to specify the mesh resolution values for a completely new cylindrical structure that was not included in the training set. The performed classification accuracy was 86.67% with a misclassification cost of just 0.028, which is quite impressive. There were only four misclassified edges (encircled in the Figure 5.7a). For all quarter circuit edges the ES proposed one finite element more than in the reference design, yet this qualified as an allowable deviation according to the construction of our training set.

With respect to the results of the ES, the FEM pre-processor built almost the same finite element mesh (Figure 5.7b) as that designed manually (Figure 5.7c). Again, a partitioning of the part into smaller sub-volumes with a maximum of six surfaces was done to satisfy the requirements of the mapped meshing procedure. This test also shows that classification accuracy may be misleading as a measure of success in this domain. The reason is that an automatic mesh generator will automatically correct some errors. This happened in the case of Figure 5.7 as follows. The mapped meshing technique assumes an equal number of finite elements on the opposite sides of the surfaces. The FEM pre-processor put 14 finite elements on the edges for which the ES specified 11 finite elements, since the total number of finite elements on the opposite side is also 14.

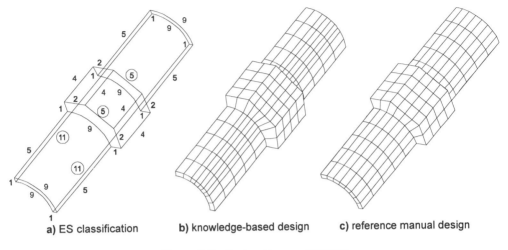

a) ES classification   b) knowledge-based design   c) reference manual design

Figure 5.7   Test on the new structure.

5.9   CONCLUSIONS

According to practical experience with FEM systems, it would be very difficult to extract the knowledge about finite element mesh design from the human expert. A lot of experience is required to design an "optimal" finite element mesh, which is hard to describe explicitly.

On the other hand, a wide range of the finite element mesh models that have been analysed in the past can be used as a source of examples for machine learning. The inductive knowledge acquisition turned out as an effective approach to solve the finite element mesh design problem. The knowledge base for finite element mesh design is not the only result of our experiments. It is also a demonstration of the strength of ILP on this particular task, as well as its potential in general.

The knowledge base presented is quite extensive, yet the architecture based on the production rules allows a relatively simple method for its enhancement if necessary. An ES for finite element mesh design, using this knowledge base, was built in Prolog. It enables efficient use of the knowledge base and adequate communication between the ES and user. One of its features is the ability to explain the inference process. Thus the ES can also be used as a teaching tool for inexperienced users. Both the time and memory space requirements of the ES are modest and do not represent any significant problem.

Considering the results of the overall ES evaluation, the following conclusions can be made:

- The classification accuracy measured by the leave-one-out test is significantly improved in comparison with all the previous experiments, which confirms that the extension of the training set was successful.
- The comparison of performance measured by the leave-one-out test and by the ten-fold cross-validation test also indicates a satisfactory distribution of the training examples. The results of the cross-validation test are somewhat higher, yet the difference is relatively small.
- The results of the ES represent a solid basis for practical application. The mesh generated according to the ES results for the example "eliminated" training model is insignificantly different from the reference mesh, although the results of the ES seemed rather low in that case. The applicability of the ES was further confirmed by the test on the completely new structure.
- In most of the cases, the results of the ES should be suited to the method for mesh generation and are therefore subject to amendments.
- When the rules in the knowledge base specify the list of the proposed classes, "the most appropriate" class should be determined. In spite of special attention that was paid to the methods for determining "the most appropriate" class out of the proposed list, the rules in the knowledge base still enable better results than those that have been achieved.

Human experts were also asked to look over the induced rules and to assess their meaningfulness in comparison with their own expert knowledge. As the most important overall conclusion of the expert evaluation of the induced rules, it has been found that the form of the rules is expected and in general matches the knowledge used by human experts.

To simplify the learning problem, the training set was designed with the aim of being representative of a particular types of structures. However, the ES presented can also be applied as a general tool for determining the mesh resolution values for structures outside the scope of these types. These values have to be adjusted subsequently according to the specific requirements of the particular analysis.

The ES application enabled the determination of an appropriate finite element mesh for a structure within the type scope in the first attempt. Such an effectiveness of the ES cannot be expected in cases of structures of different types. Yet, the resolution values specified by the ES can always serve as a basis for an initial finite element mesh, which is subject to further adaptations considering the results of the numerical analyses. It is very important to choose a good initial mesh and minimise the number of iterative steps, leading to an appropriate mesh model. The ES presented can be very helpful, especially to inexperienced users.

There are several possible directions for further improvement of the presented ES. First of all, the rules for more adequate determination of the single class out of the proposed list of classes should be found. For wide practical applicability it is also important to expand the range of available finite elements. On the other hand, the ES for mesh design should be integrated into the overall support for the key decision making during the FEM analysis process, as described in Jezernik and Dolšak (1993).

ACKNOWLEDGEMENTS

This research was financially supported by the Ministry of Science and Technology, Republic of Slovenia, and by the European Community within the action for co-operation in science and technology with Central and Eastern European countries (PECO92) - ILPNET, contract no. CIPA3510OCT920044. Researchers from several ILPNET nodes have been involved in ML applications to the finite element mesh design problem, and made their learning programs available for that purpose. S. Muggleton's GOLEM and L. De Raedt's CLAUDIEN were particularly important in our work. We would like to acknowledge Professor T.K. Hellen of Imperial College of Science, Technology and Medicine, London, M. Prašnički and R. Kogler from TAM Research & Development Institute, Maribor and S. Ulaga from the Faculty of Mechanical Sciences, Maribor for providing the learning examples. Special thanks to Professor Hellen for his willingness to carry out the expert evaluation of the induced rules.

REFERENCES

Cestnik, B., Kononenko, I. and Bratko, I. (1987). ASSISTANT 86 – A Knowledge Elicitation Tool for Sophisticated Users. In: Bratko, I. and Lavrač, N. (eds.), *Progress in Machine Learning*, Sigma Press.

De Raedt, L. and Bruynooghe, M. (1993). A Theory of Clausal Discovery. In: *Proceedings of Thirteenth International Joint Conference on Artificial Intelligence*, pages 1058–1063, San Mateo, CA, Morgan Kaufmann.

Dolšak, B. and Muggleton, S. (1992). The Application of Inductive Logic Programming to Finite Element Mesh Design. In: *Inductive Logic Programming*, pages 453–472, Academic Press.

Dolšak, B., Jezernik, A. and Bratko, I. (1994). A Knowledge Base for Finite Element Mesh Design. In: *Artificial Intelligence in Engineering* 9/94, pages 19–27, Elsevier.

Dolšak, B. (1996). A Contribution to Intelligent Mesh Design for FEM Analyses (in Slovene, with English abstract). *Ph.D. Thesis*, University of Maribor, Faculty of Mechanical Engineering, Slovenia.

Džeroski, S. (1991). Handling Noise in Inductive Logic Programming. *M.Sc. Thesis*, University of Ljubljana, Faculty of Electrical Engineering and Computer Science, Slovenia.

Fürnkranz, J. (1994a). FOSSIL: A Robust relational Learner. In: *Proceedings of the European Conference on Machine Learning*, Catania, Italy, Springer-Verlag.

Fürnkranz, J. (1994b). Top–down Pruning in Relational Learning. In: *Proceedings of the 11th European Conference on Artificial Intelligence*, pages 453–457, Amsterdam, The Netherlands.

Hellen, T. K. (1970). BERSAFE: A Computer System for Stress Analysis by Finite Elements In: *Conference Stress Analysis Today, Stress Analysis Group of Inst. of Phys. and the Phys. Soc.*, Guildford, Surrey, UK.

Jezernik, A. and Dolšak, B. (1993). Expert Systems for FEM. In: *FEM Today and the Future: Seventh World Congress on FEM*, pages 150–153, Monte Carlo.

Kononenko, I., Šimec, E. and Robnik, M. (1994). Overcoming the Myopia of Inductive Learning Algorithms. *Technical report FER-LUI-1/94*, Faculty of Electrical Eng. and Computer Science, Ljubljana, Slovenia.

Kovačič, M. (1994). MILP – A Stochastic Approach to Inductive Logic Programming. In: Wrobel, S. (ed.), *Proceedings of the Fourth International Workshop on Inductive Logic Programming (ILP-94)*, pages 123–138, GMD-Studien Nr. 237, Germany.

Lavrač, N. and Džeroski, S. (1993). *Inductive Logic Programming: Techniques and Applications*. Ellis Horwood.

Michalski, R. S. (1983). A Theory and Methodology of Inductive Learning. In: Michalski, R. S., Carbonell, J. G. and Mitchell, T. M. (eds.), *Machine Learning – An Artificial Intelligence Approach*, volume 1, pages 83–134, Morgan Kaufmann.

Muggleton, S. and Feng, C. (1990). Efficient Induction of Logic Programs. In: *Proceedings of the First Conference on Algorithmic Learning Theory*, Tokyo, Japan.

Plotkin, G. D. (1969). A Note on Inductive Generalisation. In: Meltzer, B. and Michie, D. (eds.), *Machine Intelligence 5*, pages 153–163, Edinburgh University Press.

Quinlan, J. R. (1996). Induction of Decision Trees. In: *Machine Learning* 1 (1), pages 81–106.

Van Laer, W., De Raedt, L. and Dehaspe, L. (1994) Applications of a Logical Discovery Engine, *Report CW 195*, Department of Computing Science, KU Leuven, Belgium.

Zienkiewicz, O. C. and Taylor, R. L. (1988). *The Finite Element Method – Basic Formulation and Linear Problems*, London, McGRAW-HILL Book Company.

I-DEAS Master Series™ (1993), *Exploring I-DEAS Simulation, Second Edition*, Structural Dynamic Research Corporation.

6

Application of Inductive Learning and Case-Based Reasoning for Troubleshooting Industrial Machines

Michel Manago and Eric Auriol

ABSTRACT

"Data is a burden, knowledge is an asset". Equipment manufacturers often collect a lot of data about the equipment they have to support (either internally or through their partners): technical follow-up files, breakdown files, intervention reports, preventive maintenance reports and records of requests from their clients or distributors. Unfortunately, this information is usually not well exploited and corporate databases predominantly work in write-only mode:

1. The data is not used because it is so difficult to access, but no one invests in making it easy to retrieve because it is not used.

Machine Learning and Data Mining: Methods and Applications
Edited by R.S. Michalski, I Bratko and M. Kubat
© 1997 John Wiley & Sons Ltd

2. The data is not trusted, because many errors have been recorded, but no one cares to verify the accuracy of the data because it is not trusted.

This is sad because this material could often reveal strategic knowledge for the company: Diagnosis of breakdowns, repair actions, the cost and duration of interventions, breakdown recurrence, etc. The collection and exploitation of this information permits a notable improvement of the after sales service and maintenance of the equipment. The term "Data Mining", which is part of a process called "Knowledge Discovery in Databases", refers to a set of techniques that are used to extract decision knowledge from data. "Data Mining" covers a wide variety of techniques such as neural nets, statistical analysis as well as sophisticated graphical visualization tools.

6.1   INTRODUCTION

Inductive learning and Case-Based Reasoning (CBR) are different methods for utilizing past information in solving problems. Inductive learning [Qui83] creates a general description of past examples, and then applies this description to new data. Case-based reasoning stores past examples, and assigns decisions to new data by relating it to past cases. A case is defined as the description of a problem that has been successfully solved in the past, along with its solution. When a new problem is encountered, CBR recalls similar cases and adapts the solutions that worked in the past for the current problem. Inductive learning extracts a decision tree from the whole case history and then uses this general knowledge for problem solving. Inductive learning and CBR are complementary techniques and their integration improves their capabilities [AABM95, AMAWD95]. The number of applications in various domains is growing impressively [AWAMT95]. The most convincing systems are fielded in the help-desk areas, particularly for troubleshooting complex equipment. The troubleshooting of CFM56 engines for the BOEING 737 and the diagnosis of problems of robots axis position developed by AcknoSoft respectively for Cfm International and Sepro Robotique, are two examples of successful applications in this field.

6.2   INDUCTIVE LEARNING AND CASE-BASED REASONING

The inductive method employed here creates a decision tree from case history, and then uses this tree for problem solving. Inductive learning requires that the data is structured, for example by using classes of objets with slots. A standard relational database schema can easily be mapped onto this object model. It allows one to define the vocabulary used to describe the cases. For example, an error code on a control panel, the state of a pipe, the I/O state of a relay (Table 6.1), etc. Inductive learning also requires that a target decision slot is defined (for example, the diagnosis of the fault). This target slot may also be a list of spare parts that have been changed in order to solve the problem. Given the data model, the target class and the case data, a fault tree is automatically generated (Figure 6.1). Inductive learning thus extracts relevant decision knowledge from case history.

Table 6.1 A sample case library

diagnosis	IO state	error code	cable state	pipe[valve 5y2]	...
IO card	high	I53	OK	dense	...
pipe system	low	I53	OK	leaking	...
Tool gripper	high	none	?	?	...

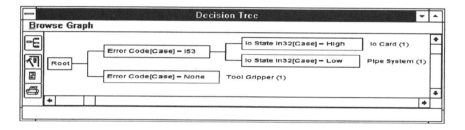

Figure 6.1 Decision tree generated from the sample case library of Table 6.1.

Unlike inductive learning, case-based reasoning does not require that a tree structure be generated before problem solving. A new problem is solved by finding similar, past cases and adapting their solutions. CBR offers flexible indexing and retrieval, and fuzzy matching. For applications where safety is important, the conclusions can be further confirmed, or refuted, by entering additional parameters that may modify the similarity values. CBR appeals to those professionals who solve problems by recalling what they did in similar situations. It works well even in domains that are poorly understood or where rules have many exceptions. Some of the characteristics that indicates if CBR technology is suitable for a particular domain are:

- experience is as valuable as textbook knowledge: CBR makes direct use of past experience;
- historical cases are viewed as an asset that should be preserved and it is intuitively clear that remembering past experience is useful;
- specialists talk about their domain by giving examples.

A critical issue when developing an application using inductive learning or CBR is performance. The following comparative evaluations, performed on a standard 486 DX2/66 PC, demonstrate that pure CBR retrieval is fast for databases with fewer than 10,000 cases. Retrieval time using a tree, once the tree has been generated, is instantaneous. When retrieval performances are required on larger case bases, CBR can be combined with a tree generated by inductive learning that is used as an indexing mechanism. Both techniques allow one to improve the decision making process by using prior experiences and to perform "what-if" analysis.

Table 6.2 Comparison of performance of case-based and inductive approaches

Domain	# of cases	# of parameters		% unknowns	# of decision classes	Time for tree generation (s)	Time for pure CBR retrieval (s)
		Numeric	Symbolic				
Car insurance	205	14	11	few	7	< 5	< 0.5
Credit assessment	735	12	12	80%	7	< 8	< 2
Travel agency	1,470	1	7	none	93	< 7	< 2
Engine maintenance	3,610	7	18	20%	59	< 18	< 3

6.3 OBTAINING BETTER FEEDBACK FROM EXPERIENCE

Today, it is becoming increasingly difficult to sell industrial machines without reliable customer support. The "cost of ownership" of long lasting equipment often far exceeds its initial value, and maintenance costs are increasingly becoming a decision criterion in buyers' minds. By increasing the quality of customer support with help-desk software and by bundling diagnostic software together with his equipment, a supplier will score points against his competitors. CBR and inductive learning help to:

- improve after-sale support (telephone hotline) with help-desk software;
- develop diagnosis and fault analysis decision support systems;
- regularly update troubleshooting manuals from observed faults;
- capture and reuse the experience of the most talented maintenance specialists, transfer expertise amongst personnel and build a corporate memory;
- perform experience feedback to increase reliability and maintainability.

CBR helps engineers relate current problems to past experiences. A new problem is solved by finding similar cases and adapting the solution that worked in the past for the current problem. CBR optimises the number of tests required for troubleshooting, reduces the cost of repair and minimises the downtime of mission critical equipment. The technology has an intuitive appeal for support engineers and adapts to their mode of reasoning: "Have I ever seen a similar problem before and if so, what did I do about it?".

One active market for CBR technology is decision support software for help desks. A help desk is located in a call center, usually at the equipment manufacturer's site, to assist customers when they have problems with equipment, such as failure of equipment at the customer's site. One of the missions of the help desk staff is to troubleshoot the manufacturer's equipment and decide if the client can solve the problem by himself, in which case a list of spare parts that must be replaced by him on the equipment is identified, or if a field technician that belongs to the manufacturer must be sent to solve the problem on the customer's site (in which case, a decision about which spare parts have to be sent is also made).

6.4   APPLICATIONS

There is a growing number of applications within the CBR market. Using AcknoSoft's KATE systems a number of applications have been developed to perform experience feedback in safety for nuclear power plants at the French Electricity company EDF, for troubleshooting large marine diesel engines at New Sulzer Diesel in Switzerland, for experience feedback in manufacturing and rapid assessment of production costs for a leading manufacturer of electrical supplies in France, for diagnosis of electronic boards at GICEP electronics, for train maintenance at Ansaldo Trasporti in Italy, for quality management of mission critical equipment in the oil industry at Schlumberger in Italy and Norsk Hydro in Norway, for reliabilty analysis of gas meters at French Gas GDF and German Gas Ruhrgas, in the aircraft industry at Aerospatiale in France, etc. In this chapter, we present two applications. The first one, called CASSIOPEE, helps troubleshooting the CFM56-3 engines of the Boeing 737. The second one, called LADI, is installed at the after-sale service of SEPRO Robotique, a French company that exports plastic injection press robots world-wide. LADI troubleshoots axis positioning defects for these three axis robots.

6.4.1   Troubleshooting CFM 56-3 Engines

Cfm-international has developed the Cfm 56 engine family for Boeing and Airbus planes. Cfm international is a joint venture of General Electric aircraft engines and France's Snecma. One of the goals of Cfm-international is to improve engine maintenance technology in order to reduce the cost of ownership of its engines for its customers. The Cassiopée project was launched in August 1993 to perform engine troubleshooting. The starting point was a reliability and maintainability database on an IBM mainframe from which 23,000 cases were extracted.

Using a combination of inductive and case-based reasoning techniques, a decision support system for the technical maintenance of the Cfm56-3 aircraft engines was developed. All Boeing 737s are equiped with Cfm56-3 engines. The system assists Cfm engineers in offering quicker and better advice to the maintenance crews of the airlines who perform on-line troubleshooting (i.e., when the airplane is at the departure gate). It is also being tested in several airlines including British Airways in the UK. The system was developed to:

- reduce downtime of the engines and avoid delays for the airlines;
- minimise the cost of diagnosis;
- reduce errors in diagnosis;
- record and document the experience of the most skilled maintenance specialists in order to build a corporate memory and help transfer know-how from the expert to the novice.

The time required for diagnosis represents about 50% of downtime (the remaining time is used for repair). We aim at dividing this figure by a factor of two.

To build a decision support system from case histories, one must first gather case data. The application data that we have used originally came from the legacy database mentioned above. However, a lot of the information required to support the technical activity of maintenance was not formatted using the fields of the database, but was provided in free-text narratives. Because of the size of the database, and in order to optimize the performance of the system in everyday use, we decided not to apply any text retrieval techniques. Instead, we have supplemented the "model" of the case databases (i.e., list of parameters used to describe a case) with the technical parameters and pre-processed the data. The pre-processing of the data was performed by a maintenance engineer who reviewed the cases at the rate of 15 per hour.

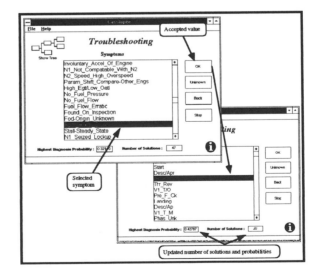

Figure 6.2 Troubleshooting a Cfm 56-3 engine.

The consultation process runs as follows. New fault trees have been generated by inductive learning. Unlike standard fault trees, that are often built during the design stage and which are based on faults that should occur in theory, the fault trees that are built automatically are based on observed faults and can be updated as new faults appear. When browsing such a fault tree, the operator is requested to answer the questions that are in close relationship with the original problem's symptom (Figure 6.2). At the end of the consultation a list of possible solutions is proposed to the operator, with their relative frequency. The procedure (test to perform on the engine), to confirm that the selected solution is the accurate one, is obtained by selecting that solution from the list. This is done to improve the accuracy of the system and not to replace the official maintenance documents (it is an add-on to the procedure that is certified by the authorities). Then the cases that support the conclusions are retrieved, and the user can browse them in order to confirm or refute the solution.

The system is fully integrated in the end-user environment. Thus, some important achievements are not directly tied to the technology *per se*: link of the system to an Illustrated Part Catalogue (IPC) to take into account engine configuration evolution (Figure 6.3), interface the IPC with EXCEL to perform statistics on reliability and maintainability, support electronic mail to collect events world-wide through the X400 network, etc.

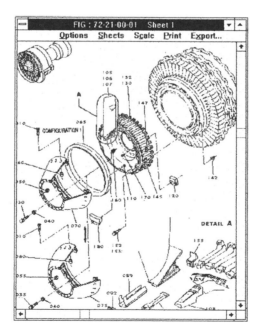

Figure 6.3 The part nomenclature is used graphically to design the faulty component.

The IPC makes extensive use of hypermedia facilities to navigate between the drawings of the parts and their nomenclature.

6.4.2 Troubleshooting Robots Axis

SEPRO Robotique is a French SME of over 100 employees that has been manufacturing robots for plastic injection presses for over 10 years. SEPRO has sold over 2600 such robots world-wide (over 65% of its production is now exported to foreign countries in Europe, Asia and in the US (Konair distributes these robots in the USA). The robots are heavy duty machines (see Figure 6.4) that automate the process of grabbing plastic parts from a plastic injection moulding press and manipulate them in a variety of ways (place some inserts, load and unload peripheral devices, etc.).

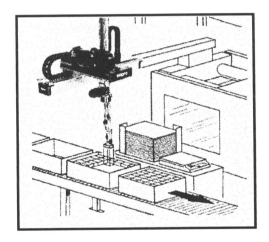

Figure 6.4 Sepro robots manipulate parts for plastic injection mouldsı.

Each robot is customized to meet the needs of specific clients and is made out of three major modules: the mechanical module, the motor, and the command and control box. Customer support engineers and field technicians at SEPRO Robotique often work by making a correlation between the faults of these robots based on the generic modules. One difficulty is that plastic injection moulding robots have a long life cycle. Robots installed ten years ago are still in operation and require support by SEPRO. New support technicians can no longer gain "in-house" experience with robots of the older families that are no longer manufactured by SEPRO and that are still in operation at the client's site. This is the case, for example, with SEPRO's Elec 88-SZ family. Thus, the customer support call center of SEPRO (four support technicians at the same time) often has problems troubleshooting this type of equipment when a technician with experience on these old robots is not on duty.

Because of the increasing cost of customer service, caused by their larger installed base, SEPRO has set a high priority on improving the efficiency of its after-sale division. In January 1995, SEPRO started to work jointly with AcknoSoft to install a CBR help-desk. A help desk system, called LADI, troubleshoots axis positioning defects (Figure 6.5). A standalone prototype was first delivered in June 1995 and went live on a five user network in the after-sale division in the spring of 1996.

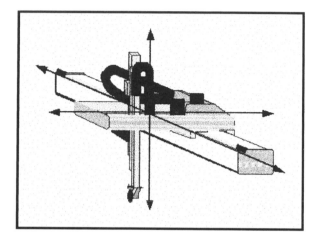

Figure 6.5 The most complex troubleshooting problems deal with the axis positioning defects1.

Axis positioning defects represent about 20 ≈ 30% of the problems that are the most difficult to solve. The system originally contained about 150 typical cases that have been reconstructed from the information available in the engineering department. The call tracking module that records incoming calls is shared on a network by the four support technicians. The case library is also shared on a local TCP/IP network of PCs. An internal organisation (case steering committee) meets on a monthly basis to monitor the quality of incoming cases before they are included in the reference case library. The case database is enriched at the rate of about 10 cases a month. The steering committee is also useful to provide better and quicker feedback to the R&D department to improve design.

The system uses a combination of CBR and inductive learning in order to suit the technicians' method of working . When a new call arrives at the after-sale service, it is pre-processed through an induction tree that has been previously built on the database, in order to eliminate the most common problems. 75% of the calls are solved at this stage. The size of the induction tree is intentionally left small (three to six questions) so that the call duration remains short. If the problem is not solved, for instance if there is still more than one diagnosis pending, the system automatically generates a list of relevant questions by "dynamic induction" (i.e., by using the same criterion as the inductive procedure:

however the list of questions is not static as in the tree). A report containing the current conclusions and the list of questions is automatically generated and sent by fax to the client site. The client is asked to answer them before calling back. As the system is connected to the Interleaf document databases on a SUN workstation, the support technician is able to access an illustrated parts catalogue, to cut and paste parts descriptions, and include troubleshooting reports in the fax before sending it to his client. When the client calls back, his former problem is retrieved and missing information is completed with respect to the questions answered. The system then performs a nearest-neighbour search on the relevant cases and returns the most similar ones together with their associated diagnosis (Figure 6.6).

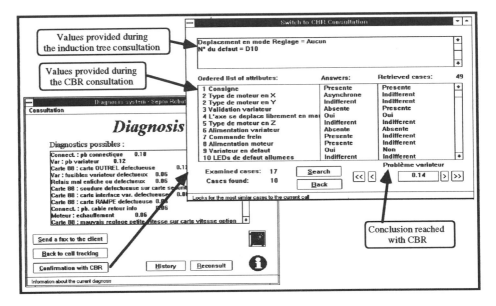

Figure 6.6 Diagnosis of a robot axis default.

The system:

- reduces the time required to solve problems that do require highly specialised technicians;
- reduces the number of wrong diagnoses done by the help desk which results in shipping the wrong spare parts and introduces additional delays when the field technician has to wait for the right spares to be shipped. This is becoming increasingly important because SEPRO Robotique is now supporting more and more clients in far away countries;

- formalises the diagnosis process by choosing the most discriminant tests in order to identify the fault. The training department of SEPRO is actively involved in the project as well as the after sales support division;
- saves training costs by transferring experience from the specialists to the novice. This is becoming more and more important since old versions of their robots, such as the Elec 88 family, are no longer produced and new technicians cannot gain experience with these. As time goes by, the new technicians will have to support more and more equipment at the help-desk for which they are not experienced (the turnover time for technicians is about four years, but robots that have been installed 15 years ago are still operating). This is a general problem for all manufacturers of equipment that has a long life span;
- to increase the quality of service support and reduce the number of call backs to a client by doing some call tracking and having immediate access to fault histories for each of their clients.

REFERENCES

[AABM95] ALTHOFF, K.-D., AURIOL, E., BARLETTA, R. & MANAGO, M. *A Review of Industrial Case-Based Reasoning Tools*. A. Goodall (ed.), AI Intelligence, Oxford, 1995.

[AWAMT95] AURIOL, E., WESS, S., ALTHOFF, K.-D., MANAGO, M. & TRAPHÖNER, R. "INRECA: A seamlessly integrated system based on inductive inference and case-based reasoning". ICCBR 95, First International Conference on Case-Based Reasoning, Veloso M. & Aamodt A. (eds.), Springer-Verlag, Heidelberg, 1995.

[AMAWD95] AURIOL, E., MANAGO, M., ALTHOFF, K.-D., WESS, S. & DITTRICH, S. "Integrating Induction and Case-Based Reasoning: Methodological Approach and First Evaluations", in *Advances in Case Based Reasoning* Haton J. P., Keane M. & Manago M. (eds.), Springer-Verlag, Heidelberg, 1995.

[Qui83] QUINLAN, J.R. "Learning Efficient Classification Procedures and their Application to Chess End Games", in *Machine Learning 1: an Artificial Intelligence Approach*, Michalski R. S., Carbonell J. G. & Mitchell T. M. (eds.), Morgan Kaufmann, Redwood City, CA, 1983.

7

Empirical Assembly Sequence Planning: A Multistrategy Constructive Learning Approach

Heedong Ko

ABSTRACT

Assembly sequence planning is a rich domain to explore learning and planning issues with a strong prospect for real world application in manufacturing industry. The problem is to find a sequence of assembly steps so that a goal assembly structure is built by carrying out the sequence. Unfortunately, a weak method that systematically explores all the alternatives is not practical because the number of possible sequences grows exponentially with the number of components, and there are few constraints or heuristics to tame the search process. Furthermore, the final assembly sequence is generated and selected in the context of a manufacturing environment that differs from one industry to another and from one job shop to another. As a result, the assembly sequence planning problem is solved by an experienced manufacturing engineer who is familiar with the production environment. Hence, the key to building an assembly sequence planner is assimilating the assembly episodes in memory which reflect the production environment. Here, the final assembly sequence is derived by bringing the previously experienced assembly episodes in memory by a multistrategy constructive learning approach in order to realize the planning methodology.

7.1 INTRODUCTION

It is a common practice in manufacturing industry to create and maintain a product model in a computer using a Computer-Aided Design (CAD) system. The product model is shared by many activities before producing the final product. For example, it is a common practice that a designer creates a model of a mechanical component using

Machine Learning and Data Mining: Methods and Applications
Edited by R.S. Michalski, I Bratko and M. Kubat
© 1997 John Wiley & Sons Ltd

a CAD system, and the commands for a Numerical Controlled (NC) machine are directly generated to manufacture the component in the NC machine by a Computer-Aided Manufacturing (CAM) system. The CAD and CAM systems are linked by a Computer-Aided Process Planning (CAPP) system which derives the cut regions of a blank stock material, their sequences, cutter locations and machining conditions, as well as fixture set ups. Commercial CAPP systems for such tasks have recently been introduced.

By analogy with NC machining of a component, a CAPP system for assemblies would benefit the manufacturing process even more, since most products are assemblies. With the CAPP system for assemblies, the commands for an industrial robot to assemble the product are generated as a designer creates a model of an assembly using a CAD system. As industrial robots come into wider use in assembly applications, there is a growing interest in systems that can automatically generate a robot program for an assembly task. The development of robot programming languages has moved consistently toward higher levels of abstraction and greater use of world knowledge. From joint level, manipulator level, to task level, robot programming languages have been proposed. To realize a CAPP system for assemblies, it is necessary to solve a still higher level of planning problem, an assembly sequencing problem (De Fazio and Whitney, 1988).

The assembly sequencing problem is how to generate a sequence of mating operations whose initial subsequence does not construct a subassembly structure that prevents a collision-free path for a mating component belonging to the latter subsequence. To create such a sequence, the planner must follow precedence constraints when generating an assembly sequence. When one cannot assemble a component because of some blocking components already in place (a base subassembly), the planner must follow a precedence constraint that some of the blocking components in the base subassembly must be assembled after the mating component. Detecting such precedence constraints requires checking whether there is no collision-free path for the component to maneuver among the components of the base subassembly. This maneuvering problem is called a FIND-PATH problem, with the base subassembly as obstacles. The algorithm for solving the FIND-PATH problem in 3D with all six degrees of freedom is not polynomially bound (Donald, 1984). Because the moving component can be an assembly structure like the base subassembly, the FIND-PATH problem must be solved for every pair of the power sets of the components in the assembly (Ko, 1989), an exponential number of FIND-PATH problems to solve.

A naive state space search approach is of little use to solve the doubly exponential assembly sequencing problem. We cope with the complexity by grouping the base and the moving subassemblies into an assembly hierarchy. Hierarchical structuring of an assembly sequencing problem is powerful world knowledge to make the sequencing problem more tractable. First of all, components within a subassembly are assembled before the components of its parent subassembly. Furthermore, sibling subassemblies are assembled independently: that is, the components across neighboring sibling subassemblies do not interfere during their respective assembly operations within each subassembly. In short, an assembly hierarchy imposes additional precedence constraints as well as locality of interactions to reduce the number of FIND-PATH problems to be solved.

In some manufacturing industries, there are long established traditions. In the automobile industry, an engine subassembly is separately designed and manufactured from the transmission subassembly. They are even manufactured in different factories. The separation may be due to the distinct roles played by the engine and transmission in the operation of the automobile. Their interactions are mediated by a cam shaft. The engine, transmission, and the cam shaft form sibling subassemblies in the final assembly hierarchy. Then, one might conclude that a functional decomposition of a product corresponds to its assembly hierarchy.

Unfortunately, this is not the case: some interactions are intentionally allowed to optimize the design. Some components are designed to play multiple roles to reduce the component count while maintaining the same functionality (Ulrich and Seering, 1988). These shared components cause interactions between their respective subassemblies. Furthermore, unexpected subassembly interactions may arise depending on the use of the hierarchy. For example, when a car was manufactured, no significant problem was encountered but the car may be hard to maintain, e.g., changing an oil filter may require the mechanic to dismount the engine subassembly to access the oil filter.

When creating a new assembly hierarchy, there is no stable heuristic or world knowledge to avoid all these interactions beforehand. Instead, through a long history of production experience in the automotive, aerospace, and ship building industries, there are widely accepted hierarchical structures, reflecting the collective knowledge of the respective industrial practices. Likewise, the world knowledge for constructing an effective assembly hierarchy brings previous assembly planning episodes to bear in a new assembly sequencing problem because they have already been subject to field tests and these design bugs have been filtered out. We hypothesize that the designer's experience and industrial practices are fundamental sources of knowledge for a planner to make the assembly sequencing problem tractable.

Hence, the key to building an effective planner is a learning issue: how to assimilate previously experienced assembly episodes, and how to bring them to bear in solving a new assembly problem. The former is a learning issue while the latter is a planning issue, and their coupling is a fundamental leverage towards solving the assembly sequence planning problem. We called such a planning paradigm an empirical assembly planning methodology to emphasize the heavy dependence on the learning mechanism to construct a plan.

Here, the learning situation is a multi-concept learning where the memory contains both assembly structure and sequencing concepts. Furthermore, success or failure of applying each assembly episode is recorded into memory incrementally, a closed-loop learning. In this chapter, we explain the Multistrategy Constructive Learning (MCL) (Michalski, 1993) system to address the learning situation using an empirical assembly planning system called NOMAD (NOrmative Mechanical Assembling Device). Before introducing the learning element, we introduce how NOMAD is given an assembly problem to solve, how to represent the assembly planning experience in memory, and the planning process.

7.2 REPRESENTATION AND PLANNING IN NOMAD

An assembly structure in CAD systems consists of components and mating conditions. A solid model of a component in a CAD system consists of faces at their boundaries between the inside and outside of a component. Then, a face is bounded by edges, and an edge is bounded by a pair of vertices. In addition, these bounding entities are associated with geometric entities, e.g. a planar face is associated with a plane. From the component models, an assembly is represented by assigning mating conditions between a pair of components at their respective bounding entities: an "against" mating condition specifies that a planar face of a component is in contact with a planar face of another component (their respective faces are facing each other and are coplanar); an "aligned" mating condition specifies that a cylindrical rod of a component is "co-cylindrical" with a cylindrical hole of the mating component. An assembly structure is represented by a labeled graph, called a mating graph (Ko and Lee, 1987), where nodes represent components and links represent mating conditions.

Figure 7.1 illustrates a Bell Head assembly structure with three components, the Bell Head, the Pin, and the Ring, while the mating graph is shown in Figure 7.2 (a). In this chapter, the examples are illustrated in 2D where the bounding elements of the components are lines and points, although NOMAD has a 3D solid modeling kernel for the assembly modeling. The Global Frame is a reference coordinate system of all the components in the environment: the z axis is pointing vertically upward. Each component has its own local reference frame, called a base frame. Figure 7.1 shows the base frame of the Pin.

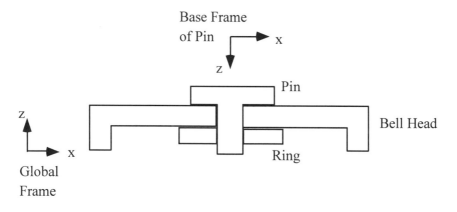

Figure 7.1 Bell Head assembly.

The assembly structure is represented by a mating graph, shown in Figure 7.2 (a). To assemble the Bell Head, the mating graph is used as a goal specification by the planner to determine the sequence of assembly steps. In general, each assembly step may consist of grasping, positioning, mating and various sensor commands to a robot. This makes it difficult to compare among the plan structures. Here, each assembly step may satisfy one or more mating conditions in the mating graph, assuming that each mating operation includes positioning, grasping and other robotic operations as its sub-operations during the operationalization process (Mostow, 1983).

In addition to the simplification of each assembly step, the plan structure must be canonicalized into elementary chunks in memory to store and compare multiple plan structures, an essential step of an empirical learning element. These elementary chunks are called *assembly episodes*. An assembly episode is a plan segment consisting of a sequence and an assembly structure. Corresponding to the assembly structure, we define a grouping as a canonical chunk from which the memory structure is built. The grouping is a set of components with a single distinguished component, called a base component, and others as satellite components. When assembling the grouping, the base component stays fixed while the satellite components are moved to mate with the base component.

In the context of a grouping, it is sufficient to represent an assembly sequence as a sequence of satellite components. As a result, an assembly episode is a combination of a grouping and a sequence of satellite components. Figure 7.2 (b) shows an assembly episode after planning for the mating graph in Figure 7.2 (a), where the Pin is the base component (a square node). The Bell Head and the Ring as satellite components are assembled to the Pin in sequence, which is represented by "<" notation between the Bell Head and the Ring.

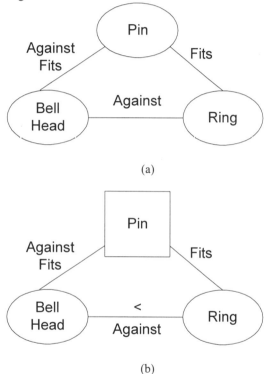

(a)

(b)

Figure 7.2   Mating graph with two assembly episodes.

The final assembly plan may consist of one or more assembly episodes. The results of carrying out the final plan are categorized as either positive or negative applications of the assembly episodes in memory. These exemplars are input to a learning element that generates a new schema using an instance-to-class generalization method (Michalski, Ko and Chen, 1987). A schema is a generalized description of a set of domain objects, e.g. in the assembly domain, a component schema for a set of components and a grouping schema for a set of groupings. The grouping schema consists of a base component schema and satellite component schemas. The ordering relations among the satellite component schemas are described by one or more precedence constraints. They are stored in a precedence schema using a part-to-whole generalization method (Michalski, Ko and Chen, 1987). Because there can be multiple ways to assemble the satellite components of a grouping, a grouping schema may have multiple precedence schemas. In short, the memory structure of NOMAD consists of two types of interrelated domain concepts: precedence and grouping schemas.

With these domain concepts in memory, the planning process proceeds in three phases: recollection, combination, and *post mortem* analyses. The recollection process decomposes the mating graph into assembly episodes. An assembly episode is identified in two steps: first by a grouping schema where the base and the satellite component schemas are identified with the components in the mating graph; second by a precedence schema where the assembly steps between the base and satellite components identified by the grouping schema in the first step are ordered into a sequence. These sequence segments are posted as candidate sequence segments to be considered as a part of the final assembly sequence.

After the recollection step, the planner combines the candidate assembly episodes into a hierarchical structure that is consistent and complete. An assembly hierarchy is complete if it contains assembly steps involving all the components in the mating graph and consistent if all the precedence relations imposed by the candidate sequence segments are not contradictory with each other. An assembly hierarchy represents an abstraction hierarchy for the assembly planner in deriving an assembly sequence. That means, when deriving an assembly sequence for the root of a hierarchy, only its immediate children subassemblies are considered for ordering with an assumption that an assembly step of a subassembly may not interact with the assembly steps of a sibling subassembly (subassembly independence law, SIL). Furthermore, assembly steps within a subassembly must be assembled before the assembly steps of the parent subassembly (subassembly precedence law, SPL). The constraints imposed by SPL and SIL, as well as assembly episodes invoked from memory, are used by the credit assignment process during the *post mortem* analysis.

After an assembly hierarchy is constructed, the final assembly sequence is derived from the precedence relations of the sequence segments as well as SPL and SIL constraints from the hierarchy. An assembly step in the sequence may fail if there is no collision-free trajectory in reaching the desired configuration of the step. For example, there is no collision-free path for the Bell Head in reaching the mating configuration after the Ring is already assembled because of spatial interference, as shown in Figures 7.3 (a) and (b) with alternative approach directions. Hence, the application of this assembly episode is a negative experience, and then the planner succeeds with the alternative episode of Figure 7.2 (b).

To learn from the planning experience involving multiple concepts in memory, the learner conducts *post mortem* analysis of which concept in memory is responsible for the failure or success in applying the assembly episodes. Then, the plan structure must be a dependency structure (de Kleer, 1986), where each precedence relation in the assertional database is supported by an assembly episode, SPL, SIL constraints or their combination.

Because both precedence and grouping schema's are used to create the assembly episode, the *post mortem* analysis must identify which of the two types of concepts are responsible. In the previous example, a precedence schema is identified as the responsible concept when the failure or success is localized within the assembly episode. On the other hand, when a subassembly of the hierarchy violates SPL or SIL constraints, or both, the grouping used to construct the subassembly is identified as the culprit. The credit assignment process identifies which concept in memory is responsible for the outcome, and hence is to be learned. The credit assignment problem is made possible by the dependency support structure between the assembly precedence relation of the final assembly sequence and the assumptions introduced by instantiating the schema in memory. The next section introduces multistrategy constructive learning as an extension of previous learning concepts to cope with the multi-concept learning situation of NOMAD.

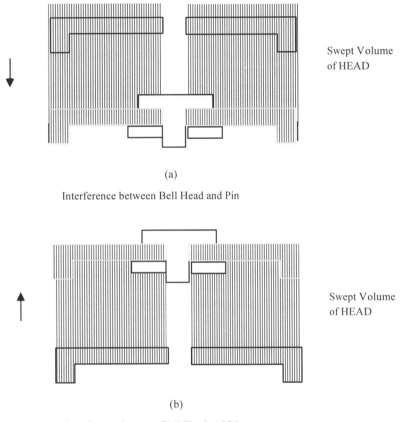

Swept Volume
of HEAD

(a)

Interference between Bell Head and Pin

Swept Volume
of HEAD

(b)

Interference between Bell Head and Ring

Figure 7.3 Spatial interference.

7.3 MULTISTRATEGY CONSTRUCTIVE LEARNING

Learning from planning experience is multi-concept learning: the planning experience may highlight more than one concept to learn. For assembly sequence planning, there are two types of concepts to learn, grouping and precedence schemas. Then, the learner must determine which concept to learn, as well as the corresponding training instances. Previous learning systems have mostly been single-concept incremental learning systems. For example, it is reported that INDUCE (Larson, 1977) is given multiple exemplars of west-bound or east-bound trains as two classes of a single concept (directionality of the train heading). In this case, indexing the memory for which concept to learn is trivial, e.g. this is determined by the class of the exemplar in INDUCE.

In a multi-concept learning situation, the system should determine which concept or concepts in memory to learn. The *post mortem* analysis using the dependency support structure of the assembly sequence in the previous section, identifies which concept (grouping or precedence schema) is responsible for the failure or success and hence which to learn. Here, the planning experience is decomposed into assembly episodes as applications of grouping and precedence schemas in memory, and their application results as training instances for the corresponding schemas. In the previous example, the precedence schema used to construct the assembly episode in Figure 7.3 is identified as a concept to learn, and the precedence constraints imposed by the assembly episode as training instances to incrementally refine the concept description of the chosen schema. Such an incremental learning in a multi-concept learning situation is called *closed-loop* learning, where the concept to learn is determined before, and incrementally updating the concept.

Initially, the concept description with little background knowledge (schemas) in memory is generated by inductive generalization of experimental observations. In empirical inductive learning, the learner generalizes examples observed to form their consistent and complete description. In machine learning, programs constructing empirical generalizations typically uses only descriptive concepts that are selected from among those used in describing the original observations. Such surface induction is called *selective induction*. In constructive induction (Michalski, 1983), the learner uses domain dependent as well as domain independent background knowledge to elaborate the input observations with new descriptors in order to search for inductive hypotheses in the preferred description space of the domain concepts. Here, the learner elaborates the training instances with relative spatial relations such as "higher-than" or "lower-than" among the components.

Finally, the system should evaluate the constructed knowledge in order to decide if it is to be stored in memory or not. Using the dependency structure, the learning episodes are combined into "more" useful knowledge before storing the experience. This step is similar to a constructive induction step, but it is called *deductive restructuring* to distinguish the fact that this step is to generate new "interesting" instances by combining multiple training instances rather than inserting new descriptors to each training instances. To learn from planning experience, these three learning steps must be combined. We call the integrated learning mechanism Multistrategy Constructive Learning (MCL):

MCL = Constructive Induction + Closed-loop + Deductive Restructuring

The next section illustrates the concepts introduced in this section with a learning scenario.

7.4 LEARNING SCENARIO BY NOMAD

Here, the multistrategy constructive learning approach of NOMAD is described as follows:
1. generate candidate grouping and precedence schemas inductively;
2. maintain the credibility of each candidate schema's by their applications; and
3. apply promising schema(s) in new assembly situations.

Suppose a user specifies the Bell Head assembly structure of Figure 7.1 when NOMAD has no experience. The Global Frame is a reference coordinate system of all the components in the environment: the z axis is pointing vertically upward. Initially, NOMAD has no schemas for the Bell Head assembly when given it as a task. So, the user may specify the grouping in Figure 7.2 (a): the Pin as a base and the Ring and the Bell Head as satellites. Then, the system may experiment with alternative plans randomly because it does not have any experience to guide the planning process.

From the successful planning episode of Figure 7.2 (b), using a constructive induction rule, the following descriptors are generated from the locations of individual satellite components with respect to the two reference frames, the global frame (dloc-g) and the base frame of the base component, the Pin (dloc-b):

● the location of the Bell Head is higher than the Ring with respect to the Global Frame: [dloc-g (Ring, Bell Head) < 0]
● the location of the Ring is higher than the Bell Head with respect to the base frame of the base component, Pin: [dloc-b(Ring, Bell Head) > 0)]

In addition, the base component, Pin, is T-shaped and the satellite components, Bell Head and Ring, are ring-shaped.

Then, NOMAD generates alternative schemas from the planning episode, using the "dropping a conjunct" inductive generalization rule (Michalski, 1983). Among alternative generalizations, two candidate precedence schemas are presented here, P1 and P2, with respect to the grouping schema as shown in Figure 7.4 and 7.5, respectively. In Figure 7.4, the base component schema, $p1, is aligned with satellite component schemas, $p2, and $p3, with respect to the global reference frames (dloc-g). Like the assembly episode, the square denotes the base component schema.

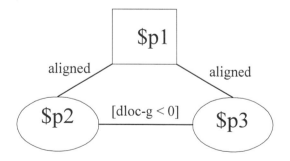

Figure 7.4 Candidate precedence schema P1.

Figure 7.5 shows that the base component schema, $p1, is aligned with satellite schemas, $p2 and $p3, and $p2 is assembled before $p3 because $p2 is lower than $p3 with respect to $p1. In addition, the component schemas of Figure 7.4 and 7.5 store the component shapes, $p1 is pin-shaped and $p2 and $p3 are ring-shaped.

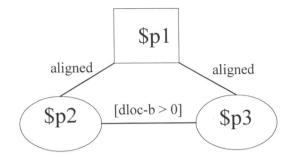

Figure 7.5 Candidate precedence schema P2.

With the two candidate precedence schemas, P1 and P2, and their grouping schema in memory, the system is given a bracket mounting assembly as a new problem to solve, as shown in Figure 7.6. Now, NOMAD applies these candidate schemas in solving the new problem. This problem is very similar to the Bell Head assembly in Figure 7.3: the Bolt is pin-shaped and the Nut and the Bracket are ring-shaped. From the grouping schema of P1 and P2, NOMAD identifies the Bolt as the base component and the Bracket and the Nut as satellite components.

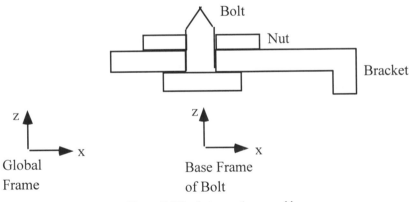

Figure 7.6 Bracket mounting assembly.

Using P1, the system plans that the Nut is attached to the Bolt first because the Nut is higher than the Bracket, as shown in Figure 7.7. However, the plan (or a hypothesis) fails for a similar reason as the case shown in Figure 7.3: the Bracket cannot be assembled if the Nut is attached first because of the spatial interference between the bracket with both the Bolt and the Nut. This failed planning episode weakens the credibility of P1.

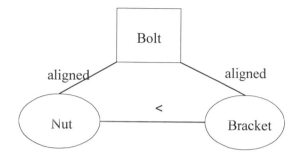

Figure 7.7 Failed application of the candidate schema P1.

An alternative plan using P2 says that the Bracket is attached to the Bolt first, as shown in Figure 7.8, because the Bracket is lower than the Nut with respect to the Bolt. This planning episode is successful and enforces the belief of P2. As an end result, P2 is going to be applied in future planning situations over invoking P1 with higher confidence.

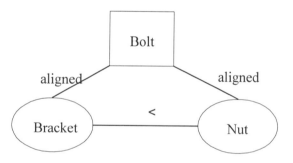

Figure 7.8 Successful application of the candidate schema P2.

Consider a screw assembly, shown in Figure 7.9. Using the grouping schema, the system recognizes the screw as a base component because it is pin-shaped. The Washers 1 and 2 are satellite components of the grouping because they are ring-shaped. Among the precedence schemas of the grouping schema, NOMAD invokes P2 over P1 from the previous planning experience. Using P2, the Washer 1 is assembled before the Washer 2 because the Washer 2 is higher than the Washer 1 with respect to the Screw. This planning episode is shown in Figure 7.10.

This learning scenario shows how the base and satellite components of an assembly are recognized, and the candidate descriptions of precedence relations are maintained or pruned in memory by actively experimenting with them in a new planning situation. The learning scenario has shown the closed-loop and constructive induction aspects of MCL by NOMAD. Now, the next example will demonstrate the use of the deductive restructuring in MCL by NOMAD. With the empirically validated schema P2, the system is presented with a new and more complicated screw assembly with three washers, as shown in Figure 7.11.

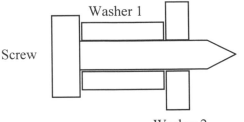

Figure 7.9. Screw assembly.

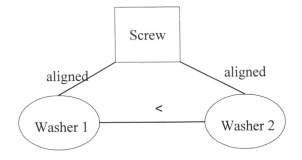

Figure 7.10 Screw assembly episode with P2.

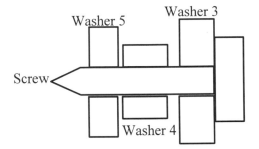

Figure 7.11 Screw assembly with three washers.

Using the grouping schema of P2, the Screw is the base component because it is pin-shaped. All the Washers 3, 4, and 5 are ring-shaped. Then, there are six possible bindings between the washers and the satellite schemas, $p2 and $p3. However, using the precedence of P2, only three of them are possible and the rest are pruned. They are shown in Figure 7.12. Episode 1 instructs assembly of the Washer 3 before Washer 4, because Washer 4 is higher than Washer 3 with respect to the Screw; Episode 2 states that Washer 3 should be assembled before Washer 5 because Washer 5 is higher than Washer 3 with respect to the Screw; likewise for the Episode 3, Washer 4 before Washer 5. These precedence constraints are all equally correct and non-conflicting with each other, but none of them by themselves are *complete* in planning for the assembly structure of Figure 7.11.

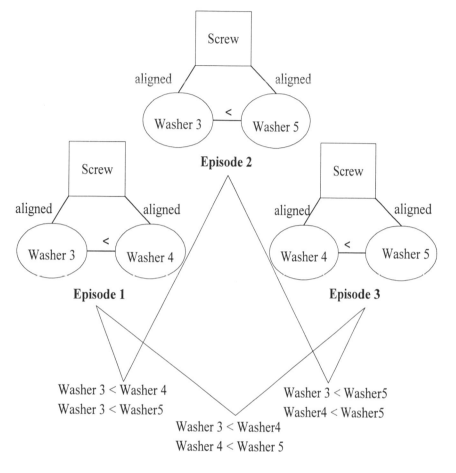

Figure 7.12 Three assembly episodes with the candidate schema P2.

When creating a complete assembly sequence plan, it is not necessary to combine all three episodes of Figure 7.12; Episodes 1 and 3 are sufficient to predict the precedence constraint of Episode 2, and therefore it is redundant. The remaining candidate assembly episodes are merged by a collapsing operator, an instance of a deductive restructuring step of MCL. Here, the collapsing operator is given two episodes at a time. From the collapse of Episodes 1 and 2, the system can predict that Washer 3 is the very first washer to assemble, but there is no precedence between Washers 4 and 5. From the collapse of Episodes 2 and 3, the system can predict that Washer 5 is the last washer to assemble, but there is no precedence relation between Washers 3 and 4. From the collapse of Episodes 1 and 3, the system predicts Washers 3, 4, and 5 are assembled in sequence. Figure 7.13 shows the collapsed structure as a new training instance. The

collapsed structure is used by NOMAD to apply a part-to-whole generalization method
of the individual episodes.

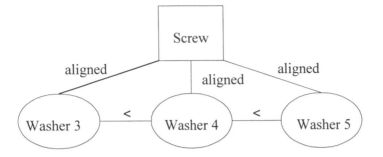

Figure 7.13 The collapsed assembly episode.

7.5 COMPARISON WITH PREVIOUS RESEARCH

Most previous planning research assumed a heuristic state space search method as a
basic problem solving mechanism: plan actions as state transition operators and the plan
structure as a sequence of operators to make the transitions from the initial to the goal
state. This transition process turned out to be an exponential search process, and a
learning component was introduced as an after-thought to reduce the search time in
reaching the goal state from the initial state. In the assembly task domain, the states
represent partially assembled components, the goal state represents fully assembled
components, and the operators are assembly steps involving grasping, moving, stacking
and others. Then, the learning component can reduce the search process in two ways:

1. by inventing a powerful heuristic that can avoid the assembly steps that are not part
   of the final assembly procedure, or
2. by memorizing the planning episodes as macro operators so that the search process
   can reduce the number of individual operator invocations.

In the former case, little is known about formulating a powerful strategic knowledge
for the assembly task domain in general. In the second approach, a macro-operator
schema was compiled away by a deductive generalization of a planning episode,
Explanation-Based Learning (EBL) (Mitchell, Keller and Kedar-Cabelli, 1986; De Jong
and Mooney, 1986). The constants of a plan episode were generalized minimally so
that the operator schemas, together with the background knowledge, logically implies
the macro-operator schema after the generalization. The generalization was deductive;
hence, the learning process is called *analytic macro-operator schema learning*.
Unfortunately, these compiled macro-operators are considered during the searching
process in addition to the primitive operators, and they may create an additional burden
on the search procedure. Hence, EBL macro-operator learning is too conservative to
yield a new form of knowledge that can make the assembly sequencing problem
tractable.

Empirical assembly planning gains fundamentally new knowledge from experience
by inductively generalizing the planning episodes. The main learning task here is to

find a plausible generalization covering all the positive instances of a concept but none of the negative instances. Here, a basic learning mechanism is to compare objects as instances or non-instances of a concept to uncover common similarities and dissimilarities among the instances. Hence, the learning mechanism requires an efficient means of comparing one instance with the next.

When each instance is described by attributes, the inner structure of an instance object is abstracted out with no component objects: it is represented by a single object, namely by itself. Then, comparing one instance to the next is trivial because there is always one component object to compare. There have been numerous inductive learning methods from attribute-based training instances (Michalski, 1973; Quinlan, 1983). Unfortunately, an assembly plan structure is a highly structured object consisting of spatial and temporal relations. Therefore, an attribute-based learning technique is not directly applicable.

The comparison procedure is complicated for structured objects where a structured object consists of component objects and their relations. When comparing two structured objects, a component object from one structured object corresponds with one from the other structured object. This problem is known as the *object-correspondence* problem. When there are M distinct objects in each of two instances; there are $M!$ possible object correspondences between them, assuming one-to-one mapping (the complexity is worse otherwise). Therefore, comparing two structured objects is an inherently explosive process. To compound the difficulties, many instances should be compared to uncover regularities.

Winston's seminal work (Winston, 1970) developed a domain-independent method for learning structural concepts from the visual scene. It divided the objects of the scene into groups based on observed similarities and dissimilarities, a grouping procedure. Each grouping as a structured object is compared with an other structured object as instances or non-instances of a structural concept, a comparison procedure. The grouping procedure was later improved by CLUSTER (Stepp, 1984). It developed a number of useful similarity metrics for the clustering criteria, and an heuristic control algorithm for the hierarchical cluster formation. The comparison procedure was improved by INDUCE (Larson, 1977). It introduced an explicit two-phase approach for comparing between objects where the structural relations (links) were matched before the object attributes were compared to find the object correspondences. Each structured object is represented by a labeled graph, and used a network matching algorithm of the subgraph isomorphism problem. Although assembly structures and plans are structured objects, the domain-independent method for learning structural concepts from them is not directly applicable to learning from assembly planning experience either.

The domain independent structural concept learning systems above handle temporally structured objects like sequences no differently from any other structures. Learning a sequential pattern was studied in SPARC (Sequential PAttern ReCognition) (Michalski, Ko and Chen, 1987) as a distinct learning problem requiring a part-to-whole generalization, as opposed to an instance-to-class generalization in the previous structural concept learning systems. Here, each element of the sequence is a manifestation of some underlying process as an instance, and the learning task is to induce a sequence generating rule to explain the sequence and to predict the future continuation of the sequence as a symbolic process prediction. Hence, the learning mechanism is focused on the sequential relationships among the instances. Depending on the types of sequential relationships, SPARC has three rule models (decomposition, periodic, and disjunctive), where each rule model is looking for its distinct type of sequential pattern. The rule model is similar to the grouping and the precedence schemas in NOMAD.

The structured concept learning systems were applied to the recognition of spatial structures like assemblies, Winston's Arch problem; the sequential pattern learning systems were applied to the symbolic process prediction. NOMAD is learning from a sequence of spatial structures (assembly structures) because the assembly sequence planning domain involves both spatially and temporally structured domain objects.

7.6 CONCLUSION

Empirical assembly planning introduces an inductive learning mechanism in an assembly planning context. Learning from planning experience must determine which concept to learn as well as the corresponding training instances from the planning experience. NOMAD decomposes the planning experience into grouping and precedence relations as assembly episodes from the grouping and precedence schemas in memory. The credibility of these schemas is incrementally updated and modified from the planning experience. Such an incremental learning in the multi-concept learning situation is a closed-loop learning. Furthermore, the learning element introduced a deductive restructuring of the episodes when generating the final assembly sequence. The deductive restructuring generates more "interesting" training instances that are not covered by the current schemas in memory so that the learner can shift the focus of its working hypothesis to a new one guided by the new instance. With the addition of a constructive induction step, these three learning steps are combined by the multistrategy constructive learning element in NOMAD.

To extend the current implementation to practical industrial use, NOMAD must have a large store of effective grouping and precedence schemas summarizing experienced planning cases in memory. As an efficient means of presenting a large body of planning cases to the learning system, a virtual assembly simulation system is being developed. Here, the teacher provides an assembly description as well as the process of assembly procedure graphically using a Virtual Reality (VR) interface, a visual robot programming environment. Then, the teacher may provide a large store of assembling episodes which are the basis of applying the multi-concept learning scenario introduced in this chapter in the more practical industrial setting. When the virtual assembly system is complete, it will be a part of an intelligent CAD-based assembly modeling and simulation system for a concurrent product development and deployment environment.

ACKNOWLEDGEMENTS

I would like to express the deepest regard for the guidance given by my thesis advisor, Professor Ryszard S. Michalski. In addition, I would like to express my deepest gratitude to the members of the Machine Learning Group at the University of Illinois at Urbana-Champaign, who provided intellectual challenges and helpful feedback while I was a Ph.D. student there.

REFERENCES

De Fazio, T.L. and Whitney, D.E. (1988). Simplified Generation of All Mechanical Assembly Sequences. *IEEE Journal of Robotics and Automation*.

DeJong, G. and Mooney, R. (1986). Explanation-Based Learning: An Alternative View. *Machine Learning Journal*, vol. 2.

de Kleer, J. (1986). An Assumption-Based Truth Maintenance System. *Artificial Intelligence*, vol. 28, no. 1.

Donald, B.R. (1984). Motion Planning with Six Degrees of Freedom. *TR-91*, Massachusetts Institute of Science and Technology, Artificial Intelligence Laboratory.

Ko, H. and Lee, K. (1987). Automatic Assembly Sequence Generation. *Computer Aided Design* vol. 19, no. 1, pp. 3–10.

Ko, H. (1989). Empirical Assembly Planning: A Learning Approach. *PhD Thesis*, Department of Computer Science, Univerisity of Illinois, Urbana.

Larson, J.B. (1977). Inductive Inference in Variable-valued Predicate Logic System VL21: A Methodology and Computer Implementation. *Ph.D. Thesis, Report No. 869*, Department of Computer Science, Univerisity of Illinois, Urbana.

Michalski, R.S. (1973). Using Classifcation Rules using Variable-valued Logic System VL1. *Proceedings of the Third International Joint Conference on Artificial Intelligence*, Stanford.

Michalski, R. S. (1983). Theory and Methodology of Inductive Learning. Chapter in R.S. Michalski, J.G. Carbonell, T. M. Mitchell (Eds.), *Machine Learning: An Artificial Intelligence Approach,* Tioga Publishing.

Michalski, R. S., Ko, H. and Chen, K. (1987). Qualitative Prediction: The SPARC/G Methodology for Describing and Predicting Discrete Processes. Chapter in P. Dufour and A. Van Lamsweede (eds.), *Expert Systems*, Academic Press, pp. 125–158.

Michalski, R. S. (1993). Toward a unified theory of learning: Multistrategy task-adaptive learning. *Readings in Knowledge Acquisition and Learning* edited by B.G. Buchanan & D. Wilkins, Morgan Kaufmann.

Mitchell, T. M., Keller, T. and Kedar-Cabelli, S. (1986). Explanation-Based Generalization: A Unifying View. *Machine Learning Journal*, vol. 1.

Mostow, J. (1983). Machine Transformation of Advice into a Heuristic Search Procedure. Chapter in R. S. Michalski, J. G. Carbonell and T. M. Mitchell (eds.), *Machine Learning: An Artificial Intelligence Approach, Vol. I*, pp. 367–403, Morgan Kaufmann, Los Altos, CA.

Quinlan, J. R. (1979). Discovering Rules from Large Collections of Examples: A Case Study. Chapter in D. Michie (Ed.), *Expert Systems in the Microelectronic Age*, Edinburgh University Press, Edinburgh.

Stepp, R. E. (1984). Conjunctive Conceptual Clustering: A Methodology and Experimentation. *Ph.D. Thesis, UIUCDCS-R-84-1189*, Department of Computer Science, University of Illinois, Urbana.

Ulrich, K.T. and Seering W.P. (1988). Function Sharing in Mechanical Design. *Draft*, Massachusettes Institute of Technology, Artificial Intelligence Laboratory.

Winston, P. H. (1970). Learning Structural Descriptions from Examples. *Ph.D. Thesis, MAC TR-76*, Massachusetts Institute of Technology.

8

Inductive Learning in Design: A Method and Case Study Concerning Design of Antifriction Bearing Systems

Wojciech Moczulski

ABSTRACT

This chapter concerns problems of applying inductive rule learning to engineering design. The specific case study concerns the design of assemblies and the completion of subassemblies regarding the given design criteria. We describe a method for learning design rules based on the AQ-15 rule learning system, and illustrate it by an example of designing antifriction bearing systems. An important aspect of this application domain is that in many design situations there may be more than one recommended solution. Therefore, a learning system has to be able to build descriptions that can logically intersect. Most existing learning systems, however, do not have this feature. Another requirement is that the learned descriptions should be easy to interpret and understand by an expert. Both these requirements are satisfied by the AQ15c learning program that was employed in this study. The preliminary results were very encouraging. The method seems useful for automating or aiding a designer in the presented class of routine design tasks.

Keywords: Machine Learning, Machine Learning in Design, Design Knowledge Acquisition, Inductive rule learning, AQ learning system, Antifriction Bearing Systems.

Machine Learning and Data Mining: Methods and Applications
Edited by R.S. Michalski, I. Bratko and M. Kubat
© 1997 John Wiley & Sons Ltd

8.1 INTRODUCTION

Designing is a creative process involving reasoning with abstract concepts to determine a solution that satisfies given criteria and constraints. The output of a design process includes a brief pre-design and design concept. A design concept consists of an outline of the problem solution, which is generated by applying design operators (Dietrych, 1985) to input data (a description of needs). These operators represent different design methods and techniques. Knowledge and skill required for design may be acquired by the designer during his/her technical studies and practical work.

If we consider the whole design process, we find that it usually requires a great amount of creative effort (Dietrych, 1985). Such an effort is too complex to be successively aided by a knowledge-based system at the present level of development of this technology (Waldron and Waldron, 1992). However, once the designer has found a preliminary design configuration, it is usually easy for him/her to determine design subtasks that can be helped by means of knowledge-based or machine learning technologies. Many such design (sub)tasks require a routine rather than innovative effort (Tong and Sriram, 1992). As such, they can be relatively easy to partially or completely automate. Such help could significantly reduce the designer's total effort. To determine tasks amenable for automation, it is important to recognize pieces of *design knowledge* that can be easily represented in the form of rules (Tong and Sriram, 1992). Once this is done, machine learning methods can be applied.

This chapter presents a method for learning design rules using an inductive rule learning system AQ15c (Wnek *et al.,* 1995). The case study concerns the design of assemblies and the completion of subassemblies with respect to a set of criteria and input data (brief pre-design). Specific problem to which we applied a learning method concerns the development of rules for selecting anti-friction bearing systems. In the first step, an experienced designer defines attributes that are used for characterizing design examples. Subsequently, he/she describes the design examples with the selected attributes. These examples are the input to the learning program. We discuss a method of representing the design features of elements, and then describe the process of determining training and testing examples (events). These examples were supplied to the AQ15c learning program, which hypothesized the rules needed (Wnek *et al.,* 1995). The rules learned were evaluated using the testing data, and empirical error estimates have been determined. The conclusion indicates issues for further research.

8.2   A METHOD FOR LEARNING DESIGN RULES

8.2.1   General Issues

There is growing interest in applying inductive learning to problems of design knowledge acquisition (e.g., Arciszewski, 1994; Tong and Sriram, 1992). One of the important aspects of this application area is that design knowledge is often ambiguous, in the sense that there can be more than one solution of any given design task. Thus, a learning system has to be able to adequately represent such ambiguous situations. Most existing learning programs, however (e.g., decision tree learning [Quinlan, 1986]) are not suitable for this task, because they produce class (concept) descriptions that are mutually exclusive.

A powerful method for representing ambiguous knowledge is implemented in the AQ family of learning programs. These programs are based on the A^q algorithm (Michalski, 1969) for generating covers (rulesets) for given sets of examples (Michalski, 1983). For each concept to be learned, the program produces a set of rules (a ruleset) that can logically intersect with rulesets for one or more other concept, if this does not lead to the contradiction regarding existing examples. If a new case (example) satisfies more than one rule, then all classes indicated by these rules are presented as alternatives.

To make possible the inductive learning, a set of training data is determined for each decision class. If we consider learning of design rules, each class corresponds to some design solution (e. g. the bearing type). Each training example describes an object belonging to the class and is represented by means of values of several attributes. *Positive* examples for the class shall be covered by the classification rule which is to be learned for this class, while *negative* examples shall not be covered by this rule and therefore prevent any excessive generalization of the rule.

Some examples may belong to more than one class (i. e. there are some classes that overlap); such examples are called the *ambiguous examples*. Two ways of handling such examples are possible: it may be treated either as a *positive* example for the current class or a *negative* one. If the ambiguous example is handled as a negative example, it is not covered by any classification rule. Otherwise, this example is covered by more than one rule. The latter is suitable for learning design rules, where more than unique solution of the task is often possible.

To start the inductive learning using the A^q method the learning system must be supplied with background knowledge, which concerns specifications of:

- attribute domains (types of attributes, variables and their value sets);
- input hypotheses (optional), whose meaning is twofold: they represent the initial knowledge contained in the learning system, or as rulesets that are to be optimized during the course of learning.

As a result of learning we obtain a ruleset (which is a special kind of a classifier), one rule for each class.

8.2.2 Empirical Errors of The Learned Ruleset

To estimate the accuracy of the rules we use testing examples, other than those used for training. There are several methods suitable to estimate the accuracy of rules, as (Weiss and Kapouleas, 1990): *leave-one-out* cross-validation or *k-fold* cross-validation.

To evaluate the performance of the ruleset we have only a small sample from the population of all possible design solutions available. We can only calculate empirical error rates which estimate true error rates (attributable to the population). The following empirical error rates are considered (Weiss and Kapouleas, 1990):

- the overall empirical error rate which may be treated as a measure of the quality of all the rules:

$$E_{ov} = \frac{\text{number of errors}}{\text{number of testing events}} \tag{8.1}$$

where an error occurs if a given testing event is misclassified;

- the empirical omission error rate:

$$E_{om} = \frac{1}{n} \sum_{k=1}^{n} E^{k}{}_{om}, \quad \text{where} \quad E^{k}{}_{om} = \frac{\text{number of omission errors for class } k}{\text{number of } positive \text{ examples for class } k} \tag{8.2}$$

where an omission error occurs if a positive example for the given class is classified as a negative one;

- the empirical comission error rate:

$$E_{cm} = \frac{1}{n} \sum_{k=1}^{n} E^{k}{}_{cm}, \quad \text{where} \quad E^{k}{}_{cm} = \frac{\text{number of } comission \text{ errors for class } k}{\text{number of } negative \text{ examples for class } k} \tag{8.3}$$

where a comission error occurs if a negative example for the given class is classified as a positive one.

8.2.3 Application of Learned Rules to New Examples

Once we have learned accurate rules from the training examples, we may apply them to the classification of new, unseen examples. To determine to which class the example belongs we can calculate the degree of match between the example to be classified and the rules corresponding to each class. This value is called the degree of confidence (that the given example belongs to the class). We compared empirically different measures and actually we use the measure based on the INLEN method (Michalski et al., 1992). For each class k we evaluate the degree of confidence DC_k. For some pre-set threshold value T, $0 < T < 1$ it is possible to define the following concluding scheme:

1. If there exists k such that $DC_k > T$ and DC_k is substantially greater than other DC values, then it is very likely that the classified example belongs to the class k. Such a case corresponds to 'sharp' result of classification, i.e., there exists only one unique design solution adequate to the input data.
2. If for each k we have $DC_k \leq T$, there does not exist any solution (the result of classification is unknown). It is likely that our knowledge base is incomplete and it is expedient to supply additional data for the induction of a more comprehensive ruleset.

3. If condition $DC_k > T$ is satisfied by several values of k, none of them being essentially greater than the others, an ambiguous result of classification occurs: we are not able to decide to which class the object belongs.

The presented concluding method is advantageous in the case of design problems where we are faced with tasks which have multiple solutions.

8.3 DESCRIPTION OF AN EXEMPLARY PROBLEM

The method described above may be implemented as shown in the example concerning the learning of rules connected with the designing of anti-friction bearing arrangements in typical drives. Figure 8.1 shows one of the possible solutions of this task. However, there is a relatively large extent of possible design solutions and a lack of generally acknowledged design rules that might be used to solve the task. Let's consider the way of designing the driving shaft support in the car's final drive by various manufacturers. We find a lot of solutions and each of them has been successfully applied in hundred thousands of cars. Thus, usually there is no unique solution of the design task and we need to represent many solutions, only advising the user on which of them is the most 'popular' among the designers.

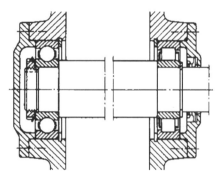

Figure 8.1 A concept of design of a bearing arrangement (SKF: General catalogue).

The design task is a kind of routine design (Tong and Sriram, 1992) and may be solved in several stages. The task being discussed is not trivial and there is no algorithm of selecting the design features that describe the solution and may be subsequently represented by means of a drawing. The design stages are shown in Figure 8.2.

The knowledge on designing anti-friction bearing arrangements is well developed. There are multiple knowledge sources available (e.g. textbooks, catalogues of anti-friction ball-bearings – see e.g. [SKF: General catalogue], skilled designers, etc.). The domain knowledge is a subject of lectures on each faculty of mechanical engineering. However, as has been explained previously, design knowledge is in some sense ambiguous: one may observe that in response to one definite set of input data there often exist more than one bearing type to be applied.

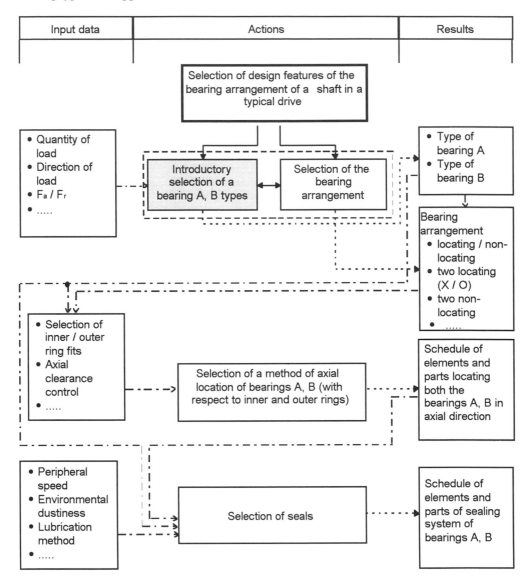

Figure 8.2 Stages of the selection of design features of a shaft with two rolling bearings A, B (Moczulski, 1995).

It is ought to be stressed that some stages of this design process are closely related with each other. There is a sequence of defined tasks, but we can find more complicated relationships between several tasks and in some cases it is impossible to distinguish between them. For example, if from input data it follows that an application of taper roller bearings is needed, one has to choose simultaneously the configuration of the bearing system. The results of several stages are the input data for other ones. For example, the results of the introductory stages are input data for designing a sealing system.

If it were possible to acquire knowledge in the form of design rules, it would subsequently be possible to develop software capable of substituting a human designer in solving routine tasks concerning the design of bearing arrangements and representing the design features by drawing. Therefore the problem is quite important and may be classified as a method of computer-aided design.

In the following we present some introductory results obtained during research on the selection of anti-friction bearing types according to input data. The interrelationships of this task are presented in Figure 8.2 (this task is represented by the shaded area). To select the bearing, we first take into account the expected life of the product, load, rotating speed and environmental conditions, as well as necessary servicing. The type of bearing is usually determined based upon the designer's prior knowledge taking into consideration the relative radial and axial load, geometric constraints, expected alignment, serviceability, etc. Then, the designer may evaluate the size of the bearing, using well-defined formulae, contained for example in accessible publications (e.g. anti-friction bearing catalogues [SKF: General catalogue]).

We wanted to learn rulesets that might be applied in the same manner as the designer uses if he/she determines the features of the bearing arrangement. Hence, we must obtain the dataset that describes the situation (location of the machine, its environment, etc.) and quantitative data (radial and/or axial load, rotating speed, shaft diameter, etc.) that both constitute input data to the design process. The ruleset learned during the course of machine learning will act as the design operator (Dietrych, 1985) in transforming the input data into the solution, which in our case is the name of the bearing type.

8.4 APPLICATION OF THE INDUCTION METHOD

We applied heuristics and knowledge available in accessible sources in order to decide which domains and domain types are suitable to represent data on the examples to be used for the machine learning stage. In the following we address the more important problems we were faced with.

We decided to use qualitative values of variables instead of quantitative ones. Such a solution is motivated by the general character of a learned ruleset that might be applied broadly in the design of bearing arrangements, independently of the particular values of variables such as: numerical value of the load, shaft diameter, rotating speed, etc. Hence, each domain will contain only a few possible values of attributes defined in this domain.

The selected domains of attributes together with a number of values and value names are presented in Table 8.1. The subsequent values of the 'condition of load' denote the percentage of the ratio of axial to radial load values (e.g. rd/25ax denotes that the value of the axial load amounts to 25% of the radial load). The qualitative attribute is linear, if it is possible to order its values (introducing the relationship $\leq$), unless the attribute is a nominal one (besides equality there are no relationships between the values of attributes).

Table 8.1   Domains of attributes

#	Type	Size	Attribute name	Attribute description	Attribute values
1	linear	3	sh_dia	Shaft diameter	small, med, great
2	nominal	2	rd_spc	Radial space limitations	yes, no
3	nominal	2	ax_spc	Axial space limitations	yes, no
4	linear	3	mag_ld	Magnitude of load	small, med, heavy
5	linear	13	cnd_ld	Condition of load	radial, rd/25ax, ... , axial
6	linear	3	misalg	Possible occurrence of misalignment	small, med, heavy
7	linear	4	rot_sp	Rotating speed	small, med, high, v_high
8	linear	3	frictn	Magnitude of friction	small, med, high
9	linear	3	stiffn	Stiffness	small, med, great
10	nominal	2	maintn	Necessity of maintenance	useless, allowed

8.4.1 Qualitative Values of Variables

The representation of continuous variables by qualitative values is a difficult problem which is always connected with a loss of information. It is usually performed by clustering the quantitative values of attributes. The system developed should be able to convert continuous variables into qualitative values before using them as input data to infer on bearing type(s). In the research reported we applied an approach based on heuristics inferred from the background knowledge of machine design.

Taking into consideration the attributes included in Table 8.1 one can distinguish two groups of attributes (Moczulski, 1995):

- attributes (bearing features) independent of the bearing load and its dimensions: e.g. the attribute 'peripheral speed of a shaft against a seal' may take the following qualitative values (heuristic approach – with respect to the application of a specific type of seal; here the value v denotes the peripheral speed of a shaft):
  - *small* for $v < 4$ m/s (possible application of rubbing felt seals if the operating temperatures are up to 100 °C – a type of seal that is simple and inexpensive),
  - *medium* for $v < 8$ m/s (possible use of radial lip-type seals),
  - *large* for $v \geq 8$ m/s (a non-rubbing seal should be applied);
- attributes dependent on the magnitudes of the bearing load, size and type of the bearing: e.g. the attribute 'magnitude of load' may take the following values (where: P = equivalent dynamic bearing load, C = basic dynamic load rating, see [SKF: General catalogue]):
  - *light*, if $P \leq 0.06\ C$,
  - *normal*, if $0.06\ C < P \leq 0.12\ C$,
  - *heavy*, if $P > 0.12\ C$.

It ought to be emphasized, that the representation of an attribute belonging to the second group of attributes may cause difficulties. For instance, in the example presented the limits of values of the attribute 'magnitude of load' are implicit in such a sense, that one has to use the properties of the bearing to be selected (basic dynamic load rating C) in order to obtain qualitative input data that may be used in the selection of this unknown bearing.

8.5 TRAINING AND TESTING EVENTS

The machine learning method based on induction requires a quite numerous set of training examples (so-called 'events'). Each example is represented by n-tuple of values of attributes, one of them being the decision attribute value, i.e. the name of the class the example belongs to. Bearing the design goal in mind, we shall use such a set of attributes, which describe the situation of the bearing in the context of the machine and which can represent qualitative data as well. These attributes were represented by qualitative values. The database of events which we applied during the course of this research was described in Maniak (1995).

8.5.1 Design Knowledge Sources

Knowledge on the design of bearing arrangements was found in accessible bibliography, as: catalogues of rolling bearings (e.g. [SKF: General catalogue]) and special publications issued by producers of bearings, textbooks on machine design, etc. These knowledge sources contain numerous examples and figures that are information carrier on design knowledge (cf. Figure 8.1).

Such examples, usually represented by a schematic figure and accompanied with a description, have been coded as events (Maniak, 1995). The conversion of quantitative values into qualitative ones was performed according to the opinion of the person who prepared the events. Then the collected events were put down into a file in the format accepted by the machine learning software.

It should be emphasized that we spent a lot of time in order to optimize a set of attributes that would be able to distinguish a dozen classes of bearings.

In the next stages of the research we are going to acquire knowledge from skilled and experienced designers, too.

8.5.2 Database of Examples

We collected examples that correspond to the following bearing types: deep grove ball bearings, angular contact ball bearings (single and double-row), self-aligning ball bearings, cylindrical roller bearings (type NU), spherical roller bearings, taper roller bearings, needle roller bearings, thrust ball bearings, cylindrical roller thrust bearings and spherical roller thrust bearings. For each of these bearing types (classes) we collected from 10 up to 26 events (total 200 events). Some examples are shown in Table 8.2. The entire representation space contains 101088 possible events and the collected examples represent only 0.2 % of all events. In our opinion the number of collected events is far too small to provide reliable knowledge on the problem domain and thus the research performed should be interpreted as a feasibility study rather than the final stage. Therefore it would be expedient to undertake further research concerning more numerous events.

The examples are represented by data describing the situation of the bearing (location of the machine, its environment, etc.) and quantitative data (radial and/or axial load, rotating speed, shaft diameter, etc.) which both constitute input data for the real design process concerning bearing systems.

Table 8.2 Exemplary training events of the class 'deep groove ball bearing'

sh_dia	rd_spc	ax_spc	mag_ld	cnd_ld	misalg	rot_sp	frictn	stiffn	maintn
med	yes	yes	med	rd/25ax	small	v_high	small	great	useless
small	yes	no	med	rd/50ax	med	high	small	small	allowed
med	no	yes	med	rd/25ax	med	high	small	med	allowed
med	yes	yes	small	radial	med	med	small	med	useless
med	no	yes	heavy	radial	small	med	small	med	useless
great	no	yes	small	rd/25ax	small	small	small	small	useless
med	no	yes	small	rd/25ax	small	small	small	small	allowed
great	no	no	med	radial	med	v_high	small	small	useless
med	no	no	med	rd/25ax	small	small	small	great	useless
small	no	yes	med	radial	med	v_high	small	med	useless
. . . . .									

8.6 RESULTS OBTAINED

In the following we present the results obtained by means of the selective induction machine learning program AQ15c (Wnek *et al.,* 1995). Conducting several trials we found optimal parameter values that control the operation of the program:

- We generate a minimum number of possible extended selectors and a minimum number of values contained in the selectors. That enables us to learn as simple rules as possible.
- Ambiguous examples we take as positive examples for each class to which they are assigned, thus they can be covered by more than one classification rule. This mode corresponds to the specificity of the application domain.
- We apply a default set of criteria used to define a lexicographic functional (LEF [Michalski, 1983]). This set contains the mincost (minimum cost of attributes) and minsel (minimization of the number of extended selectors) criteria.

8.6.1 Learning Rules From Training Examples

The introductory results obtained seem very encouraging. We optimized the representation space (both chosen domains and possible values of attributes that describe the events) with respect to the accuracy of the ruleset obtained, that made it possible to achieve the accuracy of the classification into 13 classes amounting to 92 %. For each class we obtained a rule in the form of a disjunction of complexes represented in VL_1 (Michalski, 1983). This form of representation enables the reader to understand easily the rules generated by the machine learning program AQ15c. An exemplary rule obtained during the course of research (represented in VL_1) is shown (Table 8.3). In each line we see one complex that is a conjunction of simplexes (simple conditional terms). The rule is a disjunction of several complexes. In the column 'strength' we present for each complex: t = total number of examples that support the rule, and u = number of examples that are unique. A translation of this rule into natural language is shown in Table 8.4.

Table 8.3 Exemplary rule concerning deep groove ball bearings

deepGrooveBall-outhypo		
#	complexes	strength
1	[cnd_ld=rd/25ax]	(t:10,u:10)
2	[mag_ld=med] [cnd_ld=radial,rd/50ax] [misalg=med] [rot_sp=high..v_high] [stiffn=small]	(t:4, u:4)
3	[rd_spc=yes] [ax_spc=yes] [cnd_ld=radial] [stiffn=small..med]	(t:4, u:3)
4	[ax_spc=yes] [cnd_ld=radial] [rot_sp=med] [stiffn=med]	(t:4, u:3)
5	[rd_spc=no] [ax_spc=no] [mag_ld=small] [cnd_ld=radial] [misalg=small..med]	(t:3, u:3)
6	[ax_spc=yes] [cnd_ld=radial] [rot_sp=v_high]	(t:2, u:2)

The summary of results of tests is presented in Table 8.5. The contents of this table may be used to determine the figures of empirical error rates. Following Eq. (8.1) the overall empirical error rate $E_{ov} = 0.080$, hence the accuracy of the ruleset presented here amounts to 92 %. From Table 8.5 we obtained the empirical omission error rate $E_{om} = 0.066$ and empirical comission error rate $E_{cm} = 0.007$ according to Eq. (8.2) and (8.3), respectively.

Moreover, we have enough background domain knowledge to investigate the quality of the learned design rules. To evaluate the results, we analyzed cases of misclassification using an heuristic approach. All these cases occur for such events, which describe situations where multiple types of bearings may be applied (e.g. if a radial load is expected with a medium rotating speed and a medium or low friction coefficient, we can usually apply either a deep groove ball bearing or cylindrical roller bearing). These events are then ambiguous from the designer's point of view, too. Hence, an explicit result of classification would be unexpected.

8.6.2 Assessment of Prepared Examples by Means of Incremental Learning

We conducted another test in order to evaluate the correctness and completeness of the database of examples. *Incremental learning* (Wnek *et al.,* 1995) was applied. As initial rules we used the ruleset published in the anti-friction ball bearing catalogue [SKF: General catalogue].

Table 8.4 Translation of the exemplary rule into natural language

Apply the deep groove ball bearing, if:

1. the condition of the load is radial with axial up to 25% of radial, or

2. the magnitude of the load is medium and the condition of load is radial or (radial with axial up to 50% of radial) and the misalignment is medium and the rotating speed is high to very high and the stiffness of the bearing is small, or

3. the radial space is limited and the axial space is limited and the condition of the load is radial and the stiffness is small to medium, or

4. the axial space is limited and the condition of the load is radial and the rotating speed is medium and the stiffness is medium, or

5. the radial space is unlimited and the axial space is unlimited and the magnitude of the load is small and the condition of the load is radial and the misalignment is small to medium, or

6. the axial space is limited and the condition of the load is radial and the rotating speed is very high.

Table 8.5 Summary of testing results using the 'leave-one-out' method

Class No.	Bearing type	Number of			
		positive examples	correctly classified	omission errors	comission errors
1	deep groove ball bearing	26	20	6	4
2	angular contact ball bearings, single row	12	12	0	0
3	angular contact ball bearings, double row	10	10	0	0
4	self-aligning ball bearings	13	11	2	0
5	cylindrical roller bearings of type NU	13	10	3	8
6	cylindrical roller bearings of type NUP	21	16	5	4
7	cylindrical roller bearings, double row	15	15	0	0
8	needle roller bearings	10	10	0	0
9	taper roller bearings	17	17	0	0
10	spherical roller bearings	25	25	0	0
11	thrust ball bearings	16	16	0	0
12	cylindrical roller thrust bearings	10	10	0	0
13	spherical roller thrust bearings	12	12	0	0
	Total	200	184	16	16

To verify the correctness of the examples we assumed, that the rules published in the catalogue are sound. The hypothesis formulated by the author was as follows: if a prepared set of examples were 'compatible' with the initial rules (coming from the acknowledged source), then the rules learned by 'refining' the initial rules by means of learning examples (to be evaluated) would be 'significantly better' (i.e. we would obtain a significantly greater number of correctly classified examples) than the rules learned only from these examples alone.

Table 8.6 Evaluation of training examples by means of incremental learning

Class No	Bearing type	Accuracy (%) of		Accuracy gain (%)
		previous learning	incremental learning	
1	Deep groove ball bearing	76.9	84.6	+7.7
2	Angular contact ball bearing, single-row	100.0	58.3	-41.7
3	Angular contact ball bearing, double-row	100.0	70.0	-30.0
4	Self-aligning ball bearing	84.6	100.0	+15.4
5	Cylindrical roller bearing of type NU	76.9	38.5	-38.5
6	Cylindrical roller bearing of type NUP	76.2	57.1	-19.1
7	Cylindrical roller bearing, double-row	100.0	26.7	-73.3
8	Needle roller bearing	100.0	100.0	0.0
9	Taper roller bearing	100.0	88.2	-11.8
10	Spherical roller bearing, double-row	100.0	84.0	-16.0
11	Thrust ball bearing	100.0	100.0	0.0
12	Cylindrical roller thrust bearing	100.0	100.0	0.0
13	Spherical roller thrust bearing	100.0	100.0	0.0
	Total	92.0	77.0	-15.0

In Table 8.6 we present selected results of the research, described in Maniak (1996). The overall accuracy of the set of rules obtained this stage is smaller than that discussed previously. However, both a gain and loss of the accuracy of the rules corresponding to the class concepts may be observed:

- The gain of accuracy for classes 1, 4. The training examples refine the prior ruleset and the obtained ruleset better classifies the unseen testing examples. We suppose that additional knowledge has been learned from the training examples which is compatible with the input hypotheses.
- No change in the accuracy for classes 8, 11, 12 and 13 that corresponds to the full agreement of the data and the initial rules. However, it is very likely that we learn no new knowledge within this learning process.
- The loss of the accuracy for remaining classes (especially for the class 7, but also for classes 2, 5, 3): here the examples are incompatible with the rules and we conclude that these examples are not representative to the concepts of these classes or even incorrect.

From the last case we conclude that our examples representing these classes are inadequate for the common domain knowledge (they poorly represent this concept). Thus, we should correct these examples in order to better represent the corresponding concept.

8.6.3 Confidence in Results Obtained

In the example discussed we obtained very promising results. Using the results of the classification of examples of deep groove ball bearings (Table 8.7) we show how it is possible to apply confidence figures to evaluate the learned ruleset.

We applied three values of the constant T (see Section 8.2.3): 0.25, 0.50 and 0.75. Using these threshold values we get worse accuracy values of the whole ruleset equal to 86.5 %, 66.0 % and 56.0 %, respectively. The influence of the value of the constant T may be better identified from an example corresponding to a single class (see Table 8.7). Analyzing the results contained in this table we find, then, that for the given values of T the number of correctly classified examples decreases to 18, 8 and 8, respectively.

If there were no requirements regarding the value of confidence, we would obtain very rough conclusions, because some training examples feature very low confidence. For instance (see Table 8.7) the example 8 was classified incorrectly to the class 6 with the low confidence of 0.05, while the example 12 was classified correctly to the class 1 with the confidence of 0.08. Both these examples should be rejected. The rejection could take place when the maximal confidence in belonging to some class would be less than the given threshold value T.

Another case of an ambiguous outcome of classification is represented by numerous examples (number 3, 4, 6, 7, 11, 14, 16, 21 – see Table 8.7) which belong to the class 1 with confidences amounting to 1.0 but it is likely that they could belong to some other classes as well. In this case both solutions are also possible: not only do we have examples properly classified (as example 3), but also incorrectly classified ones (as example 4). However, in this case we can deal with a very interesting opportunity – there is more than one solution of the task, which exactly corresponds with the problems the designer is faced with when he/she solves the design task.

8.7 RECAPITULATION AND CONCLUSIONS

The research confirms the feasibility of the application of machine learning to problems of deriving useful design knowledge in order to aid designers in solving routine design tasks. The selective induction method may be effectively applied to learn design rules from examples. The research presented here has made it possible to verify this approach in the case of selecting the type of bearing. The ruleset obtained features high degree of accuracy (up to 92 %), that it was possible to achieve during the course of optimizing the representation space against the accuracy criterion. This optimization may be interpreted as adding a great amount of background knowledge into the learning system.

We proposed a scheme of concluding where confidence figures were applied. This method is in good agreement with the design practice and enables the expert system to suggest several solutions of a task to the designer. The decision has to be made by the designer him/herself using his/her own background knowledge to solve the task.

Table 8.7 Exemplary degrees of confidence concerning examples of deep groove ball bearings (class 1; INLEN method)

event #	belongs to class	Degree of match an example to the class (confidence):													Max deg. of confd.	Threshold T		
		cl1	cl2	cl3	cl4	cl5	cl6	cl7	cl8	cl9	cl10	cl11	cl12	cl13		0.25	0.50	0.75
1		0.41	0.00	0.00	0.00	0.00	0.00	0.00	0.00	0.00	0.00	0.00	0.00	0.00	0.41	+	-	-
2		0.36	0.00	0.00	0.00	0.00	0.00	0.00	0.00	0.00	0.00	0.00	0.00	0.00	0.36	+	-	-
3		1.00	0.67	0.50	0.96	0.98	0.99	0.95	0.75	0.67	0.75	0.50	0.00	0.00	1.00	+	+	+
4	cl7	0.93	0.33	0.50	0.94	0.90	0.96	0.98	0.50	0.33	0.44	0.50	0.00	0.00	0.98	+	+	+
5		0.36	0.00	0.00	0.00	0.00	0.00	0.00	0.00	0.00	0.00	0.00	0.00	0.00	0.36	+	-	-
6	cl7	0.88	0.67	0.75	0.98	0.99	0.96	0.99	0.50	0.67	0.88	0.50	0.00	0.00	0.99	+	+	+
7		1.00	0.50	0.50	0.96	0.99	0.99	0.94	0.50	0.67	0.94	0.50	0.00	0.00	1.00	+	+	+
8	cl6	0.00	0.00	0.00	0.00	0.00	0.05	0.00	0.00	0.00	0.00	0.00	0.00	0.00	0.05	-	-	-
9		0.36	0.00	0.00	0.00	0.00	0.00	0.00	0.00	0.00	0.00	0.00	0.00	0.00	0.36	+	-	-
10		0.36	0.00	0.00	0.00	0.00	0.00	0.00	0.00	0.00	0.00	0.00	0.00	0.00	0.36	+	-	-
11	cl6	0.97	0.67	0.00	0.94	0.99	0.96	0.98	0.50	0.33	0.91	0.50	0.00	0.00	0.99	+	+	+
12		0.08	0.00	0.00	0.00	0.00	0.00	0.00	0.00	0.00	0.00	0.00	0.00	0.00	0.08	-	-	-
13		0.36	0.00	0.00	0.00	0.00	0.00	0.00	0.00	0.00	0.00	0.00	0.00	0.00	0.36	+	-	-
14	cl6	1.00	0.83	0.25	0.81	1.00	0.99	0.91	0.50	0.67	0.91	0.50	0.00	0.00	1.00	+	+	+
15		0.12	0.00	0.00	0.00	0.00	0.00	0.00	0.00	0.00	0.00	0.00	0.00	0.00	0.12	-	-	-
16		0.98	0.50	0.25	0.83	0.89	0.98	0.96	0.50	0.33	0.91	0.50	0.00	0.00	0.98	+	+	+
17		0.36	0.00	0.00	0.00	0.00	0.00	0.00	0.00	0.00	0.00	0.00	0.00	0.00	0.36	+	-	-
18		0.36	0.00	0.00	0.00	0.00	0.00	0.00	0.00	0.00	0.00	0.00	0.00	0.00	0.36	+	-	-
19		0.12	0.00	0.00	0.00	0.00	0.00	0.00	0.00	0.00	0.00	0.00	0.00	0.00	0.12	-	-	-
20		0.36	0.00	0.00	0.00	0.00	0.00	0.00	0.00	0.00	0.00	0.00	0.00	0.00	0.36	+	-	-
21	cl6	0.99	0.33	0.50	0.98	0.98	0.94	0.98	0.25	0.33	0.97	0.50	0.00	0.00	0.99	+	+	+
22		0.00	0.00	0.00	0.00	0.00	0.05	0.00	0.00	0.00	0.00	0.00	0.00	0.00	0.05	-	-	-
23		0.12	0.00	0.00	0.00	0.00	0.00	0.00	0.00	0.00	0.00	0.00	0.00	0.00	0.12	-	-	-
24		0.12	0.00	0.00	0.00	0.00	0.00	0.00	0.00	0.00	0.00	0.00	0.00	0.00	0.12	+	-	-
25		0.36	0.00	0.00	0.00	0.00	0.00	0.00	0.00	0.00	0.00	0.00	0.00	0.00	0.36	+	-	-
26	cl6	0.08	0.00	0.00	0.08	0.23	0.00	0.00	0.00	0.00	0.00	0.00	0.00	0.00	0.23	-	-	-
Total number of correctly classified examples of this class for different values of threshold T																18	8	8

We preliminary proved that the AQ-15 system is a powerful means of learning and representing ambiguous knowledge, which case is common in the domain of machine design.

Further verification of results obtained during the course of this research requires co-operation with skilled designers, which is intended in the next stages of the project. We are going to find rulesets for other sub-tasks of the problem domain, particularly for the application of seals, the design of bearing arrangements and axial location of bearings with respect to the shaft and housing. The corresponding research was initiated by the author and is already conducted by P. Maniak.

The conversion of continuous attributes into discrete ones with qualitative values may be performed using heuristic foundations (background knowledge of the problem domain).

The results obtained indicate that the method described can be useful for building the knowledge based systems that aid designers in solving routine machine design tasks.

ACKNOWLEDGEMENTS

The author would like to express his gratitude to Prof. Ryszard S. Michalski, George Mason University (USA), who has kindly provided the inductive learning program AQ15c (Wnek et al., 1995) that was used in our study, as well as for his helpful suggestions and comments which have a great influence on the final version of this text. The author also would like to thank Janusz Wnek and Eric Bloedorn for their suggestions concerning suitable methods for empirical error estimation.

The author would like to acknowledge the contribution of Piotr Maniak, who prepared training and testing examples, and obtained estimates of overall empirical errors for different rulesets.

This research was conducted in the Department of Foundations of Machine Design, Technical University of Silesia, Gliwice, Poland and was partially supported by the National Scientific Research Foundation under grant KBN (No. 8 T 11 F 020 09).

REFERENCES

Arciszewski, T. (1994): Machine Learning in Engineering Design. *3rd International Symposium 'Intelligent Information Systems'*. Institute of Computer Science, Polish Academy of Sciences, Warsaw–Wigry, pp. 40–54.

Arciszewski, T., Dybala T. and Wnek J. (1992): A Method for Evaluation of Learning Systems. *HEURISTICS, The Journal of Knowledge Engineering*, Special Issue on Knowledge Acquisition and Machine Learning, Vol. 5, No. 4, Winter 1992.

Dietrych, J. (1985): *System and Design* (in Polish). WNT, Warsaw.

Maniak, P. (1995): Application of Machine Learning Methods to Knowledge Acquisition on the Design of Machinery (in Polish). *M. Sc. Thesis*, Technical University of Silesia, Department of Fundamentals of Machine Design, Gliwice.

Maniak, P. (1996): Example of Induction of Rules Concerning Selection of Rolling Bearings. *Computer Integrated Manufacturing. Proc. of Int. Conference*, Vol. II, pp. 221-228. Faculty of Mechanical Engineering, Technical University of Silesia, Gliwice-Zakopane.

Michalski, R. S. (1969): Recognition of Total or Partial Symmetry in a Completely or Incompletely Specified Switching Function. *Proc. of the IV IFAC Congress*, Vol. 27, pp. 109–129, Warsaw.

Michalski, R. S. (1983): A Theory and Methodology of Inductive Learning. *Artificial Intelligence*, Vol. 20, pp. 111–116.

Michalski, R. S. (1993): Inferential Theory of Learning: Developing Foundations for Multistrategy Learning. In: Michalski R. S. and Tecuci G. (Eds.), *Machine Learning: A Multistrategy Approach*, Vol. 4, Morgan Kaufman.

Michalski, R. S., Kerschberg, L., Kaufman, K. and Ribeiro, J. (1992): Mining for Knowledge in Databases: The INLEN Architecture, Initial Implementation and First Results. *Journal of Intelligent Information Systems: Integrating AI and Database Technologies*, Vol. 1, No. 1, August 1992, pp. 85–113.

Moczulski, W. (1995): A Method of Identifying the Design Rules Concerning Subassemblies of Machines (in Polish). *Proc. of the 17th Symposium on Fundamentals of Machine Design*, Vol. II, pp. 603–608, Technical University of Lublin.

Moczulski, W. (1995a): Example of Design Knowledge Acquisition Using Induction. *Proceedings of V Workshop on Intelligent Systems*. Institute of Computer Science, Polish Academy of Sciences, Warsaw–Augustow.

Quinlan, J. R. (1986): Induction of Decision Trees, *Machine Learning*, Vol. 1 (1986), pp. 81–106.

SKF: General catalogue.

Tong, Ch. and Sriram, D. (Eds.) (1992): *Artificial Intelligence in Engineering Design*. Academic Press.

Waldron, M. B. and Waldron, K. J. (1992): A Knowledge Transfer Methodology in Selection of Mechanical Design Components. In: Tong and Sriram, 1992, Vol. III, pp. 57–77.

Weiss, S. M. and Kapouleas, I. (1990): An Empirical Comparison of Pattern Recognition, Neural Nets, and Machine Learning Classification Methods. In: Shavlik, J. W. and Dietterich, T. G. (Eds.), *Readings in Machine Learning*, Morgan Kaufmann, San Mateo, CA, 1990, pp. 177–183.

Wnek, J., Kaufman, K., Bloedorn, E. and Michalski, R. S. (1995): Selective Induction Learning System AQ15c: The Method and User's Guide. *Reports of Machine Learning and Inference Laboratory*, MLI 95-4, George Mason University, Fairfax, VA.

## PART III

Detection of Patterns in Texts, Images and Music

9

Finding Associations in Collections of Text

Ronen Feldman and Haym Hirsh

ABSTRACT

This chapter describes the FACT system for finding associations – patterns of co-occurrence – amongst the keywords labeling items in a collection of textual documents. FACT takes a query-centered view of knowledge discovery, in which an association-discovery request is viewed as a query over the implicit set of possible associations supported by a collection of documents. Further, when background knowledge is available about the keywords labeling the documents, FACT is able to use this information in its discovery process, permitting a user to specify constraints on the desired results of the query in terms of the background knowledge. Moreover, execution of an association-discovery query is structured so that these background-knowledge constraints can be exploited in the search for possible results. Finally, rather than requiring a user to specify an explicit query expression in the knowledge-discovery query language, FACT presents the user with a simple-to-use graphical interface to the query language, with the language providing a well-defined semantics for the discovery actions performed by a user through the interface.

9.1 INTRODUCTION

The incredible growth over the last few years of information available from online sources has been both a blessing and a curse. Although we now have vast amounts of information cheaply available at our fingertips, the quantity and heterogeneity of the information has

Machine Learning and Data Mining: Methods and Applications
Edited by R.S. Michalski, I Bratko and M. Kubat
© 1997 John Wiley & Sons Ltd

made exploring and comprehending this information very difficult and time-consuming. The development of tools to help users access and understand large quantities of multimodal information is crucial to harnessing the immense amount of online information that is now available to us.

This is one of the main motivations for much of the work in Knowledge Discovery from Databases (KDD). The general problem has been described as the "nontrivial extraction of implicit, previously unknown, and potentially useful information from data" (Frawley *et al.*, 1992). Unfortunately, work in this area has focused primarily on structured data, and little attention has been placed on unstructured forms of data. This chapter addresses the problem of Knowledge Discovery from Text (KDT) (Dagan and Feldman, 1995; Feldman, 1996), whose goal is the extraction of information from collections of unstructured textual documents.

A key idea in this work is to take a lesson from research in the information-retrieval community that shows that shallow representations of information often provide sufficient support for a range of information-access tasks (Salton and McGill, 1983, Frakes and Baeza-Yates, 1992). Our approach is therefore to analyze and manipulate documents by annotating them with collections of domain-level keywords. Knowledge discovery then takes place by finding correlations – associations (Agrawal *et al.*, 1993, 1995; Mannila *et al.*, 1994) – amongst the keywords labeling each document. Thus, for example, if given a collection of newswire articles one can ask for interesting patterns of co-occurrence amongst the keywords of each article, such as country names that often label a document whenever some other country names also label the document.

This chapter describes FACT (Finding Associations in Collections of Text), a KDD tool focused specifically on the discovery of associations in collections of labeled textual documents. Central to this work is a query-centered view of the discovery process (Imielinski *et al.,* 1996). Given a collection of data, there is a corresponding implicit collection of possible results supported by the data. FACT provides a query language for the discovery process in which a user can specify queries over this implicit collection of possible results supported by the data. However, rather than requiring the specification of an explicit query expression in this language, FACT presents the user with a simple-to-use graphical interface in which a user's various discovery tasks are specified, with the underlying query language providing a well-defined semantics for the discovery actions performed by the user through the interface.

Further, FACT is able to exploit some forms of background knowledge that may be available to the system. For example, in the preceding newswire context, a system trying to find associations amongst the keywords labeling newswire articles should be able to exploit knowledge about countries – such as a country's population, size, export commodities, or organizational memberships (NATO, G7, Arab League, etc.) – as well as information about relationships between countries – such as whether they are neighbors, are trading partners, or have a common language. Such background knowledge can come from many different sources, such as from databases of facts about the domain, or even from other textual information sources (as is the case in this work). FACT allows a user to include in a query constraints over the set of desired results in terms of background knowledge about the keywords labeling the documents. Moreover, FACT will exploit these constraints in how it structures its search for possible results. This background knowledge could thus enable FACT to, for example, discover associations between a G7 country that appears as a label of a document and some other non-bordering G7 countries that also appear as a label of the document.

We begin this chapter with an overview of the FACT system architecture. We then describe the general problem of finding associations, our association-discovery query language, our algorithms for executing queries in this language, and our tool for presenting discovered associations. We next discuss the use of FACT on a collection of Reuters newswire stories using background knowledge automatically extracted from the CIA World Factbook. Finally, once the work has been described, we conclude the chapter by briefly situating the work in the larger context of other KDD efforts.

9.2 THE FACT SYSTEM ARCHITECTURE

Figure 9.1 presents the overall architecture of the FACT system. Along the top are the three sources of information given to FACT. On the far right is the collection of textual data on which the discovery process takes place. Since our approach begins with the assumption borrowed from the Information Retrieval literature that each document is labeled with a set of keywords, the input text collections must either already be labeled with such keywords (as is the case for the Reuters data discussed in Section 9.7), or must be fed through a text categorization system (e.g., Iwayama and Tokunaga, 1994; Apte *et al.*, 1994) that augments documents with such keywords.

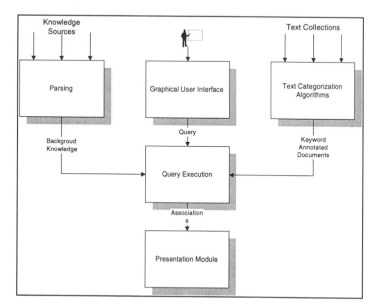

Figure 9.1 — Architecture of the FACT system.

On the far left are the knowledge sources that serve as additional background knowledge for the discovery process. To be usable by FACT, such knowledge must define unary and binary predicates over the keywords labeling the documents, representing properties of the entities represented by each keyword and relationships between them. Thus for the Reuters newswire data, for example, FACT is told for each country-keyword the organizations of which that country is a member, thereby defining a set of unary predicates over the country-keywords (one per organization). FACT is also given information about which countries neighbor one another, defining a set of binary predicates over the country-keywords. Since such information is rarely available in the precise form needed by the FACT system, it will usually be necessary to develop tools that understand the format of an information source and can translate into the necessary format for FACT. For example, the background knowledge used in our Reuters newswire experiments comes from the CIA World Factbook, a structured textual document with information about the various countries of the world. To make it possible for FACT to use this knowledge we had to develop a tool that parses the Factbook's well-structured text and converts it into the format used by FACT.

One of the difficulties faced in the conversion of the CIA World Factbook into unary and binary predicates was the fact that the vocabulary of the Factbook and of the keywords labeling documents don't always match. For example, in many of the articles mentioning Oman we have as a keyword the word "crude". However, in the CIA world factbook when describing the Export Commodities of Oman, we have fish, petroleum, copper, and textiles. Clearly, if a user poses a query for associations between Oman and topics that are not in its Export Commodities, an association between Oman and crude will be returned, since crude is not mentioned in the Export Commodities of Oman. For this reason FACT supports an additional source of background knowledge, a dictionary that defines synonyms between the unary and binary predicates defined in the first source of background knowledge discussed above and the keywords labeling documents. Figure 9.2 shows the utility that allows a user to pick a word defined by the background knowledge (in this case, predicates extracted from the CIA World Factbook), and then select a list of keywords that are its synonyms. When a user subsequent defines a query using background predicates, FACT is able to relate the predicates to the keyword vocabulary labeling documents. (And although the definition of synonyms could potentially be aided by the use of thesauri, we have not explored that yet in this work.)

Finally, the center input is the user's specification of a knowledge-discovery task, which is acquired from the user via a simple graphical user interface. The interface knows about the various keywords that can label a document, as well as the various unary and binary predicates defined by the background knowledge that can be applied to these keywords, and allows the user to specify a query using this keyword and predicate vocabulary via a collection of menus. The user specifies the knowledge-discovery query via building blocks that are represented as listboxes and radio-buttons. Figure 9.3 gives an example of a query specified via the graphical user interface for the Reuters data discussed in Section 9.7. In this query we asked for associations that have a support of at least five documents (support set threshold) and with probabilistic accuracy of at least 10% (confidence threshold).

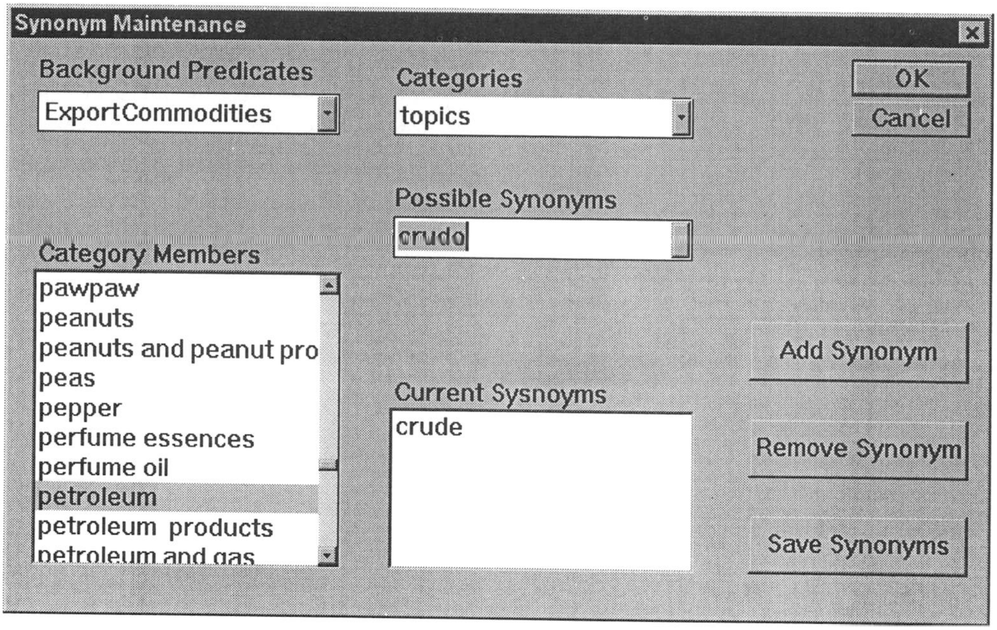

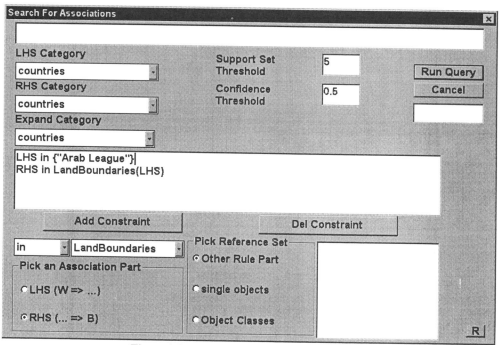

Figure 9.2 — Synonym definition utility.

Figure 9.3 — The Query specification front-end.

These three sources of information — a text collection, background knowledge, and a knowledge-discovery query — are the inputs to FACT to be used by its query execution code, depicted in the center of the figure. The results of this discovery process are then passed on to a tool, shown at the bottom of the figure, that can effectively present the results and allow the user to browse them. This component of FACT filters out redundant results (Feldman *et al.*, 1996), organizes them hierarchically, identifies commonalties amongst them, sorts results in decreasing order of confidence, and enables the user to access and browse those documents that support each of the individual results that it presents to the user. Figure 9.4 shows the association browser on the results of the query shown in Figure 9.3. Finally, the user can point on any of the associations generated by the system (such as those shown in Figure 9.4) and by double-clicking on the associations the system will provide the titles of all documents that support that association. Figure 9.5, for example, shows the titles of the documents that support the association Iraq $\Rightarrow$ Iran (i.e., all the documents that are annotated with the keywords Iraq and Iran.

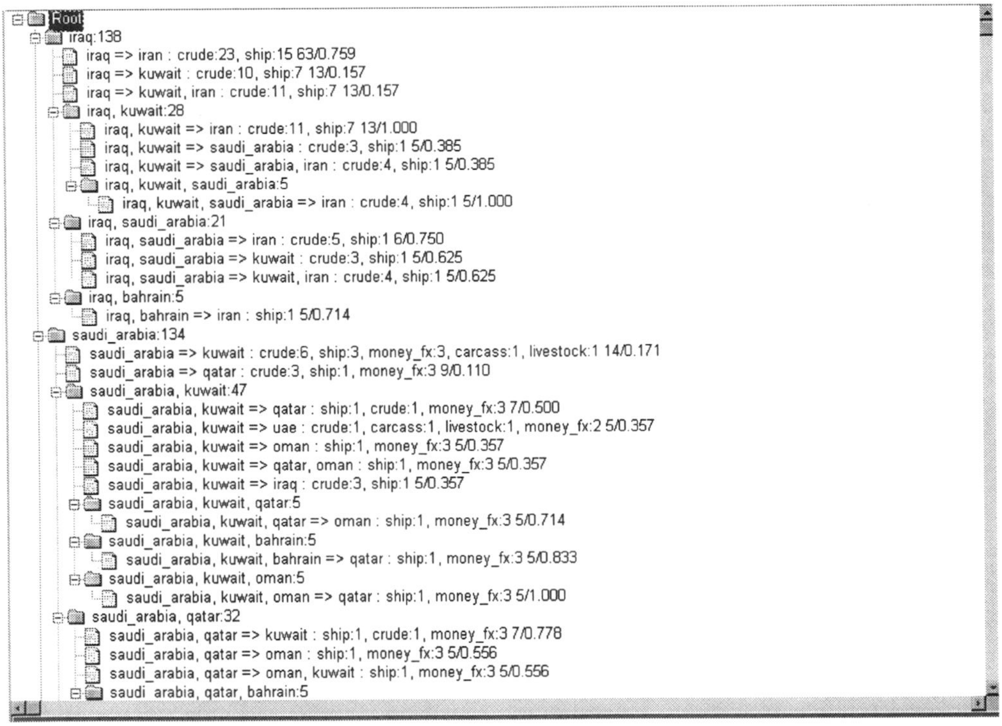

Figure 9.4 — The association browser showing association of Arab League countries with countries sharing a land boundary.

9.3 ASSOCIATIONS

FACT focuses specifically on the task of finding association in collections of text. We begin by presenting the definition of associations, based on Agrawal *et al.*, (1993, 1995) and Mannila *et al.*, (1994), as well as additional definitions and notation that will be useful for the remainder of the chapter.

Let $r = \{t_1,...,t_n\}$ be a collection of documents, each labeled with some subset of keywords from the m-keyword set $R = \{I_1, I_2,...,I_m\}$. Given a keyword A and document t, we write $t(A) = 1$ to represent the fact that A is one of the keywords labeling t, and $t(A) = 0$ otherwise. If W is a subset of the keywords in R, we use the notation $t(W) = 1$ to represent the case that $t(A) = 1$ for every keyword $A \in W$. Given a set X of keywords from R, define $(X) = \{i \mid t_i(X) = 1\}$ — (X) is the set of all documents t_i that are labeled (at least) with all the keywords in X. Given some number σ, X is called a σ-covering if $|(X)| \geq \sigma$.

We say that $W \Rightarrow B$ is an association rule over r if $W \subseteq R$ and $B \subseteq R\backslash W$. We refer to W as the left-hand side (LHS) of the association, and B as the right-hand side (RHS) of the association. We say that r satisfies $W \Rightarrow B$ with respect to $0 < \gamma \leq 1$ (the confidence threshold) and σ (the support threshold) if $W \cup B$ is a σ-covering (i.e., $|(W \cup B)| \geq \sigma$) and $|(W \cup B)|/|(W)| \geq \gamma$. Intuitively, this says that of all documents that are labeled with the keywords in W, at least a proportion γ of them are also labeled with the keywords in B, and further, this rule is based on at least σ documents that are labeled with all the keywords in both W and B.

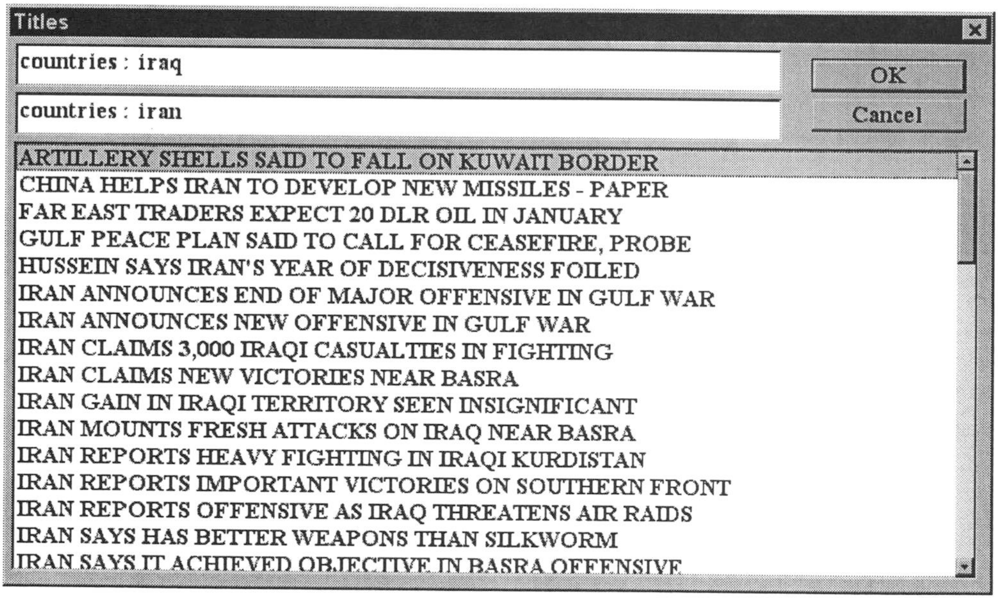

Figure 9.5 — The titles of all documents which are annotated with the keywords Iran and Iraq.

9.4 THE QUERY LANGUAGE

To execute an association-discovery task a user specifies a query in FACT's association query language – the association-discovery process should only return results that satisfy the query (much as Klemettinen *et al.*, (1994) filter out associations that do not match a user-specified template).

Each association-discovery query has three parts. The first part specifies what types of keywords are desired in the left-hand and right-hand sides of any found associations, as well as what support and confidence the association should have. Thus, for example, a user can express an interest in associations that relate a set of countries labeling a document to a person also labeling the document, as long as the association has sufficient support and confidence in the collection.

The second (possibly empty) part of a query specifies constraints – in terms of the predicates defined by the background knowledge – that the user wants any found association to satisfy. There are two types of background knowledge that can be used in queries. The first are unary predicates over keywords. In specifying a query, each unary predicate is viewed as a class of keywords, specifying the set of keywords for which it is true. Thus, for example, the unary predicate EC that is true if a keyword is the name of a country that is a member of the European Community is viewed as a class whose members are those keywords that are European-Community countries. A user can request that a unary predicate be true of some keyword in an association by specifying that the keyword be a member of the class defined by the unary predicate.

The second type of background knowledge that can be used in queries are binary predicates, which define relationships between keywords. Thus, for example, the background knowledge might define the binary predicate Nationality, which is true whenever the first argument is the name of some person whose nationality is the country appearing as the second argument of the predicate. For the query language each binary predicate is viewed as a function: given the value of the first argument, it returns the set of values for the second argument that would make the predicate true. The predicate Nationality, for example, would be viewed as a function that takes a person's name as input and returns the country that is that person's nationality; the predicate ExportCommodity becomes a function that takes a country keyword as input and outputs the keywords representing that country's export commodities. Further, whenever a function is applied to a set of keywords, the function returns all second arguments that make the predicate true for any element in the input set of keywords. A user can request that a binary predicate be true of some keywords in an association by specifying that one keyword be amongst the values returned by the function when it is applied to some other keyword in the association.

Finally, the third (also possibly empty) part of a query specifies constraints on the size of the various components of the association. Thus, for example, a user can request associations that have only one keyword on their right-hand side, or that mention at most five country keywords.

Figure 9.6 gives a BNF grammar of our association-discovery query language, where nonterminals are written in angle brackets, the nonterminal "<integer>" represents an integer, "(0,1)" represents the set of reals between 0 (noninclusive) and 1 (inclusive), and

"<CategoryType>" is defined as appropriate for a given domain, dividing the keywords labeling the documents into subclasses (such as "country", "person", etc., in the Reuters newswire data). The use of the "*" operator represents zero or more copies of the nonterminal preceding it; the "+" token is a terminal within the language (which says that a variable is set-valued, taking on one or more keywords of the category type preceding it). Finally, any expansion for "<Arg>" to "<Var>" must be a variable that was previously defined in "<Pattern>" for that query (i.e., this is a context-sensitive portion of the language that cannot be represented in BNF).

<Query> ::= *Find* (<support>/<confidence>) <Pattern>
        Where: <BackgroundConstraint>*
                <KeywordConstraint>*

<support> ::= <integer>
<confidence> ::= (0,1)
<Pattern> ::= <VarList> $\Rightarrow$ <VarList>
<VarList> ::= <VarExp> | <VarExp>, <VarList>
<VarExp> ::= <Var> : <TypeExp>
<TypeExp> ::= <CategoryType> | <CategoryType>+

<BackgroundConstraint> ::= <Arg> <Operator> <Arg>
<Operator> ::= $\in$ | $\notin$ | $\subseteq$ | $\not\subseteq$ | = | $\neq$
<Arg> ::= <Var> | <Keyword> | <Class> | <BgExpression> | LHS | RHS | All
<BgExpression> ::= <BackgroundFunction>(<Arglist>)
<Arglist> ::= <Arg> | <Arg>,<Arglist>

<KeywordConstraint> ::= <#Exp> <CompOperator> <#Exp>
<#Exp> ::= <numeric constant> | #(<category>) | #(LHS) | #(RHS) | #(All)

<CompOperator> ::= > | $\geq$ | < | $\leq$ | = | $\neq$

Figure 9.6 — BNF grammar of the query language of FACT.

We conclude this section with some examples of queries in this language, together with their English meanings.

    Find: (5/0.5) c1:country, c2:country $\Rightarrow$ t:topic
    Where: c1 $\in$ G7, c2 $\in$ {Arab League}, t $\notin$ ExportCommodities(c1).

This query requests associations where, at least half the time, whenever a G7 country and an Arab League country label a document, the document is labeled by some topic that is not an export commodity of the G7 country, and this occurs at least 5 times in the collection.

    Find: (10/0.2) c:country+ $\Rightarrow$ p:person

Where: Nationality(p) $\not\subset$ c, #(LHS) $\leq$ 3.

This query requests associations where, at least 20% of the time, whenever some set of at most three countries labels a document it is also labeled with some person whose nationality is not one of those countries, and this occurs at least 10 times in the collection.

> *Find:* (10/0.8) c1:country+ $\Rightarrow$ c2:country+
> *Where:* c1 $\subseteq$ {Arab League}, c2 $\subseteq$ LandBoundaries(c1), #(RHS) $\leq$ 2, #(country) $\leq$ 5.

This query requests associations where, at least 80% of the time, whenever some set of Arab-League countries labels a document, one or two other countries – each of which borders one of the Arab-League countries in the right-hand side of the association – also label the document, as long as this is true for at least 10 cases, and as long as the total number of countries mentioned in the association does not exceed five.

9.5 QUERY EXECUTION

Our algorithms for executing association-discovery queries in the presence of background knowledge are based on those described by Agrawal and Srikant (1994) and Mannila *et al.,* (1994). The basic approach is first to find all σ-covers X and then find subsets B $\subseteq$ X for which X\B $\Rightarrow$ B holds with confidence γ. The algorithm exploits the observation that every subset of a σ-cover is a σ-cover, and hence a set is a σ-cover only if all its subsets are σ-covers.

The set of candidate σ-covers is built incrementally, starting from singleton σ-covers and adding elements to a set so long as the set stays a σ-cover – a new set will be added to the set of candidate σ-covers only if all its subsets are included in the candidate set. The general algorithm for finding σ covers is given in Figure 9.7.

Note that, in contrast to the previously mentioned algorithms, this algorithm only checks whether sets have the necessary support after all candidates are generated, since database lookup is the most time-consuming step and in this way it is performed only once per tuple. Further, to improve efficiency further, we actually do not begin with all singleton sets as described in the figure, but rather start with the collection of all s-covers of size two, obtainable as the result of a pre-computation of keyword pairs on the documents in the collection (Feldman and Dagan, 1995), filter out candidates with insufficient support, and continue with the algorithm from there. This has the effect of starting up the algorithm as if it had already gone through the loop once to create Cand2 with those candidates with insufficient support removed. Empirically, these two ideas considerably reduce the needed computation time.

```
Cand₁ = {{A}| (A) ≥ σ}
i = 1
While Cand₁ ≠ ∅ do
          Cand_{i+1} = {S1 ∪ S2 | S1 ,S2 ∈ Cand₁, |S1 ∪ S2| = i + 1,
                         All subsets of S1 ∪ S2 are in Cand₁}
          i=i+1
     end do
Evaluate ⋃ Cand_i
         i
```

Figure 9.7 — The basic algorithm for finding σ-covers.

Once a collection of all σ covers has been found, the traditional association-discovery process attempts to find all subsets B for each σ-cover X for which X\B ⇒ B hold with the desired confidence γ. The straight-forward way to extend this algorithm to handle the "where" constraints in a query is first to use the algorithm to find all associations, ignoring the constraints, and only then remove those associations that do not satisfy the constraints. However, to limit the search to those associations satisfying the constraints we use the σ-cover algorithm in a different way, so as to use the constraints to reduce the search space and make the association-generation process more efficient.

To do this, we divide the constraints on possible associations into two classes. The first class contains those "simple" constraints that refer to only one side of the association, such as LHS ⊆ Arab League, or Iran ∈ RHS, as well as those constraints that require some property to hold on the whole association, such as #(All) < 5. The second class contains those "complex" constraints that require some relationship to hold between elements of the two sides of the association, such as RHS ⊆ LandBoundaries(LHS). We use both classes of constraints to reduce the space of possible σ-covers that must be considered.

As an example of how the first class of constraints can reduce the search space, consider the constraint LHS ⊆ Arab League. Rather than looking for σ-covers involving every possible country, only those that include Arab-league countries need be considered. This can reduce considerably the number of potential σ-covers.

The second class of constraints can also reduce the search space, only in a more subtle fashion. For example, consider the constraint, RHS ⊆ LandBoundaries(LHS). This constraint can only be evaluated once we know the exact value of the LHS of the association. However, in some cases knowing some constraint on the possible values of LHS can reduce the number of possibilities for RHS. For example, if this constraint were also specified with a constraint on LHS, such as LHS ⊆ G7, the constraint RHS ⊆ LandBoundaries(LHS) would be equivalent to RHS ⊆ LandBoundaries(G7). These sorts of constraints can be discovered before the σ-cover search begins, reducing further the search space.

Of course, in some cases there will not be any constraints on the LHS of the association and thus no such reduction will be possible. To handle this case we use the σ-cover algorithm in a slightly different fashion, to generate possible sets of keywords for the left-hand side of the association, and only then attempt to extend them to complete associations. By having the potential left-hand side completely specified, it becomes possible to filter out possible keywords for the right-hand side using constraints from the second class of constraints.

Figure 9.8 gives an outline of this algorithm for finding associations in the presence of such constraints. It takes as input the collection of documents, Ds; $K(D)$ is used to refer to the collection of keywords labeling document D. The algorithm finds all possible LHS candidates, only searching through those that satisfy the simple constraints on the LHS. For each such result the algorithm considers which other keywords could appear as the RHS of the association, constrained according to whatever additional constraints are present. At the end of the process it determines which associations satisfy the support and confidence from those that were created satisfying the given constraints. Note that, although the algorithm maintains counters for all subsets of each set B it generates, empirically we find that B is quite small after satisfying all constraints.

```
Use the σ-cover algorithm to create Ls, the set of all left-hand
sides   that   could   satisfy   the   association-discovery   query,
constrained to only consider those keywords satisfying the simple
constraints on the LHS.
For all D ∈ Ds
        For all X ∈ Ls do
               if X ⊆ K(D) then
                          B = The keywords in K(D)\X  that satisfy the
                          constraints on RHS (either simple constraints or
                          composite constraints) and that appear with the
                          required support.
                          Update  co-occurrence  counters  for  X  and  all
                          subsets of B
               end if
        end do
end do

Form associations based on the accumulated co-occurrence counters.
Remove those associations that do not satisfy the required support
and confidence.
```

Figure 9.8 — Query evaluation algorithm.

9.6 PRESENTATION OF ASSOCIATIONS

Even when data are moderately sized, association-finding methods will often generate substantial numbers of results. The problem for an association-discovery tool is to help a user identify the interesting results out of all those it generates. FACT's approach to this problem is to provide a browsing tool that helps the user easily focus on the subset of results that are potentially relevant.

The key idea underlying this association-browsing tool is to cluster together associations with identical left-hand sides, and to display the clusters in decreasing order of the generality of their left-hand side. Associations that have more general left-hand side will be listed before more specific associations. The top-level nodes in the hierarchical tree are sorted in decreasing order of the number of documents that support all associations in which they appear.

For example, Figure 9.4 depicts the presentation of results for the query shown in Figure 9.3. Iraq appeared in these associations more than any other country and hence it is listed first in the tree. Next all associations that include only Iraq on their left-hand side are presented, then we see a node for Iraq and Kuwait that lists all associations that contain only Iraq and Kuwait on their left-hand side, and finally this chain is ended in the associations that contain Iraq and Kuwait and Saudi Arabia on their left-hand side. After this chain was completed, a new branch of Iraq is starting, Iraq and Saudi Arabia. Every association appears only once in this hierarchical structure. Each terminal-node entry in this hierarchy also presents the support and confidence for the found association, as well as a list of keywords that appear frequently amongst the documents satisfying the antecedent and consequent of the association.

9.7 APPLYING FACT TO NEWSWIRE DATA

To investigate the use of FACT to find associations in text we used it on the Reuters newswire data often used in research in Information Retrieval. It has the advantage of being a well-investigated collection of textual documents, and importantly for this work, it was not necessary to use text categorization on the collection since it already comes with a set of keywords labeling the various documents. More specifically, we used the Reuters-22173 text categorization test collection, a collection of documents that appeared on the Reuters newswire in 1987. The 22173 documents were assembled and indexed with categories by personnel from Reuters Ltd. and Carnegie Group, Inc. in 1987, and further formatting and data file production was done in 1991 and 1992 by David D. Lewis and Peter Shoemaker. Each document was tagged by the Reuters personnel with a subset of 135 keywords that fell into five categories: countries, topics, people, organizations and stock exchanges.

Our goal is not just the discovery of associations in text, but doing so in the presence of background knowledge of the domain. To investigate the role of background knowledge in association discovery for the Reuters-22173 collection we used background knowledge extracted from the 1995 CIA World FactBook, a structured textual document containing information about each of the countries in the world. The information about each country is divided to 6 sections: Geography, People, Government, Economy, Communications, and Defense Forces. For our experiments with the Reuters-22173 data we extracted the following background information about each country C:

- **MemberOf:** all organizations of which C is a member (e.g., G7, Arab League, EC)
- **Land Boundaries:** the countries that have a land border with C
- **Natural Resources:** the natural resources of C (e.g., crude, coal, copper, gold)
- **ExportCommodities:** the main commodities exported by C (e.g., meat, wool, wheat)

- **Export Partners:** the principal countries to whom C exports its ExportCommodities
- **Import Commodities:** the main commodities imported by C (e.g., meat, wool, wheat)
- **Import Partners:** the principal countries from which C imports its Import Commodities
- **Industries:** the main industries of C (e.g., iron, steel, machines, textiles, chemicals)
- **Agriculture:** the main agriculture products of C (e.g., grains, fruit, potatoes, cattle)

The first defines a unary predicate and the rest binary predicates over the set of keywords that can label the documents in the Reuters-22173 collection. Figure 9.9 shows a portion of this background knowledge, using a utility that is part of FACT that enables a user to browse the background knowledge given to the system.

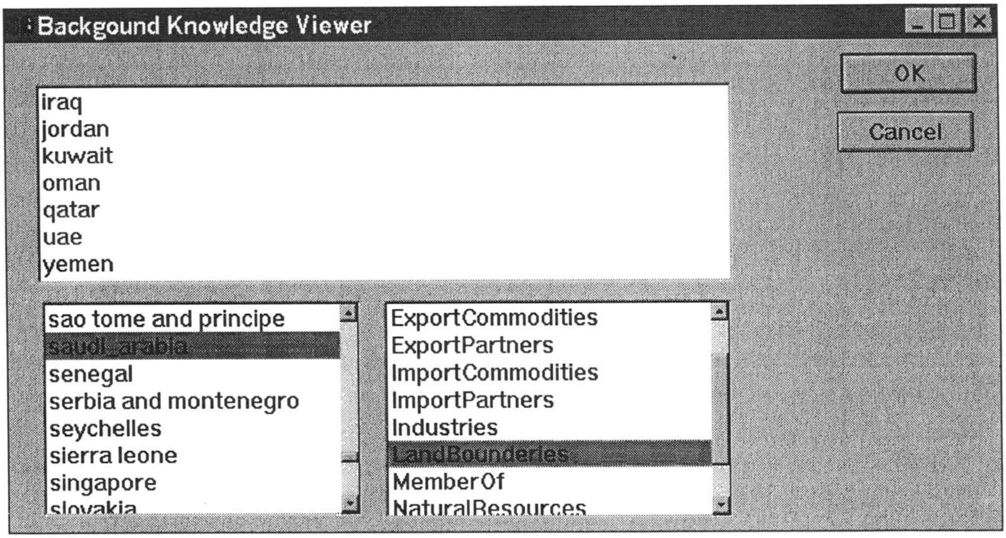

Figure 9.9 — The background knowledge viewer showing the countries with land boundaries with Saudi Arabia.

Figure 9.3 gave an example of a user query on the Reuters data using this background knowledge, specified using FACT's graphical user interface. In the Edit Control located at the top of the screen the user can see the accumulated query (converted into "pseudo-English") and can change it by directly editing the query. Figure 9.4 showed the associations that were found by FACT in response to this query in FACT's association browser.

As a further example, given a query to find all associations between a set of countries including Iran and any person, FACT returns the results

$$\{Iran, Nicaragua, USA\} \Rightarrow Reagan\ 6/1.000$$
$$\{Iran, USA\} \Rightarrow Reagan\ 18/0.692$$

The first association – which has a confidence of 100% – makes sense given that the Reuters data spans the period of time in which the "Irangate" affair took place. The documents that support this association talk about the testimony given by Ronald Reagan in the Senate.

The query to find all associations between a set of topics including Gold and any country yields the results

{gold, copper} ⇒ Canada 5/0.625
{gold, silver} ⇒ USA 12/0.571
{gold , gbond} ⇒ Switzerland 5/1.0
{gold, gbond} ⇒ Belgium 5/1.0

In this case we can see that there was no single country that was highly associated with gold, although adding more conditions to the left-hand side allowed FACT to find 4 associations. For example, in documents that are annotated with "gold" and "gbond" we will always find both Switzerland and Belgium.

As a crude measure of the efficiency of our algorithms, we ran a series of queries using FACT and compared the CPU time (on a 486/50) and the number of associations found for each query. Each query was created by instantiating one of two query templates. The first template (T1) includes a background-knowledge constraint that requires the right-hand side of any found association to be in the LandBoundaries of the left-hand side:

T1 *Find:* (5/0.1) c1:country+ ⇒ c2:country+
***Where:* c1 ⊆ CountryGroup, c2 ⊆ LandBoundaries(c1).**

To generate a query **CountryGroup** is replaced in this template by some country organizations defined in the background knowledge. The second query is generated in the same way from an identical template (T2), only without the LandBoundaries constraint:

T2 *Find:* (5/0.1) c1:country+ ⇒ c2:country+
***Where:* c1 ⊆ CountryGroup.**

Figure 9.10 shows a graph giving the CPU time it took FACT to evaluate each of the queries for all country organizations. Figure 9.11 gives a graph that shows for each country organization the number of associations produced for that query. (Organizations listed on the X axis are ordered identically for both graphs, according to the number of associations generated for its instantiation of template T2.) These results show that, rather than slowing down the association-discovery process, the specification of background-knowledge constraints actually provides information that is exploited by our discovery algorithms, speeding up the association-discovery process. Similar results were obtained with many other query templates that used other background knowledge predicates.

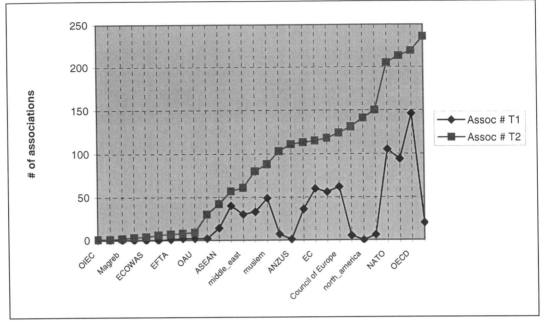

Figure 9.10 — # of associations for two sets of queries.

9.8 FINAL REMARKS

This chapter has described the FACT system for knowledge discovery in collections of text. It is specifically designed for the problem of finding associations between the various keywords labeling documents, and is able to utilize information about the keywords in this association-discovery process.

The system takes a query-centered perspective on the discovery process, in which the data are viewed as specifying an implicit collection of possible results supported by the data, and in which the user mines the data via queries over this implicit collection of results. It thus sits at a midpoint between discovery tools that do little more than database queries ("Find me all employees that make more than their bosses") and ill-defined discovery tools with ill-defined goals ("Find me something interesting"). Moreover, rather than forcing the user to specify queries in some arcane query language, FACT presents the user with an easy-to-use graphical interface in which discovery tasks can be specified.

FACT also sits at a convenient midpoint between interactive analysis tools in which the user bears all the responsibility for proposing possible interesting patterns in the data, and autonomous machine learning tools that can exploit no information from the user about the goals of the discovery process. Here, instead, the user specifies the general parameters for the discovery process, leaving it to the FACT system to discovery any interesting patterns that satisfy the user's general goal for the discovery process.

Although FACT was developed to find associations in collections of text, very little precludes its application to structured data as well. The keywords labeling textual articles can be viewed as binary attributes describing objects, and as such FACT is finding associations amongst the various attributes of each object. In future work we plan to extend the FACT system to apply to structured databases, to find associations amongst the attributes labeling objects in the database, thereby developing a tool for finding associations in data in the presence of background knowledge, as well as investigating the merit of a FACT-like query-based graphical tool for knowledge discovery in databases.

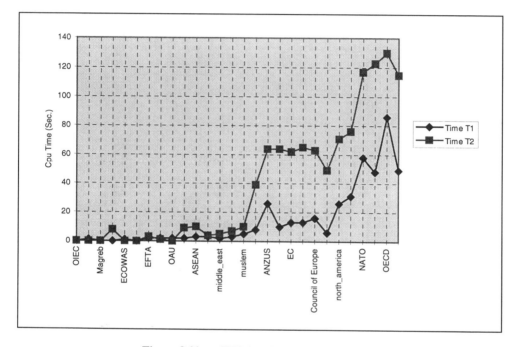

Figure 9.11 — CPU time for two sets of queries.

ACKNOWLEDGEMENTS

This research was supported by NSF grant IRI-9509819 and by grant 8615-1-96 from the Israeli Ministry of Sciences.

The authors would like to thank Ido Dagan, Tomasz Imielinski, and Willi Kloesgen for helpful discussions and comments given on drafts of this paper. Amir Zilberstien wrote the Perl program for converting the CIA World Fact Book into a set of Prolog facts.

REFERENCES

Agrawal R., Mannila H., Srikant R., Toivonen H., and Verkamo I. (1995). Fast Discovery of Association Rules. In *Advances in Knowledge Discovery and Data Mining*, Eds. U. Fayyad, G. Piatetsky-Shapiro, P. Smyth, and R. Uthurusamy, pages 307–328, AAAI Press.

Agrawal A., and Srikant R. (1994) Fast algorithms for mining association rules. In *Proceedings of the VLDB Conference*, Santiago, Chile.

Agrawal A., Imielinski T., and Swami A. (1993). Mining association rules between sets of items in large databases. In *Proc. of the ACM SIGMOD Conference on Management of Data*, pages 207–216.

Apte C., Damerau F., and Weiss S. (1994). Towards language independent automated learning of text categorization models. In *Proceedings of ACM-SIGIR Conference on Information Retrieval*.

Dagan I., Feldman R., and Hirsh H. (1996). Keyword-Based Browsing and Analysis of Large Document Sets. In *Proceedings of the 4th Symposium on Document Analysis and Information Retrieval*, Las Vegas, Nevada.

Feldman R. (1996). The KDT System – Using Prolog for KDD, In *Proceedings of the 4th Conference on Practical Applications of Prolog*, London, April 1996.

Feldman R., Dagan I., and Kloesgen W. (1996) Efficient Algorithms for Mining and Manipulating Associations in Texts. In *Proceedings of the 13th European Meeting on Cybernetics and Research,* Vienna, Austria.

Feldman R. and Dagan I. (1995). KDT – knowledge discovery in texts. In *Proceedings of the First International Conference on Knowledge Discovery (KDD-95).*

Frakes W. B. and Baeza-Yates. R. (1992). *Information Retrieval: Data Structures and Algorithms*. Prentice Hall, Englewood Cliffs, NJ.

Imielinski T., Virmani A., and Abdulghani A. (1996). DataMine: Application Programming Interface and Query Language for Database Mining. In *Proceedings of the Second International Conference on Knowledge Discovery (KDD-96).*

Iwayama M. and Tokunaga T. (1994). A probabilistic model for text categorization based on a single random variable with multiple values. In *Proceedings of the 4th Conference on Applied Natural Language Processing*.

Klemettinen M., Mannila H., Ronkainen P., Toivonen H., and Verkamo A. (1994). Finding Interesting Rules from Large Sets of Discovered Association Rules. *In Proceedings of the 3rd International conference on Information and Knowledge Management.*

Mannila H., Toivonen H., and Verkamo A. (1994). Efficient Algorithms for Discovering association rules. In *KDD-94: AAAI workshop on Knowledge Discovery in Databases*, pages 181–192.

Salton G. and McGill. M. J. (1983). *Introduction to Modern Information Retrieval*. McGraw-Hill, New York.

10

Learning Patterns in Images

Ryszard S. Michalski, Azriel Rosenfeld, Zoran Duric, Marcus Maloof
and Qi Zhang

ABSTRACT

This chapter concerns problems of learning patterns in images and image sequences, and using the obtained patterns for interpreting new images. The chapter concentrates on three problem areas: (i) semantic interpretation of color images of outdoor scenes, (ii) detection of blasting caps in x-ray images of luggage,
and (iii) recognizing actions in video image sequences. It discusses the image formation processes in these problem areas, and the choices of representation spaces
used in our approaches to solving these problems. The results presented indicate
the advantages of applying machine learning to vision.

10.1 INTRODUCTION

The underlying motivation of this research is that vision systems need learning capabilities for handling problems for which algorithmic solutions are unknown or difficult
to obtain. Learning capabilities can also make vision systems more easily adaptable to
different vision problems, and more flexible and robust in handling variable perceptual
conditions [MRA94].

Much of the current research on learning in vision systems has concentrated on neural network applications — for example, road navigation [Pom91] and object detection and recognition in various types of images (visible, SAR, etc.) [FeB96, RBP96,
RBK96]. Advantages of these methods include their generality and their ability to

Machine Learning and Data Mining: Methods and Applications
Edited by R.S. Michalski, I Bratko and M. Kubat
© 1997 John Wiley & Sons Ltd

learn continuous transformations. Disadvantages include the difficulty of incorporating prior knowledge (especially relational knowledge), the difficulty of learning complex structural knowledge, slow learning rates, and lack of comprehensibility of the learned knowledge [MRA94].

While symbolic learning methods suffer much less from these problems, they have been applied mostly in areas other than computer vision. In computer vision, they may be particularly useful for new feature generation, learning visual surface descriptions like textures, learning complex shape descriptions, acquisition of structural or relational models of objects, construction and updating of model databases, scene segmentation, learning the "context" in which an algorithm can be successfully applied, and so forth [GrP96, MDMR96, MRADMZ96, StF95]. Applications of symbolic approaches to vision problems remain an insufficiently explored but potentially fruitful domain of research.

Multistrategy learning systems combine different representations and/or different learning algorithms. One particular multistrategy system combines neural network and symbolic learning. This method induces rules which are used to structure a neural network architecture. A secondary learning step refines the network's weights. This method provides generality and very fast recognition rates [BMP94, MZMB96]. One can also use neural networks for lower-level vision processes and symbolic methods for higher-level visual processes. These methods are potentially very powerful and promising directions of research.

We have been studying the application of symbolic, neural net and multistrategy learning methods to such problems as interpreting outdoor scenes, recognizing objects in cluttered environments, and recognizing actions in video image sequences. The following sections summarize specific results obtained on a project on "Computer vision through learning" being conducted jointly by George Mason University and the University of Maryland [MRADMZ96].

In Section 10.2 we review previous work on machine learning in computer vision. In Section 10.3 we address the problem of conceptually segmenting color images of outdoor scenes. For this purpose we use the Multi-level Image Sampling and Transformation (MIST) methodology; a detailed description of this methodology can be found in [MZMB96]. In Section 10.4 we address the problem of detecting blasting caps in x-ray images of luggage; the details can be found in [MaM96, MDMR96]. Finally, in Section 10.5 we address the problem of recognizing a function of an object from its motion; the technical details can be found in [DFR96, DRR96].

10.2 PREVIOUS WORK ON MACHINE LEARNING IN COMPUTER VISION

Michalski [Mic72, Mic73] examined how symbolic AQ rule learning could be used for discrimination between textures or between simple structures. These seminal papers presented the Multi-Level Logical Template (MLT) methodology in which windowing operators scanned an image and extracted local features. These features were used to learn rules describing textures (or simple structures); the rules were then used for texture (or simple structure) recognition.

Shepherd [She83], encoding examples as feature vectors, learned decision trees for an industrial inspection task — specifically, classification of the shapes of chocolates. Comparisons of classification accuracy were made between decision tree, k-nearest neighbor (k-nn), and minimum distance classifiers. Experimental results for these classifiers were similar, with the minimum distance classifier producing the highest accuracy, 82%.

Channic [Cha89] extended the MLT methodology [Mic72, Mic73] by using convolution operators in conjunction with the original set of windowing operators for feature extraction. Using the AQ learning system, Channic investigated incremental learning and iterative learning from sequences of images using ultrasound images of laminated objects.

Instead of representing examples using feature vectors, Connell and Brady [CoB87] learned generalized semantic networks from images of classes of hammers and of overhead views of commercial aircraft. Training examples were generated by a vision system that took gray scale images as input and produced semantic networks for the objects. A learning system, which was a modified version of Winston's [Win84] ANALOGY program, learned by generalizing the training examples. The learning system was extended to learn disjunctive concepts and to learn from only positive examples. These generalized representations were used to classify unknown objects.

Cromwell and Kak [CrK91] proceeded as Shepherd did, using feature vectors to characterize shapes. Electrical component shapes were learned using a symbolic induction methodology based on that developed by Michalski [Mic80]. They reported that their method achieved 72% on testing data, but no comparisons were made to other learning methods.

Pachowicz and Bala [PaB91] also used the MLT methodology, following Michalski [Mic72, Mic73] and Channic [Cha89], but added a modified set of Laws' masks for texture feature extraction. They also applied techniques for handling noise in symbolic data. These techniques included optimizing learned symbolic descriptions by truncating rules [MMHL86], as well as removing training examples covered by weak rules and re-learning. The PRAX method for learning a large number of classes was introduced by Bala, Michalski, and Wnek [BMW92, BMW93].

Segen [Seg94] used a hybrid shape representation consisting of a hierarchical graph that takes into account local features of high curvature, and the angles and distances between these local features. This representation is invariant to both planar rotation and translation. Shapes were silhouettes of hand gestures. Segen's system runs in real time and has been applied to airplane simulator control as well as to control of a graphics editor program. Error rates were between 5% and 10%, but most errors were unknowns rather than misclassifications.

Cho and Dunn [ChD94] described a new learning algorithm for learning shape. This algorithm memorizes property lists and updates associated weights as training proceeds. Forgetting mechanisms remove useless property lists. Shapes are modeled by a series of line segments. Using the orientations of these segments, local spatial measures are computed and form a property list for a shape. The system was used to classify tools and hand gestures and achieved predictive accuracies of 92% and 96% on these problems.

Dutta and Bhanu [DuB94] presented a 3D CAD-based recognition system in which genetic algorithms are used to optimize segmentation parameters. Qualitative experimental results were presented for indoor and outdoor motion sequences in which the system recognized images of wedges (traffic cones) and cans from gray scale and depth map images.

Sung and Poggio [SuP94] worked on automatic human face detection. An example-based learning approach was tested for locating unoccluded frontal views of human faces in complex scenes. The space of human faces was represented by a few "face" and "non-face" pattern prototypes. At each image location, a two-valued distance measure was computed between the local image pattern and each prototype. A trained classifier was used to determine whether a human face is present. The authors showed that their distance metric is critical for the success of their system.

Zheng and Bhanu [ZhB96] examined how Hebbian learning mechanisms could be used to improve the performance of an image thresholding algorithm for automatic target detection and recognition. Qualitative results were presented in which the adaptive thresholding algorithm was shown to be superior to the classical thresholding algorithm for both SAR and FLIR images.

Rowley *et al.* [RBK96] built a neural network-based face detection system by using a retinally connected neural network to examine small windows of an image and decide on the existence of a face. A bootstrap algorithm was implemented during training so as to add false detection into the training set and as a consequence, eliminate the difficult task of manually selecting non-face training examples. Experimental results showed better performance in terms of detection and false-positive rates.

Romano *et al.* [RBP96] built a real-time system for face verification. Experiments showed that simple correlation strategies on template-based models are sufficient for many applications in which the identity of a face in a novel image must be verified quickly and reliably from a single reference image. The authors suggested that this automatic real-time face verification technique could be put to use in such human-machine interface applications as automated security systems. The technique has been integrated into a screen locking application which permits access to workstations by performing face verification in lieu of password authentication.

The MLT methodology [Mic72, Mic73] has recently been extended into the Multi-Level Image Sampling and Transformation (MIST) methodology. MIST has been applied to a variety of problems including natural scene segmentation [MZMB96] and identification of blasting caps in x-ray images [MDMR96]. For classifying natural scenes, three learning techniques were compared: AQ15c [WKBM95], a backpropagation neural network [Zur92], and AQ-NN [BMP94].

AQ-NN is a multistrategy learning technique in that it uses two different representations and two different learning strategies. Specifically, the AQ learning algorithm is used to learn attributional decision rules from training examples. These decision rules are then used to structure a neural network architecture. A backpropagation algorithm is then used as a learning step to further optimize the AQ induced descriptions. In such a system, learning times and recognition rates are often significantly decreased, while predictive accuracy is improved, with respect to conventional neural network learning. To learn classes such as ground, grass, trees and sky, hue, intensity, and convolution operators are used to extract features from a user-designated training area. These examples are then presented to the learning system, which induces a class description. AQ15c, used alone, achieved a predictive accuracy of 94%, while AQ-NN and a standard neural network achieved predictive accuracies near 100%. The training time of AQ-NN was approximately two orders of magnitude shorter than the training time of the standard NN.

10.3   SEMANTIC INTERPRETATION OF COLOR IMAGES OF OUTDOOR SCENES

The MIST methodology (Multi-level Image Sampling and Transformation) provides an environment for applying diverse machine learning methods to problems of computer vision. The methodology is illustrated here in connection with a problem of learning how to semantically interpret natural scenes. In the experiments described here, three learning programs were used: AQ15c for learning decision rules from examples; NN, neural network learning; and AQ-NN, multistrategy learning combining symbolic and neural network methods.

The results presented below illustrate the performance of the learning programs for the chosen problem of natural scene interpretation in terms of predictive accuracy, training time, recognition time, and complexity of the induced descriptions. The MIST methodology has proven to be very useful for this application. Overall, the experiments indicate that the multistrategy learning program AQ-NN appears to be the most promising approach.

This section briefly describes the MIST methodology and illustrates it by an application to natural scene interpretation. As pointed out in [FiS88, StF91], the semantic interpretion of natural scenes and recognition of natural objects is one of the most challenging open vision problems. The MIST methodology offers a new approach to these problems.

10.3.1   The MIST Methodology

The MIST methodology works in two basic modes: *Learning mode* and *Interpretation mode*. In Learning mode, the system builds or updates the Image Knowledge Base (IKB), which contains class descriptions and the background knowledge relevant to image interpretation. A description (or model) of a visual category is developed by inductive inference from examples specified by a trainer. Class descriptions are arranged into procedures defining sequences of image transformation operators.

In Interpretation mode, a learned (or predefined) image transformation procedure is applied to a given image to produce an Annotated Symbolic Image (ASI). In an ASI, areas that correspond to the locations of recognized classes in the original image are marked by symbols (e.g., colors) denoting these classes, and linked to annotations (text containing additional information about the classes, such as degree of certainty

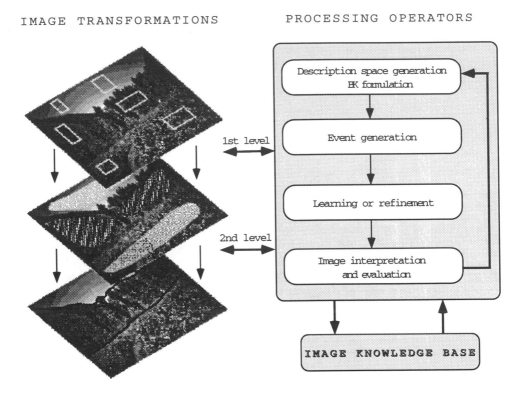

Figure 10.1   The MIST learning mode.

of recognition, properties of the class, relations to other classes, etc.). (Although developed independently, MIST's concept of an ASI is similar to the concept of a class map in the ALISA system [HoB94].) The following paragraphs describe the two modes in greater detail.

10.3.1.1   TRAINING MODE

This mode (see Figure 10.1) is executed in four phases: **LP1**—description space generation and background knowledge formulation; **LP2**—event generation; **LP3**—learning or refinement; and **LP4**—image interpretation and evaluation. These four phases can be repeated iteratively, creating images at different levels.

LP1: *Description space generation and background knowledge formulation*
A trainer assigns class names to areas in the image(s) that contain objects to be learned. These areas are divided into training and testing areas. Objects to be learned are presented in different poses and with different appearances (by changing perceptual conditions) so the system can learn a description that is invariant to class-preserving transformations. The trainer also defines the initial description space, i.e., initial attributes and/or terms to be measured on image samples, and specifies their value sets

(measurement scale) and their types. This phase also involves an optimization of the image volume, that is, a reduction of the image resolution and intensity levels (hue and saturation, in color images) according to the needs of the given problem. The trainer may also define constraints on the description space, initial recognition rules, and possibly forms for expressing the descriptions (e.g., conjunctive rules, DNF, the structure of the neural network, etc.). Procedures for the measurement of attributes/terms are selected from a predefined collection.

LP2: *Event generation*
Using the chosen procedures, the system generates initial training examples ("training events") from each area. The areas are sampled exhaustively or selectively.

LP3: *Learning or refinement*
The system applies a selected machine learning program to the training examples to generate a class description. Currently, we have the following programs available: AQ15c for learning general symbolic rules from examples; NN, neural network learning with backpropagation; and AQ-NN, a system that integrates AQ rule learning with neural network learning.

LP4: *Image interpretation and evaluation*
The developed descriptions are applied to the testing areas to generate an *Annotated Symbolic Image* (ASI). In an ASI, the areas corresponding to given classes are marked by symbols representing these classes (numbers, colors, etc.). These areas are also linked to text that includes additional information about the class descriptions. The quality of the generated descriptions is determined by comparing the ASI with testing areas in the original image. Depending on the results, the system may stop, or may execute a new learning process (iteration), in which the ASI is the input (hence the term "multilevel" in the name of the methodology). If the generated descriptions need no further improvement, the process is terminated. This occurs when the obtained symbolic image is "sufficiently close" to the target image labeling (indicating the "correct" labeling of the image). Complete object descriptions are sequences of image transformations (defined by descriptions obtained at each iteration) that produce the final ASI. Learning errors are computed by comparing the target labeling (made by the trainer) with the learned labeling (produced by the system).

10.3.1.2   INTERPRETATION MODE

In this mode, the system applies descriptions from the Image Knowledge Base to semantically interpret a new image. To do so, the system executes a sequence of operators (defined by the description) that transform the given image into an ASI. A given "pixel" in the ASI is assigned a class on the basis of applying operators to a single event, or to a sample of events, and applying majority voting (typically within a 3×3 window). In ASI, different classes are denoted by different colors and/or textures. The simplest form of annotation used in the ASI is to associate degrees of confidence with the ASI pixels denoting a given class.

Figure 10.2   A typical image of a natural scene used in experiments.

10.3.2   Implementation and Experimental Results

The current MIST methodology has been implemented with the following learning systems:

- Symbolic rule learning program AQ15c [MMHL86, WKBM95].
- Multistrategy learning system AQ-NN combining decision rule learning with neural network learning [BMP94].
- Multistrategy learning system AQ-GA that combines decision rule learning with a genetic algorithm [MBP93].
- Class similarity-based learning for building descriptions of large numbers of classes (PRAX) [BMW92, BMW93].

An earlier version of MIST has been applied to learning descriptions of classes of surfaces [MBP93]. The core part of the descriptions was in the form of decision rules, which were determined by the inductive learning program AQ15 [MMHL86] and represented in the VL_1 logic-style language (Variable-Valued Logic System 1) [Mic73]. Such decision rules can be applied to an image in parallel or sequentially.

A simple version of the MIST methodology was applied to problems of semantically interpreting outdoor scenes using several learning methods. In the experiments, we used a collection of images representing selected mountain scenes around Aspen, Colorado (see Figure 10.2).

The input to the learning process was a training image in which selected examples of the visual classes to be learned had been labeled by a trainer — for example, trees,

Table 10.1 A summary of results from learning to interpret the image in Figure 10.3.2a. Data computed for 161 training events and 150 testing events selected from the 10×10 training area

Learning method	Training time	Recognition time	Accuracy (%)
AQ15c	0.43s	1.000s	94.00
AQ-NN	10.93s	0.016s	99.98
NN	4.38s	0.033s	99.97

sky, ground, road, and grass. We experimented with different sets of attributes defining the description space, images obtained under different perceptual conditions, different sizes of training areas, and different sources of training and testing image samples (from different parts of the same image area, from different areas of the same image, from different images).

In the experiments described here, the description space was defined by such attributes as hue, saturation, intensity, horizontal and vertical gradients, high frequency spots, horizontal and vertical V-shapes, and Laplacian operators. These attributes were computed for the 5×5 windowing operator (sample size) that scanned the training area. Vectors of attribute values constituted training events. Three learning methods were used: AQ15c, AQ-NN, and NN. Three different sizes of training areas were used: 10×10, 20×20, and 40×40 pixels. The validation methodology used here was a hold-out method in which a random selection of 60% of the samples from the training area were used for training, while the remaining 40% were used for testing [WeK92].

Table 10.3.2 gives results from an experiment involving only one level of image transformation using different learning programs. In this experiment, the training area for each class was only 10×10 pixels. When the training area was enlarged to 20×20, the training time was significantly longer, but the correctness of the interpretation of the areas of the image was approximately the same.

Figure 10.3.2 presents an example of a training image and an ASI obtained by applying the learned one-level descriptions to the whole image using a majority voting evaluation scheme. As can be seen from Figure 10.3.2b, most of the areas in the image were correctly interpreted, although the system learned class descriptions from relatively small training areas (Figure 10.3.2a). In this experiment, AQ-NN produced a slightly smaller neural network and the interpretation time was about 50% shorter than with the NN method.

We also tested the data-driven constructive induction method (AQ17-DCI) in this experiment; this resulted in some new attributes, but it gave comparable results [BWMK93].

10.4 DETECTION OF BLASTING CAPS IN X-RAY IMAGES OF LUGGAGE

This section presents work on an approach to the problem of recognizing blasting caps in x-ray images. This problem is an instance of a class of problems in which a vision

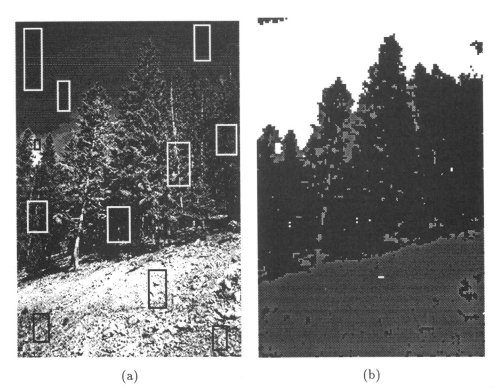

(a)   (b)

Figure 10.3 An example of the image interpretation process based on the rules learned from the indicated training areas. (a) An image with training areas for sky, tree, and ground. (b) ASI obtained using a majority voting scheme.

system must inspect a sequence of images for known objects. Unfortunately, the fact that the objects are known is often of little or no help. If there is little standardization of the class of known objects, it becomes impractical to attempt to model the objects geometrically. What often constrains a class of objects is functionality [FrN71, StB91a, RDR95]. Learning can be useful for acquiring the relationship between image characteristics and object functionality [WCHBS95].

Our primary focus is on investigating how vision and learning can be combined to find blasting caps, as well as objects that could occlude blasting caps, in x-ray images. In a previous study [MaM94, MaM96], learning was used to acquire descriptions of blasting caps. Simple segmentation techniques were used to isolate objects from their background; they were then represented using intensity and geometric features.

In the work presented here, an analysis of functional properties of blasting caps was conducted to design the representation space for learning, which combines intensity and shape features. Experimental results demonstrate the ability of the inductive learning system to acquire the relationship between image characteristics and object functionality.

This research provides an opportunity to study the interplay between vision and

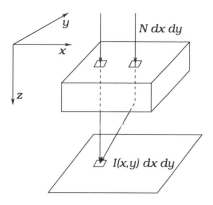

Figure 10.4   The geometry of x-ray imaging [Dan88].

learning processes [MRA94], especially as it relates to learning object functionality. A vision system capable of reliably recognizing blasting caps or objects that could occlude blasting caps could be used to aid airport security personnel in luggage screening.

10.4.1   Preliminaries

In this section we review the image formation process and imaging model in x-ray images.

A typical x-ray imaging system consists of an x-ray tube (photon source), an anti-scatter device, and a receptor (photon detector) [Dan88]. The photons emitted by the x-ray tube enter the objects, where they may be scattered, absorbed or transmitted without interaction. The primary photons recorded by the image receptor form the image, but the scattered photons create a background signal (i.e., noise) that degrades contrast. In most cases, the majority of the scattered photons can be removed by placing an anti-scatter device between the objects and the image receptor.

What follows is a simple mathematical model of the imaging process. We start by considering a monochromatic x-ray source that emits photons of energy E and is sufficiently far from the objects (luggage) being inspected that the photon beam can be considered to be parallel (see Figure 10.4). The incident photon beam is parallel to the z direction and the image is recorded in the xy plane. We assume that each photon interacting with the receptor is locally absorbed and that the response of the receptor is linear, so that the image may be considered as a distribution of absorbed energy. If N photons per unit area are incident on the object and $I(x,y)\,dx\,dy$ is the energy absorbed in area $dx\,dy$ of the detector, then

$$I(x,y) = \exp\left(-\int \mu(x,y,z)dz\right) \cdot N\,\varepsilon(E,0)\,E\,(1+R)$$

where the line integral is over all materials along the path of the primary photons reaching the point (x,y), $\mu(x,y,z)$ is the linear attenuation coefficient, $\varepsilon(E,0)$ is the energy absorption efficiency of the receptor for the photon energy level E at an incident

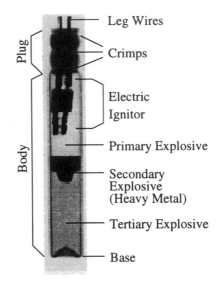

Figure 10.5   Detailed x-ray of a blasting cap.

angle of 0, and R is the ratio between the scattered and primary radiation (which is usually very small).

We assume orthographic image projection (see Figure 10.4). The image of the object point (X, Y, Z) is the point (x, y) such that

$$x = s\,X, \quad y = s\,Y,$$

where s is a constant. The image intensity at the pixel (x, y) is obtained by integrating $I(x, y)$ over the area of the pixel in the image receptor.

The intensity in an x-ray image is proportional to the number of x-ray photons that pass through objects on their way from the source to the receptor. Since different materials have different transparency properties, the intensity of an x-ray image depends on both the thickness and the type of material between the source and the receptor. Moreover, any x-ray photon that is not absorbed by one object on its path may be absorbed by another. Thus, a thick layer of semi-transparent material can have the same effect on the image receptor as a thin layer of opaque material.

10.4.2   Problem Statement

Although blasting caps are manufactured objects, there is enough variability in their manufacture to make a CAD-based recognition system impractical. What is common to all blasting caps, however, is their functionality. Ultimately, blasting caps are defined by their functional properties, not by their shapes.

A typical blasting cap (see Figure 10.5) consists of a cylindrical metal shell filled primarily with the explosive. In its approximate middle, there is a small globule of heavy metal secondary explosive. Finally, leg wires from the electric ignitor extend from one of the ends. The most dense (opaque to x-rays) part of a blasting cap is the concentration of the heavy metal explosive, which is approximately centrally symmetric. The leg wires also produce dense features, but are very thin. Finally, the copper or aluminum tube filled with explosive, which is axially symmetric, is typically more dense than the surrounding areas of the luggage.

To understand images of blasting caps, we begin by considering a generic blasting cap that is not occluded by opaque material. Let l be the length of an approximately cylindrical blasting cap, r be its radius, and σ be the angle between the axis of the cap and the image receptor. Consider the length of the path p of an x-ray photon as it passes through the blasting cap. When $\sigma = 0$, p ranges from $2r$ at the axis to 0 at the occluding contour. In general, p is multiplied by $\sec \sigma$; however, p cannot be longer than l. From the equation of $I(x, y)$, we see that the number of photons passing through the blasting cap decreases exponentially as p grows. From the image projection equations, we see that the image of a blasting cap is rectangularly shaped; its width is approximately $2rs$, and its length is approximately $ls \sec \sigma$. Its intensity is lowest along its axis, and highest along its occluding contour, which produces a low-contrast boundary. Also, the image of the heavy metal secondary explosive (see Figure 10.5) appears as a small, approximately symmetric blob on the axis of the blasting cap. The center of the blob is nearly opaque and thus its intensity is near zero. The boundary of the blob is lighter, but still has a very low intensity. The leg wires are strong features, but are not clearly visible in the images. (In our examples, the image resolution is 565×340 and the leg wires are barely visible. Currently, we are attempting to obtain images of higher resolution so that the leg wires can be more easily detected.)

Therefore, the strongest feature of a blasting cap is the low-intensity blob in the center of a rectangular ribbon of higher intensity. The intensities of both the blob and the ribbon are lowest along the axis of the blasting cap and highest along the occluding contour. Finally, if a blasting cap is occluded by any object, its image will be darker than the image of a blasting cap that is not occluded.

10.4.3   The Method and Experimental Results

We present a two-phase, bottom-up and top-down learning approach to recognizing blasting caps in x-ray images. In the first phase, low intensity blobs, which serve as attention-catching devices, are used to generate object hypotheses. These blobs correspond to the secondary high explosive, which is typically a heavy metal compound, located near the middle of the blasting cap (see Figure 10.5).

In the second phase, each generated hypothesis spawns a process that attempts to fit a local model to ribbon-like features surrounding the blob. These features correspond to the metal body of the blasting cap (see Figure 10.5). The local model is acquired using the inductive learning system AQ15c and captures intensity and geometric features of both the low intensity blob and the surrounding ribbons. A flexible matching routine is used to match the local model to the image characteristics; this not only produces an object identification, but also yields a confidence in the identification.

The x-ray images used for experimentation were of luggage containing blasting caps

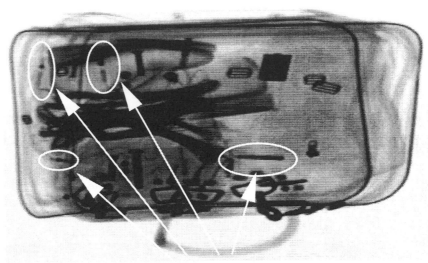

Blasting Caps

Figure 10.6   Sample image used for experimentation.

Table 10.2   Summary of quantitative experimental results

Average Predictive Accuracy (%)		
Overall	Correct	83.51±1.3
	Incorrect	16.49±1.3
Blasting Cap	Correct	85.82±2.1
	Incorrect	14.18±2.1
Non-Blasting Cap	Correct	81.19±2.4
	Incorrect	18.81±2.4

appearing in varying orientations and under varying amounts of clutter, which included clothes, shoes, calculators, pens, batteries, and the like. The luggage was imaged much as it would be in an airport scenario: flat in relation to the x-ray source, but rotated in the image plane. Five images were selected from a set of 30 which were of low to moderate complexity in terms of clutter and positional variability of the blasting cap. Figure 10.6 shows one of the images used for experimentation.

Regions of interest were interactively determined, and contained low intensity blobs and ribbons corresponding to positive and negative examples of blasting caps. From each of the 64 selected regions, 27 geometric (e.g., compactness and proximity measures) and intensity-based (e.g., minimum, maximum, and average) features were computed, resulting in 28 blasting cap and 38 non-blasting cap objects. The AQ15c [WKBM95] inductive learning system was used to learn descriptions of blasting caps and non-blasting caps.

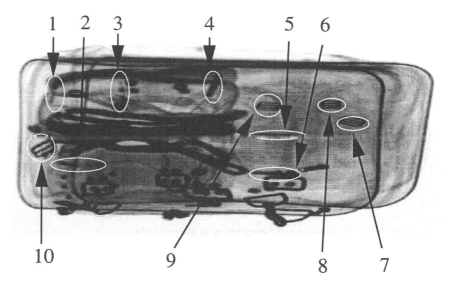

Figure 10.7   Test image for applying learned class definitions.

Induced descriptions from AQ15c were validated using 100 iterations of two-fold cross-validation. This validation method involves 100 learning and recognition runs. For each run, the extracted image data was randomly partitioned into a training set and a testing set. After learning from examples in the training set, the induced class definitions were tested using examples in the testing set. We can compute the predictive accuracy for each run based on the correct or incorrect classification of the examples in the testing set. The overall predictive accuracy for the experiment is the average of the accuracies computed for each run. These results are summarized in Table 10.2 and show the average predictive accuracy with a 95% confidence interval for the overall experiment and for each class.

As a qualitative demonstration of the method, the learned class definitions were also applied to an unseen image. The learned class definitions from AQ15c using training data from four images were tested on objects extracted from a fifth, unseen image, which is shown in Figure 10.7. Objects 1–6 are blasting caps, objects 7–10 are not. Object 5, which is a blasting cap, was mis-classified. All other objects in this image were classified correctly.

10.5   RECOGNIZING ACTIONS IN VIDEO IMAGE SEQUENCES

Recognizing the functions of objects is often a prerequisite to interacting with them. The functionality of an object can be defined as the usability of the object for a particular purpose [BoB94].

There has been considerable recent research on the problem of recognizing object functionality; for a short survey see [BoB94]. Early work on functional recognition can be found in [FrN71, SoB83, WBKL83]. The goal of this research has been to determine functional capabilities of an object based on characteristics such as shape, physics and causation. More recently, Stark and Bowyer [StB91a, StB91b, SHGB93] used this approach to solve some of the problems presented by more traditional model-based methods of object recognition. This work has dealt only with stationary objects; no motion is involved. In more recent work Green *et al.* [GESB94] discuss the recognition of articulated objects, using motion to determine whether the object possesses the appropriate functional properties. Little attention has been given to the problem of determining or learning the functionality of an object from its motion. In fact, however, motion provides a strong indication of function. In particular, velocity, acceleration, and force of impact resulting from motion strongly constrain possible function. As in other approaches to recognition of function, the object (and its motion) should not be evaluated in isolation, but in context. The context includes the nature of the agent making use of the object and the frame of reference used by the agent.

In this section, we address the following problem: How can we use the motion of an object, while it is being used to perform a task, to determine its function? Our method of answering this question is based on the extraction of a few motion descriptors from the image sequence. These descriptors are compared with stored descriptors that arise in known motion-to-function mappings to obtain function recognition.

Since many objects can display similar motion characteristics an object model is necessary to determine the functions of objects from their motion characteristics. Our work is based on segmenting the object into primitive parts and analyzing their motions.

10.5.1   Function from Motion

10.5.1.1   PRIMITIVE SHAPES AND PRIMITIVE MOTIONS

Following [Bie85, RRP93, RDR95] we regard objects as composed of primitive parts. On the coarsest level we consider four types of primitive parts: sticks, strips, plates, and blobs, which differ in the values of their relative dimensions. As in [RDR95] we let a_1, a_2, and a_3 represent the length, width, and height of a volumetric part. We can then define the four classes as follows:

$$Stick :\quad a_1 \simeq a_2 \ll a_3 \vee a_1 \simeq a_3 \ll a_2 \vee a_2 \simeq a_3 \ll a_1$$
$$Strip :\quad a_1 \neq a_2 \wedge a_2 \neq a_3 \wedge a_1 \neq a_3$$
$$Plate :\quad a_1 \simeq a_2 \gg a_3 \vee a_1 \simeq a_3 \gg a_2 \vee a_2 \simeq a_3 \gg a_1$$
$$Blob :\quad a_1 \simeq a_2 \simeq a_3$$

If all three dimensions are about the same, we have a blob. If two are about the same, and the third is very different, we have two cases: if the two are bigger than the one, we have a plate, and in the reverse case we have a stick. When no two dimensions are about the same we have a strip. For example, a knife blade is a strip, because no two of its dimensions are similar.

Primitives can be combined to create compound objects. In [RDR95] the different qualitative ways in which primitives can be combined were described—for example, end to end, end to side, end to edge, etc. In addition to specifying the two attachment surfaces participating in the junction of two primitives, we could also consider the angles at which they join, and classify the joints as perpendicular, oblique, tangential, etc. Another refinement would be to describe qualitatively the position of the joint on each surface; an attachment can be near the middle, near a side, near a corner, or near an end of the surface. We can also specialize the primitives by adding qualitative features such as axis shape (straight or curved), cross-section size (constant or tapered), etc.

Functional recognition is based on compatibility with some action requirement. Some basic "actions" are static in nature (supporting, containing, etc.), but many actions involve using an object while it is moving. To illustrate the ways in which a primitive shape can be used, consider the action of "cutting" with a sharp strip or plate. Here a sharp edge is interacting with a surface. The interaction can be described from a kinematic point of view. The direction of motion of the primitive relative to its axis defines the type of action—for example, stabbing, slicing or chopping. These actions all involve primitive motions, which we define to be motions (translations or rotations) along, or perpendicular to, the main axes of the primitive. In this section we will use the detection of primitive motions to infer an object's function.

10.5.1.2 INFERRING OBJECT FUNCTION FROM PRIMITIVE MOTIONS

Given a moving object as seen by an observer, we would like to infer the function being performed by the object. The object is given as a collection of primitives. For example, a knife can be described as consisting of two primitives: a handle (a stick) and a blade (a strip). Given this model, the system estimates the pose of the object (as in [RDR95]) and passes this information to the motion estimation module. The model and the results of the motion estimation enable the system to infer the function that is being performed by the object.

The function being performed by an object depends on the object's motion both in the object's coordinate system and relative to the object it acts on (the "actee"). This information gives us the relationships between the direction of motion, the main axis of the object, and the surface of the actee, and these relationships can be used to determine the intended function. For example, we would expect the motion of a knife that is being used to "stab" to be parallel to the main axis of the knife, whereas if the knife is being used to "chop" we would expect motion perpendicular to the main axis. In both cases, the motion is perpendicular to the surface of the actee. If the knife is being used to slice, we would expect back-and-forth motion parallel to its main axis and also parallel to the surface of the actee.

10.5.2   Computing Motion

10.5.2.1   MOTIONS OF STICKS AND STRIPS

Consider a moving object $\mathcal{B}$. There is an *ellipsoid of inertia* associated with $\mathcal{B}$. The center of the ellipsoid is at the center of mass C of $\mathcal{B}$; the axes of the ellipsoid are called the *principal axes*. We associate the coordinate system $Cx_1y_1z_1$ with the ellipsoid and choose the axes of $Cx_1y_1z_1$ to be parallel to the principal axes. Let $\vec{\imath}_1$ be the unit vector in the direction of the longest axis l_c (this axis corresponds to the smallest principal moment of inertia); let $\vec{k}_1$ be the unit vector in the direction of the shortest principal axis (this axis corresponds to the largest moment of inertia); and let $\vec{\jmath}_1$ be the unit vector in the direction of the remaining principal axis with the direction chosen so that the vectors $(\vec{\imath}_1, \vec{\jmath}_1, \vec{k}_1)$ form a right-handed coordinate system.

Here we consider only objects that are approximately planar, straight strips and sticks. For a planar strip the axis of the maximal moment of inertia is orthogonal to the plane of the strip; if the strip is approximately straight, the axis of the minimal moment of inertia is approximately parallel to the medial axis l_c of the strip. In the case of a straight stick, similarly, l_c corresponds to the longest principal axis of the ellipsoid of inertia; the other two principal axes are orthogonal to l_c and can be chosen arbitrarily. We assume that the motion of the stick or strip is planar and that the plane is "visible" to the observer. (The "visibility" constraint allows an oblique view as long as the angle between the surface normal and the z-axis of the camera is $\leq 30°$ (say).) When the object is a strip we assume that the motion is in the plane of the strip; the translational velocity is then parallel to the plane of the strip and the rotational velocity is orthogonal to the plane of the strip. When the object is a stick the consecutive positions of the stick define the motion plane; the translational velocity lies in the plane and the rotational velocity is orthogonal to the plane. In this case we choose the axis of minimal moment of inertia to be orthogonal to the plane of the motion.

10.5.2.2   COMPUTING PRIMITIVE MOTIONS

We now briefly review our method of computing primitive motions of sticks and strips. A complete description of the method can be found in [DRR96, DFR96].

We associate two rectangular coordinate frames with a rigidly moving body $\mathcal{B}$, one $(Oxyz)$ fixed in space (the camera frame), the other $(Cx_1y_1z_1)$ fixed in the body $\mathcal{B}$ and moving with it (the object frame). The position of the moving frame at any instant is given by the position $\vec{d}_c = (X_c \ Y_c \ Z_c)^T$ of the origin C (the center of mass of $\mathcal{B}$), and by the nine direction cosines of the axes of the moving frame with respect to the fixed frame. The pair $(\vec{\omega}, \vec{T})$, where $\vec{\omega} = (A \ B \ C)^T$ is the rotational velocity of the moving frame and $\dot{\vec{d}}_c = (\dot{X}_c \ \dot{Y}_c \ \dot{Z}_c)^T \equiv (U \ V \ W)^T \equiv \vec{T}$ is the translational velocity of the point C, defines the motion of $\mathcal{B}$. The rotational velocity in the moving frame is $\vec{\omega}_1 = (A_1 \ B_1 \ C_1)^T$; we can write $\vec{\omega} = R\vec{\omega}_1$ and $\vec{\omega}_1 = R^T\vec{\omega}$, where R is the matrix of the direction cosines. From our assumptions about the motion of $\mathcal{B}$ we have $\vec{\omega}_1 = C_1\vec{k}_1$ and $\vec{T}_1 = U_1\vec{\imath}_1 + V_1\vec{\jmath}_1$.

Let f be the focal length of the camera and let Z_c be the depth of the center of mass C of $\mathcal{B}$. The weak perspective projection of the scene point (X, Y, Z) onto the image point (x, y) is given by

$$x = \frac{X}{Z_c}f, \quad y = \frac{Y}{Z_c}f.$$

For the instantaneous velocity of the image point (x, y) under weak perspective projection we have [DFR96]

$$\dot{x} = \frac{Uf - xW}{Z_c} - C_1(y - y_c)N_z - C_1[(x - x_c)N_x N_y/N_z + (y - y_c)N_y^2/N_z],$$

$$\dot{y} = \frac{Vf - yW}{Z_c} + C_1(x - x_c)N_z + C_1[(x - x_c)N_x^2/N_z + (y - y_c)N_x N_y/N_z],$$

where (x_c, y_c) is the image of (X_c, Y_c) and $\vec{N} = (N_x \ N_y \ N_z)^T = R\vec{k}_1$ is the normal to the plane of motion; we have also used the fact that $\vec{\omega} = R\vec{\omega}_1$.

If we choose a unit direction vector $\vec{n}_r = n_x\vec{i} + n_y\vec{j}$ (usually the direction of the image intensity gradient) at the image point (x, y) and call it the normal direction, then the *normal motion field* at (x, y) is $\dot{\vec{r}}_n = (\dot{\vec{r}} \cdot \vec{n}_r)\vec{n}_r$. We then have $\dot{\vec{r}}_n = (\dot{x}n_x + \dot{y}n_y)\vec{n}_r$.

Let $I(x, y, t)$ be the image intensity function. Given the image gradient ∇I and the partial derivative in time I_t of I we have

$$\vec{u}_n = \frac{-I_t \nabla I}{\|\nabla I\|^2}$$

where $\vec{u}_n$ is called the *normal flow*.

The magnitude of the difference between $\vec{u}_n$ and the normal motion field $\dot{\vec{r}}_n$ is inversely proportional to the magnitude of the image gradient. Hence $\dot{\vec{r}}_n \approx \vec{u}_n$ when $\|\nabla I\|$ is large. Expression for the normal flow thus provides an approximate relationship between the 3-D motion and the image derivatives. In [DFR96, DRR96] the normal flow (an observable quantity) was used as an approximation of the projected motion field. The method of least squares estimation was used to obtain the estimates of C_1, U/Z_c, V/Z_c, and W/Z_c. These estimates and the fact that the object was "visible" were then used to obtain the values of U_1/Z_c and V_1/Z_c.

10.5.2.3 PARAMETRIZING THE MOTION OF A STICK OR STRIP

We use three angles α, β, and θ to parametrize the motions of sticks and strips.

The direction α of the medial axis is found using the following algorithm:

1 - Make a sorted (circular) list of all edge elements (sorted by their orientations modulo π) for which the normal flow is computed.

2 - Find the shortest segment $[\gamma_1, \gamma_2]$ such that more than $3/4$ of the orientations in the list are contained within it.

3 - Find the median orientation α in the sorted sublist chosen in the previous step.

4 - If α does not approximately agree with the pose that was estimated earlier, then $\alpha \leftarrow \alpha + \pi$.

5 - Use α as the orientation of the medial axis.

We estimate (x_c, y_c) — the image position of C (the reference point and the center of mass of the object)—as the average of the coordinates of all edge points for which the normal flow is computed.

We define β as the angle between the vector $(U_1 \ \ V_1 \ \ 0)^T$ and the Cx_1 axis of the tool coordinate system; thus

$$\beta = \arctan \frac{V_1}{U_1}.$$

We define θ to be the total rotation angle as a function of time:

$$\theta = \int_0^t C_1 dt.$$

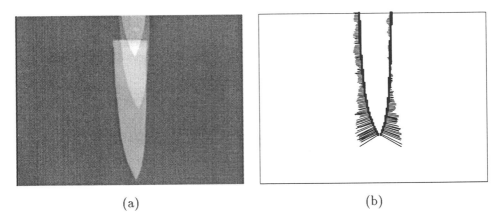

(a)   (b)

Figure 10.8   (a) Stabbing motion. (b) Flow vectors for Stabbing.

10.5.3 Experiments

In our experiments we observed the motion of a knife performing a task. The vision system took images at 25 frames per second for 5 seconds, yielding 125 images per experiment. After each image sequence was recorded, a representative sampling of the 125 images was used for further processing. Eleven evenly spaced samples, each composed of three consecutive images, were used. (For instance, samples 1 and 2 in any given experiment used images 0–2 and 10–12, respectively.) This resulted in 33 images for each experiment.

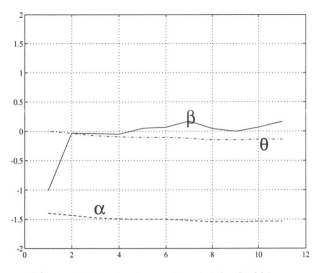

Figure 10.9   Angles α, β, and θ for Stabbing.

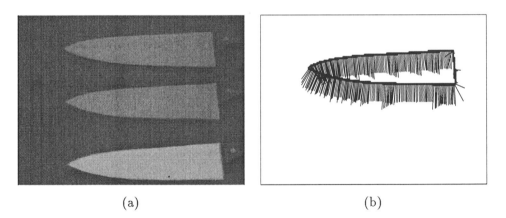

(a)   (b)

Figure 10.10   (a) Chopping motion. (b) Flow vectors for Chopping.

10.5.3.1   STABBING

Stabbing is defined as the cutting motion of a knife in which α (the angle between the projection of l_c onto the plane $Z = Z_c$ and the Ox axis) is close to either $-\pi/2$ or $\pi/2$, β is approximately 0, and θ is small and approximately constant.

Figure 10.8 shows the flow vectors taken from the 6th sample and a composite image of the knife taken from the 1st, 6th and 11th samples of the stabbing experiment. Figure 10.9 shows a plot of the triple (α, β, θ) with respect to time (frame numbers).

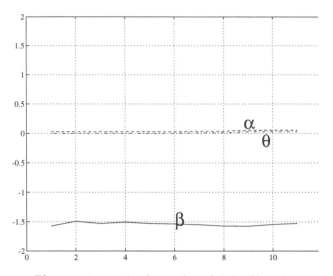

Figure 10.11   Angles α, β, and θ for Chopping.

(a)   (b)

Figure 10.12   (a) Slicing motion. (b) Flow vectors for Slicing.

We see that as was expected, the values of α are very close to $-\pi/2$, β is close to 0, and θ is close to 0. A VL_1 rule (Michalski [Mic72]) describing stabbing would be

$$< stabbing > \; <:: \; [\alpha = -1.55 \, .. \, -1.35] \, \& \, [\beta = -1 \, .. \, 0.2] \, \& \, [\theta = -0.2 \, .. \, 0].$$

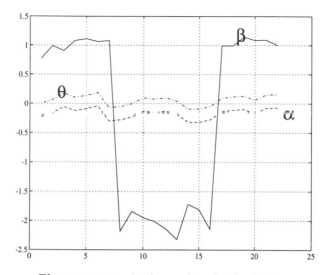

Figure 10.13   Angles α, β, and θ for Slicing.

10.5.3.2   CHOPPING

Chopping is defined as the cutting motion of a knife in which α (the angle between the projection of l_c onto the plane $Z = Z_c$ and the Ox axis) is close to either 0 or π, β is close to $\pi/2$ (when $\alpha \approx \pi$) or $-\pi/2$ (when $\alpha \approx 0$), and θ is small and approximately constant.

Figure 10.10 shows the flow vectors taken from the 6th sample and a composite image of the knife taken from the 1st, 6th and 11th samples of the chopping experiment. Figure 10.11 shows a plot of the triple (α, β, θ) with respect to time (frame numbers). We see that, as was expected, the values of α are very close to 0, β is close to $-\pi/2$, and θ is close to 0. A VL_1 rule describing chopping would be

$$< chopping > \ <::\ [\alpha = 0] \ \& \ [\beta = -1.6 \ .. \ -1.5] \ \& \ [\theta = 0].$$

10.5.3.3   SLICING

Slicing is defined as the cutting motion of a knife in which α is approximately 0 (or $< \pi/2$), β oscillates between approximately 0 and approximately π, and θ is small and approximately constant.

Figure 10.12 shows the flow vectors taken from the 6th sample and a composite image of the knife taken from the 1st, 6th and 11th samples of the slicing experiment. (The mass of vectors at the left end of Figure 10.12a come from the motion of the hand, which is visible in the images.) Figure 10.13 shows a plot of the triple (α, β, θ) with respect to time (frame numbers). We see that, as was expected, the values of α are very close to 0, and that β oscillates between approximately $\pi/2$ and approximately $-3\pi/2$ (note that the two approximate values differ by π). A VL_1 rule describing slicing would be

$$< slicing > \quad <:: \quad [\alpha = -0.25 .. 0] \; \& \; [\beta = -2.25 .. -1.75, \; 0.75 .. 1.25] \; \&$$
$$[\theta = -0.2 .. 0] \; \& \; [T_\beta = 8..12]$$

where T_β is the period of β (β changes between two ranges with the period T_β).

10.6   CONCLUSIONS AND FUTURE RESEARCH

10.6.1   Semantic Interpretation of Color Images of Outdoor Scenes

In Section 10.3 we showed that the MIST methodology can be very useful in applying machine learning methods to problems of natural scene interpretation. The results obtained so far have been promising, as they indicate a high level of performance accuracy even when only a single level of image transformation was applied. Particularly good results have been obtained with the AQ-NN method, which combines symbolic rule learning and a neural network.

There are several important advantages of this methodology. They include the ease of applying and testing diverse learning methods and approaches in a uniform manner, the potential for implementing advanced and complex learning processes, the use of background knowledge in learning and interpreting images, the suitability for parallel image learning and interpretation, and the ease of testing the performance of the methods.

Current research involves a systematic investigation of the methodology using different types of initial attributes and taking training and testing areas from images obtained under significantly different perceptual conditions.

10.6.2   Detection of Blasting Caps in X-ray Images of Luggage

In Section 10.4 we presented work in progress on the problem of recognizing blasting caps in x-ray images. In the first phase of a two-phase learning approach, low-intensity blobs were used as attention-catching devices. This bottom-up process was followed by a top-down recognition process in which a learned local model was matched to ribbon-shaped image regions surrounding a low-intensity blob. An analysis of the functional properties of blasting caps was used to design the representation space for learning, which combined intensity and geometric features. The experimental results suggest that learning can be used to acquire functional descriptions of objects. This is important for classes of objects for which geometric modeling is impractical.

Future work in this area will involve further automation of the feature extraction process and object labeling functions. In addition, other functional properties present in blasting caps still require exploitation. An example is the presence of leg wires (see Figure 10.5). Unfortunately, the current image set is not of a resolution that allows for the detection of these functional properties. We hope to acquire additional images that will be better suited for this type of analysis.

10.6.3   Recognizing Actions in Video Image Sequences

Perceiving function from motion provides an understanding of the way an object is being used by an agent. To accomplish this we combined information about the shape of the object, its motion, and its relation to the actee (the object it is acting on). Assuming a decomposition of the object into primitive parts, we analyzed a part's motion relative to its principal axes. Primitive motions (translation and rotation relative to the principal axes of the object) were dominating factors in the analysis. We used a frame of reference relative to the actee. Once such a frame is established, it can have major implications for the functionality of an action.

Several image sequences were used to demonstrate our approach. In the three sequences shown in Section 10.5, motion was used to discriminate between three cutting actions: stabbing, chopping, and slicing. In other sequences, not shown here [DFR96], we used motion information to differentiate between two different functionalities of the same object: scooping and hitting with a shovel, and hammering and tightening with a wrench.

Natural extensions of this work include the analysis of more complex objects. Complexity can be expressed in terms of either the shapes of the parts or the way in which the parts are connected. An interesting area is the analysis of articulated objects. The different types of connections between the parts constrain the possible relative motions of the parts. A pair of pliers or a pair of scissors is a simple case, with only a single articulated connection (one degree of freedom in the relative motion of the parts).

10.6.4   Advantages of Incorporating Learning into Vision Systems

We have given three illustrations of how a learning system can be used to help in handling vision problems for which algorithmic solutions are unknown or difficult to obtain. Specifically, we have studied the application of symbolic, neural network and multistrategy learning methods to the problems that involved interpreting outdoor scenes, recognizing objects in cluttered environments, and recognizing actions in video image sequences. The first problem involved segmentation of an image into regions corresponding to grass, trees, etc.; since these categories do not have simple definitions, optimal algorithms for discriminating them cannot easily be defined. The other two problems involved classes of objects or actions that do not have simple geometrical definitions, but are defined only functionally: detecting blasting caps in x-ray images of luggage, and recognizing types of cutting (stabbing, chopping, slicing) in video image sequences. In each of these cases we have been able to design an appropriate representation space to make learning (and recognition) feasible.

ACKNOWLEDGEMENTS

This research was supported in part by the Defence Advanced Research Projects Agency under grants F49620-92-J-0549 and F49620-95-1-0462 administered by the Air Force Office of Scientific Research, in part by the Air Force Office of Scientific Research under grant F49620-93-1-0039, in part by the Defence Advanced Research Projects Agency under grant No. N00014-91-J-1854 administered by the Office of Naval Research, in part by the Office of Naval Research under grant N00014-91-J-1351, and in part by the National Science Foundation under grants DMI-9496192 and IRI-9510644.

REFERENCES

[BMP94] Bala, J.W., Michalski, R.S., and Pachowicz, P.W., "Progress on vision through learning at George Mason University", in *Proc. ARPA Image Understanding Workshop*, 191–207, 1994.

[BMW92] Bala, J., Michalski, R.S., and Wnek, J., "The principal axes method for constructive induction", in *Proc. International Conference on Machine Learning*, D. Sleeman and P. Edwards (Eds.), Aberdeen, Scotland, 1992.

[BMW93] Bala, J., Michalski, R.S., and Wnek, J., "The PRAX approach to learning a large number of texture concepts", in *Proc. Machine Learning in Computer Vision: What, Why and How?, AAAI Fall Symposium on Machine Learning in Computer Vision*, 1993.

[Bie85] Biederman, I., "Human image understanding: Recent research and a theory", *Computer Vision, Graphics and Image Processing*, **32**:29–73, 1985.

[BWMK93] Bloedorn, E., Wnek, J., Michalski, R.S., and Kaufman, K., "AQ17 — A multistrategy learning system: The method and user's guide", *Reports of the Machine Learning and Inference Laboratory*, MLI 93-12, George Mason University, Fairfax, VA, 1993.

[BoB94] Bogoni, L. and Bajcsy, R., "Active investigation of functionality", in *Proc. CVPR Workshop on Visual Behaviors*, June 1994.

[BABC84] Brady, M., Agre, P.E., Braunegg, D.J., and Connell, J., II, "The mechanic's mate" in *Proc. European Conference on Artificial Intelligence*, 79–94, 1984.

[Cha89] Channic, T., "TEXPERT: An application of machine learning to texture recognition", *Reports of the Machine Learning and Inference Laboratory*, MLI 89-27, George Mason University, Fairfax, VA, 1989.

[ChD94] Cho, K. and Dunn, S.M., "Learning shape classes", *IEEE Transactions on Pattern Analysis and Machine Intelligence*, **16**:882–888, 1994.

[CrK91] Cromwell, R.L. and Kak, A.C., "Automatic generation of object class descriptions using symbolic learning techniques", in *Proc. National Conference on Artificial Intelligence*, 710–717, 1991.

[CoB87] Connell, J.H. and Brady, M., "Generating and generalizing models of visual objects", *Artificial Intelligence*, **34**:159–183, 1987.

[Dan88] Dance, D.R., "Diagnostic radiology with x-rays", in *The Physics of Medical Imaging*, S. Webb (Ed.), 20–73, IOP Publishing, Philadelphia, PA, 1988.

[DFR96] Duric, Z., Fayman, E., and Rivlin, E., "Function from motion", *IEEE Transactions on Pattern Analysis and Machine Intelligence*, 579–591, 1996.

[DRR96] Duric, Z., Rivlin, E., and Rosenfeld, A., "Learning an object's function by observing the object in action", in *Proc. ARPA Image Understanding Workshop*, 1437–1445, 1996.

[DuB94] Dutta, R. and Bhanu, B., "A learning system for consolidated recognition and motion analysis", in *Proc. ARPA Image Understanding Workshop*, 773–776, 1994.

[Fah88] Fahlman, S.E., "An empirical study of learning speed in back-propagation networks",

Report CMU-CS-88-182, Carnegie-Mellon University, Pittsburgh, PA, 1988.

[FeB96] Ferryman, A. and Bhanu, B., "A Bayesian approach for the segmentation of SAR images using dynamically selected neigborhoods", in *Proc. ARPA Image Understanding Workshop*, 891–895, 1996.

[FiS88] Fischler, M.A. and Strat, T.M., "Recognizing trees, bushes, rocks and rivers", in *Proc. AAAI Spring Symposium Series: Physical and Biological Approaches to Computational Vision*, 62–64, 1988.

[FrN71] Freeman, P. and Newell, A., "A model for functional reasoning in design", in *Proc. International Joint Conference on Artificial Intelligence*, 621–640, 1971.

[GESB94] Green, K., Eggert, D., Stark, L., and Bowyer, K., "Generic recognition of articulated objects by reasoning about functionality", in *Proc. AAAI Workshop on Represening and Reasoning about Device Function*, 56–64, 1994.

[GrP96] Grimson, W.E.L. and Poggio, T., "Progress in image understanding at MIT", in *Proc. ARPA Image Understanding Workshop*, 65–74, 1996.

[HoB94] Howard, C.G. and Bock, P., "Using a hierarchical approach to avoid over-fitting in early vision", in *Proc. International Conference on Pattern Recognition*, 826–829, 1994.

[MDMR96] Maloof, M.A., Duric, Z., Michalski, R.S., and Rosenfeld, A., "Recognizing blasting caps in x-ray images", in *Proc. ARPA Image Understandning Workshop*, 1257–1261, 1996.

[MaM94] Maloof, M.A. and Michalski, R.S., "Learning descriptions of 2D blob-like shapes for object recognition in x-ray images: An initial study", *Reports of the Machine Learning and Inference Laboratory*, MLI 94-4, George Mason University, Fairfax, VA, 1994.

[MaM96] Maloof, M.A. and Michalski, R.S, "Learning descriptions of shape for object recognition in x-ray images", *Expert Systems with Applications*, in press, 1996.

[Mic72] Michalski, R.S., "A variable-valued logic system as applied to picture description and recognition", in F. Nake and A. Rosenfeld (Eds.), *Graphic Languages*, North-Holland, Amsterdam, 21–47, 1972.

[Mic73] Michalski, R.S., "AQVAL/1: Computer implementation of a variable-valued logic system VL$_1$ and examples of its application to pattern recognition", in *Proc. International Joint Conference on Pattern Recognition*, 3–17, 1973.

[Mic80] Michalski, R.S., "Pattern recognition as rule-guided inductive inference", *IEEE Transactions on Pattern Analysis and Machine Intelligence*, 2:349–361, 1980.

[MBP93] Michalski, R.S., Bala, J.W. and Pachowicz, P.W., "Progress on vision through learning at George Mason University", in *Proc. ARPA Image Understanding Workshop*, 191–207, 1993.

[MMHL86] Michalski, R.S., Mozetic, I., Hong, J., and Lavrac, N., "The multipurpose incremental learning system AQ15 and its testing application to three medical domains", in *Proc. National Conference on Artificial Intelligence*, 1041–1045, 1986.

[MRA94] Michalski, R.S., Rosenfeld, A., and Aloimonos, Y., "Machine vision and learning: Research issues and directions — A report on the NSF/ARPA Workshop on Learning and Vision, Harpers Ferry, WV, October 15-17, 1992", *Reports of the Machine Learning and Inference Laboratory*, MLI 94-6, George Mason University, Fairfax, VA, 1994.

[MRADMZ96] Michalski, R.S., Rosenfeld, A., Aloimonos, Y., Duric, Z., Maloof, M.A., and Zhang, Q., "Progress on vision through learning: A collaborative effort of George Mason University and the University of Maryland", in *Proc. ARPA Image Understandning Workshop*, 177–187, 1996.

[MZMB96] Michalski, R.S., Zhang, Q., Maloof, M.A., and Bloedorn, E., "The multi-level image sampling and transformation methodology and its application to natural scene interpretation", in *Proc. ARPA Image Understandning Workshop*, 1473–1479, 1996.

[PaB91] Pachowicz, P.W. and Bala, J.W., "Texture recognition through machine learning and concept optimization", *Reports of the Machine Learning and Inference Laboratory*, MLI 95-4, George Mason University, Fairfax, VA, 1991.

[Pom91] Pomerleau, D.A., "Efficient training of artificial neural networks for autonomous navigation", *Neural Computation*, 3:88–97, 1991.

[RDR95] Rivlin, E., Dickinson, S.J., and Rosenfeld, A., "Recognition by functional parts", *Computer Vision and Image Understanding*, **62**:164–176, 1995.

[RRP93] Rivlin, E., Rosenfeld, A., and Perlis, D., "Recognition of object functionality in goal-directed robotics", in *Proc. AAAI Workshop on Reasoning about Function*, 126–130, 1993.

[RBP96] Romano, R., Beymer, D., and Poggio, T., "Face verification for real-time applications", in *Proc. ARPA Image Understanding Workshop*, 747–756, 1996.

[RBK96] Rowley, H.A., Baluja, S., and Kanade, T., "Neural network-based face detection", in *Proc. ARPA Image Understanding Workshop*, 725–735, 1996.

[Seg94] Segen, J., "GEST: A learning computer vision system that recognizes hand gestures", in R.S. Michalski and G. Tecuci, (Eds.), *Machine Learning: A Multistrategy Approach*, Vol. IV, 621–634, Morgan Kaufmann, San Francisco, CA, 1994.

[She83] Shepherd, B.A., "An appraisal of a decision tree approach to image classification", in *Proc. International Joint Conference on Artificial Intelligence*, 473-475, 1983.

[SoB83] Solina, S. and Bajcsy, R., "Shape and function", in *Proc. SPIE Conference on Intelligent Robots and Computer Vision*, Vol. 726, 284–291, 1983.

[StB91a] Stark, L. and Bowyer, K., "Achieving generalized object recognition through reasoning about association of function to structure", *IEEE Transactions on Pattern Analysis and Machine Intelligence*, **13**:1097–1104, 1991.

[StB91b] Stark, L. and Bowyer, K., "Generic recognition through qualitative reasoning about 3-D shape and object function", in *Proc. IEEE Conference on Computer Vision and Pattern Recognition*, 251–256, 1991.

[StB92] Stark, L. and Bowyer, K., "Indexing function-based categories for generic recognition", in *Proc. IEEE Conference on Computer Vision and Pattern Recognition*, 795–797, 1992.

[SHGB93] Stark, L., Hoover, A., Goldgof, D., and Bowyer, K., "Function-based recognition from incomplete knowledge of shape", in *Proc. IEEE Workshop on Qualitative Vision*, 11–22, 1993.

[StF91] Strat, T. and Fischler, M., "Natural object recognition: A theoretical framework and its implementation", in *Proc. International Joint Conference on Artificial Intelligence*, 1991.

[StF95] Strat, T. and Fischler, M., "The role of context in computer vision", in *Proc. ICCV Workshop on Context-Based Vision*, 1995.

[SuP94] Sung, K. and Poggio, T., "Example-based learning for view-based human face detection", in *Proc. ARPA Image Understanding Workshop*, 747–756, 1994.

[WeK92] Weiss, S.M., and Kulikowski, C.A., *Computer Systems that Learn: Classification and Prediction Methods from Statistics, Neural Nets, Machine Learning and Expert Systems*, Morgan Kaufmann, San Mateo, CA, 1992.

[Win84] Winston, P.H., *Artificial Intelligence*, 2nd ed., Addison-Wesley, Reading, MA, 1984.

[WBKL83] Winston, P.H., Binford, T.O., Katz, B., and Lowry, M., "Learning physical descriptions from functional descriptions, examples, and precedents", in *Proc. National Conference on Artificial Intelligence*, 433–439, 1983.

[WKBM95] Wnek, J., Kaufman, K., Bloedorn, E., and Michalski, R.S., "Inductive learning system AQ15c: The method and user's guide", *Reports of the Machine Learning and Inference Laboratory*, MLI 95-4, George Mason University, Fairfax, VA, 1995.

[WCHBS95] Woods, K., Cook, D., Hall, L., Bowyer, K., and Stark, L, "Learning membership functions in a function-based object recognition system", *Journal of Artificial Intelligence Research*, **3**:187–222, 1995.

[ZhB96] Zheng, Y. and Bhanu, B., "Performance improvement by input adaptation using modified Hebbian learning", in *Proc. ARPA Image Understanding Workshop*, 1381–1387, 1996.

[Zur92] Zurada, J.M., *Introduction to Artificial Neural Systems*, West Publishing, St. Paul, MN, 1992.

11

Applications of Machine Learning to Music Research: Empirical Investigations into the Phenomenon of Musical Expression

Gerhard Widmer

ABSTRACT

This chapter describes an application of machine learning techniques to the study of a fundamental phenomenon in tonal music. Learning algorithms are described that induce general rules of *expressive music performance* from examples of real performances by musicians. Motivated by the insight that general knowledge about music plays an essential role in the way humans learn this task, we present two alternative approaches to knowledge-based learning. In both cases, the domain knowledge provided to the learner is based on established theories of tonal music. Experimental results show that both approaches lead to a significant improvement of the learning results, compared to purely inductive learning. However, this project is more than basic machine learning research. Due to its thorough grounding in music theory, the project can also be viewed as a contribution to the scientific field of music research or musicology; it has produced results that have also found their way into the literature of that scientific discipline. These will also be touched on in this chapter.

Machine Learning and Data Mining: Methods and Applications
Edited by R.S. Michalski, I Bratko and M. Kubat
© 1997 John Wiley & Sons Ltd

11.1 INTRODUCTION

This chapter describes an application of machine learning that may at first sight seem somewhat unusual or even esoteric: learning algorithms are applied to problems of tonal music. In a project that has evolved over several years, we have used machine learning methods to study the foundations of a fundamental musical skill that lies at the heart of music as an art form, namely, *expressive music performance*. Several learning systems have been developed that try to learn general rules of expressive performance from examples of performances by human musicians.

The project started as basic machine learning research in the area of knowledge-based learning. The initial aim was to investigate various ways of introducing domain knowledge into the learning process and to study the general nature and impact of such knowledge. Music was selected as a test domain because it provided a set of difficult learning tasks and, more specifically, because music theory is a rich source of domain knowledge that is general, well-developed, yet far from precise and complete. As the domain analysis progressed and more and more emphasis was put on a principled and musically plausible modelling of domain knowledge, the project gradually turned into a truly interdisciplinary endeavor. It began to produce results of interest to musicology that have in the meantime found their way also into the literature of that scientific discipline (see, e.g., Widmer, 1993a, 1995a, 1995b, 1996).

What this chapter presents, then, is a genuine application of machine learning — not to a "practical" (e.g., industrial) problem, but to another branch of *science*. The potential of machine learning as a contributing technique for other scientific domains — notably, biochemistry and molecular biology — has been demonstrated by a number of researchers (e.g., Lindsay *et al.*, 1980; Hunter, 1993; King *et al.*, 1992; Muggleton *et al.*, 1992; Shavlik *et al.*, 1992). This chapter attempts to show that also more 'informal' domains like music can benefit from machine learning experiments.

As an interdisciplinary project, our work was guided by questions from, and has produced results of interest to both fields involved. From a machine learning perspective, our objective was to study various types of weak (i.e., imprecise and incomplete) domain knowledge, and ways of using it to bias a learner towards better hypotheses. The results that will be presented here are two alternative approaches to knowledge-based learning: in the first approach, an inductive learning algorithm takes advantage of explicitly represented qualitative domain knowledge to guide its search for generalizations (section 11.4). Section 11.5 describes an alternative strategy. Domain knowledge is used to transform the entire learning task to a higher abstraction level where relevant regularities become more readily apparent. Essentially, this is a form of knowledge-driven contructive induction (Wnek and Michalski, 1994). Experimental results show that both approaches lead to an improvement of the learning results.

From the viewpoint of musicology, the central problem to be investigated was the notion of musical knowledge. Relevant questions included: What kind of general musical knowledge do music listeners possess? How can it be formalized? What is the relation between this knowledge and expressive performance? What structural aspects of music pieces determine or influence the acceptability of performances? It was our belief that machine learning can shed new light into these matters, and the results of our experiments are indeed informative. A comprehensive presentation and analysis of the experiments from a music-theoretic point of view is, of course, beyond the scope of this article. In sections 11.6 and 11.7, we will at least try to hint at some of the most interesting results.

This chapter can only give a broad overview of our projects, the algorithms and results, but we do hope to give the reader an appreciation of the promise that machine learning holds for scientific fields like musicology and, not least, we hope to convey some of the fascination of AI-based music research.

11.2   THE OBJECT OF STUDY: EXPRESSIVE MUSIC PERFORMANCE

When played exactly as written, most pieces of music would sound utterly mechanical and lifeless. *Expressive performance* (or *interpretation*) is the art of 'shaping' a piece of music by playing it not exactly as given in the written score, but continuously varying certain musical parameters during a performance, e.g., speeding up or slowing down, growing louder or softer, placing micro-pauses between events, etc. There are numerous parameter dimensions that can be affected by a performer, some of which are limited to particular instruments (e.g., *vibrato*). In this project, we concentrate on the two most important expression dimensions, *dynamics* (variations of loudness) and *rubato* or *expressive timing* (variations of local tempo). Our programs will be shown the melodies of pieces as written and recordings of these melodies as played expressively by a human pianist. From that they will have to learn general principles of expressive interpretation (in the form of rules), which should enable them to play new pieces more or less expressively.

Sometimes composers place explicit expression marks in the score (e.g., the command *cresc* underneath a musical passage), but more often than not expressive form is left implicit, to be decided by the performer on the basis of his/her musical understanding. Our systems will be shown only the notes of a piece, with no explicit expression marks.

More precisely, input to the learner are *melodies* of musical pieces (i.e., sequences of notes), where each note in a melody is associated with two numeric values: the exact *loudness* with which the note was played by a performer (the *dynamics* dimension) and the precise *tempo* (i.e., the ratio of the duration as actually played vs. the duration as prescribed by the score). The learner's task is to induce rules that allow it to determine exactly how loud and how fast any note in a new given pieces should be played. The problem is thus a *numeric prediction task*. Section 11.4.3 will present a knowledge-based algorithm for this type of induction problem, but first we take a closer look at what music theory can tell us about the problem.

11.3   THE NATURE AND IMPORTANCE OF BACKGROUND
KNOWLEDGE

Consider again the abstract learning task: training examples are melodies, i.e., sequences of notes, where each note is associated with a numeric value that represents the precise degree of loudness or local tempo that has been applied to the note by a musician in a particular performance. These numeric values can be viewed as defining a curve (a *performance curve*, in music-technical terms) above the melody. The task is to learn to 'draw' 'correct' or at least 'sensible' curves above new melodies, i.e., new sequences of notes.

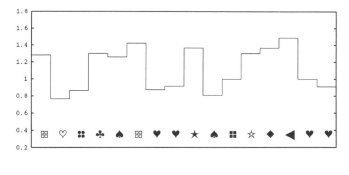

Figure 11.1 An abstract training example.

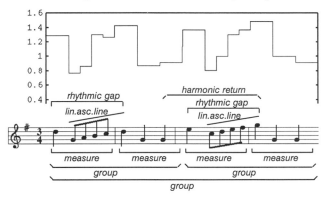

Figure 11.2 The problem as perceived by a human learner.

Figure 11.1 tries to give the reader an intuition of what the problem looks like to a learner without any knowledge of music: to a naive learner, the individual notes are simply generic *symbols* with various intrinsic characteristics or features. This abstract representation illustrates the difficulty of the learning task. It is quite evident that one of the main problems is that of *context*: one symbol alone does not uniquely determine the numeric value (the height of the curve) associated with it. It is not at all clear, however, what the relevant context is, whether there are only local or also nonlocal context influences.

It is a fact that humans (e.g., music students) learn general principles of expressive performances quite effectively, from rather few examples. The reason is, of course, that we as humans possess additional *knowledge* about the *meaning* of the symbols. To us, this is music, and that gives us an *interpretation framework* for the symbols. Listeners do not perceive a presented piece as a simple sequence of unrelated symbols or events, but they immediately and automatically interpret it in structural terms. For instance, they segment the flow of events into 'chunks' (motives, groups, phrases, etc.); they intuitively hear the *metrical structure* of the music, i.e., identify a regular alternation of strong and weak beats and know where to tap their foot. Linearly ascending or descending melodic lines are often heard as one group, and so are typical rhythmic figures and other combinations of notes. To a human learner, then, the above training example would look more like Figure 11.2.

Many more dimensions of musical structure can be identified, and it has been shown that acculturated listeners extract these structures in a highly consistent manner, and mostly without being aware of it (see, e.g., Deutsch, 1982; Sloboda, 1985). All these structures and patterns are related to the rise and fall of loudness or tempo that are observed (heard) in a performance. That is the (unconscious) musical 'knowledge' that listeners and musicians automatically bring to bear when listening to or playing a piece.

Results from musicology support this hypothesis. Numerous recent studies tell us that expression is not arbitrary, but highly correlated with the structure of music as it is perceived by performers and listeners. In fact, expression is a means for the performer to emphasize certain structures and maybe de-emphasize others, thus conducing the listener to 'hearing' the piece as the performer understands it.[1]

The following sections describe two different approaches towards providing the learning algorithm with general background knowledge about musical structure and its possible relation to expressive performance. The knowledge itself will be based in both cases on two well-known theories of tonal music — Lerdahl and Jackendoff's (1983) *Generative Theory of Tonal Music* and Eugene Narmour's (1977) *Implication-Realization Model*. Both theories postulate certain types of structures that are claimed to be perceivable by human listeners.

That is also where the project becomes interesting to musicology: experimental results with these learning systems can provide empirical evidence for or against the relevance of various parts of the underlying music theories and will generally help us identify those structural dimensions of music that seem to have the most 'explanatory power' with respect to given expressive performances.

11.4 APPROACH I: LEARNING AT THE NOTE LEVEL

The first approach we pursued was very much in the tradition of what is generally known as *knowledge-based* or *knowledge-intensive learning*: knowledge about musical structure perception was formulated in an explicit (albeit abstract, incomplete, and partly inconsistent) *domain theory* (Mitchell *et al.*, 1986). A learning algorithm by the name of IBL-SMART was developed that can use the knowledge to advantage.

11.4.1 The Target Concepts

Learning proceeds at the level of notes. Each individual note is a training example, and the induced rules refer to individual notes as well. The goal is to learn rules that determine the precise degrees of loudness and tempo to be applied to each note in a piece. We have thus two separate (numeric) learning tasks — dynamics and tempo — and accordingly, the system will learn two sets of rules.

---

[1] A clarifying remark to readers who feel that we are trivializing the artistic phenomenon of expressive performance by reducing it to a function of structural patterns in the music: We are not talking here about the highly artistic details that distinguish a great pianist or other performer, and that derive in part from his/her deep understanding of music history, experience with styles, social circumstances, and artistic intentions. What is being investigated here is the "rational" component of expression, the types of musical behavior and understanding that are more or less common and agreed upon among musicians — in other words, what a music student must learn in order to produce acceptable performances. Even a virtuoso's performance is constrained by and large by such common norms of interpretation.

To make the problem accessible to a symbolic, knowledge-based induction algorithm, we split it into a symbolic classification task and a numeric prediction task. In both expression dimensions, we distinguish two classes of notes: those that are associated with a *rise* of the performance curve (relative to the previous note), and those that witness a *fall* of the curve. In the dynamics dimension, the relevant musical terms for the two classes are *crescendo* (an increase in loudness) and *decrescendo* (a decrease), and in the tempo dimension, *accelerando* (an increase in tempo, i.e., speeding up) and *ritardando* (slowing down). These are common musical concepts.

The learner induces classification rules that distinguish between instances of the two classes. In addition, for each of these rules it learns a scheme to predict precise numeric values, i.e., by *how much* the dynamics or tempo curve should rise or fall at a particular point. The learning algorithm IBL-SMART, which was developed for this class of problems, is described in section 11.4.3.

11.4.2 The Qualitative Domain Theory

The musical examples are initially described only through intrinsic features of the individual notes (e.g., pitch (tone height), duration, relative position in the piece) and some simple relations between pairs of adjacent notes (the interval between two notes, and the direction of the interval). As we have tried to show in section 11.3, this is hardly sufficient for effective learning. Knowledge about relevant musical structure is needed. We have devised a structured symbolic *domain theory* that represents what we consider general musical intuitions that ordinary human listeners possess. Most of this knowledge is only approximate and uncertain, and that is made explicit in the formulation of the theory. Figure 11.3 sketches the general structure of the theory. A more detailed discussion can be found in Widmer (1993a, 1995a).

The model consists of two major components. The lower part, named *model of structural hearing* in Figure 11.3, is basically a set of programs that perform a structural analysis of a given melody and explicitly annotate the melody with various musical structures that we believe are perceived by human listeners. This part of the model is based on the well-known music theories by Lerdahl and Jackendoff (1983) and Narmour (1977). Essentially, the purpose is to construct meaningful higher-level descriptors that capture aspects of musical context. These can then be referred to in the induction process.

The upper part of the theory (the *qualitative dependency network*) expresses our intuitions concerning possible relations between structural aspects of the music and appropriate expressive performance decisions (i.e., the symbolic target concepts). It is similar in structure to the 'classical' domain theories as used in *Explanation-Based Generalization (EBG)* (Mitchell *et al.*, 1986). It is a hierarchy of statements relating non-operational predicates (including the target concepts) to more operational, specific conditions. However, these statements may describe relations of various strength and specificity:

- **Strict (deductive) rules:**
  As in EBG, the domain theory contains some strict deductive rules of the form $Q : -P_1, P_2, \ldots$ that specify sufficient conditions ($P_1, P_2, \ldots$) for some (non-operational) predicate Q to be true.

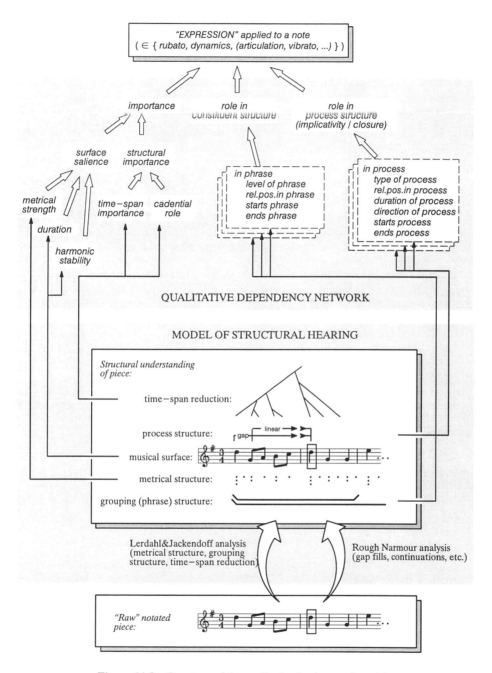

Figure 11.3 Structure of the qualitative background model.

- **Directed qualitative dependencies:**
  A statement of the form q+(A, B) can be paraphrased as "the values of attributes A and B are positively proportionally related" or "high (or low) values of A tend to produce high (or low) values of B, all other things being equal". Negative dependency q−(A, B) is defined analogously. Obviously, this kind of knowledge is less precise and logically weaker than strict rules. It does not permit deductive reasoning. A number of similar types of knowledge items have been proposed in the literature, among them Michalski's (1983) M- and R-descriptors and the positive and negative dependencies of Collins and Michalski (1989).

- **Undirected qualitative dependencies:**
  A statement depends_on(Q, [P₁, P₂, ...]) denotes an unspecific, undirected relation between the set of predicates P_i and the (non-operational) predicate Q. Basically, it says that the value (or truth value) of Q depends somehow on the values (or truth values) of the P_i, but we do not know the exact function that defines this dependency. Similar types of general knowledge items have been described in Russell (1989) and Bergadano *et al.* (1989). They are used to focus the learner on sets of relevant predicates or attributes in the search for rule refinements.

Most of the arrows in Figure 11.3 represent qualitative dependencies. For instance, the following statement at the top level of the theory relates the phenomenon of loudness variations to some abstract musical notions:

```
depends_on( crescendo(Note,X),
    [importance(Note,I),
     goal_directedness(Note,G),
     closure(Note,C)]).
```

"Whether crescendo should be applied to a note (and if so, the exact amount X) depends, among other things, on the importance I of the note, on its degree G of melodic 'goal-directedness', and on its degree C of melodic 'closure'."

Abstract notions like importance, goal_directedness, and closure are then again related to lower-level musical effects, all the way down to some surface features of training instances, for example:

```
q+( metrical_strength(Note,X),  stability(Note,Y)).
q+( harmonic_stability(Note,X), stability(Note,Y)).
```

"The perceived degree of stability Y of a note is positively proportionally related to (among other things) the metrical strength X of the note" etc.

where metrical_strength is a numeric and harmonic_stability is a symbolic attribute (with a discrete, ordered domain of qualitative values). Both are defined as operational and are computed by the lower part of the domain theory — the *model of structural hearing*.

11.4.3   The Learning Algorithm IBL-SMART

A knowledge-based learning algorithm by the name of IBL-SMART was developed for the purpose of this project (Widmer, 1993b). According to the two-part structure of the learning

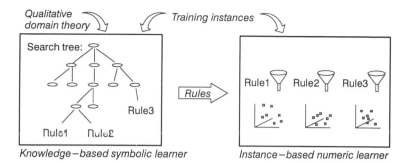

Figure 11.4 Integration of symbolic learning and numeric learning in IBL-SMART.

task as defined in section 11.4.1, IBL-SMART is composed of two major components (see Figure 11.4)[2]: a *symbolic learning component* that learns to distinguish between the symbolic target concepts (e.g., *crescendo* and *decrescendo*) and can utilize domain knowledge in the form of a qualitative model, and an *instance-based* component that stores the instances with their precise numeric attribute values and can predict the target value for some new note by numeric interpolation over known instances. The connection between these two components is as follows: each rule (conjunctive hypothesis) learned by the symbolic component describes a subset of the instances; these are assumed to represent a subtype of the target concept (e.g., some particular type of *crescendo* situations). All the instances covered by a rule are given to the instance-based learner to be stored together in a separate instance space. Predicting the target value for some new note in a new piece then involves matching the note against the symbolic rules and using only those numeric instance spaces (interpolation tables) for prediction whose associated rules are satisfied by the note.

IBL-SMART's symbolic component is a non-incremental discrimination algorithm that learns classification rules in disjunctive normal form (DNF). It has been specifically designed to be able to use imprecise, qualitative background knowledge as contained in our domain theory. The algorithm starts with a nonoperational definition of the target concept (e.g., *crescendo*) and performs stepwise top-down operationalization (specialization) by growing a heuristic best-first search tree. Expressions (nodes of the tree) are refined by operationalizing non-operational predicates or by inductively adding new conditions that discriminate between positive and negative examples. A node becomes a leaf when it covers only positive training instances; it then represents one conjunct (rule) in the final DNF hypothesis. The search terminates when a certain percentage of the positive examples are covered.

Operationalization steps that reduce a non-operational predicate to more basic ones are based on rules or dependency statements given in the domain theory. In the case of strict rules, this is identical to the method used in Explanation-Based Generalization (Mitchell *et al.*, 1986). In the case of a qualitative dependency, say, $q+(A, B)$, the operationalization step consists in replacing the non-operational predicate B with A. The algorithm creates successor nodes by replacing $B(X, .)$ with $A(X, a_i)$ for all values a_i appearing in positive instances covered by the current node. Which of these node expansions is most promising and will most

---

[2] The name IBL-SMART reflects the two components: IBL stands for *Instance-Based Learning* (Aha *et al.*, 1991) and characterizes the numeric component, and SMART is a tribute to the ML-SMART algorithm (Bergadano and Giordana, 1988), which provided some of the ideas for the search strategy of the symbolic learner.

Figure 11.5 Beginnings of three little minuets by J.S.Bach.

likely be expanded further is then determined by a heuristic *evaluation function*, which guides the search. The function takes into account empirical measures like the 'purity' of the current node, i.e., the ratio of positive / negative instances covered by the expression, but also semantic criteria, like the degree to which the attribute values involved in the operationalization observe the proportionality relation postulated by some dependency statement in the domain theory.

By taking into account both such inference-dependent plausibility measures and information about the numbers of instances covered, the search heuristic combines weak, imprecise background knowledge with empirical information from the training data, producing hypotheses that tend to correspond to the background knowledge as much as the data permits and overriding the background knowledge if the data is in conflict with the knowledge. A more detailed description of the search strategy can be found in Widmer (1993b).

11.4.4 An Experiment

The system has been tested with pieces from various musical epochs and styles (Bach minuets, Chopin waltzes, even jazz standards). Here we present two typical results.

Figure 11.5 shows the beginnings of three well-known minuets from J.S.Bach's *Notenbüchlein für Anna Magdalena Bach*. All three pieces consist of two parts. The second parts of the pieces were used for training: they were played on an electronic piano by the author, and recorded through a MIDI interface. After learning, the system was tested on the first parts of the same pieces. In this way, we combined some variation in the training data (three different pieces) with some uniformity in style (three pieces from the same period and with similar characteristics; test data from the same pieces as training data, though different).

The training input consisted of 212 examples (notes), of which 79 were examples of crescendo, and 120 were examples of decrescendo (the rest were played in a neutral way). The system learned 14 rules and, correspondingly, 14 interpolation tables characterizing crescendo situations, and 15 rules for decrescendo. Quite a number of instances were covered by more than one rule.

Applying these rules to new pieces produces expressive performances. The quality of these

Figure 11.6 Beginning of a training piece as played by teacher (*dynamics* curve).

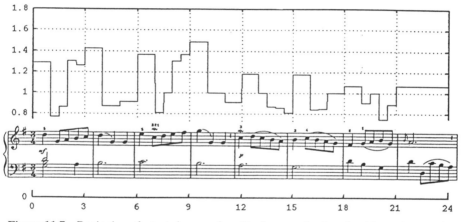

Figure 11.7 Beginning of a test piece as played by learner after learning (*dynamics* curve).

is not easy to measure, as there is no precise criterion to decide whether some performance is right or wrong. Judging the correctness is a matter of listening. Unfortunately, we cannot attach a recording to this article so that the reader can appreciate the results. Instead, Figure 11.6 depicts a part of one of the training pieces (the second part of the first minuet in G major as played by the author), and Figure 11.7 shows the performance generated by the system for a test piece (the first part of the same minuet) after learning. The figures plot the relative loudness with which the individual notes were played; a level of 1.0 represents average loudness.

The reader familiar with standard music notation may appreciate that there are strong similarities in the way similar types of phrases are played by the human teacher and the learner. Note, for instance, the crescendo in lines rising by stepwise motion, and the decrescendo patterns in measures with three quarter notes. Note also the consistent pattern of accents (loud notes) at the beginnings of measures. Given the limited amount of training data, the degree

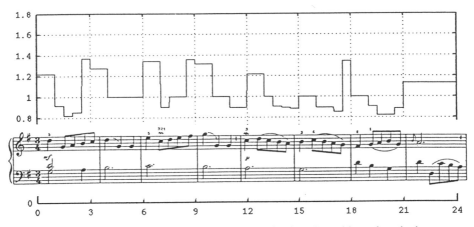

Figure 11.8 Beginning of test piece as played after learning without domain theory.

of generalization achieved is quite remarkable. In addition, an inspection of the symbolic rules learned in this experiment reveals that the system had re-discovered some expression principles that had been formulated years ago by music theorists (see section 11.7).

When we perform the same experiment *without* the domain theory, we get an impression of the importance of the musical background knowledge. Without the domain model, IBL-SMART is reduced to a purely empirical discrimination algorithm.

Figure 11.8 shows the system's performance of the same test piece after learning from the Bach minuets in this way. There is a marked deterioration in the resulting performance from learning *with* knowledge (Figure 11.7) to learning *without* knowledge (Figure 11.8). The variations applied by the restricted system are of rather mixed quality. In some cases (e.g., the decrescendo patterns in measures 4 and 5), they do make sense, in others (e.g., the stress on the last notes in measures 1, 3, and 6) the system's decisions run counter to musical intuition. Obviously, the domain theory contributes significantly to successful learning, especially when the number of available training examples is rather small, as in the current case.

Apart from such qualitative evaluations, we have also performed some quantitative measurements to establish beyond doubt the benefits of the knowledge-based approach. Section 11.7.1 has more to say on that.

11.5   APPROACH II: LEARNING AT THE STRUCTURE LEVEL

Despite some encouraging results with the first approach, it became clear eventually that the note level is not really appropriate from a musical point of view. For one thing, though the performances produced by the system were in large part musically sensible, they lacked a certain smoothness and a sense of both local and global form. Second, it is psychologically implausible that performers think and decide on a purely local level in terms of single notes; rather, they tend to comprehend music in terms of higher-level abstract forms like phrases etc. And finally, as observed by Sloboda (1985), expression is a *multi-level* phenomenon: expressive shapes, like musical structures, appear at multiple levels. Local expression patterns may

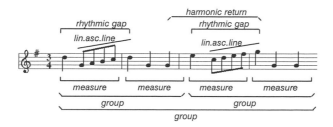

Figure 11.9   Structural interpretation of part of Bach minuet.

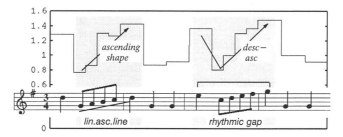

Figure 11.10   Two of the expressive shapes found in Bach recording.

be embedded within larger patterns (e.g., shaping of ornaments within an overall crescendo). A sensible formalization of musical expression should reflect that.

Consequently, we have developed an alternative approach that abandons the note level and tries to learn expression rules directly at the level of musical structures. The essence of the approach is a *knowledge-based abstraction strategy* that transforms the training examples and the entire learning problem to a musically plausible abstraction level. The induced expression rules will then also relate to that abstraction level.

The problem transformation proceeds in two stages. The system first performs a musical analysis of the given melody. Analysis routines, based again on selected parts of the theories by Lerdahl and Jackendoff (1983) and Narmour (1977), identify various structures in the melody that might be heard as units or 'chunks' by a listener or musician. The result is a rich annotation of the melody with identified structures. Figure 11.9 exemplifies the result of this step with an excerpt from one of the Bach minuets. Among the perceptual chunks identified here are four *measures* heard as rhythmic units, three *groups* heard as melodic units or "phrases" on two different levels, two *linearly ascending melodic lines*, two rhythmic patterns called *rhythmic gap fills* (a concept derived from Narmour's theory), and several others. Note that these musical structures can be of widely varying scope — some consist of two or three notes only, others may span several measures. As training examples will be defined by such structures, the system will learn to recognize and apply expression at multiple levels.

In the second step, the abstract *target concepts* for the learner are identified. The system tries to find prototypical *shapes* in the given expression (dynamics and tempo) curves that can be associated with these structures. Prototypical shapes are rough trends that can be identified in the curve. The system distinguishes five kinds of shapes: `even_level` (no recognizable rising or falling tendency of the curve in the time span covered by the structure), `ascending` (an ascending tendency from the beginning to the end of the time span), descending, asc_desc (first ascending up to a certain point, then descending), and desc_asc (first descending, then ascending). The system selects those shapes that minimize the deviation between the actual curve and an idealized shape defined by straight lines.

Figure 11.10 illustrates this step for the dynamics curve associated with the Bach example (derived from a performance by the author). We take a look at two of the structures found in Figure 11.9: the ascending melodic line in measures 1–2 has been associated with the shape ascending, as the curve shows a clear ascending (*crescendo*) tendency in this part of the recording. And the 'rhythmic gap fill' pattern in measures 3–4 has been played with a desc_asc (*decrescendo – crescendo*) shape.

The results of the transformation phase are passed on to IBL-SMART.[3] Each pair <*musical structure, expressive shape*> is a training example. Each such example is further described by a quantitative characterization of the shape (the precise loudness/tempo values, relative to the average loudness and tempo of the piece, of the curve at the extreme points of the shape) and a description, in terms of music-theoretic features, of the structure and the notes contained in it (e.g., note duration, harmonic function, metrical strength, . . .). As different types of musical structures are in part described by different attributes, the learning task is split into corresponding sub-tasks; prediction of expressive shapes is learned separately for each type of musical structure.

The *output* of IBL-SMART is then a set of general rules that decide, given the type and description of a musical structure, what kind of expressive shape should be applied to it, and exactly *how much* crescendo, accelerando, etc. should be applied.

Applying learned rules to new problems is rather straightforward: given the score of a new piece (melody) to play expressively, the system again first transforms it to the abstract structural level by performing its musical analysis. For each of the musical structures found, the learned rules are consulted to suggest an appropriate expressive shape (for dynamics and rubato). The interpolation tables associated with the matching rules are used to compute the precise numeric details of the shape. Starting from an even shape for the entire piece (i.e., equal loudness and tempo for all notes), expressive shapes are applied to the piece in sorted order, from shortest to longest. Expressive shapes are overlayed over already applied ones by averaging the respective dynamics and rubato values. The result is an expressive interpretation of the piece that pays equal regard to local and global expression patterns, thus combining micro- and macro-structures.

Note that in this abstraction approach to learning, the level of individual notes is abandoned completely. Only expressive shapes associated with entire musical structures are considered, single notes are never examined as such. Thus, our approach II does not subsume approach I (note-level learning). The results of our experiments — some of which are briefly described below — indicate that the potential danger of the abstraction method (loss of information at a detailed level) is clearly outweighed by increased noise tolerance. Also, the abstraction approach generally produces more well-structured and balanced results.

---

[3] Since there is no explicit domain theory any more in this approach, we have used FOIL (Quinlan, 1990) as the symbolic learning component of IBL-SMART in all the experiments described below.

11.5.1 An Experiment

Here are some results of an experiment with waltzes by Frédéric Chopin. The training pieces were five rather short excerpts (about 20 measures on average) from the three waltzes Op.64 no.2, Op.69 no.2, and Op.70 no.3, played by the author on an electronic piano and recorded via MIDI. The results of learning were then tested by having the system play other excerpts from Chopin waltzes.

As an example, Figure 11.11 shows the system's performance, in terms of both loudness and tempo variations, of the beginning of the waltz Op.18 after learning from the five training pieces. Again, values of 1.0 mean average loudness or tempo, higher values mean that a note has been played louder or faster, respectively. The arrows have been added by the author to indicate various structural regularities in the performance. Note that while the written musical score contains some explicit expression marks added by the composer (e.g., commands like

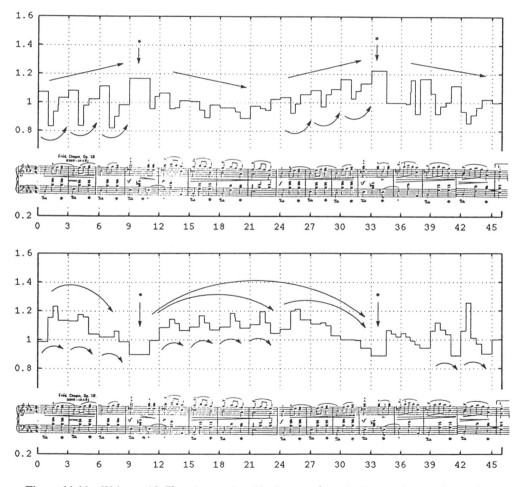

Figure 11.11 Waltz op.18, E♭ major, as played by learner: *dynamics* (top) and *tempo* (bottom).

cresc (*crescendo*), *sf* (*sforzato*) or *p* (*piano*) and graphical symbols calling for large-scale crescendo and decrescendo), the system was not aware of these; it was given the notes only.

In a qualitative analysis, the results look and sound musically convincing. The graphs suggest a clear understanding of musical structure and a musically sensible shaping of these structures, both at micro and macro levels. At the macro level (arrows above the graphs), for instance, both the dynamics and the tempo curve mirror the four-phrase structure of the piece. In the dynamics dimension, the first and third phrase are played with a recognizable crescendo culminating at the end point of the phrases (the B♭ at the beginning of the fourth and twelfth measures — see positions (beats) 9 and 33 in the plot). In the tempo dimension, phrases (at least the first three) are shaped by giving them a roughly parabolic shape — speeding up at the beginning, slowing down towards the end. That agrees well with theories of rubato published in the music literature (e.g., Todd, 1989).

At lower structural levels, the most obvious phenomenon is the phrasing of the individual measures, which creates the distinct waltz 'feel': in the dynamics dimension, the first and metrically strongest note of each measure is emphasized in almost all cases by playing it louder than the rest of the measure, and additional melodic considerations (like rising or falling melodic lines) determine the fine structure of each measure. In the tempo dimension, measures are shaped by playing the first note slightly longer than the following ones and then again slowing down towards the end of the measure.

The most striking aspect is the close correspondence between the system's variations and Chopin's (or the score editor's) explicit expression marks (which were not visible to the system!). The reader trained in reading music notation may appreciate how the system's dynamics curve closely parallels the various crescendo and decrescendo markings and also the *p* (*piano*) command in measure 5. Two notes were deemed particularly worthy of stress by Chopin and were explicitly annotated with *sf* (*sforzato*): the B♭'s at the beginning of the fourth and twelfth measures. Elegantly enough, our program came to the same conclusion and emphasized them most extremely by playing them louder and longer than any other note in the piece; the corresponding places are marked by arrows with asterisks in Figure 11.11.

Just for comparison, Figure 11.12 shows the dynamics curve from an independent recording of the same piece by the author. There are similarities at the macro level. However, the author's own performance is embarrassingly poor: it is much less regular and controlled in the fine details (due to the poor keyboard of the electronic piano and the author's far from perfect piano technique). Note that the training pieces from which the system learned were of no better quality. That the system learns to produce smooth performances from bad examples is in part due to the abstraction of *expressive shapes* from the low-level details of an example performance.

11.6   A MACHINE LEARNING ANALYSIS OF REAL ARTISTIC PERFORMANCES

All experiments so far used performances by the author himself as training examples. One might be concerned about a possible bias in these data, intentional or inadvertent.

This section briefly describes experiments performed with *real* data, that is, performances of a complete piece by a number of internationally famous pianists. The results shed some

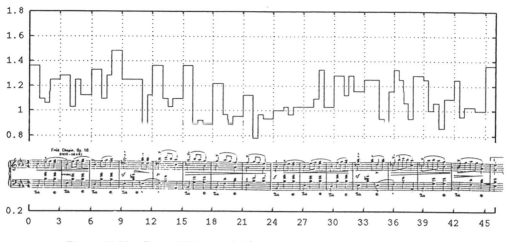

Figure 11.12 Chopin Waltz op.18, E♭ major, as played by author *(dynamics)*.

light into significant differences in personal performance styles between different artists. The experiments have also helped us pinpoint a number of weaknesses of the current approach. Appropriate refinements of the strategy and the music-theoretic vocabulary are currently under way. We cannot present a detailed discussion here — the following is only intended to give the reader an impression of the complexity of the phenomenon and a glimpse of the results we have achieved so far. Further details can be found in Widmer (1995b).

The piece in question is Robert Schumann's romantic piano piece *"Träumerei"* (from *"Kinderszenen"*, op. 15). Figure 11.13 shows the score of the entire piece. Bruno Repp (1992) has measured the tempo deviations in 28 performances of this piece by 24 well-known pianists. This data set was used as the basis for a suite of experiments. Repp's data only capture the dimension of expressive timing (tempo), dynamics was not taken into account. The learning algorithm used was IBL-SMART with knowledge-based abstraction *(approach II)*.

At the highest level, the *Träumerei* is composed of two parts of length 8 and 16 bars, respectively, where the first part is obligatorily repeated. In the experiments, we used various pianists' performances of the second part for learning. The first part of the piece was then used for testing.

Three pianists from the top of Repp's list — Claudio Arrau, Vladimir Ashkenazy, and Alfred Brendel — were chosen for the first experiment. Their performances of the second part of the *Träumerei* were used as training examples. The respective tempo curves are shown in Figure 11.14. (To facilitate an easier comparison of several curves, we are using a slightly different plot style here). As before, the labels on the x axis indicate the absolute distance from the beginning of the piece in terms of quarter notes ("score time"). The plot represents the relative tempo variations — the higher the curve, the faster the local tempo.

It is quite evident that there is significant agreement between the performances at a global level, but also a lot of differences in the fine details. All three pianists observed the major ritardandi dictated by important structural boundaries (e.g., major phrase endings) and/or prescribed by expression markings in the score. The extreme ritardando in the third to last bar is due to a *fermata* in the score.

Träumerei

Figure 11.13 "Träumerei" by Robert Schumann, from the 'Urtext Edition', W. Boetticher (ed.), G. Henle Verlag, Munich, 1977 (reproduced with kind permission).

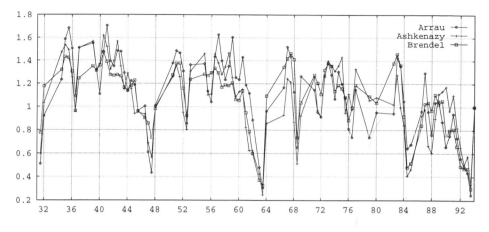

Figure 11.14   Second part of *Träumerei* as played by three pianists (tempo curves).

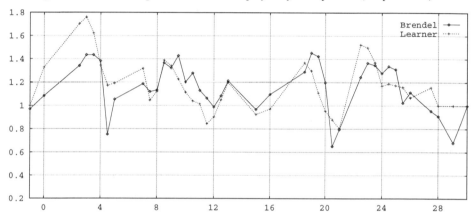

Figure 11.15   Comparison learner – Brendel on test piece (first part of "Träumerei").

Figure 11.15 shows the system's performance of the test piece (the first part of the *Träumerei*) after learning from these three examples and compares it to one of its teachers' (Brendel's) performances of the same piece.

The plot shows considerable agreement in the overall, high-level trends, but also some discrepancies in the finer details (e.g., the finer phrasing structure in measures 3 and 7). Some of these discrepancies point to shortcomings of our current system. For instance, the system fails to replicate Brendel's way of phrasing the small melodic motifs in measures 3 and 7. Deeper analysis revealed that this is due to the limited set of abstract *expressive shapes* (see section 11.5) that the learner can identify in a given performance curve. We are planning to introduce more complex abstract patterns into the learner's shape vocabulary. Generally, however, we consider the result very satisfactory, especially given that the performances of the three teachers, though fairly similar at a high level, are quite different at lower levels.

Another interesting dimension that can be explored with the help of machine learning is personal style differences between individual artists. Repp's data collection also includes three

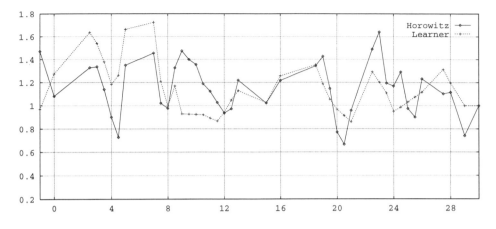

Figure 11.16   Comparison learner – Horowitz on test piece (first part of *Träumerei*).

performances by Vladimir Horowitz, who is known for his very distinctive interpretations. In another experiment, the three performances by Horowitz (again only of the second part of the piece) were used as training examples. Figure 11.16 shows the system's performance of the test piece after learning from the three Horowitz examples, and compares it to one of Horowitz's performances.

It is quite obvious that Horowitz's performance is indeed very different from, say, Alfred Brendel's (cf. Figure 11.15). The learner does seem to manage to replicate part of the Horowitz style, but not as well as that of more 'standard' interpretation styles such as Brendel's. We cannot give a conclusive explanation at this point, but one may conjecture that Horowitz's style is more idiosyncratic, his performance decisions cannot be so easily related to or 'explained' by obvious structural features of the music. We do expect that further analysis of the learned rules and more detailed experiments will provide insights into specific aspects of performance differences that may be of interest to musicology in general. In any event, we can show experimentally that the two knowledge-based approaches to learning are superior to learning without musical knowledge (see the next section).

11.7   DISCUSSION OF EXPERIMENTAL RESULTS

In the introduction to this chapter, it was claimed that, as an interdisciplinary project, our work should produce results of interest to both disciplines involved. The example results presented in the previous sections have hinted at some of these. Here, we will look at the results a bit more closely, both from a machine learning and a musicology perspective.

11.7.1   Quantitative Analysis

From the viewpoint of machine learning, the main contribution of this project is the introduction and comparison of two different approaches to knowledge-based learning: the first consists in making incomplete and very imprecise domain knowledge explicit in the form of a qualitative domain theory and devising an inductive learning algorithm that uses the theory to guide its

Table 11.1 Percentage of agreement between learner and teachers (unweighted).

	naive approach (no knowledge)	approach 1 (qual. domain theory)	approach 2 (abstraction)
matches/accelerando	58.46	61.54	55.38
matches/ritardando	50.91	54.55	78.18
Total matches	55.00	58.33	65.83

heuristic search. The alternative approach uses domain knowledge to transform the training examples and the entire learning problem to musically plausible abstraction levels. Our results with Bach minuets, briefly hinted at in section 11.4.4, weakly indicated that the introduction of additional knowledge (in that case through the first approach) does indeed improve the learning results. However, one would like to obtain quantitative results that clearly prove that hypothesis.

A fundamental problem with our application domain, at least from a machine learning point of view, is that a precise quantitative evaluation of the results is not possible. The musical quality of an expressive performance cannot be quantified. There is no one 'correct' interpretation, aesthetic judgements can depend on many extra-musical factors, and global qualities like the coherence or balance of a performance are very difficult to formalize. Nonetheless, we have performed some simple measurements in order to at least get some weak indications as to the relative merits of our learning approaches.

For instance, we experimentally compared three algorithms on the Schumann learning task: algorithm 0 (the 'naive' algorithm) is IBL-SMART *without* any domain knowledge, thus restricted to purely empirical learning. Algorithm 1 is the same system *with* the qualitative domain theory, learning at the note level as described in section 11.4, and algorithm 2 is IBL-SMART with knowledge-based abstraction as described in section 11.5. Each of the three algorithms was trained on the performances of the second piece of the *Träumerei* by the three pianists Claudio Arrau, Vladimir Ashkenazy, and Alfred Brendel. The learned rules were then applied to the first part of the piece, and the resulting performances were compared to the respective performances by the three 'teachers' by counting the number of agreements of categorical decisions (i.e., how often both the pianist and the learner applied a *ritardando* or an *accelerando* to a note). Table 11.1 summarizes these 'predictive accuracy' measurements, averaged over all three pianists. The reader should keep in mind that an agreement of 100% is strictly impossible, as the three pianists' performances differ in a lot of details.

The summary line (the total percentage of matches) indicates significant advantages of the knowledge-based systems over the learner without domain knowledge. And among the former, approach 2 (knowledge-based abstraction) clearly outperforms approach 1 (learning at the note level). That confirms our previous qualitative evaluations (by musical analysis and listening tests) and also supports the theoretic hypothesis that structure abstraction is musically more plausible than direct application of knowledge at the level of individual notes.

But such quantitative results should be taken with a grain of salt. Simply counting the number of matching decisions is far too simplistic. Not every note in a piece is equally important, and some errors are far more critical than others. All that depends in a complex way on aspects of the musical context. A musically meaningful comparison should take all the relevant factors

Table 11.2 Percentage of agreement (weighted by metrical strength).

	naive approach (no knowledge)	approach 1 (qual. domain theory)	approach 2 (abstraction)
matches/accelerando	61.93	58.88	57.87
matches/ritardando	40.83	55.03	76.92
Total matches	52.19	57.10	66.67

into account, but that would presuppose a complete theory of 'correct' interpretation, a thing which obviously does not exist (which is why we started our empirical research in the first place).

As a first approximation to a more elaborate comparison, Table 11.2 lists the results of the same experiment if we apply a simple *weighting scheme* to the counts: each match/mismatch between system and teacher is weighted by the relative *metrical strength* of the underlying note. This is meant to be a *very* rough measure of the relative importance of notes. In the weighted analysis, the differences between the three learners come out even more clearly, with the abstraction-based approach winning by a big margin. Whatever the ultimate musical validity of these measurements, they do provide strong evidence for the utility of the musical background knowledge and the effectiveness of our knowledge-based learners.

11.7.2 Useful Qualitative Results for Musicology

From the perspective of musicology, the qualitative aspects of our results are more informative. Generally, since the domain knowledge — be it in the form of a domain theory or in the form of abstraction operators — is based on two recent theories of tonal music, the musical quality of our learners' expressive performances (and the superiority over learning without knowledge) provides additional empirical evidence for the relevance of these music theories.

More detailed insights can be gained by directly inspecting the learned expression rules. For instance, an analysis of rules learned from different types of music have revealed different structural dimensions of the music to be relevant (Widmer, 1995a). Also, experiments have shown that while abstraction to the structure level generally provides better results for various types of classical music, for other styles like jazz the note level is more adequate — note level rules perform better and have more explanatory potential.

A very interesting result was that the system in effect re-discovered variations of some expression rules that were postulated by music theorists some years ago (e.g., Sundberg *et al.*, 1983; Friberg, 1991), based mainly on musical intuition and experience. For instance, one of the rules discovered by our learner reads:

```
ritardando( Note, X) :-
    interval_prev( Note, I),
    at_least( I, maj6),
    dir_prev( Note, up).
```

which may be paraphrased as *"Increase the duration (by a certain amount X) of all notes that terminate an upward melodic leap of at least a major sixth."* This is a specialization of rule 4 from Sundberg *et al.* (1983), which increases the duration of all notes that terminate a melodic leap (in either direction). Several other variants of Sundberg rules were discovered through learning. Our experiments have thus produced additional empirical support for the appropriateness of the Sundberg rules. These results are also the starting point for new investigations with various music-theoretic vocabularies that we are currently performing in cooperation with Johan Sundberg and colleagues.

11.8 CONCLUSION

This chapter has shown how machine learning can profitably be applied to the study of real problems in the field of tonal music. Compared to 'hard' sciences like physics and chemistry, music is in many ways 'softer' — many aspects are not quantifiable, and that makes it difficult to perform the kinds of precise experiments and analyses that are considered the norm in inductive learning research. Nonetheless, machine learning can make useful qualitative contributions, for instance to the empirical evaluation of existing theories of the domain. Prerequisites for the success of such projects are a thorough analysis of the application domain and existing theories thereof, and a conscious approach to domain modelling. That includes the careful design of vocabulary and representation language, which can contain (and hide) a lot of domain-specific knowledge and implicit assumptions.

Our projects have yielded a number of interesting musical results, and we view our "analysis-by-resynthesis" approach (i.e., having machine learning programs reproduce observed phenomena and analyzing the results) as a viable alternative or addition to more traditional methods in musicology (Widmer, 1994b).

From a machine learning perspective, such interdisciplinary projects can be beneficial as well: new application domains can motivate the development of new learning models and algorithms, which need not at all be domain-specific. Our algorithm IBL-SMART, for instance, is a general inductive learner that may well be useful for other classes of applications.

Future work in this project will concentrate primarily on aspects of domain modelling. Experiments with different music-theoretic vocabularies and different types of music will give us a more detailed insight into the regularities and possible explanations of performance styles. The compilation of a large collection of real performance data turns out to be difficult (mainly for copyright reasons), but it will be essential to the success of this enterprise.

ACKNOWLEDGEMENTS

The author would like to thank Bruno Repp (Haskins Laboratories, Yale University) for the permission to use his collection of Schumann performance data. Special thanks to Miroslav Kubat and Robert Holte for helpful comments and suggestions concerning this text. Financial support for the Austrian Research Institute for Artificial Intelligence is provided by the Austrian Federal Ministry for Science, Transport, and the Arts. The institute's research in the area of Knowledge Discovery and Data Mining has also been supported in part by the Austrian *Fonds zur Förderung der Wissenschaftlichen Forschung (FWF)* under grant P10489-MAT.

REFERENCES

Aha, D., Kibler, D., and Albert, M.K. (1991). Instance-Based Learning Algorithms. *Machine Learning* 6(1), pp.37–66.

Bergadano, F. and Giordana, A. (1988). A Knowledge Intensive Approach to Concept Induction. In *Proceedings of the Fifth International Conference on Machine Learning*, Ann Arbor, MI.

Bergadano, F., Giordana, A., and Ponsero, S. (1989). Deduction in Top-Down Inductive Learning. In *Proceedings of the Sixth International Workshop on Machine Learning*, Ithaca, N.Y.

Collins, A. and Michalski, R.S. (1989). The Logic of Plausible Reasoning: A Core Theory. *Cognitive Science* 13(1), pp.1–49.

Deutsch, D. (ed.) (1982). *The Psychology of Music*. New York: Academic Press.

Friberg, A. (1991). Generative Rules for Music Performance: A Formal Description of a Rule System. *Computer Music Journal* 15(2), pp.56–71.

Hunter, L. (ed.) (1993). *Artificial Intelligence and Molecular Biology*. Menlo Park, CA: AAAI Press.

King, R.D., Muggleton, S., Lewis, R.A., and Sternberg, M.J.E. (1992). Drug Design by Machine Learning: The Use of Inductive Logic Programming to Model the Structure-activity Relationship of Trimethoprim Analogues Binding to Dihydrofolate Reductase. In *Proceedings of the National Academy of Sciences*, Vol. 89, pp.11322–11326.

Lerdahl, F. and Jackendoff, R. (1983). *A Generative Theory of Tonal Music*. Cambridge, MA: MIT Press.

Lindsay, R.K., Buchanan, B.G., Feigenbaum, E.A., and Lederberg, J. (1980). *Applications of Artificial Intelligence for Organic Chemistry: The DENDRAL Project*. New York: McGraw-Hill.

Michalski, R.S. (1983). A Theory and Methodology of Inductive Learning. In R.S. Michalski, J.G. Carbonell and T.M. Mitchell (Eds.), *Machine Learning: An Artificial Intelligence Approach*, vol. I. Palo Alto, CA: Tioga.

Mitchell, T.M., Keller, R.M., and Kedar-Cabelli, S.T. (1986). Explanation-Based Generalization: A Unifying View. *Machine Learning* 1(1), pp.47–80.

Muggleton, S., King, R.D., and Sternberg, M.J.E. (1992). Protein Secondary Structure Prediction Using Logic-based Machine Learning. *Protein Engineering* 5(7), pp.647–657.

Narmour, E. (1977). *Beyond Schenkerism: The Need for Alternatives in Music Analysis*. Chicago, Ill.: Chicago University Press.

Quinlan, J.R. (1990). Learning Logical Definitions from Relations. *Machine Learning* 5(3), pp.239–266.

Repp, B. (1992). Diversity and Commonality in Music Performance: An Analysis of Timing Microstructure in Schumann's "Träumerei". *Journal of the Acoustical Society of America* 92(5), pp.2546–2568.

Russell, S.J. (1989). *The Use of Knowledge in Analogy and Induction*. London: Pitman.

Shavlik, J.W., Towell, G., and Noordewier, M. (1992). Using Neural Networks to Refine Biological Knowledge. *International Journal of Genome Research* 1(1), pp.81–107.

Sloboda, J. (1985). *The Musical Mind: The Cognitive Psychology of Music.* Oxford: Clarendon Press.

Sundberg, J., Askenfelt, A. and Frydén, L. (1983). Musical Performance: A Synthesis-by-rule Approach. *Computer Music Journal* 7(1), pp.37–43.

Todd, N. (1985). A Model of Expressive Timing in Tonal Music. *Music Perception* 3, pp.33–59

Widmer, G. (1993a). Understanding and Learning Musical Expression. In *Proceedings of the International Computer Music Conference (ICMC-93)*, Tokyo, Japan.

Widmer, G. (1993b). Combining Knowledge-Based and Instance-Based Learning to Exploit Qualitative Knowledge. *Informatica* 17, Special Issue on Multistrategy Learning, pp.371–385.

Widmer, G. (1994a). The Synergy of Music Theory and AI: Learning Multi-Level Expressive Interpretation. In *Proceedings of the 12th National Conference on Artificial Intelligence (AAAI-94)*, Seattle, WA. Menlo Park, CA: AAAI Press.

Widmer, G. (1994b). Studying Musical Expression with AI and Machine Learning: "Analysis by Resynthesis". In J. Sundberg (ed.), *Proceedings of the Aarhus Symposium on Generative Grammars for Music Performance.* Royal Institute of Technology (KTH), Stockholm, Sweden.

Widmer, G. (1995a). Modelling the Rational Basis of Musical Expression. *Computer Music Journal* 19(2), pp.76–96.

Widmer, G. (1995b). A Machine Learning Analysis of Expressive Timing in Pianists' Performances of Schumann's "Träumerei". In J. Sundberg (ed.), *Proceedings of the Stockholm Symposium on Generative Grammars for Music Performance.* Royal Institute of Technology (KTH), Stockholm, Sweden.

Widmer, G. (1996). Learning Expressive Performance: The Structure-level Approach. *Journal of New Music Research* 25(2), pp.179–205.

Wnek, J. and Michalski, R.S. (1994). Hypothesis-driven Constructive Induction in AQ17-HCI: A Method and Experiments. *Machine Learning* 14(2), pp.139–168.

PART IV

Computer Systems and Control Systems

12

WebWatcher: A Learning Apprentice for the World Wide Web

Robert Armstrong, Dayne Freitag, Thorsten Joachims and Tom Mitchell

ABSTRACT

We describe an information seeking assistant for the World Wide Web. This agent, called Web-Watcher, interactively helps users locate desired information by employing learned knowledge about which hyperlinks are likely to lead to the target information. Our primary focus to-date has been on two issues: (1) organizing WebWatcher to provide interactive advice to Mosaic users while logging their successful and unsuccessful searches as training data, and (2) incorporating machine learning methods to automatically acquire knowledge for selecting an appropriate hyperlink given the current web page viewed by the user and the user's information goal. We describe the initial design of WebWatcher, and the results of our preliminary learning experiments.

12.1   OVERVIEW

Many have noted the need for software to assist people in locating information on the world wide web. This paper[1] presents the initial design and implementation of an agent called Web-Watcher that is intended to assist users both by interactively advising them as they traverse web links in search of information, and by searching autonomously on their behalf. In interactive mode, WebWatcher acts as a *learning apprentice* [Mitchell et al., 1985, Mitchell et al., 1994],

---

[1] This paper originally appeared in the 1995 *AAAI Spring Symposium on Information Gathering from Heterogeneous, Distributed Environments,* March, 1995. For a more recent description of WebWatcher, see [Joachim, et al., 1997].

providing interactive advice to the Mosaic user regarding which hyperlinks to follow next, then learning by observing the user's reaction to this advice as well as the eventual success or failure of the user's actions. The initial implementation of WebWatcher provides only this interactive mode, and it does not yet possess sufficient knowledge to give widely useful search advice. In this paper we present WebWatcher as a case study in the design of web-based learning agents for information retrieval. We focus in particular on the interface that enables WebWatcher to observe and advise any consenting user browsing any location on the web, and on results of initial experiments with its learning methods.

12.2   WEBWATCHER

This section presents the design of WebWatcher through a scenario of its use. WebWatcher is an information search agent that is "invoked" by following a web hyperlink to its web page, then filling out a Mosaic form to indicate what information is sought (e.g., a publication by some author). WebWatcher then returns the user to (a copy of) the web page from which he or she came, and assists the user as they follow hyperlinks forward through the web in search of the target information. As the user traverses the web, WebWatcher uses its learned knowledge to recommend especially promising hyperlinks to the user by highlighting these links on the user's display. At any point, the user may dismiss WebWatcher, by clicking one of two indicators on the WebWatcher icon, indicating either that the search has succeeded, or that the user wishes to give up on this search.

The sequence of web pages visited by the user in a typical scenario is illustrated in Figures 12.1 through 12.5. The first screen shows a typical web page,[2] providing information about machine learning. Notice in the third paragraph, this page invites the user to try out WebWatcher. If the user clicks on this link, he or she arrives at the front door WebWatcher page (Figure 12.2), which allows the user to identify the type of information he seeks. In this scenario the user indicates that the goal is to locate a paper, so he is shown a new screen (Figure 12.3) with a form to elaborate this information request. Once completed, the user is returned to the original page (Figure 12.4), with WebWatcher now "looking over his shoulder". Notice the WebWatcher icon at the top of the screen, and the highlighted link (bracketed by the Web-Watcher eyes icon) halfway down the screen. This highlighted link indicates WebWatcher's advice that the user follow the link to the *University of Illinois / Urbana (UIUC) AI / ML Page*. The user decides to select this recommended link, and arrives at the new web page shown in Figure 12.5, which contains new advice from WebWatcher. The search continues in this way, with the user directing the search and WebWatcher highlighting recommended links, until the user dismisses WebWatcher by clicking on "I found it" or "I give up".

From the user's perspective, WebWatcher is an agent with specialized knowledge about how to search outward from the page on which it was invoked. While WebWatcher suggests which hyperlink the user should take, the user remains firmly in control, and may ignore the system's advice at any step. We feel it is important for the user to remain in control, because

---

[2] This is a copy of the web page
http://www.ai.univie.ac.at/oefai/ml/ml-ressources.html, to which we have added the third
paragraph inviting the user to invoke WebWatcher.

```
┌────────────────────────────────────────────────────────────────────┐
│ ▣ NCSA Mosaic: Document View ████████████████████████████      回   │
├────────────────────────────────────────────────────────────────────┤
│ File    Options    Navigate    Annotate    Documents          Help  │
├────────────────────────────────────────────────────────────────────┤
│ Document Title:  ML related (27-Apr-1994)                   ┌─────┐ │
│                                                             │  ⊛  │ │
│ Document URL:  file://localhost/afs/cs/project/theo-6/web-ag│     │ │
└────────────────────────────────────────────────────────────└─────┘─┘
```

Machine Learning Information Services

This list is being maintained by the ML Group at the Austrian Research Institute for Artificial Intelligence (OFAI), Vienna, Austria.

It is far from complete and is being updated on an irregular basis. Please direct comments / suggestions / ... to Gerhard Widmer (gerhard@ai.univie.ac.at)

To try out our experimental WebWatcher search assistant, click here.

General ML Information Sources

University of California–Irvine (UCI) Machine Learning Page.
University of Illinois / Urbana (UIUC) AI / ML Page.
ML Mailing List Archive (moderated by M.Pazzani).
MLNet – Network of Excellence in Machine Learning (GMD server).
MLNet Mailing List Archive (Amsterdam --- NOT YET INSTALLED).
ILPNET, the Inductive Logic Programming Pan–European Scientific Network.
Programme "Learning in Humans and Machines" (European Science Foundation).

Various ML Program and Data Sources

GMD Machine Learning Repository.
UC Irvine Repository of ML Databases.
UC Irvine Repository of ML Programs.
MLC++ – A Machine Learning Library in C++ (R. Kohavi, Stanford Univ.).
Proben1 --- A Set of Neural Network Benchmark Problems (Size: ~2Mb !!).
Proben1 --- Description (Tech Report).
MLT – Machine Learning Toolbox (Esprit Project).
STATLOG (Esprit Project).
EconData – Economic Time Series Data (Univ. of Maryland).
United States Census Bureau.
Imperial College Prolog 1000 Database.

Inductive Logic Programming (ILP)

```
┌──────┐┌───────┐┌────┐┌──────┐┌────┐┌────────┐┌─────┐┌──────────┐┌────────────┐
│ Back ││Forward││Home││Reload││Open...││Save As...││Clone││New Window││Close Window│
└──────┘└───────┘└────┘└──────┘└────┘└────────┘└─────┘└──────────┘└────────────┘
```

Figure 12.1   Original page.

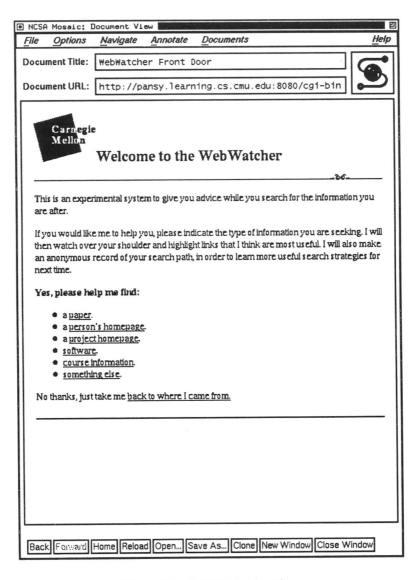

Figure 12.2   WebWatcher front door.

```
┌──────────────────────────────────────────────────────────────────────┐
│ ■ NCSA Mosaic: Document View ▓▓▓▓▓▓▓▓                               ▣ │
│ ─────────────────────────────────────────────────────────────────────│
│  File   Options   Navigate   Annotate   Documents              Help    │
│ ─────────────────────────────────────────────────────────────────────│
│  Document Title: │ Learning Web Apprentice Paper Agent          │  ┌──┐│
│                  └───────────────────────────────────────────────┘  │S ││
│  Document URL: │ http://pansy.learning.cs.cmu.edu:8080/cgi-bin │   └──┘│
│ ─────────────────────────────────────────────────────────────────────│
│                                                                        │
│     Let's find a paper!                                                │
│     ─────────────────────────────────────────────────────────         │
│                                                                        │
│     I'll try to help you find it. Please fill in any of the following  │
│     that might help me narrow your search. Use keywords in any format: │
│                                                                        │
│        Author:            ┌──────────────────────────────────┐        │
│                           └──────────────────────────────────┘        │
│        Author's institution: │ illinois                      │        │
│        Title:             ┌──────────────────────────────────┐        │
│                           └──────────────────────────────────┘        │
│        Conference:        ┌──────────────────────────────────┐        │
│                           └──────────────────────────────────┘        │
│        Subject area:      │ Machine Learning                  │        │
│                                                                        │
│     OK, let's │get started│. We'll start with the page you came from.  │
│     From now on I will look over your shoulder and highlight links for │
│     you whenever I think I have good advice.                           │
│                                                                        │
│                                                                        │
│                                                                        │
│                                                                        │
│  ◄│                                                                 │► │
│  ┌────┐┌───────┐┌────┐┌──────┐┌────┐┌───────┐┌─────┐┌──────────┐┌──────┐│
│  │Back││Forward││Home││Reload││Open...││Save As...││Clone││New Window││Close Window││
└──────────────────────────────────────────────────────────────────────┘
```

Figure 12.3   Paper search form.

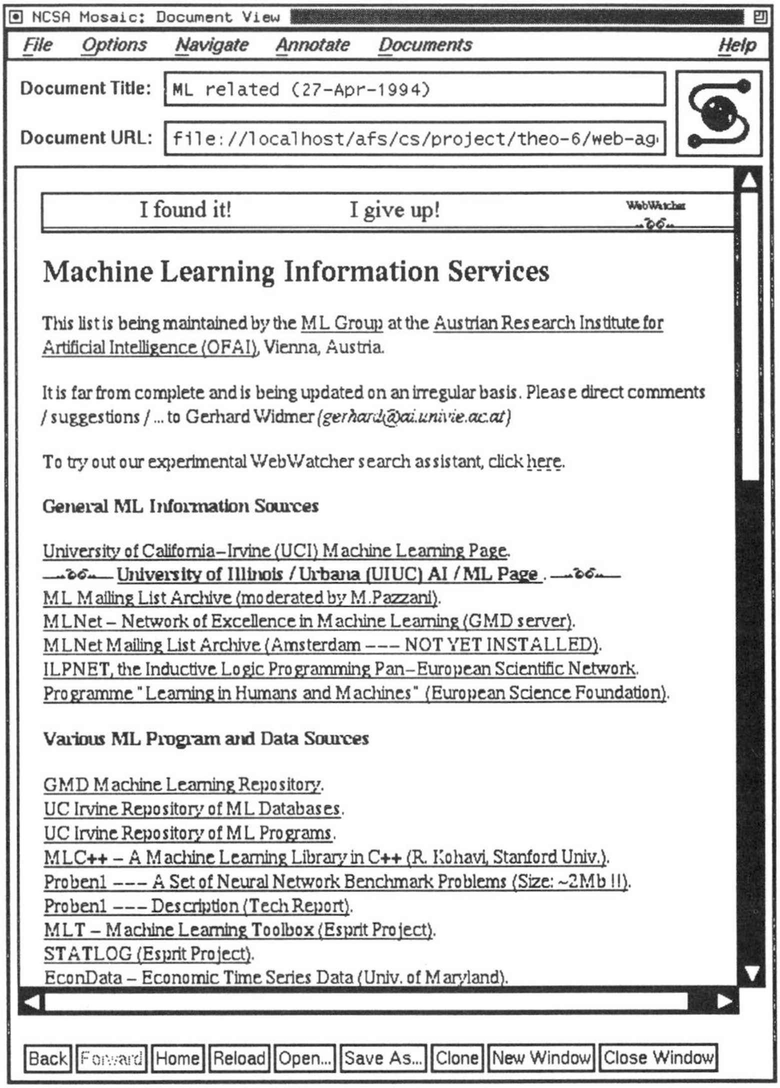

Figure 12.4   Copy of original page with WebWatcher advice.

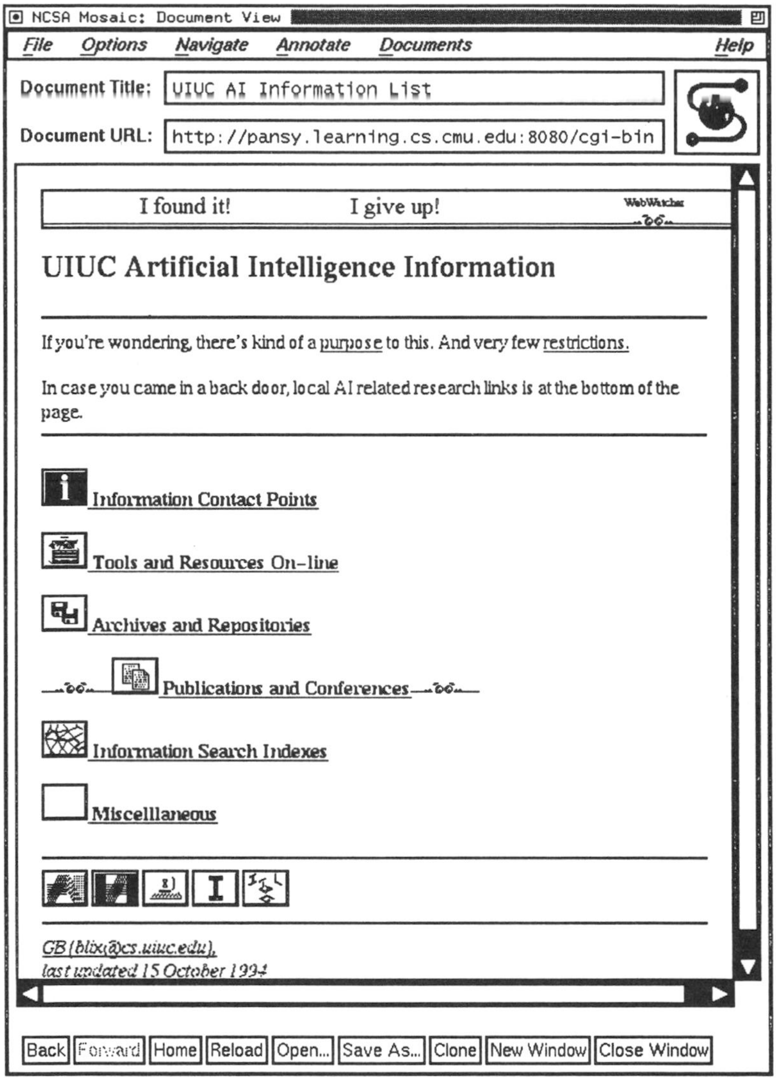

```
┌─────────────────────────────────────────────────────────────┐
│ ⊙ NCSA Mosaic: Document View ▓▓▓▓▓▓▓▓▓▓▓▓▓▓▓▓▓▓▓▓▓▓      回  │
├─────────────────────────────────────────────────────────────┤
│  File   Options   Navigate   Annotate   Documents      Help   │
│                                                               │
│  Document Title:  │ UIUC AI Information List          │       │
│                                                               │
│  Document URL:    │ http://pansy.learning.cs.cmu.edu:8080/cgi-bin │ │
│                                                               │
│   ┌─────────────────────────────────────────────────┐        │
│   │       I found it!          I give up!    WebWatcher│       │
│   ├─────────────────────────────────────────────────┤        │
│   │                                                   │        │
│   │  UIUC Artificial Intelligence Information         │        │
│   │  ─────────────────────────────────────────────   │        │
│   │  If you're wondering, there's kind of a purpose to this. And very few restrictions. │
│   │                                                   │        │
│   │  In case you came in a back door, local AI related research links is at the bottom of the │
│   │  page.                                            │        │
│   │  ─────────────────────────────────────────────   │        │
│   │                                                   │        │
│   │  [i]  Information Contact Points                  │        │
│   │                                                   │        │
│   │  [▦]  Tools and Resources On-line                 │        │
│   │                                                   │        │
│   │  [▦]  Archives and Repositories                   │        │
│   │                                                   │        │
│   │       [▦]  Publications and Conferences           │        │
│   │                                                   │        │
│   │  [▦]  Information Search Indexes                  │        │
│   │                                                   │        │
│   │  [ ]  Misclellaneous                              │        │
│   │  ─────────────────────────────────────────────   │        │
│   │  [▦][▦][▦][I][▦]                                  │        │
│   │  ─────────────────────────────────────────────   │        │
│   │  GB (blix@cs.uiuc.edu),                           │        │
│   │  last updated 15 October 1994                     │        │
│   └─────────────────────────────────────────────────┘        │
│                                                               │
│  [Back][Forward][Home][Reload][Open...][Save As...][Clone][New Window][Close Window] │
└─────────────────────────────────────────────────────────────┘
```

Figure 12.5   Next page (user has followed WebWatcher's advice).

WebWatcher's knowledge may provide imperfect advice, and because WebWatcher might not perfectly understand the user's information seeking goal.

From WebWatcher's perspective, the above scenario looks somewhat different. When first invoked it accepts an argument, encoded in the URL that accesses it, which contains the user's "return address". The return address is the URL of the web page from which the user came. Once the user fills out the form specifying his or her information seeking goal, WebWatcher sends the user back to a copy of this original page, after making three changes. First, the WebWatcher banner is added to the top of the page. Second, each hyperlink URL in the original page is replaced by a new URL that points back to the WebWatcher. Third, if the WebWatcher finds that any of the hyperlinks on this page are strongly recommended by its search control knowledge, then it highlights the most promising links in order to suggest them to the user. It sends this modified copy of the return page to the user, and opens a file to begin logging this user's information search as training data. While it waits for the user's next step, it prefetches any web pages it has just recommended to the user, and begins to process these pages to determine their most promising outgoing hyperlink. When the user clicks on the next hyperlink, WebWatcher updates the log for this search, retrieves the page (unless it has already been prefetched), performs similar substitutions, and returns the copy to the user.

This process continues, with WebWatcher tracking the user's search across the Web, providing advice at each step, until the user elects to dismiss the agent. At this point, the WebWatcher closes the log file for this session (indicating either success or failure in the search, depending on which button the user selected when dismissing WebWatcher), and returns the user to the original, unsubstituted copy of the web page he is currently at.

The above scenario describes a typical interaction with the current WebWatcher. We plan to extend the initial system in several ways. For example, WebWatcher could be made to search several pages ahead, by following its own advice while waiting for the user's next input, in order to improve upon the quality of advice it provides. In addition, if it encounters an especially promising page while searching ahead, it might suggest that the user jump directly to this page rather than follow tediously along the path that the agent has already traversed.

12.3 LEARNING

The success of WebWatcher depends crucially on the quality of its knowledge for guiding search. Because of the difficulty of hand-crafting this knowledge, and because we wish for many different copies of WebWatcher to become knowledgeable about many different regions of the Web, we are exploring methods for automatically learning this search control knowledge from experience.

12.3.1 What Should be Learned?

What is the form of the knowledge required by WebWatcher? In general, its task is to suggest an appropriate link given the current user, goal, and web page. Hence, one general form of knowledge that would be useful corresponds to knowledge of the function:

$$LinkUtility : Page \times Goal \times User \times Link \rightarrow [0, 1]$$

where *Page* is the current web page, *Goal* is the information sought by the user, *User* is the identity of the user, and *Link* is one of the hyperlinks found on *Page*. The value of *LinkUtility* is the probability that following *Link* from *Page* leads along a shortest path to a page that satisfies the current *Goal* for the current *User*.

In the learning experiments reported here, we consider learning a simpler function for which training data is more readily available, and which is still of considerable practical use. This function is:

$$UserChoice? : Page \times Goal \times Link \to [0, 1]$$

Where the value of *UserChoice?* is the probability that an arbitrary user will select *Link* given the current *Page* and *Goal*. Notice here the *User* is not an explicit input, and the function value predicts only whether users tend to select *Link* – not whether it leads optimally toward to the goal. Notice also that information about the search trajectory by which the user arrived at the current page is not considered.

One reason for focusing on *UserChoice?* in our initial experiments is that the data automatically logged by WebWatcher provides training examples of this function. In particular, each time the user selects a new hyperlink, a training example is logged for each hyperlink on the current page, corresponding to the *Page*, *Goal*, *Link*, and whether the user chose this *Link*.

12.3.2 How Should Pages, Links and Goals be Represented?

To learn and utilize knowledge of the target function *UserChoice?*, it is necessary to first choose an appropriate representation for *Page* × *Goal* × *Link*. This representation must be compatible with available learning methods, and must allow the agent to evaluate learned knowledge efficiently (i.e., with a delay negligible compared to typical page access delays on the web). Notice that one issue here is that web pages, information associated with hyperlinks, and user information goals are all predominantly text-based, whereas most machine learning methods assume a more structured data representation such as a feature vector. We have experimented with a variety of representations that re-represent the arbitrary-length text associated with pages, links, and goals as a fixed-length feature vector. This idea is common within information retrieval systems [Salton and McGill, 1983]. It offers the advantage that the information in an arbitrary amount of text is summarized in a fixed length feature vector compatible with current machine learning methods. It also carries the disadvantage that much information is lost by this re-representation.

The experiments described here all use the same representation. Information about the current *Page*, the user's information search *Goal*, and a particular outgoing *Link* is represented by a vector of approximately 530 boolean features, each feature indicating the occurrence of a particular word within the text that originally defines these three attributes. The vector of 530 features is composed of four concatenated subvectors:

1. *Underlined words in the hyperlink.* 200 boolean features are allocated to encode selected words that occur within the scope of the hypertext link (i.e., the underlined words seen by the user). These 200 features correspond to only the 200 words found to be most informative over all links in the training data (see below.)

2. *Words in the sentence containing the hyperlink.* 200 boolean features are allocated to indicate the occurrence of 200 selected words within the sentence (if any) that contains `Link`.

3. *Words in the headings associated with the hyperlink.* 100 boolean features are allocated to indicate selected words that occur in the headings (if any) under which `Link` is found. This includes words occurring in headings at any level of nesting, as long as `Link` is within the scope of the heading. For example, in Figure 12.4 any of the words in the headings *Machine Learning Information Services* and *General ML Information Sources* may be used as features to describe the link that was highlighted.

4. *Words used to define the user goal.* These features indicate words entered by the user while defining the information search goal. In our experiments, the only goals considered were searches for technical papers, for which the user could optionally enter the title, author, organization, etc. (see Figure 12.3). All words entered in this way throughout the training set were included (approximately 30 words, though the exact number varied with the training set used in the particular experiment). The encoding of the boolean feature in this case is assigned a 1 if and only if the word occurs in the user-specified goal *and* occurs in the hyperlink, sentence, or headings associated with this example.

To choose the encodings for the first three fields, it was necessary to select which words would be considered. In each case, the words were selected by first gathering every distinct word that occurred over the training set, then ranking these according to their mutual information with respect to correctly classifying the training data, and finally choosing the top n words in this ranking.[3] Mutual information is a common statistical measure (see, e.g., [Quinlan, 1993]) of the degree to which an individual feature (in this case a word) can correctly classify the observed data.

Table 12.1 summarizes the encoding of information about the current $Page$, $Link$, and $Goal$.

Table 12.1   Encoding of selected information for a given *Page, Link,* and *Goal*

200 words	200 words	100 words	≈ 30 words
Underlined	Sentence	Heading	User goal

12.3.3   What Learning Method Should be Used?

The task of the learner is to learn the general function $UserChoice?$, given a sample of training data logged from users. To explore possible learning approaches and to determine the level of competence achievable by a learning agent, we applied the following four methods to training data collected by WebWatcher during 30 information search sessions:

- `Winnow` [Littlestone, 1988] learns a boolean concept represented as a single linear threshold function of the instance features. Weights for this threshold function are learned using a multiplicative update rule. In our experiments we enriched the original 530 attributes by a transformation. Each attribute a of an example vector was transformed into two attributes $a, \bar{a}$. One attribute is equivalent with the original, the other is its negation. After the learning

---
[3] The appendix lists the words selected by this procedure using one of our training sets.

phase we removed the threshold and used the output of the learned linear function as an evaluation for instances.

- Wordstat attempts to make a prediction whether a link is followed based directly on the statistics of individual words. For each feature in the $Page \times Goal \times Link$ vector, it keeps two counts: a count of the number of times this feature was set over all training examples ($total$), and a count of the number of times this feature was set *and* the instance was classified as positive (pos). The ratio $pos/total$ provides an estimate of the conditional probability that the link will be followed, given that this feature occurs. We experimented with various ways of combining these ratios. Of the approaches we tried, the one that worked best in our experiments, the results of which we report here, involves assuming that these single-word estimates are mutually independent. This assumptions allows us to combine individual estimates in a straightforward way. If $p_1, ..., p_n$ are the individual probabilities, and I is the set of indexes for which a bit is set in a given test vector, then the probability that the corresponding link was followed is determined by $1 - \prod_{i \in I}(1 - p_i)$.

- TFIDF with cosine similarity measure [Salton and McGill, 1983], [Lang, 1995] is a method developed in information retrieval. In the general case at first a vector V of words is created. In our experiments it is already given by the representation described above. Every instance can now be represented as a vector with the same length as V, replacing every word by a number. These numbers are calculated by the formula $V_i = Freq(Word_i) * [log_2(n) - log_2(DocFreq(Word_i))]$, with n being the total number of examples, $Freq(Word_i)$ the number of occurrences of $Word_i$ in the actual example and $DocFreq(Word_i)$ the number of examples $Word_i$ appears in. The length of the vector is normalized to 1. Prototype vectors for each class of the target concept are created by adding all training vectors of this class. In our case we had a target concept with two classes: positive (link was followed by the user), and negative (link was not followed by the user). The evaluation of an instance is calculated by subtracting the cosine between the instance vector and the negative prototype vector from the cosine between the instance vector and the positive prototype vector.

- Random To provide a baseline measure against which to compare the learning methods, we also measured the performance achieved by randomly choosing one link on the page with uniform probability. The mean number of links per page over the data used here is 16, ranging from a minimum of 1 to a maximum of 300.

12.4 RESULTS

To explore the potential of machine learning methods to automatically acquire search control knowledge for WebWatcher, we collected a set of data from 30 sessions using WebWatcher to search for technical papers. In each session the user began at the web page shown in Figure 12.1, and searched for a particular type of technical paper following links forward from there. Searches were conducted by three different users. The average depth of a search was six steps, with 23 of the 30 searches successfully locating a paper. Each search session provided a set of training examples corresponding to all the $Page \times Link$ pairs occurring on each page visited by the user.

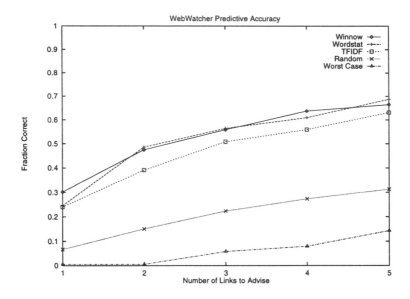

Figure 12.6   Accuracy of advice for different methods. The vertical axis indicates the fraction of pages for which the recommended hyperlinks included the link chosen by the user. The horizontal axis indicates the number of hyperlinks recommended per page. The worst case line shows the fraction of pages having N or fewer links total.

12.4.1   How Accurately Can $UserChoice$? be Learned?

Given the above representation and learning method, the obvious question is "How well can WebWatcher learn to advise the user?" To estimate the answer to this question, the available data was split into training and testing sets. Each learning method was applied to the set of training sessions and evaluated according to how frequently it recommended the hyperlink taken by the user in the separate testing sessions.

In order to obtain more statistically significant estimates of learning accuracy, the training data was separated into 29 training sessions and one test session, in each of the 30 possible ways. Each learning method was then applied to each training session collection and evaluated on the test session. The results of these 30 experiments were averaged. This procedure was run for each of the four learning methods.

Figure 12.6 plots the results of this experiment. The vertical axis indicates the fraction of test cases in which the user-selected hyperlink was among those recommended by the learned knowledge. The horizontal axis indicates the number of hyperlinks that the learner was allowed to recommend for each page. Thus, the leftmost point of each line indicates the fraction of cases in which the user chose the learner's highest-rated link. The second point to the left indicates the fraction of cases in which the user chose one of the two highest-rated links, and so on.

Notice that all three learning methods significantly outperform randomly generated advice. For example, `Winnow` recommends the user-selected link as its first choice in 30% of the test cases, and among its top three choices in 54% of the cases. Given the mean of 16 links per page in this data, random advice chooses the user-selected link only 6% of the time.

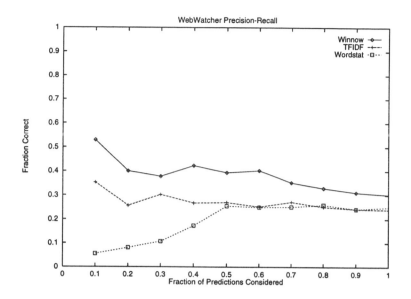

Figure 12.7   Increasing accuracy by reducing coverage. The vertical axis indicates the fraction of test pages for which the learner's top recommendation was taken by the user. The horizontal axis indicates the fraction of test cases covered by advice as the confidence threshold is varied from high confidence (left) to low (right).

12.4.2   Can Accuracy be Improved by Sacrificing Coverage?

Some users may prefer that the agent provide more accurate advice, even if this requires that it make recommendations more sparingly. To determine the feasibility of increasing advice accuracy by reducing coverage, we experimented with adding a threshold on the confidence of the advice. For each of the learning methods considered here, the learner's output is a real-valued number that can be used to estimate its confidence in recommending the link. Therefore, it is easy to introduce a confidence threshold in each of these cases.

Figure 12.7 shows how advice accuracy varies with coverage, as the confidence threshold is varied. For high values of the confidence threshold, the agent provides advice less often, but can usually achieve higher accuracy. In this case, accuracy is measured by the fraction of test cases for which the learner's top ranked hyperlink is the link selected by the user. Thus, the rightmost points in the plots of Figure 12.7 correspond exactly to the leftmost plots in Figure 12.6 (i.e., 100% coverage).

Notice that the accuracy of Winnow's top-ranked recommendation increases from 30% to 53% as its coverage is decreased to a more selective 10% of the cases. Interestingly, while Wordstat's advice is relatively accurate in general, its accuracy degrades drastically at higher thresholds. The presence of features which occur very infrequently in the training set, resulting in poor probability estimates, and the inter-feature independence assumption, which the training set by no means justifies, appear to account for this phenomenon.

12.5   CONCLUSIONS

Software assistance is already needed to deal with the growing flood of information available on the WWW. The design of WebWatcher is based on the assumption that knowledge about how to search the web can be learned by interactively assisting and watching searches performed by humans. If successful, different copies of WebWatcher could easily be attached to any web page for which a specialized search assistant would be useful. Over time, each copy could learn expertise specializing in the types of users, information needs, and information sources commonly encountered through its page.

In the preliminary learning experiments reported here, WebWatcher was able to learn search control knowledge that approximately predicts the hyperlink selected by users, conditional on the current page, link, and goal. These experiments also showed that the accuracy of the agent's advice can be increased by allowing it to give advice only when it has high confidence. While these experimental results are positive, they are based on a small number of training sessions, searching for a particular type of information, from a specific web page. We do not yet know whether the results reported here are representative of what can be expected for other search goals, users, and web localities.

Based on our initial exploration, we are optimistic that a learning apprentice for the world wide web is feasible. Although learned knowledge may provide only imperfect advice, even a modest reduction in the number of hyperlinks considered at each page leads to an exponential improvement in the overall search. Moreover, we believe learning can be made more effective by taking advantage of the abundant data available from many users on the web, and by considering methods beyond those reported here.

ACKNOWLEDGEMENTS

We thank Ken Lang for providing much of the software for learning over pages of text, and for suggesting the idea of implementing the agent by dynamically editing web pages. Thanks to Michael Mauldin for software and advice on the construction of a web-based text-retrieval system. We are grateful to Rich Caruana and Ken Lang for helpful comments on this paper. This research is supported by a Rotary International fellowship grant, an NSF graduate fellowship, and by Arpa under grant number F33615-93-1-1330.

APPENDIX

The following lists show the words used to encode *Page* × *Link* × *Goal* into a feature vector as summarized in Figure 12.1. Words are listed in order, beginning with the word with highest mutual information.

Underlined words: papers, uci, other, publications, learning, algorithm, www, illigal, page, illinois, related, ted, belding, mitchell, people, approaches, california, soar, tom, ronny, unit, readme, genetic, symbolic, sources, comparison, explanation, laboratory, cmu's, with, cmu, abstract, machine, pazzani, avrim, more, what, j, systems, michael, project, dortmund, my, subject, personal, institute, conference, their, tf3, our, lhm, esf, do, indexes, characterizing, handouts, information.html, fourier, articifial, tracking, ntrs, weakly, 26, readings, software, information, knowledge, 95, lab, language, esprit, lists, html, dnf, staff, rl, reinforcement, univ, services, pub, links, irvine, on, home, report, cognitive, list, international, that, discovery, data, z, publication, agenda, original, discussed, there, between, tex2html2, tex2html1, method, does, tcb, perception, 468, blum, illigals, actually, it, workshop94, newell, bibilography, bottom, heck, rosenbloom, relationship, mine, ciir, germany, uc, tech, net, middle, engineering, sigart, reports, mailing, network, reasoning, michigan, 10, robotics, cs, groups, online, encore, next, low, tr, 4k, pape, return, preprints, new, programs, kohavi, etc, m, group, computing, department, document, postscript, is, proben1, complete, summary, see, ls8, cultural, director, professor, references, index, problems, gmd, dept, ml, applied, vision, clifford, pan, level, faculty, introduction, call, integrated, sciences, brunk, ofai, general, college, digest, neural, ml94, applications, mit, service, databases, abstracts, austrian, issues, from, top, electronic, w, homepage, emde, starting, image

Sentence words: other, illigal, uci, papers, publications, related, algorithm, page, www, lists, people, learning, soar, ted, belding, illinois, kohavi, unit, selected, ronny, california, bottom, laboratory, symbolic, sites, mitchell, approaches, sources, avrim, comparison, more, cmu's, with, genetic, abstract, home, pazzani, systems, document, email, abstracts, institute, conference, machine, dortmund, next, led, view, their, subject, do, tf3, lhm, esf, background, handouts, recommend, ntrs, carry, indexes, tracking, articifial, 468, 26, thrun, language, explanation, what, lab, same, staff, manner, reinforcement, knowledge, cmu, cognitive, my, tom, html, web, there, services, organized, pub, on, irvine, esprit, 95, links, list, international, middle, tech, readme, personal, sigart, net, ml94, are, our, engineering, bibilography, maybe, discussed, september, actually, quick, illigals, listed, heck, tex2html2, tex2html1, relationship, agenda, event, method, does, newell, rosenbloom, tcb, publication, original, blum, z, germany, ciir, that, rl, uc, information, reasoning, know, report, software, to, department, new, groups, encore, reports, test, previous, further, level, pape, preprints, tr, clusters, readings, 4k, low, return, link, or, group, neural, postscript, discovery, computing, gmd, michigan, robotics, is, issues, maintained, mine, general, proben1, check, fields, investigations, images, complete, director, volumes, ls8, cultural, sciences, colt94, at, mailing, edu, network, stanford, college, want, applications, back, pan, online, 10, faculty, integrated, between, jump, brunk, ofai, problems, electronic, digest

Heading words: ga, personal, pages, computing, organization, lab, this, some, of, other, evolutionary, public, neural, data, knowledge, me, to, information, and, various, program, the, nlp, nets, nn, home, institutions, doing, depts, on, ai, reinforcement, about, return, ntrs, illigal, representation, kr, readings, integrated, science, language, intelligence, departments, processing, links, school, 11, systems, 94, meetings, first, try, mining, soar, html, computer,

3k, applications, possibly, ftp, aug, involved, networks, subjects, page, 10, cognitive, natural, relevant, interpretation, tf3, esf, rules, indirect, lhm, act, interest, robotics, txt, colt94, workshop, david, programmatic, you, goldberg, e, director, professor, apps, cogsci, 15, 681, list, handouts, journal, starting, logic, talks, interests

User goal words: university, carnegie, learning, pazzani, explanation, tom, cmu, genetic, information, machine, irvine, decision, reinforcement, soar, stanford, inductive, mistake, curvilinear, gigus, pattern, steffo, ilp, ronny, higher, goldberg, holland, first, rise, phoebe, avrim, mit, occams, emde, gmd, illinois, dnf, koza, berkeley, quinlan, computational, josef, average, salton

REFERENCES

T. Joachims, D. Freitag, and T. Mitchell, "WebWatcher: A Tour Guide for the World Wide Web," *Proceedings of the 1997 International Joint Conference on Artificial Intelligence*, Morgan Kaufmann Publishers: San Francisco, August 1997.

K. Lang, "NewsWeeder: Learning to Filter Netnews", *Proceedings of the International Conference on Machine Learning*, 1995.

N. Littlestone, "Learning quickly when irrelevant attributes abound," *Machine Learning*, **2:4**, pp. 285–318.

T. Mitchell, S. Mahadevan, and L. Steinberg, "LEAP: A Learning Apprentice for VLSI Design," *Ninth International Joint Conference on Artificial Intelligence*, August 1985.

T.M. Mitchell, R. Caruana, D. Freitag, J. McDermott, and D. Zabowski, " Experience with a Learning Personal Assistant," *Communications of the ACM*, Vol. 37, No. 7, pp. 81–91, July 1994.

G. Salton and M.J. McGill, *Introduction to Modern Information Retrieval*, McGraw-Hill, Inc., 1983.

J.R. Quinlan, *C4.5: Programs for Machine Learning*, Morgan Kaufmann, 1993.

13

Biologically Inspired Defences against Computer Viruses

J.O. Kephart, G.B. Sorkin, W.C. Arnold, D.M. Chess, G.J. Tesauro and S.R. White[1]

ABSTRACT

Today's anti-virus technology, based largely on analysis of existing viruses by human experts, is just barely able to keep pace with the more than three new computer viruses that are written daily. In a few years, intelligent agents navigating through highly connected networks are likely to form an extremely fertile medium for a new breed of viruses. At IBM, we are developing novel, biologically inspired anti-virus techniques designed to thwart both today's and tomorrow's viruses. Here we describe two of these: a neural network virus detector that learns to discriminate between infected and uninfected programs, and a computer immune system that identifies new viruses, analyzes them automatically, and uses the results of its analysis to detect and remove all copies of the virus that are present in the system. The neural-net technology has been incorporated into IBM's commercial anti-virus product; the computer immune system is in prototype.

---

[1] Originally published in *Proceedings of IJCAI '95*, Montreal, August 19-25, 1995. ©1995 International Joint Conferences on Artificial Intelligence, Inc.

Machine Learning and Data Mining: Methods and Applications
Edited by R.S. Michalski, I Bratko and M. Kubat
© 1997 John Wiley & Sons Ltd

13.1   INTRODUCTION

Each day, an army of perhaps a few hundred virus writers around the world produces three or more new computer viruses.[2] An army of comparable size, the anti-virus software developers (representing an approximately $100 million per year industry), works feverishly to analyze these viruses, develop cures for them, and frequently distribute software updates to users.

Currently, the battle is roughly even. Our statistics, based on observation of a sample population of several hundred thousand machines for several years [KW93, KWC93], suggest that in medium to large businesses roughly 1% of all computers become infected during any given year. The world's computer population has been inconvenienced, but despite dire predictions [Tip91] it has not been incapacitated. Most of the anti-virus products in common usage have been reasonably effective in detecting and removing viruses. Within our sample population, only 10% of all known viruses (about 360 of 4000 at the time of writing) have been observed "in the wild" — in real incidents. Several viruses that used to be relatively common now qualify for inclusion on an endangered species list. Today, computer viruses are a manageable nuisance.

Several worrisome trends threaten to turn the balance in the favor of computer virus authors. First, the rate at which new viruses are created, already on the verge of overwhelming human experts, has the potential to increase substantially. Second, continued increases in interconnectivity and interoperability among the world's computers, designed to benefit computer users, are likely to be a boon to DOS and Macintosh viruses as well. Theoretical epidemiological studies indicate that the rate at which computer viruses spread on a global scale can be very sensitive to the rate and the degree of promiscuity of software exchange [KW91, KW93, KWC93, Kep94b]. Anticipated increases in both factors threaten to increase substantially the speed of spread and the pervasiveness of these traditional types of virus. In addition, mobile intelligent agents [CGH+95, HCK94] will soon navigate the global network, potentially serving as a fertile medium for a new breed of rapidly-spreading virus that exploits the itinerancy of its host by leaving behind copies of itself wherever its host goes. Traditional methods of detecting and removing viruses, which rely upon expert analysis by humans and subsequent distribution of the cure to users, would be orders of magnitude too slow to deal with viruses that spread globally within days or hours.

To address these problems, we have developed a variety of biologically inspired antivirus algorithms and techniques that replace many of the tasks traditionally performed by human virus experts, thus permitting much faster, automatic response to new viruses.

The term "computer virus", coined by Adleman in the early 1980s [Coh87], is suggestive of strong analogies between computer viruses and their biological namesakes. Both attach themselves to a small functional unit (cell or program) of the host individual (organism or computer), and co-opt the resources of that unit for the

---

[2] This figure is based on the number of distinct new viruses that have been received by us during the last year.

purpose of creating more copies of the virus. By using up materials (memory[3]) and energy (CPU[4]), viruses can cause a wide spectrum of malfunctions in their hosts. Even worse, viruses can be toxic. In humans, diptheria is caused by a toxin produced by virally-infected bacteria [Lev92]. Some computer viruses are similarly toxic, being deliberately programmed to cause severe harm to their hosts. One notorious example, the Michelangelo virus, destroys data on a user's hard disk whenever it is booted on March 6th.

It is therefore natural to seek inspiration from defense mechanisms that biological organisms have evolved against diseases. The idea that biological analogies might be helpful in defending computers from computer viruses is not original to us [Mur88]. But to our knowledge we are the first to take these analogies seriously, to deliberately design and implement anti-virus technology that is inspired by biology, and incorporate it into a commercial anti-virus product.

First, we will briefly describe what computer viruses are, how they replicate themselves, and why their presence in a system is undesirable. Then, we shall describe the typical procedures used by human experts to analyze computer viruses, and explain why these methods are unlikely to remain viable a few years from now. Then, we shall discuss two complementary anti-virus techniques that are inspired by biological systems that learn: a neural-network virus detector and a computer immune system.

13.2   BACKGROUND

13.2.1   Computer Viruses and Worms

Computer viruses are self-replicating software entities that attach themselves parasitically to existing programs. They are endemic to DOS, Macintosh, and other microcomputer systems. When a user executes an infected program (an executable file or boot sector), the viral portion of the code typically executes first. The virus looks for one or more victim programs to which it has write access (typically the same set of programs to which the user has access), and attaches a copy of itself (perhaps a deliberately modified copy) to each victim. Under some circumstances, it may then execute a payload, such as printing a weird message, playing music, destroying data, etc. Eventually, a typical virus returns control to the original program, which executes normally. Unless the virus executes an obvious payload, the user is unlikely to notice that anything is amiss, and will be completely unaware of having helped a virus to replicate. Viruses often enhance their ability to spread by establishing themselves as resident processes in memory, persisting long after the infected host finishes its execution (terminating only when the machine is shut down). As resident processes, they can monitor system activity continually, and identify and infect executables and boot sectors as they become available.

Over a period of time, this scenario is repeated, and the infection may spread to

---

[3] The Jerusalem virus increases the size of an executable by 1813 bytes each time it infects it, eventually causing it to be too large to be loaded into memory [Hig90].

[4] The Internet worm caused the loads on some Unix machines to increase by two orders of magnitude [ER89, Spa89].

several programs on the user's system. Eventually, an infected program may be copied and transported to another system electronically or via diskette. If this program is executed on the new system, the cycle of infection will begin anew. In this manner, computer viruses spread from program to program, and (more slowly) from machine to machine. The most successful PC DOS viruses spread worldwide on a time scale of months [KW93].

Worms are another form of self-replicating software that are sometimes distinguished from viruses. They are self-sufficient programs that remain active in memory in multi-tasking environments, and they replicate by spawning copies of themselves. Since they can determine when to replicate (rather than relying on a human to execute an infected program), they have the potential to spread much faster than viruses. The Internet worm of 1988 is said to have spread to several thousand machines across the United States in less than 24 hours [ER89, Spa89].

13.2.2   Virus Detection, Removal and Analysis

Anti-virus software seeks to detect all viral infections on a given computer system and to restore each infected program to its original uninfected state, if possible.

There are a variety of complementary anti-virus techniques in common usage; tax-onomies are given in [Spa91, KWC93]. *Activity monitors* alert users to system activity that is commonly associated with viruses, but only rarely associated with the behavior of normal, legitimate programs. *Integrity management systems* warn the user of suspicious changes that have been made to files. These two methods are quite general, and can be used to detect the presence of hitherto unknown viruses in the system. However, they are not often able to pinpoint the nature or even the location of the infecting agent, and they can sometimes flag or prevent legitimate activity, disrupting normal work or leading the user to ignore their warnings altogether.

Virus scanners search files, boot records, memory, and other locations where executable code can be stored for characteristic byte patterns (called "signatures") that occur in one or more known viruses. Providing much more specific detection than activity monitors and integrity management systems, scanners are essential for establishing the identity and location of a virus. Armed with this very specific knowledge, *disinfectors*, which restore infected programs to their original uninfected state, can be brought into play. The drawback of scanning and repair mechanisms is that they can be applied only to known viruses, or variants of them. Furthermore, each individual virus strain must be analyzed in order to extract both a signature and information that permits a disinfector to remove the virus. Scanners and disinfectors require frequent updates as new viruses are discovered, and the analysis can entail a significant amount of effort on the part of human virus experts.

Whenever a new virus is discovered, it is quickly distributed among an informal, international group of anti-virus experts. Upon obtaining a sample, a human expert disassembles the virus and then analyzes the assembler code to determine the virus's behavior and the method that it uses to attach itself to host programs. Then, the expert selects a "signature" (a sequence of perhaps 16 to 32 bytes) that represents a sequence of instructions that is guaranteed to be found in each instance of the virus, and which (in the expert's estimation) is unlikely to be found in legitimate programs. This signature can then be encoded into the scanner. The attachment method and a description of the machine code of the virus can be encoded into a verifier, which verifies the identity of a virus that has been found by the scanner. Finally, a reversal of the attachment method can be encoded into a disinfector.

Virus analysis is tedious and time-consuming, sometimes taking several hours or days, and even the best experts have been known to select poor signatures — ones that cause the scanner to report false positives on legitimate programs. Alleviation of this burden is by itself enough to warrant a serious attempt to automate virus analysis. The anticipated speed with which viruses of the future may spread is an even stronger argument in favor of endowing anti-virus software with the ability to deal with new viruses on its own.[5] The rest of this paper describes two techniques for achieving this goal.

13.3   GENERIC DETECTION OF VIRUSES

Two methods of computer virus identification have already been introduced: the overly broad, *ex post facto* detection provided by activity monitors and integrity management systems, and the overly specific detection offered by virus scanners. Somewhere in between is the ideal "generic detector": taking a program's code as input, it determines whether the program is viral or non-viral. Perfect generic detection is an algorithmically "undecidable" problem: as observed by [Coh87], it is reducible to the halting problem. However, imperfect generic detection that is good in practice is possible, and is naturally viewed as a problem in automatic pattern classification. Standard classification techniques encompass linear methods and non-linear ones such as nearest-neighbor classification, decision trees, and multi-layer neural networks.

Within the problem of the generic detection of viruses, detection of "boot sector viruses" is both an important and relatively tractable sub-problem. A boot sector is a small sequence of code that tells the computer how to "pick itself up by its bootstraps". For IBM-compatible PCs, boot sectors are exactly 512 bytes long; their main function is to load and execute additional code stored elsewhere.

Although there are over 4000 different file-infecting viruses and only about 250 boot-sector viruses, of the 20 viruses most commonly seen 19 are boot viruses, and account for over 80% of all virus incidents. Boot viruses similarly dominate the rolls of newly observed viruses, so an ability to detect new boot sector viruses is significant in the war against viruses.

Detecting boot viruses is a relatively limited pattern classification task. Legitimate boot sectors all perform similar functions. Viral boot sectors also all perform similar functions, before passing control to a legitimate boot sector loaded from elsewhere.

For this application, false positives are critical. False negatives mean missed viruses,

---

[5] At the very least, anti-virus software must handle a majority of viruses well enough to prevent them from spreading. For the foreseeable future, it will continue to be important for human virus experts to analyze carefully any viruses that appear in the wild to corroborate the results of the automated analysis and to determine any side effects that the virus may cause in infected systems.

and since viruses occur fairly rarely, so will false negatives. Also, if a classifier does let a virus slip by, the outcome is no worse than if no virus protection were in place. On the other hand, false positives can occur any time, and will leave a user worse off than she would have been without virus protection. Moreover, a false positive on one legitimate boot sector will mean false-positive events on thousands of computers. False positives are not tolerable.

Nearest-neighbor classification might seem to be a simple, attractive approach to the classification of legitimate and viral boot sectors. Natural measures of the difference between two boot sectors include the Hamming distance between them (considered as 512-element vectors), or the edit distance [CR94] between them (considered as text strings). To classify a new boot sector, the procedure would find the "nearest" of the 250 known boot sector viruses and 100 legitimate boot sectors (a representative if not comprehensive set that we have collected), and classify the new boot sector as viral if its nearest neighbor is viral, legitimate if its nearest neighbor is legitimate.

Unfortunately, nearest-neighbor classification performs poorly for this problem. A viral boot sector can be just a short string of viral code written over a legitimate boot sector, so in any overall comparison, the virus will be more similar to the legitimate boot sector it happened to overwrite than to any other virus. This says that what makes viral boot sectors viral is not any overall quality but the presence of specific viral functions.

These functions can be used to construct a virus classifier. For example, one common action is for a virus to reduce the apparent size of available memory so that space taken up by the virus will not be noticed. Although this action may be variously implemented in machine code, most machine code implementations match one of a few simple patterns. (A fictitious pattern typifying the form is C31B****AC348F**90D3D217 — about 10 fixed bytes and some wildcards.) Of the viruses that lower memory in less conventional ways, most still contain a 2-byte pattern weakly indicative of the same function, but more prone to false positives. Similar strong and weak patterns describe other common viral functions.

Using expert knowledge of viral and non-viral boot sectors and several days of extensive experimentation, we hand-crafted an *ad hoc* classifier (see Figure 13.1). The classifier scans a boot sector for the presence of patterns that provide strong or weak evidence for any of four viral functions. One point is credited for weak evidence, and two points for strong evidence. A boot sector is classified as viral if its total score is 3 or higher. This classifier performed well on the 350 examples, with a false-negative rate of about 18% and a false-positive rate too small to measure over the 100 negative examples. That is, 82% of viruses were detected, and no legitimate boot sector was classified as viral.

We hoped to develop a procedure for automatically constructing a virus classifier, using similar features as inputs to a neural network. Since the *ad hoc* classifier incorporated knowledge of all of the available boot sectors, there was a possibility that it suffered from overfitting, in which case it would generalize poorly on new data. It would be much easier to assess the generalization performance of an automatically constructed classifier. Also, we hoped that algorithmic extraction of features and optimization of network weights might give even better classification performance, espe-

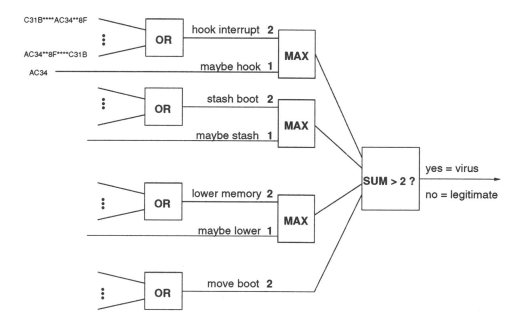

Figure 13.1 A hand-crafted multi-level classifier network. Eliminating the "MAX" boxes produces a more conventional neural network, but it is inferior, even when the seven weights are optimized.

cially in the false-positive measure. Finally, we believed that an automated procedure would adapt much more readily to new trends in boot sector viruses. If substantially new types of boot sector viruses became common, we could simply retrain the classifier — a much easier task than hacking on an *ad hoc* classifier, or re-writing it from scratch.

Essentially, what we did was this. We extracted a set of 3-byte strings, or "trigrams", appearing frequently in viral boot sectors but infrequently in legitimate ones. The presence (1) or absence (0) of the strings defined the input vector to a single-layer neural network. (See Figure 13.2.) Its weights were "trained" over about half the

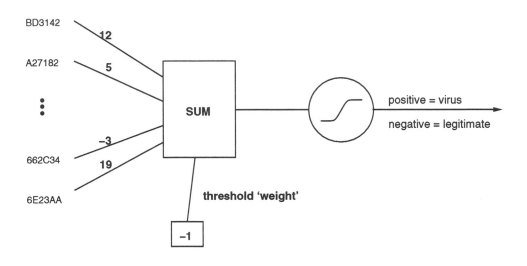

Figure 13.2 Single-layer neural classifier with about 50 input features and weights determined algorithmically. The trigrams and weights are fictitious.

examples, and the resulting network's performance tested on the other half. During the development of the automatic classifier, we encountered novel challenges in *feature pruning* and *ill-defined learning* that we think represent interesting general issues in learning. These will be introduced in the course of a more detailed description of the classifier's construction.

13.3.1   Feature Selection

The first step in the construction was the selection of byte strings to act as features. Where a human expert is able to use high-level understanding of viruses, knowledge of machine code, and natural intelligence to select complex feature patterns containing wildcards, for algorithmic feature generation we contented ourselves with simple 3-byte features. A training set with 150 512-byte viral boot sectors includes 76,500 "trigrams", of which typically 25,000 are distinct.

This is where the first challenge, *feature pruning*, comes in. A well known principle in machine learning states that the number of training examples must be considerably larger than the number of adjustable parameters to reliably give good generalization to test examples [HKP91]. With 150 viral and 45 non-viral training examples, a network must have well fewer than 195 weights — say about 50 — implying a lesser or equal number of inputs. Somehow the 25,000 trigrams must be winnowed down to 50.

Since what is desired are trigrams that are indicative of viral as opposed to legitimate behavior, it is natural to remove trigrams appearing too frequently in legitimate boot sectors. Eliminating all trigrams which appear even once in the 45 legitimate training examples reduces the 25,000 candidate trigrams by only about 8%. On the reasoning that trigrams occurring frequently in PC programs in general are analogous to the English word "the" and not salient features, further winnowing can be done. Eliminating trigrams with frequency over 1/200,000 (occurring on average more than once in 200,000 bytes) again reduces the number about 8%, leaving about 21,000 of the original 25,000 candidate features. Much more drastic pruning is required.

It is provided by selecting trigram features which figure importantly in the viral training set. One way to do this would be to select trigrams occurring at least some number of times in the viral training set, but this leaves some viral samples unrepresented by any trigrams. A better approach comes from selecting a "cover" of trigrams: a set of trigrams with at least one trigram representing each of the viral samples. In fact, we can afford something close to a 4-cover, so that each viral sample is represented by four different trigrams in the set. (A few samples have fewer than four representatives in the full set of 21,000 trigrams, in which case they are only required to be 3-covered, 2-covered, or singly covered, as possible.) Four-covering produces a set of about 50 trigram features, few enough to be used as input to a neural net.

(Even so, a complete two-layer network with h hidden nodes would have h times as many weights as inputs, which here is prohibitive even for an h of 2 or 3; this is why we used a single-layer network.)

Reassuringly, most of the trigrams were substrings of or otherwise similar to the more complex patterns of the *ad hoc* classifier. However, there were a few trigrams that could not be related to any of these patterns, and on expert inspection they turned out to define a meaningful new feature class.

13.3.2 Classifier Training and Performance

By construction, the selected trigrams are very good features: within the training set, no legitimate boot sector contains any of them, and most of the viral boot sectors contain at least 4. Paradoxically, the high quality of the features poses the second challenge, what we have called the problem of *ill-defined learning*. Since no negative example contains any of the features, any "positive" use of the features gives a perfect classifier.

Specifically, the neural network classifier of Figure 13.2 with a threshold of 0 and any positive weights will give perfect classification on the training examples, but since even a single feature can trigger a positive, it may be susceptible to false positives on the test set and in real-world use. The same problem shows up as an instability when the usual back-propagation [RHW86] training procedure is used to optimize the weights: larger weights are always better, because they drive the sigmoid function's outputs closer to the asymptotic ideal values of -1 and 1.

In fact all that will keep a feature's ideal weighting from being infinite is the feature's presence in some negative example. Since none of the features were present in any negative example, our solution was to introduce new examples. One way is to add a set of examples defined by an identity matrix. That is, for each feature in turn, an artificial negative example is generated in which that feature's input value is 1 and all other inputs are 0. This adds one artificial example for each trigram feature; it might be better to emphasize features which are more likely to appear by chance.

To do so, we used 512 bytes of code taken from the initial "entry point" portions of many PC programs to stand in as artificial legitimate boot sectors; the thought was that these sections of code, like real boot sectors, might be oriented to machine setup rather than performance of applications. Of 5000 such artificial legitimate boot sectors, 100 contained some viral feature. (This is about as expected. Each selected trigram had general-code frequency of under 1/200,000, implying that the chance of finding any of 50 trigrams among 512 bytes is at most 13%; the observed rate for the artificial boot sectors was 5%.) Since not all of the 50 trigrams occurred in any artificial boot sector, we used this approach in combination with the "identity matrix" one.

At this point the problem is finally in the form of the most standard sort of (single-layer) feed-forward neural network training, which can be done by back-propagation. In typical training and testing runs, we find that the network has a false-negative rate of 10–15%, and a false-positive rate of 0.02% as measured on artificial boot sectors.[6] (Given the trigrams' frequencies of under 1/200,000, if their occurrences were statistically independent, the probability of finding two within some 512 bytes would be at most 0.8%.) Consistent with the 0.02% false-positive rate, there were no false positives on any of the 100 genuine legitimate boot sectors.

There was one eccentricity in the network's learning. Even though all the features are indicative of viral behavior, most training runs produced one or two slightly negative weights. We are not completely sure why this is so, but the simplest explanation is that if two features were perfectly correlated (and some are imperfectly correlated), only their total weight is important, so one may randomly acquire a negative weight and the other a correspondingly larger positive weight.

For practical boot virus detection, the false-negative rate of 15% or less and false-positive rate of 0.02% are an excellent result: 85% of new boot sector viruses will be detected, with a tiny chance of false positives on legitimate boot sectors. In fact the classifier, incorporated into IBM AntiVirus, has caught several new viruses. There has also been at least one false positive, on a "security" boot sector with virus-like qualities, and not fitting the probabilistic model of typical code. Rather than specifically allowing

---

[6] Comparison of this classifier's 85% detection rate on test data with the 82% rate of the hand-crafted one is more favorable than the numbers suggest. The rate for the neural net was measured over an independent test set, where for the hand-crafted detector there was no training–testing division. Measured over all examples (and especially if trained over all examples), the network's detection rate exceeds 90%.

that boot sector, less than an hour of re-training convinced the neural network to classify it negatively; this may help to reduce similar false positives.

Of the 10 or 15% of viruses that escape detection, most do so not because they fail to contain the feature trigrams, but because the code sections containing them are obscured in various ways. If the obscured code is captured by independent means, the trigrams can be passed on to the classifier and these viruses too will be detected.

13.4   A COMPUTER IMMUNE SYSTEM

Although generic virus detection works well for boot-sector viruses, and may eventually prove useful for file infectors as well, at least two drawbacks are inherent in the technique:

1. New viruses can be detected only if they have a sufficient amount of code in common with known viruses.
2. The method is appropriate for viral detection only; it is incapable of aiding in the removal of a virus from an infected boot sector or file. The only way to eliminate the infection is to erase or replace the infected boot sector or file.

The generic classifier could be viewed as an analog of the "innate", or non-adaptive, non-specific immune system that is present in both vertebrates and lower animals. One important component of this innate immunity can be viewed as a sort of generic classifier system, in which the features on which recognition is based include:

1. the presence of certain proteins that are always present on self-cells, but usually not on foreign cells,[7]
2. the presence of double-strand RNA, which appears in much larger concentrations in a particular class of viruses than it does in mammalian cells [MK93], and
3. the presence of a peptide that begins with an unusual amino acid (formyl methionine) that is produced copiously by bacteria, but only in minute amounts by mammals [MK93].

This generic classification is coupled with a generic response to a pathogen that either disables it or kills it.

However, vertebrates have evolved a more sophisticated, adaptive immune system that works in concert with the innate immune system, and is based on recognition of *specific* pathogens.[8] It exhibits the remarkable ability to detect and respond to previously unencountered pathogens, regardless of their degree of similarity to known pathogens. This is precisely the sort of defensive capability that we seek against computer viruses.

---

[7] These proteins inactivate complement, a class of proteins that bind to cells, and attract the attention of other components of the immune system, which kill the cell [Jan93].

[8] This extra sophistication pits the quick adaptability of the immune system, which occurs within a single individual over the course of a few days, against the similarly quick evolutionary adaptability of pathogens (due to their short life-cycles). Due to their much slower life-cycles, it is doubtful that vertebrates could hold their own if their immune systems had to rely on evolution alone.

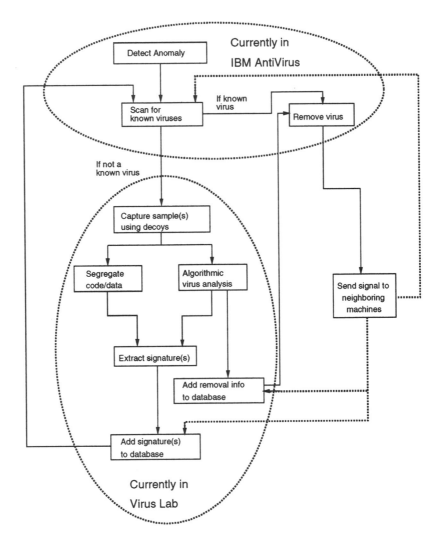

Figure 13.3 The main components of the proposed immune system for computers and their relationship to one another.

Figure 13.3 provides an overview of our design for an adaptive computer immune system. The immune system responds to virus-like anomalies (as identified by various activity and integrity monitors) by capturing and analyzing viral samples. From its analysis, it derives the means for detecting and removing the virus. Many components of the computer immune system are working in the laboratory, and are providing useful data that is incorporated into IBM AntiVirus, IBM's commercial anti-virus product.

The remainder of this section will be devoted to a discussion of the various components of the immune system design, along with their relationship to analogous biological principles. Further exploration of some biological analogies can be found in [Kep94a]. First, we shall consider the set of components that are labeled as being currently in IBM AntiVirus: anomaly detection, scanning for known viruses, and removal of known viruses. Then, we shall discuss some of the components that are labeled as being currently in the virus lab: sample capture using decoys, algorithmic virus analysis, and signature extraction. These components are all functioning prototypes. Finally, we shall discuss a mechanism by which one machine can inform its neighbors about viral infections.

13.4.1   Anomaly Detection

The fundamental problem faced by both biological and computer immune systems is to distinguish between malignant and benign entities that enter the individual. Due to the high degree of stability of body chemistry in individual vertebrates during their lifetimes, their immune systems can replace this difficult task with the much simpler one of distinguishing self from non-self. This is a nice hack, because "self" is much easier to define and recognize than "benign". The biological immune system can simply implement the xenophobic strategy: "Know thyself (and reject all else)." This strategy errs on the side of false positives (i.e. false rejection of benign entities), but except in cases of blood transfusions and organ transplants, these mistakes are of little consequence.[9]

In computers, the same xenophobic strategy is an important component of anomaly detection. Integrity monitors can use checksums or other methods[10] to determine whether an existing executable has changed. However, this is only a partial solution. The nature of "self", i.e. the collection of software on an individual computer, is continually shifting over time — much more so than in biological organisms. People continually add new software to their system, and update existing software by buying new versions or compiling new source code. The fact that an executable is new or has changed is not nearly enough to warrant suspicion. An array of other monitors and heuristics employ a complementary "Know thine enemy" strategy: the nature of the anomaly must be strongly indicative of a virus. Some components of the anomaly detector trigger on suspicious dynamical behaviors (such as one process writing to an executable or boot record, or unusual sequences of operating system calls, perhaps

---

[9] Another important class of false positives are auto-immune reactions, which are sometimes induced by biochemical changes that occur at puberty (thus changing the nature of "self").

[10] A novel method for integrity monitoring that is based on a close analogy to T cells is described in [FPAC94].

involving interception of particular interrupts); others trigger on static properties having to do with the exact nature of a change that has been identified by the integrity monitor.

13.4.2 Scanning for Known Viruses

If the anomaly detector has been triggered, the system is scanned for all known viruses. Since there are currently at least 4000 known PC DOS viruses, this means that exact or slightly inexact matches to approximately 4000 signatures, each in the range of roughly 16 to 32 bytes long, are searched in parallel. This is in itself an interesting string matching problem, and efficient search methods are an active area of research for us. Much more impressive than any string matching algorithm we could ever hope to devise, however, is the parallel search carried out by the vertebrate immune system, in which roughly 10 million different types of T-cell receptors and 100 million different types of antibodies and B-cell receptors are continually patrolling the body in search of antigen [Jan93]. Just as a computer virus scanner recognizes viruses on the basis of (perhaps inexact) matches to a fragment of the virus (the signature), T-cell and B-cell receptors and antibodies recognize antigen by binding (strongly or weakly, depending on the exactness of the match) to fragments of the antigen (consisting of linear sequences of 8 to 15 amino acids, in the case of T cells [Jan93]).

Matching to fragments rather than the entire antigen is a physical necessity in the biological immune system; in computers, this strategy is not absolutely necessary, but it has some important advantages. Matching to fragments is more efficient in time and memory, and permits the system to recognize slight variants, particularly when some mismatches are tolerated. These issues of efficiency and variant recognition are relevant for biology as well.

For both biological and computer immune systems, an ability to recognize variants is essential because viruses tend to mutate frequently. If an exact match were required, immunity to one variant of a virus would confer no protection against a slightly different variant. Similarly, vaccines would not work, because they rely on the biological immune system's ability to synthesize antibodies to tamed or killed viruses that are similar in form to the more virulent one that the individual is being immunized against.

13.4.3 Virus Removal

In the biological immune system, if an antibody encounters antigen, they bind together, and the antigen is effectively neutralized. Thus recognition and neutralization of the intruder occur simultaneously. Alternatively, a killer T cell may encounter a cell that exhibits signs of being infected with a particular infecting agent, whereupon it kills the host cell. This is a perfectly sensible course of action, because an infected host cell is slated to die anyway, and its assassination by the killer T cell prevents the viral particles from reaching maturation.

A computer immune system can take the same basic approach to virus removal: it can erase or otherwise inactivate an infected program. However, an important difference between computer viruses and biological viruses raises the possibility of a much gentler alternative.

In biological organisms, most infected cells would not be worth the trouble of saving even if this were possible, because cells are an easily-replenished resource.[11]

In contrast, each of the applications run by a typical computer user is unique in function and irreplaceable (unless backups have been kept, of course). Since a user would be likely to notice any malfunction, all but the most ill-conceived computer viruses attach themselves to their host in such a way that they do not destroy its function. Viruses tend to merely rearrange or reversibly transform their hosts. Thus an infected program is usually expressible as a reversible transformation of the uninfected original.

When the scanner identifies a particular program as being infected with a particular virus, the first step in our removal procedure is to verify that the virus is identical to a known strain. Verification is based upon checksums of regions of viral code that are known to be invariant (perhaps after an appropriate decryption operation) across different instances of the virus. The exact location and structure of the virus must have been derived beforehand, and expressed in terms of a language understood by the verification algorithm. If the verification does not succeed, an attempt to remove the virus by this means is considered too risky, and another more generic virus removal method (beyond the scope of this paper) is brought into play. If the verification succeeds, a repair algorithm carries out the appropriate sequence of steps required for removing that virus, expressed in a simple repair language. The sequence of steps is easily derived from an analysis of the locations (and transformations, if any) of all of the portions of the original host.

Although the analysis required to extract verification and removal information has traditionally been performed by human experts, we shall discuss in a later subsection an automated technique for obtaining this information.

13.4.4 Decoys

Suppose that the anomaly detector has found evidence of a virus, but that the scanner cannot identify it as any of the known strains. Most current anti-virus software will not be able to recover the host program unless it was deliberately stored or analyzed[12] prior to becoming infected. Ideally, one would like to have stronger evidence that the system really is infected, and to know more about the nature of the virus, so that all instances of it (not just the one discovered by the anomaly detector) can be found and eliminated from the system.

In the computer immune system, the presence of a previously unknown virus in the system can be established with much greater certainty than can be provided by the anomaly detector. The idea is to lure the virus into infecting one or more members of a diverse suite of "decoy" programs. Decoys are designed to be as attractive as

---

[11] Neurons are a notable exception, but they are protected from most infections by the blood-brain barrier [Sei95].

[12] Generic disinfection methods can store a small amount of information about an uninfected program, and use this information to help reconstruct it if it subsequently becomes infected.

possible to those types of viruses that spread most successfully. A good strategy for a virus to follow is to infect programs that are touched by the operating system in some way. Such programs are most likely to be executed by the user, and thus serve as the most successful vehicle for further spread. Therefore, the immune system entices a putative virus to infect the decoy programs by executing, reading, writing to, copying, or otherwise manipulating them. Such activity attracts the attention of many viruses that remain active in memory even after they have returned control to their host. To catch viruses that do not remain active in memory, the decoys are placed in places where the most commonly used programs in the system are typically located, such as the root directory, the current directory, and other directories in the path. The next time the infected file is run, it is likely to select one of the decoys as its victim. From time to time, each of the decoy programs is examined to see if it has been modified. If any have been modified, it is almost certain that an unknown virus is loose in the system, and each of the modified decoys contains a sample of that virus. These virus samples are stored in such a way that they will not be executed accidentally. Now they are ready to be analyzed by other components of the immune system.

The capture of a virus sample by the decoy programs is somewhat analogous to the ingestion of antigen by macrophages [Pau91]. Macrophages and other types of cells break antigen into small peptide fragments and present them on their surfaces, where they are subsequently bound by T cells with matching receptors. A variety of further events can ensue from this act of binding, which in one way or another play essential roles in recognizing and removing the pathogen. Capture of an intruder by computer decoys or biological macrophages allows it to be processed into a standard format that can be interpreted by other components of the immune system, provides a standard location where those components can obtain information about the intruder, and primes other parts of the immune system for action.

13.4.5 Automatic Virus Analysis

Typically, a human expert applies a deep understanding of machine instruction sequences to virus analysis. Sometimes, this is combined with observation of the effects of the virus on a program.

Our automatic virus analysis algorithm is much less sophisticated in its knowledge of machine code, but makes up for this deficiency by making use of more data: specifically, several samples of the virus. Once a few samples of the virus have been captured, the algorithm compares the infected decoys with one another and with the uninfected decoys to yield a precise description of how the virus attaches to any host. The description is completely independent of the length and contents of the host, and to some extent can accommodate self-encrypting viruses. A pictorial representation of one particularly simple infection pattern is presented in Fig. 13.4.

Automatic virus analysis provides several useful types of information:

1. The location of all of the pieces of the original host within an infected file, independent of the content and length of the original host. This information is automatically

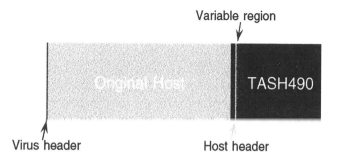

Figure 13.4 Pictorial representation of attachment pattern and structure of the TASH490 virus, derived completely automatically.

converted into the repair language used by the virus removal component of IBM AntiVirus.

2. The location and structure of all components of the virus. Structural information includes the contents of all regions of the virus that are invariant across different samples. This information has two purposes:

(a) It is automatically converted into the verification language used by the verification component of IBM AntiVirus.

(b) It is passed to the automatic signature extraction component for further processing.

13.4.6   Automatic Signature Extraction

The basic goal of automatic signature extraction is to choose a signature that is very likely to be found in all instances of the virus, and very unlikely to be found accidentally in uninfected programs. In other words, we wish to minimize false negatives and false positives. False negatives are dangerous because they leave the user vulnerable to attack. False positives are extremely annoying to customers, and so infuriating to vendors of falsely-accused software that they have led to at least one lawsuit.

To minimize false negatives, we first start with the contents of the invariant regions that have been identified by the automatic virus analysis procedure. However, it is quite conceivable that not all of the potential variation has been captured within the samples. As a general rule, non-executable "data" portions of programs, which can include representations of numerical constants, character strings, work areas for computations, etc., are inherently more likely to vary from one instance of the virus to another than are "code" portions, which represent machine instructions. The origin of the variation may be internal to the virus, or a virus hacker might deliberately change a few data bytes in an effort to elude virus scanners. To be conservative, "data" areas are excluded from further consideration as possible signatures. Although the task of separating code from data is in principle somewhat ill-defined, there are a variety of methods, such as running the virus through a debugger or virtual interpreter, which perform reasonably well.

At this point, there are one or more sequences of invariant machine code bytes from which viral signatures could be selected. We take the set of candidate signatures to be all possible contiguous blocks of S bytes found in these byte sequences, where S is a signature length that is predetermined or determined by the algorithm itself. (Typically, S ranges between approximately 12 and 36.) The remaining goal is to select from among the candidates one or perhaps a few signatures that are least likely to lead to false positives.

We have formulated the problem of minimizing the false positive probability as follows. For each candidate signature, estimate the probability for it to match a random sequence of length S that is generated by the same probability distribution that generates legitimate software on the relevant platform. (Of course, machine code is written by people or compilers, not probability distributions, so such a probability distribution is a theoretical and somewhat ill-defined construct, but we estimate its statistics from a set of over 10,000 DOS and OS/2 programs, constituting half a gigabyte of code.) Then, we select the candidate signature for which the estimated probability is the smallest.

In slightly more detail, the key steps of the algorithm are as follows:

1. Form a list of all n-grams (sequences of n bytes; $1 \le n \le n_{max}$) contained in the input data. (n_{max} is typically 5 or 8.)
2. Calculate the frequency of each such n-gram in the "self" collection.
3. Use a simple formula that chains together conditional probabilities based on the measured n-gram frequencies to form a "false-positive" probability estimate for each candidate signature, i.e. the probability that it matches a random S-byte sequence chosen from code that is statistically similar to "self".
4. Select the signature with the lowest estimated false-positive probability.

Characterizations of this method [KA94] show that the probability estimates are poor on an absolute scale, due to the fact that code tends to be correlated on a longer scale than 5 or 8 bytes. However, the relative ordering of candidate signatures is rather good, so the method generally selects one of the best possible signatures. In fact, judging from the relatively low false-positive rate of the IBM AntiVirus signatures (compared with that of other anti-virus vendors), the algorithm's ability to select good signatures may be *better* than that achieved by human experts.

In a sense, the signature extraction algorithm combines elements of outmoded and current theories of how the vertebrate immune system develops antibodies and immune-cell receptors to newly encountered antigen. The *template* theory, which held sway from the mid-1930s until the early 1960s, was that antibodies and receptors molded themselves around the antigen. The *clonal selection* theory holds that a vast, random repertoire of antibodies and receptors is generated, and those that recognize self are eliminated during the maturation phase. Of the remaining antibodies and receptors, at least a few will match any foreign antigen that is encountered. The clonal selection theory gained favor in the 1960s, and is currently accepted [Pau91].

Our automatic signature extraction method starts out looking like the template theory. Instead of generating a large random collection of signatures that might turn out to be useful someday, we take the collection of code for a particular virus as our starting point in choosing a signature. However, we do share one important element with the clonal selection theory: elimination of self-recognizing signatures. In fact, the automatic signature extraction method is even more zealous in this endeavor than clonal selection, in that it only retains the "best" signature.

13.4.7   Immunological Memory

The mechanisms by which the vertebrate immune system retains a lifelong memory of viruses to which it has been exposed are quite complex, and are still the subject of study and debate.

By contrast, immunological memory is absolutely trivial to implement in computers. During its first encounter with a new virus, a computer system may be "ill", i.e. it will devote a fair amount of time and energy (or CPU cycles) to virus analysis. After the analysis is complete, the extracted signature and verification/repair information can be added to the appropriate known-virus databases. During any subsequent encounter, detection and elimination of the virus will occur very quickly. In such a case the computer can be thought of as "immune" to the virus.

13.4.8   Fighting Self-replication with Self-replication

In the biological immune system, immune cells with receptors that happen to match a given antigen reasonably well are stimulated to reproduce themselves. This provides a very strong selective pressure for good recognizers, and by bringing a degree of mutation into play, the immune cell is generally able to come up with immune cells that are extremely well-matched to the antigen in question.

One can view this as a case in which self-replication is being used to fight a self-replicator (the virus) in a very effective manner. One can cite a number of other examples in nature and medical history where this strategy has been employed, such as the deliberate use of the myxoma virus in the 1950s to curtail an exploding rabbit population in Australia [W.H76, Lev92].

The self-replicator need not itself be a virus. In the case of the worldwide campaign against smallpox, launched by the World Health Organization in 1966, those who were in close contact with an infected individual were all immunized against the disease. Thus immunization spread as a sort of anti-disease among smallpox victims. This strategy was amazingly successful: the last naturally occurring case of smallpox occurred in Somalia in 1977 [Bai75].

We propose to use a similar mechanism, which we call the "kill signal", to quell viral spread in computer networks. When a computer discovers that it is infected, it can send a signal to neighboring machines. The signal conveys to the recipient the fact that the transmitter was infected, plus any signature or repair information that might be of use in detecting and eradicating the virus. If the recipient finds that it is infected, it sends the signal to *its* neighbors, and so on. If the recipient is not infected, it does not pass along the signal, but at least it has received the database updates, effectively immunizing it against that virus.

Theoretical modeling has shown the kill signal to be extremely effective, particularly in topologies that are highly localized or sparsely connected [KW93, Kep94b].

13.5   CONCLUSION AND PERSPECTIVE

The development of the generic virus detector and the computer immune system were primarily motivated by practical concerns: human virus experts are on the verge of being overwhelmed, and we need to automate as much of what they do as possible.

The generic virus detector was incorporated into IBM AntiVirus in May 1994, and since that time it has successfully identified several new boot viruses. It is the subject of a pending patent. Most of the components of the computer immune system are functioning as very useful prototypes in our virus isolation laboratory; we use them every day to process the large sets of new viruses that arrive in the mail from other virus experts around the world. The immune system itself is the subject of a pending patent, as are several of its components, including automatic virus analysis and automatic signature extraction.

Our eventual goal is to incorporate the immune system into IBM AntiVirus and, a few years from now, in networks inhabited by itinerant software agents. More implementation and more invention, guided in part by the biological metaphor, lie ahead.

Although our primary motivation for developing a computer immune system is practical, it is interesting to adopt a more philosophical perspective.

Consider the history of how humans have handled disease. For millions of years, our sole defense against infectious disease was our immune system, and it has done a good job of defending us from most infectious diseases. When we are suffering from the common cold, we may experience a few days of discomfort while the immune system figures out how to recognize and eradicate the virus, but we usually survive the attack. However, a minority of diseases, like smallpox or AIDS, are not handled effectively by the immune system. Fortunately, during the last few centuries, we have made tremendous advances in our understanding of infectious diseases at both the macroscopic and microscopic levels, and medical practices based on this understanding now augment the capabilities of our natural immune system.

A few hundred years ago, disease began to be understood at the macroscopic level. In 1760, Daniel Bernoulli, the founder of mathematical physics, was interested in determining whether a particular form of inoculation against smallpox would be generally beneficial or harmful to society. Formulating and solving a mathematical model, he found that inoculation could be expected to increase the average life expectancy by three years. His work founded the field of mathematical epidemiology [Bai75]. Observational epidemiology received a major boost from John Snow, who in 1854 was able to deduce the origin of a severe cholera outbreak in London by plotting the addresses of victims on a city map [Bai75].

The macroscopic approaches of Snow and Bernoulli proved fruitful even before bacteria and viruses were identified as the underlying cause of infectious disease in the late 19th century. During the 20th century, research at the microscopic level has supplemented epidemiology. Electron microscopy and X-ray crystallography brought the structure of viruses into view in the 1930s, and the fascinating complexities of their life cycle and biochemistry began to be studied intensively in the mid-1940s. These advances established *terra firma* on which mathematical epidemiologists could build their models.

Today, epidemiologists, in the detective role pioneered by John Snow, discover new viruses [Car04]. Biochemists, molecular biologists, and geneticists work to elucidate the secrets of viruses, and to create safe and effective vaccines for them. Epidemiologists use intuition and mathematics to develop plans for immunizing populations with these vaccines. The eradication of smallpox from the planet in 1977 is probably the greatest triumph of this multi-disciplinary collaboration.

Interestingly, the history of man's defense against computer viruses is almost exactly reversed. Computer viruses were first understood at the microscopic level, thanks to the pioneering work of Fred Cohen in the early 1980s [Coh87]. As soon as the first DOS viruses began to appear in 1987 [Hig90], they were dissected in great detail, and the first primitive anti-virus software was written. It was not until 1990 that the first real attempts were made to understand the spread of computer viruses from a macroscopic perspective [KW91, KW93, Tip90, Tip91]. Finally, in the mid-1990s, we are proposing to give computers what humans and other vertebrates have always relied upon as a first line of defense against disease: an immune system.

The Center for Disease Control does not get worked up when a new strain of the common cold sweeps through a population. Instead, they concentrate their limited resources on finding cures for horrible diseases such as AIDS. Currently, the world community of anti-virus researchers (the computer equivalent of the CDC) squanders lots of time analyzing the computer equivalents of the common cold. Our hope is that a computer immune system will deal with most of the standard, run-of-the-mill viruses quietly and effectively, leaving just a small percentage of especially problematic viruses for human experts to analyze.

REFERENCES

[Bai75]   Norman T.J. Bailey. *The Mathematical Theory of Infectious Diseases and Its Applications*. Oxford University Press, second edition, 1975.

[CGH⁺95] David Chess, Benjamin Grosof, Colin Harrison, David Levine, and Colin Parris. Itinerant agents for mobile computing. *IEEE Personal Communications Magazine*, 1995. submitted.

[Coh87] Fred Cohen. Computer viruses, theory and experiments. In *Computers and Security*, volume 6, pages 22–35, 1987.

[CR94]   Maxime Crochemore and Wojciech Rytter. *Text Algorithms*. Oxford University Press, 1994.

[ER89]   M.W. Eichin and J.A. Rochlis. With microscope and tweezers: An analysis of the internet virus of november 1988. In *Proceedings of the 1989 IEEE Symposium on Security and Privacy*, pages 326–343, 1989.

[FPAC94] Stephanie Forrest, Alan S. Perelson, Lawrence Allen, and Rajesh Cherukuri. Self – nonself discrimination in a computer. In *Proceedings of the 1994 IEEE Computer*

Society Symposium on Research in Security and Privacy, May 1994.

[Gar94]   Laurie Garrett. *The Coming Plague: Newly Emerging Diseases in a World Out of Balance*. Farrar, Straus and Giroux, 1994.

[HCK94] Colin Harrison, David Chess, and Aaron Kershenbaum. Mobile agents: Are they a good idea? Technical Report 19887, IBM Research Report, 1994. http://www.research.ibm.com/massdist/rc20010.ps.

[Hig90]   Harold J. Highland. *Computers and Security's Computer Virus Handbook*. Elsevier, 1990.

[HKP91] J. Hertz, A. Krogh, and R. G. Palmer. *Introduction to the Theory of Neural Computation*. Addison-Wesley, 1991.

[Jan93]   Charles A. Janeway, Jr. How the immune system recognizes invaders. *Scientific American*, 269(3):72–79, September 1993.

[KA94]   Jeffrey O. Kephart and William C. Arnold. Automatic extraction of computer virus signatures. In R. Ford, editor, *Proceedings of the Fourth International Virus Bulletin Conference*, pages 179–194. Virus Bulletin, Ltd., September 1994.

[Kep94a] J.O. Kephart. A biologically inspired immune system for computers. In R. Brooks and P. Maes, editors, *Artificial Life IV: Proceedings of the Fourth International Workshop on the Synthesis and Simulation of Living Systems*, pages 130–139. MIT Press, 1994.

[Kep94b] J.O. Kephart. How topology affects population dynamics. In C. Langton, editor, *Artificial Life III: Studies in the Sciences of Complexity*, pages 447–463. Addison-Wesley, 1994.

[KW91]   J.O. Kephart and S.R. White. Directed-graph epidemiological models of computer viruses. In *Proceedings of the 1991 IEEE Computer Society Symposium on Research in Security and Privacy*, pages 343–359, May 1991.

[KW93]   J.O. Kephart and S.R. White. Measuring and modeling computer virus prevalence. In *Proceedings of the 1993 IEEE Computer Society Symposium on Research in Security and Privacy*, pages 2–15, May 1993.

[KWC93] J.O. Kephart, S.R. White, and D.M. Chess. Computers and epidemiology. *IEEE Spectrum*, 30(5):20–26, May 1993.

[Lev92]   Arnold J. Levine. *Viruses*. Freeman, 1992. Scientific American Library.

[MK93]   Philippa Marrack and John W. Kappler. How the immune system recognizes the body. *Scientific American*, 269(3):81–89, September 1993.

[Mur88]   W.H. Murray. The application of epidemiology to computer viruses. In *Computers and Security*, volume 7, pages 130–150, 1988.

[Pau91]   William E. Paul, editor. *Immunology: Recognition and Response ... Readings from Scientific American*. Freeman, 1991.

[RHW86] D. E. Rumelhart, G. E. Hinton, and R. J. Williams. Learning internal representations by error propagation. In *Parallel Distributed Processing*, volume 1, pages 318–362. MIT Press, 1986.

[Sei95]   Philip E. Seiden. Note on auto-immunity. Private communication, 1995.

[Spa89]   E.H. Spafford. The internet worm program: An analysis. *Computer Comm. Review*, 19, 1989.

[Spa91]   E.H. Spafford. Computer viruses: A form of artificial life? In D. Farmer, C. Langton, S. Rasmussen, and C. Taylor, editors, *Artificial Life II: Studies in the Sciences of Complexity*, pages 727–747. Addison-Wesley, 1991.

[Tip90]   Peter S. Tippett. Computer virus replication. *Comput. Syst. Eur.*, 10:33–36, 1990.

[Tip91]   Peter S. Tippett. The kinetics of computer virus replication: A theory and preliminary survey. In *Safe Computing: Proceedings of the Fourth Annual Computer Virus and Security Conference*, pages 66–87, March 1991.

[W.H76]   W.H. McNeill. *Plagues and Peoples*. Doubleday, 1976.

14

Behavioural Cloning of Control Skill

Ivan Bratko, Tanja Urbančič and Claude Sammut

ABSTRACT

Controlling a complex dynamic system, such as a plane or a crane, usually requires a skilled operator. Typically, such a control skill is acquired through experience and is sub-cognitive. Thus, it is hard to access and difficult to rationally reconstruct through introspection. In this chapter we describe experiments in the reconstruction of control skill from operators' control traces by means of machine learning. Problem domains include pole-balancing, operating a crane, and flying a plane.

14.1 INTRODUCTION

Controlling a complex dynamic system usually requires an operator who has acquired a high degree of skill through experience. Although these tasks may be critical to human safety or commercial advantage, they are to a large extent performed without thinking, because many skills involved are sub-cognitive. The operator is usually only capable of describing it incompletely and approximately. Such descriptions can be used as basic guidelines for constructing automatic controllers but, as discussed, for example, in [UB94b], they are not operational in the sense of being directly translatable into an automatic controller. Still, the motivation for automatic or semi-automatic control in such areas is strong and manifold. Economic requirements go hand-in-hand with the need for assistance to human operators in order to perform reliably, effectively and safely in many different and sometimes unexpected circumstances.

Michie *et al.* suggested the use of standard machine learning techniques to learn control rules from traces of human performance. They reported successful experiments in pole-

Machine Learning and Data Mining: Methods and Applications
Edited by R.S. Michalski, I Bratko and M. Kubat
© 1997 John Wiley & Sons Ltd

balancing [MBHM90]. Their pioneering study was followed by others in more practical domains: piloting a simulated aircraft [SHKM92, MC94], operating a crane [UB94b], and production scheduling [KK94]. The approach was termed *behavioural cloning* [Mic93]. Here we survey experiments in the domains mentioned, and summarize the experience from these experiments.

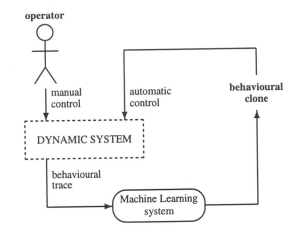

Figure 14.1   Behavioural cloning of control skill.

The basic idea, illustrated in Figure 14.1, is to a certain extent similar to some other, more "classical" applications of inductive learning, such as medical diagnosis. For example, medical records of patients' symptoms and accompanying diagnoses made by physicians are entered into an induction program which constructs rules that will automatically diagnose new patients on the basis of previous data. Just as diagnostic rules can be learned by observing a physician at work, we should be able to learn how to control a system by watching a human operator at work. In this case, the data provided to the induction program are logs of the actions taken by the operator in response to changes in the system. An induced rule-set constitutes a kind of classifier that maps state records into action names, rather than mapping patient records into disease names.

Unlike some problems that directly suit standard ML techniques, behavioural cloning requires extra effort in formulating the problem as a ML task, including designing a suitable target concept representation for learning, choosing good training examples from recorded human behaviours and interpreting the results of ML. In the absence of a general methodology, these questions have to be carefully investigated for the particular problem at hand. Although the process is still far from routine, some guidelines can be given based on the experience in the following domains: pole balancing, piloting aircraft, driving container cranes and production line scheduling. All the domains are of interest for potential applications. Even pole balancing, which is useful as experimental domain, has much in common with the control of space craft.

In all the experiments described in this chapter, simulators of the dynamic systems were used. The flight simulator used in [SHKM92] was provided by Silicon Graphics Incorporated. In [MC94], the authors used the ACM public-domain simulation of an F-16 combat aircraft.

For pole balancing and crane control, the simulators were developed specifically for these studies. In a more recent application [Kar95], a clone has been induced for controlling the electric discharge machining process (see also [BMK97], this volume). In that case, the cloning was done on the actual electric discharge machine, and not on a simulator.

14.2   BEHAVIOURAL CLONING

Some specific features distinguish learning to control dynamic systems as an atypical ML application. We are presented with the whole sequence of control actions, normally without a clear indication of

- which actions are crucial for the success of the sequence,
- which are suboptimal but compensated by the effect of other actions, or
- what was the actual stimulus for a particular action, etc.

The usual ML-based approach to behavioural cloning has been as follows. The "behaviour trace", that is, a sequence of the states of the controlled system and the operator's control actions, is viewed as a set of examples of correct control decisions. Each example consists of a pair $(State, Action)$ where $State$ is an attribute-value vector and $Action$ is a "class value" for a learning program. In such a formulation, attribute-based learning techniques can be applied to induce a functional relation

$$Action = f(State)$$

Both the attributes of $State$ and the class value $Action$ can be discrete or continuous. The learned function f then represents an artificial controller, or behavioural clone, which is supposed to mimic the original operator.

Sometimes a time delay is introduced between $State$ and $Action$. The reason is that the current $Action$ is not viewed as the operator's response to the current $State$, but to some *previous* state. This delay between the state and the action is assumed to be due to the time needed for state recognition and physical manipulation of the controls by the operator. The functional relation to be learned in such a case is

$$Action(Time) = f(State(Time - Delay))$$

In some domains there are several control variables. In piloting, for example, the throttle, flaps, ailerons, etc. can be manipulated simultaneously. In such domains the learning problem is partitioned into several sub-problems, each of them dealing with one control variable. These may be dependent, so the decision regarding one control variable may be used as an attribute for a decision regarding another control variable.

One way of structuring the learning problem is to divide the behaviour traces into phases. For example, a flight may be divided into take-off, straight-and-level flight, turn to a specified heading, etc. Separate controllers are induced from the traces for each phase of the flight. To carry out the control task, these controllers are invoked according to the particular phase of the flight plan. The phases, the plan, and the phase recognition conditions are hand crafted and not learned automatically.

Table 14.1   Characteristics of the domains and parameters of learning

	Pole and cart	Cessna	F-16	Crane
# state variables	4	15	15	6
# control variables	1	4	9	2
# types of control variables	boolean	real, integer	real, integer	integer
# subjects	10	3	1	6
# traces	1	90	20	450
# events in data set	3500	90.000	25.000	450.000
length of a trace	5 min	5 min	18 min	1 - 3 min
# phases	1	7	8	1
learning program	C4.5	C4.5	C4.5	Retis, M5
delay [seconds]	0.4 - 0.5	1 - 3	1	0 - 0.1
preprocessing of data needed	no	yes	yes	no
predefined plan needed	no	yes	yes	no

In the following sections we give a comparative analysis of some of the phenomena observed in behavioural cloning, taking into account the results in all the domains mentioned above. In order to place the results in context, in Table 14.1 we present some characteristics of the problem domains and the corresponding cloning tasks, as well as some parameters of human and machine learning in each particular case. The table gives some idea of the complexity of the tasks. However, some qualifying comments are required. One informative characteristic for a domain is the time a human operator requires to master the task. Since individual differences can be very large (see, e.g., [UB94b]), this should be treated only as a rough approximation. For pole-balancing, human learning time was around one hour. For performing a simple crane operating cycle, approximately ten hours of training were needed. The F-16 piloting problem was more demanding than the Cessna variant. Also the meaning of event should be clarified. In the flying domains, an event corresponds to a *change* in control action, while in the crane problem, events are actually snapshots, recorded at regular time intervals.

14.3   POLE BALANCING

14.3.1   The Problem

The well-known problem of balancing a pole on a cart moving on a track of limited length has often been used to demonstrate new approaches in control synthesis, e.g. in [WS64, MC68, BSA83, And87, VUF93]. For cloning, a "line-crossing" variant was used by Michie and coworkers [MBHM90]. Here, subjects are asked to make as many crossings of the mid-line of the track as possible, within the test period, without crashing.

14.3.2   Choice of Examples

One question that must be answered when designing a behavioural cloning system is which traces to choose for learning among all the available example traces. Michie *et al* state:

20 psychology student volunteers ... learned by trial and error to control with a joystick the pole-and-cart system displayed in dynamic simulation on a PC screen. The object was (1) to get an idea of the human learnability of the easiest, and the hardest of the three human-learnable grades of the task, and (2) to find at least one subject capable of being trained to a level of full mastery, analogous to the pre-selection procedures applied before simulator-training of airplane pilots. He or she would then become the subject of more intensive study of machine learning by imitation.

14.3.3   Time Delay

In some domains, it appears that a time delay is required between the system's state and the control action. Such a delay seems necessary because an operator cannot react to a stimulus, that is system state, instantaneously. Thus, an example to the induction program consists of a set of attributes, representing the state of the system and the dependent variable is the action taken, some time *after* the state represented by the attributes.

In the pole balancing study, Michie *et al.* experimented with a variety of delays, finally settling on 400 milliseconds. This appeared to give the best results.

14.3.4   Clean-up Effect

Michie and Camacho [MC94] described the *clean-up effect* as follows. "When induction-extracted rules were installed in the computer as an 'auto-pilot', performance on the task was similar to that of the trained human who had generated the original behaviour trace, but more dependable ..." They continue with an explanation of this effect. "A trained human skill, ..., is obliged to execute via an error-prone sensory-motor system. Inconsistency and moments of inattention would then be stripped away by the averaging effect implicit in inductive generalisation, thus restoring to the experimenters a cleaned-up version of the original production rules."

Chambers and Michie [CM69] were the first to report the clean-up effect which they observed in the pole-balancing domain. Michie, Bain and Hayes-Michie [MBHM90] also gave a quantitative assessment of clean-up. When a clone induced from an operator's traces is used as a *predictor* of the operator's actions, the prediction error rate often exceeds 20%. Michie and Camacho interpret this error rate simply as indicative of the cumulative sum of human perceptual and execution errors. These errors are presumably filtered out by the induction program. (They used Quinlan's C4.5 [Qui87]). As a result, the clone's behaviour is much smoother than that of the human operator. Michie and colleagues [MBHM90] measured this *performance* (not prediction!) clean-up in terms of ranges visited by the four system variables: position, angle, and their velocities. In general, better control results in smaller ranges. The ranges achieved by the clone were much tighter than those achieved by the human trainer. They were reduced by the clone to between 17% and 45% of the original human's ranges (depending on the system variable). This result is very illustrative although the simple measure of clean-up is debatable as it considers each of the state variables separately. The *fitness* function introduced in [VUF93] is probably a better measure of performance and is more in the spirit of traditional control engineering.

14.3.5   Brittleness

The initial pole balancing study made no serious attempt at measuring the robustness of the clone that was produced. That is, can the clone perform its task in a wide range of conditions. However, a subsequent study [BU] showed that robust controllers could be constructed for pole balancing, provided that traces showed examples of a variety of starting conditions. As described in [BU], Andrej Zalar was able to reliably induce completely robust clones from two operator's traces starting from two opposite positions on the track, one at $x = 2$m and one at $x = $ -2m. As an illustration, here is a rule obtained from these traces with the tree regression program Retis [Kar92], under rather high degree of tree pruning:

if $x \leq -0.1259$ then $F1$ else
  if $x \leq 0.8005$ then $F2$
  else $F3$

The three functions $F1$, $F2$ and $F3$ are:
$F1 = \text{sign}(0.0194x + 0.6442\dot{x} + 7.1169\varphi + 0.8020\dot{\varphi} - 0.3500)$
$F2 = \text{sign}(0.5621x + 0.4577\dot{x} + 6.6172\varphi + 0.7367\dot{\varphi} + 0.0164)$
$F3 = \text{sign}(1.0599x + 1.5700\dot{x} + 7.3821\varphi + 1.4439\dot{\varphi} + 2.4343)$

14.3.6   Transparency of Induced Rules

One of the goals of Michie *et al.* was to "deliver an articulate account of the given acquired skill in the form of a rule-structured expression". They succeeded in that a small number of readable rules were generated and could successfully accomplish the task. This has been confirmed independently by other researchers as illustrated by the control rule above.

The transparency of the induced rules remains a goal of all behavioural learning research. However, we will see that, in more complex domains, there is still much work to be done.

14.4   LEARNING TO FLY

14.4.1   The Problem

Two studies have been reported: piloting a Cessna [SHKM92] and piloting an F-16 [MC94]. In both cases, the task is to fly according to a predefined flight plan, including take-off, climbing to a specified altitude, straight and level flight, turning and landing.

In both studies, the source code of a flight simulation program was modified to log actions taken by pilots during a number of flights on the simulator. These logs were used to construct, by induction, a set of rules that could fly the aircraft through the same flight plan that the pilots flew. The data collected consisted of the settings of particular controls such as the elevator, ailerons, flaps, etc., and the values of the state variables of the simulator such as pitch, roll, yaw, climb rate, air speed, etc.

The data from each flight were segmented into stages, for example, take-off and climb, straight and level flight, turn, descend and line up on runway, land. For each stage separate decision trees were constructed for each of the possible control actions, e.g., elevators, ailerons, flaps, etc. A program filters the flight logs generating input files for the induction program corresponding to each control action. The attributes of a training example are the flight parameters of the simulator. The dependent variable is the attribute describing a control action.

Several induction programs have been used, including C4.5 (Quinlan, 1993) and the CART regression tree algorithm (Breiman et al., 1984). To test the induced rules, the original autopilot code in the simulator is replaced by the rules. A post-processor converts the induction programÕs output into if-statements in C so that they can be incorporated into the flight simulator easily. Hand crafted C code determines which stage the flight has reached and decides when to change stages. The appropriate rules for each stage are then selected in a switch statement. Each stage has several, independent if-statements, one for each action. The rules that have been synthesised are successful in the sense that the plane follows the flight plan just as the human trainer would and lands safely on the runway.

When applying C4.5 to this domain a technical problem had to be overcome. Control variables are either real or integer. However, C4.5 can only output discrete class values. To handle this, continuous class variables are discretised prior to submission to C4.5. Discretisation is done on the basis of clustering on the frequency histograms for the class values. Experiments have also been conducted with regression trees which can output continuous values. The results have been comparable to C4.5.

Motivation for behavioural cloning in this domain may seem dubious in the light of competition with very good existing autopilots. However, cloning is still worth doing at least for the following reasons:

1. To reconstruct the skill in symbolic form so that it is inspectable.
2. To build autopilots for cases where traditional methods fail, e.g. handling wind shear.

14.4.2 Choice of Examples

The styles and control strategies vary significantly from pilot to pilot [SHKM92]. For example, some "heavy-handed" pilots exercise the controls to a large extent in order to keep the aircraft on course. Others use gentle corrections to eventually bring the place back on track. Commercial airlines prefer the second type of pilot since they tend to cause passengers less discomfort.

Mixing data from different pilots had the tendency to "confuse" the induction algorithm since the decision tree had to try to account for different ways of achieving the same goal. Therefore, auto-pilots were constructed from traces of individual pilots. These auto-pilots mimic the style of the trainer, hence the term 'behavioural clone', coined by Donald Michie.

14.4.3 Time Delay

Sammut et al. [SHKM92] in their experiments used a delay that varied between 1 and 3 seconds. Their choice of the delay was pragmatic and determined experimentally. The choice was not made in a principled way although they paid considerable attention to this question in their discussion. They believed that the delay was important, but did not have a firm theoretical basis for determining appropriate delays. The length of the delay did not appear to be critical, provided that some delay was present. Since the pilot data were recorded with a delay, the

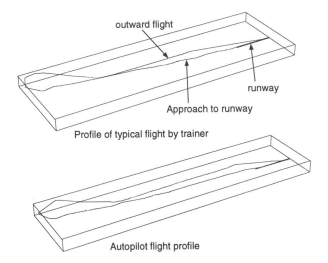

Figure 14.2   Human execution of a fixed flight plan (upper trajectory) and the clone's execution of the same plan (lower trajectory).

rules that were induced could only work if delay also existed between the execution of the rule and the execution of the action specified by that rule.

14.4.4   Clean-up Effect

Michie and Camacho [MC94] also report on clean-up in flying the simulated F-16 aircraft. They considered the error in straight and level flight measured as the plane's deviation from a straight line. The clone's deviation was only about 15% of the human's deviation.

In learning to fly the Cessna [SHKM92], the clean-up effect was also observed. Figure 14.2 shows the trajectories in three dimensions of two flights, one by a human operator and the other one induced from the same operator's traces. Both flights accomplish the same flight plan. Clean-up is easily noticeable in the approach to the runway.

14.4.5   Brittleness

Successful clones perform similarly to the human subjects, although the clones' trajectories are of course not literal reproductions of the original trajectories. However, in complex domains, such as flying and crane driving, the original experiments produced clones that were usually very brittle with respect to changes and were only successful within a fixed plan. They were sensitive to small changes in the task or the parameters of the problem domain.

These problems can be cured by training in a noisy environment. For example, the first piloting clones were built using a flight simulator that did not include turbulence or wind disturbances. Therefore, when flying straight and level, it was sufficient to leave the controls alone and the aircraft would continue along its original altitude and heading. A trace of such a flight provides no examples of what to do when the aircraft either begins off its desired course or what to do if it is pushed off course. This can be corrected by introducing turbulence and wind drift. The human pilot must now generate examples of corrections which can be used to train a more robust clone. Arentz [Are94] performed just such experiments and found that clones can be constructed that are quite robust to substantial disturbances. Clearly, if the disturbances encountered by the clone are greater than those encountered by the trainer, we can expect loss of control since circumstances have been created that are outside the clone's range of experience.

14.4.6 Transparency of Induced Rules

So far, the rules that have been generated for piloting simulated aircraft have been large and opaque. There are several conjectures as to why this is so.

The attributes that have been used for induction are simply the state variables of the simulator. They do not necessarily reflect what the pilot attends to when making control decisions. In particular, they do not give any information about the visual scene being displayed by the simulator. It is possible that high-level attributes, constructed from the primitive attributes may lead to more concise decision trees.

Although the amount of information collected from these experiments is large, the data are still sparse, relative to the size of the domain. In such circumstances, it is possible for an induction program to find spurious correlations and thus the splitting critieria become less effective. Experiments are currently underway to determine how strong this effect is.

When a pilot is tryng to fly straight and level is below the desired altitude, it is most likely that his or her goal is to achieve a positive climb rate. This may be done by a combination of increasing the throttle and pitching up. The present cloning method does not take into account this two-stage process of determining a goal and then determining how to achieve it. Thus another conjecture for the large size of the decisions trees is that there is a confusion of goal structuring and execution of control actions.

14.5 CONTAINER CRANES

14.5.1 The Problem

The world market requires cranes with as high a capacity as possible. Here, capacity is measured as the total load transported within some allotted time. Developing bigger and faster cranes is one solution, but due to undesirable effects at high operating speeds, this trend is limited in practice [Gri90]. An alternative is better use of existing cranes, especially in minimising the time needed to transport a container from a starting position to a target position. This requires good coordination of the operations: positioning the trolley and changing the rope length. Appropriate positioning of the trolley above the target load position prevents subsequent corrections that significantly degrade performance. It is also very important, for both safety and efficiency, to control the load swing. An anti-swaying capability permits greater acceleration, so if properly controlled, load swinging can be an advantage in some stages of the working cycle and skilled operators actually make use of it. Of course, the swing must be kept as small as possible when approaching the target position. A considerable amount of training is needed for an operator to become an efficient and reliable crane driver, moreover some of them never achieve top performance. It is also difficult to drive for many hours with the same degree of attention. Computer-aided assistance in this process would be highly beneficial.

Several attempts at automating crane operation are known, but according to experts in the crane building industry [Nov], there is still no controller as good as as a well trained human operator. Some research has been done with classical automatic control, e.g. [SS82]. However, ineffectiveness in the presence of unpredictable factors and opaqueness of these controllers led to the increased interest in alternative methods, such as predictive fuzzy control [YH86]. This method involves steps such as describing human operator strategies, defining the meaning of linguistic performance indices, etc. This process can be very time consuming and is a strong motivation for the synthesis of control rules directly from the recorded performance of well-trained operators.

In behavioural cloning study [UB94a], the task is to transport a container from an initial position to a target position. Performance requirements include basic safety constraints, stop-gap accuracy and as high a capacity as possible. A group of volunteers first learned to control a simulator of a container crane. Then control rules were generating with two regression tree programs RETIS [Kar92] and M5 [Qui93] from recordings of the subjects' behaviours. Clones that performed successfully were induced by both RETIS and M5.

14.5.2   Choice of Examples

The styles and control strategies of subjects in this domain varies just as much as they do among pilots. For example, some subjects tended towards fast and less reliable operation, others were slower, more conservative, and more reliable. Some were avoiding large angular accelerations at the expense of time. Such strategies produce reliable, but slow performance. This is in contrast with some operators strategies that tend to achieve faster times, but require higher accelerations of the trolley which causes large angles and requires very delicate balancing of the load at the end of the trace. There were also differences between the operators in the order of attaining the subgoals.

To avoid mixing individual styles, the commonly agreed practice in behavioural cloning has been to combine training examples from the same subject only. However, even the example trajectories of the same subject may vary considerably. For example in the crane domain, the same subject using the same control style will produce trajectories whose finishing times are quite different. According to this, when trying to induce the most "tutorial" and "unadventurous" clones, the most conservative example trajectories have been found to be by far the most useful.

14.5.3   Time Delay

Experiments were carried out with various delays [UB94a]. It appears in this domain, that zero delay does not produce inferior results compared to other delays. Some discussions lead to the belief that the operator's delay in fact varies and depends on the situation. There are quick, purely reactive decisions, and there are also strategic, longer term decisions that have to do with setting new intermediate goals, for example start accelerating until a goal speed is attained. Also, it seems that a skilled operator is capable of compensating for delays in reaction time by predicting short term future states of the system. In extreme case this would even indicate that a "negative delay" would make sense. So straightforward adoption of reaction time delays to unpredicted events, known from psychology, does not seem to be appropriate. To conclude, there seems to be no clear indication, either theoretical or experimental, of what would be an appropriate delay.

14.5.4 Clean-up Effect

The clean-up effect has also been observed in the crane domain. In the container crane, there are six system variables: position of the trolley and its velocity, rope length and its velocity, and rope inclination angle and its velocity. The task is to move the load from a start position to a given goal position. When the goal position is reached, the state variables must be kept sufficiently close to the goal values for some minimum time interval. Figure 14.3 shows two

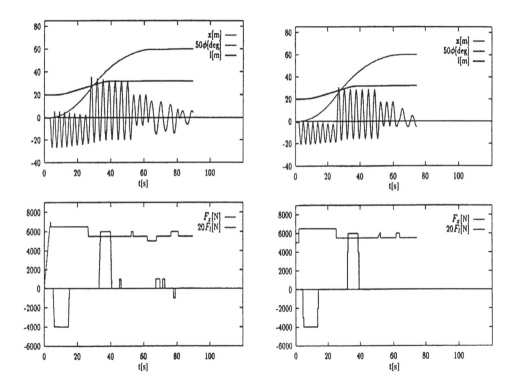

Figure 14.3 Diagrams on the left: one of the most "tutorial" traces by a human controlling the crane; on the right: the trace of a clone induced from the human's trace. The variables are: x is the position of the trolley, ϕ is the angle of the rope, l is the length of the rope, F_x is horizontal force applied to the trolley, F_l is vertical force applied to the rope.

time behaviours. One is by a human operator. This contains precisely those events that were used to induce the clone that produced the other trajectory. The clone was induced by Quinlan's M5 [Qui93] which generates regression trees that are by default drastically pruned. As in the previous cases, it can be seen in Figure 14.3 that the clone carries out the task in a style very similar to the original. The clean-up here is reflected in that the clone is noticeably more successful than the original with respect to the time required to complete the task (75 seconds for the clone compared to 90 seconds for the original).

14.5.5 Brittleness

As opposed to the above optimistic results, there is also a more negative side to the experimental findings in this domain. Brittleness was noticed at two levels:

- Cloning by straightforward learning from the traces does not reliably produce successful clones; it is very sensitive to the choice of particular traces for training and to the learning program settings;
- The clones are not robust with respect to changes in the control task (e.g. different starting or ending position of the load), even if they outperform the originals in the sense of time needed to accomplish the task.

The clones generated from more than one trace are slightly more robust but at the cost of decreased transparency due to the dimensions of the trees.

14.5.6 Transparency of Induced Rules

In the study [UB94a], special attention was devoted to the generation of transparent rules, which would help make the human operator's skill explicit, in symbolic form. This is of great practical importance for being able to capture an excellent operator's skill and transfering to less gifted operators. The authors believe that a major task in behavioural cloning is establishing the correspondence between the clones induced from an operator's traces and the instructions provided by the operator. Therefore they compared the induced clones to the operators' verbal description of their control skills.

Straightforward learning for controlling the force on the rope, F_l, using the original six attributes produced regression trees that were very hard to compare conceptually with the instructions. The trees tended to be large and the attributes appearing in the tree were different from those in the human instructions. However, with the help of the instructions it was possible to find a set of attributes that enabled the learning system to induce a more understandable clone, such as one shown in Figure 14.4.

In the case of F_x, the force applied to the trolley, it was even harder to establish the conceptual similarity between the clone and the instructions. For example, instructions involve time ordering which is not mentioned at all in the clones. Therefore, the time order of execution of various parts of the tree during replay were considered in order to identify their correspondence with particular parts of verbal instructions. Such a comparison can help in operationalising verbal instructions which are normally too incomplete and imprecise to be directly translatable into a control program. In particular, some thresholds are given very imprecisely by humans,

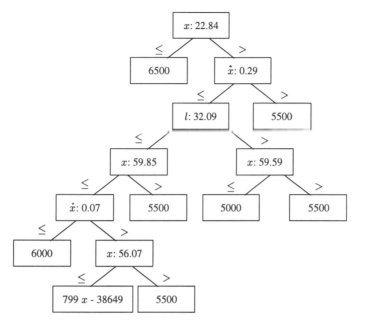

Figure 14.4 A controller for force F_x induced from the example trace in Figure 14.3.

but can be precisely identified with the help of the clone. Furthermore, ML-based analysis in this case revealed that the operator was actually not doing what she believed she was doing.

The analysis yielded a new behavioural cloning scheme which includes the operators' incomplete verbal instructions as a source of background knowledge. This can substantially improve machine learning results. The result of learning can be, in turn, used to better understand and improve the instructions themselves.

14.6 PRODUCTION LINE SCHEDULING

14.6.1 The Problem

Kerr and Kibira [KK94] claim that "the complexity and variability in manufacturing systems make it difficult to develop automated scheduling systems using analytic methods". Therefore, they attempted to schedule resources for a telephone manufacturing system using behavioural cloning. The problem is to determine an optimum or near optimum allocation of labor for a period of time on a production line at any time during a shift. This domain is atypical in that it requires control decisions at time points separated by several hours. Figure 14.5 gives an overview of the process. Between each step in the manufacturing process, buffers store the components output from one stage, ready for input to the next. The buffer levels are the key attributes in deciding how to allocate labour. Four decision trees are constructed, each determining the labour requirements at four workstation.

14.6.2 Choice of Examples

Separate example sets for induction were derived from individual human schedulers who were trained to be expert in scheduling a simulation of the plant.

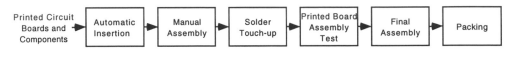

Figure 14.5   Basic stages in manufacturing process.

14.6.3   Time Delay

Time delay was not a significant factor in this problem since scheduling decisions are made at regular intervals, some hours apart. The decisions are based on the buffer levels and production volumes at the time of the scheduling decision.

14.6.4   Clean-up Effect

In this domain, the goal is that at the end of an 8.5 hour shift, the buffer levels of currently available subassemblies at the various stages of the line are as close as possible to specified goal levels (500 in Kibira's experiments). The buffer levels at the start of the shift deviated grossly from the target levels. Kerr and Kibira [KK94] give the time behaviour of the queue sizes at various points in the assembly line for both human expert scheduler and the clone. The clean-up effect is reflected in the fact that the clone's final level (at 8.5 hours) is always closer to 500 than the human's final level.

14.6.5   Brittleness

The human scheduler provided several traces under different conditions. These lead to an automatic scheduler which was quite robust. Tests were done to compare the performance of the automatic scheduler with a human and an analytically derived capacity allocator. The analytic solution was very brittle in the face of variations common in real manufacturing systems, where as the cloned scheduler was at least as good as the human.

14.6.6   Transparency of Induced Rules

The rules produced by induction in this task are understandable by a human expert. In contrast to the other domains discussed in this chapter, the attributes here are relatively simple and have few dependencies.

14.7   DISCUSSION

Experience in behavioural cloning described in this paper indicates some elements of an emerging methodology which we summarise in the following paragraphs.

1. *Choice of example traces for learning.* Style and control strategies vary significantly from operator to operator. To avoid mixing individual styles, the commonly agreed practice in behavioural cloning has been to use training examples from the same subject only. However, even the example trajectories of the same subject may vary considerably. When trying to induce the most reliable and "unadventurous" clones, the most conservative example trajectories were found to be by far the most useful.

2. *Time delay between state and action*. Human response times for sudden stimuli do not necessarily give any indication of an appropriate delay for behavioural cloning. A reasonable method is to try first with zero delay and increase the delay gradually, looking for the best performance.

3. When *designing the representation*, i.e. choosing attributes, it is useful to take into account the operator's verbal description of his/her skill. The introduction of such a descriptions into the "cloning cycle" is discussed in [UB94b].

In all the work until now the clones have taken the form of decision or regression trees or rule sets. These clones are purely reactive and inadequately structured as conceptualisations of the human skill (unless embedded in a hand-crafted fixed plan). They lack the conceptual structure typical in human control strategies: goals and subgoals, phases and causality. The simple form of the clones as mappings from system states to actions does not suffice to express such a conceptual structure. This conceptual difference between the clones and the humans' own descriptions of their skill is analysed in [UB94b].

Here we note some requirements for the representation of human-like controllers. First, such a controller should have some internal memory to maintain the current goals and phase of task. Furthermore, to enable the learning program to discover conceptual structure in a behavioural trace, the program should have access to some background knowledge about the domain.

In his work on improving yield in process control, Leech [Lee86] developed a two-stage method in which variables critical to the yield were first identified by induction. A further inductive step was used to construct control rules to achieve desired values for the critical variables. Michie [Mic] has suggested that an analogous scheme might be used in behavioural cloning. This approach is currently under investigation in the piloting domain. Initial results suggest that it may, indeed, be possible to construct more goal-oriented clones. However, there is still much work to be done.

Regardless of the representation, we believe that the study of human skill should take into account the constraints that humans must live with. One constraint is that the human can only look at a small number of state variables a time. Here are comments from one of our crane operators: "At this stage I only look at x very little; I never look at θ. [Later:] Here I never look at $\dot{x}$; if I do I get very confused". This suggests that at any given time the operator's decision only depends on a very small number of attributes. An important part of human strategy is to know what instruments to look at at various stages of the task.

ACKNOWLEDGEMENTS

We thank Donald Michie for the many helpful discussions and suggestions that have contributed to our experiments. We acknowledge Marko Grobelnik for providing the crane simulator and Matjaž Siegl for his help in crane experiments. Mike Bain helped with clarifying comments on the pole balancing experiments.

REFERENCES

[And87]   C.W. Anderson. Strategy learning with multilayer connectionist representations. In P. Langley, editor, *Proceedings of the 4th International Workshop on Machine Learning*, pages 103–114. Morgan Kaufmann, 1987.

[Are94]   D. Arentz. Experiments in learning to fly, 1994. Computer Engineering Thesis, School of Computer Science and Engineering, University of New South Wales.

[BMK97]   I. Bratko, S. Muggleton, and A. Karalič. Applications of inductive logic programming. In *Machine Learning and Data Mining: Methods and Applications*. Wiley, 1997. (This volume.)

[BSA83]   A.G. Barto, R.S. Sutton, and C.W. Anderson. Neuronlike adaptive elements that can solve difficult learning control problems. *IEEE Transactions on Systems, Man and Cybernetics*, SMC-13(5):834–846, 1983.

[BU]   I. Bratko and T. Urbančič. Skill reconstruction: machine learning *vs.* handcrafting. In D. Michie, S. Muggleton, and K. Furukawa, editors, *Machine Intelligence 15*. Clarendon Press, Oxford. To appear.

[CM69]   R.A. Chambers and D. Michie. Man-machine co-operation on a learning task. In R.D. Parslow, R.W. Prowse, and R.E. Green, editors, *Computer Graphics – Techniques and Applications*, pages 179–185, 1969. Plenum Press.

[Gri90]   D. Griffiths. Virtuoso performance: Pdi container crane survey 90. *Cargo Systems*, 17:XI–XII, 1990.

[Kar92]   A. Karalič. Employing linear regression in regression tree leaves. In *Proceedings of the 10th European Conference on Artificial Intelligence*, pages 440–441. John Wiley & Sons, 1992. Vienna, Austria.

[Kar95]   A. Karalič. *First Order Regression*. 1995. Ljubljana University, Faculty of El. Eng. and Computer Sc.: Ph. D. Thesis.

[KK94]   R.M. Kerr and D. Kibira. Intelligent reactive scheduling by human learning and machine induction. In *IFAC Symposium On Intelligent Manufacturing*, 1994. Vienna.

[Lee86]   W.J. Leech. A rule-based process control method with feedback. In *Proceedings of the ISA/86 International Conference and Exhibit*, 1986. Houston, Texas.

[MBHM90]   D. Michie, M. Bain, and J. Hayes-Michie. Cognitive models from subcognitive skills. In M. Grimble, J. McGhee, and P. Mowforth, editors, *Knowledge-Based Systems in Industrial Control*, pages 71–90, Stevenage, 1990. Peter Peregrinus.

[MC68]   D. Michie and R.A. Chambers. Boxes: an experiment in adaptive control. In E. Dale and D. Michie, editors, *Machine Intelligence 2*, pages 137–152. Edinburgh University Press, 1968.

[MC94]   D. Michie and R. Camacho. Building symbolic representations of intuitive real-time skills from performance data. In K. Furukawa, S. Muggleton, and D. Michie, editors, *Machine Intelligence 13*, 1994. Oxford: Clarendon Press.

[Mic]   D. Michie. Personal communication.

[Mic93]   D. Michie. Knowledge, learning and machine intelligence. In L.S. Sterling, editor, *Intelligent Systems*, New York, 1993. Plenum Press.

[Nov]   A. Novak. Personal communication.

[Qui87]   R. Quinlan. Simplifying decision trees. *International Journal of Man-Machine Studies*, 27(3):221–234, 1987.

[Qui93]   R. Quinlan. Combining instance-based and model-based learning. In *Proceedings of the 10th International Conference on Machine Learning*, pages 236–243. Morgan Kaufmann, 1993.

[SHKM92]   C. Sammut, S. Hurst, D. Kedzier, and D. Michie. Learning to fly. In D. Sleeman and P. Edwards, editors, *Proceedings of the Ninth International Workshop on Machine Learning*, pages 385–393. Morgan Kaufmann, 1992.

[SS82]   Y. Sakawa and Y. Shinido. Optimal control of container crane. *Automatica*, 18(3):257–266, 1982.

[UB94a]   T. Urbančič and I. Bratko. Learning to control dynamic systems. In D. Michie, D. Spiegel-halter, and C. Taylor, editors, *Machine Learning, Neural and Statistical Classification*, pages 247–269. Ellis Horwood, 1994.

[UB94b]   T. Urbančič and I. Bratko. Reconstructing human skill with machine learning. In A. Cohn, editor, *Proceedings of the 11th European Conference on Artificial Intelligence*, pages 498–502. John Wiley & Sons, Ltd., 1994.

[VUF93]   A. Varšek, T. Urbančič, and B. Filipič. Genetic algorithms in controller design and tuning. *IEEE Transactions on Systems, Man and Cybernetics*, SMC-23(6):1330–1339, 1993.

[WS64]   B. Widrow and F.W. Smith. Pattern recognising control systems. In J.T.Tou and R.H.Wilcox, editors, *Computer and Information Sciences*. Clever Hume Press, 1964.

[YH86]   S. Yasunobu and T. Hasegawa. Evaluation of an automatic container crane operation system based on predictive fuzzy control. *Control-Theory and Advanced Technology*, 2(3):419–432, 1986.

15

Acquiring First-order Knowledge About Air Traffic Control

Yves Kodratoff and Christel Vrain

ABSTRACT

This chapter presents an application of knowledge intensive generalization to knowledge acquisition, in the domain of air traffic control. We explain why knowledge intensiveness and first order logic are sometimes necessary, as in the application field studied here. An obvious advantage of first order knowledge is its power of expression, while an obvious drawback is large computation time. We also describe some less obvious advantages and drawbacks of first order logic, especially when the knowledge must be expressed as Horn clauses to retain some computational efficiency. Finally, we emphasize the large translation problem that must be solved in order to allow an efficient interaction with the expert. Two translation phases are necessary. One goes from the expert's language to Horn clauses, the second goes back from Horn's clauses to the expert's language. The former is necessary to ensure automatic learning, while the latter allows the expert to understand what has been learned. Both phases are far from trivial and ask for choices that must be carefully done in order to avoid losing significant information. One of our unexpected results is that the second translation phase plays the role of a validation step. It thus becomes a very efficient way to acquire knowledge the expert has problems formalizing. Using first order logic does complicate things, but it provides, as a reward, a powerful way for extracting and validating the acquired knowledge, especially when the field expert is unable to express his knowledge in a simple way.

15.1 INTRODUCTION

In the field of Air Traffic Control (ATC), the central problem is obviously avoiding the crash of an aircraft, and much work deals with this problem. Each controller is in charge of a part of the space, called a sector. The controller practically ignores everything outside his sector.

Machine Learning and Data Mining: Methods and Applications
Edited by R.S. Michalski, I. Bratko and M. Kubat
© 1997 John Wiley & Sons Ltd

When a plane enters his sector, he is in charge of verifying that this new plane will not collide with planes already in the sector. If he suspects that such a case is possible (called a conflict), he must modify the route of the planes, thus resolving the conflict. Some attempts have been made (Shively and Schwamb, 1984; Planchon and Berrada, 1988) to try and model the controller task by means of an expert system (ES). It must nevertheless be pointed out that the different applications of this technique to ATC do not seem to be powerful enough to allow automation, which shows that many problems are still to be solved. The complexity of the domain and the lack of formalism of the expertise prevent us from modeling correctly the behavior of the expert. The goal of the PERSPICACE[1] project (Cannat and Vrain, 1988) is the application of machine learning (ML) techniques to learn ATC rules that cannot be obtained by a direct discussion with the expert. It seems easier for an expert to give examples rather than rules of his behavior. Therefore, we planned to make use of some of the ML achievements (Michalski, 1983; Kodratoff et al., 1984; Kodratoff and Ganascia, 1986; Kodratoff and Tecuci, 1988) relative to concept learning, in order to learn expert's behavior rules.

To learn rules for an ES, the classical Knowledge Acquisition (KA) approach consists in interviewing an expert of the field. Conversely, our approach consists in observing sequences of good expert behavior, in our case the steps taken by an air controller in order to solve conflict situations. Our system generalizes over these examples the conditions in which each action has been performed. One thus obtains general rules that have to be validated by the field expert. If he does, the learning is completed, and the rule is inserted into the rule-base. If the expert rejects the rule, he is requested to provide explanations for his rejection, in the form of new positive or negative examples, or by improving the Background Knowledge (BK), or by refining the concept.

The dialogue with the expert will thus be divided into four main steps. At the beginning of the process, we need three steps to acquire BK, to determine the concepts to learn, and to gather positive and negative examples illustrating the concepts. The process of generalization is inductive and cannot guarantee the validity of its results. Therefore, we need a fourth step to validate the knowledge that has been learned. We shall not take up this question in this chapter. The simplest method to achieve it, perhaps a little inefficiently, is to present the results to the expert; another way is to test them on examples. In any case, if some result is wrong, due to errors in the examples, or in BK, or due to the formalism used, we presently have no way to correct them automatically, and we must find the errors by an interactive discussion with the expert.

The method suggested by learning a generalization can be summed up by the scheme shown in Figure 15.1.

Actually, the application of ML techniques is not as straightforward as suggested by this scheme. Collecting the examples is an easy task for an expert—in the application to ATC, a month's work delivered roughly 100 examples—but building up the BK is a difficult task. Beside the dialogue with the expert, we have to find a language of representation adapted to the domain and to the generalization tool, and to translate BK and the examples into this language. In Section 15.3, we treat the problem of translating BK and examples into a first order logic formalism, then translating back our results into a language understandable to the field expert.

---

[1] PERSPICACE: (from the French "Prototype d'Expert en Résolution de Situations, Problème Intéressant le Contrôle Aérien et Conçu à partir d'Exemples") contract C.E.N.A./L.R.I., October 1986–1988.

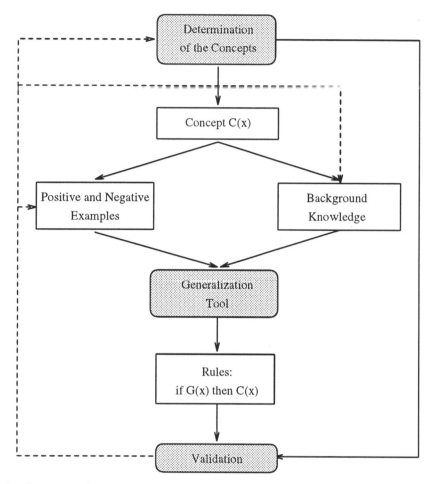

It can be decomposed into several steps:
– determination of the concepts to learn,
– determination of the background knowledge,
– determination of positive and negative examples for each concept to learn,
– generalization,
– validation.
According to the results of the validation module, we might have to modify the concepts, or the background knowledge, or the examples.

Figure 15.1 The cycle of acquisition/validation of knowledge.

In this paper, we intend to show the problems that have arisen, mostly due to the need to use first order logics. They have been partly solved and we explain the solutions that we have adopted. The knowledge learned can take many different forms. Our system learns knowledge expressed as production rules

$$\textit{if <conditions> then perform <actions>},$$

where the actions to perform are very often the addition of new facts to the database. In rule-based ESs, there are different ways of representing the conditions and the conclusions of the rules (Shortliffe, 1976; Forgy and McDermott, 1977). Most often, the representation is based on a logical formalism, propositional or first order logics. Unfortunately, no representation is completely satisfactory. Zero order logic enables very quick inferences but is restricted, while first order logic has a very high power of expression but matching operations between the knowledge base and the database may be costly, mainly when using a forward chaining deduction mechanism. To avoid some of these problems, people use often a representation (attribute, value), that can be viewed as intermediate between zero and first order logics. In this representation, it is difficult to represent different objects and relations between these objects. In our application, we had to choose a first order formalism; we shall explain the reasons for this choice and show the problems that have arisen due to it.

This chapter uses a technique of generalization that can be described as *knowledge intensive relational generalization*. We now introduce what relational generalizations are, stress their importance to accurately represent the learned knowledge, and present the new problems they raise in knowledge acquisition, namely the proper definition of predicates and the definition of "Skolem function" (the quotations are necessary and will be explained later on) by the expert.

15.2   KNOWLEDGE INTENSIVE RELATIONAL GENERALIZATION

We have already mentioned that ESs show a trade-off between the expressive power of relational logic and its lack of speed at computing. This problem also shows up in ML. For instance, in similarity-based learning, first order knowledge enables the representation of complex events, involving different objects and their relations, but knowledge intensive generalization tools are difficult to implement and have to face combinatorial problems.

Let us now give some more details about the problem of using first versus zero order logic representations. This will explain why we need a relational representation for our ATC application.

15.2.1   Zero Versus First Order Representation

15.2.1.1   Variables

In theory, first order logic allows the presence of universally or existentially quantified variables. As an example, think of the description of a chemical molecule. Some molecules may have the property that all carbons are linked to at least one hydrogen. This is a typical property that cannot be described except with a universally quantified variable. Another molecule might be described by the fact that it contains at least one oxygen molecule. This is a typical property that cannot be described except with an existentially quantified variable.

In practice, we would like to draw here some of the consequences of such representation choices. More generally, first order logic expresses well such relations, while zero order logic is very poor at it. This example shows a second consequence of first order logic of high practical importance: all combinations of instances that satisfy a given relation are tried out. This feature is desirable since it exhausts the possibilities of the patterns to be recognized. This feature becomes unbearable whenever there are too many possibilities. Then, one has to choose heuristics in order to cut down the complexity.

In the context of learning, this exploration of combination takes also place at the moment a recognition function is invented. For instance, suppose that we want to learn about fathers, and that we have three examples of fathers, John, Peter, and Tom. Suppose that John and Peter have A grade type children, and that John and Tom have sports fanatics children. If we start generalizing on John and Peter, we lose the knowledge that John's children are also sports fanatics. Generalization to first order techniques must thus include mechanisms that optimize the choices done in the ordering of the examples.

In conclusion, the main practical features of first order logic (as opposed to zero order representations) are that

1. it allows the expression of relations among the features,
2. it takes into account the possible combinations of the predicates expressing the same relation, in order to generate recognition functions.

In the application to ATC, we have only a few objects, at least the two aircraft in conflict, but we have many relations between them. It may even happen that other planes play a part in the decision of the expert. The expert will forget some of these relations; he will represent only the pieces of knowledge that he has in mind at present. This means that we cannot express all the knowledge in the initial representation of the examples; we need theorems that will repair the expert's description of the examples. Besides, most of the knowledge of the expert is first order knowledge, such as the relation between speed, time, and distance.

15.2.1.2 Functions

First order logic representations enable functional expressions. For instance, consider the relation between speed, distance, and time. We are unable to express it in a zero logic representation, whereas we can write in first order logic:

$$\forall x \ \forall t \ [distance(x) \wedge time(t) \Rightarrow speed(x/t)],$$

i.e., if the distance is x and the time is t then the speed is x/t.

In fact, we shall see that in the application to ATC we did not take advantage of this last point because the current version of our generalization tool did not treat numeric values. Numeric values are replaced by symbolic ones and we use a kind of very naive qualitative physics to perform the computations. For instance, we replace the numeric operation / by a symbolic one, called $/_s$ defined by:

$$/_s(large, small) = large,$$
$$/_s(small, large) = small,$$
$$otherwise \qquad /_s(x, y) = undefined.$$

We give two theorems expressing the graph of $/_s$,

$$distance(large) \wedge times(small) \Rightarrow speed(large),$$
$$distance(small) \wedge times(large) \Rightarrow speed(small).$$

15.2.1.3   Clauses and their Skolemization

First order logic is able to express a large variety of knowledge. Nevertheless, it has a well-known drawback, namely the undecidability of the proof procedure. Since we want to use a theorem prover that is efficient enough to be applied iteratively on the examples, we have to restrict ourselves to the simpler case of Horn clauses.

Transforming a theorem into a set of clauses includes a step known as skolemization; it happens because in a clause all variables have to be universally quantified. Therefore, all existentially quantified variables have to be deleted.

If the existential quantification is not under the scope of a universal quantifier, as when there are only existentially quantified variables, then they must be replaced by a *new* constant. If the existential quantification is under the scope of one or several universal quantifiers, then the existentially quantified variables must be replaced by a *new* function, depending on these universally quantified variables whose $\forall$ occurs ahead of the $\exists$ concerned. In other words, suppose that we have a formula of the form $\forall x \, \forall y \, \exists u \, \forall z \, \exists v \, F(x, y, z, u, v)$, then it can be transformed into $\forall x \, \forall y \, \forall z \, F(x, y, z, h(x, y), g(x, y, z))$ where h and g are new symbols of function. Notice that u has been replaced by a function of x and y because it is under the scope of x and y, while v, which is under the scope of x, y, and z, has to be replaced by a function of x, y, and z. The constant or function introduced are new symbols; skolemization does not transform a formula into an equivalent one. Consider now that when this operation is performed by an expert, as happens in AI, he will not introduce a new symbol which would be meaningless for him. On the contrary, he will insist on finding the "good" symbol that will keep the truth value of his clauses. In other words, the operation performed by a human is a pseudo-skolemization (hence the quotations we have been using above when speaking of skolemization) in which the pseudo-Skolem function is related to the existing knowledge.

Let us exemplify the skolemization problem on the clause representation of the sentence *Everybody makes mistakes*. In first-order logic it reads:

$$\forall x \, \exists y \, [human(x) \Rightarrow (does(x, y) \wedge mistake(y))].$$

The variable y is under the scope of the $\forall$ quantifier that quantifies x, therefore y has to be skolemized as a function of x. We can bring in an arbitrary Skolem function and transform our theorem into:

$$\forall x \, [human(x) \Rightarrow (does(x, g(x)) \wedge mistake(g(x)))]$$

where g is a new function symbol. In practice, it is awkward to neglect any information we have about the function g, which tells us that what is done is a misfit action. An expert would even insist on making explicit the kind of actions that are misfit in the considered field of expertise. Suppose that we are in the context of a school class, and that the teacher wants to insist on the fact that lack of attention brings mistakes, then he would attribute these errors to unthoughtfulness, and write, instead of $g(x)$, *unthoughtful_action(x):*

$$\forall x \, [human(x) \Rightarrow$$
$$(does(x, unthoughtful\_action(x)) \wedge mistake(unthoughtful\_action(x)))],$$

To complete the example, let us point out that the expert would also dislike the presence of functions in his predicates, he would then rather give to the theorem the form:

$$\forall x \, \forall y \, [(human(x) \wedge unthoughtful\_action\_pred(x, y)) \Rightarrow$$
$$(does(x, y) \wedge mistake(y))],$$

where *unthoughtful_action_pred(x,y)* represents the graph of the function *unthoughtful_action(x)* and can be expressed in a logic with equality by:

$$\forall x \, \forall y \, [unthoughtful\_action\_pred(x, y) \Leftrightarrow y = unthoughtful\_action(x)].$$

This last version is no longer equivalent at all to the general theorem we started from. In theory, this is an abomination. In practice, we want the expert satisfied with the knowledge he has transmitted into the system. The skolemization process has forced him to clarify his thought, which is a very positive feature of knowledge acquisition.

The choice of an appropriate replacement for a Skolem function is a problem which nobody has envisaged an automatic solution to, as far as we know. However, as the following examples clearly show, it is quite all right to convert a sentence expressing a feature into a theorem when its conversion into a clause (or rule) requires a pseudo-skolemization which can only be done well by a domain expert. Techniques for acquiring knowledge to construct ESs must not fail to get the expert to point out the right supplementary information that allows us to solve the problem of skolemization.

In the next section we shall explain how OGUST works, with which we will be able to explain the representation that has been chosen.

15.2.2   A presentation of OGUST

The OGUST system is a generalization tool which learns a recognition function of a concept from a set of examples. It is based on a simplified version of structural matching (Kodratoff and Ganascia, 1986), and it is knowledge intensive.

15.2.2.1   Language of Representation

The representation language of the examples and of the generalization is restricted to a subset of first order logic, in which we allow only variables, predicate symbols and constants, the latter two being considered as functions with no arguments. Other functions of arity greater or equal to 1 are not allowed. An atom is therefore an expression $p(t_1, \ldots, t_n)$ where p is a predicate of arity n and $t_1, \ldots, t_n$ are either constants or variables.

Examples are written as conjunctions of ground atoms, i.e., without variables. For instance, suppose that a car insurance company wants to learn the concept of a "costly driver", prone to be expensive for the insurance company. Let us work on the following two examples.

E_1: John and Mary are married, they have their driving license, John has a car and Mary uses it only on holidays.

E_2: Peter has a son Bob. Bob just obtained his driving license; sometimes he borrows his father's car.

There are many ways of translating these two sentences into predicate logic, depending, on the one hand, on the pieces of implicit information that we want to express, and on the other hand, on the choice of the predicate symbols and of the constants. We shall not discuss this problem now, since we show in Section 15.3 how the choices have been made for the application to ATC. Following these choices, E_1 and E_2 are translated in the following way, where RE_1 and RE_2 denote the representation of E_1 and E_2.

$RE_1 = $ married(JOHN,MARY) $\wedge$ driving_license(JOHN) $\wedge$ driving_license(MARY) $\wedge$ owns(JOHN, C1) $\wedge$ car(C1) $\wedge$ uses_on_holiday(MARY, C1).

$RE_2 = $ son(BOB, PETER) $\wedge$ new_driver(BOB) $\wedge$ owns(PETER, C2) $\wedge$ car (C2) $\wedge$ borrows(BOB, C2, PETER).

In these examples, *married, driving_license, owns, car, uses_on_holiday, son, new_driver, borrows* are predicates, whereas JOHN, MARY, BOB, PETER, C1 and C2 are constants. We notice here that we have represented only the knowledge explicitly expressed in the sentences. We could also represent that JOHN, PETER AND BOB are men, whereas MARY ia a woman, since this information is implicit in the sentences. Due to the fact that functions are not allowed, some properties of the examples cannot be expressed directly. Techniques for the transformation of clauses with functions into clauses without functions have been developed (Rouveirol, 1991).

Background knowledge is expressed as Horn clauses. For instance, we have:

$$
\begin{array}{llll}
R_1 : & \forall x & man(x) & \Rightarrow person(x) \\
R_2 : & \forall x & woman(x) & \Rightarrow person(x) \\
R_3 : & \forall x\,\forall y & married(x,y) & \Rightarrow family\_relation(x,y) \\
R_4 : & \forall x\,\forall y & son(x,y) & \Rightarrow family\_relation(x,y) \\
R_5 : & \forall x\,\forall y & family\_relation(x,y) & \Rightarrow family\_relation(y,x) \\
R_6 : & \forall x & new\_driver(x) & \Rightarrow driving\_license(x) \\
R_7 : & \forall x\,\forall y & uses\_on\_holidays(x,y) \wedge car(y) & \Rightarrow driver(x,y) \\
R_8 : & \forall x\,\forall y & owns(x,y) \wedge car(y) & \Rightarrow driving\_license(x) \\
R_9 : & \forall x\,\forall y\,\forall z & borrows(x,y,z) \wedge car(y) & \Rightarrow driver(x,y) \\
R_{10} : & \forall x\,\forall y & uses\_on\_holidays(x,y) \wedge car(y) & \Rightarrow unskilled\_driver(x) \\
R_{11} : & \forall x & new\_driver(x) & \Rightarrow unskilled\_driver(x) \\
R_{12} : & etc. \\
\end{array}
$$

15.2.2.2 Algorithm

The generalization algorithm can be decomposed into two main steps: a deductive one followed by an inductive one (see Algorithm 15.1).

In the first step, the examples are put into structural matching (Kodratoff and Ganascia, 1986), that is to say, their representations are transformed using the background knowledge until they match or until no more transformations can be applied to improve the matching. The second step generalizes the two representations we have obtained by structural matching.

To understand the first step, we can imagine that examples are a collection of objects, each object being characterized by its own properties and its relations with other objects. For instance, the example E_1 is composed of three objects JOHN, MARY, and C1. JOHN is characterized by the property that he has a driving license and by some relations with MARY and with C1. To apply structural matching to the examples, we first have to find among the objects those that are in some sense the most similar, i.e., the most promising for the future generalization. We have then to make the common properties between these objects explicit.

In other words, structural matching can be decomposed into two steps (Algorithm 15.2)

- choose an object in each example and replace all its occurrences by a variable of generalization,
- for those properties that do not match, improve their matching as much as possible, using the given BK.

These two steps iterate in a cycle which is repeated until there are no more objects to choose in the examples. Once this cycle has been completed, the deductive generalization step can be performed.

To exemplify these notions, let us consider again our concept of "costly driver", and examples E_1 and E_2.

Inputs:
- $E_1, \ldots, E_n$: examples of the concept C expressed as conjunctions of ground atoms,
- BK: background knowledge expressed by Horn clauses,

Output: A generalization of the examples expressed as a conjunction of atoms.

1. put the examples into structural matching (deductive step): transform the examples E_1, $\ldots, E_n$ into $E'_1, \ldots, E'_n$ so that for $i = 1 \ldots n$,

   - $E_i \leftrightarrow E'_i$,
   - $E'_i = F(x_1, \ldots, x_p) \wedge G_i(x_1, \ldots, x_p) \wedge (x_1 = C_i^1) \wedge \ldots \wedge (x_p = C_i^p)$, where:
     - F : a formula composed of the variables $x_1, \ldots, x_p$, common to all the examples,
     - G_i : a conjunction of atoms such that for each atom there exists at least an example $E'_j, j \neq i$, in which it does not appear,
     - $C_i^1, \ldots, C_i^p$: constants appearing in E_i.

2. generalization (inductive step): the formula F common to all the examples

---

Algorithm 15.1   A simplified version of the generalization algorithm. *In this version, we suppose that:*
– in all the examples, the number of constants is p,
– we do not use the "renaming rule": $P(x) \leftrightarrow (P(y) \wedge (x = y))$

Definition: an occurrence of a variable x in an example E_i is **discriminating** if it appears in a predicate $P(\ldots, x, \ldots)$ of E_i at position p_k and there exists an example E_j, $j \neq i$, in which x does not appear at position p_k in an atom composed with the predicate P.

Inputs:
- $E_1, \ldots, E_n$: examples of the concept C expressed as conjunctions of ground atoms,
- BK : background knowledge expressed as Horn clauses,

Output: $E_1', \ldots, E_n'$ so that for $i = 1, \ldots, n$

▷ $E_i \leftrightarrow E_i'$,

▷ $E_i' = F(x_1, \ldots, x_p) \wedge G_i(x_1, \ldots, x_p) \wedge (x_1 = C_i^1) \wedge \ldots \wedge (x_p = C_i^p)$,

where:

- F : a formula composed of the variables $x_1, \ldots, x_p$, common to all the examples,
- G_i : a conjunction of atoms such that for each atom there exists at least an example E_j', $j \neq i$, in which it does not appear,
- $C_i^1, \ldots, C_i^p$: constants appearing in E_i.

Initially, $VAR = \emptyset$

1. Choose a constant C_i^j in each example E_i and replace all the occurrences of C_i^j by a variable x, $x \notin VAR$: $E_i \leftrightarrow E_i' \wedge (x = C_i^j)$; $VAR \leftarrow VAR \cup \{x\}$;
2. Compare the occurrences of x in the examples:

   - Find the discriminating occurrences of the variable x :
   - For each discriminating occurrence $P(\ldots, x, \ldots)$ of an example E_i,
     1- if possible, using BK, introduce an occurrence of $P(\ldots, x, \ldots)$ in the examples where there is no such occurrence,
     2- if it is not possible, try to deduce in E_i from $P(\ldots, x, \ldots)$ using BK a new occurrence of x, that is not a discriminating one.

3. Repeat steps 1 and 2 until there are no more constants in the examples.

Algorithm 15.2   A simplified version of the structural matching algorithm.

15.2.2.3   Example

Structural matching (deductive step)

In E_1, there are three constants, JOHN, MARY, and C1. In E_2, there are also three constants, BOB, PETER, and C2. To determine which objects are the most similar, OGUST uses a heuristic that compares the explicit properties of the objects and computes a similarity between these objects. Algorithm 15.3 describes a possible process to choose the best constants to match according to a given measure of similarity *sim*. This algorithm gives the best choice according to *sim* but is intractable when the numbers of constants and of examples are large. In our example, we have to compare JOHN and PETER, JOHN and BOB, JOHN and C2, MARY and PETER, MARY and BOB, etc. To decrease the number of comparisons to be performed, the constants of the examples can be typed. For instance, here we could say that it is uninteresting to compare a person with a car, which will lower the number of comparisons from nine to four. To type the constants is another way of introducing knowledge in the process of generalization; it constrains the space of possible generalizations by discarding "uninteresting" over-generalizations. Other heuristics as well as an incremental version of the algorithm (Vrain and Lu, 1988), have been developed to decrease its complexity.

Inputs:
- $E_1, \ldots, E_n$: examples,
- sim a function of arity n; $sim(C_1, \ldots, C_n)$ computes the similarity between the constants $C_1, \ldots, C_n$.

Output: a combination of constants $(C_1, \ldots, C_n)$ where C_i is a constant of $E_i, i = 1, \ldots, n$, that maximizes sim.

1. for each combination of constants $(C_1, \ldots, C_n)$, where $C_i, i = 1, \ldots, n$, is a constant of E_i, compute $sim(C_1, \ldots, C_n)$.
2. choose a combination that realizes the maximum

Algorithm 15.3   The choice of constants.

If we do suppose that the constants are typed, we have only to compare JOHN and PETER, JOHN and BOB, MARY and PETER, MARY and JOHN. We shall not detail the similarity measure, but simply give an intuitive feeling of the way it has been built. Intuitively, we can say that JOHN and PETER are the persons who seem the most similar, since they both own a car. Thus, we replace all the occurrences of JOHN and PETER by the same variable of generalization, here called vg_1. In other words, we can say that JOHN and PETER will be generalized in the inductive step by the variable vg_1. We get

RE$_1$ =   **married**(vg_1, MARY) $\wedge$ **driving_license**(vg_1) $\wedge$ driving_license (MARY) $\wedge$ owns(vg_1, C1) $\wedge$ car(C1) $\wedge$ uses_on_holiday(MARY, C1) $\wedge$ [(= vg_1 JOHN)]

RE$_2$ =   **son**(BOB, vg_1) $\wedge$ **new_driver**(BOB) $\wedge$ owns(vg_1, C2) $\wedge$ car(C2) $\wedge$ **borrows**(BOB, C2, vg_1) $\wedge$ [(= vg_1 PETER)]

In each example, vg_1 satisfies the underlined property of owning an object. Since these occurrences are common to both examples, they are said to be not discriminating. On the contrary, in E$_1$, vg_1 has a driving license and is married, whereas in E$_2$, vg_1 has a son and someone borrows something from him or her. In that case, since vg_1 occurs in atoms that do not belong to both examples, they are called discriminating occurrences of the variable vg_1. They are written in bold in RE$_1$ and RE$_2$. The work of OGUST is to try canceling these differences by using the available BK. We give here no details about the algorithm that performs this task; it is carefully described in Vrain (1990). We rather give an intuitive presentation of the way it works.

- Occurrence of vg_1 in the atom *driving_license*(vg_1). We can prove in E$_2$ that vg_1 has a driving license, by means of theorem R_8. Therefore, this occurrence, which was discriminating in the "raw" examples, is proven not to be by using BK. It will be treated as a non-discriminating occurrence in the next steps.
- Occurrence of vg_1 in the atom married(vg_1, MARY). We cannot prove that in E$_2$, vg_1 is married, but we can prove that in E$_1$ and in E$_2$, vg_1 satisfies a family relation. Therefore, the discriminating occurrence stays as such, but we introduce new atoms, stemming from BK,

that are consequences of the information contained in the raw examples, and that decrease the discrimination between E_1 and E_2.

- Occurrence of vg_1 in the atom $son(\text{BOB}, vg_1)$. We cannot prove that in E_1, vg_1 has a son, we can only prove again that vg_1 in E_1 and in E_2 satisfies a family relation. This does not decrease any more the discrimination between the two examples.
- Occurrence of vg_1 in the atom $borrows(\text{BOB}, \text{C2}, vg_1)$. We cannot prove this property in E_1 and we can prove no new properties satisfied by vg_1 in each example. Therefore, these occurrences remain discriminating, and nothing new is acquired from the use of BK.

We now write in simple italics the discriminating occurrences that are left; this gives

$\text{RE}_1 =$ *married*(vg_1, MARY) $\wedge$ driving_license(vg_1) $\wedge$ driving_license (MARY) $\wedge$ owns(vg_1, C1) $\wedge$ car(C1) $\wedge$ uses_on_holiday(MARY, C1) $\wedge$ family_relation(vg_1, MARY) $\wedge$ [(= vg_1 JOHN)]

$\text{RE}_2 =$ *son*(BOB, vg_1) $\wedge$ new_driver(BOB) $\wedge$ owns(vg_1, C2) $\wedge$ car(C2) $\wedge$ *borrows*(BOB, C2, vg_1) $\wedge$ driving_license(vg_1) $\wedge$ family_relation(vg_1, BOB) $\wedge$ [(= vg_1 PETER)]

The same process is iterated. There is a person and a car in each example. Since we have supposed that we cannot compare a person and a car, we have to choose either BOB and MARY, or C1 and C2. Let us choose BOB and MARY and replace their occurrences by a new variable of generalization vg_2. We write the new discriminating occurrences in bold, and the new occurrences that are not discriminating are underlined. This yields

$\text{RE}_1 =$ **married**(vg_1, vg_2) $\wedge$ driving_license(vg_1) $\wedge$ **driving_license**(vg_2) $\wedge$ owns(vg_1, C1) $\wedge$ car(C1) $\wedge$ **uses_on_holiday**(vg_2, C1) $\wedge$ family_relation(vg_1, vg_2) $\wedge$ [(= vg_1 JOHN)(= vg_2 MARY)]

$\text{RE}_2 =$ **son**(vg_2, vg_1) $\wedge$ **new_driver**(vg_2) $\wedge$ owns(vg_1, C2) $\wedge$ car(C2) $\wedge$ **borrows**(vg_2, C2, vg_1) $\wedge$ driving_license(vg_1) $\wedge$ family_relation(vg_1,vg_2) $\wedge$ [(= vg_1 PETER)(= vg_2 BOB)]

Using again BK to erase as much as possible the discriminating occurrences, we obtain

$\text{RE}_1 =$ *married*(vg_1,vg_2) $\wedge$ driving_license(vg_1) $\wedge$ driving_license(vg_2) $\wedge$ owns(vg_1, C1) $\wedge$ car(C1) $\wedge$ *uses_on_holiday*(vg_2, C1) $\wedge$ family_relation(vg_1, vg_2) $\wedge$ driver(vg_2, C1) $\wedge$ unskilled_driver(vg_2) $\wedge$ [(= vg_1 JOHN)(= vg_2 MARY)]

$\text{RE}_2 =$ *son*(vg_2, vg_1) $\wedge$ *new_driver*(vg_2) $\wedge$ owns(vg_1, C2) $\wedge$ car(C2) $\wedge$ *borrows*(vg_2, C2, vg_1) $\wedge$ driving_license(vg_1) $\wedge$ family_relation(vg_1, vg_2) $\wedge$ driver(vg_2, C2) $\wedge$ unskilled_driver(vg_2) $\wedge$ [(= vg_1 PETER)(= vg_2 BOB)]

There is now a single constant left in each example. We replace all its occurrences by a variable vg_3.

$\text{RE}_1 =$ married(vg_1, vg_2) $\wedge$ driving_license(vg_1) $\wedge$ driving_license(vg_2) $\wedge$ owns(vg_1, vg_3) $\wedge$ car(vg_3) $\wedge$ **uses_on_holiday**(vg_2,vg_3) $\wedge$ family_relation(vg_1, vg_2) $\wedge$ driver(vg_2, vg_3) $\wedge$ unskilled_driver(vg_2) $\wedge$ [(= vg_1 JOHN)(= vg_2 MARY)(= vg_3 C1)]

$\text{RE}_2 =$ son(vg_2, vg_1) $\wedge$ new_driver(vg_2) $\wedge$ owns(vg_1, vg_3) $\wedge$ car(vg_3) $\wedge$ **borrows**(vg_2, vg_3, vg_1) $\wedge$ driving_license(vg_1) $\wedge$ family_relation(vg_1, vg_2) $\wedge$ driver(vg_2, vg_3) $\wedge$ unskilled_driver(vg_2) $\wedge$ [(= vg_1 PETER)(= vg_2 BOB)(= vg_3 C2)]

We try again to treat the discriminating occurrences using the domain knowledge. In that case, we learn no new common properties, therefore

$RE_1 = $ married$(vg_1, vg_2) \land$ driving_license$(vg_1) \land$ driving_license$(vg_2) \land$ owns$(vg_1, vg_3) \land$ car$(vg_3) \land$ uses_on_holiday$(vg_2, vg_3) \land$ family_relation$(vg_1, vg_2) \land$ driver(vg_2, vg_3) $\land$ unskilled_driver$(vg_2) \land [(= vg_1$ JOHN$)(= vg_2$ MARY$)(= vg_3$ C1$)]$

$RE_2 = $ son$(vg_2, vg_1) \land$ new_driver$(vg_2) \land$ owns$(vg_1, vg_3) \land$ car$(vg_3) \land$ borrows$(vg_2, vg_3, vg_1) \land$ driving_license$(vg_1) \land$ family_relation$(vg_1, vg_2) \land$ driver$(vg_2, vg_3) \land$ unskilled_driver$(vg_2) \land [(= vg_1$ PETER$)(= vg_2$ BOB$)(= vg_3$ C2$)]$

We have no more constants in the examples and we have tried to remove as much as possible the discriminating properties, given our BK. Thus, the structural matching step is completed.

Inductive step

We generalize the two examples in a straightforward way, by keeping their common properties. This yields the recognition function G:

$G = $ owns$(vg_1, vg_3) \land$ car$(vg_3) \land$ driving_license$(vg_1) \land$ family_relation$(vg_1, vg_2) \land$ driver$(vg_2, vg_3) \land$ unskilled_driver(vg_2)

15.2.2.4 Conclusion

The positive features of OGUST are:

- its representation language; predicate logic is richer than an attribute-value representation, since it efficiently represents several objects and the relations between them,
- its systematic use of BK to find a recognition function of the concept as specific as possible,
- its ability to generate explanations of its results.

The drawbacks of OGUST are:

- its exponential complexity; to find a generalization of the examples, it studies all the alternate choices of objects to match,
- its inability to deal with negative examples; heuristics have been elaborated to choose the constants to match according to the negative examples, but they do not enable us to treat all of them, and the recognition function we learn may not be consistent, i.e., it may confuse negative examples for positive ones.

In this application of ATC, OGUST has been chosen for the following reasons. We have already shown the importance of first order knowledge for ATC. Moreover, we know that in the domain of ATC there exists a BK. It is not explicit, and it is part of the engineering work to obtain this knowledge from the expert. Finally, we need explanations of the behavior of the system, for at least two reasons:

- we have to validate the learned rules; and
- the BK acquired from the expert may contain errors and we have to debug it.

A negative example in this domain would be a crash between two aircraft due to a decision of ATC, and no such negative examples were made available to us. The limitation of OGUST, due to its inability to treat negative examples, was not a large problem in this application.

15.3   APPLICATION OF ATC

15.3.1   Introduction

The application to a real domain of the knowledge acquisition scheme proposed in Section 15.1 is not as straightforward as suggested by this scheme. At the start of the project, we thought that the main problem would be the use of first order knowledge. Actually, our generalization tool is well adapted to ATC knowledge. The main problems come from the extraction of BK and, surprisingly, from the definition of the predicates, i.e., the expert shows an unexpected propensity to provide wrong definitions of his own vocabulary.

We describe here the problems that we had to face, and we point out the solutions adopted. For each of them, we will distinguish whether they were inherent to the process of learning expert rules, or to the application of our particular generalization tool.

The complete acquisition cycle must include steps necessary to transform knowledge in order to allow some understanding between the expert and the system. The knowledge (i.e., examples + BK) given by the expert must be translated into a representation adapted to the generalization tool. To make the validation step easier, the learned knowledge must be translated back into a representation understandable by the expert.

In the following sections, we describe the complete knowledge acquisition task.

15.3.2   Choosing the Language Representation

This problem can be divided into two linked subproblems:

1. choosing the basic vocabulary,
2. choosing the formalism, logical, propositional or predicate, attribute-value representation, etc.

The representation problem is a basic one in AI. In our application, the formalism is forced by the domain and by the choice of the generalization tool; it is a subset of first order logic. OGUST, as many symbolic learning systems, is unable to deal with numeric values, which thus need a preliminary transformation into symbolic ones. Besides, due to the particular behavior of OGUST, we have to take great care in determining the constants and the predicates of the representation language. This last point is developed in Section 15.3.4.2.

15.3.3   Determining the Concepts to Learn

The aim of this application is to learn decision rules used by a human controller, from examples of his behavior when solving a conflict. We have defined six actions that can be performed on aircraft to avoid an impending accident between them.

- Do nothing: the action is performed on the other aircraft.
- Change of direction, which is a temporary modification of the route of the aircraft.
- Change of route of the aircraft.
- Stabilization of the aircraft to a given height.
- Speed regulation.

- Change in the height regulation, that is, a change of the vertical speed.

A solution of a conflict between two aircraft is a combination of two of these actions performed on each aircraft.

For each solution, we want to learn a description of the situations for which it is advisable to again use this solution. To that purpose, we have to cluster all the examples showing the same solution and to generalize them, using OGUST. The recognition function that we will obtain using OGUST might be too general and even perhaps empty. This may happen because OGUST learns a pure conjunctive recognition function of a concept, and the concepts defined at first were actually disjunctions of more specific concepts. For instance, the solution *stabilization*, after further discussions with the expert, has been decomposed into two kinds of solutions. It may be a *steady stabilization* of the aircraft to the height it should retain during its flight in the sector[2] concerned, or a *temporary stabilization* to avoid the conflict[3]. Besides, any stabilization can be performed in two ways, either directly or by means of some intermediate levels.

An important task was therefore to define the intermediary concepts to learn.

15.3.4   Obtaining the Examples and Rewriting Them

Once the language representation and the concepts to learn have been set, the problem is to obtain examples of these concepts and to rewrite them into the desired formalism. In most applications, a questionnaire is established and the expert fills up this questionnaire in real situations. The questionnaire can be viewed as a list of attributes with their possible values; the attributes are determined from the basic vocabulary. For a given situation, the expert checks for each attribute the right value, and mentions whether it is a positive or a negative example of the concept. The examples are then translated into the right formalism.

15.3.4.1   Obtaining "Raw" Examples

In our application, we had problems to solve before obtaining usable examples. A questionnaire was set up, but experimentation showed that it was impossible to fill it up in real situations, so much short is the time between the occurrence of a conflict situation and its solution. The expert prefers to work in two steps.

In the first step, he draws a blueprint representing the conflict situation, and adds to it the convenient verbal information not represented on the drawing. Figures 15.2 and 15.3 picture a conflict situation written during the control task of the expert. We can see that the attributes which are added to the scheme, for instance the convergence angle of the aircraft before the conflict point, have numerical values.

In the second step, he transcribes the blueprint and the comments into answers to the questionnaire (see Figure 15.4). In this questionnaire, all the numeric values have been translated into symbolic ones. For example, the numeric domain of the descriptor *encounter angle of the*

---

[2] Aircraft controllers work on a well-defined area of space, called a sector. They take in charge a plane entering their sector, and pass it along to a colleague when the plane exits their sector.

[3] When controllers recognize that two or more planes are on a possible collision course within their sector, they say that these planes are in a situation of conflict.

aircraft after the conflict point has been restricted to the following values: *same route* and *divergent route*.

The questionnaire is composed of different kind of attributes.

- Attributes describing the global working environment of the controller, as his *present work load,* his *foreseen work load,* etc. Each of these attributes has three possible values: *low, steady* and *high.* They will influence the decision of the controller. For instance, when the attribute *present work load* is high, the controller is much more cautious and often changes the route of an aircraft before a real conflict situation occurs.
- Attributes describing the characteristics of each aircraft. For instance, the attribute *type* takes the values *superjet, jet, turbo* or *propeller;* the attribute *trajectory in vertical plane inside the sector* takes three possible values *steady, up* and *down.* The controller gives the values of the attributes for each aircraft. A special attribute here is the solution applied to the aircraft to solve the conflict. This attribute is the only one which is multi-valued and describes the way the aircraft route has been changed.
- Attributes describing relations between aircraft, which can be divided into two kinds.

    - Attributes describing oriented relations between the two conflicting aircraft. For instance, the relative position between the two aircraft can take the values *ahead, slightly ahead, equidistant from conflict occurrence, just above each other.*
    - Attributes describing non-oriented relations between the aircraft; for instance, the *angle of the foreseen routes of the aircraft just before conflict occurrence, their angle after conflict occurrence,* etc.

A first module has been written to transform the commented printouts into a formalism similar to the one adopted in the questionnaire. The second step is then to translate the questionnaire into a formalism adapted to OGUST.

15.3.4.2 Rewriting the Examples in OGUST Formalism

1. *How to translate a questionnaire into a first order representation*
   In most applications, an expert describes a situation he has to face by using attributes and relations between objects. The attributes represent either global descriptors of the context in which the situation occurs, for instance, the weather, or descriptors of the objects appearing in the situation, for instance, the temperature of the patient, the color of an object, etc. In other terms, the description provided by the expert is composed of

    - some pairs *(attribute, value)* characterizing the environment, for instance *(weather, fine),*
    - some triplets *(attribute, object, value),* for instance *(temperature,* BOB, *high),*
    - some relations *(relation, object$_1$, object$_2$, ...)* which may be oriented. In this case, the order of the objects occurring in the list is important. Most often, the relations are binary ones.

Present work load: high, steady, low
Foreseen work load: high, steady, low

Estimation of the angle of the routes just before conflict occurrence: | 10 deg |

	AF2470	BR1667
Estimation of the angle of the routes after conflict occurrence:	0 deg	0 deg
Relative position of the aircraft:		
equidistant	....	....
slightly ahead	....	.....×.....
ahead	....	....
doubtful	....	....
Rate of raise:		
high	....	....
standard	....×....	....
low	....	....
Relative ground speed, relative air speed:	470/0.79	410/0.64
Qualitative trajectory in vertical plane at the time of entering the sector:		
steady	....	.....×.....
evolutive	....↑....	....
Qualitative trajectory in vertical plane in the sector:		
steady	....	.....×.....
evolutive	....↑....	....
Qualitative trajectory in vertical plane at the time of exiting the sector:		
steady	....×....	.....×.....
evolutive	....	....
Destination:		
close	....	.....×.....
West-European	....×....	....
far away	....	....
Environmental limitations:		
active zone	....×....	....
other flight	....	....
nearby sector	....	.....×.....
Parameters describing how much an environmental limitation hinders:		
change of direction to the left, value, distance or beacon	....	.....×.....
change of direction to the right, value, distance or beacon	× > 10 deg	....
change of route to the left, value, distance	....	....
change of route to the right, value, distance	....	....
Uncertainty:		
poor radar contact	....	....
poor readibility of radar image	....	....
unstable information	....	....
Distance of the flights from the conflict point at the time of actualization of the solution:	40 NM	40 NM

Solution:
    steady stabilization
    temporary stabilization
    change of direction
        parallelization of routes
        moving away conflict point
        bringing closer the conflict point
        crossing behind
        crossing ahead
    change of route
    speed regulation
    height regulation
    left to pilot's estimation

| AF 2470, $right$ 10 deg |
| BR1667, direction unchanged |

Figure 15.2   Information about a conflict situation between two aircraft.

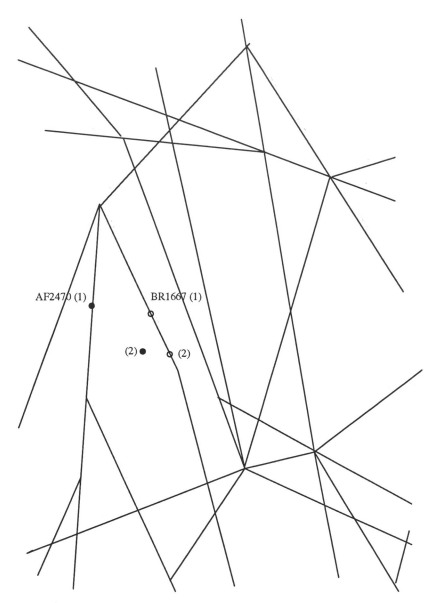

The positions of the aircraft AF2470 are written using a black circle.
The positions of the aircraft BR1667 are written using a white circle.

Figure 15.3   A blueprint representing a conflict situation.

	AF2470		BR1667

Present work load   high   <u>steady</u>   low
Foreseen work load   high   <u>steady</u>   low
Number of simultaneous conflicts
Estimation of the angle of the routes of the aircraft just before conflict occurrence
    – same routes
    – <u>sharp convergence</u>
    – convergence
    – broad convergence
    – front encounter
Estimation of the angle of the routes of the aircraft after conflict occurrence
    – <u>same routes</u>
    – routes branching off
Estimation of the angle between the present route and the route for direct exit
    – <u>null</u>   – <u>null</u>
    – small change   – small change
    – large change   – large change
    – left   – left
    – right   – right
Relative position of the aircraft as seen from the conflict point
                equidistant
    – slightly ahead   – slightly ahead
    – ahead   – <u>ahead</u>
            – overhead
Rate of raise
    – high   – high
    – <u>standard</u>   – standard
    – low   – low
Relative ground speed
            – same
    – <u>faster</u>   – faster
    – much faster   – much faster
Relative air speed
            – same
    – faster   – faster
    – <u>much faster</u>   – much faster
Type
    – <u>superjet</u>   – superjet
    – <u>jet</u>   – <u>jet</u>
    – turbo   – turbo
    – propeller   – propeller
Qualitative trajectory in vertical plane at the time of conflict analysis
    – steady   – steady
    – <u>up</u>   – <u>up</u>
    – down   – down
Qualitative trajectory in vertical plane at the time of entering the sector
    – steady   – <u>steady</u>
    – <u>up</u>   – up
    – down   – down

Figure 15.4   (upper part).

Qualitative trajectory in vertical plane in the sector

– steady	– steady
– up	– up
– down	– down

Qualitative trajectory in vertical plane at the time of exiting the sector

– steady	– steady
– up	– up
– down	– down

Destination

– close	– close
– West-European	– West- European
– far away	– far away

Forbidden Actions

– active zone	– active zone
– other flight	– other flight
– slight change allowed	– slight change allowed
– small change allowed	– small change allowed
– left	– left
– right	– right

Action forbidden unless special authorizing

– nearby sector	– nearby sector
– other flight	– other flight
– slight change allowed	– slight change allowed
– small change allowed	– small change allowed
– left	– left
– right	– right

Uncertainty

– poor radar contact	– poor radar contact
– poor readability of radar image	– poor readability of radar image
– unstable information	– unstable information

Distance of the flights from the conflict point at the time of actualization of the solution
- far away
- mean distant
- nearby

Solution

– steady stabilization	– steady stabilization
– temporary stabilization	– temporary stabilization
– change of direction	– change of direction
– change of route	– change of route
– slight	– slight
– small	– small
– left	– left
– right	– right
– parallelization of routes	– parallelization of routes
– moving away conflict point	– moving away conflict point
– bringing closer the conflict point	– bringing closer the conflict point
– crossing behind	– crossing behind
– crossing ahead	– crossing ahead
– speed regulation	– speed regulation
– height regulation	– height regulation
– left to pilot's estimation	– left to pilot's estimation

Figure 15.4   (lower part): the transcription of the conflict situation of Figure 15.3 into a questionnaire.

We can see at least four ways of transforming a pair *(attribute, value)* into a first order representation, but the list is not exhaustive. Let us first consider the case of global descriptors, represented by pairs *(attribute, value)*, for instance, the pair *(weather, fine)* which means that for the given situation, the weather is fine:

- 1st representation:
  *attribute(*VALUE*), attribute* becomes a predicate and VALUE becomes a constant. This representation is the closest to the attribute-value one. In this case, the word *weather* becomes a predicate of the underlying first order language and the word FINE becomes a constant. In terms of logics, in order to define a semantic interpretation of this formula, we have to give a non empty set D, an interpretation of the constant FINE and of the predicate *weather* over D. Intuitively, we interpret the constant FINE as an object, and this is not very natural.
- 2nd representation:
  *value(*ATTRIBUTE*), value* becomes a predicate and ATTRIBUTE becomes a constant. In this representation, we transform the pair *(weather, fine)* into *fine(*WEATHER*)*. In that case, WEATHER becomes a constant and *fine* a predicate. Intuitively, WEATHER is interpreted as an object which satisfies the property of being fine.
- 3rd representation:
  *pred(*ATTRIBUTE, VALUE*), pred* is a new symbol of predicate; ATTRIBUTE and VALUE are constants. In this representation, a type has been attributed to the pair *(attribute, value)* and *pred* is a new symbol of predicate that represents the type. For instance, we can say that the pair *(weather, fine)* represents a weather forecast by *forecast(*WEATHER, FINE*)*.
- 4th representation:
  *attribute(*C*) ∧ value(*C*), attribute* and *value* become predicates and C is a new symbol of constant.
  This last representation is close to an object-oriented one. For instance, in our example, we express that there is an object, say W, which satisfies the two following properties. W represents the weather of the given situation and W is fine. This reads *weather(*W*) ∧ fine(*W*)*. The words *fine* and *weather* both become predicates, and we introduce a new constant W. This idea of introducing a fictitious object is quite classical. It is used to transform facts written in first order logic into structured object representations (Nilsson, 1980). For instance, to translate the atom *gives(*PETER, MARY, BOOK1*)*, we introduce a new object G which is an instance of the action *give,* for which the actor is PETER, the receiver is MARY, and the object is BOOK1, and we obtain *give(*G*) ∧ actor(*G, PETER*) ∧ receiver(*G, MARY*) ∧ object(*G, BOOK1*)*.

We can extend these four representations to descriptions of objects, that is to say, to triplets *(attribute, object, value)*, for instance, the triplet *(color_eyes,* JOHN, BROWN*)*.

- 1st representation:
  *attribute(*OBJECT, VALUE*)* gives *color_eyes(*JOHN, BROWN*)*.
- 2nd representation:
  *value(*OBJECT, ATTRIBUTE*)* gives *brown(* JOHN, COLOR_EYES*)*.
- 3rd representation:
  *pred(*OBJECT, ATTRIBUTE, VALUE*)* gives *physical_descr(*JOHN, COLOR_EYES, BROWN*)*.

- 4th representation:
  attribute(OBJECT, C) $\wedge$ *value*(C) gives *color_eyes*(JOHN,C) $\wedge$ *brown*(C) where C is a new symbol of constant.

The choice of the objects and predicates depends on the behavior of the generalization tool, and it is essential to learn good generalizations. We will now show why we have chosen the fourth representation.

2. *The use of the 1st or of the 3rd representation would lead* OGUST *to learn absurd recognition functions, when two different attributes share the same value*
For example, let us suppose that according to the first representation we represent the case when the present work load of the controller and his foreseen work load are high by *present_work*(HIGH)) $\wedge$ *foreseen_work*(HIGH).

OGUST is not able to make a distinction between the value HIGH of the present work load and that of the foreseen work load. They represent for OGUST the same object and they are generalized by the same variable, yeilding *present_work*(vg_1) $\wedge$ *foreseen_work*(vg_1). The variable vg_1 represents an object which is together the present work load and the foreseen work load. Of couse, such a representation is nonsense, since it merges into a unique variable two different objects.

The same argument can be given against the 3rd representation. The previous example would be written, for instance, *work*(PRESENT_WORK, HIGH) $\wedge$ *work*(FORESEEN_WORK, HIGH), and the generalization of the constant HIGH into the variable vg_1 would lead to *work*(PRESENT_WORK, vg_1) $\wedge$ *work*(FORESEEN_WORK, vg_1).

This problem does not appear with the 2nd and the 4th representations. With the 2nd representation, the example would be written as *high*(PRESENT_WORK) $\wedge$ *high*(FORESEEN_WORK), and the two distinct constants PRESENT_WORK and FORESEEN_WORK would be generalized into two distinct variables *high*(vg_1) $\wedge$ *high*(vg_2) [(= vg_1 PRESENT_WORK)(= vg_2 FORESEEN_WORK)].

With the 4th representation, the example becomes *present_work*(C1) $\wedge$ *high*(C1) $\wedge$ *foreseen_work*(C2) $\wedge$ *high*(C2).

3. *The 2nd and 3rd representations could prevent* OGUST *from using BK correctly, thus leading to over-generalizations*
For example, suppose that in E_1 the foreseen work load is high, and that in E_2 the present work load is high. The 2nd representation gives

$E_1 = high$(FORESEEN_WORK).
$E_2 = high$(PRESENT_WORK).

Suppose also that the attributes *present_work* and *foreseen_work* can be generalized into the attribute *amount_work*. OGUST uses BK on the predicates, but does not on the constants. Therefore, it generalizes the two constants FORESEEN_WORK and PRESENT_WORK into the variable of generalization vg_1 and learns $G = high$ (vg_1). It does not use the previous piece of knowledge and loses the information that vg_1 is an amount of work. The same argument can be applied to the 3rd representation.

This problem arises neither with the 1st representation nor with the 4th. Let us consider, for instance, the 4th one. The examples are written

$E_1 = foreseen\_work$(C1) $\wedge$ *high*(C1)
$E_2 = present\_work$(C2) $\wedge$ *high*(C2),

The constants HIGH are replaced in each example by a variable of generalization, called vg_1.

$E_1 = foreseen\_work(vg_1) \wedge high(vg_1)[(= vg_1 \; C1)]$

$E_2 = present\_work(vg_1) \wedge high(vg_1) \; [(= vg_1 \; C2)]$

OGUST uses its BK to suppress the discriminating occurrences of the variable vg_1 in the examples, and we obtain the generalization

$G = amount\_work(vg_1) \wedge high(vg_1)$

The only representation that solves these two problems is the 4th one; this is why we have been using it.

4. *Description of the actual representation*

Each aircraft is represented by a constant. For the sake of simplicity, in the following, the symbol AIRCRAFT$_i$ will represent the i-th aircraft.

For each attribute describing the environment, a fictitious object represented by a constant, here called AT$_1$, is created and is described by the conjunction

$$attr(\text{AT}_1) \wedge val(\text{AT}_1)$$

where *attr* is the name of the concerned attribute describing the environment and *val* its value.

For each attribute describing the i-th aircraft, a fictitious object, called ATTR$_i$, is created and is described by the conjunction

$$attr(\text{AIRCRAFT}_i, \text{ATTR}_i) \wedge val(\text{ATTR}_i),$$

where *val* represents the value of the attribute *attr* for the i-th aircraft of the given example. In other words, we create a fictitious object which represents the attribute *attr* of the i-th aircraft and which has the value *val*.

For instance, we write as follows the information that the trajectory inside the sector of the first aircraft is steady:

$$traj\_in(\text{AIRCRAFT}_1, \text{TRAJ\_IN}_1) \wedge steady(\text{TRAJ\_IN}_1).$$

If the solution to the conflict consists in changing the course of the first aircraft to the right, we shall write

$$solution(\text{AIRCRAFT}_1, \text{SOLUTION}_1) \wedge$$
$$change\_course(\text{SOLUTION}_1) \wedge to\_the\_right(\text{SOLUTION}_1).$$

The information that the type of the second aircraft is a jet is written

$$type(\text{AIRCRAFT}_2, \text{TYPE}_2) \wedge jet(\text{TYPE}_2).$$

For each attribute representing an oriented relation between two aircraft, the attribute is directly written as a predicate. Therefore,

$$attr(\text{AIRCRAFT}_i, \text{AIRCRAFT}_j)$$

represents that in the example, the relation *attr* is satisfied between the i-th and the j-th aircraft. For instance, we have

$$ahead(\text{AIRCRAFT}_i, \text{AIRCRAFT}_j).$$

For each attribute representing a non-oriented relation between two aircraft, first order logic is ill-suited, since it compels the orientation of the relations. To prevent this, in our application they are treated as global descriptors and they have the same representation as that used to describe the environment. Therefore, we introduce a fictitious object ATTR_1, and we write

$$attr(\text{ATTR}_1) \wedge val(\text{ATTR}_1)$$

where *attr* is the name of the concerned non-oriented relation.

For instance, to express that in a given example the meeting angle of the routes of the two aircraft before the conflict point is minimal, we write

$$angle\_before\ (\text{ANGLE\_BEFORE}_1) \wedge minimal(\text{ANGLE\_BEFORE}_1).$$

For instance, the example described in Figures 15.2, 15.3 and 15.4 are translated into:

```
(∧ (present_work_load PRESENT_WORK_LOAD₁) (steady PRESENT_WORK_LOAD₁)
   (foreseen_work_load FORESEEN_WORK_LOAD₁) (steady FORESEEN_WORK_LOAD₁)
   (angle_routes_before ANGLE_ROUTES_BEFORE₁) (sharp ANGLE_ROUTES_BEFORE₁)
   (angle_routes_after ANGLE_ROUTES_AFTER₁) (same ANGLE_ROUTES_AFTER₁)
   (direct_route AF2470 DIRECT_ROUTE₁) (null DIRECT_ROUTE₁)
   (direct_route BR1667 DIRECT_ROUTE₂) (null DIRECT_ROUTE₂)
   (rate_raise AF2470 RATE_RAISE₁) (null RATE_RAISE₁)
   (rate_raise BR1667 RATE_RAISE₂)
   (type AF2470 TYPE₁) (superjet TYPE₁)
   (type BR1667 TYPE₂) (jet TYPE₂)
   (traj_init AF2470 TRAJ_INIT₁) (up TRAJ_INIT₁)
   (traj_init BR1667 TRAJ_INIT₂) (steady TRAJ_INIT₂)
   ...
   (destination AF2470 DESTINATION₁) (west_european DESTINATION₁)
   (destination BR1667 DESTINATION₂) (far_away DESTINATION₂)
   (solution AF2470 SOLUTION₁) (change_direction SOLUTION₁)
   (parallelization_routes SOLUTION₁)
   (right SOLUTION₁)
   (slight SOLUTION₁)
   (solution BR1667 SOLUTION₂)),
```

where the predicate symbol is the first inside the parenthesis.

To conclude on this problem, we can say that the representation chosen is a structured-object one, written in first order logic. We deal with some basic objects such as the *present work load of the controller* and we have structured objects, the aircraft, composed of basic objects representing, for instance, their *type* or their *profile in the sector*, and so on. Moreover, all the objects are implicitly typed, so that we cannot match, for instance, the present work load and the foreseen one. Algorithm 15.4 explains how this change of representation is implemented. In our application, this algorithm was a little simplified since we had only two structured objects, namely the two aircraft in conflict. The non-oriented relations between the two aircraft were treated as global descriptors and written in the list LIST_ENV.

Inputs:
- A list LIST_ENV of pairs *(Attribute, Value)* describing the global environment.
- A list LIST_OBJ $= (L_1, \ldots, L_p)$ where each list L_i represents a structured object and has the form $(Name_i \ Type_i \ (Attribute_i^1, Value_i^1), \ldots, (Attribute_i^n, Value_i^n))$
- A list LIST_REL giving the relations existing between objects.

Output: a conjunction of ground atoms representing the example

1. for each element $(Attribute, Value)$ of LIST_ENV,
   - create a new name by adding to the name of the attribute, a number (1 for instance)
   - transform $(Attribute, Value)$ into $Attribute(\text{ATTRIBUTE}_1) \land Value(\text{ATTRIBUTE}_1)$
2. for each list L_i of LIST_OBJ describing the object of name $Name_i$ and type $Type_i$ and for each element $(Attribute_i^j, Value_i^j)$ of this list
   - create the atom $type_i(\text{NAME}_i)$
   - create a new name by adding to the name of the attribute, a number (1 for instance),
   - transform $(Attribute_i^j, Value_i^j)$ into $attribute_i^j(\text{NAME}_i, \text{ATTRIBUTE}_{i1}^j) \land value_i^j(\text{ATTRIBUTE}_{i1}^j)$
3. keep unchanged each element of LIST_REL

Algorithm 15.4 Change of representation.

15.3.5 Rewriting BK as Horn lauses

15.3.5.1 Influence of the Representation of the Examples

The choice for the representation of the examples has a great influence on the writing of BK. For instance, let us suppose that we want to express the following knowledge:

> IF a given plane has a steady trajectory when entering, exiting the sector and inside the sector, THEN it is on cruise.

The qualitative trajectories of a plane, within the sector, when entering it, and when exiting it, are attributes given in the questionnaire. On the contrary, the characteristic of the flight, that is to say *on cruise*, is a new one. To be coherent with our structured representation, we must define a new attribute characterizing the flight, and which can take three values: *cruising, moving from cruise state, partially moving out of cruise state.* Let us call this new attribute *flight.* The theorem is then written

$$TH_1 : \forall x \, \forall y \, \forall z \, \forall t \, [[traj\_enter(x, y) \land steady(y) \land traj\_init(x, z) \land steady(z) \land$$
$$traj\_exit(x, t) \land steady(t)] \Rightarrow \exists \, fl \, [flight(x, fl) \land cruising(fl)]]$$

The conclusion of the theorem expresses that there exists an object which represents the flight of x and which satisfies the property of being cruising.

15.3.5.2   Horn Clauses

Theorems must be expressed as Horn clauses: the conclusion of a theorem must be a single atom and we do not allow existential variables. To solve the first problem, we replace the previous theorem by the two following ones:

$$TH_{21} : \forall x \, \forall y \, \forall z \, \forall t \, [[traj\_enter(x,y) \wedge steady(y) \wedge traj\_in(x,z) \wedge steady(z) \wedge$$
$$traj\_exit(x,t) \wedge steady(t)] \Rightarrow \exists \, fl[flight(x,fl)]]$$

$$TH_{22} : \forall x \, \forall y \, \forall z \, \forall t \, \forall fl \, [traj\_enter(x,y) \wedge steady(y) \wedge traj\_in(x,z) \wedge steady(z) \wedge$$
$$traj\_exit(x,t) \wedge steady(t) \wedge flight(x,fl)] \Rightarrow cruising(fl)]$$

In the first theorem, we say that, under some conditions, we can introduce a new object, which is the *flight* of the aircraft. In the second one, we say that with the same conditions, and if the flight of the aircraft is represented by the variable fl, then we can deduce that the flight fl is a cruise.

TH_1 is a logical consequence of $TH_{21} \wedge TH_{22}$ but the reverse is not true, and therefore the two formulas are not equivalent. In fact, TH_{21} does not exactly express our knowledge, since we know that there exists a unique object which represents the flight of x. We should use the quantifier $\exists!$ but we did not allow this formalism in our implementation.

To solve the problem of the existential quantifiers in TH_{21}, we skolemize it. Thus, we introduce a new symbol of function f and we can rewrite it

$$TH_{31} : \forall x \, \forall y \, \forall z \, \forall t \, [[traj\_enter(x,y) \wedge steady(y) \wedge traj\_in(x,z) \wedge steady(z) \wedge$$
$$traj\_exit(x,t) \wedge steady(t)] \Rightarrow flight(x,f(x,y,z,t))]$$

15.3.5.3   Introduction of a Functional Term

The application of a theorem on an example can, as in TH_{31}, introduce a functional term. In this case, we replace the functional symbol by a new constant, if possible by a constant bearing a meaning for the expert. This is our crude way of solving the problem of skolemization studied in Section 15.2.1.3. In the following example, the function introduced by TH_{31}, f(AIRCRAFT, TRAJ_ENT, TRAJ_IN, TRAJ_OUT), will be replaced by a new constant NFL, about which nothing special is known, unfortunately, since our expert cannot say anything about it.

For instance, let us suppose that our example is

$E = traj\_enter$(AIRCRAFT,TRAJ_ENT) $\wedge$ $steady$(TRAJ_ENT) $\wedge$
    $traj\_in$(AIRCRAFT,TRAJ_IN) $\wedge$ $steady$(TRAJ_IN) $\wedge$
    $traj\_exit$(AIRCRAFT,TRAJ_OUT) $\wedge$ $steady$(TRAJ_OUT) $\wedge \ldots$

When applying theorem TH_{31}, we introduce a new constant, NFL, and we obtain

$E = traj\_enter$(AIRCRAFT,TRAJ_ENT) $\wedge$ $steady$(TRAJ_ENT) $\wedge$
    $traj\_in$(AIRCRAFT,TRAJ_IN) $\wedge$ $steady$(TRAJ_IN) $\wedge$
    $traj\_exit$(AIRCRAFT,TRAJ_OUT) $\wedge$ $steady$(TRAJ_OUT) $\wedge$
    $flight$(AIRCRAFT,NFL) $\wedge \ldots$

We do not write the information that

$$\text{NFL} = f(\text{AIRCRAFT,TRAJ\_ENT,TRAJ\_IN,TRAJ\_OUT})$$

because our expert cannot say anything about this f.

15.3.5.4 Symbolic Representations

As mentioned in Section 15.2.1, the solution adopted in our implementation was not entirely satisfactory, since the solution was to represent a numeric function by a crude qualitative representation, with a very restricted definition domain. For instance, we are unable to determine the value of the speed when the distance is small and the time is small.

15.3.6 Adaptation of the Algorithm to Structured Objects

Let us first recall the principle developed in OGUST to choose the constants to match. In OGUST, a constant represents an object and we look for the most similar objects, in order to find their common properties. In the application to ATC, the only real objects we have are the aircraft but, as seen in Section 15.3.4.2, we introduce fictitious objects to represent the examples. We can single out two among these fictitious objects,

- the objects describing the global environment and independent of the other objects, such as the present work load of the controller,
- the objects representing properties of the aircraft, such as their types, their qualitative trajectories.

To compute the similarity between two aircraft, we must take into account the common properties related to the last type of fictitious objects.

Let us consider the two simplified examples:

$E_1 = traj\_init(\text{AIRCRAFT}_1^1,\text{TRAJ\_IN}_1^1) \wedge steady(\text{TRAJ\_IN}_1^1) \wedge$
$\quad type(\text{AIRCRAFT}_1^1,\text{TYPE}_1^1) \wedge jet(\text{TYPE}_1^1) \wedge$
$\quad solution(\text{AIRCRAFT}_1^1,\text{SOLUTION}_1^1) \wedge change\_course(\text{SOLUTION}_1^1) \wedge$
$\quad to\_the\_right(\text{SOLUTION}_1^1) \wedge$
$\quad traj\_in(\text{AIRCRAFT}_1^2,\text{TRAJ\_IN}_1^2) \wedge steady(\text{TRAJ\_IN}_1^2) \wedge$
$\quad type(\text{AIRCRAFT}_1^2,\text{TYPE}_1^2) \wedge jet(\text{TYPE}_1^2) \wedge$
$\quad solution(\text{AIRCRAFT}_1^2,\text{SOLUTION}_1^2) \wedge change\_course(\text{SOLUTION}_1^2) \wedge$
$\quad to\_the\_left(\text{SOLUTION}_1^2)$

$E_2 = traj\_init(\text{AIRCRAFT}_2^1,\text{TRAJ\_IN}_2^1) \wedge steady(\text{TRAJ\_IN}_2^1) \wedge$
$\quad type(\text{AIRCRAFT}_2^1,\text{TYPE}_2^1) \wedge jet(\text{TYPE}_2^1) \wedge$
$\quad solution(\text{AIRCRAFT}_2^1,\text{SOLUTION}_2^1) \wedge change\_course(\text{SOLUTION}_2^1) \wedge$
$\quad to\_the\_right(\text{SOLUTION}_2^1) \wedge$
$\quad traj\_in(\text{AIRCRAFT}_2^2,\text{TRAJ\_IN}_2^2) \wedge steady(\text{TRAJ\_IN}_2^2) \wedge$
$\quad type(\text{AIRCRAFT}_2^2,\text{TYPE}_2^2) \wedge super\_jet(\text{TYPE}_2^2) \wedge$
$\quad solution(\text{AIRCRAFT}_2^2,\text{SOLUTION}_2^2) \wedge speed\_regulation(\text{SOLUTION}_2^2)$

In each example, we have two aircraft and there are four ways to match them by choosing an aircraft in each example. To know which aircraft to match, OGUST searches for the common properties of the aircraft of each combination. The only way it has to find the properties of an aircraft is to search among the examples for the occurrences of the constant representing this aircraft. Let us, for instance, consider the first aircraft of the first example, AIRCRAFT_1^1. This constant occurs in the atoms $traj\_init(\text{AIRCRAFT}_1^1, \text{TRAJ\_IN}_1^1)$, $type(\text{AIRCRAFT}_1^1, \text{TYPE}_1^1)$ and $solution(\text{AIRCRAFT}_1^1, \text{SOLUTION}_1^1)$. In other words, the properties of this aircraft are the following: it has a trajectory in the sector, it has a type and its course has been changed. All aircraft of the two examples share the same properties. The important piece of information with our representation is not, for instance, the fact that the aircraft has a type, but the fact that the type is a jet. Therefore, to compute the similarities between two aircraft, we must take into account the similarities of the fictitious objects representing their properties.

To take into account this notion of structured objects, we have modified the computation of the similarity between two objects, in the following way:

- For two basic objects O_1 and O_2 of the same type
  $$new\_sim(O_1, O_2) = sim(O_1, O_2),$$
- For two structured objects O_1 and O_2 of the same type and composed of the objects $(O_1^1, \ldots, O_1^n)$ and $(O_2^1, \ldots, O_2^n)$,
  $$new\_sim(O_1, O_2) = \Sigma_i sim(O_1^i, O_2^i).$$

Let us notice that in this application we had only one type of structured object: the aircraft. Each aircraft is composed of the same type of basic objects, such as its trajectory in the vertical plane in the sector, its trajectory when exiting the sector, and so on. There is, therefore, a one-to-one correspondence between the basic objects of two aircraft. In general cases, the computation of $new\_sim(O_1, O_2)$ could be more complicated [4].

Once the constants to match have been chosen, we replace the two constants by a variable vg and we have to start a structural matching as described in Section 15.2. Two cases are still possible:

- The two constants O_1, O_2 represent basic objects, and the structural matching starts at once.
- The two constants O_1, O_2 represent structured objects. The structural matching takes place on the basic objects that they are composed of. Let us call $(O_1^1, \ldots, O_1^n)$ and $(O_2^1, \ldots, O_2^n)$ the basic objects comprising O_1 and O_2. For each pair of objects (O_1^j, O_2^j) of the same type, we introduce a new variable vg_j and we start the structural matching.

The cycle previously developed in OGUST and applied to all the constants of the examples is now only applied to the structured objects representing the aircraft, and to the basic objects representing the global environment. This new cycle could be easily extended to more complex structures.

15.3.7 Rewriting the Generalization

The formalism that is used to represent the learned rules is not natural for the expert. To show them to the expert, we are forced to translate the concepts learned by OGUST in a more familiar representation. The representation we use is that of the questionnaire. A module has been implemented to automate this step (Algorithm 15.5). It reverses the process described in Section 15.3.4.

---

[4] For a general solution in more complicated cases see Bisson (1992).

Inputs:
- a list ATT_ENV of the attributes used to describe the global environment,
- a list TYPE_OBJ composed of lists L_i $(type_i, att_i^1, \ldots, att_i^n)$ where $type_i$ is the name of a type and $att_i^1, \ldots, att_i^n$ are the attributes used to describe an object of this type,
- a list SYM_REL giving the name of the oriented relations that can exist between objects,
- a conjunction E of atoms describing an example.

Outputs:
- a list LIST_ENV of pairs *(Atttributo, Valuo)* describing the global environment,
- a list LIST_OBJ $= (L_1, \ldots, L_p)$ where each list L_i represents a structured object and has the form $(Name_i \ Type_i \ (Attribute_i^1, Value_i^1), \ldots, (Attribute_i^n, Value_i^n))$,
- a list LIST_REL giving the relations existing between objects.

Initially, LIST_ENV = LIST_OBJ = LIST_REL = $\emptyset$

1. for each attribute *att* of ATT_ENV,

   - search for an atom, written *att(O)*, the predicate of which is *att*,
   - search for an atom *val(O)*, *val* $\neq$ *att*, *val* is the value of the attribute,
   - take off *att(O)* $\wedge$ *val(O)* from E,
   - add the pair *(att,val)* to LIST_ENV,

2. for each list L_i : $(type_i, att_i^1, \ldots, att_i^n)$ of TYPE_OBJ,

   - search for the objects $O_i^1, \ldots, O_i^k$ of type $type_i$ present in E, i.e., search for the atoms $type_i(O_i^j)$, take off $type_i(O_i^j)$ from E, add to LIST_OBJ the new lists $L_i^1, \ldots, L_i^k$, where $L_i^j = (O_i^j, type_i)$,
   - for each object O_i^j,
     - search for the atoms $p_l(O_i^j, V_l)$ and then for the atoms $val_l(V_l)$,
     - add to the list $L_i^j = (O_i^j, type_i)$ the pairs (p_l, val_l),
     - take off $p_l(O_i^j, V_l) \wedge val_l(V_l)$ from E

3. LIST_REL is composed of the remaining atoms (we can check whether each predicate belongs to SYMB_REL).

Algorithm 15.5 Change of representation.

For instance, a generalization of the example illustrated by Figures 15.2, 15.3 and 15.4 with another example for which a change of direction was also proposed to solve the conflict is:

$G = (\wedge \ (present\_work\_load \ vg_3) \ (steady \ vg_3) \ (foreseen\_work\_load \ vg_4) \ (steady \ vg_4)$
$(angle\_routes\_before \ vg_5) \ (sharp \ vg_5) \ (angle\_routes\_after \ vg_6) \ (same \ vg_6)$
$(direct\_route \ vg_1 \ vg_7) \ (direct\_route \ vg_2 \ vg_8) \ (null \ vg_8) \ (rate\_raise \ vg_1 \ vg_9)$
$(rate\_raise \ vg_2 \ vg_{10}) \ (type \ vg_1 \ vg_{11}) \ (superjet \ vg_{11}) \ (type \ vg_2 \ vg_{12}) \ (jet \ vg_{12})$
$(traj\_init \ vg_1 \ vg_{13}) \ (up \ vg_{13}) \ (traj\_init \ vg_2 \ vg_{14}) \ (steady \ vg_{14}) \ (traj\_enter \ vg_1$
$vg_{15}) \ (up \ vg_{15}) \ (traj\_enter \ vg_2 \ vg_{16}) \ (steady \ vg_{16}) \ (traj\_in \ vg_1 \ vg_{17}) \ (up \ vg_{17})$
$traj\_in \ vg_2 \ vg_{18}) \ (steady \ vg_{18}) \ (traj\_exit \ vg_1 \ vg_{19}) \ (steady \ vg_{19}) \ (traj\_exit \ vg_2$
$vg_{20}) \ (steady \ vg_{20}) \ (destination \ vg_1 \ vg_{21}) \ (destination \ vg_2 \ vg_{22}) \ldots (solution \ vg_1$
$vg_{26}) \ (change\_direction \ vg_{26}) \ (parallelization\_routes \ vg_{26}) \ (solution \ vg_2 \ vg_{27}))$

The first order representation is translated back into a representation close to the one familiar to the expert:

Foreseen work load
  – steady
Estimation of the angle of the routes of the aircraft just before conflict occurrence
  – sharp convergence
Estimation of the angle of the routes of the aircraft after conflict occurrence
  – same routes
Estimation of the angle between the present route and the route for direct exit
  – vg_1:
  – vg_2: zero
Type
  – vg_1: superjet
  – vg_2: jet
Qualitative trajectory in vertical plane at the time of conflict analysis
  – vg_1: up
  – vg_2: steady
Qualitative trajectory in vertical plane at the time of entering the sector
  – vg_1: up
  – vg_2: steady
Qualitative trajectory in vertical plane in the sector
  – vg_1: up
  – vg_2: steady
Qualitative trajectory in vertical plane at the time of exiting the sector
  – vg_1: steady
  – vg_2: steady
Solution
  – vg_1: change of direction, parallelization of routes

It means: if the foreseen work load of the controller is steady and if we have two aircraft vg_1 and vg_2 such that:

- their angle of convergence before conflict occurrence is a sharp convergence,
- their routes after conflict occurrence are the same,
- for the aircraft vg_2, the angle between the present route and the route for direct exit is zero,
- vg_1 is a superjet,
- vg_2 is a jet,
- the qualitative trajectory in the vertical plane at the time of conflict analysis is up for vg_1 and steady for vg_2
- the qualitative trajectory in the vertical plane at the time of entering the sector is up for vg_1 and steady for vg_2,
- the qualitative trajectory in the vertical plane in the sector is up for vg_1 and steady for vg_2,
- the qualitative trajectory in the vertical plane at the time of exiting the sector is steady for vg_1 and vg_2,

then we should apply a change of direction on vg_1 parallelizing the routes.

15.4 CONCLUSION

We have shown that knowledge intensive generalization techniques need even more than a generalization tool making use of the field expert's knowledge (called BK throughout this chapter). The very use of BK entails a first order logic representation, which is not friendly to the expert. Thus, besides the generalization tools, we need other tools to perform the transformation of the examples and the expert's knowledge in first order, and, once the learning has taken place, we need to translate it back into a representation that is acceptable to the expert. All these translation steps are far from trivial, and they contain choices that must be carefully discussed with the expert since they can strongly influence the learning.

The success of the learning process often relies on a proper choice of the formalism used to represent knowledge, and this includes the choice of the basic vocabulary. It is obvious that if a concept depends on a factor and if we have no way to represent this factor with the primitives of the language we have defined, we shall not be able to learn a good definition of the concept. The choice of the primitives of the language is very much domain dependent, so that we have no hope of making this step automatic and we can only get them through a dialog with the expert. The latter will certainly be improved by using techniques stemming from knowledge acquisition. In the application to ATC, this choice has led to the elaboration of a questionnaire containing those language primitives which seemed important for the decision of the controller. We also had to choose a logical formalism, and we chose first order formalism against a more classical attribute-value representation. The expressive power of first order logic is higher than that of an attribute-value representation, but most existing systems did not choose it because the processes that use it lack efficiency. We have shown that in some cases, as in ATC, we are compelled to use it. Once first order is chosen, we have shown that we have to determine which primitives of the language will become predicates, and which must play the role of constants. In our application, our choice simulates an object-oriented representation. Another task is obtaining the positive and negative examples and their translation into the formalism we have chosen. For ATC, this task can itself be divided into several steps. The expert in real situations has no time to fill the pre-determined questionnaire. Therefore, he writes only the information which is necessary to remember the conflict, and the way it has been solved. Afterwards, he transcribes it into answers to a questionnaire. A friendly interface enables one to store the answers, and a module translates them from their attribute-value representation into the first order representation.

The most difficult problem is certainly obtaining the BK base. We did it through discussions with the expert, but we are conscious that it was far from satisfactory. When expressing *if ...then ...* rules, the expert very often forgets some conditions, thus delivering relevant but actually false rules. Moreover, he does not give all the rules, and we thus obtain an incomplete BK. The falsity of some pieces of knowledge leads to erroneous generalizations, and the lack of pieces of knowledge leads to over-generalizations. The validation step, by the field expert, of the rules learned is therefore of great importance. When an expert rejects a rule, we have to find where the errors are, in the definition of the concept, in the examples, or in the BK.

Another problem, which has been only partially solved here, is that of numeric values. This application shows the necessity of introducing numeric values into the first order generalization tool.

A last problem, partially solved, is that of skolemization. In this particular application, the expert did not know the relations entailed by the existence of the functions we have been meeting. This is why we had to use the most trivial solution, and replace the Skolem functions by fictitious constants, the actual value of which will be computed by applying other theorems.

Among all the tasks that we had to solve during this application to air traffic control, those implemented, that is, the generalization tool, the interface to store the examples into an attribute_value representation, and the translation modules, have been written in Lelisp version 15.2.

To the best of our knowledge, there is still no full automation of air traffic control. We cannot thus claim that our work has been directly applied in a system. Once our contract finished, its results were the property of CENA, which has been using it for research to come.

ACKNOWLEDGEMENTS

This work has been partially sponsored by a CENA contract, and we thank J.J. Cannat and G. Bisson who worked on this contract at LRI. We also acknowledge the continuous support of the GRECO-PRC IA of the French ministry for the scientific research.

Reprinted from *Knowledge Acquisition*, Volume 5, Y. Kodratoff, C. Vrain, Acquiring first-order knowledge about air-traffic control, 1–36, 1993, by permission of the publisher Academic Press Limited, London.

REFERENCES

Avizienis A., Ball D.E.(1987). On the Achievement of a Highly Dependable and Fault-Tolerant Air Traffic Control System. *Computer,* February 1987, Volume 20, Number 2, pp. 84-92.

Bisson G. (1992). Learning in FOL with a similarity measure. Proceedings of AAAI, San Jose, California, 13-17 July 1992.

Bleistein S., Goettge R., Petroski F., Wiseman R. (1987). Capacity Management of Air Traffic Control Computer Systems. *Computer,* February 1987, Volume 20, Number 2, pp. 73-83.

Bratko I., Lavrac N. (1987). *Progress in Machine Learning,* Proceedings of the 2nd European Working Session on Learning, Bled, Yugoslavia, May 1987, Sigma Press.

Buchanan B.G., Shortliffe E.H. (1984). *Rule-Based Expert Systems: The MYCIN Experiments of the Stanford Heuristic Programming Project,* Addison-Wesley, 1984.

Cannat J.J., Vrain C. (1988). Machine Learning applied to air traffic control. Colloque International Homme-Machine et Intelligence Artificielle dans les domaines de l'Aéronautique et de l'Espace, Toulouse, France, 28-30 September 1988, pp. 265-274.

Chaib-draa B., Mandiau R., Millot P. (1988). CIS: Cooperating Intelligent System. Colloque International Homme-Machine et Intelligence Artificielle dans les domaines de l'Aéronautique et de l'Espace, Toulouse, France, 28-30 September 1988, pp. 315-329.

Forgy C., McDermott J. (1977). OPS, a domain independant production system language. Proceedings 5th International Joint Artificial Intelligence Conference, Cambridge, Massachusetts, 1977, pp. 933-939.

Hunt V.R., Kloster G.V. (1987). The FAA's Advanced Automation System: Strategies for Future Air traffic Control Systems. *Computer*, February 1987, Volume 20, Number 2, pp. 19-32.

Kloster G.V., Zellweger A. (1987). Engineering the Man-Machine Interface for Air Traffic Control. *Computer*, February 1987, Volume 20, Number 2, pp. 47-62.

Kodratoff, Y., Ganascia J. G., Clavieras B., Bollinger T. (1984). Careful generalization for concept learning. Proceedings ECAI-84, Pisa, 1984, pp. 483-492.

Kodratoff Y., Ganascia J. G. (1986). Improving the Generalization Step in Learning. *Machine Learning: An Artificial Intelligence Approach*, Vol.2, Michalski R.S., Carbonell J.G. and Mitchell T.M. (Eds.), Morgan Kaufmann, 1986, pp. 215-244.

Kodratoff Y., Tecuci G. (1988). Learning based on conceptual distance. *IEEE Trans. on Pattern Anal. and Mach. Int.* 10, 1988, pp. 897-909.

Kodratoff Y. (1988). *Introduction to Machine Learning*, Pitman, 1988.

Langley P. (1986). The terminology of Machine Learning. *Machine Learning Journal*, Volume 1, Number 2, 1986, pp. 141-144.

Levi R., Shalin V.L., Wisniewskii E.J., Scott P.D. (1987). An Analysis of Machine Learning Applications for Pilot Aiding Expert Systems. Interim Report for period October 1986 - July 1987, Contract N^o F33615-86-1125, Honeywell Systems and Research Center, Minneapolis.

Michalski R.S. (1983). A Theory and Methodology of Inductive Learning. *Artificial Intelligence*, Volume 20, Number 2, February 1983.

Michalski R.S., Kodratoff Y. (1990). Research in Machine Learning; Recent Progress, Classification of Methods, and Future Directions. *Machine Learning: An Artificial Intelligence Approach*, Vol. 3, Kodratoff Y. and Michalski R. S., (Eds.), Morgan Kaufmann, 1990, pp. 3-30.

Nilsson N. (1980). Structured object representation. *Principles of Artificial Intelligence*, Chapter 9, Tioga, pp. 361-414.

Onken R. (1988). Automatic pilot aid for situation awareness and flight planning. Colloque International Homme-Machine et Intelligence Artificielle dans les domaines de l'Aéronautique et de l'Espace, Toulouse, France, 28-30 September 1988, pp. 125-137.

Phillips M.D. (1987). The Quantification of Operational Suitability. *Computer*, February 1987, Volume 20, Number 2, pp. 63-72.

Planchon P., Berrada J. (1988). ANTICO: an anti-collision system in air traffic control. Colloque International Homme-Machine et Intelligence Artificielle dans les domaines de l'Aéronautique et de l'Espace, Toulouse, France, 28-30 September 1988, pp. 331-346.

Quinlan J.R. (1983). Learning Efficient Classification Procedures and their Application to Chess End Games. *Machine Learning, an Artificial Intelligence Approach*, Michalski R.S., Carbonell J.G. and Mitchell T.M. (Eds.), Morgan Kaufmann, 1983, chap. 15, pp. 463-482.

Rouveirol C. (1991). ITOU: Induction of First Order Theories, First Inductive Learning Programming Workshop, Viana de Castelo, 2-4 mars 1991, S. Muggleton (Ed.), pp 127-158.

Shively C., Schwamb K.B. (1984). AIRPAC: Advisor for the Intelligent Resolution of Predicted Aircraft Conflicts. October 1984, MTR-84W164, the MITRE Corporation.

Shortliffe E.H. (1976). Computer-Based Medical Consultations: MYCIN. *Artificial Intelligence Series 2*, Elsevier Computer Science Library.

Speyer J.J. (1988). Towards design-induced error tolerance. Colloque International Homme-Machine et Intelligence Artificielle dans les domaines de l'Aéronautique et de l'Espace, Toulouse, France, 28-30 September 1988, pp. 69-94.

Vrain C. (1987). Un outil pour la Généralisation Utilisant Systématiquement les Théorèmes: le système OGUST. Thèse de troisième cycle, L.R.I., Université Paris-Sud, Orsay, France, Février 1987.

Vrain C., Lu C.R. (1988). An Analogical Method to Do Incremental Learning of Concepts, *proceedings of the third European Working Session on Learning*, Turing Institute, Glasgow, 3-5 October 1988, D. Sleeman (Ed.), Pitman, pp. 227-235.

Vrain C., Kodratoff Y. (1989). The use of Analogy in incremental SBL. *Knowledge Representation and Organization in Machine Learning*, K. Morik (Ed.), Lecture Notes in Artificial Intelligence 347, Springer-Verlag, pp. 231-246.

Vrain C. (1990). OGUST : A System that Learns Using Domain Properties Expressed as Theorems. *Machine Learning, an Artificial Intelligence Approach*, Vol. 3, Y. Kodratoff, R. S. Michalski (Eds.), Morgan Kaufman, pp. 360-382.

Vrain C., Kodratoff Y. (1991). Acquiring first-order knowledge about air traffic control. Proceedings of KAW 91, Banff, 6-11 October 1991.

PART V

Medicine and Biology

16

Application of Machine Learning to Medical Diagnosis

Igor Kononenko, Ivan Bratko and Matjaž Kukar

ABSTRACT

Although machine learning may induce reliable diagnostic algorithms from the limited description of the patient, such diagnostic tools definitely cannot, and also are not intended to, replace the physicians, but should rather be considered as helpful tools that can improve the physicians' performance. The results in this chapter and from other experiments convincingly demonstrate that the physicians' diagnostic accuracy should be possible to improve with the aid of machine learning. When applying a machine learning system in medical diagnosis there are several specific requirements that the system must meet. This chapter is not a comprehensive review of medical applications of machine learning, but it discusses several issues related to the use of machine learning in medical diagnosis and prognosis problems, and illustrates the problematic issues within several applications that were developed in the past. We discuss advantages and disadvantages of different machine learning algorithms when used in medical diagnosis.

16.1 INTRODUCTION

Machine learning algorithms can be classified into three major groups (Michie *et al.*, 1994): statistical or pattern recognition methods (such as the k-nearest neighbours, discriminant analysis, and Bayesian classifiers), inductive learning of symbolic rules (such as top-down induction of decision trees, decision rules, and induction of logic programs), and artificial neural networks (such as the multilayered feedforward neural network with backpropagation learning, the Kohonen's self-organizing network, and the Hopfield's associative memory).

It seems that the machine learning technology is well suited for medical diagnosis in small specialized diagnostic problems. Data about correct diagnoses are often available in the form of medical records in specialized hospitals or their departments. All that has to be done is to input the records of the patients with known correct diagnosis into the computer, and run the learning algorithm. This is, of course, an oversimplification, but in principle, the medical diagnostic knowledge can be automatically derived from the description of cases solved in the past. The derived classifier can then be used either to assist the physician when diagnosing new patients in order to improve the diagnostic speed, accuracy and/or reliability, or to train the students or physicians non-specialists to diagnose the patients in some special diagnostic problem.

Machine learning systems were actually applied in many medical domains, e.g. in oncology (Bratko and Mulec, 1980; Zwitter et al., 1983; Kononenko et al., 1984; Bratko and Kononenko, 1987; Elomaa and Holsti, 1989), liver pathology (Lesmo et al., 1982), prognosing the survival in hepatitis (Kononenko et al., 1984), urology (Kononenko et al., 1984; Bratko and Kononenko, 1987; Roškar et al., 1986), diagnosis of thyroid diseases (Horn et al., 1985; Hojker et al., 1988; Quinlan et al., 1987), rheumatology (Kononenko et al., 1988; Karalič and Pirnat, 1990; Kern et al.1990), diagnosing craniostenosis syndrome (Baim, 1988), dermatoglyptic diagnosis (Chan and Wong, 1989), cardiology (Bratko et al., 1989; Clark and Boswell, 1991; Catlett, 1991), neuropsychology (Muggleton, 1990), gynaecology (Nuñez, 1990), and perinatology (Kern et al., 1990).

However, not all the learning systems are equally appropriate. When applying a machine learning system in medical diagnosis, there are several specific requirements that the system must meet. This chapter discusses several issues related to the use of machine learning in medical diagnostic and prognostic problems, such as reliability and transparency of decisions. We illustrate the problematic issues within several different applications that were developed in the past: localization of the primary tumor, predicting the recurrence of the breast cancer, diagnosis of thyroid diseases, diagnosis in rheumatology, and prediction of complications in the femoral neck fracture recovery. We discuss advantages and disadvantages of several different machine learning algorithms when used in medical diagnosis: top down induction of decision trees, the naive and the semi-naive Bayesian classifier, the k-nearest neighbors (k-NN) algorithm, multilayered feedforward neural networks with backpropagation and weight elimination learning algorithm, and Lookahead Feature Construction (LFC).

The chapter is organized as follows. In the next section we describe a typical process of diagnosing a patient and describe results obtained in the past by applying machine learning algorithms in several medical problems. Section 16.3 compares the diagnostic performance of physicians to that of machine learning systems. Section 16.4 describes specific requirements for ML systems to be applied in medical diagnosis and compares seven ML algorithms with respect to those requirements. Section 16.5 disccusses the issue of why ML applications in medical diagnosis are (not) accepted in practice.

16.2   MEDICAL DIAGNOSIS

A typical diagnostic process is the following. During the interview of the patient the anamnestic data is obtained and immediately afterwards during the preliminary examination of the patient the physician records the status data. Depending on the anamnestic and the status data, the patient takes additional laboratory examinations. The diagnosis is then determined by the physician, who takes into account the whole available description of the patient's state of health. Depending on the diagnosis, the treatment is prescribed and, after the treatment, the whole process may be repeated. In each iteration the diagnosis may be confirmed, refined, or rejected. The definition of the final diagnosis depends on the medical problem. In some problems the first diagnosis is also the final; in some others the final diagnosis is determined after the results of the treatment are available; and in some problems there is no way to obtain a 100% reliable final diagnosis. For example, in the problem of localization of the primary tumor the final diagnosis can always be obtained with an operation where the location of the primary tumor is verifed, although this *examination* is avoided and replaced with other laboratory tests unless it is really necessary to obtain the verified diagnosis. In the problem of predicting the recurrence of the breast cancer after the removal of the breast with an operation, the final verification of the prediction is impossible until five years after the operation. And in urology, in the problem of diagnosing the type of incontinence, in practice the final diagnosis is never obtained as there is no practical way to verify the diagnosis.

Medical diagnosis is known to be subjective, and depends not only on the available data but also on the experience of the physician, his or her intuition and biases, and even on the psycho-physiological condition of the physician. Several studies have shown that the diagnosis of a patient can differ significantly if the patient is examined by different physicians or even by the same physician at different times (different day of the week or different hour of the day).

Machine learning can be used to automatically derive diagnostic rules from the descriptions of the patients treated in the past for which the final diagnoses were verified. Automatically derived diagnostic knowledge may assist physicians to make the diagnostic process more objective and more reliable.

16.3 DIAGNOSTIC PERFORMANCE OF PHYSICIANS VS. MACHINE LEARNING

Typically, automatically generated diagnostic rules slightly outperform the diagnostic accuracy of physicians specialists when physicians have available exactly the same information as the machine. Table 16.1 provides a comparison of the performance of two machine learning algorithms, the naive Bayesian classifier and Assistant (Cestnik *et al.*, 1987), with the average perfomance of four physicians specialists in each of four different medical diagnostic problems. The problems include: the localization of the primary tumor, the prediction of the recurrence of the breast cancer, the diagnostics of thyroid diseases, and rheumatology. The data used in our experiments was collected at the University Medical Center in Ljubljana. The following are brief descriptions of the diagnostic problems.

- **Localization of primary tumor:** the medical treatment of patients with metastases is much more successful if the location of the primary tumor in the body of the patient is known. The diagnostic task is to determine one of 22 possible locations of the primary tumor on the basis of age, sex, histological type of carcinoma, the degree of differentiation and 13 possible locations of discovered metastases. From the Institute of Oncology in Ljubljana,

Table 16.1   The comparison of performance of different classifiers in four medical domains

classifier	primary tumor		breast cancer		thyroid		rheumatology	
naive Bayes	49%	1.60bit	78%	0.08bit	70%	0.79bit	67%	0.52bit
Assistant	44%	1.38bit	77%	0.07bit	73%	0.87bit	61%	0.46bit
physicians	42%	1.22bit	64%	0.05bit	64%	0.59bit	56%	0.26bit

the data for 339 patients with known location of the primary tumor was provided which was used in our experiments.

- **Prediction of recurrence of breast cancer:** among patients with removed breast cancer the disease recurs in five years after the operation in about 20% of cases. For better treatment it is necessary to predict the possibility of the recurrence on the basis of age, size and location of the tumor and the data about lymphatic nodes. The problem is rather difficult for physician specialists, as due to long time observations (five years), little practical experience can be obtained. From the Institute of Oncology in Ljubljana, the data for 288 patients with known recurrence of the breast cancer five years after the operation was used in our experiments.

- **Thyroid diseases:** the diagnostic problem is to determine one of four possible diagnoses from age, sex, histological data, and results of laboratory tests. However, in everyday practice physicians use much more additional information for diagnostics, which was not available for computer processing. From the Clinic for Nuclear Medicine in the University Medical Center in Ljubljana, the data for 884 patients with known final diagnoses was obtained and used in our experiments.

- **Rheumatology:** the diagnostic problem is to select one of six groups of possible diagnoses from anamnestic data and status data. There are over 200 diagnoses used by physician specialists in rheumatology. However, general practitioners have to decide among rheumatological and orthopedical diseases for patients to be further investigated and treated by specialists. Such decisions are unreliable and, in the opinion of the physician specialist in rheumatology, in more than 30% of cases wrong. From the Clinic for Rheumatology in the University Medical Center in Ljubljana, the data for 355 patients with known final diagnoses was provided for our experiments. All diagnoses were verified with additional observations, laboratory tests, and X-ray.

The characteristics of the data sets used in our experiments are summarized in Table 16.2. (PRIM, BREA and RHEU, respectively). Entropy together with the number of classes (diagnoses) shows the difficulty of the diagnostic problem. The number of attributes approximately tells us how well the patients are described. The majority class percentage approximates the prior probability of the most probable diagnosis. This is in fact the classification accuracy of the *default* classifier which, regardless of the patient, always selects the same most probable diagnosis.

In our experiments one run was performed by randomly selecting 70% of instances for learning and 30% for testing. The results in Table 16.1 are averages of 10 runs. The average accuracy is given along with the average *information score per answer* (Kononenko and Bratko, 1991). Information score is a performance measure that eliminates the influence of prior probabilities of classes and can be applied to various kinds of incomplete and proba-

Table 16.2 Basic description of medical data sets

domain	#class	#atts.	#val/att.	# instances	maj.class (%)	entropy(bit)
THYR	4	15	9.1	884	56	1.59
PRIM	22	17	2.2	339	25	3.89
BREA	2	10	2.7	288	80	0.73
LYMP	4	18	3.3	148	55	1.28
RHEU	6	32	9.1	355	66	1.73
BONE	2	19	4.5	270	65	0.93
HEPA	2	19	3.8	155	79	0.74
DIAB	2	8	8.8	768	65	0.93
HEART	2	13	5.0	270	56	0.99

bilistic answers. For completeness, its definition is provided in the Appendix. This measure is necessary as in each domain the default classifier would achieve high classification accuracy.

Four physician specialists in each domain were tested to estimate their diagnostic accuracy. From a set of training data a subset of patients was randomly selected and their description printed on paper without the diagnosis. The physicians were asked to select the most probable diagnosis for each patient. The performances of physicians in Table 16.1 are the averages of four physician specialists in each domain. The physicians were tested in the University Medical Center in Ljubljana. While in breast cancer and rheumatology, diagnosing a patient on paper is somewhat unnatural, for the other two domains it often occurs in practice.

Both algorithms significantly outperform the diagnostic performance of the physicians in terms of the classification accuracy and the average information score of the classifier. However, these results need a qualification. It should be emphasized that in these experiments both the physicians and the computer had exactly the same information available. This is often unrealistic in medical practice. During the examination of the patient the physician often observes the patient's condition in terms of intuitive impressions which cannot be formally described and therefore cannot be typed into the computer. The lack of such information may in some cases be of crucial importance for the (in)ability to obtain more reliable diagnosis. The accuracy results in Table 16.1 should therefore be understood as an estimate of how well the algorithms perform, and not necessarily how badly the physicians diagnose. Although machine learning may induce more reliable diagnostic algorithms from the limited description of the patient, such diagnostic tools definitely cannot, and also are not intended to, replace the physicians, but should rather be considered as helpful tools that can improve the physicians' performance. The results in this chapter and from other experiments convincingly demonstrate that the physicians' diagnostic accuracy should be possible to improve with the aid of machine learning.

16.4 SELECTING THE APPROPRIATE ML SYSTEM

In this section we give a description of specific requirements that any machine learning system has to satisfy in order to be used in the developement of applications in medical diagnosis. Several learning algorithms are then briefly described. We compare the performance of all the algorithms on several medical diagnostic and prognostic problems, and their appropriateness for applications in medical diagnosis is discussed.

16.4.1   Specific Requirements for ML Systems

For ML system to be useful in solving medical diagnostic tasks the following features are desired: good perfomance, the ability to appropriately deal with missing data and with noisy data (errors in data), the transparency of diagnostic knowledge, the ability to explain decisions, and the ability of the algorithm to reduce the number of tests necessary to obtain a reliable diagnosis.

In this section we first discuss these requirements. Then we present a comparison study of seven representative ML algorithms to illustrate more concretely the points made.

- **Good performance:** the algorithm has to be able to extract significant information from the available data. The diagnostic accuracy on new cases has to be as high as possible. Typically, most of the algorithms perform at least as well as the physicians, and often the classification accuracy of machine classifiers is better than that of physicians when using the same description of the patients. Therefore, if there is a possibility to measure the accuracy of physicians, their perfomance can be used as a lower bound on the required accuracy of the ML system in the given problem.

  In the majority of learning problems, various approaches typically achieve similar performance in terms of classification accuracy, although in some cases some algorithms may perform significantly better than the others (Michie *et al.*, 1994). Therefore, *a priori* almost none of the algorithms can be excluded with respect to the performance criterion. Rather, several learning approaches should be tested on the available data, and one or few with the best estimated performance should be considered for the developement of the application.
- **Dealing with missing data:** in medical diagnosis very often the description of patients lacks certain data. ML algorithms have to be able to deal appropriately with such incomplete descriptions of patients.
- **Dealing with noisy data:** medical data typically suffers from uncertainty and errors. Therefore machine learning algorithms, appropriate for medical applications, have to have an effective means for handling noisy data.
- **Transparency of diagnostic knowledge:** the generated knowledge and the explanation of decisions should be transparent to the physician. He or she should be able to analyse and understand the knowledge generated. Ideally, the automatically generated knowledge would provide the physicans with a novel point of view on the given problem, and may reveal new interrelations and regularities that the physician did not see before in an explicit form.
- **Explanation ability:** the system must be able to explain decisions when diagnosing new patients. When faced with the curious solution of the new problem the physician will require further explanation, otherwise he or she will not seriously consider the system's suggestions. The only possibility that physicians would accept a *black box* classifier is in the situation where such a classifier would outperform by a very large margin all other classifiers, including the physicians themselves, in terms of classification accuracy. However, such a situation is highly improbable, and the authors of this chapter are not aware of any such example.
- **Reduction of the number of tests:** in medical practice the collection of patients' data is

often expensive, time consuming, and harmful for the patients. Therefore, it is desirable to have a classifier that is able to reliably diagnose with a small amount of data about the patients. This can be verified by providing all candidate algorithms with the limited amount of data. However, the process of determining the right subset of data may be time consuming, as it is essentially a combinatorial problem. Some of the ML systems are themselves able to select the appropriate subset of attributes, i.e. the selection is done during the learning process and may be more appropriate than others that lack this facility.

16.4.2 Description of the Tested Algorithms

In this subsection we briefly describe seven algorithms that were used in our experiments: Assistant-R, Assistant-I, LFC, the naive and the semi-naive Bayesian classifier, backpropagation with weight elimination, and the k-nearest neighbors algorithm.

- **Assistant-R:** is a reimplementation of the Assistant learning system for top down induction of decision trees (Cestnik et al., 1987). The basic algorithm goes back to CLS (Concept Learning System) developed by Hunt et al.(1966) and was reimplemented and improved by several authors (see Quinlan (1986) for an overview). The main features of Assistant are binarization of attributes, decision tree prepruning and postpruning, incomplete data handling, and the use of the naive Bayesian classifier to calculate the classification in *null leaves*.

  The main difference between Assistant and its reimplementation, Assistant-R, is that ReliefF is used for attribute selection (Kononenko, 1994). ReliefF is an extended version of Relief, developed by Kira and Rendell (1992), which is a non-myopic heuristic measure that is able to estimate the quality of attributes even if there are strong conditional dependencies between attributes. For example, Relief can efficiently estimate the quality of attributes in parity problems. In addition, wherever appropriate, instead of the relative frequency, Assistant-R uses the m-estimate of probabilities, which was shown to often improve the performance of machine learning algorithms (Cestnik,1990).

- **Assistant-I:** a variant of Assistant-R that instead of ReliefF uses information gain for the selection criterion, as does original Assistant. However, the other differences to Assistant remain (m-estimate of probabilities).

- **LFC:** Ragavan et al.(1993; Ragavan and Rendell, 1993) use limited lookahead in their LFC (Lookahead Feature Construction) algorithm for top down induction of decision trees to detect significant conditional dependencies between attributes for constructive induction. They show interesting results on some data sets. Robnik (1993) developed a reimplementation of their algorithm which was then used in our experiments. LFC generates binary decision trees. At each node, the algorithm constructs new binary attributes from the original attributes, using logical operators (conjunction, disjunction, and negation). From the constructed binary attributes, the best attribute is selected and the process is recursively repeated on two subsets of training instances, corresponding to two values of the selected attribute. For constructive induction a limited lookahead is used. The space of possible useful constructs is restricted, due to the geometrical representation of the conditional entropy which is the estimator of the attributes' quality. To further reduce the search space, the algorithm also limits the breadth and the depth of search.

  As LFC uses lookahead it is less myopic than the greedy algorithm of Assistant. The comparison of experimental results of LFC and Assistant-R contrasts the performance of the greedy search in combination with ReliefF versus the lookahead strategy. To make results comparable to Assistant-R we equipped LFC with the same pruning and probability estimation facilities. All tests were performed with a default set of parameters (depth of the lookahead 3, beam size 20), although in some domains better results may be obtained by parameter tuning. However, higher values of the parameters may combinatorially increase the search space of LFC, which makes the algorithm impractical.

- **Naive Bayesian Classifier:** a classifier that uses the naive Bayesian formula to calculate the probability of each class C given the values V_i of all the attributes for an instance to be classified, assuming the conditional independence of the attributes given the class:

$$P(C|V_1..V_n) = P(C) \prod_i \frac{P(C|V_i)}{P(C)}$$

A new instance is classified into the class with maximal calculated probability. We used the m-estimate of probabilities (Cestnik, 1990). For prior probabilities the Laplace's law of succession was used:

$$P(C) = \frac{N(C)+1}{N + \#\_of\_classes}$$

where N is the number of all examples and $N(C)$ is the number of examples of class C. These prior probabilities are then used in the m-estimate of conditional probabilities:

$$P(C|V_i) = \frac{N(C\&V_i) + m \times P(C)}{N(V_i) + m}$$

The parameter m trades off between the contributions of the relative frequency and the prior probability. In our experiments, the parameter m was set to 2.0 (this setting is usually used as default and, empirically, gives satisfactory results (Cestnik, 1990)).

The relative performance of the naive Bayesian classifier can serve as an estimate of the conditional independence of attributes.

- **Semi-naive Bayesian Classifier:** Kononenko (1991) developed an extension of the naive Bayesian classifier that explicitly searches for dependencies between the values of different attributes. If such dependency is discovered between two values V_i and V_j of two different attributes, then they are not considered as conditionally independent. Accordingly, the term

$$\frac{P(C|V_i)}{P(C)} \times \frac{P(C|V_j)}{P(C)}$$

in the naive Bayesian formula is replaced with

$$\frac{P(C|V_i,V_j)}{P(C)}$$

For such replacement a reliable approximation of the conditional probability $P(C|V_i,V_j)$ is required. Therefore, the algorithm trades off between the non-naivety and the reliability of approximations of probabilities.

- **Backpropagation with weight elimination:** the multilayered feedforward artificial neural network is a hierarchical network consisting of two or more fully interconected layers of processing units – neurons. The task of the learning algorithm is to determine the appropriate weights on the interconnections between neurons. Backpropagation of error in multilayered feedforward neural networks (Rumelhart and McClelland, 1986) is a well known learning algorithm, and also the most popular among algorithms for training artificial neural networks. Well known problems with backpropagation are the selection of the appropriate topology of the network and overfitting the training data. An extension of the basic algorithm that uses the weight elimination technique (Weigand *et al.*, 1990) addresses both problems. The idea is to start with too many hidden neurons and to introduce into the criterion function a term that penalizes large weights on the connections between neurons. With such a criterion function the algorithm, during training, eliminates an appropriate number of weights and neurons in order to obtain the appropriate generalization on the training data.
- *k*-**NN:** the *k*-nearest neighbor algorithm. For a given new instance the algorithm searches for *k* nearest training instances and classifies the instance into the most frequent class of these *k* instances. The results presented in the next section were obtained with Manhattan-distance. The results using Euclidian distance are practically the same. The best results with respect to parameter *k* are presented, although for fair comparison such parameter tuning should be allowed only on the training and not the testing sets of data.

16.4.3   Comparing the Performance of Algorithms on Medical Problems

We compared the performance of the algorithms on several medical data sets:

- Data sets obtained from the University Medical Center in Ljubljana, Slovenia: the problem of locating the primary tumour in patients with metastases (PRIM), the problem of predicting the recurrence of breast cancer five years after the removal of the tumour (BREA), the problem of determining the type of the cancer in lymphography (LYMP), diagnosis in rheumatology (RHEU), and the problem of prediction of the femoral neck fracture recovery (BONE).
- HEPA: prognosis of survival for patients suffering from hepatitis. The data was provided by Gail Gong from Carnegie-Mellon University.
- Data sets obtained from the StatLog database (Michie *et al.*,1994): diagnosis of diabetes (DIAB) and diagnosis of heart diseases (HEART).

The basic characteristics of the above medical data sets are given in Table 16.2. The results of experiments on these data sets are in Tables 16.3 and 16.4. The results are averages and standard deviations over 10 runs for each domain. In each run, the dataset was randomly partitioned into 70% of data for learning, and 30% for testing.

16.4.4   Appropriateness for Medical Diagnosis

In this section we discuss how various algorithms fit the requirements described in Section 16.1. Table 16.5 summarizes the comparison of algorithms with respect to the appropriateness for developing applications in medical diagnostic and prognostic problems.

Table 16.3   Classification accuracy of learning systems on medical data sets

domain	LFC	Assist.-I	Assist.-R	naive Bayes	semi-naive	backprop.	k-NN
PRIM	37.1±4.9	40.8±5.1	38.9±4.7	49.2±3.9	48.2±4.3	43.4±4.4	42.1±5.0
BREA	76.1±4.3	76.8±4.6	78.5±3.9	77.3±4.2	78.9±3.6	76.4±4.1	79.5±2.7
LYMP	82.4±5.2	77.0±5.5	77.0±5.9	84.2±2.7	84.5±2.5	82.5±4.5	82.6±5.7
RHEU	60.6±4.7	64.8±4.0	63.8±4.9	67.1±4.7	68.0±3.6	68.7±4.1	66.0±3.6
BONE	69.4±4.6	72.1±4.1	70.8±6.2	69.7±5.7	70.6±4.5	71.1±4.1	69.0±4.0
HEPA	79.0±5.3	77.2±5.3	82.3±5.4	85.3±3.9	86.4±2.9	80.2±3.6	82.6±4.9
DIAB	69.2±3.0	71.1±2.8	71.5±2.6	77.0±1.8	77.1±2.0	72.2±2.2	73.9±2.5
HEART	77.3±5.2	75.4±4.0	77.6±4.5	84.5±3.1	84.5±3.6	80.4±2.9	82.9±3.7

Table 16.4   Average information score of learning systems on medical data sets

domain	LFC	Assist.-I	Assist.-R	naive Bayes	semi-naive	backprop.	k-NN
PRIM	1.02±.14	1.19±.11	1.07±.11	1.61±.14	1.52±.15	1.41±.15	1.15±.11
BREA	0.01±.09	0.02±.08	0.05±.06	0.06±.06	0.07±.04	0.07±.07	0.02±.02
LYMP	0.79±.10	0.62±.09	0.61±.09	0.78±.08	0.77±.08	0.77±.10	0.53±.08
RHEU	0.41±.10	0.43±.08	0.41±.08	0.53±.06	0.54±.08	0.58±.08	0.43±.05
BONE	0.41±.09	0.23±.08	0.25±.06	0.29±.07	0.36±.06	0.35±.06	0.40±.07
HEPA	0.19±.14	0.13±.09	0.22±.11	0.35±.10	0.40±.10	0.25±.07	0.21±.05
DIAB	0.26±.06	0.26±.04	0.27±.04	0.38±.03	0.38±.03	0.34±.05	0.24±.02
HEART	0.52±.10	0.45±.07	0.46±.07	0.64±.05	0.64±.06	0.58±.06	0.46±.04

Among the algorithms compared, only decision tree builders are able to select the appropriate subset of attributes. With respect to the criterion of reduction of the number of tests, these algorithms have a clear advantage over other algorithms.

With respect to the performance criterion, the algorithms are more similar. The best performance was achieved by naive and semi-naive Bayesian classifiers. In medical data sets, attributes are typically relatively conditionally independent given the class. Physicians try to define conditionally independent attributes. Humans tend to think linearly, and independent attributes make the diagnostic process easier. Therefore, it is not surprising that the Bayesian classifiers show clear advantage on medical data sets. It is interesting that the performance of the k-NN algorithm is also good in these domains.

The information score (Table 16.4) for the BREA data set indicates that no learning algorithm was able to solve this problem. This suggests that the attributes are not relevant. That conclusion was also confirmed by physician specialists. The prediction of the recurrence of breast cancer five years after the operation is currently an unsolved medical problem.

Both versions of Assistant have similar performance, except in the HEPA domain, where Assistant-R has significantly better performance (99.95% confidence level using two tailed t-test). A detailed analysis showed that in this problem, ReliefF discovered a significant conditional interdependency between two attributes given the class. These two attributes score poorly when considered independently. That is why Assistant-I was not able to discover this regularity in data. On the other hand, other (redundant) attributes are available in this domain that contain similar information as these two attributes together. This is the reason why the naive Bayesian classifier performs better. We tried to provide the naive Bayesian classifier with an additional attribute by joining the two conditionally dependent attributes. However, the performance remained the same.

For the DIAB data set, Ragavan and Rendell (1993) report 78.8% classification accuracy with their LFC algorithm. They also report poor performance of several other algorithms without constructive induction (up to 58%). However, our results (see below) and results of the StatLog project (Michie *et al.*,1994) show that the poor results of the other algorithms in this domain are not due to the lack of constructive induction. In our experiments on the DIAB dataset, all classifiers perform equally well, with the exception of the Bayesian classifiers which are significantly better. LFC achieved significantly better results than the other two inductive algorithms in the LYMP domain, where constructive induction seems to be useful. However, LFC performed significantly worse in the RHEU domain, while in the other domains the three inductive algorithms perform equally well.

With respect to the transparency and the explanation ability criteria, there are great differences between the algorithms:

- **k-nearest neighbours:** as k-NN does no generalization, the transparency of knowledge representation is poor. However, to explain the decision of the algorithm, a predefined number (k) of nearest neighbours from the training set is shown. This approach is analogous to the approach used by domain experts, who make decisions on the basis of previously known similar cases. Such an explanation ability is estimated by physicians as acceptable.
- **Naive and semi-naive Bayes:** here, knowledge representation consists of a table of conditional probabilities which seems to be of interest to physicians. Therefore such knowledge representation is estimated as good. On the other hand, the decisions of Bayesian classi-

Table 16.5   The appropriateness of various algorithms for medical diagnosis

classifier	perfor- mance	trans- parency	explanations	reduction	miss. data handling
Assistant-R	good	very good	good	good	acceptable
Assistant-I	good	very good	good	good	acceptable
LFC	good	good	good	good	acceptable
naive Bayes	very good	good	very good	no	very good
semi-naive Bayes	very good	good	very good	no	very good
backpropagation	very good	poor	poor	no	acceptable
k-NN	very good	poor	acceptable	no	acceptable

fiers can be naturally interpreted as the sum of information gains (Kononenko, 1993). The amount of information necessary to find out that an instance belongs to class C is given by:

$$-\log_2 P(C|V_1,...,V_n) = -\log_2 P(C) - \sum_i (-\log_2 P(C) + \log_2 P(C|V_i))$$

Therefore, the decisions of the Bayesian classifiers can be explained with the sum of information gains from all attributes in favor or against the given class. In the case of the semi-naive Bayesian classifier, the process is exactly the same, except when the tuples of joined attribute/value pairs occur. In this case, instead of simple attribute values, the joined values are used.

Such information gains can be listed in a table to sum up the evidence for/against the decision. Table 16.6 provides a typical explanation of one decision. Each attribute has an associated strength, which is interpreted as the amount of information in bits provided by that attribute. It can be in favor or against the classifier's decision. One of the main advantages of such explanation is that it uses all the available attributes. Such explanation was found by physicians to be very good, and they feel that Bayesian classifiers solve the task in a similar way to which they diagnose. Namely, they also sum up the evidence for/against a given diagnosis.

- **Backpropagation neural networks** have non-transparent knowledge representation and in general cannot easily explain their decisions. This is due to the large number of real-valued weights which all influence the result. In some cases it is possible to extract symbolic rules from the trained neural network. However, the rules tend to be large and relatively complex. Craven and Shavlik (1993) compare rules extracted from a neural network with rules produced by Quinlan's (1993) C4.5 system. The rules for a *NetTalk* data set extracted from a neural network have on average over 30 antecedents per rule compared to two antecedens for C4.5. Such rules are too complicated and hardly offer a useful explanation to a non-technically oriented domain expert.
- **Decision trees (Assistant-I and Assistant-R):** can be used without the computer and are fairly easy to understand. Positions of attributes in the tree, especially the top ones, often directly correspond to the domain expert's knowledge. However, to produce general rules, these methods use pruning which drastically reduces the tree sizes. Correspondingly, the paths from the root to the leaves are shorter, contaning only a few, although the most informative, attributes. In many cases the physicians feel that such a tree too poorly describes

Table 16.6 Semi-naive Bayes: an explanation of a decision in the femoral neck fracture recovery problem. Decision = No complications (correct)

Attribute value	For decision (bit)	Against decision (bit)
Age = 70 - 80	0.07	
Sex = Female		-0.19
Mobility before injury = Fully mobile	0.04	
State of health before injury = Other	0.52	
Mechanism of injury = Simple fall		-0.08
Additional injuries = None	0.00	
Time between injury and operation > 10 days	0.42	
Fracture classification acc. to Garden = Garden III		-0.30
Fracture classification acc. to Pauwels = Pauwels III		-0.14
Transfusion = Yes	0.07	
Antibiotic profilaxis = Yes		-0.32
Hospital rehabilitation = Yes	0.05	
General complications = None		-0.00
Combination: Time between injury and examination < 6 hours AND Hospitalization time between 4 and 5 weeks	0.21	
Combination: Therapy = Artroplastic AND Anticoagulant therapy = Yes	0.63	

the diagnoses, and is therefore not sufficiently informative (Pirnat *et al.*, 1989). In several promlems the physicians have preferred the decision trees generated by Assistant-R. It seems that the estimates of ReliefF correspond to the way in which the physicians estimate the importance of attributes. In fact, the structure of trees generated by Assistant-I are often considered by physicians as strange and unnatural.

- **Lookahead feature construction (LFC)** also generates decision trees. However, in each node a potentially complex logical expression is used instead of a simple attribute value. The generated trees can therefore be smaller. The expressions may represent valid concepts from the domain. However, on the lower levels of the tree the expressions are often very specific and typically meaningless. Due to complex logical expressions in nodes, the number of attributes used to classify an instance can be higher than in usual decision trees.

16.5 ACCEPTANCE IN PRACTICE

Although the results of applying various machine learning algorithms in medical diagnosis seem excellent, this technology has not been widely accepted in medical practice. Reasons usually given by physicians themselves are diverse:

- Inflexibility of the knowledge representation. The set of attributes that describe the patients must be fixed. The information that is used by the rules to derive the final diagnosis is limited to strictly defined parameters while subjective, informal, and fuzzy notions (like intuition, impression, etc.) cannot be represented in a formal and symbolic way.

- Physicians often claim that if they are not sure about the final diagnosis, usually further examinations (e.g. laboratory tests) may be performed to verify the diagnosis. In situations where further examinations are easy, the physicians do not feel the need for assistance in diagnostic process. In prognosis there is no possibility for further examination that would confirm the prediction. For that reason the prognostic problems are even more attractive for machine learning than diagnostic problems (Zwitter *et al.*, 1983).

- Physicians often claim that they are too busy to use any additional tool for decision making. In everyday practice it is too time and/or energy consuming to type in the data into the computer in order to use the computer support in the diagnostic process.

- Non-negligible is also the subjective resistance of physicians to new diagnostic technology. It is often felt that the diagnosis problem, considered as perhaps the most critical and sensitive task, will be left to machines, thereby leaving the physicians without power to control and without responsibility.

- We have also rather frequently encountered quite irrational reasons for resisting computer diagnosis. These have actually been described by some physicians as follows. Diagnosis is regarded by some physicians as the premium intellectual task of their profession. As such, this task requires in-depth knowledge, unexpected ideas, and in particular, intuition. Therefore diagnosis is a bit of an art that is impossible to explain and formalise. How can it then be done by computers? And if computers could do it, that would destroy all the magic and professional pride.

In the past we developed several applications in medical diagnostic problems using decision tree technology (Kononenko *et al.*, 1984; Roškar *et al.*, 1986; Hojker *et al.*, 1988). Besides the above-mentioned problems, decision trees suffer also from the following defficiencies:

- Learning and classification is sensitive to missing data (Quinlan, 1989), which is often the case in medical data.

- The generated decision rules typically include too few attributes (Pirnat *et al.*, 1989). The explanation of decisions is therefore poor and does not support typically exact decisions of generated diagnostic rules.

To solve those two problems and to increase the reliability and transparency of automatically generated classifiers, a multistrategy approach is becoming important (Michalski and Tecuci, 1994). One idea is to develop several classifiers using different approaches and then use *all* the classifiers on new problems by combining their decisions. This approach is analogous to decision making in hospitals, where the decisions for harder cases are left to be solved by the group of physicians rather than by one physician alone. We used this idea in the prediction of the femoral neck fracture recovery problem (Kukar *et al.*, 1996). In this study the results of different classifiers were combined (using the naive Bayesian formula) to make the final decision which can be explained as a weighted sum of single decisions. Physicians indeed felt that with a multistrategy approach, the reliability and the comprehensibility of the system was much better than when using decision trees only.

One of our goals is also to make machine learning systems easier to use by non-ML experts. This includes making the tools more intuitive and equipped with functional and visually attractive user interfaces. Since for many algorithms there is a need to set certain numeric parameters in order to achieve best performance, a method for automatic parameter setting would be highly desirable. To make the preparation of data easier for users, the ML systems should be able to interface to industry-standard databases (such as dBase).

16.6 CONCLUSION

Our experiments show that in medical domains various classifiers perform roughly the same. So the important factor when choosing which classifier to apply is its explanation ability. Our experiments show that the physicians prefer explanations as provided by the Bayesian classifiers and decision tree classifiers: Assistant-R and LFC. However, instead of selecting a single best classifier, it seems that the best solution is to use all of them and combine their decision when solving new problems. The physicians found combination of classifiers to be the appropriate way of improving the reliability and comprehensibility of diagnostic systems.

Regarding the future role of machine learning in medical diagnosis, our views are as follows:

- Machine learning technology has not been accepted in the practice of medical diagnosis to an extent that the clearly demonstrated technical possibilities indicate. However, it is hard to expect that this disproportion between the technical possibilities and practical exploitation will remain for very much longer.
- Among the reasons for this slow acceptance, perhaps the most reasonable one is that introduction of machine learning technology will further increase the abundance of tools and instrumentation available to physicians. Any new tool thus has an undesirable side effect of further increasing the complexity of the physician's work, which is already sufficiently complicated. Therefore machine learning technology will have to be integrated into the existing instrumentation that makes its use as simple and natural as possible.
- Machine learning-based diagnostic programs will be used as any other instrument available to physicians: as just another source of possibly useful information that helps to improve diagnostic accuracy. The final responsibility and judgement whether to accept or reject this information will, as usual, remain with the physician.

ACKNOWLEDGEMENTS

Collecting and assembling the experimental data would not be possible without the invaluable help of physician specialists Dr. Matjaž Zwitter, Dr. Sergej Hojker, Dr. Tomaž Silvester, and Dr. Vlado Pirnat from the University Medical Center in Ljubljana. We thank them for providing and interpreting the data, for testing the diagnostic performance of physician specialists from the University Medical Center, for the interpretation of results, and for the estimation of the explanation abilities of different classifiers. This research was supported by the Slovenian Ministry of Science and Technology.

APPENDIX: INFORMATION SCORE

Besides the classification accuracy, in our experiments we measured also the average information score (Kononenko and Bratko, 1991). This measure eliminates the influence of prior probabilities and appropriately treats probabilistic answers of the classifier. The average information score is defined as:

$$Inf = \frac{\sum_{i=1}^{\#testing\ instances} Inf_i}{\#testing\ instances}$$

where the information score of the classification of i-th testing instance is defined by:

$$Inf_i = \begin{cases} -\log_2 P(C_i) + \log_2 P'(C_i), & P'(C_i) \geq P(C_i) \\ -\left(-\log_2(1 - P(C_i)) + \log_2(1 - P'(C_i))\right), & P'(C_i) < P(C_i) \end{cases}$$

C_i is the class of the i-th testing instance, $P(C)$ is the prior probability of class C and $P'(C)$ the probability returned by a classifier. If the returned probability of the correct class is greater than the prior probability the information score is positive, as the obtained information is correct. It can be interpreted as the prior information necessary for correct classification minus the posterior information necessary for correct classification. If the returned probability of the correct class is lower than the prior probability the information score is negative, as the information obtained is wrong. It can be interpreted as the prior information necessary for incorrect classification minus the posterior information necessary for incorrect classification.

The main difference between the classification accuracy and the information score can be illustrated with the following example. Let the prior distribution of classes be $P(C_1) = 0.2$ and $P(C_2) = 0.8$ and let the posterior distribution returned by the classifier be $P(C_1) = 0.4$ and $P(C_2) = 0.6$. If the correct class is C_1 then the information score is positive, while the classification accuracy treats the given posterior distribution as a wrong answer. If the correct class is C_2 then the information score is negative, while the classification accuracy treats the given posterior distribution as a correct answer.

Classification accuracy may in some special cases exhibit high variance while information score is much more stable. In a very special case where we have a data set with irrelevant attributes and exactly 50% of instances from one class and 50% of instances from the other class, the leave-one-out testing for a probabilistic classifier would give the approximate accuracy of 50%, while for the *default* classifier, that classifies every instance into the majority class, the accuracy would be 0%. A slight modification of the distribution of training instances would drastically change the latter accuracy to approximately 50%. A more drastic modification of the distribution, say 80% of cases for one class and 20% for the other, would increase the accuracy of the *default* classifier to 80%, while the accuracy of the probabilistic classifier would be approximately $0.8 \times 0.8 + 0.2 \times 0.2 = 68\%$. However, for both classifiers the information score would in all scenarios remain approximately 0 bits, which would correctly indicate that both classifiers are unable to extract any useful information from the attributes.

REFERENCES

Baim P.W., A Method for Attribute Selection in Inductive Learning Systems, *IEEE Trans. on PAMI*, Vol. 10, No. 6, 1988, pp. 888-896.

Bratko I., Kononenko I., Learning Rules from Incomplete and Noisy Data, in B. Phelps (ed.), *Interactions in Artificial Intelligence and Statistical Methods*, Hampshire: Technical Press, 1987.

Bratko I., Mozetič I., Lavrač N., *KARDIO: A Study in Deep and Qualitative Knowledge for Expert Systems*, Cambridge, MA: MIT Press, 1989.

Bratko I., Mulec P., An Experiment in Automatic Learning of Diagnostic Rules, *Informatica*, Ljubljana, Vol. 4, No. 4, 1980, pp. 18-25.

Catlett J., On changing continuous attributes into ordered discrete attributes, *Proc. European Working Session on Learning-91*, Porto, March 4-6 1991, pp. 164-178.

Cestnik B., Estimating Probabilities: A Crucial Task in Machine Learning, *Proc. European Conf. on Artificial Intelligence*, Stockholm, August, 1990, pp. 147-149.

Cestnik B., Kononenko I. and Bratko I., ASSISTANT 86: A knowledge elicitation tool for sophisticated users, in: I. Bratko, N. Lavrac (eds.): *Progress in Machine learning*, Wilmslow: Sigma Press, 1987.

Chan K.C.C., Wong A.K.C., Automatic Construction of Expert Systems from Data: A Statistical Approach, *Proc. IJCAI Workshop on Knowledge Discovery in Databases*, Detroit, Michigan, August, 1989, pp. 37-48.

Clark P., Boswell R., Rule Induction with CN2: Some Recent Improvements, *Proc. European Working Session on Learning-91*, Porto, Portugal, March, 1991, pp. 151-163.

Craven M.W., Shavlik J.W., Learning symbolic rules using artificial neural networks, *Proc. 10th Intern. Conf. on Machine Learning*, Amherst, MA, Morgan Kaufmann, 1993, pp. 73-80.

Elomaa T., Holsti N., An Experimental Comparison of Inducing Decision Trees and Decision Lists in Noisy Domains, *Proc. 4th European Working Session on Learning*, Montpeiller, Dec. 4-6 1989, pp. 59-69.

Hojker S., Kononenko I., Jauk A., Fidler V., Porenta M., Expert System's Development in the Management of Thyroid Diseases, *Proc. European Congress for Nuclear Medicine*, Milano, Sept., 1988.

Horn K.A., Compton P., Lazarus L., Quinlan J.R., An Expert System for the Interpretation of Thyroid Assays in a Clinical Laboratory, *The Australian Computer Journal*, Vol. 17, No.

1, 1985, pp. 7-11.

Hunt E., Martin J., Stone P., *Experiments in Induction*, New York, Academic Press, 1966.

Karalič A., Pirnat V., Significance Level Based Classification with Multiple Trees, *Informatica*, Ljubljana, Vol. 15, No. 1, 1991, pp. 54-58.

Kern J., Deželič G., Težak-Benčič M., Durrigl T., Medical Decision Making Using Inductive Learning Program (in Croatian), *Proc 1st Congress on Yugoslav Medical Informatics*, Beograd, Dec. 6-8 1990, pp. 221-228.

Kira K., Rendell L., A practical approach to feature selection, *Proc. Intern. Conf. on Machine Learning*, (Aberdeen, July 1992), D. Sleeman, P. Edwards (eds.) Morgan Kaufmann, 1992a, pp. 249-256.

Kira K., Rendell L., The feature selection problem: traditional methods and new algorithm. *Proc. AAAI'92*, San Jose, CA, July 1992b.

Kononenko I., Semi-naive Bayesian classifier, *Proc. European Working Session on Learning-91*, Y. Kodratoff (ed.), Springer-Verlag, Porto, March 4-6 1991, pp. 206-219.

Kononenko I., Inductive and Bayesian learning in medical diagnosis. *Applied Artificial Intelligence*, Vol. 7, pp. 317-337, 1993.

Kononenko I., Estimating attributes: Analysis and extensions of Relief. *Proc. European Conf. on Machine Learning* (Catania, April 1994), L. De Raedt, F.Bergadano (eds.), Springer Verlag, 1994, pp. 171-182.

Kononenko I., Bratko I., Information based evaluation criterion for classifier's performance, *Machine Learning*, Vol. 6, No. 1, 1991, pp. 67-80.

Kononenko I., Bratko I., Roškar E., Experiments in automatic learning of medical diagnostic rules, *International School for the Synthesis of Expert's Knowledge Workshop*, Bled, Slovenia, August 1984.

Kononenko I., Jauk A., Janc T., Induction of reliable decision rules, *International School for the Synthesis of Expert's Knowledge Workshop*, Udine, Italy, 10-13 Sept. 1988.

Kukar M., Kononenko I., Silvester T., Machine learning in prognosis of the femoral neck fracture recovery, *Artificial Intelligence in Medicine*, Vol. 8, 1996, pp. 431-451.

Lesmo L., Saitta L., Torasso P., Learning of Fuzzy Production Rules for Medical Diagnoses, In Gupta M.M., Sanchez E.(eds.) *Approximate Reasoning in Decision Analysis*, North-Holland, 1982.

Michalski R., Tecuci G., *Machine Learning: A Multistrategy Approach*, Vol. 4, Morgan Kaufmann, 1994.

Michie D., Spiegelhalter D.J., Taylor C.C (eds.) *Machine Learning, Neural and Statistical Classification*, Ellis Horwood, 1994.

Muggleton S., *Inductive Acquisition of Expert Knowledge*, Turing Institute Press and Addison-Wesley, 1990.

Nuñez M., Decision Tree Induction Using Domain Knowledge, In Wielinga B. et al. (eds.), *Current Trends in Knowledge Acquisition*, IOS Press, 1990.

Pirnat V., Kononenko I., Janc T., Bratko I., Medical Estimation of Automatically Induced Decision Rules, *Proc. of 2nd Europ. Conf. on Artificial Intelligence in Medicine*, City University, London, August 29-31 1989, pp. 24-36.

Quinlan J.R., Induction of Decision Trees. *Machine Learning*. Vol. 1, No. 1, 1986, pp. 81-106.

Quinlan J.R., Unknown attribute values in induction, *Proc. 6th Int. Workshop on Machine Learning*, Cornell University, Ithaca, June 26-27 1989, pp. 164-168.

Quinlan J.R., *C4.5: Programs for Machine Learning*, San Mateo, CA, Morgan Kaufmann, 1993.

Quinlan R., Compton P., Horn K.A., Lazarus L., Inductive knowledge acquisition: A case study, in J.R. Quinlan (ed.), *Applications of Expert Systems*, Turing Institute Press and Addison Wesley, 1987. (Also: *Proc. 2nd Australian Conf. on Applications of Expert Systems*, Sydney, May 14-16 1986.)

Ragavan H., Rendell L., Lookahead feature construction for learning hard concepts. *Proc. 10th Intern. Conf. on Machine Learning*. (Amherst, MA, June 1993), Morgan Kaufmann, pp. 252-259.

Ragavan H., Rendell L., Shaw M., Tessmer A., Learning complex real-world concepts through feature construction. *Technical Report UIUC-BI-AI-93-03*. The Beckman Institute, University of Illinois, 1993.

Robnik M., Constructive induction with decision trees. *B.Sc. Thesis*, University of Ljubljana, Faculty of Electrical Eng. and Computer Science, Ljubljana, Slovenia (In Slovene), 1993.

Roškar E., Abrams P., Bratko I., Kononenko I., Varšek A., MCUDS – An expert system for the diagnostics of lower urinary tract disorders, *Journal of Biomedical Measurements, Infor-*

matics and Control, Vol. 1, No. 4, 1986, pp. 201-204.

Rumelhart D.E., McClelland J.L. (eds.), *Parallel Distributed Processing, Vol. 1: Foundations*. MIT Press, 1986.

Weigand S., Huberman A., Rumelhart D.E., Predicting the future: a connectionist approach, *International Journal of Neural Systems*, Vol. 1, No. 3, 1990.

Zwitter M., Bratko I., Kononenko I., Rational and irrational reservations against the use of computer in medical diagnosis and prognosis, *Proc. 3rd Mediterranean Conf. on Medical and Biological Engineering*, Portorož, Slovenia, Sept. 5-9 1983.

17

Learning to Classify Biomedical Signals

Miroslav Kubat, Irena Koprinska and Gert Pfurtscheller

ABSTRACT

Medical doctors analyze biological signals such as EEG, ECG, heart rate, or respiration, with the objective of detecting patterns indicating specific pathophysiological states. The costs of this analysis, as expressed in terms of the time and effort of a highly qualified professional, motivate attempts to partially automate the process. This chapter focuses on two domains where a learning system has been employed to induce, from examples, the knowledge necessary for pattern recognition purposes. The complicated nature of these domains makes it difficult to use symbolic machine-learning techniques such as rules or decision trees. Likewise, the use of neural networks poses serious problems pertaining to the idiosyncracies of the backpropagation algorithm. However, it has turned out that initializing neural networks by way of decision trees side-steps most of the caveats, and facilitates significantly better performance in terms of the classification accuracy on testing examples.

17.1 INTRODUCTION

From the machine-learning perspective, this chapter is concerned with *concept learning*. The system is expected to induce internal representations (*models*) of two or more concepts so as to facilitate *classification:* when a new, nonclassified, example is presented to the computer, the machine checks its properties against the models stored in the memory and labels the example with the concept name of the closest model.

In symbolic machine learning, recognition of a concept is often accompanied by an explanation that is indispensable in applications where the decision is followed by irreversible consequences like those in medical surgery. In these domains the model is best expressed in

Machine Learning and Data Mining: Methods and Applications
Edited by R.S. Michalski, I Bratko and M. Kubat
© 1997 John Wiley & Sons Ltd

symbolic terms that are easy to interpret such as rules or decision trees. In contrast, many other applications emphasize the recognition in its own right, without the need for explanations. A system evaluating postal codes should maximize the number of correctly identified digits and the operator will not insist on knowing the reasons for the classifications of the thousands of instances. This is also the case of the two research projects reported here. In the classification of sleep stages and in the prediction of brain-issued motor commands, the system is expected to carry out numerous identifications based on variables that cannot be straightforwardly interpreted.

A brief characterization of both domains is presented in the next section. Then, the specific learning techniques are studied. Section 17.3 describes the tree-based neural networks (TBNN) and Section 17.4 describes the tree-based radial-basis-function networks (TB-RBF). Section 17.5 reports experimental results documenting the strengths of these learners in the given domains and Section 17.6 summarizes the contribution as viewed from both of the involved perspectives: initialization of neural networks and the classification of medical data.

17.2   TWO MEDICAL DOMAINS

To give the reader an idea of the background of our research, we briefly characterize the two medical domains, where the machine-learning techniques proved useful.

17.2.1   Sleep Classification

In human sleep, medical experts distinguish three or four basic stages plus the stage when the subject dreams. This last stage is accompanied by rapid eye movements below the eye-lids, and is therefore called the REM-stage. Disturbances in the distribution of these stages during the night can indicate a sleep disorder such as insomnia or sleep apnea in adult sleepers and the risk of sudden infant death syndrome (SIDS) in infants. To detect such disturbances, the expert analyzes a *hypnogram*—a graph where the horizontal axis represents time and the vertical axis visualizes the different sleep stages. A simplified idealized example is shown in Figure 17.1.

To draw a hypnogram, the expert uses an 8-hours' night recording of electroencephalogram (EEG), electrooculogram (EOG), and electromyogram (EMG) that monitor brain activities (EEG), eye movements (EOG), and muscle contractions (EMG). Each individual stage manifests itself in characteristic patterns of these signals. The fact that drawing the hypnogram for one-night sleep of a single sleeper requires several hours of concentrated effort of a highly qualified specialist (who is expensive and sometimes even unavailable) makes the idea of automating the process by a computer program attractive. This is the task of the first case study reported in this chapter: to develop a classifier that will be able to indentify the individual sleep stages based on the above signals, and that will be able to do so with accuracy comparable to that of human experts.

To develop and test the system, eight different data files have been used, each representing 8-hours' recording on one subject. The sleepers are 6-months-old children that are, for the needs of scientific publication, given the names BR, KR, RA, KL, BU, PR, GO, and FR. The data files contain 780–960 examples, each example being described by 15 numeric attributes.

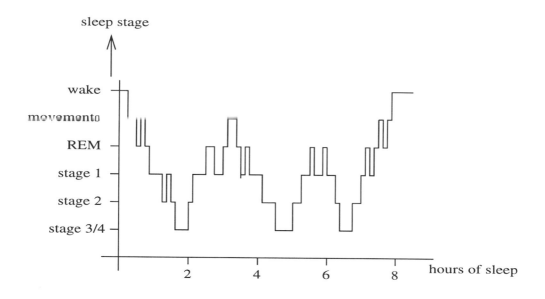

Figure 17.1 Idealized hypnogram. In adult sleepers, the stage 3/4 splits into two different stages. In small children, another state, 'movements,' is also considered.

The examples are classified by an expert into seven sleep stages (these include, apart from three non-REM stages and REM stage, also 'movements,' 'awake state' and 'artifact').

Importantly, the learning program will see different attributes than the medical expert. The reason for this arrangement is that human experts perform their classifications based on specific shapes of the signals. These shapes, albeit being easy to detect for a trained professional, are difficult to formalize for the needs of computer implementation. The attributes describing the examples for the needs of machine learning include respiratory variability from nasal and thoracic signals, 1–4 Hz power from EEG, EOG, heart rate and its variability, actogram (microvibration) of the left and right hands, EMG, and Hjorth parameters (activity, mobility, and complexity) of EEG signals from two different electrodes. Hence, 15 numeric attributes describe a single measurement—one sample taken every 30 seconds throughout the whole-night sleep. For learning, these 15-dimensional vectors are classified by an expert that has access also to the aforementioned more sophisticated features not included in the vectors. The expert classified the examples using the rules of Guilleminault and Souquet (1979).

Several aspects of the data complicate learning. First, the expert's sleep classifications can be inconsistent because the sleep stages are not accurately defined. Moreover, the attributes are noisy in the sense that on some occasions (3 − 5%) they acquire arbitrary values. Another complication is a strong covariance among the attributes. Finally, previous studies have shown that the attributes do not have equal importance and that some of them will probably be redundant or completely irrelevant (in this particular study, though, we assume that the relevances are not *a priori* known).

Early experiments revealed that learning from examples obtained from one subject, and then applying the induced knowledge to classify another subject is not viable because the requisite medical signals are strongly sleeper dependent (Kubat, Pfurtscheller, and Flotzinger, 1994). Therefore, a weaker objective was defined: the expert classifies a subset of examples obtained from a single sleeper. The system learns from them and, later, classifies all the remaining data of the same sleeper automatically. Even this weaker scenario provides significant savings in the expensive human expertise.

17.2.2   Recognition of Motor Commands from EEG Signals

An ambitious project being currently pursued at the University of Technology in Graz aims at establishing the grounds that will permit the development of a direct Brain-Computer Interface. The idea is to provide a new communication channel for patients with severe amyothropic lateral sclerosis or those suffering from the so-called *locked-in syndrome*. These patients are totally paralyzed and, having lost the command of motor functions, they cannot even move their pupils. However, the fact that their brains function and that cerebral activity is accompanied by specific electrical signals motivate the surmise that some clearly defined mental states can perhaps be detected in the EEG signals and that these states could be used for trivial communication.

Although one cannot expect a machine to read thoughts, simple commands such as 'move the right hand' or 'move the left hand' are known to manifest themselves by significant desynchronisation of EEG as measured in the area over the sensorimotor cortex. This phenomenon has been extensively studied by one of the authors (for a review and pointers to literature see Pfurtscheller, Flotzinger, and Neuper, 1994). Since the desynchronisation is present even in the brain of paralyzed subjects (the command leaves the brain but fails to reach muscles), a study of the relation between specific EEG patterns and particular motor commands in healthy subjects (that are more easily available for experimentation) can provide crucial hints for subsequent patient-oriented research. Early experiments in this direction strongly support this hypothesis (Pfurtscheller, Flotzinger, and Kalcher, 1992)

The procedure to obtain the learning and testing examples is organized as follows. The subject is seated in a comfortable chair in a dark room (to minimize the activity of unrelated cortical areas) and is instructed to carry out, in a random order, the following motor commands: 'move the right hand,' 'move the left hand,' 'move a foot,' and 'move the tongue.' The scenario is depicted in Figure 17.2. Upon being alerted with the warning signal (WS), the subject receives a cue (CUE) telling him or her which movement should be carried out. The subject makes the movement shortly after the response stimulus (RS).

A cap placed tightly on the subject's head holds several electrodes recording EEG signals that are then band-pass filtered and subjected to some additional data processing techniques irrelevant from the perspective of machine learning. A detailed discussion of the data acquisition and preprocessing would exceed the needs and scope of this chapter but, in principle, each movement (classified as belonging to one of four classes) is described by a vector characterizing the power of EEG prior to the movement. The electrodes are arranged on the cap in accordance with international standards (Figure 17.3). From the total of 56 electrodes, only 11 have been selected by a neurophysiologist as potentially relevant for our study.

The task of the machine-learning program is to induce models of the four classes and use them for the classification of future measurements. Should this recognition turn out to be viable, then a good basis for future work in the field of brain-computer interface has been

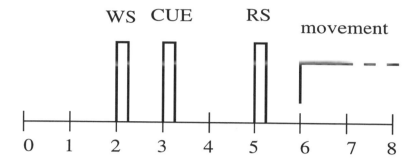

Figure 17.2 Experimental paradigm.

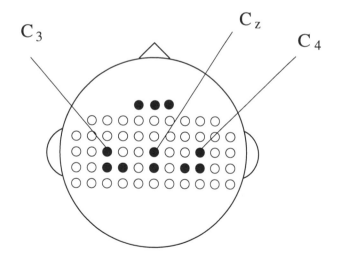

Figure 17.3 Electrode locations (C3, Cz, C4 according to the international 10-20 system). The 11 black electrode positions were selected for classification.

established. For instance, such concepts as 'move right' or 'move left' can be employed to control the movement of a cursor on a computer monitor. The cursor's pointing to letters on the screen can spell out the patient's wishes.

The data available to the learning program are far from perfect because the signals are strongly affected not only by the given concept, but also by the different degree of attention of the subjects, by the instability of their 'mental setting,' by changes in vigilance, by artifacts during recording, by not using the optimal frequency band, and by many other factors. Considering the large number of attributes in the measurement vectors, the learning examples are sparse and, moreover, lack any guarantee of representativeness. Further on, some of the attributes are probably irrelevant for classification, whereas some important attributes might have been ignored because they were unknown to the experimenters. The attributes are strongly intercorrelated, which further complicates the learning task.

17.3 DECISION-TREE BASED INITIALIZATION OF NEURAL NETWORKS

The quantity that perhaps most determines the success or failure of a concept-learning program in real-world applications is the richness of the representation language and its appropriateness to the given problem. For illustration, consider two popular representations commonly used in concept learning: neural networks and decision trees.

The representation language of *neural networks* is rich because of the large number of free parameters (usually weights). Theoreticians have proved theorems stating that a neural network can represent *any* mapping from an m-dimensional space to a unit hypercube, $f : R^m \rightarrow [0,1]^n$ (Cybenko, 1989). However, whether this mapping can be discovered by a learning algorithm is another question. Neural networks can be trained to model complicated decision surfaces, but they also suffer from countless pitfalls such as local minima, saddle points, and the danger of overtraining. Further on, if the learning program is to have a chance to converge on a hypothesis that will provide high classification performance on independent testing examples, then really *many* training examples must be provided.

Decision trees, too, are universal approximators—they can carry out any mapping defined by the training set, provided that this set does not contain contradictions. Moreover, they do not require as many examples as the neural networks. On the other hand, the fact that decision trees typically delineate the concept by a set of axis-parallel hyperplanes will in realistic problems constrain the classification accuracy on independent testing sets. For instance, 2-dimensional concepts can only be approximated by a disjunction of appropriately sized rectangles, and such models can turn out to be too coarse if the tree is small. Large trees, though, can easily overfit the training set, which means poor generalization to examples that have not been seen during learning.

These considerations motivate the idea to combine the two approaches into a single system: a decision-tree generator approximates the concept, and this approximation is then further tuned by neural-network training. Neural-network training starts from a point that is already very close to the global minimum, well beyond a majority of local minima and saddle points. This substantially reduces the number of examples required for successful learning in neural networks while offering a representation language with higher capabilities than that provided by decision trees.

The objective of this section is to present one possible implementation of this idea in multilayer neural networks. The next section will then show how to use decision trees to initialize another popular connectionist formalism, the radial-basis-function networks.

17.3.1   General Idea of TBNN

A simple algorithm to map decision trees to neural networks was proposed by Sethi (1990) and, since then, several alternative solutions have appeared in the literature—see Brent (1991), Park (1994), Ivanova and Kubat (1995), and Sahami (1995). Most of these algorithms build on the fact that a decision tree actually represents a set of d logically disjoint rules, where d is the number of different class labels.

Figure 17.4 describes, and Figure 17.5 illustrates, a simple mechanism to map disjunctive normal forms to neural networks with two hidden layers. The OR-layer contains one neuron per concept and the number of neurons in the AND-layer is equal to the number of leaves in the decision tree. The task of the first hidden layer, located between the input and the AND-layer, is to carry out the tests suggested by the decision-tree generator. The reader will easily check that the example described by $at1 = 0.8 \wedge at2 = 0.4 \wedge at3 = 0.9$ will activate the output neuron that shares the label with the rightmost leaf of the decision tree. All other output neurons will be off. Note that, for this particular example, the value of $at2$ does not affect the class label assigned by the tree or the network.

The mapping of the tree to a neural net merely turns one representation mechanism into another. The point is that the neural-network scheme possesses many more degrees of freedom than the original decision tree, and the newly emerged parameters can be used to 'fine-tune' the concept model. To fully exploit the richness of the connectionist paradigm, the system TBNN (Tree-Based Neural Net, Ivanova and Kubat, 1995) extends the representational flexibility by the following three steps. (1) Initialization of the weights and full interconnection of adjacent layers to ensure that the network labels the examples with the same concepts as the original decision tree. To this end, formulae for the initial weight setting are needed. (2) Softening the rigid attribute-value tests. And, (3) tuning the synaptic weights by means of the backpropagation algorithm.

The individual steps are detailed in the upcoming subsections. Figure 17.6 illustrates a few conventions that will be used in the sequel. Weights along links leading to the i-th hidden unit are denoted by $w_{i\alpha}$; weights along links leading to the i-th output unit are denoted by $w_{i\beta}$.

---

1. Induce a decision tree with some tree induction algorithm;
2. Turn the tree into a multilayer perceptron where the output layer performs the disjunctions, the second hidden layer carries out the conjunctions, and the first hidden layer determines which of the attribute-intervals is satisfied;
3. Soften the boundaries of the intervals and tune the network by means of the backpropagation algorithm.

Figure 17.4   The algorithm of the system TBNN.

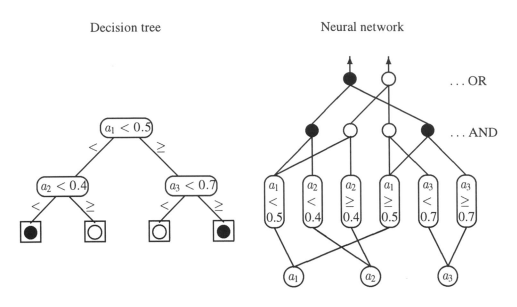

Figure 17.5   Translation of a decision tree into a neural net.

Lowercase n will denote the number of positive weights and lowercase m will denote the number of negative weights. Note that $w_{i\alpha}$ and $w_{i\beta}$ denote absolute values. The thresholds of the neurons are denoted by $t_{i\alpha}$ and $t_{i\beta}$, respectively. An important part will be played by the *activation constant A* that is defined as a threshold above which the neuron is assumed to be in the active state. A neuron is active (has output $> A$) if the sum of its inputs exceeds some

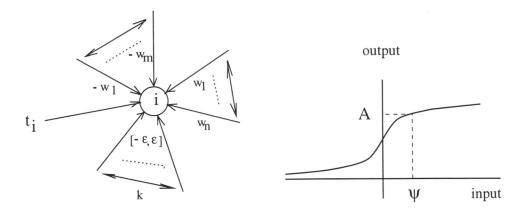

Figure 17.6   Input links of a neuron and definition of the activation constant A.

critical value ψ. Solving the equation $A = 1/(1+\exp(-h\psi))$ for ψ will establish that for the neuron to be active, the sum of its inputs must be $\psi > \frac{1}{h} \ln \frac{A}{1-A}$.

17.3.2 Initialization of the Weights and Full Interconnection of Adjacent Layers

In virtue of the logic encoded in the decision tree, the OR-layer has only positive inputs. Suppose that, after the tree-to-net mapping, k additional links with small random weights from the interval $[-\epsilon; \epsilon]$ have been added to a neuron to make it fully interconnected with the previous layer. Two conditions must be satisfied if the OR-layer is to model the original disjunction of leaves.

First, the i-th OR-neuron must become *active* under the same conditions for which the original tree yields the respective classification. This means that its input, decreased by the threshold $t_{i\beta}$, should be larger than ψ if at least one of the AND-neurons along the regular links is active (feeding the OR-neuron with input $(1 \cdot A \cdot w_{i\beta})$, even if all other regular links provide zero input $((n - 1) \cdot 0 \cdot w_{i\beta})$ and if the additional links provide maximally negative inputs $(-k \cdot \epsilon)$.

Second, the i-th OR-neuron must be *inactive* under the same conditions for which the original tree yields the respective classification. This means that its input, decreased by the threshold $t_{i\beta}$, should be smaller than $-\psi$ if all AND-neurons along the regular links output the maximum value for which they are still considered inactive $(n \cdot (1 - A) \cdot w_{i\beta})$, even if the additional links provide maximally positive inputs $(k \cdot \epsilon)$.

It can be shown (Ivanova and Kubat, 1995) that these requirements are satisfied when the weights and thresholds are set to the following values:

$$w_{i\beta} \leq \frac{2(\psi + k\epsilon)}{A(n + 1) - n} \tag{17.1}$$

$$t_{i\beta} \leq (\psi + k\epsilon)\frac{n - A(n - 1)}{A(n + 1) - n} \tag{17.2}$$

under the assumption that A has been chosen so that $A(n + 1) - n > 0$.

Similar considerations apply also for the AND-neurons which can have $m \geq 0$ negative weights. The following three conditions must be satisfied if the AND-layer is to model the original conjunction of intervals in the presence of additional links.

First, the i-th AND-neuron must be *active* when the example is propagated down the respective branch in the tree. This means that its input, decreased by the threshold $t_{i\alpha}$, should be larger than ψ if all previous neurons along the positive regular links output the minimum value for which they are considered active $(n \cdot A \cdot w_{i\alpha})$, even if all previous neurons along the negative regular links output the maximum value for which they are still considered inactive $(m \cdot (1 - A)(-w_{i\alpha}))$ and even if all additional links provide maximally negative inputs $(-k \cdot \epsilon)$.

Second, the i-th AND-neuron must become *inactive* if at least one positive regular input is inactive $(1 \cdot (1 - A) \cdot w_{i\alpha})$, even if all other positive regular inputs have maximum values $((n - 1) \cdot 1 \cdot w_{i\alpha})$, and even if all negative regular inputs are zero $(m \cdot 0 \cdot (-w_{i\alpha}))$ and the additional links provide maximally positive inputs $(k \cdot \epsilon)$.

Third, the i-th AND-neuron must be *inactive* if at least one negative regular input provides the minimum value for which it is considered as active $(1 \cdot A \cdot (-w_{i\alpha}))$, even if all positive regular inputs are maximally active $(n \cdot 1 \cdot w_{i\alpha})$, even if all other negative regular inputs are zero $((m-1) \cdot 0 \cdot (-w_{i\alpha}))$ and even if the additional links provide maximally positive inputs $(k \cdot \epsilon)$.

These requirements are satisfied when the weights and thresholds are set to the following values:

$$w_{i\alpha} \leq \frac{2(\psi + k\epsilon)}{A(n+m+1) - (n+m)} \tag{17.3}$$

$$t_{i\alpha} \leq (\psi + k\epsilon) \frac{A(n+m-1) + (n-m)}{A(n+m+1) - (n+m)} \tag{17.4}$$

The denominators are positive if $A(n+m+1) - (n+m) > 0$. The current implementation of TBNN uses the same A for all neurons and the constant is set to the minimum value that satisfies the inequality at each neuron.

17.3.3   Softening the Intervals and Neural-Network Tuning

Each branch of a decision tree defines a rule that divides the entire universe into two parts: one in which the rule is true and one in which the rule is false. The rule is mapped to an AND-neuron by the principle depicted in Figure 17.7. Note how the tests in a single branch partition the domain of an attribute to two or three intervals. For instance, if the tests on attribute a_1 in a branch are $a_1 \geq 0.4$, and $a_1 < 0.7$, then an example arrives at the leaf assigned to this branch if $a_1 \in [0.4, 0.7)$. If the values of a_1 are all from $[0,1]$, then the tests in the branch define the following intervals in the domain of a_1: $[0,0.4),[0.4,0.7)$ and $[0.7,1]$.

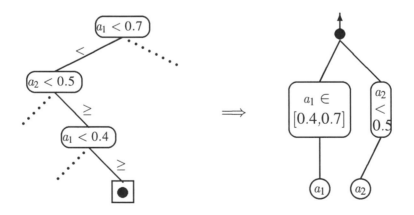

$$\{a_1 \in [0.4,0.7)) \wedge (a_2 \in [0.5,1]\} \rightarrow \quad \bullet$$

Figure 17.7   Decision-tree branch described in logic and turned into an AND-neuron. The ranges of a_1 and a_2 are $[0,1]$.

Previous work in decision-tree based initialization of neural nets has shown that improvement in the network's classification performance can be achieved if the crisp tests on attribute
values are softened. Put another way, values close to interval boundaries should somehow be
considered as belonging to both of the neigboring intervals.

If the example is described by the vector $\mathbf{a} = \{a_1, \ldots, a_n\}$, then the softening is accomplished by replacing each attribute a_i with its soft value $y_i = 1/(1 + e^{v_i})$ where v_i is the
closeness to the center of the respective interval, calculated as:

$$v_i = \frac{R_i - 2 \, |\mu_i - a_i|}{2 R_i} \tag{17.5}$$

where μ_i is the mean value of the interval, R_i is the size of the interval, and a_i is the actual
value of the given attribute.

For further tuning of the concept model, TBNN applies the *backpropagation algorithm*
with momentum function as suggested by Rumelhart, Hinton, and Williams (1986). After
the example presentation, the weights are updated according to the usual formula $w_{t+1} =
w_t + \eta \cdot \Delta \cdot o + \alpha(w_t - w_{t-1})$, where w_t is the weight at time t, Δ is the backpropagated error,
o is the previous neuron's output, η is the learning rate, and α is the momentum constant.

To prevent the network's *overtraining*, the backpropagation part of TBNN employs the
following mechanism: the training examples are divided into two subsets: two thirds of the
examples are used for training and one third of the examples are used for on-line testing of the
model's current version. The latter subset is called 'training test set'. After each pass through
the training examples (i.e. after each *epoch*), the system tests the performance on the training
test set. The training stops when the classification accuracy on the training test set declines,
even if the mean square error on the training set still improves.

In all experiments, the following parameter settings were used: learning rate $\eta = 0.2$,
momentum constant $\alpha = 0.5$.

17.4   TREE-BASED INITIALIZATION OF RBF NETWORKS

Another representation formalism that can benefit from being initialized by a decision tree is
the Radial-Basis-Function (RBF) network. The next section explains the general strategy of
learning in RBF and then suggests a modification that follows a similar line of thought as in
the previous system.

17.4.1   RBF Networks and their Parameters

The rationale behind the idea of *basis functions* is anchored in the mathematical finding that
numeric vectors are more likely to be linearly separable if they are *nonlinearly mapped* to a
space with *higher dimensionality* (Cover, 1965). Even though certain theoretical and practical
considerations indicate that the concrete selection of the nonlinear function to carry out this
mapping is not critical for the resulting performance (Powell, 1988), a common practice is to
use gaussian bell functions, defined for our needs as follows.

Suppose that p examples, described by vectors $\mathbf{x_i} = [x_{i1}, \ldots, x_{in}]^T$, are available for
learning and that functions $\varphi_j : R^n \longrightarrow R^m$ are defined as follows:

$$\varphi_j(\mathbf{x_i}) = \frac{1}{(2\pi)^{n/2}\,|\Sigma_j|^{(1/2)}}\exp\{-\frac{1}{2}(\mathbf{x_i}-\boldsymbol{\mu}_j)^T\Sigma_j^{-1}(\mathbf{x_i}-\boldsymbol{\mu}_j)\} \qquad (17.6)$$

where Σ_j^{-1} is the inverse of the covariance matrix of the input vectors and $|\Sigma_j|$ is the determinant of this matrix. Equation 17.6 describes an n-dimensional gaussian surface characterized by the covariance matrix Σ and the center $\boldsymbol{\mu}_j = [\mu_{j1}, \ldots \mu_{jn}]^T$. The larger the distance between $\mathbf{x_i}$ and $\boldsymbol{\mu}_j$, the smaller the value of $\varphi_j(\mathbf{x_i})$. Each function $\varphi_j(\mathbf{x_i})$ outputs a scalar value and the i-th example is thus redescribed by the vector $\varphi(\mathbf{x_i}) = [\varphi_1(\mathbf{x_i}), \ldots, \varphi_m(\mathbf{x_i})]$.

Figure 17.8 shows how to implement this mapping in the hidden layer of a neural network (radial-basis functions were first cast in the neural network setting by Broomhead and Lowe, 1988). The transfer functions of the neurons in this layer are defined by Equation 17.6, whereas the output neurons have linear transfer functions. Only the output layer of weights are trained. The extra input, permanently set to $\varphi_0 = 1$, provides offsets for the linear functions at the output layer. Park and Sandberg (1991) proved the universality of RBF networks: given sufficient number of hidden-layer neurons with properly defined gaussian centers and covariance matrices, the network can approximate any continuous function with arbitrary accuracy. We will use RBF for the concept recognition task that can be conceived as a special case of function approximation: each output neuron stands for one concept and the example is labeled with the l-th concept if the l-th output neuron has the highest output.

A RBF network is defined by its topology and by a set of trainable parameters. The system TB-RBF addresses both of these issues. Trainable *parameters* of an RBF network are: the gaussian centers, covariance matrices, and the weights w_{ij}. The weights can easily be trained

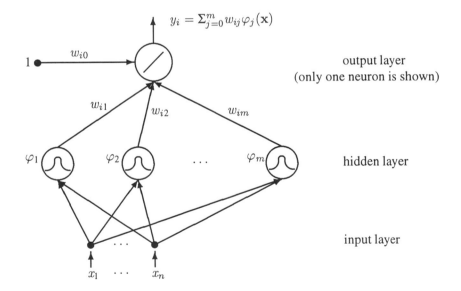

Figure 17.8   Radial-basis function network. Functions $\varphi_j(\mathbf{x_i})$ are defined by the centers and standard deviations. The transfer functions at the output-layer neurons are linear.

by the delta rule (Widrow and Hoff, 1960) and the covariance matrices can be computed directly from the input vectors or, to simplify the task, replaced by standard deviations.

Under *topology* we understand the number of hidden neurons and their interconnection with the other layers. In many realistic domains, only a subset of the attributes are relevant for each of the concepts. Sanger (1991) selects these attributes by a method implementing a tree-like structure of RBF units in multiple hidden layers. This approach leads to very large trees if the number of attributes is large. Andrew, Kubat, and Pfurtscheller (1995) describe a system that reduces the number of input-to-hidden connections by means of a hill-climbing search but this technique is computationally expensive.

As for the gaussian centers, Poggio and Girosi (1990) locate them at the coordinates of the input vectors, x_i, and conceive the task as a function interpolation problem. When the examples abound, the network becomes large and, therefore, Lowe (1989) uses a random subset of the examples. The idea to include in the network only the most relevant examples motivated Cheng and Lin (1994) to apply a search technique with operators 'add a neuron' and 'delete a neuron.' Likewise, Chen, Cowan, and Grant (1991) apply a single operator, 'add a neuron,' and use the orthogonal least square criterion to select the next candidate. Methods for adding one neuron at a time with subsequent *tuning* of the coordinates of the centers were presented by Wettschereck and Dietterich (1992) as well as by Fritzke (1994). Alternative attempts to reasonably reduce the number of hidden neurons capitalize on statistical clustering techniques (Musavi *et al.*, 1992) and place the gaussian centers at the centers of gravity of the clusters.

17.4.2   Decision Tree Based Parameter Setting

The system TB-RBF employs a decision-tree induction technique to optimize both the number of input-to-hidden-layer connections and the number of hidden neurons in a computationally effective way. The parameters of the gaussians are determined without the necessity to compute the inverse of the covariance matrix, Σ^{-1}.

The principle is illustrated in Figure 17.9. The decision tree, induced from the learning data by a standard decision-tree generator, partitions the entire two-dimensional space to four disjoint regions. The idea is to locate at the center of each of these regions one hidden unit. The fact that the regions defined by the decision tree are hyperrectangular with axis-parallel sides underlies the assumption of zero intercorrelations among attributes inside the individual regions. This makes it possible to replace the covariance matrix in Equation 17.6 with standard deviations that are then determined by means of a simple heuristic (for notational convenience, we will omit, in the next considerations, the index j and will write, for instance, φ instead of φ_j).

Suppose the input space has only one dimension ($n = 1$). It can be shown that if M_φ denotes the maximum of φ (in the gaussian center), then at distance $1.5\sigma^2$ from the center the value of φ drops to $\varphi = 0.3125M_\varphi$. Similarly, at distance σ^2 the value drops to $\varphi = 0.6250M_\varphi$. Let us now generalize this idea to $n > 1$ dimensions. Denote by L_k the length of the k-th side of the hyperrectangle and define $P_k = L_k/\sigma_k$. Then, Equation 17.6 can be reformulated as:

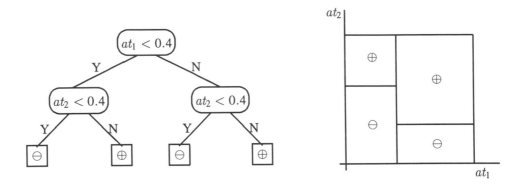

Figure 17.9   Hyperrectangular regions defined by a decision tree. Each branch of the tree, understood as as sequence of tests, defines one such region.

$$\varphi(\mathbf{x_i}) = \prod_{k=1}^{n} \frac{P_k}{L_k \sqrt{2\pi}} \exp\{-\frac{P_k^2 (x_{ik} - c_k)^2}{2L_k^2}\} \qquad (17.7)$$

The parameter P_k determines the value of φ at the hyperrectangle's boundary along a single dimension. In our experiments, we used a fixed value of P_k for all dimensions k. The algorithm of TB-RBF is summarized in Figure 17.10.

---

1. Induce a decision tree with some tree induction algorithm;
2. Turn the tree into a RBF network. Each hyperrectangle, defined by the tree, is represented by one hidden neuron with the transfer function given by Equation 17.7;
3. Train the output-layer weights by the delta rule on the same training examples.

Figure 17.10   The algorithm of the system TB-RBF.

17.5   EXPERIMENTS

The objective of the experiments is to investigate whether neural networks can really profit from being initialized by machine-learning techniques as described in the previous sections, and whether the resulting systems compare favorably with other learning techniques in terms of classification performance.

   As already mentioned, previous research in both of our domains indicated that it might be very difficult to induce classification rules that would generalize to subjects unseen during the learning session. For this reason, we adopted the following scenario: a subset of measurements taken on a subject are classified by an expert and supplied to the learning system. The induced classifier is then used to classify the sleep stages or motor commands only in this particular subject.

For the experimental assessment of the performance of the two learning systems, eight data files from the domain of sleep classification and three files from the domain of the brain-computer-interface project have been used. The data files differ in their sizes. The sleep-data files contain 770–960 examples, described by 15 attributes and classified into seven classes. The brain-data files contain 150–250 examples, described by 11 attributes (in the case of A4) or 44 attributes (in the case of B6 and B8) and classified into four classes.

The estimation of the classification accuracy on unseen data has been carried out by the *random subsampling* strategy as suggested, for instance, by Weiss and Kapouleas (1989). A set of examples is randomly split into two nonoverlapping subsets. One subset is used for learning and the other subset is used for testing. The experiments are repeated (in our case 10 times) for different splits and the results averaged. This procedure has been carried out for each data file and for each learning system, so that each entry in the tables reporting our results represents the average and standard deviation as calculated from 10 random runs. Each training set contained 60% of the examples of the given data file and the corresponding testing set contained the remaining 40% examples.

Table 17.1 Classification accuracy achieved by various learners on the sleep data

%	MNN	CN2	ID3	C4.5	LVQ	TBNN
BR	60.0 ± 2.8	72.8 ± 1.7	77.3 ± 3.0	78.1 ± 1.8	81.0 ± 1.5	85.5 ± 3.6
KR	39.7 ± 5.3	56.7 ± 2.6	64.0 ± 1.6	61.7 ± 3.8	66.5 ± 2.5	68.3 ± 4.9
RA	68.3 ± 11.0	75.6 ± 2.4	77.5 ± 1.5	76.8 ± 1.9	78.5 ± 2.5	80.8 ± 0.6
KL	72.6 ± 1.4	70.4 ± 3.3	77.3 ± 1.7	76.6 ± 2.1	78.1 ± 1.4	80.2 ± 1.7
BU	66.4 ± 2.1	63.4 ± 2.9	65.5 ± 4.6	69.7 ± 2.3	72.9 ± 1.5	73.1 ± 1.8
PR	62.8 ± 3.0	61.8 ± 1.7	63.9 ± 2.6	64.2 ± 2.4	65.9 ± 2.1	66.8 ± 2.0
GO	56.8 ± 3.8	54.7 ± 1.8	63.0 ± 2.2	61.1 ± 1.9	65.8 ± 2.4	66.3 ± 2.7
FR	73.4 ± 4.6	74.9 ± 2.0	75.5 ± 1.8	78.8 ± 2.8	79.9 ± 1.5	81.3 ± 1.8

Table 17.2 Classification accuracy achieved by various learners on the brain data

%	MNN	CN2	ID3	C4.5	LVQ	TBNN
A4	43.2 ± 6.3	41.0 ± 3.1	48.3 ± 3.4	46.9 ± 2.5	50.5 ± 3.3	55.1 ± 1.8
B6	43.0 ± 6.7	35.6 ± 16.9	46.2 ± 5.1	42.0 ± 6.5	48.0 ± 5.3	54.1 ± 3.3
B8	35.6 ± 5.9	35.1 ± 7.5	38.1 ± 5.8	31.0 ± 7.0	42.4 ± 5.2	49.2 ± 3.4

For the needs of comparison, Tables 17.1 and 17.2 summarize the classification performances of various learners on the sleep data and on the brain data, respectively. The column headed with MNN contains the results achieved by a multilayer neural network when initialized by small random weights as suggested by the inventors of the backpropagation algorithm, Rumelhart, Hinton, and Williams (1986). We experimented with various numbers of hidden neurons and the results in the tables are those that have been obtained from the architecture that provided the best classification accuracy. CN2 is a popular machine-learning program invented by Clark and Niblett (1989). Its output has the form of production rules. Two generators of decision trees have been run on the data: ID3 (Quinlan, 1986) and C4.5 (Quinlan, 1993). However, only ID3 was used for the initialization of the neural network in TBNN. The algorithm LVQ, developed by Kohonen (1990), optimizes the coordinates of a set of prototypes for each class and the prototypes are then used for classifications on the nearest-neighbor basis.

The somewhat disappointing results of the randomly initialized MNN can be explained by the fact that whereas MNNs with small numbers of hidden neurons are exposed to various risks (most importantly local minima), increased number of hidden neurons can eliminate this shortcoming but the price is the great number of free parameters and thus the need for prohibitively many training examples. LVQ, that only approximates the concept by piecewise linear boundaries, scores much better and a similar observation can be made in the decision trees.

In summary, if the MNN is initialized randomly, then the initial weights will very likely be much too distant from the solution to facilitate convergence. In contrast, initializing the weights by way of mapping from the decision tree will ensure that the backpropagation algorithm will start from a good initial position and will be able to reach a relatively accurate approximation of the concept even given the limited number of examples.

Table 17.3 Performance and characteristics of the RBF networks—sleep data

	C4.5r	TB-RBF	units	connections	trainable
BR	78.4 ± 1.7	81.4 ± 1.3	40.2 ± 2.9	106.8 ± 12.2	20.2 ± 2.1
KR	62.2 ± 2.3	66.0 ± 2.1	39.1 ± 3.4	88.4 ± 14.8	18.9 ± 2.8
RA	75.7 ± 3.0	80.1 ± 2.2	40.0 ± 2.8	94.7 ± 11.8	19.9 ± 2.0
KL	75.5 ± 2.6	78.8 ± 3.0	39.9 ± 3.3	89.7 ± 15.7	18.8 ± 2.6
BU	69.4 ± 1.8	73.7 ± 1.9	51.2 ± 3.1	157.7 ± 13.3	29.6 ± 3.0
PR	63.4 ± 2.7	70.7 ± 2.5	51.0 ± 3.1	154.4 ± 20.3	29.4 ± 3.3
GO	62.0 ± 1.7	68.8 ± 2.3	43.2 ± 2.5	116.9 ± 13.2	21.5 ± 2.4
FR	78.5 ± 2.0	82.8 ± 1.9	39.9 ± 1.7	96.9 ± 6.9	19.1 ± 1.3

Table 17.4 Performance and characteristics of the RBF networks—brain data

	C4.5r	TB-RBF	units	connections	trainable
A4	47.2 ± 4.0	57.6 ± 2.9	39.9 ± 1.7	54.5 ± 12.4	12.2 ± 3.3
B6	40.5 ± 5.3	49.6 ± 5.2	25.6 ± 2.9	96.9 ± 6.8	6.2 ± 2.1
B8	31.2 ± 6.6	47.5 ± 4.3	39.9 ± 1.7	96.6 ± 6.8	19.1 ± 1.3

Tables 17.3 and 17.4 summarize the results achieved in the two domains by TB-RBF. Preliminary experiments seemed to indicate that the decision trees generated by C4.5 might heavily overfit the training set. Hence, we decided to take advantage of the fact that C4.5 contains an option turning the decision tree to production rules that are further optimized. As

the rules turned out to be much more compact, we used them to initialize the network. The principle, though, remained the same: each rule defined a hyperrectangular region hosting one hidden neuron.

Careful comparison of the results with those in Tables 17.1 and 17.2 will reveal that both TBNN and TB-RBF outperform their opponents while the difference between the performance of TBNN and TB-RBF is statistically insignificant. TB-RBF is by far more economical of the two in terms of the involved parameters. This is due not only to the more compact representation of the radial-basis functions but also has to do with the way the system was implemented. The reader will recall that unlike TBNN, that generated fully interconnected networks, the system TB-RBF minimized the number of connections between the input and the hidden layers.

For this reason, Tables 17.3 and 17.4 also give the average number of units and the average number of neural links of the RBF network. The networks produced by TB-RBF are fairly efficient during the classification phase. Indeed, a fully connected RBF network would typically have—by the same number of hidden units and by the 15 attributes in the sleep domain—$40 \times 15 = 600$ connections, which is much more than in TB-RBF. In the brain domain, this phenomenon is even more pronounced: in the case of A4, the full interconnection will amount to about $40 \times 11 = 440$ connections as compared to the average 54 connections in TB-RBF; in the case of B8, this will even mean $40 \times 44 = 1760$ instead of about 100. Furthermore, by the essence of the radial-basis functions, the weights of all input-to-hidden links are set to 1. Only the hidden-to-output weights are actually trained, which makes the learning very fast (the number of trained parameters is provided in the rightmost column of the tables).

17.6 DISCUSSION

Researchers that sought experimental evidence of the superiority of their favored learning techniques usually observed that each learner was suited for a distinct task. Neural networks seem to outperform traditional rule-generating techniques in domains with complicated decision surfaces and with abundant training examples. Weiss and Kapouleas (1989) observed that symbolic methods offered better classifications than randomly initialized MNN trained with the backpropagation algorithm whenever the underlying concept could be described by a few simple rules. Similar observation is discussed at length by Wnek and Michalski (1994). However, when Fisher and McKusick (1989) and Fisher *et al.* (1989) experimented with more sophisticated concepts, they realized that MNN compared favorably with decision trees (especially in noisy domains) if provided with a sufficient number of training examples and if trained for a sufficient number of epochs.

Atlas *et al.* (1990) report that in three realistic domains MNN clearly outperformed decision trees. Experiments reported by Ivanova, Kubat, and Pfurtscheller (1994) suggest that for very complicated concepts, neural networks can become prohibitively sensitive to proper initialization of the topology and weights. Whereas the backpropagation algorithm tends to get trapped in local minima if initialized randomly, TBNN can outstrip decision trees when the training begins at an appropriate initial state.

Ivanova and Kubat (1995) distinguish two generic approaches to determine the topology of a neural network for a given task. *Search-based* strategies either grow networks by gradually adding one neuron at a time (Fahlman and Lebiere, 1990; Frean, 1990) or prune large networks by removing neurons or connections (Mozer and Smolensky, 1989; Le Cun, Denker, and Solla, 1990). In contrast, *informed* strategies initialize neural networks by way of knowledge expressed in terms of production rules (Towell, Shavlik, and Noordewier, 1990; Goodman *et al.*, 1992; Bala, Michalski, and Pachowicz, 1994) or decision trees (Sethi, 1990; Ivanova and Kubat, 1995; Sahami, 1995; Bioch, Carsouw, and Potharst, 1995).

This chapter reported a case study where a decision-tree generator was employed to initialize MNN and RBF networks. After much faster training, the networks compare favorably (in the given domains) with several alternative learners. Induction of decision trees can be used to determine the number of hidden neurons in MNN and to initialize the weights. In the case of RBF, the decision tree determined the number of radial-basis functions, their interconnection and parameters. The contribution of the tree-based initialization is twofold: increased classification accuracy on unseen examples and, in the case of RBF neworks, also a compact network. This second goal was not investigated in the case of TBNN because previous results reported by Ivanova and Kubat (1995) demonstrated the merit of making the MNN fully interconnected.

The two learning systems reported in this chapter can be used to assist specialists in the domain of sleep classification, which significantly reduces the costs of hypnogram drawing. The accuracy achieved by TBNN and TB-RBF in the sleep domain is not worse than that of human experts—Kemp *et al.* (1987) report that the agreement among six human classifiers does not exceed 75%, which is in accordance with our own experience. The learning systems reached about the same level of accuracy and this performance can be further improved by postprocessing techniques whose study, though, would exceed the scope of this paper. Human experts confirmed that the hypnograms produced by TBNN and RBF are fully usable.

The second domain, the brain-computer interface, can profit from having at hand a simple tool for the classification of EEG signals relevant to motor commands issued by the human brain. Here, the utility is obvious because the patterns of desynchronization of EEG are difficult to describe by rules, and learning appears to be the only way to accomplish the task.

ACKNOWLEDGEMENTS

The medical data used in this research belong to the Department of Medical Informatics, Technical University in Graz, Austria. The sleep classification data have been recorded and classified under a grant from 'Fonds zur Förderung der wissenschaftlichen Forschung,' project S49/03. The brain data have been recorded and classified under grants from 'Fonds zur Förderung der wissenschaftlichen Forschung,' projects P9043 and P11208 in Austria.

REFERENCES

L. Atlas, R. Cole, Y. Muthusamy, A. Lippman, J. Connor, D. Park, M. El-Sharkawi, and R.J. Marks (1990). A Performance Comparison of Trained Multilayer Perceptrons and Trained Classification Trees. *Proceedings of the IEEE*, 70, 1614–1619.

J.W. Bala, R.S. Michalski, and P.W. Pachowicz (1994). Progress on Vision through Learning at George Mason University. *Proceedings of ARPA Image Understadning Workshop* 191–207.

J.C. Bioch, R. Carsouw, and R. Potharst (1995). On the use of simple classifiers for the initialization of one-hidden-layer neural nets, *Proceedings of the IEEE International Conference on Neural Networks (ICNN95)*, Vol.4, 1739–1743.

R.P. Brent (1991). Fast Training Algorithms for Multilayer Neural Nets. *IEEE Transactions on Neural Networks* 2, 346–354.

S. Chen, C.F.N. Cowan, and P.M. Grant (1991). Orthogonal Least Squares Learning Algorithm for Radial Basis Function Networks. *IEEE Transactions on Neural Networks* 2, 302–309.

Y.-H. Cheng and C.-S. Lin (1994). A Learning Algorithm for Radial Basis Function Networks: with the Capability of Adding and Pruning Neurons. *Proceedings of the IEEE*, 797–801.

P. Clark and T. Niblett (1989), The CN2 Induction Learning. *Machine Learning*, 3, 261–283.

T.M. Cover (1965). Geometrical and Statistical Properties of Systems of Linear Inequalities with Applications in Pattern Recognition. *IEEE Transactions on Electronic Computers*. EC-14, 326–334.

G. Cybenko (1989). Approximation by Superposition of Sigmoidal Function. *Mathematics of Control, Signals, and Systems*, 2, 303–314.

S.E. Fahlman and C. Lebiere (1989). Cascade-Correlation Learning Architecture. In D.S. Touretzky (ed.) *Advances in Neural Information Procession Systems* Vol.2, Morgan Kaufmann 524–532.

D.H. Fisher and K.B. McKusick (1989). En Empirical Comparison of ID3 and Back-propagation. *Proceedings of the 11th International Joint Conference on AI, IJCAI'89*, Detroit, MI, 788–793.

D.H. Fisher, K.B. McKusick, R. Mooney, J.W. Shavlik, and G. Towell (1989). Processing Issues in Comparisons of Symbolic and Connectionist Learning Systems. *Proceedings of the 6th International Machine-Learning Workshop*, Ithaca, NY, 169–173.

M. Frean (1990). The Upstart Algorithm: A Method for Constructing and Training Feedforward Neural Networks. *Neural Computation*, 2, 198–209.

B. Fritzke (1994). Fast Learning with Incremental RBF Networks. *Neural Processing Letters*, 1, 2–5.

R.M. Goodman, C.M. Higgins, J.W. Miller, and P. Smyth (1992). Rule-Based Neural Networks for Classification and Probability Estimation. *Neural Computation*, 4, 781–804.

C. Guilleminault and M. Souquet (1979). Sleep States and Related Pathology. In: Korobkin, R., and Guilleminault, C. (eds.), *Advances in Perinatal Neurology*, S.P. Medical and Scientific Books, New York, 225–247.

I. Ivanova, M. Kubat, and G. Pfurtscheller (1994). The System TBNN for the Learning of 'Difficult' Concepts. *Proceedings of the 4th Belgian-Dutch Conference on Machine Learning, BENELEARN'94* (pp. 230–241), Rotterdam, The Netherlands.

I. Ivanova and M. Kubat. (1995). Initialization of Neural Networks by Means of Decision Trees. *Knowledge-Based Systems 8*, 333–344.

B. Kemp, E.W. Gröneveld, A.J.M.W. Janssen, and J.M. Franzen (1987) A Model-Based Monitor of Human Sleep Stages. *Biological Cybernetics*, 57, 365–378.

T. Kohonen (1990). The self-organizing map. *Proceedings of the IEEE*, 78, 1464–1480.

M. Kubat and I. Ivanova (1995). Initialization of RBF Networks with Decision Trees. *Proceedings of the 5th Belgian-Dutch Conference on Machine Learning, BENELEARN'95* (pp. 61–70) Leuven, Belgium.

M. Kubat, G. Pfurtscheller, and D. Flotzinger(1994). AI-Based Approach to Automatic Sleep Classification. *Biological Cybernetics*, 79, 443–448.

Y. Le Cun, J.S. Denker, and S.A. Solla (1990). Optimal Brain Damage. In D.S. Touretzky (ed.) *Advances in Neural Information Processing Systems*, Vol.2. Morgan Kaufmann, 598–605.

D. Lowe (1989). Adaptive Radial Basis Function Nonlinearities and the Problem of Generalization. *1st International Conference on Artificial Neural Networks* (171–175), London, UK.

M.C. Mozer and P. Smolensky (1990). Skeletonization: A Technique for Trimming the Fat from a Network via Relevance Assessment. In D.S. Touretzky (ed.) *Advances in Neural Information Procession Systems* Vol.1, Morgan Kaufmann, 107–115.

J. Park and I.W. Sandberg (1991). Universal Approximation Using Radial-Basis-Function Networks. *Neural Computation*, 3, 246–257.

Y. Park (1990). A Mapping from Linear Tree Classifiers to Neural Net Classifiers. *Proceedings of IEEE International Conference on Neural Networks* (Vol. I, 94–100), Orlando, Florida.

G. Pfurtscheller, D. Flotzinger, and K. Matuschik (1992). Sleep Classification in Infants Based on Artificial Neural Networks. *Biomedizinische Technik*, 37, 122-130.

G. Pfurtscheller, D. Flotzinger, and J. Kalcher (1992). Brain-Computer Interface—A New Communication Device for Handicapped Persons. In W. Zagler (ed.): *Computer for Handicapped Persons: Proceedings of the 3rd International Conference* (pp. 409–415), Vienna.

G. Pfurtscheller, D. Flotzinger, and C. Neuper (1994). Differentiating Between Finger, Toe, and Tongue Movement in Man, Based on 40 Hz EEG. *Electroencephalography and Clinical Neurophysiology*, 90, 456–460.

T. Poggio and F. Girosi (1990). Regularization Algorithms for Learning that are Equivalent to Multi-layer Networks. *Science*, 247, 987–982.

M.D.J. Powell (1988). Radial Basis Function Approximations to Polynomials. *Numerical Analysis 1987 Proceedings*, 223–241, Dundee, UK.

J.R. Quinlan (1986). Induction of Decision Trees. *Machine Learning*, 1, 81–106.

J.R. Quinlan (1993). *C4.5: Programs for Machine Learning.* Morgan Kaufmann, San Mateo.

D. Rumelhart, G. Hinton, and J. Williams (1986). Learning Internal Representations by Error Propagation. In: D. Rumelhart and J. McClelland (eds.), *Parallel Distributed Processing*, MIT Press, Cambridge, Vol.1, 318–362.

M. Sahami (1995), Generating Neural Networks Through the Induction of Threshold Logic Unit Trees. em Proceedings of the 8th Europen Conference on Machine Learning, 339–342.

I.K. Sethi (1990). Entropy Nets: From Decision Trees to Neural Networks. *Proceedings of the IEEE*, 78, 1605–1613.

J.R. Smith and I. Karacan (1971). EEG Sleep Stage Scoring by an Automatic Hybrid System. *Electroencephalography and Clinical Neurophisiology*, 31, 321–237.

G.G. Towell, J.W. Shavlik, and M.O. Noordewier (1990). Refinement of Approximate Domain Theories by Knowledge-Based Neural Networks. *Proceedings of the 8th National Conference on Artificial Intelligence, AAAI'90*, 861–866.

S.M. Weiss and I. Kapouleas (1989). An Empirical Comparison of Pattern Recognition, Neural Nets, and Machine Learning Classification Methods. *Proceedings of the 11th International Joint Conference on Artificial Intelligence, IJCAI'89* (pp.781–787), Detroit, MI.

D. Wettschereck and T.G. Dietterich (1992). Improving the Performance of Radial Basis Function Networks by Learning Center Locations. *Advances in Neural Information Processing Systems 4*, (J.E. Moody, S.J. Hanson, and R.P. Lippmann, eds.), 1133–1140. San Mateo, CA: Morgan Kaufmann.

B. Widrow and M.E. Hoff (1960). Adaptive Switching Circuits. *IRE WESCON Convention Record*, 96–104.

J. Wnek and R.S. Michalski (1994). Comparing Symbolic and Subsymbolic Learing: Three Studies. In: R.S. Michalski and G. Tecuci (Eds.), *Machine Learning: A Multistrategy Approach*, Vol. IV, Morgan Kaufmann, San Francisco, CA, 489–519.

J. Zhang (1991): Integrating Symbolic and Subsymbolic Approaches in Learning Flexible Concepts. *Proceedings of the 1st International Workshop on Multistrategy Learning* (pp. 289–304), Harpers Ferry, U.S.A.

18

Machine Learning Applications in Biological Classification of River Water Quality

Sašo Džeroski, Jasna Grbović and William J. Walley

ABSTRACT

We present several applications of machine learning, in particular rule induction, to the area of biological classification of river water quality. These applications aim at reducing the subjectivity of currently used classification methods based on biological indices. Rules for biological classification of British rivers based on bioindicator data are induced from expert classified samples. Data acquired through a monitoring programme for Slovenian rivers are analyzed to determine the influence of physical and chemical parameters on selected bioindicator organisms in Slovenian rivers. This methodology can be used to determine the ecological requirements of organisms that are not sufficiently well understood. Rules are also induced for biological classification of Slovenian rivers based on physical and chemical parameters as well as bioindicator data. In all three cases, valuable knowledge is extracted from data acquired through environmental monitoring and/or expert interpretation of the acquired samples.

Machine Learning and Data Mining: Methods and Applications
Edited by R.S. Michalski, I Bratko and M. Kubat
© 1997 John Wiley & Sons Ltd

18.1   INTRODUCTION

Rivers are the most important freshwater resource for man, being used for a variety of purposes, including potable water supply, irrigation of agricultural land, industrial and municipal water supplies, industrial and municipal waste disposal, navigation, fishing, and body-contact recreation (Friedrich *et al.*, 1992). River water managers thus require high quality scientific information on the quantity and the quality of the waters under their control. The quality of surface waters, including rivers, depends on their physical, chemical and biological properties. The latter are reflected by the types of living organisms present in the water and their density (this includes the structure of the community and its diversity). Based on the above properties, surface waters are classified into (one of) several quality classes which indicate the suitability of the water for different kinds of use.

It is well known that the physical and chemical properties give a limited picture of water quality at a particular point in time, while the biota (living organisms) act as continuous monitors of water quality over a period of time (Cairns *et al.*, 1968). This has increased the importance of biological methods for monitoring water quality (De Pauw and Hawkes, 1993). Since Kolkwitz and Marsson (1902), who first proposed the use of biota as a means of monitoring the quality of natural waters, many different methods for mapping biological data to discrete quality classes or continuous scales have been developed (for overviews, see Friedrich *et al.*, 1992; De Pauw and Hawkes, 1993; Grbović, 1994). Most of these approaches use indicator organisms (bioindicators), which have well known ecological requirements and are selected for their sensitivity / tolerance to various kinds of pollution. Given a biological sample, information on the presence and density of all indicator organisms present in the sample is usually combined to derive a biological index that reflects the quality of the water at the site where the sample was taken.

An example of a well known biological index is the Saprobic Index (Pantle and Buck, 1955), based on the Saprobic System of Kolkwitz and Marsson (1902), which is used in many countries of Central Europe, including Germany and Slovenia. A bioindicator is assigned a saprobic zone preference s, which specifies the water quality class where the bioindicator is most frequently found, and a weighting factor g, which depends on how spread across different quality classes the presence of the bioindicator is (a single organism can be present in waters of different quality). The frequency of occurrence h (number of organisms found in the sample) of the bioindicator is also taken into account. The Saprobic Index SI at a given sampling point is calculated as

$$SI = \frac{\sum_{i=1}^{n} s_i g_i h_i}{\sum_{i=1}^{n} g_i h_i}$$

where i ranges over all bioindicators present in the sample.

Bioindicators can be identified at different taxonomical levels, e.g., at the species level or the family level. A family, a species or any other taxonomical group can be referred to as a taxon (plural taxa). In the Saprobic System, bioindicators are identified at the species level, which is more demanding in terms of sample processing effort, but also gives a more precise picture of the water quality. Family level identification is used in the Biological Monitoring Working Party Score (ISO-BMWP, 1979), abbreviated as BMWP, and its derivative Average Score Per Taxon (ASPT). Both are in use in the United Kingdom. A single number (score), is assigned to each bioindicator. Only the presence/absence of bioindicators is taken into account. The scores of all bioindicators present in the sample are summed to yield the BMWP score and this is divided by the number of bioindicators present to obtain the ASPT. Unlike the Saprobic Index, which includes both plant and animal taxa, the BMWP score relies on animals only, more specifically macrobenthic invertebrates, i.e., invertebrates that live in the river bed.

The main problem with the biological indices described above is their subjectivity (Walley, 1993). Namely, the assignment of saprobic zone preferences, weighting factors, and BMWP scores, to individual bioindicators was done by expert biologists and ecologists or committees thereof. The numbers assigned are based on the experts' knowledge about the ecological requirements of the bioindicator taxa, which is not always complete. The assigned bioindicator values are thus often inappropriate, as suggested by a recent reappraisal of the BMWP scores using data acquired through biological monitoring (Walley and Hawkes, 1996). An additional layer of subjectivity is added by combining the scores of the individual bioindicators through ad-hoc procedures based on sums, averages, and weighted averages instead of using a sound method of combination.

The subjectivity of the aforementioned biological indices cannot be completely avoided. Water quality has thousands of dimensions, not all of which are relevant to all users. A general water quality index must therefore, by virtue of its very nature, be subjective. However, subjectivity should be minimized: it should only enter into the methodology where it cannot be avoided, i.e., in relation to the target classifications. The subjectivity introduced at intermediate levels as described in the previous paragraph can and should be minimized. The chapter describes our efforts to apply machine learning techniques towards this end.

We first applied machine learning to induce rules for biological classification of water quality from samples taken from British rivers and classified by an expert river ecologist. The classification of samples by an ecologist is definitely a subjective process, but this is the only phase where subjectiveness appears: machine learning is used to identify a set of rules that mimic the expert behavior without using the intermediate stages of assigning scores to bioindicators and combining these scores through weighted averaging. Section 18.2 describes this application of machine learning.

Given data acquired through a monitoring programme for Slovenian rivers, we induced rules that describe the influence of physical and chemical parameters on selected bioindicator organisms. This helps identify the ecological requirements of the organisms and thus helps reduce the subjectivity of assigning saprobic zone preferences and weighting factors. Rules were also induced for biological classification of Slovenian rivers based on physical and chemical parameters as well as bioindicator data. These applications of machine learning are described in Section 18.3. Finally, Section 18.4 concludes with a summary, discussion and pointers to related work.

18.2 LEARNING RULES FOR BIOLOGICAL CLASSIFICATION OF BRITISH RIVERS

To arrive at a suitable method for biological water quality classification, one could use the following approach. Suppose we had a set of samples (that list the present bioindicators and their abundance) and their correct classifications. We could then use a rule induction method to capture the knowledge needed to classify samples correctly. Correct classification may be provided by an expert in riverine ecology. This section describes how this approach was applied to obtain a method for biological classification of British rivers.

18.2.1 The Data

The data considered here consist of 292 samples of benthic macroinvertebrates collected as part of a biological monitoring programme of the British National Rivers Authority. They originate from the upper Trent catchment in England. They are given in the form of a site by species matrix, where the rows correspond to samples (sites) and the columns correspond to eighty different macroinvertebrate families (or taxa, in some cases). For each sample, the abundances are given for each of the eighty families of invertebrates.

The abundance of animals found is recorded as an integer between 0 to 6. Zero denotes that no members of the particular family were found in the sample, 1 denotes the presence of 1–2 members, 2 denotes 3–9 members present, 3 denotes 10–49, 4 denotes 50–99, 5 denotes 100–999, and 6 denotes more than 1000. There is a large number of zeros in the matrix (it is quite sparse), as most of the families are absent from any given sample. In our experiments, the abundances of all families were treated as continuous variables.

The samples were classified by the riverine ecology expert H. A. Hawkes, who is now an Honorary Reader at Aston University, Birmingham, UK. He was a member of the Biological Monitoring Working Party (ISO-BMWP, 1979), the committee which was set up by the Department of Environment to establish a biological monitoring system for the UK. He chaired the working sub-committee responsible for the allocation of the family scores, intended to reflect the relative importance and influence of individual families on the overall water quality. In other words, he is an acknowledged expert in the area of biological classification of British rivers.

The samples were classified into five classes, based on the level of organic pollution indicated by the invertebrate community. This was originally done as part of a project to develop a Bayesian-based expert system (Walley et al., 1992). The five classes were designed to mirror the five chemical classes (1a, 1b, 2, 3, and 4) presently in use in the UK, and were designated B1a, B1b, B2, B3, and B4 to distinguish them from the chemical classes (Ruck et al., 1993). Class B1a indicates least polluted (best quality) water, while class B4 represents water of the poorest quality. In machine learning terminology, the abundance of each family is an attribute, each biological sample is an example, and the classification assigned by the expert is the class.

18.2.2 The Experiments

We addressed two learning problems: predicting the water quality class from the original 80 attributes and predicting the water quality class in the presence of additional attributes that describe the diversity of the population in a given sample. A set of rules was generated for each of the problems using the methodology described above. The rules were then inspected and evaluated by a domain expert (H. A. Hawkes). Their performance was also measured in terms of classification accuracy and information content.

The rule induction system CN2 (Clark and Niblett, 1989; Clark and Boswell, 1991) as modified by Džeroski et al., (1993) was used to induce rules from the classified samples. Džeroski et al., (1993) have modified CN2 to measure the relative information score (Kononenko and Bratko, 1991) of rule sets and to use the m-estimate (Cestnik, 1990) instead of the Laplace estimate in the search heuristic. The relative information score takes into account the differences in prior probability among the classes, while the m-estimate allows for better probability estimation when learning from noisy examples.

Table 18.1 Rules for biological classification of British rivers based on the presence and frequency of occurrence of bioindicators

```
IF Hydrobiidae <= 3
AND Planorbidae <= 0
AND Gammaridae <= 5
AND Leuctridae > 0
THEN   Class = B1a
        [42 0 0 0 0]


IF Asellidae > 2
AND 0 < Gammaridae <= 4
AND Scirtidae <= 0
THEN Class = B2
       [0 0 41 0 0]


IF Planariidae <= 0
AND Tubificidae > 0
AND Lumbricidae <= 0
AND Glossiphoniidae <= 2
AND Asellidae > 0
AND Gammaridae <= 0
AND Veliidae <= 0
AND Hydropsychidae <= 0
AND Simulidae <= 0
AND Muscidae <= 0
THEN Class = B3
       [0 0 3 28 10]
```

In our experiments, CN2 was used to induce sets of unordered rules. The rules were required to be highly significant (at the 99% level). Except for the significance threshold and the search heuristic settings, described below, the parameter settings of CN2 were the default ones (see Clark and Boswell, 1991).

To select the appropriate probability estimation method, i.e., the appropriate value for the parameter m, we used the following methodology. Fifteen different values of the parameter m were tried (0, 0.01, 0.25, 0.5, 1, 2, 4, 8, 16, 32, 64, 128, 256, 512 and 1024), as suggested by earlier experiments (Cestnik, 1990; Džeroski et al., 1993). The Laplace estimate was also tried out. For a given set of examples, we thus induced 16 sets of rules and chose the best according to the following lexicographic criterion: (1) information score, (2) accuracy, (3) smaller value of the parameter m. The accuracy and the relative information score are estimated on the training set. This procedure allows us to choose the right level of fitting: overfitting is prevented by applying the significance threshold. As the parameter m increases, the accuracy and information score of the induced rules increase until an optimum is reached, then decrease (Ličan-Milošević, 1994). Note that this kind of behavior is obtained only if we use a high significance threshold. If we don't apply a significance threshold then accuracy and information score fall as m grows: we cannot choose an appropriate value of m on the training set.

CN2 (Džeroski *et al.*, 1993) induced 12 rules from the 292 samples containing 80 attribute values each. The best value of the m-parameter turned out to be $m = 32$. As indicated above, a significance threshold of 99 % was employed, enforcing the induction of reliable rules. On the average, each rule covered 25 examples and contained five conditions. These rules achieve 86.3 % accuracy on the training set, as well as 75 % information content. Three of the 12 rules are shown in Table 18.1.

The first rule in Table 18.1 predicts the water quality class B1a. It covers 42 examples of class B1a and no examples of the other four classes, as indicated by the numbers between the square brackets. The condition (IF) part states that less than 50 animals ($<= 3$) of the family Hydrobiidae are present in the sample, Planorbidae are absent ($<= 0$), there are less than 1000 animals of the family Gammaridae ($<= 5$), and there are some Leuctridae (> 0) present.

The second rule in Table 18.1 predicts the water quality class B2. It covers 41 examples of class B2. It requires the absence of Scirtidae, at least 50 members of Asellidae, and the presence of Gammaridae, which at the same time must not be overabundant (less than 100 members).

Finally, the third rule in Table 18.1 predicts the water quality class B3. Note that this rule covers ten examples of class B4 and three of class B2, in addition to the 28 examples of class B3. This fact is taken into account during the classification process, which combines all rules that match the example classified. The rule relies heavily on the absence of several families (Planariidae, Lumbricidae, Gammaridae, Veliidae, Hydropsychidae, Simulidae, and Muscidae). It requires the presence of Tubificidae and Asellidae, and restricts the number of Glossiphoniidae to be less than 10.

The induced rules mention the presence/absence or give other bounds on the abundance levels for 35 out of the 80 families. The rule induction algorithm chooses the families that are most indicative of the water quality class, mainly in conjunction with other families. This is in contrast with standard practices, which usually combine the evidence of different bioindicators in a joint index through weighted averaging, but do not refer explicitly to co-occurrences of specific taxa.

To test the consistency of the induced rules with the existing expert knowledge, the twelve rules were presented to the ecological expert without the conclusion part. The order in which the rules were presented was random. The expert was then required to specify the appropriate classes for the conclusions of the rules. Most of the time, the expert's conclusions confirmed the rules: for five rules he gave the same class, for three he specified the next worse class, for three he specified a possible range of the correct class and the next worse, and for one rule one class better than the actual. For the first rule in Table 18.1, the expert specified class B1b (actual B1a), for the second class B3 (actual B2), and for the third rule class B3 (actual B3).

While the rules were roughly consistent with expert knowledge, some criticism was expressed regarding the reliance of the rules on the absence of families from samples (see for example the last rule in Table 18.1). The absence of a taxon may often be insignificant and in many cases (but not all) provides little extra information. The main criticism, however, was that the rules use only a small number of taxa, whereas the expert takes into account the whole community when giving his classification. The diversity of the community structure is an important indication of the water quality. The expert was reluctant to interpret some of the rules because he felt that he needed more information in order to draw a proper conclusion.

Taking into account the criticism, we conducted an experiment where the learning system was given six additional attributes intended to capture the diversity of a sample. The attributes, named MoreThan0, ..., MoreThan5, reflect the number of families present over a certain abundance level: MoreThan0 is the total number of families present, while MoreThan5 is the number of families present with at least 1000 members in the sample. The same settings as above were used, except that the best value for the parameter m was $m = 64$. Thirteen rules were generated with accuracy 88.4 % (on the training set) and information content 80 %. This performance improvement suggests that the expert criticism was justified.

An example rule that exploits the additional diversity attributes is given in Table 18.2. It predicts class B4 (poorest quality). At most five different taxa are allowed in the sample (MoreThan0 $<=$ 5), and at least two of these have to be present with at least three animals each (MoreThan1 $>$ 1). Dixidae have to be absent, Asellidae may be present with up to 50 and Oligochaeta with up to 1000 animals. The rule covers 25 examples of class B4 and four examples of class B3.

Table 18.2 A rule for biological classification of British rivers that uses biodiversity information

```
IF Oligochaeta <= 5
AND Asellidae <=3
AND Dixidae <= 0
AND MoreThan0 <=5
AND MoreThan1 > 1
THEN Class = B4
        [0 0 0 4 25]
```

To estimate the performance on unseen cases, we split the set of 292 examples randomly into a training set of 195 examples (two thirds) and a testing set of 97 examples (one third). A set of rules was generated from the training set using the standard methodology and then evaluated on the testing set. For the original learning problem (80 attributes), the value of $m = 128$ turned out to be the best (on the training set). Ten rules were induced with an accuracy of 61.9% and information score of 55% on the unseen cases. For comparison, the performance on the training set was 91.3% in terms of accuracy and 80% in terms of information content. For the extended learning problem (86 attributes), $m = 32$ was the best setting. An accuracy of 68.0% and an information score of 56% were achieved on unseen cases (93.8% and 83%, respectively, on the training set) by the 12 induced rules. There is an obvious performance improvement from the original to the extended problem, especially in terms of classification accuracy on unseen cases.

For comparison to more classical classification methods, we applied the nearest neighbour algorithm to our two classification problems. The nearest neighbour (NN) algorithm is one of the most well-known classification algorithms and an enormous body of research exists on the subject, as evidenced by the survey of Dasarathy (1990). In essence, the NN algorithm treats attributes as dimensions of an Euclidean space and examples as points in this space. In the training phase, the classified examples are stored without any processing. When classifying a new example, the Euclidean distance between that example and all training examples is calculated and the class of the closest training example is assigned to the new example.

The more general kNN method takes the k nearest training examples and determines the class of the new example by majority vote. In improved versions of kNN, the votes of each of the k nearest neighbours are weighted by the respective proximity to the new example. An optimal value of k may be determined automatically from the training set by using leave-one-out cross-validation. Finally, the contribution of each attribute to the distance may be weighted by the mutual information between that attribute and the class. These so-called feature weights can also be determined automatically on the training set. For our experiments, we used the kNN algorithm as implemented by Wettschereck (1994), which includes the improvements described above.

Using the same 195 training examples and 97 testing examples as CN2, different versions of kNN performed as follows. The basic NN algorithm achieved 55.7% accuracy without and 59.8% with diversity attributes. The kNN method without feature weights achieved 55.7% accuracy in both cases, the best value of k being 3. Finally, the The kNN method with feature weights achieved 56.7% and 58.8% accuracy, respectively, the best values of k being 3 and 5, respectively. The rules induced by CN2 obviously perform better in both cases, which means that they represent useful generalizations of the training examples.

18.3   ANALYSIS OF DATA ABOUT SLOVENIAN RIVERS

According to current legislation on water classification in Slovenia (OJSFRY, 1978), the water belongs to the first (best) quality class if it is suitable for drinking, bathing and fisheries. Second class water is suitable for fisheries and recreation, including bathing; after simple treatment (coagulation, filtration, disinfection) it can be used for industrial purposes, even in the food industry. Third class waters can be used for irrigation and (after conditioning) in the industry, except the food industry. Water of the fourth (worst) quality class can be used only for purposes less demanding than the above ones and after appropriate treatment.

Slovenian water authorities use the Saprobic Index method, as introduced by Pantle and Buck (1955) and modified by Zelinka and Marvan (1961), to map biological data to a continuous water quality scale. The Saprobic Index derived from a given water sample is a single real number between one and four that reflects the quality of the water. For presentation purposes, the Saprobic Index is mapped into a discrete quality scale of four basic classes and three intermediate classes, i.e., seven discrete classes: 1, 1–2, 2, 2–3, 3, 3–4, and 4. Class 1 corresponds to clean waters where the Saprobic Index ranges between 1.00 and 1.50, while class 4 corresponds to heavily polluted waters where the Saprobic Index ranges between 3.51 and 4.00. Class 1–2 waters are designated as mildly, class 2 waters as moderately, and class 2–3 waters as critically polluted. The four basic classes correspond to the legislation defined classes, but are somewhat different, as the latter rely mainly on chemical properties.

As explained in the introductory section, the Saprobic Index is calculated as a weighted average of the saprobic zone preferences of the bioindicators that appear in a given biological sample. These are weighted with the indicator value and the frequency of occurrence of the respective bioindicator species (or other taxonomical units, in general referred to as taxa). The bioindicator taxa are such that their biology, water quality importance and ecological role is known. In a way, they reflect the overall water quality as affected by physical and chemical influences over a period of time. However, the ecological role and water quality importance is not known for many taxa (which therefore cannot be used as bioindicators) and may furthermore differ from country to country (Grbović, 1994). Little is also known about the influence of physical and chemical water properties on many taxa. From an ecological and water quality point of view, these are important research topics.

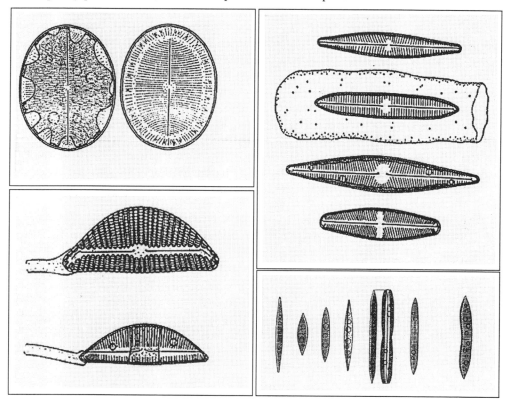

Figure 18.1 Representative individuals of four plant taxa. From top left corner clockwise: *Cocconeis placentula*, *Navicula cryptocephala*, *Nitzschia palea*, and *Cymbella sp.*

The data about Slovenian rivers come from the Hydrometeorological Institute of Slovenia (Hidrometereološki Zavod Republike Slovenije, abbreviated as HMZ) that performs water quality monitoring for most Slovenian rivers and maintains a database of water quality samples. The data provided by HMZ cover a four year period, from 1990 to 1993. Biological samples are taken twice a year, once in summer and once in winter, while physical and chemical analyses are performed several times a year for each sampling site. The physical and chemical samples include the measured values of 50 different parameters, which include for example dissolved oxygen and hardness, while the biological samples include a list of all taxa present at the sampling site and their density. The frequency of occurrence (density) of each present taxon is recorded by an expert biologist at three different qualitative levels, where 1 means the taxon occurs incidentally, 3-frequently, and 5-abundantly. Biological samples include the corresponding Saprobic Index value and the corresponding quality class as determined by the index. In total, 698 water samples were available on which both physical/chemical and biological analyses were performed: our experiments were conducted using these samples.

Given the data described above, we applied the CN2 rule induction system (Clark and Boswell, 1991; Džeroski *et al.*, 1993). We formulated several learning problems: analysis of the influence of selected physical and chemical water properties on the presence of selected taxa; water quality classification starting from a selected set of bioindicators; and water quality classification based on a a selected set of physical and chemical properties. Below, we briefly describe the methodology used to learn and evaluate rules and then present the results for each of the learning problems. The evaluation of induced rules comprises comments by Jasna Grbović, an expert biologist who performs analyses of biological samples at HMZ and has knowledge on the ecology of plants and animals found in Slovenian rivers, as well as the classification accuracy and information score of the rules (estimated on unseen cases).

CN2 was used in the same way as described in Section 18.2.2 to induce sets of unordered rules. A significance threshold of 99% was applied and the other settings were the default ones. Given a training set, the Laplace estimate and fifteen different values of m in the m-estimate were tried, yielding 16 different rule sets. The best of these was then selected according to the lexicographic criterion (1) information score, (2) accuracy, (3) smaller value of the parameter m, where the information score and accuracy were measured on the training set.

For each of the learning problems, two sets of experiments were performed. The first set induced rules from all 698 examples, aiming to find as many reliable patterns (and hopefully knowledge) as possible. The rules derived in this way were inspected by the expert biologist and evaluated in the light of existing knowledge on riverine ecology and water quality. The second batch of experiments was aimed at evaluating the performance of induced rules in terms of their accuracy and information score on unseen cases. To this end, we split the entire dataset into a training (70% – 489 cases) and testing (30% – 209 cases) set in ten different ways. For each split, we induced a set of rules according to the above methodology from the training set, then tested the performance of the rules on the test set; the results appearing in Sections 18.3.1 and 18.3.2 are the averages over the ten different splits.

18.3.1   The Influence of Physical and Chemical Parameters on Selected Organisms

Plants are mostly influenced by the following physical and chemical parameters (water properties): total hardness, nitrogen compounds (NO_2, NO_3, NH_4), phosphorus compounds (PO_4), silica (SiO_2), iron (Fe), surfactants (detergents), chemical oxygen demand (COD), and biochemical oxygen demand (BOD). The last two parameters indicate the degree of organic pollution: the first reflects the total amount of degradable organic matter, while the second reflects the amount of biologically degradable matter. Animals are influenced by different

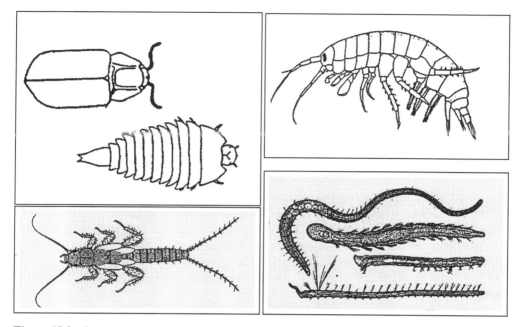

Figure 18.2   Representative individuals of four animal taxa. From top left corner clockwise: *Elmis sp.* (adult and larvae), *Gammarus fossarum*, *Tubifex sp.*, and *Plecoptera leuctra sp.*

parameters: water temperature, acidity or alkalinity (pH), dissolved oxygen (O_2, saturation of O_2), total hardness, chemical (COD), and biochemical oxygen demand (BOD).

The experiments presented in this section studied the influence of the physical and chemical parameters listed above on ten plant taxa and seven animal taxa. On the plant side, eight kinds of diatomae (BACILLARIOPHYTA) and two kinds of green algae (CHLOROPHYTA) were studied. The animal taxa chosen for study include worms (OLIGOCHAETA), crustacea (AMPHIPODA) and five kinds of insects. Figures 18.1 and 18.2 show representative individuals of eight of these taxa (four plant and four animal taxa).

For each of the selected taxa we defined an attribute-based learning problem, the attributes being the selected physical and chemical parameters (Hardness, NO2, NO3, NH4, PO4, SiO2, Fe, Detergents, COD, BOD for plants; Temperature, PH, O2, Saturation, COD, BOD for animals). The class is the presence of the selected taxon (with values Present and Absent). Seventeen different learning problems (domains) were thus defined.

We now summarize the experiments with the above learning problems, carried in accordance with the methodology specified above. We first give an overview of the performance of the induced rules, both for rules derived from the whole data set (calculated on the training set) and for rules derived from the ten splits (calculated on the testing set and averaged over the ten splits). We then give excerpts of the expert rule evaluation for selected plant and animal taxa. A detailed description of the selected taxa, the experiments, the performance of induced rules, the selected sets of rules, and the expert evaluation of these rules can be found in the BSc Thesis of Ličan-Milošević (1994).

The accuracy on the whole (training) dataset ranges between 66% and 85% (the frequency of the majority class ranges between 50% to 70%), while the information score ranges between 23% and 50%. The rule sets for different taxa comprised 10 to 20 rules, the average rule length was less than five conditions, and average rule coverage was 15 to 45 examples.

While the performance (accuracy) of the rules on the training set is not as high as might be expected, we should bear in mind that the use of a high significance threshold prevents overfitting. More importantly, the physical and chemical parameters at a certain point in time do not completely determine the presence (absence) of a particular taxon: the presence depends on the physical and chemical parameters over a longer period of time, on the life time of the taxon, the water level, and the river bed. To make the problem even harder, some taxa group together very different organisms: an example is the taxon *Chironomidae (green)*, where the lowest information score on the whole dataset (1.4%) was recorded.

The information scores of the rules induced from 70% of the dataset (measured on the remaining 30%) are much lower for all taxa, but remain positive. This means that the rules contain useful information about the influence of physical and chemical parameters on the presence of the taxa. Nevertheless, the accuracy is worse than the default for five out of the 17 taxa. In the remainder of the section, we give an excerpt from the expert evaluation of the rules for the diatom *Nitzschia palea* and the water beetle *Elmis sp.*. The rules for these taxa achieved the highest information scores of 29.2% and 26.1%, respectively, on unseen cases (average of the 10 splits 70% training–30% testing) and accuracies 69.7% and 71.0% (default accuracies 60.8% and 64.6%).

Table 18.3 Selected rules predicting the presence of the species *Nitzschia palea* from physical and chemical parameters

```
IF   PO4 > 0.065              IF   NO3 > 1.3
AND Fe < 0.595                AND NH4 < 0.97
AND COD > 25.5                AND 13.25 < COD < 16.35
THEN Taxon = Present          THEN Taxon = Present
     [58 0]                        [36 0]


IF   4.25 < NO3 < 12.35       IF   Hardness > 11.85
AND SiO2 > 1.65               AND NO2 > 0.095
AND Detergents > 0.055        AND NH4 > 0.09
THEN Taxon = Present          THEN Taxon = Present
     [50 0]                        [82 0]


IF   NO3 < 5.95               IF   NO2 < 0.005
AND SiO2 > 4.75               AND NO3 < 7.1
AND COD > 7.95                AND PO4 < 0.125
AND 1.3 < BOD < 42.05         AND Detergents < 0.055
THEN Taxon = Present          AND BOD < 2
     [59 0]                   THEN Taxon = Absent
                                   [0 39]
```

Table 18.4 Selected rules predicting the presence of the beetle *Elmis sp.* from physical and chemical parameters

```
IF   O2 < 11.45                  IF   Temperature > 12.75
AND Hardness > 10.35             AND BOD < 0.65
AND COD > 2.15                   THEN Taxon = Present
AND BOD < 1.25                       [8 0]
THEN Taxon = Present
     [36 0]                      IF   23 < COD < 46.45
                                 THEN Taxon = Absent
IF   Temperature > 11.75             [0 72]
AND 12.3 < Hardness <14.3
AND BOD < 1.75                   IF   PH > 7.05
THEN Taxon = Present             AND BOD > 12.15
     [14 0]                      THEN Taxon = Absent
                                     [0 47]
```

The diatom *Nitzschia palea* is present in 420 of the 698 samples, and is the most common species in Slovenian rivers. It is very tolerant to pollution and lives in waters of a wide quality range. It is characteristic of the water quality class 2–3 (this is its saprobic preference zone): it is used as an indicator of critically polluted waters.

The rules built from the whole dataset confirm that a larger degree of pollution is beneficial to this species. From the 18 rules, Table 18.3 lists six rules, chosen for their large coverage. The rules indicate that *Nitzschia palea* needs nitrogen compounds, phosphates, silica, and larger amounts of degradable matter (COD and BOD). The numbers in square brackets are the numbers of examples of each class covered by the respective rule. For example, [58 0] means that the corresponding rule covers 58 examples of class Present, while [0 39] means that the corresponding rule covers 39 examples of class Absent.

Beetles *COLEOPTERA*, where the taxon *Elmis sp.* belongs, are quite common on land but rare in water. From the literature and expert experiences it is known that this taxon inhabits clean waters: it is considered an indicator of the quality class 1–2

From the 17 rules induced, five selected by the expert are listed in Table 18.4. As above, the numbers in square brackets are the numbers of examples of each class covered by the respective rule. For example, [36 0] means that the corresponding rule covers 36 examples of class Present, while [0 72] means that the corresponding rule covers 72 examples of class Absent. The first rule demands a relatively low quantity of biodegradable matter (pollution) in order for *Elmis sp.* to be present; this has to be even lower as water temperature increases (see the second and the third rule). The last two rules predict that the taxon will be absent if the water is overly polluted as indicated by the high values of BOD, COD and pH. The rules confirm that *Elmis sp.* is a bioindicator of clean to mildly polluted waters.

Not all of the induced rules agree completely with existing expert knowledge. As an example, let us consider the two rules in Table 18.5 that predict the presence of the taxon *Plecoptera leuctra sp.* The first rule indicates that the taxon is found in clean waters (low COD), which is consistent with existing knowledge about its ecological requirements: *Plecoptera leuctra sp.* is used as an indicator of clean waters. The second rule, however, indicates that the taxon can be present in quite polluted waters (high COD), provided enough oxygen (high Saturation). This rule supplements existing expert knowledge in an important way as most Slovenian rivers are torrential streams and thus well aerated.

Table 18.5 Two rules predicting the presence of *Plecoptera leuctra sp.* from physical and chemical parameters

IF Temperature > 10	IF Temperature < 23
AND Saturation > 102.5	AND 120 < Saturation < 150
AND COD < 2.35	AND COD > 10.9
THEN Taxon = Present	AND BOD < 3.75
[14 0]	THEN Taxon = Present
	[8 0]

Another example are the rules that predict the presence of the taxon *Cymbella sp.*, see Table 18.6. The rules point out that the taxon can be found in moderately to critically polluted waters (as indicated by the tolerance of large quantities of biodegradable matter, cf. large values of BOD ans COD in the rules). In water monitoring practice, however, *Cymbella sp.* is used as an indicator of clean to mildly polluted waters.

Table 18.6 Two rules predicting the presence of *Cymbella sp.* from physical and chemical parameters

IF Hardness < 13.2	IF Hardness < 12.6
AND NO3 < 6.75	AND NO2 < 0.2
AND 0.13 < NH4 < 0.25	AND NO3 > 6.45
AND PO4 < 0.05	AND 0.02 < PO4 < 0.5
AND Detergents < 0.02	AND SiO2 < 1.95
AND COD < 5.25	AND BOD < 9.95
THEN Taxon = Present	THEN Taxon = Present
[29 2]	[17 0]

18.3.2 Biological Classification

This section describes the experiments in predicting the biological water quality class of Slovenian rivers, as determined by the Saprobic Index, from two different sets of attributes. The first set consists of all the physical and chemical parameters mentioned in the previous section, altogether 13 parameters. The second consists of the 17 taxa from the previous section and 10 additional taxa, altogether 27 taxa. The 13 parameters give rise to real valued attributes, while the 27 taxa give rise to discrete valued attributes with four (linearly ordered) values: 0, 1, 3, and 5. As mentioned earlier, there are seven water quality classes. The majority class 2 comprises 339 of the 698 examples, thus the default accuracy is 48.6%.

For illustration, let us take a look at the two rules in Table 18.7 that predict the water quality class from physical and chemical parameters: these are the rules with greatest coverage derived from the whole dataset. The first covers nine examples of class 1, 80 examples of class 1–2,

Table 18.7   Two rules that predict water quality from physical and chemical parameters

```
IF   Temperature < 14.35
AND  PH < 8.45
AND  NO2 < 0.235
AND  1.75 < NO3 < 7.15
AND  Detergents < 0.025
AND  COD < 4.25
AND  BOD < 2.35
THEN QualityClass = 1-2
     [9 80 2 0 0 0 0]


IF Temperature > 12.65
AND PH < 8.65
AND Saturation > 57.3
AND NO2 < 0.375
AND NH4 > 0.065
AND PO4 < 0.39
AND SiO2 < 10.75
AND COD > 2.65
AND 1.25 < BOD < 4.75
THEN QualityClass = 2
     [0 8 152 5 0 0 0]
```

and two examples of class 2. The second covers eight examples of class 1–2, 152 examples of class 2, and five examples of class 2–3.

While we would need expertise in both the chemistry and biology of water quality to thoroughly evaluate these rules, they are intuitive and understandable. Class 1–2 (first rule) requires relatively cold water and very small quantities of pollutants (NO_2, NO_3, detergents, COD, BOD). Class 2 waters (second rule) are usually warmer and somewhat larger quantities of pollutants are allowed, provided there is enough oxygen (Saturation > 57.3).

The rules induced on the entire dataset reach 81.5% classification accuracy when using physical and chemical parameters and 71.1% when using bioindicators, the information scores being 62% and 44%. When learning on 70% of the dataset, the corresponding accuracies on the testing set are 60% and 58%, the information scores being 32% and 28%. It is interesting to note that better performance is achieved when predicting from physical and chemical parameters, despite the fact that biological quality is predicted. However, to determine the quality class a much larger set of bioindicators is used than the one used in our experiments.

Let us finally take a look at the four rules in Table 18.8 that predict the water quality class from the 27 bioindicators. The first covers one example of class 1, 16 examples of class 1–2, and one example of class 2. The second covers two examples of class 1, 32 examples of class 1–2, and two examples of class 2. The third covers three examples of class 1–2, 32 examples of class 2, nine examples of class 2–3, two examples of class 3, and one example of class 4. The last covers one example of each of class 2 and 2–3, 16 examples of class 3, and two examples of class 3–4.

Table 18.8   Four rules that predict the water quality class from the frequency of occurrence of selected bioindicators

```
IF  BACILLARIOPHYTA_Navicula_cryptocephala = 0
AND CHLOROPHYTA_Scenedesmus_obliquus = 0
AND DIPTERA_Chironomidae_green = 3
AND COLEOPTERA_Elmis_sp. = 3
THEN QualityClass = 1-2
     [1 16 1 0 0 0 0]


IF  BACILLARIOPHYTA_Nitzschia_palea = 0
AND CHLOROPHYTA_Oedogonium_sp. = 0
AND OLIGOCHAETA_Tubifex_sp. = 0
AND AMPHIPODA_Gammarus_fossarum = 5
THEN QualityClass = 1-2
     [2 32 2 0 0 0 0]


IF  BACILLARIOPHYTA_Navicula_cryptocephala = 1
AND BACILLARIOPHYTA_Nitzschia_palea = 1
THEN QualityClass = 2
     [0 3 32 9 2 0 1]


IF  BACILLARIOPHYTA_Cocconeis_placentula = 0
AND BACILLARIOPHYTA_Cymbella_ventricosa = 0
AND CHLOROPHYTA_Cladophora_sp. = 0
AND TURBELLARIA_Dendrocoelum_lacteum = 0
AND OLIGOCHAETA_Tubifex_sp. = 5
AND DIPTERA_Simulium_sp. = 0
THEN QualityClass = 3
     [0 0 1 1 16 2 0]
```

The first rule predicts class 1–2 when *Elmis sp.* and *Chironomidae (green)* occur frequently (3) and the species *Scenedesmus obliquus* and *Navicula cryptocephala* are absent (0). It is in agreement with existing expert knowledge: *Elmis sp.* and *Chironomidae (green)* are indicators of clean waters, while *Navicula cryptocephala* is indicative of polluted waters (class 3). The second rule also predicts class 1–2. Note that the rule requires the absence of *Tubifex sp.*, an indicator of heavy pollution, and the abundant presence of *Gammarus fossarum*, an indicator of clean waters. In fact, four of the six rules that predict class 1–2 explicitly require the absence of *Tubifex sp.* The third rule predicts class 2 when *Navicula cryptocephala* and *Nitzschia palea* occur incidentally (1). Both species are indicative of heavily polluted waters if they occur in larger quantities: as they only occur incidentally, the rule is in agreement with expert knowledge. Finally, the last rule predicts class 3, requiring the abundant presence of *Tubifex sp.* and the absence of several taxa that indicate clean (*Cocconeis placentula*) to moderately polluted (*Simulium sp.*) waters.

18.4 DISCUSSION

We have used rule induction to address several problems in the area of biological classification of water quality. These include the synthesis of classification rules from expert classified samples and the analysis of water quality data. Data were available about British and Slovenian rivers.

For the British rivers, expert classifications of the biological samples were available. The induced rules successfully captured the knowledge of the expert. The expert also found that the rules are generally consistent with his knowledge. Information on the diversity of the population further increased the information content and the quality of the induced rules. We evaluated the performance of the induced rules on unseen cases, and demonstrated that they perform better than the kNN classification algorithm, providing further evidence that the rules embody useful generalizations of the training examples. The induced rules can be used to automate the task of interpretation of biological samples in water quality terms, i.e., to predict the water quality at a particular site given the structure of the invertebrate community at that site.

Concerning Slovenian rivers, the experiments we have performed indicate that rule induction can be used to analyze water quality data and discover different kinds of knowledge. We induced rules that describe the influence of physical and chemical properties of the water in Slovenian rivers on the presence of selected living organisms that are currently used as bioindicators of river water quality. Expert evaluation of these rules showed that they do indeed capture useful knowledge, as indicated by their positive information scores. In some cases, the rules just confirmed the expert knowledge of the biology of the bioindicator taxon concerned. In others, they revealed new aspects of the biology of the studied taxon, which extend existing knowledge without conflicting it. There were even cases when the rules indicated that the given taxon is used as an indicator for a wrong class of water quality.

While the above analysis concerned 17 taxa with relatively well known biology that are routinely used as bioindicators of water quality, we have still been able to find some new knowledge on the biology of the taxa studied and their bioindicator roles. This means that the use of rule induction can improve our knowledge about riverine biology and ecology. A promising direction for further work is thus to extend the analysis to taxa about which relatively little is known and which are currently not used as bioindicators. This could contribute new knowledge both to biology and to the practice of water quality monitoring, as some of the taxa analyzed may turn out to be very good bioindicators. An additional possibility is to induce rules that relate a time series of physical and chemical measurements to the presence of a bioindicator, as bioindicators reflect the water quality over a period of time. Techniques like inductive logic programming (ILP) (Lavrač and Džeroski, 1994) can be employed for that purpose.

We also induced rules that predict the river water quality class (as provided through the Saprobic Index) of Slovenian rivers. The rules that use bioindicator data to this end are mainly consistent with existing expert knowledge: this is understandable, as bioindicator data (albeit on a much larger set of indicators) is used to derive the Saprobic Index. The rules that predict the biological quality class from the physical and chemical water properties are surprisingly accurate and informative and deserve a more detailed further analysis by experts fluent in both biological and chemical aspects of water quality. An interesting topic for further work is to induce classification rules that use both bioindicator and chemical/physical data, as the two are complementary to a certain degree.

The applications described here were aimed at reducing the subjectivity of currently used methods for biological classification of river water quality. For the biological classification of British rivers, our approach has been to introduce subjectivity at one point only, the expert classification of a representative cross-section of samples so as to provide a set of examples. We then use rule induction to map directly from the samples to the classifications, with no (or very little) introduction of further subjectivity. For the biological classification of Slovenian rivers, subjectivity is also introduced through the classifications of the samples, obtained by using the Saprobic Index. As mentioned earlier, the subjectivity of the target classifications cannot be avoided. The analysis of the influence of physical and chemical parameters on selected organisms in Slovenian rivers helps to understand the biology of these organisms and make the assignment of saprobic preference zones and indicator values more objective. In both cases, rule induction contributes towards better, more objective methods for water quality classification.

Concerning related work, several studies exist in applying different statistical or machine learning methods to the problem of classification of British rivers. These include the studies by Walley *et al.*, (1992) and Ruck *et al.*, (1993). Walley *et al.*, use Bayesian inference, while Ruck *et al.*, use neural networks to perform biological classification of river water quality. An extension of this work is a comparison of several approaches, i.e., Bayesian, neural networks and machine learning methods (Walley and Džeroski, 1995), which also includes a comparison to traditional classification methods, such as the ASPT (Average Score per Taxon). However, this study treats water quality as a continuous variable and is not directly comparable to the present study. ILP (Lavrač and Džeroski, 1994) has also been applied to the same data, but without a comparison of performance to other methods in terms of accuracy and/or information score. However, expert evaluation of the induced rules indicates that the declarative bias facilities of ILP systems are very desirable for this application.

In a broader context, Kompare *et al.*, (1994), Kompare and Džeroski (1995), Križman *et al.*, (1995), and Karalič and Bratko (1996) apply machine learning techniques to the problem of modelling algal growth in lakes and lagoons. In particular, regression trees (Breiman *et al.*, 1984) and machine discovery techniques (Langley and Zytkow, 1989) are applied to modelling algal growth in the Lagoon of Venice (Kompare *et al.*, 1994), while ILP is applied to modelling algal growth in the Lake of Bled (Karalič and Bratko, 1996). Most notably, a difference equation model has been induced from measured data (Kompare and Džeroski, 1995; Križman *et al.*, 1995) which is able to successfully predict peaks and crashes for the algae *Ulva rigida* in the Lagoon of Venice.

To conclude, we have described several applications of rule induction in the domain of biological water quality classification. The rules produced are transparent and can be easily understood by experts. In all the problems addressed, the induced rules contained valuable knowledge about the domain studied. In some cases, this knowledge extended and complemented existing expert knowledge. Despite the need for more thorough evaluation in terms of performance, we can say that machine learning techniques can be useful tools for classification and data analysis in the domain of river water quality and other ecological domains.

ACKNOWLEDGEMENTS

Parts of this chapter were originally published in Džeroski *et al.* (1994), Džeroski and Grbović (1995) and Džeroski *et al.* (1997). The authors wish to thank H. A. Hawkes for his invaluable assistance in classifying the biological samples and providing expert comments on the rules produced. The NRA (Severn-Trent Region) provided the biological data on British rivers, while the Hydrometeorological Institute of Slovenia provided the biological, physical and chemical data on Slovenian rivers. Many thanks to Doris Ličan-Milošević, who performed the experiments with the data on Slovenian rivers as part of her BSc Thesis at the Faculty of electrical engineering and computer science, University of Ljubljana, Slovenia. Her thesis was supervised by Professor Ivan Bratko, Sašo Džeroski and Jasna Grbović. Sašo Džeroski acknowledges the financial support from the Slovenian Ministry of Science and Technology (MZT) and the European Research Consortium on Informatics and Mathematics (ERCIM).

REFERENCES

[1] Breiman, L., Friedman, J. H., Olshen, R. A., and Stone, C. J. (1984). *Classification and Regression Trees*. Wadsworth, Belmont.

[2] Cairns, J., Douglas, W.A., Busey, F., and Chaney, M.D. (1968). The sequential comparison index – a simplified method for non-biologists to estimate relative differences in biological diversities in stream pollution studies. *J. Wat. Pollut. Control Fed.*, 40: 1607–1613.

[3] Cestnik, B. (1990). Estimating probabilities: A crucial task in machine learning. In *Proc. Ninth European Conference on Artificial Intelligence*, pages 147–149. Pitman, London.

[4] Clark, P. and Boswell, R. (1991). Rule induction with CN2: Some recent improvements. In *Proc. Fifth European Working Session on Learning*, pages 151–163. Springer, Berlin.

[5] Clark, P. and Niblett, T. (1989). The CN2 induction algorithm. *Machine Learning*, 3(4): 261–283.

[6] Dasarathy, B.V., editor. *Nearest Neighbor (NN) Norms: NN Pattern Classification Techniques*. IEEE Computer Society Press, Los Alamitos, CA.

[7] De Pauw, N. and Hawkes, H.A. (1993). Biological monitoring of river water quality. In *Proc. Freshwater Europe Symposium on River Water Quality Monitoring and Control*, pages 87–111. Aston University, Birmingham.

[8] Džeroski, S. (1996). Inductive logic programming and knowledge discovery in databases. In U. Fayyad, G. Piatetsky-Shapiro, P. Smyth, and R. Uthurusamy, editors, *Advances in Knowledge Discovery and Data Mining*, pages 118–152. MIT Press, Cambridge, MA.

[9] Džeroski, S., Cestnik, B., and Petrovski, I. (1993). Using the m-estimate in rule induction. *Journal of Computing and Information Technology*, 1: 37–46.

[10] Džeroski, S., Dehaspe, L., Ruck, B., and Walley, W.J. (1994). Classification of river water quality data using machine learning. In P. Zannetti, editor, *Computer Techniques in Environmental Studies V (Proc. Fifth International Conference on the Development and Application of Computer Techniques to Environmental Studies), Vol. I: Pollution modelling*, pages 129–137, Computational Mechanics Publications, Southampton.

[11] Džeroski, S., and Grbović, J. (1995). Knowledge discovery in a water quality database. In *Proc. First International Conference on Knowledge Discovery and Data Mining*, pages 81–86. AAAI Press, Menlo Park, CA.

[12] Džeroski, S., Grbović, J., Walley, W.J., Kompare, B. (1997). Using machine learning techniques in the construction of models. II. Data analysis with rule induction. *Ecological Modelling*, 95: 95–111.

[13] Friedrich, G., Chapman, D., and Beim, A. (1992). The use of biological material. In Chapman, D., editor, *Water Quality Assessments*, pages 171–238. Chapman and Hall, London.

[14] Grbović, J. (1994). *Applicability of Various Procedures for the Assessment of Quality of Torrential Streams*. PhD Thesis, Biotechnical Faculty, University of Ljubljana, Slovenia. In Slovenian.

[15] ISO-BMWP (1979). *Assessment of the Biological Quality of Rivers by a Macroinvertebrate Score.* ISO/TC147/SC5/WG6/N5, International Standards Organization.

[16] Karalič, A. and Bratko, I. (1996). First order regression. *Machine Learning.* To appear.

[17] Kolkwitz, R. and Marsson, M. (1902). Grundsatze für die biologische Beurteilung des Wassers nach seiner Flora und Fauna. *Mitt. Prüfungsanst. Wasserversorg. Äbwasserein*, 1: 33–72.

[18] Kompare, B., Bratko, I., Steinman, F., and Džeroski, S. (1994). Using machine learning techniques in the construction of models. Part I: Introduction. *Ecological Modelling*, 75/76: 617–628.

[19] Kompare, B. and Džeroski, S. (1995). Getting more out of data: Automated modelling of algal growth with machine learning. In *Proc. International Conference on Coastal Ocean Space Utilization*, pages 209–220. University of Hawaii, Honolulu, HI.

[20] Kononenko, I. and Bratko, I. (1991). Information-based evaluation criterion for classifier's performance. *Machine Learning*, 6(1): 67–80.

[21] Križman, V., Džeroski, S., and Kompare, B. (1995). Discovering dynamics from measured data. *Electrotechnical Review*, 62(3-4): 191–198.

[22] Langley, P., and Zytkow, J. (1989). Data-driven approaches to empirical discovery. *Artificial Intelligence*, 40: 283–312.

[23] Lavrač, N. and Džeroski, S. (1994). *Inductive Logic Programming: Techniques and Applications.* Ellis Horwood, Chichester.

[24] Ličan-Milošević, D. (1994). *Analysis of water quality data by rule induction.* BSc Thesis, Faculty of electrical engineering and computer science, University of Ljubljana, Slovenia. In Slovenian.

[25] OJSFRY (1978). Regulations on water classification for interstate streams, international waters and coastal waters of Yugoslavia. *Official Journal of the Socialist Federative Republic of Yugoslavia*, No. 6.

[26] Pantle, R. and Buck, H. (1955). Die biologische Überwachung der Gewas und die Darstellung der Ergebnisse. *Gas und Wasserfach*, 96: 603.

[27] Ruck, B.M., Walley, W.J. and Hawkes, H.A. (1993). Biological classification of river water quality using neural networks. In *Proc. Eight International Conference on Artificial Intelligence in Engineering*, pages 361–372. Elsevier.

[28] Walley, W.J., Boyd, M., and Hawkes, H.A. (1992). An expert system for the biological monitoring of river pollution. In *Proc. Fourth International Conference on the Development and Application of Computer Techniques to Environmental Studies*, pages 1030–1047. Elsevier, Amsterdam.

[29] Walley, W.J. (1993). Artificial intelligence in river water quality monitoring and control. In *Proc. Freshwater Europe Symposium on River Water Quality Monitoring and Control*, pages 179–193. Aston University, Birmingham.

[30] Walley, W.J. and Džeroski, S. (1995). Biological monitoring: A comparison between Bayesian, neural and machine learning methods of water quality classification. In *Proc. International Symposium on Environmental Software Systems.* Malvern, PA. Forthcoming.

[31] Walley, W.J. and Hawkes, H.A. (1996). A computer-based reappraisal of the Biological Monitoring Working Party scores using data from the 1990 river quality survey of England and Wales. *Water Research.* To appear.

[32] Wettschereck, D. (1994). A study of distance-based machine learning algorithms. PhD Thesis, Department of Computer Science, Oregon State University, Corvallis, OR.

[33] Zelinka, M. and Marvan, P. (1961). Zur Präzisierung der biologischen Klassifikation der Reinheit fliessender Gewässer. *Arch, Hydrobiol.*, 57: 389–407.

Index

ABACUS program 80, 81
absorption 37
accuracy values 216
activity monitors 316
Air Traffic Control (ATC) 353–86, 368–77
    adaptation of algorithm to structured objects 379–81
    application 366–82
    choosing the language representation 366
    determining the concepts to learn 366–7
    obtaining and rewriting examples 367–77
    obtaining raw examples 367–8
    rewriting BK as Horn clauses 377–9
    rewriting the generalization 380–2
    see also OGUST formalism
algorithm selection 158–9
alternative representations 11–12
ambiguous examples 205
American Express UK 115
analogy-based reasoning 53–4
ANALOGY program 243
analytic macro-operator schema learning 198
AND-layer 62, 415, 417
AND-neuron 417–18
Annotated Symbolic Image (ASI) 245, 247, 249
anomalies in subgroups 101–2
anti-friction bearing systems 203–19
anti-virus software 316
AQ-algorithm 10, 25–9, 64, 97, 205
AQ15c learning program 88, 95, 204, 212, 245
AQDT–2 program 97
AQ-NN learning technique 9, 244–5
arguments 10
artificial discovery 42–53
artificial intelligence 3, 14
artificial neural networks see neural networks
assembly episodes 188, 197
assembly hierarchy 187
assembly plan structure 199
assembly sequence planning 185–201
Assistant-I 395, 400
Assistant-R 395, 400

association browser 228
associations 229
    in collections of text 223–40
    presentation 234–5
attribute-based training instances 199
attribute-value algorithms 158
attribute-value description of edges 153
attributes
    best 19–20
    dependencies 86
    domains 210
    generation 86, 99
    most relevant 98–9
    nonessential 79
    output 85
    predefined set 9
    selection 85
    structured 94–6, 102–4
attributional logic 9–10
automated interaction detection 123
automatic classification of celestial objects 116–17
automatic human face detection 244
automatic target detection and recognition 244
Average Score Per Taxon (ASPT) 430

backed-up error 22
background knowledge (BK) 39, 75, 152, 354
backpropagation, with weight elimination 397
backpropagation learning algorithm 59, 62, 63, 419
backpropagation neural networks 400
backtracking 14
BACON system 50–2, 80
banding reduction in rotogravure printing 118
base component schema 193
base concept representation (BCR) 28–9
beam-search algorithm 17
behavioural cloning of control skill 335–51
Bell Head assembly 188, 193, 194
BERSAFE package 163
best attribute 19–20

best-first search algorithm 16–17
binarization 23
biological classification of river water quality
    see river water quality biological
        classification
Biological Monitoring Working Party Score
    (BMWP) 430
biomedical signals classification 409–28
    experiments 422–5
black-box methods 5
body of clause 10
Boolean constants 8
bracket mounting assembly 194
breadth-first search 14
breast cancer, prediction of recurrence 392
British Petroleum 120

candidate precedence schemas 193, 194
CART programs 132
case-based learning 65
case-based reasoning (CBR) 173–83
    applications 177
CASSIOPEE project 177
celestial objects, automatic classification of
    116–17
Cfm 56–3 engines, troubleshooting 177–80
characteristic concept descriptions 77
characteristic description 91, 92
chemical compounds, mutagenicity prediction of
    134–5
chemical process control 114–15
chi-square analysis 98
CIA system 41–2
CIA World Factbook 226, 235
CLASS 74
classification accuracy 56
classification cost 165
classification rules 160, 164
CLAUDIEN algorithm 140, 157, 159–62
clauses 358–9
clean-up effect 339, 342, 345–6, 348
CLINT system 39–41
closed-loop learning 192
CLUSTER algorithm 44–5, 91, 199
cluster analysis 41
CLUSTER/2 program 90
clustering 86, 90–2
clusters 6
COBWEB system 48–9
cognitive perspective 6–8
color images of outdoor scenes 245–9
    future research 264

computational tractability 12
computer-aided design (CAD) system 185
computer-aided manufacturing (CAM) system
    186
computer-aided process planning (CAPP)
    system 186
computer viruses 313–34
    anomaly detection 325–6
    automatic analysis 328–9
    automatic signature extraction 329–31
    boot viruses 317, 322
    classifier 318
        training and performance 321–3
    decoys 327–8
    detection, removal and analysis 316–17
    feature selection 320–1
    function of 315–16
    generic detection 317–23
    immune system 323–32
    immunological memory 331
    removal 326–7
    scanning 316, 326
    self-replication 331–2
    use of term 314
    virus writers vs. anti-virus software
        developers 314
computer vision 242–5
concept discovery 41, 44–6
concept drift 31
concept formation 44–50
conceptual clustering 44–6, 78–9, 90
conceptual cohesiveness 78
CONDITION 74
confidence degrees 216, 217
consistent generalization 94
constructive induction 41–2, 79–80, 83
constructive induction operators 104
container cranes 343–7
context dependency 8
control skill, behavioural cloning of 335–51
CONVART 99
COPER system 80
credit assignment process 191
credit decision-making 115
crisp conceptual hierarchies 46–8
current states 16

data analysis techniques 72
data analysis tools 72
data exploration operators 76–7
data exploration tasks, classification 83–7
Data Management Operators (DMOs) 87

data mining 72–3
data refinement in program design 140
data visualization 92–4
decision rules 26, 28, 87, 97–8
decision structures 97–8
    from declarative knowledge 87
decision support system 178
decision-tree-based neural networks (TBNN)
    414–19
decision-tree-based parameter setting 421–2
decision trees 18, 62, 115, 121, 400, 414
    constructive induction 23
    for problem solving 174
    induced from numeric attributes 25
    numerica data 23–5
    pitfalls 21
    pruning 21–3
    replication problem 24
    simplification 23
decomposition model 82
deductive restructuring step 197
demographic data 99–104
depth-first search 14
descriptive models 81
design, inductive rule learning in 203–19
design knowledge acquisition 204
design knowledge sources 211
design rules, method for learning 204–7
diagnosis of mechanical devices 116
diagrammatic visualization 92
DIAV program 75, 87, 92
discriminant descriptions 77, 91–2
discrimination function 55
disinfectors 316
disjunctive normal form (DNF) model 82, 277
divide-and-conquer learning 17–25
domain 83
domain independent structural concept learning
        systems 199
domain theory 273
domains of attributes 210
dropping condition 94
dynamic systems 52–3

economic analysis 99
economic data 99–104
electrical discharge machining (EDM) 136–9
    developing the representation 136–7
electrical transformers, preventing breakdowns
    119
electroencephalogram (EEG) 410, 411
    recognition of motor commands from 412–14

electromyogram (EMG) 410, 411
electrooculogram (EOG) 410, 411
EMERALD system 74–5
empirical assembly planning 198
empirical comission error rate 206
empirical error rate 206
empirical errors 205–6
empirical omission error rate 206
entropy networks 62–3
error area 76
evolution 31
EXCEL 179
exclusive OR 57
exemplary application 99–104
exemplary problem 207–9
exhaustive search 14
expert system 113, 121, 149, 354
    addition to FEM generator 149–50
    evaluation 165
    shell 164
explanation-based learning (EBL) 65, 198
explicitly constrained languages 11
extension-against operator 94, 95

face and non-face pattern prototypes 244
face detection system 244
face verification 244
FACT system 223–40
    application to newswire data 235–7
    architecture 225–8
    association query language 230–2
    query execution 232–4
false negatives 317
false positives 317
family relations 32
fault trees 179
feature pruning 321
feedback 176–7
feedforward neural network training 322
final state 14
FIND-PATH problem 186
finite automata 11
finite element method (FEM) 147–71
    discretisation 148
    mesh design 139–40, 150
    mesh models 148, 151
    pre-processor environment 163
Finite Elements 148
first order logic 10, 355–9
First Order Regression (FORS)) program 137
first order representation 368
fitness function 60

flexible matching 29
FOIL algorithm 10, 35–6, 131, 156–7
forms, automated completion 120–1
FORS (First Order Regression) program 137
FOSSIL 157
frames 11
functional expressions 357
functions 11

GA-algorithm 61
gain ratio 86, 98
gas–oil separation 118
general data table (GDT) 83–7
generalization hierarchy 7
generalizations 12–15, 64
genetic algorithms 59–61, 244
    and neural nets 64–5
genetic search 61, 64
GENRULE operators 88
gini index 98
GLAUBER system 52
Global Frame 193
global reference frames 193
GOLEM program 154–6, 158
grammars 11
grouping schema 193, 195, 196

Hartford Steam Boiler 121
head of clause 10
Hebbian learning mechanisms 244
helicopter blades, repair 122
heuristic search 14–17
hierarchically ordered concepts 46
hill-climbing algorithm 17
Horn clauses 33–6, 121, 377–9
hybrid systems 61–5
hypnogram 410

IBL-algorithm 55
IBL-SMART 273–4, 276–8
IBM AntiVirus 332
I-DEAS computer aided design package 166
identification 37
Illustrated Part Catalogue (IPC) 179
Image Knowledge Base (IKB) 245
images, learning patterns in 241–70
incremental learning 31, 213–15
incremental rule update 86
INDUCE 191–2, 199
induced rules
    post-processing 162–4
    transparency 340, 343, 346–8

induction method, application 209–11
inductive learning 173–83
Inductive Logic Programming (ILP) 32, 131–43,
    151
    applications 139–41
    compared to other approaches to ML 132–34
    inducing program invariants 140
    learning problem 131
    results of learning and expert's evaluation
        137–9
inductive rule learning
    in design 203–19
    see also AQ15c
inferential concept interpretation (ICI) 28–9
initial state 14
INLEN system 73, 83, 85, 87–90, 96, 98–100,
    102, 105, 206
INLEN–2 103
innovative design from first principles 141
instance-based learning 54–6
    algorithm 56
instance-to-class generalization 199
integration of multiple operators 100–1
integration of qualitative and quantitative
    discovery 80–1
integrity management systems 316
intermediate concepts 63
internal disjunction 9
interpretational rule 29
inverse resolution 36–9

k-fold cross-validation 205
k-nearest neighbor 399
    algorithm 397
KBANN system 63
Kepler's Law 80
knowledge acquisition (KA) 354
knowledge base 164, 165
    fielding 125–6
    supporting maintenance 121
knowledge-based abstraction strategy 281
knowledge-based learning 273
knowledge-based neural nets 63
knowledge-based systems 113
knowledge discovery 72–3
Knowledge Discovery from Databases (KDD)
    224
Knowledge Discovery from Text (KDT)
    224
knowledge engineering process 113
knowledge evaluation 125
Knowledge Generation Operators (KGOs) 87–8

knowledge intensive relational generalization 355–65
Knowledge Management Operators (KMOs) 87
knowledge-oriented algorithms 6
knowledge-oriented methods 5
knowledge segments 86

LADI help desk system 177, 181
LAGRANCE program 52–3
Laplace estimate 22
learned rules, application to new examples 206–7
learned ruleset 205–6
learning
  classic methods 17–31
  divide-and-conquer 17–25
  from planning experience 191
  inductive essence 12–14
learning algorithms, assessment 29–31
learning operators 90–2
learning patterns in images 241–70
learning problem 150
learning process, theory revision 39–41
learning rules 85, 94–6, 205–7, 212–13
  from training events 212–13
learning scenario 195
learning set 154
learning to fly 340–3
leave-one-out method 205, 214
leave-one-out test 166–7
Leeds Permanent Building Society 120
lexicographic functional (LEF) 212
loan decisions 115
lookahead feature construction (LFC) 401
  algorithm 395
LUMO (Lowest Unoccupied Molecular Orbital) 134

machine learning
  close neighborhood 56–61
  concept of 5–12
  determining the representation 124–5
  fielded applications 113–29
  formulating the problem 124
  general framework 5
  oriented approach 82–3
  perspectives 65
  review of methods 3–69
  sources of power 126
  strategies and lessons 123
  task 5
  vs. physician 391–3
  see also under specific applications

machining learning, database of examples 211–12
maximal consistent generalization 94
mechanical devices, diagnosis of 116
medical diagnosis 389–403
  acceptance in practice 401–3
  appropriateness of algorithms 397–401
  description of tested algorithms 395–7
  diagnostic problems 391–3
  information score 404
  performance comparison of algorithms 397
  physician vs. machine learning 391–3
  selecting appropriate ML system 393–401
  specific requirements for ML systems 394–5
  typical process 390–1
medical domains 410–14
memory 86
method of outstanding representatives 80
mFOIL 157
MILP algorithm 157
minimal-error pruning 22
misclassification cost 165
missing data 86
MIST methodology 244–9
  implementation and experimental results 248–9
  Interpretation mode 245, 247–9
  Learning mode 245–7
  simple version 248
Monod model 53
most relevant attributes 98–9
multi-concept learning 191, 192
multi-layer neural network (MNN) 423–6
Multi-layer Perceptron 58
Multi-Level Image Sampling and Transformation see MIST methodology
Multi-Level Logical Template (MLT) methodology 242–3
multi-level phenomenon 280
multiple operators, integration of 100–1
multistrategy constructive learning 191–2
multistrategy data exploration 73–83
  determining general rules from specific cases 74–8
multistrategy learning 61–5, 242
music research 269–93
musical expression 269–93
  background knowledge 271–3
  experimental results 288–91
  learning at the note level 273–80
  learning at the structure level 280–4
  machine learning analysis of real artistic performances 284–8

musical performance, expressive timing 271
mutagenicity prediction of chemical compounds
    134–5
mutations 60, 61

naive Bayesian classifier 396, 399
natural laws 50–2
nearest-neighbor classification 318
nearest-neighbor principle 55
    see also k-nearest neighbor
negative examples 152, 205
neural networks 57, 59, 134, 241–2, 244
    and genetic algorithms 64–5
    backpropagation 400
    classifier 321
    feedforward training 322
    knowledge-based 63
    multi-layer (MNN) 423–6
    representation language 414
    tree-based (TBNN) 424–6
    tuning 418–19
noise 5
NOMAD 187, 200
    learning scenario 193–8
    memory structure 190
    representation and planning 187–91
nondeterminate literals 153
nonessential attribute 79
numeric prediction task 271
numerical controlled (NC) machine 186
numerical taxonomy technique 72

object-correspondence problem 199
OGUST system 359–65
    algorithm 360–1
    drawbacks 365
    formalism 368–77
    inductive step 365
    language of representation 359–61
    positive features 365
    structural matching 362–5
oil–gas separation 118
on-line pruning 22
OR-layer 62, 415, 417
OR-neuron 417
outdoor scenes, color images of 245–9
output attribute 85
overfitting 21
overgeneralization 13
overtraining 419

Palomar Observatory Sky Survey 116

partitioning layer 62
part-to-whole generalization 199
patterns 86
PEOPLE database 101–3
perceptron 57, 58
performance curve 271
periodic model 82
PERSPICACE project 354
planner building 187
planning episode 193, 194
planning experience, learning from 191
planning paradigm 187
planning research 198
pole balancing 338–40
population growth rate 103
positive examples 152, 205
post-mortem analysis 190, 192
post-processing of induced rules 162–4
post-pruning 22
PRAX method 243
predicate logic 31–42
predicates 10
preference criterion 26
preventive diagnosis 121
primary tumor localization 391–2
probabilistic conceptual hierarchies 48–50
probability estimation 21
problem solving, decision tree for 174
product model 185
production line scheduling 347–8
production rules 64
Progol system 134, 135
program design, data refinement in 140
progressive coverage 25–9
PROLOG 10, 75
PROMISE 98, 99
Promise level 86
propositional calculus 8–9
protein structures prediction 122–3

Qualitative Differential Equations (QDEs) 141
qualitative domain theory 274
qualitative prediction 81
qualitative system identification 141
qualitative values of variables 210–11
quality monitoring, rolling emulsions 117
QUANTA program 134
quantitative empirical laws 50–2
query specification front-end 227

Radial-Basis-Function (RBF) network 419–22
random subsampling strategy 423

reasoning-by-analogy algorithm 54
recombination 61
recursive descriptions 11
reference coordinate system 193
regression unfriendly compounds 135
reinforcement learning 65
Relative Least General Generalisation (RLGG)
    155
REM-stage 410
representation language 8, 12
representation spaces, automatic improvement
    98–9
representational issues 8
reproduction 61
resolution principle 37
resolvent 37
Reuters newswire data 235
rheumatology, diagnostic problem 392
river water quality biological classification 140,
    429–48
    analysis of data for Slovenian rivers 436–44
    data 432
    experiments in predicting for British rivers
        432–6
    experiments in predicting for Slovenian rivers
        442–4
    influence of physical and chemical parameters
        on selected organisms 438–42
    learning rules for British rivers 431–6
robot axis, troubleshooting 180–3
robustness
    against missing information 31
    against noise 31
rolling emulsions, quality monitoring 117
rotogravure printing, banding reduction in 118
rule induction 114–20
    applied work on 120–3
    fielded applications 119–20
rule learning 85, 94–6, 205–7, 212–13
rule preference criterion 26
rule visualization 92–4

sample case library 175
scheduling, automation in steel mill 123
screw assembly 196
search heuristics 53–4
search operators 14
search process 14–17
search space 53–6
search strategies 14, 425
second order logic 10–11
second order schemata 11

seeds 26
segmentation parameters 244
selective induction 192
semi-naive Bayesian classifier 396, 399, 401
Sendzimir mill 117
sexual reproduction 60
shape learning 243
SIA system 64
skill reconstruction in electrical discharge
    machining 136–9
Skolem function 355
Skolemization 358–9
sleep classification 410
space shuttle engine tests 121–2
SPARC 199
SPARC/G 82, 88
specialization 13
star generation procedure 26
statistical analysis 72
Stoke's Law 81
strong criterion 6
structure/activity relationships (SAR) 134
structured attributes 94–6, 102–4
structured induction 118
subassembly independence law (SIL) 190
subgroups, anomalies in 101–2
sudden infant death syndrome (SIDS) 410
supervised learning 42
supporting facts 63
'survival of the fittest' principle 59–60
symbolic learning component 277
symbolic learning methods 242
symbolic process prediction 200
synonym definition utility 227

target concept 76
task-oriented knowledge 74
TB-RBF 419–22, 424–6
TDIDT algorithm 9, 18–19, 25, 31, 61, 62
tenfold cross-validation test 167
termination criterion 14
testing events 211–12
text, finding associations in collections of 223–
    40
thunderstorms, forecasting 122
thyroid diseases, diagnostic problem 392
time delay 339, 341–2, 344–5, 348, 349
time-dependent patterns 85
topological relations between edges 153–4
training data collection 125
training events 211–12
    learning rules from 212–13

transparency of induced rules 340, 343, 346–8
tree-based neural networks (TBNN) 424–6
tree-based radial-based function (TB-RBF)
        networks 419–22, 424–6
troubleshooting
    Cfm 56–3 engines 177–80
    industrial machines 173–83
    robot axis 180–3
TRUNC method 29
two-tiered approach 28–9
type 83

ultrastrong criterion 6
UNIMEM system 46–8
unseen structure test 167–8
unsupervised learning 42
UserChoice? 305–8

variable-valued logic 10
variables 9, 355–7
Version Space algorithms 13
video image sequences
    chopping 263
    computing motion 258–60
    computing primitive motions 258–9
    experiments 260–4
    function from motion 256–7
    inferring object function from primitive
        motion 257

motions of sticks and strips 258
parametrizing motion of stick or strip
        259–60
primitive shapes and primitive motions 256–7
recognizing actions in 255–65
slicing 263–4
stabbing 261–2
vision systems 241
    advantages of incorporating learning into 265

weak criterion 6
WebWatcher 297–312
    accuracy 308–9
    design 298–304
    knowledge required by 304–5
    learning 304–7
    representation of pages, links and goals 305–6
    UserChoice? 305–8
World Wide Web 297–312
worms 316

x-ray images of luggage 249–55
    future research 264–5
    image formation process and imaging model
        251–2
    method and experimental results 253–5
    problem statement 252–3

zero-order logic 8, 355–9